The Complete Artist's Way

BY JULIA CAMERON

Books in The Artist's Way Series

The Artist's Way
Walking in This World
Finding Water

Other Books on Creativity

The Right to Write
The Sound of Paper
The Vein of Gold
The Artist's Way Workbook
The Artist's Way Morning Pages Journal
The Artist's Date Book
    (illustrated by Elizabeth Cameron)
How to Avoid Making Art (or Anything Else You Enjoy)
    (illustrated by Elizabeth Cameron)
Supplies: A Troubleshooting Guide for Creative Difficulties
Inspirations: Meditations from *The Artist's Way*
The Writer's Life: Insights from *The Right to Write*
The Artist's Way at Work
    (with Mark Bryan and Catherine Allen)
Money Drunk, Money Sober
    (with Mark Bryan)

Prayer Books

Answered Prayers
Heart Steps
Blessings
Transitions

Books on Spirituality

Prayers from a Nonbeliever
Letters to a Young Artist
God Is No Laughing Matter
God Is Dog Spelled Backwards
    (illustrated by Elizabeth Cameron)

Memoir

Floor Sample: A Creative Memoir

Fiction

Popcorn: Hollywood Stories
The Dark Room

Plays

Public Lives
The Animal in the Trees
Four Roses
Love in the DMZ
Avalon *(a musical)*
The Medium at Large *(a musical)*
Magellan *(a musical)*

Poetry

Prayers for the Little Ones
Prayers to the Nature Spirits
The Quiet Animal
This Earth *(also an album with Tim Wheater)*

Feature Film

(as writer-director) God's Will

The
Complete Artist's Way

Creativity as a Spiritual Practice

Julia Cameron

JEREMY P. TARCHER/PENGUIN

a member of Penguin Group (USA) Inc.

New York

JEREMY P. TARCHER/PENGUIN
Published by the Penguin Group
Penguin Group (USA) Inc., 375 Hudson Street, New York, New York 10014, USA •
Penguin Group (Canada), 90 Eglinton Avenue East, Suite 700, Toronto, Ontario
M4P 2Y3, Canada (a division of Pearson Penguin Canada Inc.) • Penguin Books Ltd,
80 Strand, London WC2R 0RL, England • Penguin Ireland, 25 St Stephen's Green,
Dublin 2, Ireland (a division of Penguin Books Ltd) • Penguin Group (Australia),
250 Camberwell Road, Camberwell, Victoria 3124, Australia (a division of Pearson
Australia Group Pty Ltd) • Penguin Books India Pvt Ltd, 11 Community Centre,
Panchsheel Park, New Delhi–110 017, India • Penguin Group (NZ), 67 Apollo
Drive, Rosedale, North Shore 0632, New Zealand (a division of Pearson
New Zealand Ltd) • Penguin Books (South Africa) (Pty) Ltd, 24 Sturdee Avenue,
Rosebank, Johannesburg 2196, South Africa

Penguin Books Ltd, Registered Offices:
80 Strand, London WC2R 0RL, England

Most Tarcher/Penguin books are available at special quantity discounts for bulk purchase
for sales promotions, premiums, fund-raising, and educational needs. Special books or
book excerpts also can be created to fit specific needs. For details, write Penguin Group
(USA) Inc. Special Markets, 375 Hudson Street, New York, NY 10014.

Library of Congress Cataloging-in-Publication Data
Cameron, Julia.
The complete artist's way: creativity as a spiritual practice / Julia Cameron.
p.   cm.—(The artist's way series)
ISBN 978-1-58542-630-0 (alk. paper)
1. Spiritual life. 2. Creative ability—Religious aspects.
3. Creation (Literary, artistic, etc.)—Religious aspects. 1. Title.
BL624.C33185   2007   2007028172
204'.4—dc22

Printed in the United States of America
5   7   9   10   8   6
This book is printed on acid-free paper. ∞

Book design by Claire Vaccaro, Marysarah Quinn, and Amanda Dewey

While the author has made every effort to provide accurate telephone numbers and
Internet addresses at the time of publication, neither the publisher nor the author
assumes any responsibility for errors, or for changes that occur after publication. Further,
the publisher does not have any control over and does not assume any responsibility
for author or third-party websites or their content.

ACKNOWLEDGMENTS

Elizabeth Cameron, for her commitment
Sara Carder, for her care
Carolina Casperson, for her daring
Jane Cecil, for her grace
Sonia Choquette, for her vision
Judy Collins, for her generosity
Tim Farrington, for his fortitude
Joel Fotinos, for his faith
Natalie Goldberg, for her resilience
Bernice Hill, for her sagacity
Jack Hofsiss, for his leadership
Tracy Jamar, for her grit
Linda Kahn, for her clarity
Bill Lavallee, for his strength
Laura Leddy, for her prayers
Emma Lively, for her perseverance
Larry Lonergan, for his guidance
Julianna McCarthy, for her inspiration
Robert McDonald, for his art
Bruce Pomahac, for his belief
Susan Raihofer, for her insight
Domenica Cameron-Scorsese, for her loyalty
Jeremy Tarcher, for his wisdom
Edmund Towle, for his friendship
Claire Vaccaro, for her eye
Rosemary Welden, for her enthusiasm
Elizabeth Winick, for her shepherding

To the artists who have gone before me,
leaving a trail of hope and perseverance

Contents

The Quiet Animal

Oh quiet animal, sleeping,
What dreams lie within your cells?
What ages brought you here
Through coal and ice?
Eye twitch, lip curl—
Blood dreams again.

Blood is always dreaming.
Scheming to move us forward and take us back,
Dreaming the dark places,
Caves and the backs of stars.

Your ivory bones are the tusks of time
Who eats with all our mouths.
That crescent moon? It's just a bone
Thrown beyond our reach.
The stars at night were someone's baby teeth.

The blood remembers
What the mind forgets.
The soul is a quiet animal.
Given less to thought than memory,
More to dreams than plan,
The soul owes more to half-remembered God
Than waking life as man.

—J.C.

INTRODUCTION

IT IS A GRAY, CHILL day. Manhattan is socked in. The tall buildings are wreathed in fog, almost like Taos Mountain with its shawl of clouds. I am seated at my small Chinese desk, looking north across a row of brownstones. I am twenty-odd blocks north of where I lived when I first formulated *The Artist's Way,* and I am twenty-odd years further down my own creative path. For a quarter of a century now, I have been teaching and learning the miracles of creative unblocking. I have seen lives transformed through the use of a few simple tools. My own life has been a rich garden, blossoming in many unexpected directions. Throughout this time, I have continued to write and publish on the creative process. My thinking has deepened and broadened. Each book marked another milestone: *This is what it looks like from here.* Now, for the first time, these books are being offered as a set. This is very exciting for me. I believe that the individual books stand alone, but I also believe that as a trilogy they build, one upon the other, offering substantial guidance for the creative journey. Let me tell you a little bit about each volume and the ways in which I feel they interlock.

I had been teaching a full decade before I put my theories on the page with the original text, *The Artist's Way.* In broad strokes, it laid out my thinking. All of us are creative. We can all become more creative through engaging God, the Great Creator, in our process. Creativity is the natural order of life, nothing we need to invent. Put simply, creativity is God's gift to us. Our use of it is our gift back to God. We are intended to be creative.

Laying out this simple foundation, the course built lesson by lesson for twelve weeks. A pair of basic tools, "Morning Pages" and "Artist Dates," was introduced. Each week's march contained a further ten tasks, all designed to explore and expand our personal creative territory. Entering the course with skepticism and hope, people reported back later that the book "changed my life." Of course, *they* changed their lives. They worked with the tool kit, and a creative awakening followed.

For many users, *The Artist's Way* was an into-the-water book. They moved from the embankment into the flow of a creative life. They went from not doing to doing, from not trying to trying, from stunted to flourishing. When I went out to teach, writers would hand me books, saying, "I used your tools and this is what I made." Painters would bring me photos or slides of their work. Actors would say, "I am working." It was like visiting a vast garden as people bloomed in diverse and colorful directions. Many people circled back through the book repeatedly. Some formed Artist's Way groups, creative clusters devoted to mutual unblocking. Once having found the tools, many people worked with them for years. This was very gratifying.

I, too, worked with the tools. Using them, I wrote novels, plays, poetry, even music. I began to joke that I was the "floor sample" of my own tool kit. I felt I owed my own creative flourishing to my teaching the tools of unblocking. As I moved further and further along on my own journey, I began once again to write about what I was discovering. There were so many lessons I was eager to share! I wanted to add a new wing to the Artist's Way foundation. That wing became the book *Walking in This World*. It was fulled with my newest insights, the discoveries I kept making through my own adventure as an artist. Like *The Artist's Way*, this book was grounded not in creativity theory but in creativity *practice*. I learned by going where I had to go.

If *The Artist's Way* was a manual for how to get started creatively, this second book was about coping with life in the artistic trenches. If the first book was visionary, this second book was practical. It grappled with the daily practice of an artist's life. I myself was living this life and often found it challenging. What exactly needed to be done for the daily march to go more smoothly? What stratagems could I devise to help people faced with the many obstacles of life? Asking myself these questions, I came up with answers that worked for me and for my students.

To give just one example, I discovered the value of walking, and a third basic tool was added to the kit. If Morning Pages were about "sending" and Artist Dates were about "receiving," walking seemed to be about integrating the two. I undertook a regular regimen of walking, at first through the sagebrush in New Mexico and later on the streets of New York. In both locales, the result was the same: it was nearly impossible to walk and to remain blocked. I set my students to walking, and they, too, reported breakthroughs. They felt happier and more grounded. Many reported that their "conscious contact" with a power greater than themselves dramatically improved.

Watching them and watching myself, I learned still more. For example, it was not excessive outflow that damaged artists so much as increased inflow. Without the time and space to metabolize our impressions, we could easily become flooded by too many stimuli. What could be done to normalize the turbulence we some-times experienced? The answers were often surprisingly simple.

Assembling *Walking in This World,* I paired a single task with each essay. I wanted the book to approximate walking, moving slowly enough to absorb a great deal of detail, pausing along the path to focus on what could be observed. When the book went out in the world, I was once more pleased to discover that people enjoyed working through it in clusters. It was my intention that practitioners could learn from one another as well as from the text. I wanted creativity to be a more user-friendly experience. Increasingly, students reported that as they used the tools, it was.

Creativity is an act of faith, I have long believed and taught. How do we find the faith necessary to "keep on keeping on"? That was the central question that I tried to answer in *Finding Water,* the third book of this trilogy. Like life itself, cre-ativity can be difficult. We must dig down deep to find the inner resources neces-sary to stick to our creative path. Grounded in a trying year of my own journey, the essays of *Finding Water* emphasize the importance of tenacity.

Working to bring a musical from the page to the stage, I faced despair and dis-couragement. And yet, I found that I was always given sufficient spiritual resources to meet the seemingly insurmountable challenges. Friends stepped forward to lend support. No longer isolated and alone with my creative dreams, I found a taproot in community. I began to devise tools for reaching out as well as for reaching within. Writing about the tribulations of the artistic path, I found I could conjure an optimistic tool to match each adversity. I began to believe the spiritual adage that we are never given more than we and God can handle. Once more, groups sprang into being to practice the principles my book laid out. Once more, people reported a sense of comfort and growing excitement that the trail they faced was mapped out.

It is my belief that the creative journey is at once highly individual and highly trackable. The books of the Artist's Way trilogy chart a path that artists habitually tread. There is great comfort in knowing that our path is communal. As we share the process, we receive more and more guidance. My trio of books may blaze a trail for you—or help you to recognize the trail that you are already blazing. It has been my privilege to serve as a guide and a muse. It is my hope that by using my books you will serve those functions for still others.

The Artist's Way

A Spiritual Path to Higher Creativity

MY ARTIST'S WAY GRATITUDE LIST

AT THIS POINT, WELL over a million people have contributed to *The Artist's Way*. It is truly a movement. There are, however, people without whom its safety and growth could not have occurred. I wish to thank some of them here.

Jeremy Tarcher, for publishing my work, editing and caring for it so carefully with his characteristic brilliance and vision.

Joel Fotinos, for nurturing and guarding my body of work—husbanding not only my work but my deepest heart and truest dreams with clarity and strength.

Mark Bryan, my gratitude for fighting to protect and defend my body of work, for his innovative and visionary thinking and capacity to understand and forgive our frequently—and necessarily—divergent paths.

My daughter, Domenica Cameron-Scorsese, for sharing her mother and bearing the dual pressures of second-generation fame and first-rate talent. My gratitude for being always the kind of artist and person for whom I want to write good and useful books. With admiration for her shrewdness, tenderness, and sheer creative "guts."

Emma Lively, with gratitude for her visionary strength and her bold and daring conviction in her work both with my music and my books. A true friend, not only to my creativity but also to my dreams and desires. We met through *The Artist's Way* and my musical *Avalon*, and have enjoyed combining our Artist's Ways as musical collaborators over the last four years.

Susan Schulman, with gratitude for her long years of devotion and commitment to *The Artist's Way*, with admiration for her vision and with humility for her courage throughout our parallel and difficult trials.

With gratitude to Pat Black and company, for holding a steady course as *The Artist's Way*, and I myself, grew in fits and starts.

With gratitude to David Groff, for his fine writing and thinking.

To Johanna Tani, for her graceful and acute editing.

And to Sara Carder, for her deft and careful assistance above and beyond the call of duty—all three of these creative souls.

James Navé, for his loyalty and generosity as a long-term teaching partner.

And to Tim Wheater, a special thank-you for his musical brilliance and creative and teaching partnering through multiple years and projects.

Gratitude also to Mauna Eichner and Claire Vaccaro, for their inspired and fastidious design work, remembering always that form follows function—to make my books embody that artist's formula—"Beauty is truth, and truth is beauty."

Gratitude always, too, to my sister and frequent collaborator, fine artist and cartoonist Libby Cameron, whose wit and whimsy allowed me to create additional tools to support *The Artist's Way*. She well knows the truth that laughter is the best medicine, and helped me in administering creative first aid with a spoonful of sugar to make the medicine go down. My deepest thanks for her inspired work on *The Artist's Date Book, Supplies, God Is Dog Spelled Backwards*, and the upcoming *How Not to Make Art*—or anything else that really matters.

My gratitude to Sonia Choquette and Larry Lonergan, for their love and clarity of vision as I labored to bring into fruition large dreams from small seeds.

To Edmund Towle and Robert McDonald, for their creativity and chivalry as they both protected and inspired me to do all forms of my creative work.

Finally, I wish to thank those who have gone before me and shown me the path, most especially Julianna McCarthy, Max Showalter, John Newland, and all who hold a spiritual lantern to light our Artist's Way with their artistry and generosity.

This sourcebook is dedicated to Mark Bryan.
Mark urged me to write it, helped shape it, and co-taught it.
Without him it would not exist.

CONTENTS

INTRODUCTION

WHEN PEOPLE ASK ME what I do, I usually answer, "I'm a writer-director and I teach these creativity workshops."

The last one interests them.

"How can you teach creativity?" they want to know. Defiance fights with curiosity on their faces.

"I can't," I tell them. "I teach people to *let* themselves be creative."

"Oh. You mean we're all creative?" Now disbelief and hope battle it out.

"Yes."

"You *really* believe that?"

"Yes."

"So what do you do?"

> *The primary imagination I hold to be the Living Power.*
> SAMUEL TAYLOR COLERIDGE

This book is what I do. For a decade now, I have taught a spiritual workshop aimed at freeing people's creativity. I have taught artists and nonartists, painters and filmmakers and homemakers and lawyers—anyone interested in living more creatively through practicing an art; even more broadly, anyone interested in practicing the art of creative living. While using, teaching, and sharing tools I have found, devised, divined, and been handed, I have seen blocks dissolved and lives transformed by the simple process of engaging the Great Creator in discovering and recovering our creative powers.

"The Great Creator? That sounds like some Native American god. That sounds too Christian, too New Age, too . . ." Stupid? Simple-minded? Threatening? . . . I know. Think of it as an exercise in open-mindedness. Just think, "Okay, Great Creator, *whatever that is*," and keep reading. Allow yourself to experiment with the idea there might be a Great Creator and you might get some kind of use from it in freeing your own creativity.

Because *The Artist's Way* is, in essence, a spiritual path, initiated and practiced through creativity, this book uses the word *God*. This may be volatile for some of you—conjuring old, unworkable, unpleasant, or simply unbelievable ideas about God as you were raised to understand "him." Please be open-minded.

Remind yourself that to succeed in this course, no god concept is necessary. In fact, many of our commonly held god concepts get in the way. Do not allow semantics to become one more block for you.

Man is asked to make of himself what he is supposed to become to fulfill his destiny.

PAUL TILLICH

When the word *God* is used in these pages, you may substitute the thought *good orderly direction* or *flow*. What we are talking about is a creative energy. *God* is useful shorthand for many of us, but so is *Goddess, Mind, Universe, Source,* and *Higher Power*. . . . The point is not what you name it. The point is that you try using it. For many of us, thinking of it as a form of spiritual electricity has been a very useful jumping-off place.

I myself do nothing. The Holy Spirit accomplishes all through me.

WILLIAM BLAKE

By the simple, scientific approach of experimentation and observation, a workable connection with the flow of good orderly direction can easily be established. It is not the intent of these pages to engage in explaining, debating, or defining that flow. You do not need to understand electricity to use it.

Why indeed must "God" be a noun? Why not a verb . . . the most active and dynamic of all?

MARY DALY
THEOLOGIAN

Do not call it God unless that is comfortable for you. There seems to be no need to name it unless that name is a useful shorthand for what you experience. Do not pretend to believe when you do not. If you remain forever an atheist, agnostic—so be it. You will still be able to experience an altered life through working with these principles.

I have worked artist-to-artist with potters, photographers, poets, screenwriters, dancers, novelists, actors, directors—and with those who knew only what they dreamed to be or who only dreamed of being somehow more creative. I have seen blocked painters paint, broken poets speak in tongues, halt and lame and maimed writers racing through final drafts. I have come to not only believe but know:

No matter what your age or your life path, whether making art is your career or your hobby or your dream, it is not too late or too egotistical or too selfish or too silly to work on your creativity. One fifty-year-old student who "always wanted to write" used these tools and emerged as a prize-winning playwright. A judge used these tools to fulfill his lifelong dreams of sculpting. Not all students become full-time artists as a result of the course. In fact, many full-time artists report that they have become more creatively rounded into full-time people.

Through my own experience—and that of countless others that I have shared—I have come to believe that creativity is our true nature, that blocks are an unnatural thwarting of a process at once as normal and as miraculous as the blossoming of a flower at the end of a slender green stem. I have found this process of making spiritual contact to be both simple and straightforward.

If you are creatively blocked—and I believe all of us are to some extent—it is possible, even probable, that you can learn to create more freely through your willing use of the tools this book provides. Just as doing Hatha Yoga stretches alters consciousness when all you are doing is stretching, doing the exercises in this book alters consciousness when "all" you are doing is writing and playing. Do these things and a break-through will follow—whether you believe in it or not. Whether you call *it* a spiritual awakening or not.

In short, the theory doesn't matter as much as the practice itself does. What you are doing is creating pathways in your consciousness through which the creative forces can operate. Once you agree to clearing these pathways, your creativity emerges. In a sense, your creativity is like your blood. Just as blood is a fact of your physical body and nothing you invented, creativity is a fact of your spiritual body and nothing that you must invent.

My Own Journey

I began teaching the creativity workshops in New York. I taught them because I was *told* to teach them. One minute I was walking in the West Village on a cobblestone street with beautiful afternoon light. The next minute I suddenly knew that I should begin teaching people, groups of people, how to unblock. Maybe it was a wish exhaled on somebody else's walk. Certainly Greenwich Village must contain a greater density of artists—blocked and otherwise—than nearly anyplace else in America.

"I need to unblock," someone may have breathed out.

"I know how to do it," I may have responded, picking up the cue. My life has always included strong internal directives. *Marching orders*, I call them.

In any case, I suddenly knew that I did know how to unblock people and that I was meant to do so, starting then and there with the lessons I myself had learned.

Where did the lessons come from?

In the brush doing what it's doing, it will stumble on what one couldn't do by oneself.

ROBERT MOTHERWELL

The position of the artist is humble. He is essentially a channel.

PIET MONDRIAN

In 1978, in January, I stopped drinking. I had never thought drinking made me a writer, but now I suddenly thought not drinking might make me stop. In my mind, drinking and writing went together like, well, scotch and soda. For me, the trick was always getting past the fear and onto the page. I was playing beat the clock—trying to write before the booze closed in like fog and my window of creativity was blocked again.

By the time I was thirty and abruptly sober, I had an office on the Paramount lot and had made a whole career out of that kind of creativity. Creative in spasms. Creative as an act of will and ego. Creative on behalf of others. Creative, yes, but in spurts, like blood from a severed carotid artery. A decade of writing and all I knew was how to make these headlong dashes and hurl myself, against all odds, at the wall of whatever I was writing. If creativity was spiritual in any sense, it was only in its resemblance to a crucifixion. I fell upon the thorns of prose. I bled.

If I could have continued writing the old, painful way, I would certainly still be doing it. The week I got sober, I had two national magazine pieces out, a newly minted feature script, and an alcohol problem I could not handle any longer.

I told myself that if sobriety meant no creativity I did not want to be sober. Yet I recognized that drinking would kill me *and* the creativity. I needed to learn to write sober—or else give up writing entirely. Necessity, not virtue, was the beginning of my spirituality. I was forced to find a new creative path. And that is where my lessons began.

I learned to turn my creativity over to the only god I could believe in, the god of creativity, the life force Dylan Thomas called "the force that through the green fuse drives the flower." I learned to get out of the way and let that creative force work through me. I learned to just show up at the page and write down what I heard. Writing became more like eavesdropping and less like inventing a nuclear bomb. It wasn't so tricky, and it didn't blow up on me anymore. I didn't have to be in the mood. I didn't have to take my emotional temperature to see if inspiration was pending. I simply wrote. No negotiations. Good, bad? None of my business. *I* wasn't doing it. By resigning as the self-conscious author, I wrote freely.

In retrospect, I am astounded I could let go of the drama of being a suffering artist. Nothing dies harder than a bad idea. And few ideas are worse than the ones we have about art. We can charge so many things off to our suffering-artist identity: drunkenness, promiscuity, fiscal problems, a certain ruthlessness or self-destructiveness in matters of the heart. We all know how broke-crazy-promiscuous-unreliable artists are. And if they don't have to be, then what's my excuse?

The idea that I could be sane, sober, and creative terrified me, implying, as it did, the possibility of personal accountability. "You mean if I have these gifts, I'm supposed to use them?" Yes.

Providentially, I was sent another blocked writer to work with—and on—at this time. I began to teach him what I was learning. (Get out of the way. Let *it* work through you. Accumulate pages, not judgments.) He, too, began to unblock. Now there were two of us. Soon I had another "victim," this one a painter. The tools worked for visual artists, too.

This was very exciting to me. In my grander moments, I imagined I was turning into a creative cartographer, mapping a way out of confusion for myself and for whoever wanted to follow. I *never* planned to become a teacher. I was only angry I'd never had a teacher myself. Why did I have to learn what I learned the way I learned it: all by trial and error, all by walking into walls? We artists should be more teachable, I thought. Shortcuts and hazards of the trial could be flagged.

These were the thoughts that eddied with me as I took my afternoon walks—enjoying the light off the Hudson, plotting what I would write next. Enter the marching orders: I was to teach.

Within a week, I was offered a teaching position and space at the New York Feminist Art Institute—which I had never heard of. My first class—blocked painters, novelists, poets, and filmmakers—assembled itself. I began teaching them the lessons that are now in this book. Since that class there have been many others, and many more lessons as well.

The Artist's Way began as informal class notes mandated by my partner, Mark Bryan. As word of mouth spread, I began mailing out packets of materials. A peripatetic Jungian, John Giannini, spread word of the techniques wherever he lectured—seemingly everywhere. Requests for materials always followed. Next, the creation spirituality network got word of the work, and people wrote in from Dubuque, British Columbia, Indiana. Students materialized all over the globe. "I am in Switzerland with the State Department. Please send me . . ." So I did.

> *God must become an activity in our consciousness.*
>
> JOEL S. GOLDSMITH

The packets expanded and the number of students expanded. Finally, as the result of some *very* pointed urging from Mark—"Write it *all* down. You can help a lot of people. It should be a *book*"—I began formally to assemble my thoughts. I wrote and Mark, who was by this time my co-teacher and taskmaster, told me what I had left out. I wrote more and Mark told me what I had *still* left out. He reminded me that I had seen plenty of miracles to support my theories and urged me to include those, too. I put on the page what I had been putting into practice for a decade.

The resulting pages emerged as a blueprint for do-it-yourself recovery. Like mouth-to-mouth resuscitation or the Heimlich maneuver, the tools in this book are intended as life-savers. Please use them and pass them on.

Many times, I've heard words to this effect: "Before I took your class, I was completely separate from my creativity. The years of bitterness and loss had taken their toll. Then, gradually, the miracle started to happen. I have gone back to school to get my degree in theater, I'm auditioning for the first time in years, I'm writing on a steady basis—and, most important of all, I finally feel comfortable calling myself an artist."

I doubt I can convey to you the feeling of the miraculous that I experience as a teacher, witnessing the before and after in the lives of students. Over the duration of the course, the sheer physical transformation can be startling, making me realize that the term *enlightenment* is a literal one. Students' faces often take on a glow as they contact their creative energies. The same charged spiritual atmosphere that fills a great work of art can fill a creativity class. In a sense, as we are creative beings, our lives become our work of art.

Spiritual Electricity
The Basic Principles

FOR MOST OF US, the idea that the creator encourages creativity is a radical thought. We tend to think, or at least fear, that creative dreams are egotistical, something that God wouldn't approve of for us. After all, our creative artist is an inner youngster and prone to childish thinking. If our mom or dad expressed doubt or disapproval for our creative dreams, we may project that same attitude onto a parental god. This thinking must be undone.

What we are talking about is an induced—or invited—spiritual experience. I refer to this process as a *spiritual chiropractic*. We undertake certain spiritual exercises to achieve alignment with the creative energy of the universe.

If you think of the universe as a vast electrical sea in which you are immersed and from which you are formed, opening to your creativity changes you from something bobbing in that sea to a more fully functioning, more conscious, more cooperative part of that ecosystem.

As a teacher, I often sense the presence of something transcendent—a spiritual electricity, if you will—and I have come to rely on it in transcending my own limitations. I take the phrase *inspired teacher* to be a quite literal compliment. A higher hand than just my own engages us. Christ said, "Wherever two or more are gathered together, there I am in your midst." The god of creativity seems to feel the same way.

The heart of creativity is an experience of the mystical union; the heart of the mystical union is an experience of creativity. Those who speak in spiritual terms

The music of this opera [Madame Butterfly] was dictated to me by God; I was merely instrumental in putting it on paper and communicating it to the public.

GIACOMO PUCCINI

Straightaway the ideas flow in upon me, directly from God.

JOHANNES BRAHMS

We must accept that this creative pulse within us is God's creative pulse itself.

JOSEPH CHILTON PEARCE

It is the creative potential itself in human beings that is the image of God.

MARY DALY

routinely refer to God as the creator but seldom see *creator* as the literal term for *artist*. I am suggesting you take the term *creator* quite literally. You are seeking to forge a creative alliance, artist-to-artist with the Great Creator. Accepting this concept can greatly expand your creative possibilities.

As you work with the tools in this book, as you undertake the weekly tasks, many changes will be set in motion. Chief among these changes will be the triggering of *synchronicity*: we change and the universe furthers and expands that change. I have an irreverent shorthand for this that I keep taped to my writing desk: "Leap, and the net will appear."

It is my experience both as an artist and as a teacher that when we move out on faith into the act of creation, the universe is able to advance. It is a little like opening the gate at the top of a field irrigation system. Once we remove the blocks, the flow moves in.

Again, I do not ask you to *believe* this. In order for this creative emergence to happen, you don't have to believe in God. I simply ask you to observe and note this process as it unfolds. In effect, you will be midwiving and witnessing your own creative progression.

Creativity is an experience—to my eye, a spiritual experience. It does not matter which way you think of it: creativity leading to spirituality or spirituality leading to creativity. In fact, I do not make a distinction between the two. In the face of such experience, the whole question of belief is rendered obsolete. As Carl Jung answered the question of belief late in his life, "I don't believe; I know."

The following spiritual principles are the bedrock on which creative recovery and discovery can be built. Read them through once a day, and keep an inner ear cocked for any shifts in attitudes or beliefs.

Basic Principles

1. Creativity is the natural order of life. Life is energy: pure creative energy.
2. There is an underlying, in-dwelling creative force infusing all of life—including ourselves.
3. When we open ourselves to our creativity, we open ourselves to the creator's creativity within us and our lives.
4. We are, ourselves, creations. And we, in turn, are meant to continue creativity by being creative ourselves.
5. Creativity is God's gift to us. Using our creativity is our gift back to God.
6. The refusal to be creative is self-will and is counter to our true nature.
7. When we open ourselves to exploring our creativity, we open ourselves to God: good orderly direction.
8. As we open our creative channel to the creator, many gentle but powerful changes are to be expected.
9. It is safe to open ourselves up to greater and greater creativity.
10. Our creative dreams and yearnings come from a divine source. As we move toward our dreams, we move toward our divinity.

How to Use This Book for Your Creative Recovery

There are a number of ways to use this book. Most of all, I invite you to use it creatively. This section offers you a sort of road map through the process, with some specific ideas about how to proceed. Some students have done the course solo; others have formed circles to work through the book together. (In the back of the book, you'll find guidelines about doing the work in groups.) No matter which way you choose, *The Artist's Way* will work for you.

First, you may want to glance through the book to get a sense of the territory covered. (Reading the book through is not the same as using it.) Each chapter

I paint not by sight but by faith. Faith gives you sight.

AMOS FERGUSON

Why should we all use our creative power. . . ? Because there is nothing that makes people so generous, joyful, lively, bold and compassionate, so indifferent to fighting and the accumulation of objects and money.

BRENDA UELAND

includes essays, exercises, tasks, and a weekly check-in. Don't be daunted by the amount of work it seems to entail. Much of the work is really play, and the course takes little more than one hour a day.

When I am formally teaching, I suggest students set a weekly schedule. For example, if you're going to work a Sunday-to-Sunday week, begin by reading the chapter of the week on Sunday night. After you've read the chapter, speed-write through the exercises. The exercises in each week are critical. So are the morning pages and the artist date. (More about these in the next chapter.) You probably won't have time to complete all of the other tasks in any given week. Try to do about half. Know that the rest are there for use when you are able to get back to them. In choosing which half of the tasks to do, use two guidelines. Pick those that appeal to you and those you strongly resist. Leave the more neutral ones for later. Just remember, in choosing, that we often resist what we most need.

In all, make a time commitment of about seven to ten hours a week—an hour a day, or slightly more if you choose. This modest commitment to using the tools can yield tremendous results within the twelve weeks of the course. The same tools, used over a longer period, can alter the trajectory of a lifetime.

In working with this book, remember that *The Artist's Way* is a spiral path. You will circle through some of the issues over and over, each time at a different level. There is no such thing as being done with an artistic life. Frustrations and rewards exist at all levels on the path. Our aim here is to find the trail, establish our footing, and begin the climb. The creative vistas that open will quickly excite you.

What to Expect

Many of us wish we were more creative. Many of us sense we *are* more creative, but unable to effectively tap that creativity. Our dreams elude us. Our lives feel somehow flat. Often, we have great ideas, wonderful dreams, but are unable to actualize them for ourselves. Sometimes we have specific creative longings we would love to be able to fulfill—learning to play the piano, painting, taking an acting class, or writing. Sometimes our goal is more diffuse. We hunger for what might be called creative living—an expanded sense of creativity in our business lives, in sharing with our children, our spouse, our friends.

While there is no quick fix for instant, pain-free creativity, creative recovery (or discovery) is a teachable, trackable spiritual process. Each of us is complex and highly individual, yet there are common recognizable denominators to the creative recovery process.

Working with this process, I see a certain amount of defiance and giddiness in the first few weeks. This entry stage is followed closely by explosive anger in the course's midsection. The anger is followed by grief, then alternating waves of resistance and hope. This peaks-and-valleys phase of growth becomes a series of expansions and contractions, a birthing process in which students experience intense elation and defensive skepticism.

This choppy growth phase is followed by a strong urge to abandon the process and return to life as we know it. In other words, a bargaining period. People are often tempted to abandon the course at this point. I call this a creative U-turn. Recommitment to the process next triggers the free-fall of a major ego surrender. Following this, the final phase of the course is characterized by a new sense of self marked by increased autonomy, resilience, expectancy, and excitement—as well as by the capacity to make and execute concrete creative plans.

If this sounds like a lot of emotional tumult, it is. When we engage in a creativity recovery, we enter into a withdrawal process from life as we know it. *Withdrawal* is another way of saying *detachment* or *nonattachment*, which is emblematic of consistent work with any meditation practice.

In movie terms, we slowly *pull focus*, lifting up and away from being embedded in our lives until we attain an overview. This overview empowers us to make valid creative choices. Think of it as a journey with difficult, varied, and fascinating terrain. You are moving to higher ground. The fruit of your withdrawal is what you need to understand as a positive process, both painful and exhilarating.

Many of us find that we have squandered our own creative energies by investing disproportionately in the lives, hopes, dreams, and plans of others. Their lives have

The purpose of art is not a rarified, intellectual distillate—it is life, intensified, brilliant life.

ALAIN ARIAS-MISSON

What lies behind us and what lies before us are tiny matters, compared to what lies within us.

RALPH WALDO EMERSON

obscured and detoured our own. As we consolidate a core through our withdrawal process, we become more able to articulate our own boundaries, dreams, and authentic goals. Our personal flexibility increases while our malleability to the whims of others decreases. We experience a heightened sense of autonomy and possibility.

Ordinarily, when we speak of withdrawal, we think of having a substance removed from us. We give up alcohol, drugs, sugar, fats, caffeine, nicotine—and we suffer a withdrawal. It's useful to view creative withdrawal a little differently. We ourselves are the substance we withdraw *to*, not from, as we pull our overextended and misplaced creative energy back into our own core.

We begin to excavate our buried dreams. This is a tricky process. Some of our dreams are very volatile, and the mere act of brushing them off sends an enormous surge of energy bolting through our denial system. Such grief! Such loss! Such pain! It is at this point in the recovery process that we make what Robert Bly calls a "descent into ashes." We mourn the self we abandoned. We greet this self as we might greet a lover at the end of a long and costly war.

To effect a creative recovery, we must undergo a time of mourning. In dealing with the suicide of the "nice" self we have been making do with, we find a certain amount of grief to be essential. Our tears prepare the ground for our future growth. Without this creative moistening, we may remain barren. We must allow the bolt of pain to strike us. Remember, this is useful pain; lighting illuminates.

How do you know if you are creatively blocked? Jealousy is an excellent clue. Are there artists whom you resent? Do you tell yourself, "I could do that, if only . . ." Do you tell yourself that if only you took your creative potential seriously, you might:

- Stop telling yourself, "It's too late."
- Stop waiting until you make enough money to do something you'd really love.
- Stop telling yourself, "It's just my ego" whenever you yearn for a more creative life.
- Stop telling yourself that dreams don't matter, that they are only dreams and that you should be more sensible.
- Stop fearing that your family and friends would think you crazy.
- Stop telling yourself that creativity is a luxury and that you should be grateful for what you've got.

As you learn to recognize, nurture, and protect your inner artist, you will be able to move beyond pain and creative constriction. You will learn ways to recognize and resolve fear, remove emotional scar tissue, and strengthen your confidence. Damaging old ideas about creativity will be explored and discarded. Working with this book, you will experience an intensive, guided encounter with your own creativity—your private villains, champions, wishes, fears, dreams, hopes, and triumphs. The experience will make you excited, depressed, angry, afraid, joyous, hopeful, and, ultimately, more free.

8/28/2018

The Basic Tools

THERE ARE TWO PIVOTAL tools in creative recovery: *the morning pages* and *the artist date*. A lasting creative awakening requires the consistent use of both. I like to introduce them both immediately, and at sufficient length to answer most of your questions. This chapter explains these tools carefully and in depth. Please read it with special care and begin the immediate use of both tools.

The Morning Pages

In order to retrieve your creativity, you need to find it. I ask you to do this by an apparently pointless process I call *the morning pages*. You will do the pages daily through all the weeks of the course and, I hope, much longer. I have been doing them for a decade now. I have students who have worked with them nearly that long and who would no more abandon them than breathing.

Ginny, a writer-producer, credits the morning pages with inspiration for her recent screenplays and clarity in planning her network specials. "I'm superstitious about them by now," she says. "When I was editing my last special, I would get up at 5:00 A.M. to get them done before I went in to work."

What are morning pages? Put simply, the morning pages are three pages of longhand writing, strictly stream-of-consciousness: "Oh, god, another morning. I have NOTHING to say. I need to wash the curtains. Did I get my laundry yesterday? Blah, blah, blah . . ." They might also, more ingloriously, be called *brain drain*, since that is one of their main functions.

There is no wrong way to do morning pages. These daily morning meanderings are not meant to be *art*. Or even *writing*. I stress that point to reassure the nonwriters working with this book. Writing

> *Words are a form of action, capable of influencing change.*
>
> INGRID BENGIS

> *You need to claim the events of your life to make yourself yours.*
>
> ANNE-WILSON SCHAEF

is simply one of the tools. Pages are meant to be, simply, the act of moving the hand across the page and writing down *whatever* comes to mind. Nothing is too petty, too silly, too stupid, or too weird to be included.

The morning pages are not supposed to sound smart—although sometimes they might. Most times they won't, and nobody will ever know except you. Nobody is allowed to read your morning pages except you. And you shouldn't even read them yourself for the first eight weeks or so. Just write three pages, and stick them into an envelope. Or write three pages in a spiral notebook and don't leaf back through. *Just write three pages* . . . and write three more pages the next day.

> September 30, 1991 . . . Over the weekend, for Domenica's biology project, she and I went bug hunting on the Rio Grande and Pott Creek. We collected water crawlies and butterflies. I made a crimson homemade butterfly net that was quite functional although dragonflies eluded us to our dismay. We did not catch the tarantula strolling down the dirt road near our house. We just enjoyed spotting it.

Although occasionally colorful, the morning pages are often negative, frequently fragmented, often self-pitying, repetitive, stilted or babyish, angry or bland—even silly sounding. Good!

> Oct. 2, 1991 . . . I am up and have had a headache and have taken aspirin and feel a little better although still shaky. I may have that flu after all. I am getting to the bottom of a lot of unpacking and still no teapot from Laura whom I am sorely missing. What a heartbreak . . .

All that angry, whiny, petty stuff that you write down in the morning stands between you and your creativity. Worrying about the job, the laundry, the funny knock in the car, the weird look in your lover's eye—this stuff eddies through our subconscious and muddies our days. Get it on the page.

The morning pages are the primary tool of creative recovery. As blocked artists, we tend to criticize ourselves mercilessly. Even if we look like functioning artists to the world, we feel we never do enough and what we do isn't right. We are victims of our own internalized perfectionist, a nasty internal and eternal critic, the Censor, who resides in our (left) brain and keeps up a constant stream of subversive remarks that are often disguised as the truth. The Censor says wonderful things like: "You call that writing? What a joke. You can't even punctuate. If you haven't done it by now you never will. You can't even spell. What makes you think you can be creative?" And on and on.

Make this a rule: always remember that your Censor's negative opinions are not the truth. This takes practice. By spilling out of bed and straight onto the page every morning, you learn to evade the Censor. Because there is no wrong way to write the morning pages, the Censor's opinion doesn't count. Let your Censor rattle on. (And it will.) Just keep your hand moving across the page. Write down the Censor's thoughts if you want to. Note how it loves to aim for your creative jugular. Make no mistake: the Censor is out to get you. It's a cunning foe. Every time you get smarter, so does it. So you wrote one good play? The Censor tells you that's all there is. So you drew your first sketch? The Censor says, "It's not Picasso."

A mind too active is no mind at all.

THEODORE ROETHKE

The events in our lives happen in a sequence in time, but in their significance to ourselves, they find their own order . . . the continuous thread of revelation.

EUDORA WELTY

Think of your Censor as a cartoon serpent, slithering around your creative Eden, hissing vile things to keep you off guard. If a serpent doesn't appeal to you, you might want to find a good cartoon image of your Censor, maybe the shark from *Jaws*, and put an X through it. Post it where you tend to write or on the inside cover of your notebook. Just making the Censor into the nasty, clever little character that it is begins to pry loose some of its power over you and your creativity.

More than one student has tacked up an unflattering picture of the parent responsible for the Censor's installation in his or her psyche and called that his or her Censor. The point is to stop taking the Censor as the voice of reason and learn to hear it for the blocking device that it is. Morning pages will help you to do this.

Morning pages are nonnegotiable. Never skip or skimp on morning pages. Your mood doesn't matter. The rotten thing your Censor says doesn't matter. We have this idea that we need to be in the mood to write. We don't.

Morning pages will teach you that your mood doesn't really matter. Some of the best creative work gets done on the days when you feel that everything you're doing is just plain junk. The morning pages will teach you to stop judging and just let yourself write. So what if you're tired, crabby, distracted, stressed? Your artist is a child and it needs to be fed. Morning pages feed your artist child. So write your morning pages.

Three pages of whatever crosses your mind—that's all there is to it. If you can't think of anything to write, then write, "I can't think of anything to write. . . ." Do this until you have filled three pages. *Do anything until you have filled three pages.*

When people ask, "Why do we write morning pages?" I joke, "To get to the other side." They think I am kidding, but I'm not. Morning pages do get us to the other side: the other side of our fear, of our negativity, of our moods. Above all, they get us beyond our Censor. Beyond the reach of the Censor's babble we find our own quiet center, the place where we hear the still, small voice that is at once our creator's and our own.

A word is in order here about logic brain and artist brain. *Logic brain* is our brain of choice in the Western Hemisphere. It is the categorical brain. It thinks in a neat, linear fashion. As a rule, logic brain perceives the world according to known categories. A horse is a certain combination of animal parts that make up a horse. A fall forest is viewed as a series of colors that add up to "fall forest." It looks at a fall forest and notes: red, orange, yellow, green, gold.

Poetry often enters through the window of irrelevance.

M. C. RICHARDS

Logic brain was and is our survival brain. It works on known principles. Anything unknown is perceived as wrong and possibly dangerous. Logic brain likes things to be neat little soldiers marching in a straight line. Logic brain is the brain we usually listen to, especially when we are telling ourselves to be sensible.

Logic brain is our Censor, our second (and third and fourth) thoughts. Faced with an original sentence, phrase, paint squiggle, it says, "What the hell is that? That's not right!"

Artist brain is our inventor, our child, our very own personal absent-minded professor. Artist brain says, "Hey! That is so neat!" It puts odd things together (boat equals wave and walker). It likes calling a speeding GTO a wild animal: "The black howling wolf pulled into the drive-in . . ."

Artist brain is our creative, holistic brain. It thinks in patterns and shadings. It sees a fall forest and thinks: Wow! Leaf bouquet! Pretty! Gold-gilt-shimmery-earthskin-king's-carpet! Artist brain is associative and freewheeling. It makes new connections, yoking together images to invoke meaning: like the Norse myths calling a boat "wave-horse." In *Star Wars*, the name Skywalker is a lovely artist-brain flash.

Why all this logic-brain/artist-brain talk? Because the morning pages teach logic brain to stand aside and let artist brain play.

The Censor is part of our leftover survival brain. It was the part in charge of deciding whether it was safe for us to leave the forest and go out into the meadow. Our Censor scans our creative meadow for any dangerous beasties. Any original thought can look pretty dangerous to our Censor.

The only sentences/paintings/sculptures/photographs it likes are ones that it has seen many times before. Safe sentences. Safe paintings. Not exploratory blurts, squiggles, or jottings. Listen to your Censor and it will tell you that everything original is wrong/dangerous/rotten.

Who wouldn't be blocked if every time you tiptoed into the open somebody (your Censor) made fun of you? The morning pages will teach you to stop listening to that ridicule. They will allow you to detach from your negative Censor.

It may be useful for you to think of the morning pages as meditation. It may not be the practice of meditation you are accustomed to. You may, in fact, not be accustomed to meditating at all. The pages may not seem spiritual or even meditative—more like negative and materialistic, actually—but they are a valid form of meditation that gives us insight and helps us effect change in our lives.

Let's take a look at what we stand to gain by meditating. There are many ways of thinking about meditation. Scientists speak of it in terms of brain hemispheres and shunting techniques. We move from logic brain to artist brain and from fast to slow, shallow to deep. Management consultants, in pursuit of corporate physical health, have learned to think of meditation primarily as a stress-management technique. Spiritual seekers choose to view the process as a gateway to God. Artists and creativity mavens approve of it as a conduit for higher creative insights.

> Inspiration may be a form of superconsciousness, or perhaps of subconsciousness—I wouldn't know. But I am sure it is the antithesis of self-consciousness.
>
> AARON COPLAND

All of these notions are true—as far as they go. They do not go far enough. Yes, we will alter our brain hemisphere, lower our stress, discover an inner contact with a creative source, and have many creative insights. Yes, for any one of these reasons, the pursuit is a worthy one. Even taken in combination, however, they are still intellectual constructs for what is primarily an experience of wholeness, rightness, and power.

We meditate to discover our own identity, our right place in the scheme of the universe. Through meditation, we acquire and eventually acknowledge our connection to an inner power source that has the ability to transform our outer world. In other words, meditation gives us not only the light of insight but also the power for expansive change.

Insight in and of itself is an intellectual comfort. Power in and of itself is a blind force that can destroy as easily as build. It is only when we consciously learn to link power and light that we begin to feel our rightful identities as creative beings. The morning pages allow us to forge this link. They provide us with a spiritual ham-radio set to contact the Creator Within. For this reason, the morning pages are a spiritual practice.

It is impossible to write morning pages for any extended period of time without coming into contact with an unexpected inner power. Although I used them for many years before I realized this, the pages are a pathway to a strong and clear sense of self. They are a trail that we follow into our own interior, where we meet both our own creativity and our creator.

> It always comes back to the same necessity: go deep enough and there is a bedrock of truth, however hard.
>
> MAY SARTON

Morning pages map our own interior. Without them, our dreams may remain terra incognita. I know mine did. Using them, the light of insight is coupled with the power for expansive change. It is very difficult to complain about a situation morning after morning, month after month, without being moved to constructive action. The pages lead us out of despair and into undreamed-of solutions.

The first time I did morning pages, I was living in Taos, New Mexico. I had gone there to sort myself out—into what, I didn't know. For the third time in a row, I'd had a film scuttled due to studio politics. Such disasters are routine to screenwriters, but to me they felt like miscarriages. Cumulatively, they were disastrous. I wanted to give the movies up. Movies had broken my heart. I didn't want any more brainchildren to meet untimely deaths. I'd gone to New Mexico to mend my heart and see what else, if anything, I might want to do.

Living in a small adobe house that looked north to Taos Mountain, I began a practice of writing morning pages. Nobody told me to do them. I had never heard of anybody doing them. I just got the insistent, inner sense that I should do them and so I did. I sat at a wooden table looking north to Taos Mountain and I wrote.

The morning pages were my pastime, something to do instead of staring at the mountain all the time. The mountain, a humpbacked marvel different in every weather, raised more questions than I did. Wrapped in clouds one day, dark and wet the next, that mountain dominated my view and my morning pages as well. What did it—or anything—mean? I asked page after page, morning after morning. No answer.

And then, one wet morning, a character named Johnny came strolling into my pages. Without planning to, I was writing a novel. The morning pages had shown me a way.

Anyone who faithfully writes morning pages will be led to a connection with a source of wisdom within. When I am stuck with a painful situation or problem that I don't think I know how to handle, I will go to the pages and ask for guidance. To do this, I write "LJ" as a shorthand for me, "Little Julie," and then I ask my question.

LJ: What should I tell them about this inner wisdom? (Then I listen for the reply and write that down, too.)

ANSWER: You should tell them everyone has a direct dial to God. No one needs to go through an operator. Tell them to try this technique with a problem of their own. They will.

Sometimes, as above, the answer may seem flippant or too simple. I have come to believe that *seem* is the operative word. Very often, when I act on the advice I have been given, it is exactly right—far more right than something more complicated would have been. And so, for the record, I want to say: pages are my way of meditating; I do them because they work.

A final assurance: the morning pages will work for painters, for sculptors, for poets, for actors, for lawyers, for housewives—for anyone who wants to try anyting creative. Don't think they are a tool for writers only. Hooey. These pages are not intended for writers only. Lawyers who use them swear they make them more effective in court. Dancers claim their balance improves—and not just emotionally. If anything, writers, who have a regrettable desire to *write* morning pages instead of just do them, may have the hardest time seeing their impact. What they're likely to see is that their other writing seems to suddenly be far more free and expansive and somehow easy to do. In short, no matter what your reservation or your occupation, morning pages will function for you.

> *Like an ability or a muscle, hearing your inner wisdom is strengthened by doing it.*
>
> ROBBIE GASS

> *It is in the knowledge of the genuine conditions of our lives that we must draw our strength to live and our reasons for living.*
>
> SIMONE DE BEAUVOIR

Timothy, a buttoned-down, buttoned-lip curmudgeon millionaire, began writing morning pages with a skeptic's scorn. He didn't want to do them without some proof that they would work. The damn pages had no label, no Dun and Bradstreet rating. They just sounded silly, and Timothy hated silly.

Timothy was, in street parlance, a serious player. His poker face was so straight it looked more like a fireplace poker than a mere cardsharp's defense. Practiced for years in the corporate board room, Timothy's invincible facade was as dark, shiny, and expensive as mahogany. No emotions scratched the surface of this man's calm. He was a one-man monument to the Masculine Mystique.

"Oh, all right . . ." Timothy agreed to the pages, but only because he had paid good money to be told to do them. Within three weeks, straightlaced, pin-striped Timothy became a morning-pages advocate. The results of his work with them convinced him. He started—heaven forbid—to have a little creative fun. "I bought guitar strings for this old guitar I had lying around," he reported one week. And then, "I rewired my stereo. I bought some wonderful Italian recordings." Although he hesitated to acknowledge it, even to himself, Timothy's writer's block was melting. Up at dawn, Gregorian chant on the stereo, he was writing freely.

> *Painting is just another way of keeping a diary.*
>
> PABLO PICASSO

> *Experience, even for a painter, is not exclusively visual.*
>
> WALTER MEIGS

Not everyone undertakes the morning pages with such obvious antagonism. Phyllis, a leggy, racehorse socialite who for years had hidden her brains behind her beauty and her life behind her man's, tried the morning pages with a great deal of surface cheer—and an inner conviction they would never work for her. It had been ten years since she had allowed herself to write anything other than letters and bread-and-butter lists. About a month into morning pages, seemingly out of nowhere, Phyllis got her first poem. In the three years she has used pages since, she has written poems, speeches, radio shows, and a nonfiction book.

Anton, grumpy but graceful in his use of the pages, accomplished unblocking as an actor. Laura, talented but blocked as a writer, painter, and musician, found that the morning pages moved her to her piano, typewriter, and paint supplies.

While you may undertake this course with an agenda as to what you want unblocked, the tools may free creative areas you have long ignored or even been blind to. Ingeborg, using the pages to unblock her creative writer, moved from being one of Germany's top music critics to composing for the first time in twenty years. She was stunned and made several ecstatic transatlantic calls to share her good news.

Often, the students most resistant to morning pages come to love them the best. In fact, hating the morning pages is a very good sign. Loving them is a good sign, too, if you keep writing even when you suddenly don't. A neutral attitude is the third position, but it's really just a defensive strategy that may mask boredom.

Boredom is just "What's the use?" in disguise. And "What's the use?" is fear, and fear means you are secretly in despair. So put your fears on the page. Put anything on the page. Put three pages of it on the page.

The Artist Date

The other basic tool of *The Artist's Way* may strike you as a nontool, a diversion. You may see clearly how morning pages could work yet find yourself highly dubious about something called an *artist date*. I assure you, artist dates work, too.

Think of this combination of tools in terms of a radio receiver and transmitter. It is a two-step, two-directional process: *out* and then *in*. Doing your morning pages, you are sending—notifying yourself and the universe of your dreams, dissatisfactions, hopes. Doing your artist date, you are receiving—opening yourself to insight, inspiration, guidance.

> *The most potent muse of all is our own inner child.*
>
> STEPHEN NACHMANOVITCH

> *At the height of laughter, the universe is flung into a kaleidoscope of new possibilities.*
>
> JEAN HOUSTON

But what exactly *is* an artist date? An artist date is a block of time, perhaps two hours weekly, especially set aside and committed to nurturing your creative consciousness, your inner artist. In its most primary form, the artist date is an excursion, a play date that you preplan and defend against all interlopers. You do not take anyone on this artist date but you and your inner artist, a.k.a. your creative child. That means no lovers, friends, spouses, children—no taggers-on of any stripe.

If you think this sounds stupid or that you will never be able to afford the time, identify that reaction as resistance. You cannot afford *not* to find time for artist dates.

"Do you spend quality time with each other?" troubled couples are often asked by their therapist. Parents of disturbed children are asked the same thing.

"Well . . . what do you mean, 'quality time'?" is the usual weasely response. "We spend a lot of time together."

"Yes . . . but is it quality time? Do you ever have any fun together?" the therapist may press.

"Fun?" (Whoever heard of having fun in a rotten relationship like this one?)

"Do you go on dates? Just to talk? Just to listen to each other?"

"Dates? . . . But we're married, too busy, too broke, too—"

"Too scared," the therapist may interrupt. (Hey, don't sugarcoat it.)

It *is* frightening to spend quality time with a child or lover, and our artist can be seen as both to us. A weekly artist date is remarkably threatening—and remarkably productive.

> *The creation of something new is not accomplished by the intellect but by the play instinct acting from inner necessity. The creative mind plays with the objects it loves.*
>
> C. G. JUNG

A date? With my artist?

Yes. Your artist needs to be taken out, pampered, and listened to. There are as many ways to evade this commitment as there are days of your life. "I'm too broke" is the favored one, although no one said the date need involve elaborate expenses.

Your artist is a child. Time with a parent matters more than monies spent. A visit to a great junk store, a solo trip to the beach, an old movie seen alone together, a visit to an aquarium or an art gallery—these cost time, not money. Remember, it is the time commitment that is sacred.

In looking for a parallel, think of the child of divorce who gets to see a beloved parent only on weekends. (During most of the week, your artist is in the custody of a stern, workaday adult.) What that child wants is attention, not expensive outings. What that child does not want is to share the precious parent with someone like the new significant other.

Spending time in solitude with your artist child is essential to self-nurturing. A long country walk, a solitary expedition to the beach for a sunrise or sunset, a sortie out to a strange church to hear gospel music, to an ethnic neighborhood to taste foreign sights and sounds—your artist might enjoy any of these. Or your artist might like bowling.

Commit yourself to a weekly artist's date, and then watch your killjoy side try to wriggle out of it. Watch how this sacred time gets easily encroached upon. Watch how the sacred time suddenly includes a third party. Learn to guard against these invasions.

Above all, learn to listen to what your artist child has to say on, and about, these joint expeditions. For example, "Oh, I hate this serious stuff," your artist may exclaim if you persist in taking it only to grown-up places that are culturally edifying and good for it.

Listen to that! It is telling you your art needs more playful inflow. A little fun can go a long way toward making your work feel more like play. We forget that the imagination-at-play is at the heart of all good work. And increasing our capacity for good creative work is what this book is about.

You are likely to find yourself avoiding your artist dates. Recognize this resistance as a fear of intimacy—*self*-intimacy. Often in troubled relationships, we settle into an avoidance pattern with our significant others. We don't want to hear what they are thinking because it just might hurt. So we avoid them, knowing that, once they get the chance, our significant others will probably blurt out something we do not want to hear. It is possible they will want an answer we do not have and can't give them. It is equally possible we might do the same to them and that then the two of us will stare at each other in astonishment, saying, "But I never knew you felt like that!"

It is probable that these self-disclosures, frightening though they are, will lead to the building of a real relationship, one in which the participants are free to be who they are and to become what they wish. This possibility is what makes the risks of self-disclosure and true intimacy profitable. In order to have a real relationship with our creativity, we must take the time and care to cultivate it. Our creativity will use this time to confront us, to confide in us, to bond with us, and to plan.

The morning pages acquaint us with what we think and what we think we need. We identify problem areas and concerns. We complain, enumerate, identify, isolate, fret. This is step one, analogous to prayer. In the course of the release engendered by our artist date, step two, we begin to hear solutions. Perhaps equally important, we begin to fund the creative reserves we will draw on in fulfilling our artistry.

> *Every child is an artist. The problem is how to remain an artist once he grows up.*
>
> PABLO PICASSO

> *During [these] periods of relaxation after concentrated intellectual activity, the intuitive mind seems to take over and can produce the sudden clarifying insights which give so much joy and delight.*
>
> FRITJOF CAPRA
> PHYSICIST

Filling the Well, Stocking the Pond

Art is an image-using system. In order to create, we draw from our inner well. This inner well, an artistic reservoir, is ideally like a well-stocked trout pond. We've got big fish, little fish, fat fish, skinny fish—an abundance of artistic fish to fry. As artists, we must realize that we have to maintain this artistic ecosystem. If we don't give some attention to upkeep, our well is apt to become depleted, stagnant, or blocked.

Any extended period or piece of work draws heavily on our artistic well. Overtapping the well, like overfishing the pond, leaves us with diminished resources. We fish in vain for the images we require. Our work dries up and we wonder why, "just when it was going so well." The truth is that work can dry up *because* it is going so well.

As artists, we must learn to be self-nourishing. We must become alert enough to consciously replenish our creative resources as we draw on them—to restock the trout pond, so to speak. I call this process *filling the well*.

Filling the well involves the active pursuit of images to refresh our artistic reservoirs. Art is born in attention. Its mid-wife is detail. Art may seem to spring from pain, but perhaps that is because pain serves to focus our attention onto details (for instance, the excruciatingly beautiful curve of a lost lover's neck). Art may seem to involve broad strokes, grand schemes, great plans. But it is the attention to detail that stays with us; the singular image is what haunts us and becomes art. Even in the midst of pain, this singular image brings delight. The artist who tells you different is lying.

In order to function in the language of art, we must learn to live in it comfortably. The language of art is image, symbol. It is a wordless language even when our very art is to chase it with words. The artist's language is a sensual one, a language of felt experience. When we work at our art, we dip into the well of our experience and scoop out images. Because we do this, we need to learn how to put images back. How do we fill the well?

> *Younger Self—who can be as balky and stubborn as the most cantankerous three-year-old—is not impressed by words. Like a native of Missouri, it wants to be shown. To arouse its interest, we must seduce it with pretty pictures and pleasurable sensations—take it out dining and dancing as it were. Only in this way can Deep Self be reached.*
>
> STARHAWK
> THEOLOGIAN

We feed it images. Art is an artist-brain pursuit. The artist brain is our image brain, home and haven to our best creative impulses. The artist brain cannot be reached—or triggered—effectively by words alone. The artist brain is the sensory brain: sight and sound, smell and taste, touch. These are the elements of magic, and magic is the elemental stuff of art.

In filling the well, think magic. Think delight. Think fun. Do not think duty. Do not do what you *should* do—spiritual sit-ups like reading a dull but recommended critical text. Do what intrigues you, explore what interests you; think mystery, not mastery.

A mystery draws us in, leads us on, lures us. (A duty may numb us out, turn us off, tune us out.) In filling the well, follow your sense of the mysterious, not your sense of what you should know more about. A mystery can be very simple: if I drive this road, not my usual road, what will I see? Changing a known route throws us into the now. We become refocused on the visible, visual world. Sight leads to insight.

A mystery can be simpler even than that: if I light this stick of incense, what will I feel? Scent is an often-overlooked pathway to powerful associations and healing. The scent of Christmas at any time of year—or the scent of fresh bread or home-made soup—can nourish the hungry artist within.

Some sounds lull us. Others stimulate us. Ten minutes of listening to a great piece of music can be a very effective meditation. Five minutes of barefoot dancing to drum music can send our artist into its play-fray-day refreshed.

Filling the well needn't be all novelty. Cooking can fill the well. When we chop and pare vegetables, we do so with our thoughts as well. Remember, art is an artist-brain pursuit. This brain is reached through rhythm—through rhyme, not reason. Scraping a carrot, peeling an apple—these actions are quite literally food for thought.

> *Nobody sees a flower—really—it is so small it takes time—we haven't time—and to see takes time, like to have a friend takes time.*
>
> GEORGIA O'KEEFFE

> *So you see, imagination needs moodling—long, inefficient, happy idling, dawdling and puttering.*
>
> BRENDA UELAND

Any regular, repetitive action primes the well. Writers have heard many woeful tales of the Brontë sisters and poor Jane Austen, forced to hide their stories under their needle-work. A little experiment with some mending can cast a whole new light on these activities. Needlework, by definition regular and repetitive, both soothes and stimulates the artist within. Whole plots can be stitched up while we sew. As artists, we can very literally reap what we sew.

"Why do I get my best ideas in the shower?" an exasperated Einstein is said to have remarked. Brain research now tells us that this is because showering is an artist-brain activity.

Showering, swimming, scrubbing, shaving, steering a car—so many *s-like-yes* words!—all of these are regular, repetitive activities that may tip us over from our logic brain into our more creative artist brain. Solutions to sticky creative problems may bubble up through the dishwater, emerge on the freeway just as we are executing a tricky merge . . .

The true mystery of the world is the visible, not the invisible.

OSCAR WILDE

Inside you there's an artist you don't know about . . . Say yes quickly, if you know, if you've known it from before the beginning of the universe.

JALAI UD-DIN RUMI

Learn which of these works best for you and use it. Many artists have found it useful to keep a notepad or tape recorder next to them as they drive. Steven Spielberg claims that his very best ideas have come to him as he was driving the freeways. This is no accident. Negotiating the flow of traffic, he was an artist immersed in an oncoming, ever-altering flow of images. Images trigger the artist brain. Images fill the well.

Our focused attention is critical to filling the well. We need to encounter our life experiences, not ignore them. Many of us read compulsively to screen our awareness. On a crowded (interesting) train, we train our attention on a newspaper, losing the sights and sounds around us—all images for the well.

Artist's block is a very literal expression. Blocks must be acknowledged and dislodged. Filling the well is the surest way to do this.

Art is the imagination at play in the field of time. Let yourself play.

Creativity Contract

When I am teaching the Artist's Way, I require students to make a contract with themselves, committing to the work of the course. Can you give yourself that gift? Say yes by means of some small ceremony. Buy a nice notebook for your pages; hire your babysitter ahead of time for the weekly artist dates. Read the contract below. Amend it, if you like; then sign and date it. Come back to it when you need encouragement to go on.

Contract

I, *Lana Panfilova*, understand that I am undertaking an intensive, guided encounter with my own creativity. I commit myself to the twelve-week duration of the course. I, *Lana* commit to weekly reading, daily morning pages, a weekly artist date, and the fulfillment of each week's tasks.

I, *Lana*, further understand that this course will raise issues and emotions for me to deal with. I, *Lana* commit myself to excellent self-care—adequate sleep, diet, exercise, and pampering—for the duration of the course.

_____*Lana Panfilova*_____ (signature)

_____*8/28/2018*_____ (date)

Recovering a Sense of Safety

This week initiates your creative recovery. You may feel both giddy and defiant, hopeful and skeptical. The readings, tasks, and exercises aim at allowing you to establish a sense of safety, which will enable you to explore your creativity with less fear.

Shadow Artists

ONE OF OUR CHIEF needs as creative beings is support. Unfortunately, this can be hard to come by. Ideally, we would be nurtured and encouraged first by our nuclear family and then by ever-widening circles of friends, teachers, well-wishers. As young artists, we need and want to be acknowledged for our attempts and efforts as well as for our achievements and triumphs. Unfortunately, many artists never receive this critical early encouragement. As a result, they may not know they are artists at all.

Parents seldom respond, "Try it and see what happens" to artistic urges issuing from their offspring. They offer cautionary advice where support might be more to the point. Timid young artists, adding parental fears to their own, often give up their sunny dreams of artistic careers, settling into the twilight world of could-have-beens and regrets. There, caught between the dream of action and the fear of failure, shadow artists are born.

I am thinking here of Edwin, a miserable millionaire trader whose joy in life comes from his art collection. Strongly gifted in the visual arts, he was urged as a child to go into finance. His father bought him a seat on the stock exchange for his twenty-first birthday. He has been a trader ever since. Now in his mid-thirties, he is very rich and very poor. Money cannot buy him creative fulfillment.

Surrounding himself with artists and artifacts, he is like the kid with his nose pressed to the candy-store window. He would love to be more creative but believes

*Nothing has a stronger
influence psychologically on
their environment and
especially on their children than
the unlived life of the parent.*

CARL JUNG

*I believe that if it were left to
artists to choose their own
labels, most would choose none.*

BEN SHAHN

that is the prerogative of others, nothing he can aspire to for himself. A generous man, he recently gifted an artist with a year's living expenses so she could pursue her dreams. Raised to believe that the term *artist* could not apply to him, he cannot make that same gift for himself.

Edwin's is not an isolated case. All too often the artistic urges of the artist child are ignored or suppressed. Often with the best intentions, parents try to foster a different, more sensible self for the child. "Stop daydreaming!" is one frequently heard admonition. "You'll never amount to anything if you keep on with you head in the clouds" is another.

Baby artists are urged to think and act like baby doctors or lawyers. A rare family, faced with the myth of the starving artist, tells its children to go right ahead and try for a career in the arts. Instead, if encouraged at all, the children are urged into thinking of the arts as hobbies, creative fluff around the edges of real life.

For many families, a career in the arts exists outside of their social and economic reality: "Art won't pay the electric bill." As a result, if the child is encouraged to consider art in job terms at all, he or she must consider it *sensibly*.

Erin, a gifted children's therapist, was in her mid-thirties before she began experiencing a haunting dissatisfaction in her work. Unsure what direction to take, she began adapting a children's book for the screen. Midway through the adaptation, she suddenly had a telling dream about abandoning her own artist child. Prior to becoming a therapist, she had been a gifted art student. For two decades, she had suppressed her creative urges, pouring all of her creativity into helping others. Now, nearly forty, she found herself longing to help herself.

Erin's story is all too common. Fledgling artists may be encouraged to be art teachers or to specialize in crafts with the handicapped. Young writers may be pushed toward lawyering, a talky, wordy profession, or into medical school because they're so smart. And so the child who is himself a born storyteller may be converted into a gifted therapist who gets his stories secondhand.

Too intimidated to become artists themselves, very often too low in self-worth to even recognize that they have an artistic dream, these people become shadow artists instead. Artists themselves but ignorant of their true identity, shadow artists are to be found shadowing declared artists. Unable to recognize that they themselves may possess the creativity they so admire, they often date or marry people who actively pursue the art career they themselves secretly long for.

When Jerry was still blocked as an artist, he began to date Lisa, a gifted but broke free-lance artist. "I am your biggest fan," he often told her. What he did not immediately tell her was that he himself dreamed of being a filmmaker. He had, in fact, an entire library of film books and avidly devoured special-interest magazines on filmmaking. But he was afraid to take steps to actualize his interest. Instead, he poured his time and attention into Lisa and Lisa's art career. Under his guidance, her career flourished. She became solvent and increasingly well known. Jerry remained blocked in his own behalf. When Lisa suggested he take a filmmaking course, he ran for cover. "Not everyone can be an artist," he told her—and himself.

Artists love other artists. Shadow artists are gravitating to their rightful tribe but cannot yet claim their birthright. Very often audacity, not talent, makes one person an artist and another a shadow artist—hiding in the shadows, afraid to step out and expose the dream to the light, fearful that it will disintegrate to the touch.

Shadow artists often choose shadow careers—those close to the desired art, even parallel to it, but not the art itself. Noting their venom, François Truffaut contended that critics were themselves blocked directors, as he had been when he was a critic. He may be right. Intended fiction writers often go into newspapering or advertising, where they can use their gift without taking the plunge into their dreamed-of fiction-writing career. Intended artists may become artist managers and derive a great deal of secondary pleasure from serving their dream even at one remove.

Carolyn, herself a gifted photographer, made a successful but unhappy career as a photographer's rep. Jean, who yearned to write feature films, wrote minimovies in her thirty-second commercial spots. Kelly, who wanted to be a writer but feared taking her creativity seriously, made a profitable career out of repping "really" creative people. Shadow artists all, these women needed to place themselves and their dreams stage center. They knew this, but didn't dare. They had been raised to the role of shadow artist and would need to work consciously to dismantle it.

It takes a great deal of ego strength to say to a well-meaning but domineering parent or a just plain domineering one, "Wait a minute! I am too an artist!" The dreaded

We have been taught to believe that negative equals realistic and positive equals unrealistic.

SUSAN JEFFERS

Do not weep; do not wax indignant. Understand.

BARUCH SPINOZA

response may come back, "How do you know?" And, of course, the fledgling artist does not *know*. There is just this dream, this feeling, this urge, this desire. There is seldom any real proof, but the dream lives on.

As a rule of thumb, shadow artists judge themselves harshly, beating themselves for years over the fact that they have not acted on their dreams. This cruelty only reinforces their status as shadow artists. Remember, it takes nurturing to make an artist. Shadow artists did not receive sufficient nurturing. They blame themselves for not acting fearlessly anyhow.

In a twisted version of Darwinian determinism, we tell ourselves that real artists can survive the most hostile environments and yet find their true calling like homing pigeons. That's hogwash. Many real artists bear children too early or have too many, are too poor or too far removed culturally or monetarily from artistic opportunity to become the artists they really are. These artists, shadow artists through no fault of their own, hear the distant piping of the dream but are unable to make their way through the cultural maze to find it.

> To live a creative life, we must lose our fear of being wrong.
>
> JOSEPH CHILTON PEARCE

> When you are feeling depreciated, angry or drained, it is a sign that other people are not open to your energy.
>
> SANAYA ROMAN

For all shadow artists, life may be a discontented experience, filled with a sense of missed purpose and unfulfilled promise. They want to write. They want to paint. They want to act, make music, dance . . . but they are afraid to take themselves seriously.

In order to move from the realm of shadows into the light of creativity, shadow artists must learn to take themselves seriously. With gentle, deliberate effort, they must nurture their artist child. Creativity is play, but for shadow artists, learning to allow themselves to play is hard work.

Protecting the Artist Child Within

Remember, your artist is a child. Find and protect that child. Learning to let yourself create is like learning to walk. The artist child must begin by crawling. Baby steps will follow and there will be falls—yecchy first paintings, beginning films that look like unedited home movies, first poems that would shame a greeting card. Typically, the recovering shadow artist will use these early efforts to discourage continued exploration.

Judging your early artistic efforts is artist abuse. This happens in any number of ways: beginning work is measured against the masterworks of other artists; beginning work is exposed to premature criticism, shown to overly critical friends. In short, the fledgling artist behaves with well-practiced masochism. Masochism is an art form long ago mastered, perfected during the years of self-reproach; this habit is

> *Painting is an attempt to come to terms with life. There are as many solutions as there are human beings.*
>
> GEORGE TOOKER

the self-hating bludgeon with which a shadow artist can beat himself right back into the shadows.

In recovering from our creative blocks, it is necessary to go gently and slowly. What we are after here is the healing of old wounds—not the creation of new ones. No high jumping, please! Mistakes are necessary! Stumbles are normal. These are baby steps. Progress, not perfection, is what we should be asking of ourselves.

Too far, too fast, and we can undo ourselves. Creative recovery is like marathon training. We want to log ten slow miles for every one fast mile. This can go against the ego's grain. We want to be great—immediately great—but that is not how recovery works. It is an awkward, tentative, even embarrassing process. There will be many times when we won't look good—to ourselves or anyone else. We need to stop demanding that we do. It is impossible to get better and look good at the same time.

Remember that in order to recover as an artist, you must be willing to be a bad artist. Give yourself permission to be a beginner. By being willing to be a bad artist, you have a chance to *be* an artist, and perhaps, over time, a very good one.

When I make this point in teaching, I am met by instant, defensive hostility: "But do you know how old I will be by the time I learn to really play the piano/ act/paint/write a decent play?"

Yes . . . the same age you will be if you don't.

So let's start.

YOUR ENEMY WITHIN: Core Negative Beliefs

Most of the time when we are blocked in an area of our life, it is because we feel safer that way. We may not be happy, but at least we know what we are—unhappy. Much fear of our own creativity is the fear of the unknown.

If I am fully creative, what will it mean? What will happen to me and to others? We have some pretty awful notions about what *could* happen. So, rather than find out, we decide to stay blocked. This is seldom a conscious decision. It is more often an unconscious response to internalized negative beliefs. In this week, we will work at uncovering our negative beliefs and discarding them.

Here is a list of commonly held negative beliefs:
I can't be a successful, prolific, creative artist because:

1. Everyone will hate me.
2. I will hurt my friends and family.
3. I will go crazy.
4. I will abandon my friends and family.
5. I can't spell.
6. I don't have good enough ideas.
7. It will upset my mother and/or father.
8. I will have to be alone.
9. I will find out I am gay (if straight).
10. I will be struck straight (if gay).
11. I will do bad work and not know it and look like a fool.
12. I will feel too angry.
13. I will never have any real money.
14. I will get self-destructive and drink, drug, or sex myself to death.
15. I will get cancer, AIDS—or a heart attack or the plague.
16. My lover will leave me.
17. I will die.
18. I will feel bad because I don't deserve to be successful.
19. I will have only one good piece of work in me.
20. It's too late. If I haven't become a fully functioning artist yet, I never will.

None of these core negatives need be true. They come to us from our parents, our religion, our culture, and our fearful friends. Each one of these beliefs reflects notions we have about what it means to be an artist.

Once we have cleared away the most sweeping cultural negatives, we may find we are still stubbornly left with core negatives we have acquired from our families, teachers, and friends. These are often more subtle—but equally undermining if not confronted. Our business here is confronting them.

Negative beliefs are exactly that: beliefs, not facts. The world was never flat, although everyone believed it was. You are not dumb, crazy, egomaniacal, grandiose, or silly just because you falsely believe yourself to be.

What you are is scared. Core negatives keep you scared.

The bottom line is that core negatives—personal and cultural—always go for your jugular. They attack your sexuality, your lovability, your intelligence—whatever vulnerability they can latch on to.

Some core negatives beliefs and their positive alternatives are listed below.

NEGATIVE BELIEFS	POSITIVE ALTERNATIVES
Artists are:	Artists can be:
drunk	sober
crazy	sane
broke	solvent
irresponsible	responsible
loners	user-friendly
promiscuous	faithful
doomed	saved
unhappy	happy
born, not made	discovered and recovered

For example, in a female artist, the artists-are-promiscuous cliché may have in its place a personal negative: "No man will ever love you if you are an artist. Artists are either celibate or gay." This negative, picked up from a mother or teacher and unarticulated by the young artist, can constitute grounds for a powerful block.

Similarly, a young male artist may have the personal negative "Male artists are either gay or impotent." This notion, picked up from a teacher or from reading too much about Fitzgerald and Hemingway, may again create a block. Who wants to be sexually dysfunctional?

A gay artist may have yet anther spin on the ball: "Only heterosexual art is really acceptable, so why make my art if I have to either disguise it or come out of the closet whether I want to or not?"

Stripped to their essence, our multiple negative beliefs reveal a central negative belief: we must trade one good, beloved dream for another. In other words, if

I cannot believe that the inscrutable universe turns on an axis of suffering; surely the strange beauty of the world must somewhere rest on pure joy!

LOUISE BOGAN

being an artist seems too good to be true to you, you will devise a price tag for it that strikes you as unpayable. Hence, you remain blocked.

Most blocked creatives carry unacknowledged either/or reasoning that stands between them and their work. To become unblocked we must recognize our either/or thinking. "I can either be romantically happy *or* an artist." "I can either be financially successful *or* an artist." It is possible, quite possible, to be both an artist and romantically fulfilled. It is quite possible to be an artist and financially successful.

Your block doesn't want you to see that. Its whole plan of attack is to make you irrationally afraid of some dire outcome you are too embarrassed to even mention. You know rationally that writing or painting shouldn't be put off because of your silly fear, but because it is a silly fear, you don't air it and the block stays intact. In this way, "You're a bad speller" successfully overrides all computer spelling programs. You *know* it's dumb to worry about spelling . . . so you don't mention it. And since you don't, it continues to block you from finding a solution. (Spelling fear is a remarkably common block.)

In the next part of this week, we will excavate your unconscious beliefs by using some logic-brain/artist-brain learning tricks. These may strike you as hokey and unproductive. Again, that's resistance. If internalized negativity is the enemy within, what follows is some very effective weaponry. Try it before discarding it out of hand.

YOUR ALLY WITHIN: Affirmative Weapons

As blocked creatives, we often sit on the sidelines critiquing those in the game. "He's not so talented," we may say of a currently hot artist. And we may be right about that. All too often, it is audacity and not talent that moves an artist to center stage. As blocked creatives, we tend to regard these bogus spotlight grabbers with animosity. We may be able to defer to true genius, but if it's merely a genius for self-promotion we're witnessing, our resentment runs high. This is not just jealousy. It is a stalling technique that reinforces our staying stuck. We make speeches to ourselves and other willing victims: "I could do that better, if only . . ."

You could do it better if only you would let yourself do it!

Affirmations will help you allow yourself to do it. An affirmation is a positive statement of (positive) belief, and if we can become one-tenth as good at positive self-talk as we are at negative self-talk, we will notice an enormous change.

Affirmations help achieve a sense of safety and hope. When we first start working with affirmations, they may feel dumb. Hokey. Embarrassing. Isn't this interesting? We can easily, and without embarrassment, bludgeon ourselves with negative affirmations: "I'm not gifted enough/not clever enough/not original enough/not young enough . . ." But

> *Affirmations are like prescriptions for certain aspects of yourself you want to change.*
>
> JERRY FRANKHAUSER

saying nice things about ourselves is notoriously hard to do. It feels pretty awful at first. Try these and see if they don't sound hopelessly syrupy: "I deserve love." "I deserve fair pay." "I deserve a rewarding creative life." "I am a brilliant and successful artist." "I have rich creative talents." "I am competent and confident in my creative work."

Did your Censor perk its nasty little ears up? Censors loathe anything that sounds like real self-worth. They immediately start up with the imposter routine: "Who do you think you are?" It's as though our entire collective unconscious sat up late nights watching Walt Disney's *One Hundred and One Dalmatians* and practicing Cruella DeVille's delivery for scathing indictments.

Just try picking an affirmation. For example "I, _____ (your name), am a brilliant and prolific potter [painter, poet, or whatever you are]." Write that ten times in a row. While you are busy doing that, something very interesting will happen. Your Censor will start to object. "Hey, wait a minute. You can't say all that positive stuff around me." Objections will start to pop up like burnt toast. These are your *blurts*.

Listen to the objections. Look at the ugly, stumpy little blurts. "Brilliant and prolific . . . sure you are. . . . Since when? . . . Can't spell. . . . You call writer's block prolific? . . . You're just kidding yourself . . . an idiot . . . grandiose. . . . Who are you kidding? . . . Who do you think you are?" and so on.

You will be amazed at the rotten things your subconscious will blurt out. Write them down. These blurts flag your personal negative core beliefs. They hold the key to your freedom in their ugly little claws. Make a list of your personal blurts.

It's time to do a little detective work. Where do your blurts come from? Mom? Dad? Teachers? Using your list of blurts, scan your past for possible sources. At least

> The meeting of two personalities is like the contact of two chemical substances: if there is any reaction, both are transformed.
>
> CARL JUNG

some of them will spring violently to mind. One effective way to locate the sources is to time-travel. Break your life into five-year increments, and list by name your major influences in each time block.

Paul had *always* wanted to be a writer. And yet, after a brief flurry of college creativity, he stopped showing his writing to anyone. Instead of the short stories he dreamed of, he kept journal after journal, each following the last into a dark drawer far from prying eyes. Why he did this was a mystery to him until he tried working with affirmations and blurts.

When Paul began writing his affirmations, he was immediately shaken by an almost volcanic blast of disparagement.

He wrote, "I, Paul, am a brilliant and prolific writer." From deep in his unconscious there erupted a spewing torrent of self-abuse and self-doubt. It was numbingly specific and somehow *familiar:* "You're just kidding yourself, a fool, no real talent, a pretender, a dilettante, a joke . . ."

Where did this core belief come from? Who could have said this to him? When? Paul went time-traveling to look for the villain. He located him with great embarrassment. Yes, there was a villain, and an incident he had been too ashamed to share and air. A malevolent early teacher had first praised his work and then set about a sexual seduction. Fearful that he had somehow invited the man's attention, ashamed lest the work really be rotten too, Paul buried the incident in his unconscious, where it festered. No wonder secondary motives were always a fear when someone praised him. No surprise he felt that someone could praise work and not mean it.

Boiled down to its essentials, Paul's core negative belief was that he was only kidding himself that he could write. This belief had dominated his thinking for a decade. Whenever people complimented him on his work, he was deeply suspicious of them and their motives. He had all but dropped friends once they had expressed interest in his talents; he had certainly stopped trusting them. When his girlfriend, Mimi, expressed interest in his talents, he even stopped trusting her.

Once Paul brought this monster up from the depths, he could begin to work with it. "I, Paul, have a real talent. I, Paul, trust and enjoy positive feedback. I, Paul, have a real talent. . . ." Although such positive affirmations felt very uncomfortable at first, they rapidly allowed Paul the freedom to participate in the first public

Creative Affirmations
1. I am a channel for God's creativity, and my work comes to good.
2. My dreams come from God and God has the power to accomplish them.
3. As I create and listen, I will be led.
4. Creativity is the creator's will for me.
5. My creativity heals myself and others.
6. I am allowed to nurture my artist.
7. Through the use of a few simple tools, my creativity will flourish.
8. Through the use of my creativity, I serve God.
9. My creativity always leads me to truth and love.
10. My creativity leads me to forgiveness and self-forgiveness.
11. There is a divine plan of goodness for me.
12. There is a divine plan of goodness for my work.
13. As I listen to the creator within, I am led.
14. As I listen to my creativity I am led to my creator.
15. I am willing to create.
16. I am willing to learn to let myself create.
17. I am willing to let God create through me.
18. I am willing to be of service through my creativity.
19. I am willing to experience my creative energy.
20. I am willing to use my creative talents.

reading of his work. When he was widely praised, he was able to accept the good response without discounting it.

Turn now to your own list of blurts. They are very important to your recovery. Each of them has held you in bondage. Each of them must be dissolved. For example, a blurt that runs, "I, Fred, am untalented and phony" might be converted to the affirmation "I, Fred, am genuinely talented."

Use your affirmations after your morning pages.

Also use any of the creative affirmations listed.

An affirmation is a strong, positive statement that something is already so.

SHAKTI GAWAIN

TASKS

1. Every morning, set your clock one-half hour early; get up and write three pages of longhand, stream-of-consciousness morning writing. Do not reread these pages or allow anyone else to read them. Ideally, stick these pages in a large manila envelope, or hide them somewhere. Welcome to the morning pages. They will change you.

   This week, please be sure to work with your affirmations of choice and your blurts at the end of each day's morning pages. Convert all blurts into positive affirmations.

2. Take yourself on an artist date. You will do this every week for the duration of the course. A sample artist date: take five dollars and go to your local five-and-dime. Buy silly things like gold stick-'em stars, tiny dinosaurs, some postcards, sparkly sequins, glue, a kid's scissors, crayons. You might give yourself a gold star on your envelope each day you write. Just for fun.

3. Time Travel: List three old enemies of your creative self-worth. Please be as specific as possible in doing this exercise. Your historic monsters are the building blocks of your core negative beliefs. (Yes, rotten Sister Ann Rita from fifth grade does count, and the rotten thing she said to you does matter. Put her in.) This is your monster hall of fame. More monsters will come to you as you work through your recovery. It is always necessary to acknowledge creative injuries and grieve them. Otherwise, they become creative scar tissue and block your growth.

4. Time Travel: Select and write out one horror story from your monster hall of fame. You do not need to write long or much, but do jot down whatever details come back to you—the room you were in, the way people looked at you, the way you felt, what your parent said or didn't say when you told about it. Include whatever rankles you about the incident: "And then I remember she gave me this real fakey smile and patted my head. . . ."

   You may find it cathartic to draw a sketch of your old monster or to clip out an image that evokes the incident for you. Cartoon trashing your monster, or at least draw a nice red X through it.

5. Write a letter to the editor in your defense. Mail it to yourself. It is great fun to write this letter in the voice of your wounded artist child: "To whom it may concern: Sister Ann Rita is a jerk and has pig eyes and I can too spell!"

6. Time Travel: List three old champions of your creative self-worth. This is your hall of champions, those who wish you and your creativity well. Be specific.

Every encouraging word counts. Even if you disbelieve a compliment, record it. It may well be true.

If you are stuck for compliments, go back through your time-travel log and look for positive memories. When, where, and why did you feel good about yourself? Who gave you affirmation?

Additionally, you may wish to write the compliment out and decorate it. Post it near where you do your morning pages or on the dashboard of your car. I put mine on the chassis of my computer to cheer me as I write.

7. Time Travel: Select and write out one happy piece of encouragement. Write a thank-you letter. Mail it to yourself or to the long-lost mentor.

8. Imaginary Lives: If you had five other lives to lead, what would you do in each of them? I would be a pilot, a cowhand, a physicist, a psychic, a monk. You might be a scuba diver, a cop, a writer of children's books, a football player, a belly dancer, a painter, a performance artist, a history teacher, a healer, a coach, a scientist, a doctor, a Peace Corps worker, a psychologist, a fisherman, a minister, an auto mechanic, a carpenter, a sculptor, a lawyer, a painter, a computer hacker, a soap-opera star, a country singer, a rock-and-roll drummer. Whatever occurs to you, jot it down. Do not overthink this exercise.

The point of these lives is to have fun in them—more fun than you might be having in this one. Look over your list and select one. Then do it this week. For instance, if you put down *country singer*, can you pick a guitar? If you dream of being a cowhand, what about some horseback riding?

9. In working with affirmations and blurts, very often injuries and monsters swim back to us. Add these to your list as they occur to you. Work with each blurt individually. Turn each negative into an affirmative positive.

10. Take your artist for a walk, the two of you. A brisk twenty-minute walk can dramatically alter consciousness.

CHECK-IN

You will do check-ins every week. If you are running your creative week Sunday to Sunday, do your check-ins each Saturday. Remember that this recovery is *yours*. What you think is important, and it will become increasingly interesting to you as

> *Undoubtedly, we become what we envisage.*
>
> CLAUDE M. BRISTOL

you progress. You may want to do check-ins in your morning-pages notebook. It's best to answer by hand and allow about twenty minutes to respond. The purpose of check-ins is to give you a journal of your creative journey. It is my hope that you will later share the tools with others and in doing so find your own notes invaluable: "Yes, I was mad in week four. I loved week five. . . ."

1. **How many days this week did you do your morning pages?** Seven out of seven, we always hope. How was the experience for you?
2. **Did you do your artist date this week?** Yes, of course, we always hope. And yet artist dates can be remarkably difficult to allow yourself. What did you do? How did it feel?
3. **Were there any other issues this week that you consider significant for your recovery?** Describe them.

Recovering a Sense of Identity

This week addresses self-definition as a major component of creative recovery. You may find yourself drawing new boundaries and staking out new territories as your personal needs, desires, and interests announce themselves. The essays and tools are aimed at moving you into your personal identity, a self-defined you.

Going Sane

TRUSTING OUR CREATIVITY IS new behavior for many of us. It may feel quite threatening initially, not only to us but also to our intimates. We may feel—and look—erratic. This erraticism is a normal part of getting unstuck, pulling free from the muck that has blocked us. It is important to remember that at first flush, going *sane* feels just like going crazy.

There is a recognizable ebb and flow to the process of recovering our creative selves. As we gain strength, so will some of the attacks of self-doubt. This is normal, and we can deal with these stronger attacks when we see them as symptoms of recovery.

Common self-attacks are: "Okay, so I did okay this week but it's just a temporary thing . . . Okay, so I got the morning pages done. I probably did them wrong . . . Okay, so now I need to plan something big and do it *right away!* . . . Who am I kidding? I'll never recover, not right away . . . not ever. . . ."

These attacks are groundless, but very convincing to ourselves. Buying into them enables us to remain stuck and victimized. Just as a recovering alcoholic must avoid the first drink, the recovering artist must avoid taking the first *think*. For us, that think is really self-doubt: "I don't *think* this is any good. . . ."

All sanity depends on this: that it should be a delight to feel heat strike the skin, a delight to stand upright, knowing the bones are moving easily under the flesh.

DORIS LESSING

Snipers are people who undermine your efforts to break unhealthy relationship patterns.

JODY HAYES

These attacks can come from either internal or external sources. We can neutralize them once we recognize them as a sort of creative virus. Affirmations are a powerful antidote for self-hate, which commonly appears under the mask of self-doubt.

Early in our creative recovery, self-doubt can lure us into self-sabotage. A common form for this sabotage is showing someone our morning pages. Remember, the morning pages are private and are not intended for the scrutiny of well-meaning friends. One newly unblocked writer showed his morning pages to a writer friend who was still blocked. When she critiqued them, he blocked again.

Do not let your self-doubt turn into self-sabotage.

Poisonous Playmates

Creativity flourishes when we have a sense of safety and self-acceptance. Your artist, like a small child, is happiest when feeling a sense of security. As our artist's protective parent, we must learn to place our artist with safe companions. Toxic playmates can capsize our artist's growth.

Not surprisingly, the most poisonous playmates for us as recovering creatives are people whose creativity is still blocked. Our recovery threatens them.

As long as we were blocked, we often felt that it was arrogance and self-will to speak of ourselves as creative artists. The truth is that it was self-will to refuse to acknowledge our creativity. Of course, this refusal had its payoffs.

To know what you prefer instead of humbly saying Amen to what the world tells you you ought to prefer, is to have kept your soul alive.

ROBERT LOUIS STEVENSON

We could wonder and worry about our arrogance instead of being humble enough to ask help to move through our fear. We could fantasize about art instead of doing the work. By not asking the Great Creator's help with our creativity, and by not seeing the Great Creator's hand in our creativity, we could proceed to righteously ignore our creativity and never have to take the risks of fulfilling it. Your blocked friends may still be indulging in all these comforting self-delusions.

If they are having trouble with your recovery, they are still getting a payoff from remaining blocked. Perhaps they still get an anorectic high from the martyrdom of being blocked or they still collect sympathy and wallow in self-pity. Perhaps they still feel smug thinking about how much more creative they *could* be than those who are out there doing it. These are toxic behaviors for you now.

Do not expect your blocked friends to applaud your recovery. That's like expecting your best friends from the bar to celebrate your sobriety. How can they when their own drinking is something they want to hold on to?

Blocked friends may find your recovery disturbing. Your getting unblocked raises the unsettling possibility that they, too, could become unblocked and move into authentic creative risks rather than bench-sitting cynicism. Be alert to subtle sabotage from friends. You cannot afford their well-meaning doubts right now. Their doubts will reactivate your own. Be particularly alert to any suggestion that you have become selfish or different. (These are red-alert words for us. They are attempts to leverage us back into our old ways for the sake of someone else's comfort, not our own.)

> *Every time you don't follow your inner guidance, you feel a loss of energy, loss of power, a sense of spiritual deadness.*
>
> SHAKTI GAWAIN

Blocked creatives are easily manipulated by guilt. Our friends, feeling abandoned by our departure from the ranks of the blocked, may unconsciously try to guilt-trip us into giving up our newly healthy habits. It is very important to understand that the time given to morning pages is time between you and God. You best know your answers. You will be led to new sources of support as you begin to support yourself.

Be very careful to safeguard your newly recovering artist. Often, creativity is blocked by our falling in with other people's plans for us. We want to set aside time for our creative work, but we feel we *should* do something else instead. As blocked creatives, we focus not on our responsibilities to ourselves, but on our responsibilities to others. We tend to think such behavior makes us good people. It doesn't. It makes us frustrated people.

The essential element in nurturing our creativity lies in nurturing ourselves. Through self-nurturance we nurture our inner connection to the Great Creator. Through this connection our creativity will unfold. Paths will appear for us. We need to trust the Great Creator and move out in faith.

Repeat: the Great Creator has gifted us with creativity. Our gift back is our use of it. Do not let friends squander your time.

Be gentle but firm, and hang tough. The best thing you can do your friends is to be an example through your own recovery. Do not let their fears and second thoughts derail you.

Soon enough, the techniques you learn will enable you to teach others. Soon enough, you will be a bridge that will allow others to cross over from self-doubt into self-expression. For right now, protect your artist by refusing to show your morning pages to interested bystanders or to share your artist date with friends. Draw a sacred circle around your recovery. Give yourself the gift of faith. Trust that you are on the right track. You are.

As your recovery progresses, you will come to experience a more comfortable faith in your creator and your creator within. You will learn that it is actually easier to write than not write, paint than not paint, and so forth. You will learn to enjoy the process of being a creative channel and to surrender your need to control the result. You will discover the joy of *practicing* your creativity. The process, not the product, will become your focus.

You own healing is the greatest message of hope for others.

Crazymakers

A related thing creatives do to avoid being creative is to involve themselves with *crazymakers*. Crazymakers are those personalities that create storm centers. They are often charismatic, frequently charming, highly inventive, and powerfully persuasive. And, for the creative person in their vicinity, they are enormously destructive. You know the type: charismatic but out of control, long on problems and short on solutions.

Crazymakers are the kind of people who can take over your whole life. To fixer-uppers, they are irresistible: so much to change, so many distractions. . . .

If you are involved with a crazymaker, you probably know it already, and you certainly recognize the thumbnail description in the paragraph above. Crazymakers like drama. If they can swing it, they are the star. Everyone around them functions as supporting cast, picking up their cues, their entrances and exits, from the crazymaker's (crazy) whims.

Learn to get in touch with the silence within yourself and know that everything in this life has a purpose.

ELISABETH KÜBLER-ROSS

Some of the most profoundly destructive crazymakers I have ever encountered are themselves famous artists. They are the kind of artists that give the rest of us bad names. Often larger than life, they acquire that status by feeding on the life energies of those around them. For this reason, many of the most crazy artists in America are found surrounded by a cadre of supporters as talented as they are but determined to subvert their own talent in the service of the Crazymaking King.

I am thinking of a movie set I visited several years ago. The filmmaker was one of the giants of American cinema. His stature was unmistakable, and so was his identity as a crazymaker. Given that all filmmaking is demanding, his sets are far more so: longer hours; long bouts of paranoia; intrigue and internecine politics. Amid rumors that the set was bugged, this Crazymaker King addressed his actors over a loudspeaker system while he, like the Wizard of Oz, secreted himself away in a large and luxuriously equipped trailer cave.

Over the past two decades, I have watched many directors at work. I was married to a profoundly gifted director, and I have directed a feature myself. I have often remarked how closely a film crew resembles an extended family. In the case of this Crazymaker King, the crew resembled nothing so much as an alcoholic family: the alcoholic drinker (thinker) surrounded by his tiptoeing enablers, all pretending that his outsized ego and its concomitant demands were normal.

On that crazymaker's set, the production lurched off schedule and over budget from king baby's unreasonable demands. A film crew is essentially a crew of experts, and to watch these estimable experts become disheartened was a strong lesson for me in the poisonous power of crazymaking. Brilliant set designers, costume designers, sound engineers—not to mention actors—became increasingly injured as the production ran its devastating course. It was against the crazymaking director's personal dramas that they struggled to create the drama that was meant to go onscreen. Like all good movie people, this crew was willing to work long hours for good work. What discouraged them was working those hours in the service of ego instead of art.

The crazymaking dynamic is grounded in power, and so any group of people can function as an energy system to be exploited and drained. Crazymakers can be found in almost any setting, in almost any art form. Fame may help to create them, but since they feed on power, any power source will do. Although quite frequently crazymakers are found among the rich and famous, they are common even among commoners. Right in the nuclear family (there's a reason we use that word), a resident crazymaker may often be found pitting family member against family member, undercutting anyone's agenda but his or her own.

I am thinking now of a destructive matriarch of my acquaintance. The titular head of a large and talented clan, she has devoted her extensive energies to destroying the creativity of her children. Always choosing critical moments for her sabotage, she plants her bombs to explode just as her children approach success.

The daughter struggling to finish a belated college degree finds herself saddled with a sudden drama the night before her final exam. The son with a critical job interview is gifted with a visitation just when he needs to focus the most.

"Do you know what the neighbors are saying about you?" the crazymaker will often ask. (And the beleaguered student mother will hear a horrific round of gossip that leaves her battered, facing her exam week beset by feelings of "What's the use?")

"Do you realize you're ruining your own marriage with this possible new job?" (And the son's hopeful career move is ashes before it begins.)

Whether they appear as your overbearing mother, your manic boss, your needy friend, or your stubborn spouse, the crazymakers in your life share certain destructive patterns that make them poisonous for any sustained creative work.

Crazymakers break deals and destroy schedules. They show up two days early for your wedding and expect to be waited on hand and foot. They rent a vacation cabin larger and more expensive than the one agreed upon, and then they expect you to foot the bill.

What I am actually saying is that we need to be willing to let our intuition guide us, and then be willing to follow that guidance directly and fearlessly.

SHAKTI GAWAIN

Crazymakers expect special treatment. They suffer a wide panoply of mysterious ailments that require care and attention whenever you have a deadline looming—or anything else that draws your attention from the crazymaker's demands. The crazymaker cooks her own special meal in a house full of hungry children—and does nothing to feed the kids. The crazymaker is too upset to drive right after he has vented enormous verbal abuse on the heads of those around him. "I am afraid Daddy will have a heart attack," the victim starts thinking, instead of, "How do I get this monster out of my house?"

Crazymakers discount your reality. No matter how important your deadline or how critical your work trajectory at the moment, crazymakers will violate your needs. They may act as though they hear your boundaries and will respect them, but in practice *act* is the operative word. Crazymakers are the people who call you at midnight or 6:00 A.M. saying, "I know you asked me not to call you at this time, but . . ." Crazymakers are the people who drop by unexpectedly to borrow something you can't find or don't want to lend them. Even better, they call and ask you to locate something they need, then fail to pick it up. "I know you're on a deadline," they say, "but this will only take a minute." Your minute.

Crazymakers spend your time and money. If they borrow your car, they return it late, with an empty tank. Their travel arrangements always cost you time or money. They demand to be met in the middle of your workday at an airport miles from town. "I didn't bring taxi money," they say when confronted with, "But I'm working."

Crazymakers triangulate those they deal with. Because crazymakers thrive on energy (your energy), they set people against one another in order to maintain their own power position dead center. (That's where they can feed most directly on the negative energies they stir up.) "So-and-so was telling me you didn't get to work on time today," a crazymaker may relay. You obligingly get mad at so-and-so and miss the fact that the crazymaker has used hearsay to set you off kilter emotionally.

Crazymakers are expert blamers. Nothing that goes wrong is ever their fault, and to hear them tell it, the fault is usually yours. "If you hadn't cashed that child-support check it would never have bounced," one crazymaking ex-husband told his struggling-for-serenity former spouse.

> *Slow down and enjoy life. It's not only the scenery you miss by going to fast—you also miss the sense of where you are going and why.*
>
> EDDIE CANTOR

Crazymakers create dramas—but seldom where they belong. Crazymakers are often blocked creatives themselves. Afraid to effectively tap their own creativity, they are loath to allow that same creativity in others. It makes them jealous. It makes them threatened. It makes them dramatic— at your expense. Devoted to their own agendas, crazymakers impose these agendas on others. In dealing with a crazymaker, you are dealing always with the famous issue of figure and ground. In other words, whatever matters to you becomes trivialized into mere backdrop for the crazymaker's personal plight. "Do you think he/she loves me?" they call you to ask when you are trying to pass the bar exam or get your husband home from the hospital.

Crazymakers hate schedules—except their own. In the hands of a crazymaker, time is a primary tool for abuse. If you claim a certain block of time as your own, your crazymaker will find a way to fight you for that time, to mysteriously need things (meaning you) just when you need to be alone and focused on the task at hand. "I stayed up until three last night. I can't drive the kids to school," the crazymaker will spring on you the morning you yourself must leave early for a business breakfast with your boss.

Crazymakers hate order. Chaos serves their purposes. When you begin to establish a place that serves you and your creativity, your crazymaker will abruptly invade that space with projects of his/her own. "What are all these papers, all this laundry on top of my work table?" you ask. "I decided to sort my college papers . . . to start looking for the matches for my socks . . ."

Crazymakers deny that they are crazymakers. They go for the jugular. "I am not what's making you crazy," your crazymaker may say when you point out a broken promise or a piece of sabotage. "It's just that we have such a rotten sex life."

> *Whatever God's dream about man may be, it seems certain it cannot come true unless man cooperates.*
>
> STELLA TERRILL MANN

If crazymakers are that destructive, what are we doing involved with them? The answer, to be brief but brutal, is that we're that crazy ourselves and we are that self-destructive.

Really?

Yes. As blocked creatives, we are willing to go to almost any lengths to remain blocked. As frightening and abusive as life with a crazymaker is, we find it far less threatening than the challenge of a creative life of our own. What would happen then? What would we be like? Very often, we fear that if we let ourselves be creative, we will become crazymakers ourselves and abuse those around us. Using this fear as our excuse, we continue to allow others to abuse us.

If you are involved now with a crazymaker, it is very important that you admit this fact. Admit that you are being used—and admit that you are using your own abuser. Your crazymaker is a block you chose yourself, to deter you from your own trajectory. As much as you are being exploited by your crazymaker, you, too, are using that person to block your creative flow.

If you are involved in a tortured tango with a crazymaker, stop dancing to his/her tune. Pick up a book on codependency or get yourself to a twelve-step program for relationship addiction. (Al-Anon and Sex and Love Addicts Anonymous are two excellent programs for stopping the crazymaker's dance.)

The next time you catch yourself saying or thinking, "He/she is driving me crazy!" ask yourself what creative work you are trying to block by your involvement.

Skepticism

Now that we have talked about the barrier to recovery others can present, let us take a look at the inner enemy we harbor ourselves. Perhaps the greatest barrier for any of us as we look for an expanded life is our own deeply held skepticism. This might be called *the secret doubt*. It does not seem to matter whether we are officially believers or agnostics. We have our doubts about all of this creator/creativity stuff, and those doubts are very powerful. Unless we air them, they can sabotage us. Many times, in trying to be good sports we stuff our feelings of doubt. We need to stop doing that and explore them instead.

Boiled down to their essentials, the doubts go something like this: "Okay, so I started writing the morning pages and I seem more awake and alert in my life. So what? It's just a coincidence. . . . Okay, so I have started filling the well and taking my artist on a date and I do notice I am cheering up a little. So what? It's just coincidental. . . . Okay, so now I am beginning to notice that the more I let myself explore the possibility of there being some power for good, the more I notice lucky coincidence turning up in my life. So what? I can't believe I am really being led. That's just too weird. . . ."

The reason we think it's weird to imagine an unseen helping hand is that we still doubt that it's okay for us to be creative. With this attitude firmly entrenched, we not only look all gift horses in the mouth but also swat them on the rump to get them out of our lives as fast as possible.

> *To believe in God or in a guiding force because someone tells you to is the height of stupidity. We are given senses to receive our information with. With our own eyes we see, and with our skin we feel. With our intelligence, it is intended that we understand. But each person must puzzle it out for himself or herself.*
>
> SOPHY BURNHAM

When Mike began his creative recovery, he let himself admit that he wanted to make films. Two weeks later, through a series of "coincidences," he found himself in film school with his company paying for it. Did he relax and enjoy this? No. He told himself that film school was distracting him from his real job of finding another job. And so he gave up filmmaking to look for another job.

Two years later, remembering this incident, Mike can shake his head at himself. When the universe gave him what he wanted, he gave the gift right back. Eventually, he did let himself learn filmmaking, but he made it a lot harder on himself than the universe may have intended.

One of the things most worth noting in a creative recovery is our reluctance to take seriously the possibility that the universe just might be cooperating with our new and expanded plans. We've gotten brave enough to try recovery, but we don't want the universe to really pay attention. We still feel too much like frauds to handle some success. When it comes, we want to go.

Think of yourself as an incandescent power, illuminated and perhaps forever talked to by God and his messengers.

BRENDA UELAND

No matter how slow the film, Spirit always stands still long enough for the photographer It has chosen.

MINOR WHITE

Of course we do! Any little bit of experimenting in self-nurturance is very frightening for most of us. When our little experiment provokes the universe to open a door or two, we start shying away. "Hey! You! Whatever you are! Not so fast!"

I like to think of the mind as a room. In that room, we keep all of our usual ideas about life, God, what's possible and what's not. The room has a door. That door is ever so slightly ajar, and outside we can see a great deal of dazzling light. Out there in the dazzling light are a lot of new ideas that we consider too far-out for us, and so we keep them out there. The ideas we are comfortable with are in the room with us. The other ideas are out, and we keep them out.

In our ordinary, prerecovery life, when we would hear something weird or threatening, we'd just grab the doorknob and pull the door shut. Fast.

Inner work triggering outer change? Ridiculous! (Slam the door.) God bothering to help my *own* creative recovery? (Slam.) Synchronicity supporting my artist with serendipitous coincidences? (Slam, slam, slam.)

Now that we are in creative recovery, there is another approach we need to try. To do this, we gently set aside our skepticism—for later use, if we need it—and when a weird idea or coincidence whizzes by, we gently nudge the door a little further open.

Setting skepticism aside, even briefly, can make for very interesting explorations. In creative recovery, it is not necessary that we change any of our beliefs. It is necessary that we examine them.

More than anything else, creative recovery is an exercise in open-mindedness. Again, picture your mind as that room with the door slightly ajar. Nudging the door open a bit more is what makes for open-mindedness. Begin, this week, to consciously practice opening your mind.

Attention

Very often, a creative block manifests itself as an addiction to fantasy. Rather than working or living the now, we spin our wheels and indulge in daydreams of could have, would have, should have. One of the great misconceptions about the artistic life is that it entails great swathes of aimlessness. The truth is that a creative life involves great swathes of attention. Attention is a way to connect and survive.

Develop interest in life as you see it; in people, things, literature, music—the world is so rich, simply throbbing with rich treasures, beautiful souls and interesting people. Forget yourself.

HENRY MILLER

"Flora and fauna reports," I used to call the long, winding letters from my grandmother. "The forsythia is starting and this morning I saw my first robin. . . . The roses are holding even in this heat. . . . The sumac has turned and that little maple down by the mailbox. . . . My Christmas cactus is getting ready. . . ."

I followed my grandmother's life like a long home movie: a shot of this and a shot of that, spliced together with no pattern that I could ever see. "Dad's cough is getting worse. . . . The little Shetland looks like she'll drop her foal early. . . . Joanne is back in the hospital at Anna. . . . We named the new boxer Trixie and she likes to sleep in my cactus bed—can you imagine?"

I could imagine. Her letters made that easy. Life through grandma's eyes was a series of small miracles: the wild tiger lilies under the cottonwoods in June; the quick lizard scooting under the gray river rock she admired for its satiny finish. Her letters clocked the seasons of the year and her life. She lived until she was eighty, and the letters came until the very end. When she died, it was as suddenly as her

Christmas cactus: here today, gone tomorrow. She left behind her letters and her husband of sixty-two years. Her husband, my grandfather Daddy Howard, an elegant rascal with a gambler's smile and a loser's luck, had made and lost several fortunes, the last of them permanently. He drank them away, gambled them away, tossed them away the way she threw crumbs to her birds. He squandered life's big chances the way she savored the small ones. "That man," my mother would say.

My grandmother lived with that man in tiled Spanish houses, in trailers, in a tiny cabin halfway up a mountain, in a railroad flat, and, finally, in a house made out of ticky-tacky where they all looked just the same. "I don't know how she stands it," my mother would say, furious with my grandfather for some new misadventure. She meant she didn't know why.

The truth is, we all knew how she stood it. She stood it by standing knee-deep in the flow of life and paying close attention.

My grandmother was gone before I learned the lesson her letters were teaching: survival lies in sanity, and sanity lies in paying attention. Yes, her letters said, Dad's cough is getting worse, we have lost the house, there is no money and no work, but the tiger lilies are blooming, the lizard has found that spot of sun, the roses are holding despite the heat.

My grandmother knew what a painful life had taught her: success or failure, the truth of a life really has little to do with its quality. The quality of life is in proportion, always, to the capacity for delight. The capacity for delight is the gift of paying attention.

In a year when a long and rewarding love affair was lurching gracelessly away from the center of her life, the writer May Sarton kept *A Journal of a Solitude.* In it, she records coming home from a particularly painful weekend with her lover. Entering her empty house, "I was stopped by the threshold of my study by a ray on a Korean chrysanthemum, lighting it up like a spotlight, deep red petals and Chinese yellow center. . . . Seeing it was like getting a transfusion of autumn light."

It's no accident that May Sarton uses the word *transfusion.* The loss of her lover was a wound, and in her responses to that chrysanthemum, in the act of paying attention, Sarton's healing began.

The reward for attention is always healing. It may begin as the healing of a particular pain—the lost lover, the sickly child, the shattered dream. But what is healed, finally, is the pain that underlies all pain: the pain that we are all, as Rilke phrases it, "unutterably alone." More than anything else, attention is an act of connection. I learned this the way I have learned most things—quite by accident.

When my first marriage blew apart, I took a lonely house in the Hollywood Hills. My plan was simple. I would weather my loss alone. I would see no one, and no one would see me, until the worst of the pain was over. I would take long, solitary walks, and I would suffer. As it happened, I did take those walks, but they did not go as planned.

Two curves up the road behind my house, I met a gray striped cat. This cat lived in a vivid blue house with a large sheepdog she clearly disliked. I learned all this despite myself in a week's walking. We began to have little visits, that cat and I, and then long talks of all we had in common, lonely women.

The noun of self becomes a verb. This flashpoint of creation in the present moment is where work and play merge.

STEPHEN NACHMANOVITCH

Both of us admired an extravagant salmon rose that had wandered across a neighboring fence. Both of us like watching the lavender float of jacaranda blossoms as they shook loose from their moorings. Alice (I heard her called inside one afternoon) would bat at them with her paw.

By the time the jacarandas were done, an unattractive slatted fence had been added to contain the rose garden. By then, I had extended my walks a mile farther up and added to my fellowship other cats, dogs, and children. By the time the salmon rose disappeared behind its fence, I had found a house higher up with a walled Moorish garden and a vitriolic parrot I grew fond of. Colorful, opinionated, highly dramatic, he reminded me of my ex-husband. Pain had become something more valuable: experience.

Writing about attention, I see that I have written a good deal about pain. This is no coincidence. It may be different for others, but pain is what it took to teach me to pay attention. In times of pain, when the future is too terrifying to contemplate and the past too painful to remember, I have learned to pay attention to right now. The precise moment I was in was always the only safe place for me. Each moment, taken alone, was always bearable. In the exact now, we are all, always, all right. Yesterday the marriage may have ended. Tomorrow the cat may die. The phone call from the lover, for all my waiting, may not ever come, but just at the moment, just now, that's all right. I am breathing in and out. Realizing this, I began to notice that each moment was not without its beauty.

The night my mother died, I got the call, took my sweater, and set out up the hill behind my house. A great snowy moon was rising behind the palm trees. Later that night, it floated above the garden, washing the cactus silver. When I think now about my mother's death, I remember that snowy moon.

> *The painting has a life of its own. I try to let it come through.*
>
> JACKSON POLLOCK

The poet William Meredith has observed that the worst that can be said of a man is that "he did not pay attention." When I think of my grandmother, I remember her gardening, one small, brown breast slipping unexpectedly free from the halter top of the little print dress she made for herself each summer. I remember her pointing down the steep slope from the home she was about to lose, to the cottonwoods in the wash below. "The ponies like them for their shade," she said. "I like them because they go all silvery in their green."

Rules of the Road

In order to be an artist, I must:

1. Show up at the page. Use the page to rest, to dream, to try.
2. Fill the well by caring for my artist.
3. Set small and gentle goals and meet them.
4. Pray for guidance, courage, and humility.
5. Remember that it is far harder and more painful to be a blocked artist than it is to do the work.
6. Be alert, always, for the presence of the Great Creator leading and helping my artist.
7. Choose companions who encourage me to do the work, not just talk about doing the work or why I am not doing the work.
8. Remember that the Great Creator loves creativity.
9. Remember that it is my job to do the work, not judge the work.
10. Place this sign in my workplace: Great Creator, I will take care of the *quantity*. You take care of the *quality*.

TASKS

1. Affirmative Reading: Every day, morning and night, get quiet and focused and read the Basic Principles to yourself. (See page 17.) Be alert for any attitudinal shifts. Can you see yourself setting aside any skepticism yet?

2. Where does your time go? List your five major activities this week. How much time did you give to each one? Which were what you wanted to do and which were shoulds? How much of your time is spent helping others and ignoring your own desires? Have any of your blocked friends triggered doubts in you?

   Take a sheet of paper. Draw a circle. Inside that circle, place topics you need to protect. Place the names of those you find to be supportive. Outside the circle, place the names of those you must be self-protective around just now. Place this safety map near where you write your morning pages. Use this map to support your autonomy. Add names to the inner and outer spheres as appropriate: "Oh! Derek is somebody I shouldn't talk to about this right now."

3. List twenty things you enjoy doing (rock climbing, roller-skating, baking pies, making soup, making love, making love again, riding a bide, riding a horse, playing catch, shooting baskets, going for a run, reading poetry, and so forth). When was the last time you let yourself do these things? Next to each entry, place a date. Don't be surprised if it's been years for some of your favorites. That will change. This list is an excellent resource for artist dates.

4. From the list above, write down two favorite things that you've avoided that could be this week's goals. These goals can be small: buy one roll of film and shoot it. Remember, we are trying to win you some autonomy with your time. Look for windows of time just for you, and use them in small creative acts. Get to the record store at lunch hour, even if only for fifteen minutes. Stop looking for big blocks of time when you will be free. Find small bits of time instead.

5. Dip back into Week One and read the affirmations. Note which ones cause the most reaction. Often the one that sounds the most ridiculous is the most significant. Write three chosen affirmations five times each day in your morning pages; be sure to include the affirmations you made yourself from your blurts.

6. Return to the list of imaginary lives from last week. Add five more lives. Again, check to see if you could be doing bits and pieces of these lives in the one you are living now. If you have listed a dancer's life, do you let yourself go dancing? If you have listed a monk's life, are you ever allowed to go on a retreat? If you are a scuba diver, is there an aquarium shop you can visit? A day at the lake you could schedule?

7. Life Pie: Draw a circle. Divide it into six pieces of pie. Label one piece *spirituality*, another *exercise*, another *play*, and so on with *work, friends*, and *romance/adventure*. Place a dot in each slice at the degree to which you are fulfilled in that area (outer rim indicates great; inner circle, not so great). Connect the dots. This will show you where you are lopsided.

As you begin the course, it is not uncommon for your life pie to look like a tarantula. As recovery progresses, your tarantula may become a mandala. Working with this tool, you will notice that there are areas of your life that feel impoverished and on which you spend little or no time. Use the time tidbits you are finding to alter this.

If your spiritual life is minimal, even a five-minute pit stop into a synagogue or cathedral can restore a sense of wonder. Many of us find that five minutes of drum music can put us in touch with our spiritual core. For others, it's a trip to a greenhouse. The point is that even the slightest attention to our impoverished areas can nurture them.

8. Ten Tiny Changes: List ten changes you'd like to make for yourself, from the significant to the small or vice versa ("get new sheets so I have another set, go to China, paint my kitchen, dump my bitchy friend Alice"). Do it this way:

I would like to _____.

I would like to _____.

As the morning pages nudge us increasingly into the present, where we pay attention to our current lives, a small shift like a newly painted bathroom can yield a luxuriously large sense of self-care.

9. Select one small item and make it a goal for this week.

10. Now do that item.

CHECK-IN

1. **How many days this week did you do your morning pages?** (We're hoping seven, remember.) How was the experience for you? How did the morning pages work for you? Describe them (for example, "They felt so stupid. I'd write all these itty-bitty disconnected things that didn't seem to have anything to do with one another or with anything . . ."). Remember, if you *are* writing morning pages, they are working for you. What were you surprised to find yourself

writing about? Answer this question in full on your check-in page. This will be a weekly self-scan of your moods, not your progress. Don't worry if your pages are whiny and trite. Sometimes that's the very best thing for you.

2. **Did you do your artist date this week?** Remember that artist dates are a necessary frivolity. What did you do? How did it feel?

3. **Were there any other issues this week that you consider significant for your recovery?** Describe them.

Recovering a Sense of Power

This week may find you dealing with unaccustomed bursts of energy and sharp peaks of anger, joy, and grief. You are coming into your power as the illusory hold of your previously accepted limits is shaken. You will be asked to consciously experiment with spiritual open-mindedness.

Anger

ANGER IS FUEL. We feel it and we want to do something. Hit someone, break something, throw a fit, smash a fist into the wall, tell those bastards. But we are *nice* people, and what we do with our anger is stuff it, deny it, bury it, block it, hide it, lie about it, medicate it, muffle it, ignore it. We do everything but *listen* to it.

Anger is meant to be listened to. Anger is a voice, a shout, a plea, a demand. Anger is meant to be respected. Why? Because anger is a *map*. Anger shows us what our boundaries are. Anger shows us where we want to go. It lets us see where we've been and lets us know when, we haven't liked it. Anger points the way, not just the finger. In the recovery of a blocked artist, anger is a sign of health.

Anger is meant to be acted upon. It is not meant to be acted out. Anger points the direction. We are meant to use anger as fuel to take the actions we need to move where our anger points us. With a little thought, we can usually translate the message that our anger is sending us.

"Blast him! I could make a better film than that!" (This anger says: you want to make movies. You need to learn how.)

"I can't believe it! I had this idea for a play three years ago, and she's gone and written it." (This anger says: stop procrastnating. Ideas don't get opening nights. Finished plays do. Start writing.

"This's my strategy he's using. This is incredible! I've been ripped off! I knew I should have pulled that material together and copyrighted it." (This anger says: it's time to take your own ideas seriously enough to treat them well.)

When we feel anger, we are often very angry *that* we feel anger. Damn anger!! It tells us we can't get away with our old life any longer. It tells us that old life is dying. It tells us we are being reborn, and birthing hurts. The hurt makes us angry.

Anger is the firestorm that signals the death of our old life. Anger is the fuel that propels us into our new one. Anger is a tool, not a master. Anger is meant to be tapped into and drawn upon. Used properly, anger is *use-full*.

Sloth, apathy, and despair are the enemy. Anger is not. Anger is our friend. Not a nice friend. Not a gentle friend. But a very, very loyal friend. It will always tell us when we have been betrayed. It will always tell us when we have betrayed ourselves. It will always tell us that it is time to act in our own best interests.

Anger is not the action itself. It is action's invitation.

Synchronicity

Answered prayers are scary. They imply responsibility. You asked for it. Now that you've got it, what are you going to do? Why else the cautionary phrase "Watch out for what you pray for; you just might get it"? Answered prayers deliver us back to our own hand. This is not comfortable. We find it easier to accept them as examples of synchronicity:

- A woman admits to a buried dream of acting. At dinner the next night, she sits beside a man who teaches beginning actors.
- A writer acknowledges a dream to go to film school. A single exploratory phone call puts him in touch with a professor who knows and admires his work and promises him that the last available slot is now his.
- A woman is thinking about going back to school and opens her mail to find a letter requesting her application from the very school she was thinking about going to.

- A woman wonders how to rent a rare film she has never seen. She finds it at her neighborhood *bookstore* two days later.
- A businessman who has secretly written for years vows to himself to ask a professional writer for a prognosis on his talent. The next night, over a pool table, he meets a writer who becomes his mentor and then collaborator on several successful books.

It's my experience that we're much more afraid that there might be a God than we are that there might not be. Incidents like those above happen to us, and yet we dismiss them as sheer coincidence. People talk about how dreadful it would be if there were no God. I think such talk is hooey. Most of us are a lot more comfortable feeling we're not being watched too closely.

If God—by which I do not necessarily mean a single-pointed Christian concept but an all-powerful and all-knowing force—does not exist, well then, we're all off the hook, aren't we? There's no divine retribution, no divine consolation. And if the whole experience stinks—ah well. What did you expect?

That question of expectations interests me. If there is no God, or if that God is disinterested in our puny little affairs, then everything can roll along as always and we can feel quite justified in declaring certain things impossible, other things unfair. If God, or the lack of God, is responsible for the state of the world, then we can easily wax cynical and resign ourselves to apathy. What's the use? Why try changing anything?

This is the use. If there is a responsive creative force that does hear us and act on our behalf, then we may really be able to do some things. The jig, in short, is up: God knows that the sky's the limit. Anyone honest will tell you that possibility is far more frightening than impossibility, that freedom is far more terrifying than any prison. If we do, in fact, have to deal with a force beyond ourselves that involves itself in our lives, then we may have to move into action on those previously impossible dreams.

Life is what we make of it. Whether we conceive of an inner god force or an other, outer God, doesn't matter. Relying on that force does.

> *The universe will reward you for taking risks on its behalf.*
>
> SHAKTI GAWAIN

> *A discovery is said to be an accident meeting a prepared mind.*
>
> ALBERT SZENT-GYORGYI

> *Did you ever observe to whom the accidents happen? Chance favors only the prepared mind.*
>
> LOUIS PASTEUR

"Ask and you shall receive. Knock and it shall be opened to you. . . ." These words are among the more unpleasant ones ascribed to Jesus Christ. They suggest the possibility of scientific method: ask (experiment) and see what happens (record the results).

Is it any wonder we discount answered prayers? We call it coincidence. We call it luck. We call it anything but what it is—the hand of God, or good, activated by our own hand when we act in behalf of our truest dreams, when we commit to our own soul.

Even the most timid life contains such moments of commitment: "I will get a new love seat after all!" And then, "I found the perfect one. It was the strangest thing. I was at my Aunt Bernice's and her neighbor was having a garage sale and she had this wonderful love seat her new husband was allergic to!"

In outsized lives, such moments stand out in bas-relief, large as Mount Rushmore: Lewis and Clark headed west. Isak Dinesen took off for Africa. We all have our Africas, those dark and romantic notions that call to our deepest selves. When we answer that call, when we commit to it, we set in motion the principle that C. G. Jung dubbed *synchronicity*, loosely defined as a fortuitous intermeshing of events. Back in the sixties, we called it *serendipity*. Whatever you choose to call it, once you begin your creative recovery you may be startled to find it cropping up everywhere.

Don't be surprised if you try to discount it. It can be a very threatening concept. Although Jung's paper on synchronicity was a cornerstone of his thought, even many Jungians prefer to believe it was a sort of side issue. They dismiss it, like his interest in the I Ching, as an oddity, nothing to take too seriously.

> Chance is always powerful.
> Let your hook be always cast;
> in the pool where you least
> expect it, there will be a fish.
>
> OVID

Jung might differ with them. Following his own inner leadings brought him to experience and describe a phenomenon that some of us prefer to ignore: the possibility of an intelligent and responsive universe, acting and reacting in our interests.

It is my experience that this *is* the case. I have learned, as a rule of thumb, never to ask whether you can do something. Say, instead, that you are doing it. Then fasten your seat belt. The most remarkable things follow.

"God is efficient," the actress Julianna McCarthy always reminds me. I have many times marveled at the sleight of hand with which the universe delivers its treats.

About six years ago, a play of mine was chosen for a large staged reading at the Denver Center for the Performing Arts. I had written the play with my friend Julianna in mind for the lead. She was my ideal casting, but when I arrived in Denver, casting was already set. As soon as I met my leading lady, I had a funny feeling there was a bomb ticking. I mentioned this to the director but was assured the actress was a consummate professional. Still, the funny feeling lingered in my stomach. Sure enough, a week before we were set to open, our leading lady abruptly resigned—from my play and from *Painting Churches*, the play that was in mid-run.

The Denver Center was stunned and very apologetic. They felt terrible about the damage my play would sustain by the abrupt departure. "In a perfect world, who would you cast?" they asked me. I told them, "Julianna McCarthy."

Julianna was hired and flown in from Los Angeles. No sooner did the center's directors lay eyes on her work than they asked her not only to do my play but also to take over the run of *Painting Churches*—for which she was brilliantly cast.

"God is showing off," I laughed to Julianna, very happy that she had the chance to do "her" play after all.

In my experience, the universe falls in with worthy plans and most especially with festive and expansive ones. I have seldom conceived a delicious plan without being given the means to accomplish it. Understand that the *what* must come before the *how*. First choose *what* you would do. The *how* usually falls into place of itself.

> *Desire, ask, believe, receive.*
>
> STELLA TERRILL MANN

All too often, when people talk about creative work, they emphasize strategy. Neophytes are advised of the Machiavellian devices they must employ to break into the field. I think this is a lot of rubbish. If you ask an artist how he got where he is, he will not describe breaking in but instead will talk of a series of lucky breaks. "A thousand unseen helping hands," Joseph Campbell calls these breaks. I call them synchronicity. It is my contention that you can count on them.

Remember that creativity is a tribal experience and that tribal elders will initiate the gifted youngsters who cross their path. This may sound like wishful thinking, but it is not. Sometimes an older artist will be moved to help out even against his or her own wishes. "I don't know why I'm doing this for you, but . . ." Again, I would say that some of the helping hands may be something more than human.

We like to pretend it is hard to follow our heart's dreams. The truth is, it is difficult to avoid walking through the many doors that will open. Turn aside your dream and it will come back to you again. Get willing to follow it again and a second mysterious door will swing open.

The universe is prodigal in its support. We are miserly in what we accept. All gift horses are looked in the mouth and usually returned to sender. We say we are scared by failure, but what frightens us more is the possibility of success.

Take a small step in the direction of a dream and watch the synchronous doors flying open. Seeing, after all, is believing. And if you see the results of your experiments, you will not need to believe me. Remember the maxim "Leap, and the net will appear." In his book, *The Scottish Himalayan Expedition*, W. H. Murray tells us his explorer's experience:

> Until one is committed, there is hesitancy, the chance to draw back, always ineffectiveness. Concerning all acts of initiative [or creation] there is one elementary truth, the ignorance of which kills countless ideas and splendid plans: that the moment one definitely commits oneself, then Providence moves too.
>
> All sorts of things occur to help one that would otherwise never have occurred. A whole stream of events issues from the decision, raising in one's favor all manner of incidents and meetings and material assistance which no man would have believed would have come his way.

Genuine beginnings begin within us, even when they are brought to our attention by external opportunities.

WILLIAM BRIDGES

If you do not trust Murray—or me—you might want to trust Goethe. Statesman, scholar, artist, man of the world. Goethe had this to say on the will of Providence assisting our efforts:

Whatever you think you can do or believe you can do, begin it. Action has magic, grace, and power in it.

Shame

Some of you are thinking, "If it were that easy to take an action, I wouldn't be reading this book." Those of us who get bogged down by fear before action are usually being sabotaged by an older enemy, shame. Shame is a controlling device. Shaming someone is an attempt to prevent the person from behaving in a way that embarrasses us.

Making a piece of art may feel a lot like telling a family secret. Secret telling, by its very nature, involves shame and fear. It asks the question "What will they think of me once they know this?" This is a frightening question, particularly if we have ever been made to feel ashamed for our curiosities and explorations—social, sexual, spiritual.

"How dare you?" angry adults often rage at an innocent child who has stumbled onto a family secret. (How dare you open your mother's jewelry box? How dare you open your father's desk drawer? How dare you open the bedroom door? How dare you go down in the cellar, up in the attic, into some dark place where we hide those things we don't want you to know?)

The act of making art exposes a society to itself. Art brings things to light. It illuminates us. It sheds light on our lingering darkness. It casts a beam into the heart of our own darkness and says, "See?"

When people do not want to see something, they get mad at the one who shows them. They kill the messenger. A child from an alcoholic home gets into trouble scholastically or sexually. The family is flagged as being troubled. The child is made to feel shame for bringing shame to the family. But did the child bring shame? No. The child brought shameful things to light. The family shame predated and caused the child's distress. "What will the neighbors think?" is a shaming device aimed at continuing a conspiracy of illness.

Art opens the closets, airs out the cellars and attics. It brings healing. But before a wound can heal it must be seen, and this act of exposing the wound to air and light, the artist's act, is often reacted to with shaming. Bad reviews are a prime source of shame for many artists. The truth is, many reviews do aim at creating shame in an artist. "Shame on you! How dare you make that rotten piece of art?"

> *The cost of a thing is the amount of what I call life which is required to be exchanged for it, immediately or in the long run.*
>
> HENRY DAVID THOREAU

For the artist who endured childhood shaming—over any form of neediness, any type of exploration, any expectation—shame may kick in even without the aid of a shame-provoking review. If a child has ever been made to feel foolish for believing himself or herself talented, the act of actually finishing a piece of art will be fraught with internal shaming.

Many artists begin a piece of work, get well along in it, and then find, as they near completion, that the work seems mysteriously drained of merit. It's no longer worth the trouble. To therapists, this surge of sudden disinterest ("It doesn't matter") is a routine coping device employed to deny pain and ward off vulnerability.

Adults who grew up in dysfunctional homes learn to use this coping device very well. They call it detachment, but it is actually a numbing out.

"He forgot my birthday. Oh, well, no big deal."

A lifetime of this kind of experience, in which needs for recognition are routinely dishonored, teaches a young child that putting anything out for attention is a dangerous act.

"Dragging home the invisible bone" is how one recovering artist characterized her vain search for an achievement big enough to gain approval in her family of origin. "No matter how big a deal it was, they never seemed to take much notice. They always found something wrong with it. All A's and one B and that B got the attention."

It is only natural that a young artist try to flag parental attention by way of accomplishments—positive or negative. Faced with indifference or rage, such youngsters soon learn that no bone would really meet with parental approval.

Often we are wrongly shamed as creatives. From this shaming we learn that we are wrong to create. Once we learn this lesson, we forget it instantly. Buried under *it doesn't matter*, the shame lives on, waiting to attach itself to our new efforts. The very act of attempting to make art creates shame.

This is why many a great student film is never sent off to festivals where it can be seen; why good novels are destroyed or live in desk drawers. This is why plays do not get sent out, why talented actors don't audition. This is why artists may feel shame at admitting their dreams. Shame is retriggered in us as adults because our internal artist is always our creative child. Because of this, making a piece of art may cause us to feel shame.

We don't make art with its eventual criticism foremost in mind, but criticism that asks a question like "How could you?" can make an artist feel like a shamed child. A well-meaning friend who constructively criticizes a beginning writer may very well end that writer.

Let me be clear. Not all criticism is shaming. In fact, even the most severe criticism when it fairly hits the mark is apt to be greeted by an internal *Ah-hah!* if it shows the artist a new and valid path for work. The criticism that damages is that

> *We will discover the nature of our particular genius when we stop trying to conform to our own or to other peoples' models, learn to be ourselves, and allow our natural channel to open.*
>
> SHAKTI GAWAIN

which disparages, dismisses, ridicules, or condemns. It is frequently vicious but vague and difficult to refute. This is the criticism that damages.

Shamed by such criticism, an artist may become blocked or stop sending work out into the world. A perfectionist friend, teacher, or critic—like a perfectionist parent who nitpicks at missing commas—can dampen the ardor of a young artist who is just learning to let it rip. Because of this, as artists, we must learn to be very self-protective.

Does this mean no criticism? No. It means learning where and when to seek out right criticism. As artists, we must learn when criticism is appropriate and from whom. Not only the source but the timing is very important here. A first draft is seldom appropriately shown to any but the most gentle and discerning eye. It often takes another artist to see the embryonic work that is trying to sprout. The inexperienced or harsh critical eye, instead of nurturing the shoot of art into being, may shoot it down instead.

Since you are like no other being ever created since the beginning of time, you are incomparable.

BRENDA UELAND

As artists, we cannot control all the criticism we will receive. We cannot make our professional critics more healthy or more loving or more constructive than they are. But we can learn to comfort our artist child over unfair criticism; we can learn to find friends with whom we can safely vent our pain. We can learn not to deny and stuff our feelings when we have been artistically savaged.

I have made my world and it is a much better world than I ever saw outside.

LOUISE NEVELSON

Art requires a safe hatchery. Ideally, artists find this first in their family, then in their school, and finally in a community of friends and supporters. This ideal is seldom a reality. As artists, we must learn to create our own safe environments. We must learn to protect our artist child from shame. We do this by defusing our childhood shamings, getting them on the page, and sharing them with a trusted, nonshaming other.

By telling our shame secrets around our art and telling them through our art, we release ourselves and others from darkness. This release is not always welcomed.

We must learn that when our art reveals a secret of the human soul, those watching it may try to shame us for making it.

"It's terrible!" they may say, attacking the work when the work itself is actually fine. This can be very confusing. When we are told, "Shame on you" and feel it, we must learn to recognize this shame as a re-creation of childhood shames.

"I know that work is good. . . . I thought that was good work. . . . Could I be kidding myself? . . . Maybe that critic is right. . . . Why did I ever have the nerve to think . . .?" And the downward spiral begins.

At these times, we must be very firm with ourselves and not pick up the first doubt. We simply cannot allow the first negative thinking to take hold. Taking in the first doubt is like picking up the first drink for an alcoholic. Once in our system, the doubt will take on another doubt—and another. Doubting thoughts can be stopped, but it takes vigilance to do it. "Maybe that critic was right. . . ." And, *boom*, we must go into action: "You are a good artist, a brave artist, you are doing well. It's good that you did the work. . . ."

What doesn't kill me makes me stronger.

Albert Camus

When *God's Will*, the romantic film comedy I directed, debuted in Washington, D.C., it was a homecoming for me. My earliest journalism work had been for the *Washington Post*. I was hoping for a hometown-girl-makes-good reception. But in the reviews printed prior to the opening, I did not get it.

The Post sent a young woman who watched an entire movie about theater people and then wrote that it was about movie people. She added that "Most" of my dialogue had been *stolen* from "Casablanca." I wondered what movie she had seen; not the one I made. My movie had forty odd theater jokes and a one line joke about "Casablanca." Those were the facts but they didn't do me any good.

I was mortified. Shamed. Ready to (almost) die.

Because the antidote for shame is self-love and self-praise, this is what I did. I went for a walk through Rock Creek Park. I prayed. I made a list for myself of past compliments and good reviews. I did not tell myself, "It doesn't matter." But I did tell my artist self, "You will heal."

And I showed up for my opening. It was a lot more successful than my reviews.

Three months later, my film was chosen for a prestigious European festival. They offered to fly me over. To pay my expenses. To showcase my film. I hesitated. The Washington shaming had done its slow and poisonous work. I was afraid to go.

But I knew better than to not go. My years in artistic recovery had taught me to just show up. When I did, my film sold at a great price and won a headline in *Variety*.

I share the headline because the irony of it was not lost on me. "*God's Will* Hit in Munich," it read.

It *is* "God's will" for us to be creative.

Dealing with Criticism

It is important to be able to sort useful criticism from the other kind. Often we need to do the sorting out for ourselves, without the benefit of a public vindication. As artists, we are far more able to do this sorting than people might suspect. Pointed criticism, if accurate, often gives the artist an inner sense of relief: "Ah, hah! so that's what was wrong with it." Useful criticism ultimately leaves us with one more puzzle piece for our work.

Useless criticism, on the other hand, leaves us with a feeling of being bludgeoned. As a rule, it is withering and shaming in tone; ambiguous in content; personal, inaccurate, or blanket in its condemnations. There is nothing to be gleaned from irresponsible criticism.

You are dealing with an inner child. Artistic child abuse creates rebellion creates block. All that can be done with abusive criticism is to heal from it.

There are certain rules of the road useful in dealing with *any* form of criticism.

> *The words that enlighten the soul are more precious than jewels.*
>
> HAZRAT INAYAT KHAN
>
> *Artists who seek perfection in everything are those who cannot attain it in anything.*
>
> EUGÈNE DELACROIX

1. Receive the criticism all the way through and get it over with.
2. Jot down notes to yourself on what concepts or phrases bother you.
3. Jot down notes on what concepts or phrases seem useful.
4. Do something very nurturing for yourself—read an old good review or recall a compliment.
5. Remember that even if you have made a truly rotten piece of art, it may be a *necessary* stepping-stone to your next work. Art matures spasmodically and *requires* ugly-duckling growth stages.
6. Look at the criticism again. Does it remind you of any criticism from your past—particularly shaming childhood criticism? Acknowledge to yourself that the current criticism is triggering grief over a long-standing wound.
7. Write a letter to the critic—not to be mailed, most probably. Defend your work *and* acknowledge what was helpful, if anything in the criticism proffered.
8. Get back on the horse. Make an immediate commitment to do something creative.
9. Do it. Creativity is the only cure for criticism.

Detective Work, an Exercise

Many blocked people are actually very powerful and creative personalities who have been made to feel guilty about their own strengths and gifts. Without being acknowledged, they are often used as batteries by their families and friends, who feel free to both use their creative energies and disparage them. When these blocked artists strive to break free of their dysfunctional systems, they are often urged to be sensible when such advice is not appropriate for them. Made to feel guilty for their talents, they often hide their own light under a bushel for fear of hurting others. Instead, they hurt themselves.

Take your life in your own hands and what happens? A terrible thing: no one to blame.

ERICA JONG

A little sleuth work is in order to restore the persons we have abandoned—ourselves. When you complete the following phrases, you may feel strong emotion as you retrieve memories and misplaced fragments of yourself. Allow yourself to free-associate for a sentence or so with each phrase.

1. My favorite childhood toy was . . .
2. My favorite childhood game was . . .
3. The best movie I ever saw as a kid was . . .
4. I don't do it much but I enjoy . . .
5. If I could lighten up a little, I'd let myself . . .
6. If it weren't too late, I'd . . .
7. My favorite musical instrument is . . .
8. The amount of money I spend on treating myself to entertainment each month is . . .
9. If I weren't so stingy with my artist, I'd buy him/her . . .
10. Taking time out for myself is . . .
11. I am afraid that if I start dreaming . . .
12. I secretly enjoy reading . . .
13. If I had had a perfect childhood I'd have grown up to be . . .
14. If it didn't sound so crazy, I'd write or make a . . .
15. My parents think artists are . . .
16. My God thinks artists are . . .
17. What makes me feel weird about this recovery is . . .

18.   Learning to trust myself is probably . . .
19.   My most cheer-me-up music is . . .
20.   My favorite way to dress is . . .

Growth

Growth is an erratic forward movement: two steps forward, one step back. Remember that and be very gentle with yourself. A creative recovery is a healing process. You are capable of great things on Tuesday, but on Wednesday you may slide backward. This is normal. Growth occurs in spurts. You will lie dormant sometimes. Do not be discouraged. Think of it as resting.

Very often, a week of insights will be followed by a week of sluggishness. The morning pages will seem pointless. *They are not.* What you are learning to do, writing them even when you are tired and they seem dull, is to rest on the page. This is very important. Marathon runners suggest you log ten slow miles for every fast one. The same holds true for creativity.

In this sense, *Easy does it* is actually a modus operandi. It means, "Easy accomplishes it." If you will hew to a practice of writing three pages every morning and doing one kind thing for yourself every day, you will begin to notice a slight lightness of heart.

Practice being kind to yourself in small, concrete ways. Look at your refrigerator. Are you feeding yourself nicely? Do you have socks? An extra set of sheets? What about a new house plant? A thermos for the long drive to work? Allow yourself to pitch out some of your old ragged clothes. You don't have to keep everything.

The expression "God helps those who help themselves" may take on a new and very different meaning. Where in the past it translated, "God helps only those who earn help," it will now come to signify the amazing number of small free gifts the creator showers on those who are helping themselves to a little bounty. If you do one nice thing a day for yourself, God will do two more. Be alert for support and encouragement from unexpected quarters. Be open to receiving gifts

> *There is a vitality, a life force, an energy, a quickening, that is translated through you into action, and because there is only one of you in all time, this expression is unique. And if you block it, it will never exist through any other medium and will be lost.*
>
> MARTHA GRAHAM

from odd channels: free tickets, a free trip, an offer to buy you dinner, a new-to-you old couch. Practice saying yes to such help.

The scientifically inclined among you might want to make a good, thorough list of clothes you wish you had. Very often, the items on the list come into your possession at disconcerting speed. Just try it. Experiment.

More than anything else, experiment with solitude. You will need to make a commitment to quiet time. Try to acquire the habit of checking in with yourself.

Several times a day, just take a beat, and ask yourself how *you* are feeling. Listen to your answer. Respond kindly. If you are doing something very hard, promise yourself a break and a treat afterward.

Yes, I *am* asking you to baby yourself. We believe that to be artists we must be tough, cynical, and intellectually chilly. Leave that to the critics. As a creative being, you will be more productive when coaxed than when bullied.

> *Whenever I have to choose between two evils, I always like to try the one I haven't tried before.*
>
> MAE WEST

TASKS

1. Describe your childhood room. If you wish, you may sketch this room. What was your favorite thing about it? What's your favorite thing about your room right now? Nothing? Well, get something you like in there—maybe something from that old childhood room.

2. Describe five traits you like in yourself as a child.

3. List five childhood accomplishments (straight A's in seventh grade, trained the dog, punched out the class bully, short-sheeted the priest's bed).
   And a treat: list five favorite childhood foods. Buy yourself one of them this week. Yes, Jell-O with bananas is okay.

4. Habits: Take a look at your habits. Many of them may interfere with your self-nurturing and cause shame. Some of the oddest things are self-destructive. Do you have a habit of watching TV you don't like? Do you have a habit of hanging out with a really boring friend and just killing time (there's an expression!)? Some rotten habits are obvious, overt (drinking too much, smoking, eating instead of writing). List three obvious rotten habits. What's the payoff in continuing them?

Some rotten habits are more subtle (no time to exercise, little time to pray, always helping others, not getting any self-nurturing, hanging out with people who belittle your dreams). List three of your subtle foes. What use do these forms of sabotage have? Be specific.

5. Make a list of friends who nurture you—that's *nurture* (give you a sense of your own competency and possibility), not enable (give you the message that you will never get it straight without their help). There is a big difference between being helped and being treated as though we are help-less. List three nurturing friends. Which of their traits, particularly, serve you well?

6. Call a friend who treats you like you are a really good and bright person who can accomplish things. Part of your recovery is reaching out for support. This support will be critical as you undertake new risks.

7. Inner Compass: Each of us has an inner compass. This is an instinct that points us toward health. It warns us when we are on dangerous ground, and it tells us when something is safe and good for us. Morning pages are one way to contact it. So are some other artist-brain activities—painting, driving, walking, scrubbing, running. This week, take an hour to follow your inner compass by doing an artist-brain activity and *listening* to what insights bubble up.

8. List five people you admire. Now, list five people you secretly admire. What traits do these people have that you can cultivate further in yourself?

9. List five people you wish you had met who are dead. Now, list five people who are dead whom you'd like to hang out with for a while in eternity. What traits do you find in these people that you can look for in your friends?

10. Compare the two sets of lists. Take a look at what you really like and really admire—and a look at what you think you should like and admire. Your *shoulds* might tell you to admire Edison while your heart belongs to Houdini. Go with the Houdini side of you for a while.

Creative work is play. It is free speculation using the materials of one's chosen form.

STEPHEN NACHMANOVITCH

Creativity is . . . seeing something that doesn't exist already. You need to find out how you can bring it into being and that way be a playmate with God.

MICHELE SHEA

CHECK-IN

1. **How many days this week did you do your morning pages?** How was the experience for you? If you skipped a day, why did you skip it?

2. **Did you do your artist date this week?** (Yes, yes, and it was *awful*.) What did you do? How did it feel?

3. **Did you experience any synchronicity this week?** What was it?

4. **Were there any other issues this week that you consider significant for your recovery?** Describe them.

Recovering a Sense of Integrity

This week may find you grappling with changing self-definition. The essays, tasks, and exercises are designed to catapult you into productive introspection and integration of new self-awareness. This may be both very difficult and extremely exciting for you. Warning: Do not skip the tool of reading deprivation!

Honest Changes

WORKING WITH THE MORNING pages, we begin to sort through the differences between our *real* feelings, which are often secret, and our *official* feelings, those on the record for public display. Official feelings are often indicated by the phrase, "I feel okay about that [the job loss, her dating someone else, my dad's death, . . .]."

What do we mean by "I feel okay"? The morning pages force us to get specific. Does "I feel okay" mean I feel resigned, accepting, comfortable, detached, numb, tolerant, pleased, or satisfied? *What* does it mean?

Okay is a blanket word for most of us. It covers all sorts of squirmy feelings; and it frequently signals a loss. We officially feel okay, but do we?

At the root of a successful creative recovery is the commitment to puncture our denial, to stop saying, "It's okay" when in fact it's something else. The morning pages press us to answer what else.

In my years of watching people work with morning pages, I have noticed that many tend to neglect or abandon the pages whenever an unpleasant piece of clarity is about to emerge. If we are, for example, very, very angry but not admitting it, then we will be tempted to say we feel "okay about that." The morning pages will not allow us to get away with this evasion. So we tend to avoid them.

Each painting has its own way of evolving. . . . When the painting is finished, the subject reveals itself.

WILLIAM BAZIOTES

Eliminate something superfluous from your life. Break a habit. Do something that makes you feel insecure.

PIERO FERRUCCI

If we have the creeping feeling that our lover is not being totally honest with us, the morning pages are liable to bring this creepy possibility up—and with it, the responsibility for an unsettling conversation. Rather than face this mess, we will mess up on doing the morning pages.

By contrast, if we are suddenly and madly in love, the morning pages may seem threatening. We don't want to puncture the fragile and shiny bubble of our happiness. We want to stay lost in the sea of a blissful us rather than be reminded that there is an I in the we (or an "eye" in the we) that is temporarily blinded.

In short, extreme emotions of any kind—the very thing that morning pages are superb for processing—are the usual triggers for avoiding the pages themselves.

Just as an athlete accustomed to running becomes irritable when he is unable to get his miles in, so, too, those of us accustomed now to morning pages will notice an irritability when we let them slide. We are tempted, always, to reverse cause and effect: "I was too crabby to write them," instead of, "I didn't write them so I am crabby."

Over any considerable period of time, the morning pages perform spiritual chiropractic. They realign our values. If we are to the left or the right of our personal truth, the pages will point out the need for a course adjustment. We will become aware of our drift and correct it—if only to hush the pages up.

"To thine own self be true," the pages say, while busily pointing that self out. It was in the pages that Mickey, a painter, first learned she wanted to write comedy. No wonder all her friends were writers. So was she!

Chekhov advised, "If you want to work on your art, work on your life." That's another way of saying that in order to have self-expression, we must first have a self to express. That is the business of the morning pages: "I, myself, feel this way . . . and that way . . . and this way. . . . No one else need agree with me, but this is what *I* feel."

The process of identifying a *self* inevitably involves loss as well as gain. We discover our boundaries, and those boundaries by definition separate us from our fellows. As we clarify our perceptions, we lose our misconceptions. As we eliminate ambiguity, we lose illusion as well. We arrive at clarity, and clarity creates change.

"I have outgrown this job," may appear in the morning pages. At first, it is a troubling perception. Over time, it becomes a call for action and then an action plan.

"This marriage is not working for me," the morning pages say. And then, "I wonder about couples therapy?" And then, "I wonder if I'm not just bored with me?"

In addition to posing problems, the pages may also pose solutions. "I *am* bored with me. It would be fun to learn French." Or, "I noticed a sign just down the block for a clay and fiber class. That sounds interesting."

As we notice which friends bore us, which situations leave us stifled, we are often rocked by waves of sorrow. We may want our illusions back! We want to pretend the friendship works. We don't want the trauma of searching for another job.

Faced with impending change, change we have set in motion through our own hand, we want to mutiny, curl up in a ball, bawl our eyes out. "No pain, no gain," the nasty slogan has it. And we resent this pain no matter what gain it is bringing us.

"I don't want to raise my consciousness!" we wail. "I want . . ." And thanks to the morning pages we learn what we want and ultimately become willing to make the changes needed to get it. But not without a tantrum. And not without a *kriya*, a Sanskrit word meaning a spiritual emergency or surrender. (I always think of kriyas as spiritual seizures. Perhaps they should be spelled *crias* because they are cries of the soul as it is wrung through changes.)

We all know what a kriya looks like: it is the bad case of the flu right after you've broken up with your lover. It's the rotten head cold and bronchial cough that announces you've abused your health to meet an unreachable work deadline. That asthma attack out of nowhere when you've just done a round of *care*-taking your alcoholic sibling? That's a kriya, too.

Always significant, frequently psychosomatic, kriyas are the final insult our psyche adds to our injuries: "Get it?" a kriya asks you.

Get it:

You can't stay with this abusive lover.

You can't work at a job that demands eighty hours a week.

You can't rescue a brother who needs to save himself.

Stop thinking and talking about it and there is nothing you will not be able to know.

ZEN PARADIGM

In twelve-step groups, kriyas are often called *surrenders*. People are told *just let go*. And they would if they knew what they were holding on to. With the morning pages in place and the artist dates in motion, the radio set stands half a chance of picking up the message you are sending and/or receiving. The pages round up the usual suspects. They mention the small hurts we prefer to ignore, the large successes we've failed to acknowledge. In short, the morning pages point the way to reality: this is how you're feeling; what do you make of that?

And what we make of that is often art.

People frequently believe the creative life is grounded in fantasy. The more difficult truth is that creativity is grounded in reality, in the particular, the focused, the well observed or specifically imagined.

As we lose our vagueness about our self, our values, our life situation, we become available to the moment. It is there, in the particular, that we contact the creative self. Until we experience the freedom of solitude, we cannot connect authentically. We may be enmeshed, but we are not encountered.

Art lies in the moment of encounter: we meet our truth and we meet ourselves; we meet ourselves and we meet our self-expression. We become original because we become something specific: an origin from which work flows.

As we gain—or regain—our creative identity, we lose the false self we were sustaining. The loss of this false self can feel traumatic: "I don't know who I am anymore. I don't recognize me."

All the arts we practice are apprenticeship. The big art is our life.

M. C. RICHARDS

It is not because things are difficult that we do not dare; it is because we do not dare that they are difficult.

SENECA

Remember that the more you feel yourself to be terra incognita, the more certain you can be that the recovery process is working. You are your own promised land, your own new frontier.

Shifts in taste and perception frequently accompany shifts in identity. One of the clearest signals that something healthy is afoot is the impulse to weed out, sort through, and discard old clothes, papers, and belongings.

"I don't need this anymore," we say as we toss a low-self-worth shirt into the giveaway pile. "I'm sick of this broken-down dresser and its sixteen coats of paint," as the dresser goes off to Goodwill.

By tossing out the old and unworkable, we make way for the new and suitable. A closet stuffed with ratty old clothes does not invite new ones. A house overflowing with odds and ends and tidbits you've held on to for someday has no space for the things that might truly enhance today.

When the search-and-discard impulse seizes you, two crosscurrents are at work: the old you is leaving and grieving, while the new you celebrates and grows strong. As with any rupture, there is both tension and relief. Long-seated depression breaks up like an ice floe. Long-frozen feelings thaw, melt, cascade, flood, and often overrun their container (you). You may find yourself feeling volatile and changeable. You are.

Be prepared for bursts of tears and of laughter. A certain giddiness may accompany sudden stabs of loss. Think of yourself as an accident victim walking away from the crash: your old life has crashed and burned; your new life isn't apparent yet. You may feel yourself to be temporarily without a vehicle. Just keep walking.

If this description sounds dramatic, it is only to prepare you for possible emotional pyrotechnics. You may not have them. Your changes may be more like cloud movements, from overcast to partly cloudy. It is important to know that no matter which form your growth takes, there is another kind of change, slower and more subtle, accumulating daily whether you sense its presence or not.

"Nothing dramatic is happening to me. I don't think the process is working," I have often been told by someone who from my perspective is changing at the speed of light. The analogy that I use is that once we engage in the process of morning pages and artist dates, we begin to move at such velocity that we do not even realize the pace. Just as travelers on a jet are seldom aware of their speed unless they hit a patch of turbulence, so, too, travelers on the Artist's Way are seldom aware of the speed of their growth. This is a form of denial that can tempt us to abort the recovery process that "isn't happening" to us. Oh yes it is.

When we have engaged the creator within to heal us, many changes and shifts in our attitudes begin to occur I enumerate some of them here because many of these will not be recognizable at first as healing. If fact, they may seem crazy and even destructive. At best, they will seem eccentric.

There will be a change in energy patterns. Your dreams will become stronger and clearer, both by night and by day. You will find yourself remembering your nighttime dreams, and by day, daydreams will catch your attention. Fantasy, of a benign and unexpected sort, will begin to crop up.

> *To become truly immortal, a work of art must escape all human limits: logic and common sense will only interfere. But once these barriers are broken, it will enter the realms of childhood visions and dreams.*
>
> GIORGIO DE CHIRICO

Many areas of your life that previously seemed to fit will stop fitting. Half your wardrobe may start to look funny. You may decide to reupholster a couch or just toss it out. Musical bents may alter. There may even be bursts of spontaneous singing, dancing, running.

You may find your candor unsettling. "I don't like that" is a sentence that will leave your mouth. Or "I think that's great." In short, your tastes and judgments and personal identity will begin to show through.

What you have been doing is wiping the mirror. Each day's morning pages take a swipe at the blur you have kept between you and your real self. As your image becomes clearer, it may surprise you. You may discover very particular likes and dislikes that you hadn't acknowledged. A fondness for cactuses. So why do I have these pots of ivy? A dislike for brown. So why do I keep wearing that sweater if I never feel right in it?

Conditioned as we are to accept other peoples' definitions of us, this emerging individuality can seem to us like self-will run riot. It is not.

The snowflake pattern of your soul is emerging. Each of us is a unique, creative individual. But we often blur that uniqueness with sugar, alcohol, drugs, overwork, underplay, bad relations, toxic sex, underexercise, over-TV, undersleep—many and varied forms of junk food for the soul. The pages help us to see these smears on our consciousness.

> *The center that I cannot find is known to my unconscious mind.*
>
> W. H. AUDEN

> *All you need to do to receive guidance is to ask for it and then listen.*
>
> SANAYA ROMAN

Is you look over the time you have been doing your morning writing, you will see that many changes have entered your life as a result of your willingness to clear room in it for your creator's action. You will have noticed an increased, sometimes disconcerting, sense of personal energy, some bursts of anger, some flash points of clarity. People and objects may have taken on a different meaning to you. There will be a sense of the flow of life—that you are brought into new vistas as you surrender to moving with the flow of God. This is clear already.

You may well be experiencing a sense of both bafflement and faith. You are no longer stuck, but you cannot tell where you are going. You may feel that this can't keep up. You may long for the time when there was no sense of possibility, when you felt more victimized, when you didn't realize how many small things you could do to improve your own life.

It is normal to yearn for some rest when you are moving so rapidly. What you will learn to do is rest in motion, like lying down in a boat. Your morning pages are your boat. They will both lead you forward and give you a place to recuperate from your forward motion.

It is difficult for us to realize that this process of going inside and writing pages can open an inner door through which our creator helps and guides us. Our willingness swings this inner door open. The morning pages symbolize our willingness to speak to and hear God. They lead us into many other changes that also come from God and lead us to God. This is the hand of God moving through your hand as you write. It is very powerful.

One technique that can be very reassuring at this point is to use your morning pages—or a part of them—for written affirmation of your progress.

"Put it in writing," we often say when making a deal.

There is a special power in writing out the deal we are making with our creator. "I receive your good willingly" and "Thy will be done" are two short affirmations that when written in the morning remind us to be open to increased good during the day.

"I trust my perceptions" is another powerful affirmation to use as we undergo shifts in identity. "A stronger and clearer me is emerging."

Choose affirmations according to your need. As you excavate your buried dreams, you need the assurance that such explorations are permissible: "I recover and enjoy my identity."

Buried Dreams, an Exercise

As recovering creatives, we often have to excavate our own pasts for the shards of buried dreams and delights. Do a little digging, please. Be fast and frivolous. This is an exercise in spontaneity, so be sure to write your answers out quickly. Speed kills the Censor.

1. List five hobbies that sound fun.
2. List five classes that sound fun.
3. List five things you personally would *never* do that sound fun.
4. List five skills that would be fun to have.

5. List five things you used to enjoy doing.
6. List five silly things you would like to try once.

As you may have gathered by this point in your work, we will approach certain problems from many different angles, all of them aimed at eliciting more information from your unconscious about what you might consciously enjoy. The exercise that follows will teach you enormous amounts about yourself—as well as giving you some free time in which to pursue the interests you just listed.

Reading Deprivation

If you feel stuck in your life or in your art, few jump starts are more effective than a week of *reading deprivation*.

> *We are always doing something, talking, reading, listening to the radio, planning what next. The mind is kept naggingly busy on some easy, unimportant external thing all day.*
>
> BRENDA UELAND

No reading? That's right: no reading. For most artists, words are like tiny tranquilizers. We have a daily quota of media chat that we swallow up. Like greasy food, it clogs our system. Too much of it and we feel, yes, fried.

It is a paradox that by emptying our lives of distractions we are actually filling the well. Without distractions, we are once again thrust into the sensory world. With no newspaper to shield us, a train becomes a viewing gallery. With no novel to sink into (and no television to numb us out) an evening becomes a vast savannah in which furniture—and other assumptions—get rearranged.

Reading deprivation casts us into our inner silence, a space some of us begin to immediately fill with new words—long, gossipy conversations, television bingeing, the radio as a constant, chatty companion. We often cannot hear our own inner voice, the voice of our artist's inspiration, above the static. In practicing reading deprivation, we need to cast a watchful eye on these other pollutants. They poison the well.

If we monitor the inflow and keep it to a minimum, we will be rewarded for our reading deprivation with embarrassing speed. Our reward will be a new outflow. Our own art, our own thoughts and feelings, will begin to nudge aside the sludge of blockage, to loosen it and move it upward and outward until once again our well is running freely.

Reading deprivation is a very powerful tool—and a very frightening one. Even thinking about it can bring up enormous rage. For most blocked creatives, reading is an addiction. We gobble the words of others rather than digest our own thoughts and feelings, rather than cook up something of our own.

In my teaching, the week that I assign reading deprivation is always a tough one. I go to the podium knowing that I will be the enemy. I break the news that we won't be reading and then I brace myself for the waves of antagonism and sarcasm that follow.

At least one student always explains to me—pointedly, in no uncertain terms—that he or she is a very important and busy person with duties and obligations that include reading.

> *In a dark time, the eye begins to see.*
>
> THEODORE ROETHKE

This information is inevitably relayed in a withering tone that implies I am an idiot child, an artistic flake, unable to grasp the complexities of an adult's life. I just listen.

When the rage has been vented, when all the assigned reading for college courses and jobs has been mentioned, I point out that I have had jobs and I have gone to college and that in my experience I had many times wriggled out of reading for a week due to procrastination. As blocked creatives, we can be very creative at wriggling out of things. I ask my class to turn their creativity to wriggling *into* not reading.

"But what will we do?" comes next.

Here is a brief list of some things that people do when they are not reading:

Listen to music.	Knit.	Work out.
Make curtains.	Cook.	Meditate.
Wash the dog.	Fix the bike.	Have friends to dinner.
Sort closets.	Watercolor.	Get the stereo working.
Pay bills.	Rewire the lamp.	Sort bookshelves (a dangerous one!).
Write old friends.	Paint the bedroom.	Go dancing.
Report some plants.	Rearrange the kitchen.	
Mend.		

Even at the safe remove of the written word, I can feel the shock waves of antagonism about trying this tool. I will tell you that those who have most resisted it have come back the most smugly rewarded for having done it. The nasty bottom line is this: sooner or later, if you are not reading, you will run out of work and be forced to play. You'll light some incense or put on an old jazz record or paint a shelf turquoise, and then you will feel not just better but actually a little excited.

Don't read. If you can't think of anything else to do, cha-cha.

(Yes, you can read and do this week's tasks.)

TASKS

1. Environment: Describe your ideal environment. Town? Country? Swank? Cozy? One paragraph. One image, drawn or clipped, that conveys this. What's your favorite season? Why? Go through some magazines and find an image of this. Or draw it. Place it near your working area.

2. Time Travel: Describe yourself at eighty. What did you do after fifty that you enjoyed? Be very specific. Now, write a letter from you at eighty to you at your current age. What would you tell yourself? What interests would you urge yourself to pursue? What dreams would you encourage?

3. Time Travel: Remember yourself at eight. What did you like to do? What were your favorite things? Now, write a letter from you at eight to you at your current age. What would you tell yourself?

4. Environment: Look at your house. Is there any room that you could make into a secret, private space for yourself? Convert the TV room? Buy a screen or hang a sheet and cordon off a section of some other room? This is your dream area. It should be decorated for fun and not as an office. All you really need is a chair or pillow, something to write on, some kind of little altar area for flowers and candles. This is to help you center on the fact that creativity is a spiritual, not an ego, issue.

5. Use your life pie (from Week One) to review your growth. Has that nasty tarantula changed shape yet? Haven't you been more active, less rigid, more

expressive? Be careful not to expect too much too soon. That's *raising the jumps.* Growth must have time to solidify into health. One day at a time, you are building the habit patterns of a healthy artist. Easy does do it. List ongoing self-nurturing toys you could buy your artist: books on tape, magazine subscriptions, theater tickets, a bowling ball.

6. Write your own Artist's Prayer. (See pages 210–211.) Use it every day for a week.

7. An Extended Artist Date: Plan a small vacation for yourself. (One weekend day. Get ready to execute it.)

8. Open your closet. Throw out—or hand on, or donate—one low-self-worth outfit. (You know the outfit.) Make space for the new.

9. Look at one situation in your life that you feel you should change but haven't yet. What is the payoff for you in staying stuck?

10. If you break your reading deprivation, write about how you did it. In a tantrum? A slipup? A binge? How do you feel about it? Why?

CHECK-IN

1. **How many days this week did you do your morning pages?** (Tantrums often show up as skipping the morning pages.) How was the experience for you?

2. **Did you do your artist date this week?** (Does your artist get to do more than rent a movie?) What did you do? How did it feel?

3. **Did you experience any synchronicity this week?** What was it?

4. **Were there any other issues this week that you consider significant for your recovery?** Describe them.

Recovering a Sense of Possibility

This week you are being asked to examine your payoffs in remaining stuck. You will explore how you curtail your own possibilities by placing limits on the good you can receive. You will examine the cost of settling for appearing good instead of being authentic. You may find yourself thinking about radical changes, no longer ruling out your growth by making others the cause of your constriction.

Limits

ONE OF THE CHIEF barriers to accepting God's generosity is our limited notion of what we are in fact able to accomplish. We may tune in to the voice of the creator within, hear a message—and then discount it as crazy or impossible. On the one hand, we take ourselves very seriously and don't want to look like idiots pursuing some patently grandiose scheme. On the other hand, we don't take ourselves—or God—seriously enough and so we define as grandiose many schemes that, with God's help, may fall well within our grasp.

Remembering that God is my source, we are in the spiritual position of having an unlimited bank account. Most of us never consider how powerful the creator really is. Instead, we draw very limited amounts of the power available to us. We decide how powerful God is for us. We unconsciously set a limit on how much God can give us or help us. We are stingy with ourselves. And if we receive a gift beyond our imagining, we often send it back.

Some of you may be thinking that this sounds like the magic-wand chapter: I pray and presto! Sometimes, that *is* how it will feel. More often, what we are talking

Except your every need to be met, expect the answer to every problem, expect abundance on every level, expect to grow spiritually.

EILEEN CADDY

Look and you will find it—what is unsought will go undetected.

SOPHOCLES

about seems to be a conscious partnership in which we work along slowly and gradually, clearing away the wreckage of our negative patterning, clarifying the vision of what it is we want, learning to accept small pieces of that vision from whatever source and then, one day, presto! The vision seems to suddenly be in place. In other words, pray to catch the bus, then run as fast as you can.

For this to happen, first of all, we must believe that we are allowed to catch the bus. We come to recognize that God is unlimited in supply and that everyone has equal access. This begins to clear up guilt about having or getting too much. Since everyone can draw on the universal supply, we deprive no one with our abundance. If we learn to think of receiving God's good as being an act of worship—cooperating with God's plan to manifest goodness in our lives—we can begin to let go of having to sabotage ourselves.

One reason we are miserly with ourselves is scarcity thinking. We don't want our luck to run out. We don't want to overspend our spiritual abundance. Again, we are limiting our flow by anthropomorphizing God into a capricious parent figure. Remembering that God is our source, an energy flow that *likes* to extend itself, we become more able to tap our creative power effectively.

God has lots of money. God has lots of movie ideas, novel ideas, poems, songs, paintings, acting jobs. God has a supply of loves, friends, houses that are all available to us. By listening to the creator within, we are led to our right path. On that path, we find friends, lovers, money, and meaningful work. Very often, when we cannot seem to find an adequate supply, it is because we are insisting on a particular human source of supply. We must learn to let the flow manifest itself where it will—not where we *will* it.

Cara, a writer, spent far longer than she should remaining in an abusive agent relationship because she thought it would be creative suicide to sever that professional tie. The relationship was plagued with evasions, half-truths, delays. Cara hung in, afraid to let go of her agent's prestige. Finally, after a particularly abusive phone call, Cara wrote a letter severing the relationship. She felt as if she had just jumped into outer space. When her husband came home, she tearfully told him how she had sabotaged her career. He listened and then said, "A week ago, I was in this bookstore and the owner asked me if you had a good agent. He gave me this woman's name and number. Call her."

Tearfully, Cara acquiesced. She got on the phone and connected immediately to the new agent's sensibility. They have been working together, very successfully, ever since.

To my eye, this is a story not only of synchronicity but also of right-dependence on universe as source. Once Cara became willing to receive her good from whatever source it appeared in, she stopped being victimized.

I recently had a woman artist tell me that she got her new and excellent agent by using affirmations. Even after years of artistic recovery, I still have my cynical side that says, "*Mmm.*" It is as though we want to believe God can create the subatomic structure but is clueless when faced with how to aid or fix our painting, sculpture, writing, film.

I recognize that many will balk at the simplicity of this concept. "God doesn't run the movie business," we want to say. "CAA does." I want to sound a cautionary note here for all artists who put their creative lives into solely human hands. This can block your good.

The desire to be worldly, sophisticated, and smart often blocks our flow. We have ideas and opinions about where our good should come from. As a Hollywood screenwriter, I had many rueful conversations with other screenwriters about the fact that while our agents were often invaluable, we seemed to get an awful lot of breaks from places like "my next door neighbor," "my dentist's brother," or "somebody my wife went to college with." Those breaks are God the source in action.

I have said before that creativity is a spiritual issue. Any progress is made by leaps of faith, some small and some large. At first, we may want faith to take the first dance class, the first step toward learning a new medium. Later, we may want the faith and the funds for further classes, seminars, a larger work space, a year's sabbatical. Later still, we may conceive an idea for a book, an artists' collective gallery space. As each idea comes to us, we must in good faith clear away our inner barriers to acting on it and then, on an outer level, take the concrete steps necessary to trigger our synchronous good.

> It is within my power either to serve God or not to serve him. Serving him, I add to my own good and the good of the whole world. Not serving him, I forfeit my own good and deprive the world of that good, which was in my power to create.
>
> LEO TOLSTOY

If this still sounds airy fairy to you, ask yourself bluntly what next step you are evading. What dream are you discounting as impossible given your resources? What payoff are you getting for remaining stuck at this point in your expansion?

God as my source is a simple but completely effective plan for living. It removes negative dependency—and anxiety—from our lives by assuring us that God will provide. Our job is to listen for how.

One way we listen is by writing our morning pages. At night, before we fall asleep, we can list areas in which we need guidance. In the morning, writing on these same topics, we find ourselves seeing previously unseen avenues of approach. Experiment with this two-step process: ask for answers in the evening; listen for answers in the morning. Be open to all help.

Finding the River

For four weeks now, we have been excavating our consciousness. We have seen how often we think negatively and fearfully, how frightening it has been for us to begin to believe that there might be a right place for us that we could attain by listening to our creative voice and following its guidance. We have begun to hope, and we have feared that hope.

The shift to spiritual dependency is a gradual one. We have been making this shift slowly and surely. With each day we become more true to ourselves, more open to the positive. To our surprise, this seems to be working in our human relationships. We find we are able to tell more of our truth, hear more of other people's truth, and encompass a far more kindly attitude toward both. We are becoming less judgmental of ourselves and others. How is this possible? The morning pages, a flow of stream of consciousness, gradually loosens our hold on fixed opinions and short-sighted views. We see that our moods, views, and insights are transitory. We acquire a sense of movement, a current of change in our lives. This current, or river, is a flow of grace moving us to our right livelihood, companions, destiny.

Dependence on the creator within is really freedom from all other dependencies. Paradoxically, it is also the only route to real intimacy with other human beings. Freed from our terrible fears of abandonment, we are able to live with more spontaneity. Freed from our constant demands for more and more reassurance, our fellows are able to love us back without feeling so burdened.

As we have listened to our artist child within, it has begun to feel more and more safe. Feeling safe, it speaks a little louder. Even on our worst days, a small, positive voice says, "You could still do this or it might be fun to do that. . . ."

Most of us find that as we work with the morning pages, we are rendered less rigid that we were. Recovery is the process of finding the river and saying yes to its flow, rapids and all. We startle ourselves by saying yes instead of no to opportunities. As we begin to pry ourselves loose from our old self-concepts, we find that our new, emerging self may enjoy all sorts of bizarre adventures.

Michelle, a hard-driving, dressed-for-success lawyer, enrolled in flamenco dancing lessons and loved them. Her house—formerly a sleek, careerist's high-tech showcase—suddenly began filling up with lush plants, plump pillows, sensuous incense. Tropical colors bloomed on the once-white walls. For the first time in years, she allowed herself to cook a little and then to sew again. She was still a successful lawyer, but her life took on a rounded shape. She laughed more, looked prettier. "I can't believe I am doing this!" she would announce with delight as she launched into some new venture. And then, "I can't believe I didn't do this sooner!"

By holding lightly to an attitude of gentle exploration, we can begin to lean into creative expansion. By replacing "No way!" with "Maybe," we open the door to mystery and to magic.

This newly positive attitude is the beginning of trust. We are starting to look for the silver lining in what appears to be adversity. Most of us find that as we work with the morning pages, we begin to treat ourselves more gently. Feeling less desperate, we are less harsh with ourselves and with others. This compassion is one of the first fruits of aligning our creativity with its creator.

As we come to trust and love our internal guide, we lose our fear of intimacy because we no longer confuse our intimate others with the higher power we are coming to know. In short, we are learning to give up idolatry—the worshipful dependency on any person, place, or thing. Instead, we place our dependency on the source itself. The source meets our needs through people, places, and things.

This concept is a very hard one for most of us to really credit. We tend to believe we must go out and shake a few trees to make things happen. I would not deny that shaking a few trees is good for us. In fact, I believe it is necessary. I

> *Often people attempt to live their lives backwards: they try to have more things, or more money, in order to do more of what they want so that they will be happier. The way it actually works is the reverse. You must first be who you really are, then, do what you need to do, in order to have what you want.*
>
> MARGARET YOUNG

call it *doing the footwork*. I want to say, however, that while the footwork is necessary, I have seldom seen it pay off in a linear fashion. It seems to work more like we shake the apple tree and the universe delivers oranges.

Time and again, I have seen a recovering creative do the footwork of becoming internally clear and focused about dreams and delights, take a few outward steps in the direction of the dream—only to have the universe fling open an unsuspected door. One of the central tasks of creative recovery is learning to accept this generosity.

The Virtue Trap

An artist must have downtime, time to do nothing. Defending our right to such time takes courage, conviction, and resiliency. Such time, space, and quiet will strike our family and friends as a withdrawal from them. It is.

For an artist, withdrawal is necessary. Without it, the artist in us feels vexed, angry, out of sorts. If such deprivation continues, our artist becomes sullen, depressed, hostile. We eventually became like cornered animals, snarling at our family and friends to leave us alone and stop making unreasonable demands.

We are the ones making unreasonable demands. We expect our artist to be able to function without giving it what it needs to do so. An artist requires the upkeep of creative solitude. An artist requires the healing of time alone. Without this period of recharging, our artist becomes depleted. Over time, it becomes something worse than out of sorts. Death threats are issued.

In the early stages, these death threats are issued to our intimates. ("I could kill you when you interrupt me. . . .") Woe to the spouse who doesn't take the hint. Woe to the hapless child who doesn't give you solitude. ("You're making me very angry. . . .")

Over time, if our warnings are ignored and we deem to stay in whatever circumstance—marriage, job, friendship—requires threats and warnings, homicide gives way to suicide. "I want to kill myself" replaces "I could murder you."

> *We are traditionally rather proud of ourselves for having slipped creative work in there between the domestic chores and obligations. I'm not sure we deserve such big A-pluses for that.*
>
> TONI MORRISON

"What's the use?" replaces our feelings of joy and satisfaction. We may go through the actions of continuing our life. We may even continue to produce creatively, but we are leaching blood from ourselves, vampirizing our souls. In short, we are on the treadmill of virtuous production and we are caught.

We are caught in the virtue trap.

There are powerful payoffs to be found in staying stuck and deferring nurturing your sense of self. For many creatives, the belief that they must be nice and worry about what will happen with their friends, family, mate if they dare to do what they really want to constitutes a powerful reason for nonaction.

A man who works in a busy office may crave and need the retreat of solitude. Nothing would serve him better than a vacation alone, but he thinks that's selfish so he doesn't do it. It wouldn't be nice to his wife.

A woman with two small children wants to take a pottery class. It conflicts with some of her son's Little League practices, and she wouldn't be able to attend as faithful audience. She cancels pottery and plays the good mother—seething on the sidelines with resentments.

A young father with a serious interest in photography, yearns for a place in the home to pursue his interest. The installation of a modest family darkroom would require dipping into savings and deferring the purchase of a new couch. The dark-room doesn't get set up but the new couch does.

Many recovering creatives sabotage themselves most frequently by making nice. There is a tremendous cost to such ersatz virtue.

Many of us have made a virtue out of deprivation. We have embraced a long-suffering artistic anorexia as a mar-tyr's cross. We have used it to feed a false sense of spiritual-ity grounded in being good, meaning *superior.*

I call this seductive, faux spirituality the Virtue Trap. Spirituality has often been misused as a route to an unlov-ing solitude, a stance where we proclaim ourselves above our human nature. This spiritual superiority is really only one more form of denial. For an artist, virtue can be deadly. The urge toward respectability and maturity can be stultifying, even fatal.

> *You build up a head of steam. If you're four days out of the studio, on the fifth day you really crash in there. You will kill anybody who disturbs you on that fifth day, when you desperately need it.*
>
> SUSAN ROTHENBERG

We strive to be good, to be nice, to be helpful, to be unselfish. We want to be generous, of service, of the world. *But what we really want is to be left alone.* When we can't get others to leave us alone, we eventually abandon ourselves. To others, we may look like we're there. We may act like we're there. But our true self has gone to ground.

What's left is a shell of our whole self. It stays because it is caught. Like a listless circus animal prodded into performing, it does its tricks. It goes through its routine. It earns its applause. But all of the hoopla falls on deaf ears. We are dead to it. Our artist is not merely out of sorts. Out artist has checked out. Our life is now an out-of-body experience. We're gone. A clinician might call it disassociating. I call it leaving the scene of the crime.

"Come out, come out, wherever you are," we wheedle, but our creative self no longer trusts us. Why should it? We sold it out.

Afraid to appear selfish, we lose our self. We become self-destructive. Because this self-murder is something we seek passively rather than consciously act out, we are often blind to its poisonous grip on us.

The question "Are you self-destructive?" is asked so frequently that we seldom hear it accurately. What it means is *Are you destructive of your self?* And what that really asks us is *Are you destructive of your true nature?*

> *Nobody objects to a woman being a good writer or sculptor or geneticist if at the same time she manages to be a good wife, good mother, good-looking, good-tempered, well-groomed, and unaggressive.*
>
> LESLIE M. McINTYRE

Many people, caught in the virtue trap, do not appear to be self-destructive to the casual eye. Bent on being good husbands, fathers, mothers, wives, teachers, whatevers, they have constructed a false self that looks good to the world and meets with a lot of worldly approval. This false self is always patient, always willing to defer its needs to meet the needs or demands of another. ("What a great guy! That Fred gave up his concert tickets to help me move on a Friday night . . .")

Virtuous to a fault, these trapped creatives have destroyed the true self, the self that didn't meet with much approval as a child. The self who heard repeatedly, "Don't be selfish!" The true self is a disturbing character, healthy and occasionally anarchistic, who knows how to play, how to say no to others and "yes" to itself.

Creatives who are caught in the Virtue Trap still cannot let themselves approve of this true self. They can't show it to the world without dreading the world's continued disapproval. ("Can you believe it? Fred used to be such a nice guy. Always ready to help me out. Anytime, anyplace. I asked him to help me move last week and he said he was going to a play. When did Fred get so cultured, I ask you?")

Fred knows full well that if he stops being so nice, Fabulous Fred, his outsized, nice-guy alter ego, will bite the dust. Martyred Mary knows the same thing as she agrees to round five of baby-sitting for her sister so *she* can go out. Saying no to her sister would be saying yes to herself, and that is a responsibility that Mary just can't handle. Free on a Friday night? What would she do with herself? That's a good question, and one of many that Mary and Fred use their virtue to ignore.

"Are you self-destructive?" is a question that the apparently virtuous would be bound to answer with a resounding no. They then conjure up a list proving how responsible they are. But responsible to whom? The question is *"Are* you self-destructive?" Not "Do you *appear* self-destructive?" And most definitely not "Are you nice to other people?"

We listen to other people's ideas of what is self-destructive without ever looking at whether their self and our self have similar needs. Caught in the Virtue Trap, we refuse to ask ourselves, "What are my needs? What would I do if it weren't too selfish?"

Are you self-destructive?

This is a very difficult question to answer. To begin with, it requires that we know something of our true self (and that is the very self we have been systematically destroying).

One quick way to ascertain the degree of drift is to ask yourself this question: what would I try if it weren't too crazy?

> *There is the risk you cannot afford to take, [and] there is the risk you cannot afford not to take.*
>
> PETER DRUCKER

1. Sky diving, scuba diving.
2. Belly dancing, Latin dancing.
3. Getting my poems published.
4. Buying a drum set.
5. Bicycling through France.

If your list looks pretty exciting, even if crazy, then you are on the right track. These crazy notions are actually voices from our true self. What would I do if it weren't too selfish?

1. Sign up for scuba lessons.
2. Take the Latin dancing class at the Y.
3. Buy *The Poet's Market* and make a submission a week.
4. Get the used drum set my cousin is trying to sell.
5. Call my travel agent and check out France.

By seeking the creator within and embracing our own gift of creativity, we learn to be spiritual in this world, to trust that God is good and so are we and so is all of creation. In this way, we avoid the Virtue Trap.

The Virtue-Trap Quiz

1. The biggest lack in my life is_____.
2. The greatest joy in my life is_____.
3. My largest time commitment is_____.
4. As I play more, I work_____.
5. I feel guilty that I am_____.
6. I worry that_____.
7. If my dreams come true, my family will_____.
8. I sabotage myself so people will_____.
9. If I let myself feel it, I'm angry that I_____.
10. One reason I get sad sometimes is_____.

Does your life serve you or only others? Are you self-destructive?

Forbidden Joys, an Exercise

One of the favored tricks of blocked creatives is saying no to ourselves. It is astonishing the number of small ways we discover to be mean and miserly with ourselves. When I say this to my students, they often protest that this is not true—that they are very good to themselves. Then I ask them to do this exercise.

List ten things you love and would love to do but are not allowed to do. Your list might look like this:

1. Go dancing.
2. Carry a sketch book.
3. Roller-skate.
4. Buy new cowboy boots.
5. Streak your hair blond.

6. Go on vacation.
7. Take flying lessons.
8. Move to a bigger place.
9. Direct a play.
10. Take life-drawing class.

Very often, the mere act of writing out your list of forbidden joys breaks down your barriers to doing them.

Post your list somewhere highly visible.

Wish List, an Exercise

One of the best ways we can evade our Censor is to use the technique of speed writing. Because wishes are just wishes, they are allowed to be frivolous (and frequently should be taken very seriously). As quickly as you can, finish the following phrases.

1. I wish _____.
2. I wish _____.
3. I wish _____.
4. I wish _____.
5. I wish _____.
6. I wish _____.
7. I wish _____.
8. I wish _____.
9. I wish _____.
10. I wish _____.
11. I wish _____.
12. I wish _____.
13. I wish _____.
14. I wish _____.
15. I wish _____.
16. I wish _____.
17. I wish _____.
18. I wish _____.
19. I most especially wish _____.

The specific meaning of God depends on what is the most desirable good for a person.

ERICH FROMM

TASKS

The following tasks explore and expand your relationship to the source.

1. The reason I can't really believe in a *supportive* God is . . . List five grievances. (God can take it.)

2. Starting an Image File: If I had either faith or money I would try . . . List five desires. For the next week, be alert for images of these desires. When you spot them, clip them, buy them, photograph them, draw them, *collect them somehow*. With these images, begin a file of dreams that speak to you. Add to it continually for the duration of the course.

3. One more time, list five imaginary lives. Have they changed? Are you doing more parts of them? You may want to add images of these lives to your image file.

4. If I were twenty and had money . . . List five adventures. Again, add images of these to your visual image file.

5. If I were sixty-five and had money . . . List five postponed pleasures. And again, collect these images. This is a very potent tool. I now live in a house that I *imaged* for ten years.

6. Ten ways I am mean to myself are . . . Just as making the positive explicit helps allow it into our lives, making the negative explicit helps us to exorcise it.

7. Ten items I would like to own that I don't are . . . And again, you may want to collect these images. In order to boost sales, experts in sales motivation often teach rookie salesmen to post images of what they would like to own. It works.

8. Honestly, my favorite creative block is . . . TV, over-reading, friends, work, rescuing others, overexercise. You name it. Whether you can draw or not, please cartoon yourself indulging in it.

9. My payoff for staying blocked is . . . This you may want to explore in your morning pages.

10. The person I blame for being blocked is . . . Again, use your pages to mull on this.

CHECK-IN

1. **How many days this week did you do your morning pages?** Are you starting to like them—at all? How was the experience for you? Have you

discovered the page-and-a-half *truth point* yet? Many of us find that pay dirt in our writing occurs after a page and a half of vamping.

2. **Did you do your artist date this week?** Have you had the experience of hearing answers during this leisure time? What did you do for your date? How did it feel? Have you taken an artist date yet that really felt adventurous?

3. **Did you experience any synchronicity this week?** What was it? Try inaugurating a conversation on synchronicity with your friends.

4. **Were there any other issues this week that you consider significant for your recovery?** Describe them.

Recovering a Sense of Abundance

This week you tackle a major creative block—money. You are asked to really look at your own ideas around God, money, and creative abundance. The essays will explore the ways in which your attitudes limit abundance and luxury in your current life. You will be introduced to counting, a block-busting tool for clarity and right use of funds. This week may feel volatile.

The Great Creator

"I'M A BELIEVER," Nancy declares. "I just don't believe God gets involved with money." Although she doesn't recognize it, Nancy carries two self-sabotaging beliefs. She believes not only that God is good—too good to do money—but also that money is bad. Nancy, like many of us, needs to overhaul her God concept in order to fully recover her creativity.

For many of us, raised to believe that money is the real source of security, a dependence on God feels foolhardy, suicidal, even laughable. When we consider the lilies of the fields, we think they are quaint, too out of it for the modern world. We're the ones who keep clothes on our backs. We're the ones who buy the groceries. And we will pursue our art, we tell ourselves, when we have enough money to do it easily.

And when will that be?

We want a God that feels like a fat paycheck and a license to spend as we please. Listening to the siren song of *more*, we are deaf to the still small voice waiting in our soul to whisper, "You're enough."

"Seek ye first the kingdom of heaven and all things will be added to it," we have been told, often since childhood, by people quoting from the Bible. We don't believe this. And we certainly don't believe it about art. Maybe God would feed and clothe us, in a pinch, but painting supplies? A museum tour of Europe, dance classes? God's not about to spring for those, we tell ourselves. We cling to our financial concerns as a way to avoid not only our art but also our spiritual growth. Our faith is in the dollar. "I have to keep a roof over my head," we say. "Nobody's going to pay me to be more creative."

We are awfully sure about that. Most of us harbor a secret belief that work has to be work and not play, and that anything we really want to do—like write, act, dance— must be considered frivolous and be placed a distant second. This is not true.

We are operating out of the toxic old idea that God's will for us and our will for us are at opposite ends of the table. "I want to be an actress, but God wants me to wait tables in hash joints," the scenario goes. "So if I try to be an actress, I will end up slinging hash."

Thinking like this is grounded in the idea that God is a stern parent with very rigid ideas about what's appropriate for us. And you'd better believe we won't like them. This stunted god concept needs alteration.

This week, in your morning pages, write about the god you do believe in and the god you would like to believe in. For some of us, this means, "What if God's a woman and she's on my side?" For others, it is a god of energy. For still others, a collective of higher forces moving us toward our highest good. If you are still dealing with a god consciousness that has remained unexamined since childhood, you are probably dealing with a toxic god. What would a nontoxic god think of your creative goals? Might such a god really exist? If so, would money or your job or your lover remain your higher power?

Many of us equate difficulty with virtue—and art with fooling around. Hard work is good. A terrible job must be building our moral fiber. Something—a talent for painting, say—that comes to us easily and seems compatible with us must be some sort of cheap trick, not to be taken seriously. On the one hand, we give

---

> *Money is God in action.*
>
> RAYMOND CHARLES BARKER

> *The more we learn to operate in the world based on trust in our intuition, the stronger our channel will be and the more money we will have.*
>
> SHAKTI GAWAIN

> *Money will come when you are doing the right thing.*
>
> MIKE PHILLIPS

lip service to the notion that God wants us to be happy, joyous, and free. On the other, we secretly think that God wants us to be broke if we are going to be so decadent as to want to be artists. Do we have any proof at all for these ideas about God?

Looking at God's creation, it is pretty clear that the creator itself did not know when to stop. There is not one pink flower, or even fifty pink flowers, but hundreds. Snowflakes, of course, are the ultimate exercise in sheer creative glee. No two alike. This creator looks suspiciously like someone who just might send us support for our creative ventures.

"We have a new employer," the Big Book of Alcoholics Anonymous promises recovering alcoholics. "If we take care of God's business he will take care of ours." To battered AA newcomers, such thinking is a lifeline. Desperate for a way to achieve sobriety, they cling to this thought when worried about their own precarious abilities to live effectively. Expecting divine help, they tend to receive it. Tangled lives smooth out; tangled relationships gain sanity and sweetness.

> *Always leave enough time in your life to do something that makes you happy, satisfied, even joyous. That has more of an effect on economic well-being than any other single factor.*
>
> PAUL HAWKEN

To those less desperate, such assurances sound foolish, even deceptive, like we're being conned. The God who has a job for us? The God who has fulfilling work? The God who holds abundance and dignity, who holds a million possibilities, the keys to every door? This God can sound suspiciously like a flimflam man.

And so, when it comes time for us to choose between a cherished dream and a lousy current drudgery, we often choose to ignore the dream and blame our continued misery on God. We act like it's God's fault we didn't go to Europe, take that painting class, go on that photo shoot. In truth, we, not God, have decided not to go. We have tried to be sensible—as though we have any proof at all that God is sensible—rather than see if the universe might not have supported some healthy extravagance.

The creator may be our father/mother/source but it is surely not the father/mother/church/teacher/friends here on earth who have instilled in us their ideas of what is sensible for us. Creativity is not and never has been sensible. Why should it be? Why should you be? Do you still think there is some moral virtue in being martyred? If you want to make some art, make some art. Just a little art . . . two sentences. One rhyme. A silly kindergarten ditty:

> *All substance is energy in motion. It lives and flows. Money is symbolically a golden, flowing stream of concretized vital energy.*
>
> THE MAGICAL WORK
> OF THE SOUL

God likes art.
That's the part
My parents would ignore.
God likes art,
And I make art.
That's what God likes me for!

Making art beings with making hay while the sun shines. It begins with getting into the *now* and enjoying your day. It begins with giving yourself some small treats and breaks. "This is extravagant but so is God" is a good attitude to take when treating your artist to small bribes and beauties. Remember, you are the cheapskate, not God. As you expect God to be more generous, God will be able to be more generous to you.

What we really want to do is what we are really meant to do. When we do what we are meant to do, money comes to us, doors open for us, we feel useful, and the work we do feels like play to us.

We will continue to work this week with our ideas surrounding money. We will see how our ideas about money ("It's hard to get. You have to work long hours for it. You need to worry about money first and creativity second") shape our ideas about creativity.

Luxury

For those of us who have become artistically anorectic—yearning to be creative and refusing to feed that hunger in ourselves so that we become more and more focused on our deprivation—a little authentic luxury can go a long way. The key work here is *authentic*. Because art is born in expansion, in a belief in sufficient supply, it is critical that we pamper ourselves for the sense of abundance it brings to us.

What constitutes pampering? That will vary for each of us. For Gillian, a pair of new-to-her tweed trousers from the vintage store conjured up images of Carole Lombard laughter and racy roadsters. For Jean, a single, sprightly Gerber daisy perched on her night table told her life was abloom with possibility. Matthew found that the scent of real furniture wax gave him a feeling of safety, solidity, and order. Constance found luxury in allowing herself the indulgence of a magazine subscription (a twenty-dollar gift that keeps giving for a full year of images and indulgence).

All too often, we become blocked and blame it on our lack of money. This is *never* an authentic block. The actual block is our feeling of constriction, our sense of powerlessness. Art requires us to empower ourselves with choice. At the most basic level, this means choosing to do self-care.

One of my friends is a world-famous artist of formidable talents. He is assured a place in history for his contributions to his field. He is sought after by younger artists and respected by older artists. Although not yet fifty, he has already been singled out for lifetime achievement awards. Nonetheless, this is an artist suffering in the throes of artistic anorexia. Although he continues to work, he does so at greater and greater cost to himself. Why, he sometimes wonders to himself, does his life's work now feel so much like his life's *work*?

Why? Because he has denied himself luxury.

Let me be clear that the luxury I am talking about here has nothing to do with penthouse views, designer clothes, zippy foreign sports cars, or first-class travel. This man enjoys all those privileges, but what he doesn't enjoy is his life. He has denied himself the luxury of time: time with friends, time with family, above all, time to himself with no agendas of preternatural accomplishment. His many former passions have dwindled to mere interests; he is too busy to enjoy pastimes. He tells himself he has no time to pass. The clock is ticking and he is using it to get famous.

Recently, I bought myself a horse for the first time in a decade. On hearing the good news, my accomplished friend moved immediately into his Wet Blanket mode, cautioning, "Well, I hope you don't expect to get to ride it much or even see it much. As you get older, you do less and less of the things you enjoy. Life becomes more and more about doing what you must. . . ."

> *I'd rather have roses on my table than diamonds on my neck.*
>
> EMMA GOLDMAN

Because I have learned to hear Wet Blanket messages for what they are, I was not too daunted by this prognosis. But I was saddened by it. It reminded me of the vulnerability of all artists, even very famous ones, to the shaming, "I should be working" side of themselves that discourages creative pleasures.

In order to thrive as artists—and, one could argue, as people—we need to be available to the universal flow. When we put a stopper on our capacity for joy by anorectically declining the small gifts of life, we turn aside the larger gifts as well. Those of us, like my artist friend, who are engaged in long creative works will find ourselves leaching our souls to find images, returning to past work, to tricks, practicing our craft more than enlarging our art. Those of us who have stymied the work flow completely will find ourselves in lives that feel barren and devoid of interest no matter how many meaningless things we have filled them with.

What gives us true joy? That is the question to ask concerning luxury, and for each of us the answer is very different. For Berenice, the answer is raspberries, fresh raspberries. She laughs at how easily pleased she is. For the cost of a pint of raspberries, she buys herself an experience of abundance. Sprinkled on cereal, cut up with a peach, poured over a scoop of ice cream. She can buy her abundance at the supermarket and even get it quick frozen if she has to.

"They cost $1.98 to $4.50, depending on the season. I always tell myself they are too expensive, but the truth is that's a bargain for a week of luxury. It's less than a movie. Less than a deluxe cheeseburger. I guess it's just more than I thought I was worth."

For Alan, music is the great luxury. A musician when he was younger, he had long denied himself the right to play. Like most blocked creatives, he suffered from a deadly duo: artistic anorexia and prideful perfectionism. There were no practice shots for this player. He wanted to be at the top, and if he couldn't be there he wouldn't be anywhere near his beloved music.

Stuck and stymied, Alan described his block this way: "I try to play and I hear myself, and what I can do is so far away from what I want to do that I cringe." (And then quit.)

> *Explore daily the will of God.*
> CARL JUNG

Working on his creative recovery, Alan began by allowing himself the luxury of buying a new recording a week. He stopped making music work and started making it fun again. He was to buy crazy recordings, not just high art. Forget high-minded aspirations. What sounded like fun?

Alan began exploring. He bought gospel, country and western, Indian drum music. A month of this and he impulsively bought a set of practice sticks at the music store. He let them lie and let them lie and . . .

Three months later, Alan was drumming on the handle-bars of his exercise bike while rock and roll blasted through his Walkman. Two months later, he cleared a space in the attic and acquired a secondhand drum kit.

"I thought my wife and daughter would be embarrassed by how bad I was," he explains. Catching himself in his blaming, he cops, "Actually, I was the one who was embarrassed, but now I'm just having fun with it and actually sounding a little better to myself. For an old guy, I'd say my chops are coming back."

For Laura, a dime-store set of watercolor paints was her first foray into luxury. For Kathy, it was a deluxe Crayola set, "the kind my mother would never get me. I let myself do two drawings the first night, and one of them was a sketch of me in my new life, the one I am working toward."

But for many blocked creatives, it takes a little work to even *imagine* ourselves having luxury. Luxury is a learned practice for most of us. Blocked creatives are often the Cinderellas of the world. Focused on others at the expense of ourselves, we may even be threatened by the idea of spoiling ourselves for once.

"Don't try to let go of Cinderella," my writer friend Karen advises. "Keep Cinderella but focus on giving yourself the glass slipper. The second half of that fairy tale is great."

What we are talking about when we discuss luxury is very often a shift in consciousness more than flow—although as we acknowledge and invite what feels luxurious to us, we may indeed trigger an increased flow.

Creative living requires the luxury of time, which we carve out for ourselves—even if it's fifteen minutes for quick morning pages and a ten-minute minibath after work.

Creative living requires the luxury of space for ourselves, even if all we manage to carve out is one special bookshelf and a windowsill that is ours. (My study has a window shelf of paperweights and seashells.) Remember that your artist is a youngster and youngsters like things that are "mine." My chair. My book. My pillow.

> *True life is lived when tiny changes occur.*
>
> LEO TOLSTOY

Designating a few things special and yours alone can go a long way toward making you feel pampered. Chinatown anywhere offers a beautiful teacup and saucer for under five dollars. Secondhand stores often have one-of-a-kind china plates that make an afternoon snack a more creative experience.

Much of what we do in a creative recovery may seem silly. Silly is a defense our Wet Blanket adult uses to squelch our artist child. Beware of *silly* as a word you toss at yourself. Yes, artist dates *are* silly—that's the whole point.

Creativity lives in paradox: serious art is born from serious play.

Counting, an Exercise

For the next week you will be discovering how you spend your money. Buy a small pocket notepad and write down every nickel you spend. It doesn't matter what it is for, how tiny the purchase, how petty the amount. Petty cash is still cash.

Each day, date a page and count—what you bought, what you spent, where your money went, whether it was for groceries, lunch in a diner, a cab ride, subway fares, or a loan to your brother. Be meticulous. Be thorough. And be nonjudgmental. This is an exercise in self-observation—*not* self-flagellation.

You may want to continue this practice for a full month or longer. It will teach you what you value in terms of your spending. Often our spending differs from our real values. We fritter away cash on things we don't cherish and deny ourselves those things we do. For many of us, counting is a necessary prelude to learning creative luxury.

Money Madness, an Exercise

Complete the following phrases.

1. People with money are _____.
2. Money makes people _____.
3. I'd have more money if _____.
4. My dad thought money was _____.
5. My mom always thought money would _____.
6. In my family, money caused _____.
7. Money equals _____.
8. If I had money, I'd _____.
9. If I could afford it, I'd _____.
10. If I had some money, I'd _____.
11. I'm afraid that if I had money I would _____.
12. Money is _____.
13. Money causes _____.
14. Having money is not _____.

15. In order to have more money, I'd need to_____.
16. When I have money, I usually_____.
17. I think money _____.
18. If I weren't so cheap I'd _____.
19. People think money _____.
20. Being broke tells me _____.

TASKS

1. Natural Abundance: Find five pretty or interesting rocks. I enjoy this exercise particularly because rocks can be carried in pockets, fingered in business meetings. They can be small, constant reminders of our creative consciousness.

2. Natural Abundance: Pick five flowers or leaves. You may want to press these between wax paper and save them in a book. If you did this in kindergarten, that's fine. Some of the best creative play is done there. Let yourself do it again.

> *As an artist, it is central to be unsatisfied! This isn't greed, though it might be appetite.*
>
> LAWRENCE CALCAGNO

3. Clearing: Throw out or give away five ratty pieces of clothing.

4. Creation: Bake something. (If you have a sugar problem, make a fruit salad.) Creativity does not have to always involve capital-A art. Very often, the act of cooking something can help you cook something up in another creative mode. When I am stymied as a writer, I make soups and pies.

5. Communication: Send postcards to five friends. This is not a goody-two-shoes exercise. Send to people you would *love* to hear from.

7. Reread the Basic Principles. (See page 17.) Do this once daily. Read an Artist's Prayer—yours from Week Four or mine on pages 210–211. Do this once daily.

8. Clearing: Any new changes in your home environment? Make some.

9. Acceptance: Any new flow in your life? Practice saying yes to freebies.

10. Prosperity: Any changes in your financial situation or your perspective on it? Any new—even crazy—ideas about what you would love doing? Pull images around this and add to your image file.

CHECK-IN

1. **How many days this week did you do your morning pages?** (Have you used them yet to think about creative luxury for yourself?) How was the experience for you?
2. **Did you do your artist date this week?** (Have you considered allowing yourself two?) What did you do? How did it feel?
3. **Did you experience any synchronicity this week?** What was it?
4. **Were there any other issues this week that you consider significant for your recovery?** Describe them.

Recovering a Sense of Connection

We turn this week to the practice of right attitudes for creativity. The emphasis is on your receptive as well as active skills. The essays, exercises, and tasks aim at excavating areas of genuine creative interest as you connect with your personal dreams.

Listening

THE ABILITY TO LISTEN is a skill we are honing with both our morning pages and our artist dates. The pages train us to hear past our Censor. The artist dates help us to pick up the voice of inspiration. While both of these activities are apparently unconnected to the actual act of making art, they are critical to the creative process.

Art is not about thinking something up. It is about the opposite—getting something down. The directions are important here.

If we are trying to *think something up*, we are straining to reach for something that's just beyond our grasp, "up there, in the stratosphere, where art lives on high. . . ."

When we *get something down*, there is no strain. We're not doing; we're getting. Someone or something else is doing the doing. Instead of reaching for inventions, we are engaged in listening.

When an actor is in the moment, he or she is engaged in listening for the next right thing creatively. When a painter is painting, he or she may begin with a plan, but that plan is soon surrendered to the painting's own plan. This is often expressed as "The brush takes the next stroke." In dance, in composition, in sculpture, the experience is the same: we are more the conduit than the creator of what we express.

Art is an act of tuning in and dropping down the well. It is as though all the stories, painting, music, performances in the world live just under the surface of our

In the esoteric Judaism of the Cabalah, the Deep Self is named the Neshamah, from the root of Shmhm, "to hear or listen": the Neshamah is She Who Listens, the soul who inspires or guides us.

STARHAWK

Listening is a form of accepting.

STELLA TERRILL MANN

normal consciousness. Like an underground river, they flow through us as a stream of ideas that we can tap down into. As artists, we drop down the well into the stream. We hear what's down there and we act on it—more like taking dictation than anything fancy having to do with art.

A friend of mine is a superb film director who is known for his meticulous planning. And yet he often shoots most brilliantly from the seat of his pants, quickly grabbing a shot that comes to him as he works.

These moments of clear inspiration require that we move into them on faith. We can practice these small leaps of faith daily in our pages and on our artist dates. We can learn not only to listen but also to hear with increasing accuracy that inspired, intuitive voice that says, "Do this, try this, say this. . . ."

Most writers have had the experience of catching a poem or a paragraph or two of formed writing. We consider these finds to be small miracles. What we fail to realize is that they are, in fact, the norm. We are the instrument more than the author of our work.

Michelangelo is said to have remarked that he released David from the marble block he found him in. "The painting has a life of its own. I try to let it come through," said Jackson Pollock. When I teach screenwriting, I remind my students that their movie already exists in its entirety. Their job is to listen for it, watch it with their mind's eye, and write it down.

The same may be said of all art. If painting and sculptures wait for us, then sonatas wait for us; books, plays, and poems wait for us, too. Our job is simply to get them down. To do that, we drop down the well.

Some people find it easier to picture the stream of inspiration as being like radio waves of all sorts being broadcast at all times.

With practice, we learn how to hear the desired frequency on request. We tune in to the frequency we want. Like a parent, we learn to hear the voice of our current brainchild among the other children's voices.

Once you accept that it is natural to create, you can begin to accept a second idea—that the creator will hand you whatever you need for the project. The minute you are willing to accept the help of this collaborator, you will see useful bits of help everywhere in your life. Be alert: there is a second voice, a higher harmonic, adding to and augmenting your inner creative voice. This voice frequently shows itself in synchronicity.

You will hear the dialogue you need, find the right song for the sequence, see the exact paint color you almost had in mind, and so forth. You will have the experience of finding things—books, seminars, tossed-out stuff—that happen to fit with what you are doing.

Learn to accept the possibility that the universe is helping you with what you are doing. Become willing to see the hand of God and accept it as a friend's offer to help with what you are doing. Because many of us unconsciously harbor the fearful belief that God would find our creations decadent or frivolous or worse, we tend to discount this creator-to-creator help.

Try to remember that God is the Great Artist. Artists like other artists.

Expect the universe to support your dream. It will.

Perfectionism

Tillie Olsen correctly calls it the "knife of the perfectionist attitude in art." You may call it something else. *Getting it right,* you may call it, or *fixing it before I go any further.* You may call it *having standards.* What you should be calling it is *perfectionism.*

Perfectionism has nothing to do with getting it right. It has nothing to do with fixing things. It has nothing to do with standards. Perfectionism is a refusal to let yourself move ahead. It is a loop—an obsessive, debilitating closed system that causes you to get stuck in the details of what you are writing or painting or making and to lose sight of the whole. Instead of creating freely and allowing errors to reveal themselves later as insights, we often get mired in getting the details right. We correct our originality into a uniformity that lacks passion and spontaneity. "Do not fear mistakes," Miles Davis told us. "There are none."

The perfectionist fixes one line of a poem over and over—until no lines are right. The perfectionist redraws the chin line on a portrait until the paper tears. The perfectionist writes so many versions of scene one that she never gets to the rest of the play. The perfectionist writes, paints, creates with one eye on her audience. Instead of enjoying the process, the perfectionist is constantly grading the results.

> *Cerebration is the enemy of originality in art.*
>
> MARTIN RITT

The perfectionist has married the logic side of the brain. The critic reigns supreme in the perfectionist's creative household. A brilliant descriptive prose passage is critiqued with a white-glove approach: "*Mmm.* What about this comma? Is this how you spell . . .?"

For the perfectionist, there are no first drafts, rough sketches, warm-up exercises. Every draft is meant to be final, perfect, set in stone.

Midway through a project, the perfectionist decides to read it all over, outline it, see where it's going.

And where is it going? Nowhere, very fast.

The perfectionist is never satisfied. The perfectionist never says, "This is pretty good. I think I'll just keep going."

To the perfectionist, there is always room for improvement. The perfectionist calls this humility. In reality, it is egotism. It is pride that makes us want to write a perfect script, paint a perfect painting, perform a perfect audition monologue.

Perfectionism is not a quest for the best. It is a pursuit of the worst in ourselves, the part that tells us that nothing we do will ever be good enough—that we should try again.

No. We should not.

"A painting is never finished. It simply stops in interesting places," said Paul Gardner. A book is never finished. But at a certain point you stop writing it and go on to the next thing. A film is never cut perfectly, but at a certain point you let go and call it done. That is a normal part of creativity—letting go. We always do the best that we can by the light we have to see by.

> *Living is a form of not being sure, not knowing what next or how. The moment you know how, you begin to die a little. The artist never entirely knows. We guess. We may be wrong, but we take leap after leap in the dark.*
>
> AGNES DE MILLE

Risk

QUESTION: What would I do if I didn't have to do it perfectly?

ANSWER: A great deal more than I am.

We've all heard that the unexamined life is not worth living, but consider too that the unlived life is not worth examining. The success of a creative recovery hinges on our ability to move out of the head and into action. This brings us squarely to risk. Most of us are practiced at talking ourselves out of risk. We are skilled speculators on the probable pain of self-exposure.

"I'll look like an idiot," we say, conjuring images of our first acting class, our first hobbled short story, our terrible drawings. Part of the game here is lining up the masters and measuring our baby steps against their perfected craft. We don't compare our student films to George Lucas's student films. Instead, we compare them to *Star Wars*.

We deny that in order to do something well we must first be willing to do it badly. Instead, we opt for setting our limits at the point where we feel assured of success. Living within these bounds, we may feel stifled, smothered, despairing, bored. But, yes, we do feel safe. And safety is a very expensive illusion.

In order to risk, we must jettison our accepted limits. We must break through "I can't because . . ." Because I am too old, too broke, too shy, too proud? Self-defended? Timorous?

Usually, when we say we can't do something, what we mean is that we won't do something unless we can guarantee that we'll do it perfectly.

Working artists know the folly of this stance. There is a common joke among directors: "Oh, yeah. I always know exactly how I should direct the picture—after I'm done directing it."

As blocked artists, we unrealistically expect and demand success from ourselves and recognition of that success from others. With that as an unspoken demand, a great many things remain outside our sphere of possibility. As actors, we tend to allow ourselves to be typecast rather than working to expand our range. As singers, we stay married to our safe material. As songwriters, we try to repeat a formula hit. In this way, artists who do not appear blocked to the outside eye experience themselves as blocked internally, unable to take the risk of moving into new and more satisfying artistic territory.

Once we are willing to accept that anything worth doing might even be worth doing badly our options widen. "If I didn't have to do it perfectly, I would try . . ."

1. Stand-up comedy.
2. Modern dancing.
3. Whitewater rafting.
4. Archery.
5. Learning German.
6. Figure drawing.

We cannot escape fear. We can only transform it into a companion that accompanies us on all our exciting adventures. . . . Take a risk a day—one small or bold stroke that will make you feel great once you have done it.

SUSAN JEFFERS

7. Figure skating.
8. Being a platinum blond.
9. Puppeteering.
10. Trapeze.
11. Water ballet.
12. Polo.
13. Wearing red lipstick.
14. Taking a couture class.
15. Writing short stories.
16. Reading my poetry in public.
17. A spontaneous tropical vacation.
18. Learning to shoot video.
19. Learning to ride a bike.
20. Taking a watercolor class.

In the movie *Raging Bull*, boxer Jake La Motta's manager-brother explains to him why he should shed some weight and fight an unknown opponent. After an intricate spiel that leaves La Motta baffled, he concludes, "So do it. If you win, you win, and if you lose, you win."

It is always that way with taking risks.

To put it differently, very often a risk is worth taking simply for the sake of taking it. There is something enlivening about expanding our self-definition, and a risk does exactly that. Selecting a challenge and meeting it creates a sense of self-empowerment that becomes the ground for further successful challenges. Viewed this way, running a marathon increases your chances of writing a full-length play. Writing a full-length play gives you a leg up on a marathon.

Complete the following sentence. "If I didn't have to do it perfectly, I would try . . ."

> *There is no must in art because art is free.*
>
> WASSILY KANDINSKY

> *Shoot for the moon. Even if you miss it you will land among the stars.*
>
> LES BROWN

Jealousy

Jealousy, I've often heard, is a normal human emotion. When I hear that, I think, "Maybe your jealousy—not mine."

My jealousy roars in the head, tightens the chest, massages my stomach lining with a cold fist as it searches out the best grip. I have long regarded jealousy as my greatest weakness. Only recently have I seen it for the tough-love friend that it is.

Jealousy is a map. Each of our jealousy maps differs. Each of us will probably be surprised by some of the things we discover on our own. I, for example, have never been eaten alive with resentment over the success of women novelists. But I took an unhealthy interest in the fortunes and misfortunes of women playwrights. I was their harshest critic, until I wrote my first play.

With that action, my jealousy vanished, replaced by a feeling of camaraderie. My jealousy had actually been a mask for my fear of doing something I really wanted to do but was not yet brave enough to take action toward.

Jealousy is always a mask for fear: fear that we aren't able to get what we want; frustration that somebody else seems to be getting what is rightfully ours even if we are too frightened to reach for it. At its root, jealousy is a stingy emotion. It doesn't allow for the abundance and multiplicity of the universe. Jealousy tells us there is room for only one—one poet, one painter, one whatever you dream of being.

> *With courage you will dare to take risks, have the strength to be compassionate and the wisdom to be humble. Courage is the foundation of integrity.*
>
> KESHAVAN NAIR

The truth, revealed by action in the direction of our dreams, is that there is room for all of us. But jealousy produces tunnel vision. It narrows our ability to see things in perspective. It strips us of our ability to see other options. The biggest lie that jealousy tells us is that we have no choice but to be jealous. Perversely, jealousy strips us of our will to act when action holds the key to our freedom.

The Jealousy Map, an Exercise

Your jealousy map will have three columns. In the first column, name those whom you are jealous of. Next to each name write why. Be as specific and accurate as you can. In the third column, list one action you can take to move toward creative risk and out of jealousy.

When jealousy bites, like a snakebite it requires an immediate antidote. On paper, make your jealousy map.

WHO	WHY	ACTION ANTIDOTE
My sister Libby	She has a real art studio	Fix spare room
My friend Ed	Writes good crime novels	Try writing one
Anne Sexton	Famous poet	Publish my long-hoarded poems

Even the biggest changes begin with small ones. Green is the color of jealousy, but it is also the color of hope. When you learn to harness its fierce energy on your own behalf, jealousy is part of the fuel toward a greener and more verdant future.

Archeology, an Exercise

I don't have a lot of respect for talent. Talent is genetic. It's what you do with it that counts.

MARTIN RITT

The phrases that follow are more of your sleuth work. Very often, we have buried parts of ourselves that can be uncovered by some digging. Not only will your answers tell you what you missed in the past; they will tell you what you can be doing, now, to comfort and encourage your artist child. It is not too late, no matter what your ego tells you.

Complete these phrases.

1. As a kid, I missed the chance to _____.
2. As a kid, I lacked _____.
3. As a kid, I could have used _____.
4. As a kid, I dreamed of being _____.
5. As a kid, I wanted a _____.
6. In my house, we never had enough _____.
7. As a kid, I needed more _____.
8. I am sorry that I will never again see _____.
9. For years, I have missed and wondered about _____.
10. I beat myself up about the loss of _____.

It is important to acknowledge our positive inventory as well as our shortfalls. Take positive stock of what good you have to build on in the present.

Finish these phrases.

1. I have a loyal friend in _____.
2. One thing I like about my town is_____.
3. I think I have nice _____.
4. Writing my morning pages has shown me I can _____.
5. I am taking a greater interest in_____.
6. I believe I am getting better at _____.
7. My artist has started to pay more attention to _____.
8. My self-care is _____.
9. I feel more _____.
10. Possibly, my creativity is _____.

TASKS

1. Make this phrase a mantra: *Treating myself like a precious object will make me strong.* Watercolor or crayon or calligraph this phrase. Post it where you will see it daily. We tend to think being hard on ourselves will make us strong. But it is cherishing ourselves that gives us strength.

> *Trust in yourself. Your perceptions are often far more accurate than you are willing to believe.*
>
> CLAUDIA BLACK

2. Give yourself time out to listen to one side of an album, just for joy. You may want to doodle as you listen, allowing yourself to draw the shapes, emotions, thoughts you hear in the music. Notice how just twenty minutes can refresh you. Learn to take these mini-artist dates to break stress and allow insight.

3. Take yourself into a sacred space—a church, synagogue, library, grove of trees—and allow yourself to savor the silence and healing solitude. Each of us has a personal idea of what sacred space is. For me, a large clock store or a great aquarium store can engender a sense of timeless wonder. Experiment.

4. Create one wonderful smell in your house—with soup, incense, fir branches, candles—whatever.

5. Wear your favorite item of clothing for no special occasion.

6. Buy yourself one wonderful pair of socks, one wonderful pair of gloves—one wonderfully comforting, self-loving something.

7. Collage: Collect a stack of at least ten magazines, which you will allow yourself to freely dismember. Setting a twenty-minute time limit for yourself, tear (literally) through the magazines, collecting any images that reflect your life or interests. Think of this collage as a form of pictorial autobiography. Include your past, present, future, and your dreams. It is okay to include images you simply like. Keep pulling until you have a good stack of images (at least twenty). Now take a sheet of newspaper, a stapler, or some tape or glue, and arrange your images in a way that pleases you. (This is one of my students' favorite exercises.)

8. Quickly list five favorite films. Do you see any common denominators among them? Are they romances, adventures, period pieces, political dramas, family epics, thrillers? Do you see traces of your cinematic themes in your collage?

9. Name your favorite topics to read about: comparative religion, movies, ESP, physics, rags-to-riches, betrayal, love triangles, scientific breakthroughs, sports . . . Are these topics in your collage?

10. Give your collage a place of honor. Even a secret place of honor is all right— in your closet, in a drawer, anywhere that is yours. You may want to do a new one every few months, or collage more thoroughly a dream you are trying to accomplish.

CHECK-IN

1. **How many days this week did you do your morning pages?** Have you allowed yourself to daydream a few creative risks? Are you coddling your artist child with childhood loves?

2. **Did you do your artist date this week?** Did you use it to take any risks? What did you do? How did it feel?

3. **Did you experience any synchronicity this week?** What was it?

4. **Were there any other issues this week that you consider significant for your recovery?** Describe them.

Recovering a Sense of Strength

This week tackles another major creative block: time. You will explore the ways in which you have used your perception of time to preclude taking creative risks. You will identify immediate and practical changes you can make in your current life. You will excavate the early conditioning that may have encouraged you to settle for far less than you desire creatively.

Survival

ONE OF THE MOST difficult tasks an artist must face is a primal one: artistic survival. All artists must learn the art of surviving loss: loss of hope, loss of face, loss of money, loss of self-belief. In addition to our many gains, we inevitably suffer these losses in an artistic career. They are the hazards of the road and, in many ways, its signposts. Artistic losses can be turned into artistic gains and strengths—but not in the isolation of the beleaguered artist's brain.

As mental-health experts are quick to point out, in order to move through loss and beyond it, we must acknowledge it and share it. Because artistic losses are seldom openly acknowledged or mourned, they become artistic scar tissue that blocks artistic growth. Deemed too painful, too silly, too humiliating to share and so to heal, they become, instead, secret losses.

If artistic creations are our brainchildren, artistic losses are our miscarriages. Women often suffer terribly, and privately, from losing a child who doesn't come to term. And as artists we suffer terrible losses when the book doesn't sell, the film doesn't get picked up, the juried show doesn't take our paintings, the best pot shatters, the poems are not accepted, the ankle injury sidelines us for an entire dance season.

I shall become a master in this art only after a great deal of practice.

ERICH FROMM

Taking a new step, uttering a new word is what people fear most.

FYODOR DOSTOYEVSKI

We must remember that our artist is a child and that what we can handle intellectually far outstrips what we can handle emotionally. We must be alert to flag and mourn our losses.

The disappointing reception of a good piece of work, the inability to move across into a different medium or type of role due to other people's expectations of us are artistic losses that must be mourned. It does no good to say, "Oh, it happens to everybody" or "Who was I kidding anyway?" The unmourned disappointment becomes the barrier that separates us from future dreams. Not being cast in the role that's "yours," not being asked to join the company, having the show canceled or the play unreviewed—these are all losses.

Perhaps the most damaging form of artistic loss has to do with criticism. The artist within, like the child within, is seldom hurt by truth. I will say again that much true criticism liberates the artist it is aimed at. We are childlike, not childish. *Ah-hah!* is often the accompanying inner sound when a well-placed, accurate critical arrow makes its mark. The artist thinks, "Yes! I can see that! That's right! I can change that!"

The criticism that damages an artist is the criticism—well intentioned or ill—that contains no saving kernel of truth yet has a certain damning plausibility or an unassailable blanket judgment that cannot be rationally refuted.

Teachers, editors, mentors are often authority figures or parent figures for a young artist. There is a sacred trust inherent in the bond between teacher and student. This trust, when violated, has the impact of a parental violation. What we are talking about here is emotional incest.

A trusting student hears from an unscrupulous teacher that good work is bad or lacks promise or that he, the guru-teacher, senses a limit to the student's real talent or was mistaken in seeing talent, or doubts that there is talent . . . Personal in nature, nebulous as to specifics, this criticism is like covert sexual harassment—a sullying yet hard to quantify experience. The student emerges shamed, feeling like a bad artist, or worse, a fool to try.

The Ivory Power

It has been my perilous privilege over the past decade to undertake teaching forays into the groves of academia. It is my experience as a visiting artist that many academics are themselves artistic beings who are deeply frustrated by their inability to create. Skilled in intellectual discourse, distanced by that intellectual skill from their own creative urgings, they often find the creativity of their charges deeply disturbing.

> *Imagination is more important than knowledge.*
>
> ALBERT EINSTEIN

Devoted as they are to the scholarly appreciation of art, most academics find the beast intimidating when viewed firsthand. Creative-writing programs tend to be regarded with justified suspicion: those people aren't studying creativity, they're actually practicing it! Who knows where this could lead?

I am thinking particularly of a film-department chair of my acquaintance, a gifted filmmaker who for many years had been unable or unwilling to expose himself to the rigors and disappointments of creating. Channeling his ferocious creative urges into the lives of his students, he alternately overcontrolled and undercut their best endeavors, seeking to vicariously fulfill or justify his own position on the sidelines.

As much as I wanted to dislike this man—and I certainly disliked his behaviors—I found myself unable to regard him without compassion. His own thwarted creativity, so luminous in his early films, had darkened to shadow first his own life and then the lives of his students. In the truest sense, he was a creative monster.

It took more years and more teaching for me to realize that academia harbors a far more subtle and deadly foe to the creative spirit. Outrighht hostility, after all, can be encountered. Far more dangerous, far more soul-chilling, is the subtle discounting that may numb student creativity in the academic grove.

I am thinking now of my time at a distinguished research university, where my teaching colleagues published widely and well on film topics of the most esoteric and exotic stripe. Highly regarded among their intellectual peers, deeply immersed in their own academic careers, these colleagues offered scant mirroring to the creative students who passed through their tutelage. They neglected to supply that most rudimentary nutrient: encouragement.

Surround yourself with people who respect and treat you well.

CLAUDIA BLACK

To the rationally minded the mental processes of the intuitive appear to work backwards.

FRANCES WICKES

Creativity cannot be comfortably quantified in intellectual terms. By its very nature, creativity eschews such containment. In a university where the intellectual life is built upon the art of criticizing—on deconstructing a creative work—the art of creation itself, the art of creative construction, meets with scanty support, understanding, or approval. To be blunt, most academics know how to take something apart, but not how to assemble it.

Student work, when scrutinized, was seldom *appreciated*. Far from it. Whatever its genuine accomplishments, it was viewed solely in terms of its shortfalls. Time and again I saw promising work met with a volley of should-have-dones, could-have-dones, and might-have-dones, instead of being worked with as it was.

It is not my argument that the world of academia be turned into an exalted artists' studio. It is, however, my point that artists attempting to exist, grow, even flourish, within that milieu recognize that the entire thrust of intellectualism runs counter to the creative impulse. For an artist, to become overly cerebral is to become crippled. This is not to say that artists lack rigor; rather, that artistic rigor is grounded differently than intellectual life usually admits.

Artists and intellectuals are not the same animal. As a younger artist this was very confusing to me. I myself have considerable critical gifts, and have in fact won national awards for practicing them. It was to my own rue that I discovered that these same skills were misapplied when focused on embryonic artistic endeavors—mine or others. Younger artists are seedlings. Their early work resembles thicket and underbrush, even weeds. The halls of academia, with their preference for lofty intellectual theorems, do little to support the life of the forest floor. As a teacher, it has been my sad experience that many talented creatives were daunted early and unfairly by their inability to conform to a norm that was not their own. It would be my hope that the academics who read this book and apply it would do so with an altered appreciation for the authenticity of growth for the sake of growth. In other words, as taller trees, let us not allow our darker critical powers unfettered play upon the seedling artists in our midst.

Without specific tools and sufficient ego strengths, many gifted artists languish for years in the wake of such blows. Shamed at their supposed lack of talent, shamed by their "grandiose" dreams, the young artists may channel their gifts into

commercial endeavors and then forget their dreams of doing more groundbreaking (and risky) work. They may
work as editors instead of writers, film editors instead of
film directors, commercial artists instead of fine artists, and
get stuck within shouting distance of their dreams. Often
audacity, not authentic talent, confers fame on an artist.
The lack of audacity—pinched out by critical abuse or
malnourished through neglect—may cripple many artists
far superior to those we publicly acclaim. In order to recover our sense of hope and the courage to create, we must
acknowledge and mourn the scars that are blocking us.
This process may seem both painstaking and petty, but it is
a necessary rite of passage. Just as a teenager must gain autonomy from an overbearing parent, so too an artist must gain autonomy from ma-
lignant artistic mentors.

> *Trust that still, small voice that says, "This might work and I'll try it."*
>
> DIANE MARIECHILD

> *Man can learn nothing except by going from the known to the unknown.*
>
> CLAUDE BERNARD

When Ted finished writing his first novel, he bravely sent it off to a literary
agent. He also sent a check for one hundred dollars to pay the agent for taking the
time and trouble to read it. What came back was a single page of unusable, irresponsible, and vague reaction: "This novel is half good and half bad. That's the
worst kind. I can't tell you how to fix it. I suggest pitching it out."

When I met Ted, he had been blocked for seven years. Like many beginners, he
hadn't even known to get another opinion. It was with great difficulty that he
handed his novel over to me. As Ted's friend, I was heartbroken for him that this
novel had been manhandled. As a professional, I was impressed—so impressed I
found myself with my first student to unblock.

"Please try to write again. You can do it. I know you can do it," I started in. Ted
was willing to risk unblocking. It is now twelve years since Ted began his work
with the morning pages. He has written three novels and two movies. He has an
impressive literary agent and a growing reputation.

In order to get to where he is now, Ted had to refeel and mourn the wounding
he had endured as a young writer. He had to make his peace with the lost years this
wounding had cost him. A page at a time, a day at a time, he had to slowly build
strength.

Like the career of any athlete, an artist's life will have its injuries. These go with
the game. The trick is to survive them, to learn how to let yourself heal. Just as a
player who ignores a sore muscle may tear it further, an artist who buries his pain

over losses will ultimately cripple himself into silence. Give yourself the dignity of admitting your artistic wounds. That is the first step in healing them.

No inventory of our artistic injuries would be complete without acknowledging those wounds that are self-inflicted. Many times, as artists, we are offered a chance that we balk at, sabotaged by our fear, our low self-worth, or simply our other agendas.

Grace is offered an art scholarship in another city but doesn't want to leave Jerry, her boyfriend. She turns the scholarship down.

Jack is offered a dream job in his field in a faraway city. It's a great job but he turns it down because of all the friends and family he has where he is.

Angela gets terrible reviews in a terrible play and is then offered another lead in a challenging play. She turns it down.

These lost chances often haunt us bitterly in later years. We will work more extensively later with our artistic U-turns, but for now, just counting them as losses begins the process of healing them.

Gain Disguised as Loss

Art is the act of structuring time. "Look at it this way," a piece of art says. "Here's how I see it." As my waggish friend the novelist Eve Babitz remarks, "It's all in the frame." This is particularly true when what we are dealing with is an artistic loss. Every loss must always be viewed as a potential gain; it's all in the framing.

Every end is a beginning. We know that. But we tend to forget it as we move through grief. Struck by a loss, we focus, understandably, on what we leave behind, the lost dream of the work's successful fruition and its buoyant reception. We need to focus on what lies ahead. This can be tricky. We may not know what lies ahead. And, if the present hurts this badly, we tend to view the future as impending pain.

> *I cannot expect even my own art to provide all of the answers—only to hope it keeps asking the right questions.*
>
> GRACE HARTIGAN

"Gain disguised as loss" is a potent artist's tool. To acquire it, simply, brutally, ask: "How can this loss serve me? Where does it point my work?" The answers will surprise and liberate you. The trick is to metabolize pain as energy. The key to doing that is to know, to trust, and to act as if a silver lining exists if you are only willing to look at the work differently or to walk through a different door, one that you may have balked at.

"In order to catch the ball, you have to want to catch the ball," the film director John Cassavetes once told a young director. Hearing this, I took it to mean, "Stop complaining about the lousy curves you get thrown and stretch, reach for what you *really* want." I have tried to follow this advice.

For years, I played studio roulette. Repeatedly, original scripts were bought and not made. Repeatedly, fine work languished on studio shelves, the victim of revolving studio doors. Go pictures became dead overnight, except in my filmmaker's heart—which was breaking.

"That's just the way it is," I was told repeatedly. "If you want to see your films made, you must first sell yourself as a writer and then *if* one of yours scripts is made and *if* that film is a hit and *if* the climate warms up a little, *then* you *might* get a shot at directing. . . ."

I listened to this conventional wisdom for a long time, racking up loss after loss, writing script after script. Finally, after one loss too many, I began to look for the other door, the one I had refused to walk through. I decided to catch the ball: I became an independent filmmaker.

I left Hollywood. I went to Chicago, bought a used camera and, using my *Miami Vice* writing money, shot my own feature, a romantic, forties-style comedy. It was in the can for $31,000 and it looked good. Then, incredibly, my sound tapes were stolen. I finished the film anyway, dubbing it in its entirety. (Yes, crazy, but so was Cassavetes, my role model.) The result won foreign distribution and fine reviews abroad. And I learned a lot.

Because I asked "How?" instead of "Why me?" I now have a modest first feature to my credit. It might have happened if I had not taken matters into my own hands, but it might not have, either. Since 1974, I have worked vigorously and exhaustively as a film writer. I have written—and sold—features, short films, documentaries, docudramas, teleplays, movies of the week, and that bastardized movie, the miniseries. I have directed one feature and a half dozen short films. Less visibly, I have labored as a script doctor, credited and not, for hire and for love.

> *Art is a technique of communication. The image is the most complete technique of all communication.*
>
> CLAES OLDENBURG

To boot, I have written a hundred-plus film essays, film interviews, think pieces, trend pieces, aesthetics pieces, more—all as I toiled as a writer for such diverse publications as *Rolling Stone*, the *New York Times*, the *Village Voice, New York, New West*, the *Los Angeles Times*, the *Chicago Tribune*, and, most conspicuously,

American Film, where I served as a contributing editor for many years. In short, you might say I have done my dharma to my favored art form.

Why all of this diverse, hydra-headed productivity? Because I love movies, love making them, and did not want my losses to take me down. I learned, when hit by loss, to ask the right question: "What next?" instead of "Why me?"

Whenever I am willing to ask "What is necessary next?" I have moved ahead. Whenever I have taken no for a final answer I have stalled and gotten stuck. I have learned that the key to career resiliency is self-empowerment and choice.

If you look at long and successful creative careers, you will see this principle in action. The distinguished videographer Shirley Clarke began her creative career as a dancer. She first became a filmmaker so that there would be some properly made dance films. Distinguishing herself next as a first-rate feature director, winning renown in Europe if not directing jobs in American studios, Clarke became the first American director to shoot a feature in Harlem, the first American director to explore the range of hand-held camera, the American director that John Cassavetes,

> *The world of reality has its limits; the world of imagination is boundless.*
>
> Jean-Jacques Rousseau

Martin Scorsese, and Paul Shrader all credit as seminal in their own artistic formation. Alas, she was a woman and she lived in difficult times. When her filmmaking revenues dried up, she became one of the first video artists, working with Sam Shepard, Joseph Papp, Ornette Coleman. Clarke clearly took to heart the idea that it was harder to hit a moving target. Whenever one avenue for her creativity was blocked, she found another.

Film annals abound with such stories. Elia Kazan, out of favor as a director, wrote novels. The director John Cassavetes, also a fine actor, used his acting to fund his directing efforts, which were too eclectic for studio backing. "If they won't make it as a feature, *I'll* make it," Cassavetes said, and he did. Rather than allow himself to be blocked, he looked for the other door.

We would not enjoy the wonderful series *Fairytale Theater* if actress-producer Shelley Duvall had stayed home complaining during acting droughts instead of turning her creativity elsewhere. *Non illegitimi te carborundum*, the graffiti in prisoner-of-war camps is said to have run. The rough translation, very important for artists, is "Don't let the bastards get you down."

Artists who take this to heart survive and often prevail. The key here is action. Pain that is not used profitably quickly solidifies into a leaden heart, which makes *any* action difficult.

When faced with a loss, immediately take one small action to support your artist. Even if all you are doing is buying a bunch of tulips and a sketch pad, your action says, "I acknowledge you and your pain. I promise you a future worth having." Like a small child, our artist needs mommying. "Ouch. That hurt. Here's a little treat, a lullaby, a promise . . ."

I have a director friend who tells me that on his worst nights, when he is about to open a new film and he awaits career catastrophe, sure that he will never work again, in the dark, alone, he cajoles himself to sleep: "If I can't shoot 35 mm, I could still shoot 16 mm. If I can't shoot 16 mm, then I can shoot video. If I can't shoot video, I can shoot super 8."

Age and Time: Product and Process

QUESTION: Do you know how old I'll be by the time I learn to play the piano?
ANSWER: The same age you will be if you don't.

"I'm too old for that" ranks with "I don't have money for it" as a Great Block Lie we use to prevent further exploration. "I'm too old" is something we tell ourselves to save ourselves from the emotional cost of the ego deflation involved in being a beginner.

> *Satisfaction of one's curiosity is one of the greatest sources of happiness in life.*
>
> LINUS PAULING

"I'm too old to go to film school," I told myself at thirty-five. And when I got to film school I discovered that I was indeed fifteen years older than my classmates. I also discovered I had greater creative hunger, more life experience, and a much stronger learning curve. Now that I've taught in a film school myself, I find that very often my best students are those who came to their work late.

"I'm too old to be an actor," I have heard many students complain—and dramatically, I might add. They are not always pleased when I tell them this is not the case. The splendid actor John Mahoney did not begin acting until he was nearly forty. Ten years into a highly successful career, he is now often booked three films in advance and works with some of the finest directors in the world.

"I'm too old to really be a writer" is another frequent complaint. This is more ego-saving nonsense. Raymond Chandler didn't publish until the far side of forty. The superb novel *Jules and Jim* was written as a first novel by a man in his seventies.

"I'm too old" is an evasive tactic. It is *always* used to avoid facing fear.

Now let's look at the other side: "I'll let myself try it when I'm retired." This is an interesting side trip on the same ego-saving track. As a culture, we glorify youth and allow our youth the freedom to experiment. And we disparage our old-timers but allow them the right to be a little crazy.

Many blocked creatives tell themselves they are both too old and too young to allow themselves to pursue their dreams. Old and dotty, they might try it. Young and foolish, they might try it. In either scenario, being crazy is a prerequisite to creative exploration. We do not want to look crazy. And trying something like that (whatever it is) at our age (whatever it is) would look nuts.

Yes, maybe.

Creativity occurs in the moment, and in the moment we are timeless. We discover that as we engage in a creative recovery. "I felt like a kid," we may say after a satisfying artist date. Kids are not self-conscious, and once we are actually in the flow of our creativity, neither are we.

"How long would it take me to learn to do that?" we may ask, standing on the sideline of a longed-for activity.

"Maybe a year to be pretty good," the answer comes back. "It depends."

As blocked creatives, we like to pretend that a year or even several years is a long, long time. Our ego plays this little trick to keep us from getting started. Instead of allowing ourselves a creative journey, we focus on the length of the trip. "It's such a long way," we tell ourselves. It may be, but each day is just one more day with some motion in it, and that motion toward a goal is very enjoyable.

At the heart of the anorexia of artistic avoidance is the denial of process. We like to focus on having learned a skill or on having made an artwork. This attention to final form ignores the fact that creativity lies not in the done but in doing.

"I am writing a screenplay" is infinitely more interesting to the soul than "I have written a screenplay," which pleases the ego. "I am in an acting class" is infinitely more interesting than "I took an acting class a few years ago."

In a sense, no creative act is ever finished. You can't learn to act because there is always more to learn. Arguably, you cannot even direct a film because you will always be redirecting it, even years later. You will know then what you might have done and what you will do next if you keep working. This doesn't mean that the work accomplished is worthless. Far from it. It simply means that doing the work points the way to new and better work to be done.

Focused on process, our creative life retains a sense of adventure. Focused on product, the same creative life can feel foolish or barren. We inherit the obsession with product and the idea that art produces finished product from our consumer-oriented society. This focus creates a great deal of creative block. We, as working artists, may want to explore a new artistic area, but we don't see where it will get us. We wonder if it will be good for our career. Fixated on the need to have something to show for our labors, we often deny our curiosities. Every time we do this, we are blocked.

There is a logic of colors, and it is with this alone, and not with the logic of the brain, that the painter should conform.

PAUL CÉZANNE

Our use of age as a block to creative work interlocks with our toxic finished-product thinking. We have set an appropriate age on certain activities: college graduation, going to med school, writing a first book. This artificial ego requirement asks us to be done when what we truly yearn for is to start something.

"If I didn't think I'd look like a jerk next to the young guys, I'd let myself sign up for an improv class."

"If my body looked anything the way it did twenty years ago, I'd let myself take that jazzercize class at the Y."

"If I didn't think my family would consider me a stupid old fool, I'd start playing the piano again. I still remember some of my lessons."

If these excuses are beginning to sound flimsy to you, good! Ask yourself if you haven't employed a few of them. Then ask yourself if you can acquire the humility to start something despite your ego's reservations.

The grace to be a beginner is always the best prayer for an artist. The beginner's humility and openness lead to exploration. Exploration leads to accomplishment. All of it begins at the beginning, with the first small and scary step.

Filling the Form

What do I mean by *filling the form*? I mean taking the next small step instead of skipping ahead to a large one for which you may not yet be prepared. To be very specific, in order to sell a screenplay, you must first write one. In order to write one, you must come up with an idea and then commit it to paper, a page at a time until you have about 120 pages of script. *Filling the form* means that you write your daily pages. It means that when obsession strikes—as it will—about how the damn thing is not any good, you tell yourself that this is a question for later and turn back to doing what is the next right thing. And that means you write the pages of the day.

Art? You just do it.

MARTIN RITT

If you break a screenplay down into daily increments, that small smattering of writing can get done quickly and promptly—before the dirty laundry. And it can carry you through the rest of your day guilt-free and less anxious.

Most of the time, the next right thing is something small: washing out your paintbrushes, stopping by the art-supply store and getting your clay, checking the local paper for a list of acting classes . . . As a rule of thumb, it is best to just admit that there is always *one* action you can take for your creativity daily. This daily-action commitment fills the form.

All too often, when people look to having a more creative life, they hold an unspoken and often unacknowledged expectation, or fear, that they will be abandoning life as they know it.

"I can't be a writer and stay in this marriage."

"I can't pursue my painting and stay at this dull job."

"I can't commit to acting and stay in Chicago . . . or Seattle or Atlanta . . ."

Blocked creatives like to think they are looking at changing their whole life in one fell swoop. This form of grandiosity is very often its own undoing. By setting the jumps too high and making the price tag too great, the recovering artist sets defeat in motion. Who can concentrate on a first drawing class when he is obsessing about having to divorce his wife and leave town? Who can turn toe out in modern jazz from when she is busy reading the ads for a new apartment since she will have to break up with her lover to concentrate on her art?

Creative people are dramatic, and we use negative drama to scare ourselves out of our creativity with this notion of wholesale and often destructive change. Fantasizing about pursuing our art full-time, we fail to pursue it part-time—or at all.

Instead of writing three pages a day on a screenplay, we prefer worrying about how we will have to move to Hollywood if the script gets bought. Which it can't anyway since we are too busy worrying about selling it to write it.

Instead of checking into a life-drawing class at the local culture center, we buy *Art Forum* and remind ourselves that our stuff is not in style. How can it be? It doesn't exist yet!

Instead of clearing out the little room off the kitchen so that we will have a place to work on our pottery, we complain about needing a studio—a complaint that we ourselves cannot take seriously since we do not have any work to argue our case.

Indulging ourselves in a frantic fantasy of what our life would look like if we were *real* artists, we fail to see the many small creative changes that we could make at this very moment. This kind of look-at-the-big-picture thinking ignores the fact that a creative life is grounded on many, many small steps and very, very few large leaps.

Rather than take a scary baby step toward our dreams, we rush to the edge of the cliff and then stand there, quaking, saying, "I can't leap. I can't. I can't. . . ."

No one is asking you to leap. That's just drama, and, for the purposes of a creative recovery, drama belongs on the page or on the canvas or in the clay or in the acting class or in the *act* of creativity, however small.

Creativity requires activity, and this is not good news to most of us. It makes us responsible, and we tend to hate that. You mean I have to *do* something in order to feel better?

Yes. And most of us hate to *do* something when we can obsess about something else instead. One of our favorite things to do—instead of our art—is to contemplate the odds.

In a creative career, thinking about the odds is a drink of emotional poison. It robs us of the dignity of art-as-process and puts us at the mercy of imagined powers *out there*. Taking this drink quickly leads to a severe and toxic emotional bender. It leads us to ask, "What's the use?" instead of "What next?"

As a rule of thumb, the odds are what we use to procrastinate about doing what comes next. This is our addiction to anxiety in lieu of action. Once you catch on to this, the jig is up. Watch yourself for a week and notice the way you will pick up an anxious thought, almost like a joint, to blow off—or at least delay—your next creative action.

You've cleared a morning to write or paint but then you realize that the clothes are dirty. "I'll just think about what I want to paint and fine-tune it while I fold the clothes," you tell yourself. What you really mean is, "Instead of painting anything, I will worry about it some more." Somehow, the laundry takes your whole morning.

Most blocked creatives have an active addiction to anxiety. We prefer the low-grade pain and occasional heart-stopping panic attack to the drudgery of small and simple daily steps in the right direction.

Filling the form means that we must work with what we have rather than languish in complaints over what we have not. As a director, I have noticed that the actors who get work are the actors who *work*—whether they are working or not. I am thinking specifically about Marge Kottlisky, a fine stage and film actress who has always made herself available to work and to workshop writers' materials. She worked with the young playwright David Mamet in the St. Nicholas Theater Group in Chicago and now works with the somewhat older and more accomplished David Mamet wherever he is working. Rather than rest on any creative laurels, she engages in a very healthy sort of creative restlessness. When she is not engaged in the run of a show, she often takes a class to keep her hand in, and she always is available for read-throughs of new plays. Like all actors, she suffers from the "I'll never work again" syndrome, but unlike many less-committed actors, she never allows herself to make her work something she does only for others or only when she is paid. Yes, she wants to be paid, and I am not arguing here that actors should work for free. What I am saying is that work begets work. Small actions lead us to the larger movements in our creative lives.

Many actors allow themselves the dubious luxury of handing their careers over to their agents instead of keeping their art in the custody of their souls. When an agent is in charge of your creative life, you can easily despair that "my agent doesn't do enough" instead of asking what you yourself might do to hone your craft. Fill the form. What can you do, right now, in your life as it is currently constituted? Do that thing.

Take one small daily action instead of indulging in the big questions. When we allow ourselves to wallow in the big questions, we fail to find the small answers. What we are talking about here is a concept of change grounded in respect—respect for where we are as well as where we wish to go. We are looking not to grand strokes of change—although they may come—but instead to the act of creatively husbanding all that is in the present: this job, this house, this relationship.

> *No trumpets sound when the important decisions of our life are made. Destiny is made known silently.*
>
> AGNES DE MILLE

Recovering creatives commonly undergo bouts of fierce rage and grief over their lost years. When these creative kriyas occur, we desperately want to kick over the traces and get the hell out of life as it is currently constituted. Instead, make changes, small changes, right where you are. Fill this form with creative care until it overflows into a newer, larger form—organically.

As the poet Theodore Roethke phrases it, "We learn by going/Where we have to go." We have found that when we fill the form, we do not often need to make large changes. Large changes occur in tiny increments. It is useful to think in terms of a space flight: by altering the launch trajectory very slightly, a great difference can be made over time.

Early Patternings, an Exercise

Although we seldom connect the dots, many of our present-day losses are connected to our earlier conditioning. Children may be told they can't do anything or, equally damaging, be told they should be able to do absolutely anything with ease. Either of these messages blocks the recipient. The following questions are aimed at helping you retrieve and decipher your own conditioning. Some of them may seem not to apply. Write about *whatever* they trigger for you.

> *I am in the world only for the purpose of composing.*
>
> FRANZ SCHUBERT

1. As a kid, my dad thought my art was_____. That made me feel_____.
2. I remember one time when he_____.
3. I felt very _____ and _____ about that. I never forgot it.
4. As a kid, my mother taught me that my daydreaming was _____.
5. I remember she'd tell me to snap out of it by reminding me _____.
6. The person I remember who believed in me was_____ _____.
7. I remember one time when_____.
8. I felt _____ and _____ about that. I never forgot it.
9. The thing that ruined my chance to be an artist was _____.
10. The negative lesson I got from that, which wasn't logical but I still believe, is that I can't _____ and be an artist.
11. When I was little, I learned that _____ and _____ were big sins that I particularly had to watch out for.
12. I grew up thinking artists were _____ people.
13. The teacher who shipwrecked my confidence was_____.
14. I was told_____.
15. I believed this teacher because_____.
16. The mentor who gave me a good role model was_____.
17. When people say I have talent I think they want to_____.
18. The thing is, I am suspicious that_____.
19. I just can't believe that_____.

20. If I believe I am really talented, then I am mad as hell at _____ and _____ and _____ and _____ and _____.

Affirmations

The following affirmations affirm your right to the practice of your creativity. Select five affirmations and work with them this week.

I am a talented person.
I have a right to be an artist.
I am a good person and a good artist.
Creativity is a blessing I accept.
My creativity blesses others.
My creativity is appreciated.
I now treat myself and my creativity more gently.
I now treat myself and my creativity more generously.
I now share my creativity more openly.
I now accept hope.
I now act affirmatively.
I now accept creative recovery.
I now allow myself to heal.
I now accept God's help unfolding my life.
I now believe God loves artists.

TASKS

1. Goal Search: You may find the following exercise difficult. Allow yourself to do it anyway. If multiple dreams occur to you, do the exercise for each one of them. The simple act of imagining a dream in concrete detail helps us to bring it into reality. Think of your goal search as a preliminary architect's drawing for the life you would wish to have.

The Steps

1. Name your dream. That's right. Write it down. "In a perfect world, I would secretly love to be a _____."

2. Name one concrete goal that signals to you its accomplishment. On your emotional compass, this goal signifies true north.
   (Note: two people may want to be an actress. They share that dream. For one, an article in *People* magazine is the concrete goal. To her, glamour is the emotional center for her dream; glamour is true north. For the second actress, the concrete goal is a good review in a Broadway play. To her, respect as a creative artist is the emotional center of her dream; respect is true north. Actress one might be happy as a soap star. Actress two would need stage work to fulfill her dream. On the surface, both seem to desire the same thing.)

3. In a perfect world, where would you like to be in five years in relation to your dream and true north?

4. In the world we inhabit now, what action can you take, this year, to move you closer?

5. What action can you take this month? This week? This day? Right now?

6. List your dream (for example, to be a famous film director). List its true north (respect and higher consciousness, mass communication.) Select a role model (Walt Disney, Ron Howard, Michael Powell). Make an action plan. Five years. Three years. One year. One month. One week. Now. Choose an action. *Reading this book is an action.*

> *Your desire is your prayer. Picture the fulfillment of your desire now and feel its reality and you will experience the joy of the answered prayer.*
>
> DR. JOSEPH MURPHY

2. New Childhood: What might you have been if you'd had perfect nurturing? Write a page of this fantasy childhood. What were you given? Can you reparent yourself in that direction now?

3. Color Schemes: Pick a color and write a quick few sentences describing yourself in the first person. ("I am silver, high-tech and ethereal, the color of dreams and accomplishment, the color of half-light and in between, I feel serene." Or "I am red. I am passion, sunset, anger, blood, wine and roses, armies, murder, lust, and apples.") What is your favorite color? What do you have that is that color? What about an entire room? This is your life and your house.

4. List five things you are not allowed to do: kill your boss, scream in church, go outside naked, make a scene, quit your job. Now do that thing on paper. Write it, draw it, paint it, act it out, collage it. Now put some music on and dance it.

5. Style Search: List twenty things you like to do. (Perhaps the same twenty you listed before, perhaps not.) Answer these questions for each item.

Does it cost money or is it free?

Expensive or cheap?

Alone or with somebody?

Job related?

Physical risk?

Fast-paced or slow?

Mind, body, or spiritual?

6. Ideal Day: Plan a perfect day in your life as it is now constituted, using the information gleaned from above.

7. Ideal Ideal Day: Plan a perfect day in your life as you *wish* it were constituted. There are no restrictions. Allow yourself to be and to have whatever your heart desires. Your ideal environment, job, home, circle of friends, intimate relationship, stature in your art form—your wildest dreams.

8. Choose one festive aspect from your ideal day. Allow yourself to live it. You may not be able to move to Rome yet, but even in a still-grungy apartment you can enjoy a homemade cappuccino and a croissant.

CHECK-IN

1. **How many days this week did you do your morning pages?** (Have you been very tempted to abandon them?) How was the experience for you?

2. **Did you do your artist date this week?** (Have you been allowing workaholism or other commitments to sabotage this practice?) What did you do? How did it feel?

3. **Did you experience any synchronicity this week?** What was it?

4. **Were there any other issues this week that you consider significant for your recovery?** Describe them.

Recovering a Sense of Compassion

This week finds us facing the internal blocks to creativity. It may be tempting to abandon ship at this point. Don't! We will explore and acknowledge the emotional difficulties that beset us in the past as we made creative efforts. We will undertake healing the shame of past failures. We will gain in compassion as we reparent the frightened artist child who yearns for creative accomplishment. We will learn tools to dismantle emotional blocks and support renewed risk.

Fear

ONE OF THE MOST important tasks in artistic recovery is learning to call things—and ourselves—by the right names. Most of us have spent years using the wrong names for our behaviors. We have wanted to create and we have been unable to create and we have called that inability *laziness*. This is not merely inaccurate. It is cruel. Accuracy and compassion serve us far better.

Blocked artists are not lazy. They are blocked.

Being blocked and being lazy are two different things. The blocked artist typically expends a great deal of energy—just not visibly. The blocked artist spends energy on self-hatred, on regret, on grief, and on jealousy. The blocked artist spends energy on self-doubt.

The blocked artist does not know how to begin with baby steps. Instead, the blocked artist thinks in terms of great big scary impossible tasks: a novel, a feature film, a one-person show, an opera. When these large tasks are not accomplished, or even begun, the blocked artist calls that laziness.

Do not call the inability to start laziness. Call it fear.

Fear is the true name for what ails the blocked artist. It may be fear of failure or fear of success. Most frequently, it is fear of abandonment. This fear has roots in childhood reality. Most blocked artists tried to become artists against either their parents' good wishes or their parents' good judgment. For a youngster this is quite a conflict. To go squarely against your parents' values means you'd better know what you're doing. You'd better not just be an artist. You better be a *great* artist if you're going to hurt your parents so much. . . .

Parents do act hurt when children rebel, and declaring oneself an artist is usually viewed by parents as an act of rebellion. Unfortunately, the view of an artist's life as an adolescent rebellion often lingers, making any act of art entail the risk of separation and the loss of loved ones. Because artists still yearn for their creative goals, they then feel guilty.

This guilt demands that they set a goal for themselves right off the bat that they must be great artists in order to justify this rebellion.

The need to be a great artist makes it hard to be an artist.

The need to produce a great work of art makes it hard to produce any art at all.

Finding it hard to begin a project does not mean you will not be able to do it. It means you will need help—from your higher power, from supportive friends, and from yourself. First of all, you must give yourself permission to begin small and go in baby steps. These steps must be rewarded. Setting impossible goals creates enormous fear, which creates procrastination, which we wrongly call laziness.

Do not call procrastination laziness. Call it fear.

Fear is what blocks an artist. The fear of not being good enough. The fear of not finishing. The fear of failure and of success. The fear of beginning at all. There is only one cure for fear. That cure is love.

Use love for your artist to cure its fear.

Stop yelling at yourself. Be nice. Call fear by its right name.

Enthusiasm

"It must take so much discipline to be an artist," we are often told by well-meaning people who are not artists but wish they were. What a temptation.

What a seduction. They're inviting us to preen before an admiring audience, to act out the image that is so heroic and Spartan—and false.

As artists, grounding our self-image in military discipline is dangerous. In the short run, discipline may work, but it will work only for a while. By its very nature, discipline is rooted in self-admiration. (Think of discipline as a battery, useful but short-lived.) We admire ourselves for being so wonderful. The discipline itself, not the creative outflow, becomes the point.

That part of us that creates best is not a driven, disciplined automaton, functioning from willpower, with a booster of pride to back it up. This is operating out of self-will. You know the image: rising at dawn with military precision, saluting the desk, the easel, the drawing board . . .

Over any extended period of time, being an artist requires enthusiasm more than discipline. Enthusiasm is not an emotional state. It is a spiritual commitment, a loving surrender to our creative process, a loving recognition of all the creativity around us.

Enthusiasm (from the Greek, "filled with God") is an ongoing energy supply tapped into the flow of life itself. Enthusiasm is grounded in play, not work. Far from being a brain-numbed soldier, our artist is actually our child within, our inner playmate. As with all playmates, it is joy, not duty, that makes for a lasting bond.

True, our artist may rise at dawn to greet the typewriter or easel in the morning stillness. But this event has more to do with a child's love of secret adventure than with ironclad discipline. What other people may view as discipline is actually a play date that we make with our artist child: "I'll meet you at 6:00 A.M. and we'll goof around with that script, painting, sculpture . . ."

Our artist child can best be enticed to work by treating work as play. Paint is great gooey stuff. Sixty sharpened pencils are fun. Many writers eschew a computer for the comforting, companionable clatter for a solid typewriter that trots along like a pony. In order to work well, many artists find that their work spaces are best dealt with as play spaces.

Dinosaur murals, toys from the five-and-dime, tiny miniature Christmas lights, papier-mâché monsters, hanging crystals, a sprig of flowers, a fish tank . . .

> *It don't mean a thing if it ain't got that swing.*
>
> DUKE ELLINGTON
> AND IRVING MILLS

> *Art evokes the mystery without which the world would not exist.*
>
> RENÉ-FRANÇOIS-GHISLAIN
> MAGRITTE

As attractive as the idea of a pristine cell, monastic in its severity, is to our romanticized notion of being a real artist, the workable truth may be somewhat messier than that. Most little kids would be bored silly in a stark, barren room. Our artist child is no exception.

Remember that art is process. The process is supposed to be fun. For our purposes, "the journey is always the only arrival" may be interpreted to mean that our creative work is actually our creativity itself at play in the field of time. At the heart of this play is the mystery of joy.

Creative U-Turns

Recovering from artist's block, like recovering from any major illness or injury, requires a commitment to health. At some point, we must make an active choice to relinquish the joys and privileges accorded to the emotional invalid. A productive artist is quite often a happy person. This can be very threatening as a self-concept to those who are used to getting their needs met by being unhappy.

"I'd love to, but you see . . . I have these crippling fears . . ." can get us a lot of attention. We get more sympathy as crippled artists than as functional ones. Those of us addicted to sympathy in the place of creativity can become increasingly threatened as we become increasingly functional. Many recovering artists become so threatened that they make U-turns and sabotage themselves.

We usually commit creative hara-kiri either on the eve of or in the wake of a first creative victory. The glare of success (a poem, an acting job, a song, a short story, a film, or any success) can send the recovering artist scurrying back into the cave of self-defeat. We're more comfortable being a victim of artist's block than risking having to consistently be productive and healthy.

An artistic U-turn arrives on a sudden wave of indifference. We greet our newly minted product or our delightful process with "Aw, what does it matter anyhow? It's just a start. Everybody else is so much further ahead. . . ."

Man is not free to refuse to do the thing which gives him more pleasure than any other conceivable action.

STENDHAL

Yes, and they will stay that way if we stop working. The point is we have traveled light-years from where we were when we were blocked. We are now on the road, and the road is scary. We begin to be distracted by roadside attractions or detoured by the bumps.

- A screenwriter has an agent interested in repping a script with just a few changes. He doesn't make the changes.
- A performance artist is offered a space to use for work-shopping his new material. He does it once, doesn't like his mixed reception indicating more work is needed, then stops working on new material at all.
- An actor is told to get his head shots together and check back in with a prestigious agent. He doesn't get his head shots, doesn't check back in.
- An actress-producer with a solid script is offered a studio deal to further develop her project. She finds fault with the deal and then shelves the project entirely.
- A painter is invited into a group show, his first, but picks a fight with the gallery owner.
- A poet reads some poems to very good public reception at a neighborhood open mike. Instead of continuing at this level and gaining strength, the poet enters a *slam* (a sort of boxing match for poets judged by nonpoets), loses, and stops reading publicly altogether.
- A lyricist hooks up with a new composer, and they literally make beautiful music together. They demo three songs, which get enthusiastic response, and then stop working together.
- A fledgling photographer is greatly encouraged by her teacher's interest in her work. She botches developing one roll of film and then quits the class, claiming it was boring.

In dealing with our creative U-turns, we must first of all extend ourselves some sympathy. Creativity is scary, and in *all* careers there are U-turns. Sometimes these U-turns are best viewed as recycling times. We come up to a creative jump, run out from it like a skittish horse, then circle the field a few times before trying the fence again.

> *Life shrinks or expands in proportion to one's courage.*
>
> ANAÏS NIN

Typically, when we take a creative U-turn we are doubly shamed: first by our fear and second by our reaction to it. Again, let me say it helps to remember that *all* careers have them.

For two years in my mid-thirties I wrote arts coverage for the *Chicago Tribune*. In this capacity, I talked to Akira Kurosawa, Kevin Klein, Julie Andrews, Jane Fonda, Blake Edwards, Sydney Pollack, Sissy Spacek, Sigourney Weaver, Martin Ritt,

Gregory Hines, and fifty-odd more. I talked to most of them about discouragement—which meant talking to them about U-turns. As much as talent, the capacity to avoid or recoup from creative U-turns distinguished their careers.

A successful creative career is always built on successful creative failures. The trick is to survive them. It helps to remember that even our most illustrious artists have taken creative U-turns in their time.

Blake Edwards has directed some of the funniest and most successful comedy of the past three decades. Nonetheless, he spent seven years in self-imposed exile in Switzerland because a script that he felt was his best was taken away from him in preproduction when his take on the material differed from that of the star the studio had acquired to enhance it.

Fired from his own project, Edwards sat on the sidelines watching as his beloved film was made by others and botched badly. Like a wounded panther, Edwards retired to the Alps to nurse his wounds. He wound up back directing seven long years later—when he concluded that creativity, not time, would best heal his creative wounds. Sticking to this philosophy, he has been aggressively productive every since. Talking about this time-out to me, he was rueful, and pained, about the time it cost him.

Have compassion. Creative U-turns are always born from fear—fear of success or fear of failure. It doesn't really matter which. The net result is the same.

To recover from a creative U-turn, or a pattern involving many creative U-turns, we must first admit that it exists. Yes, I did react negatively to fear and pain. Yes, I do need help.

Think of your talent as a young and skittish horse that you are bringing along. This horse is very talented but it is also young, nervous, and inexperienced. It will make mistakes, be frightened by obstacles it hasn't seen before. It may even bolt, try to throw you off, feign lameness. Your job, as the creative jockey, is to keep your horse moving forward and to coax it into finishing the course.

First of all, take a look at what jumps make your horse so skittish. You may find that certain obstacles are far more scary than others. An agent jump may frighten you more than a workshop jump. A review jump may be okay while a rewrite jump scares your talent to death. Remember that in a horse race, there are other horses in the field. One trick a seasoned jockey uses is to place a green horse in the slipstream of an older, steadier, and more seasoned horse. You can do this, too.

- Who do I know who has an agent? Then ask them how they got one.
- Who do I know who has done a successful rewrite? Ask them how to do one.
- Do I know anyone who has survived a savage review? Ask them what they did to heal themselves.

Once we admit the need for help, the help arrives. The ego always wants to claim self-sufficiency. It would rather pose as a creative loner than ask for help. Ask anyway.

Bob was a promising young director when he made his first documentary. It was a short, very powerful film about his father, a factory worker. When he had a rough cut together, Bob showed it to a teacher, a once-gifted filmmaker who was blocked himself. The teacher savaged it. Bob abandoned the film. He stuck the film in some boxes, stuck the boxes in his basement, and forgot about them until the basement flooded. "Oh well. Just as well," he told himself then, assuming the film was ruined.

I met Bob half a decade later. Sometime after we became friends, he told me the story of his film. I had a suspicion that it was good. "It's lost," he told me. "Even the lab lost the footage I gave them." Talking about the film, Bob broke down— and through. He began to mourn his abandoned dream.

A week later, Bob got a call from the lab. "It's incredible. They found the footage," he related. I was not too surprised. I believe the creator keeps an eye on artists and was protecting that film. With the encouragement of his screenwriter girlfriend, now his wife, Bob finished his film. They have gone on to make a second, innovative documentary together.

Faced with a creative U-turn, ask yourself, "Who can I ask for help about this U-turn?" Then start asking.

Blasting Through Blocks

In order to work freely on a project, an artist must be at least functionally free of resentment (anger) and resistance (fear). What do we mean by that? We mean that any buried barriers must be aired before the work can proceed. The same holds true for any buried payoffs to not working. Blocks are seldom mysterious. They are, instead, recognizable artistic defenses against what is perceived (rightly or wrongly) as a hostile environment.

Remember, your artist is a creative child. It sulks, throws tantrums, holds grudges, harbors irrational fears. Like most children, it is afraid of the dark, the bogeyman, and any adventure that isn't safely scary. As your artist's parent and guardian, its big brother, warrior, and companion, it falls to you to convince your artist it is safe to come out and (work) play.

Beginning any new project, it's a good idea to ask your artist a few simple questions. These questions will help remove common bugaboos standing between your artist and the work. These same questions, asked when work grows difficult or bogs down, usually act to clear the obstructed flow.

1. List any resentments (anger) you have in connection with this project. It does not matter how petty, picky, or irrational these resentments may appear to your adult self. To your artist child they are real big deals: grudges.

   Some examples: I resent being the second artist asked, not the first. (I am too the best.) . . . I resent this editor, she just nitpicks. She never says anything nice. . . . I resent doing work for this idiot; he never pays me on time.

2. Ask your artist to list any and all fears about the projected piece of work and/or anyone connected to it. Again, these fears can be as dumb as any two-year-old's. It does not matter that they are groundless to your adult's eye. What matters it that they are big scary monsters to your artist.

   Music is your own experience, your thoughts, your wisdom. If you don't live it, it won't come out your horn.

   CHARLIE PARKER

   Some examples: I'm afraid the work will be rotten and I won't know it. . . . I'm afraid the work will be good and they won't know it. . . . I'm afraid all my ideas are hackneyed and outdated. . . . I'm afraid my ideas are ahead of their time. . . . I'm afraid I'll starve. . . . I'm afraid I'll never finish. . . . I'm afraid I'll never

   Be really whole And all things will come to you.

   LAO-TZU

   start. . . . I'm afraid I will be embarrassed (I'm already embarrassed). . . . The list goes on.

3. Ask yourself it that is all. Have you left out any itsy fear? Have you suppressed any "stupid" anger? Get it on the page.

4. Ask yourself what you stand to gain by not doing this piece of work.

Some examples: If I don't write the piece, no one can hate it. . . . If I don't write the piece, my jerk editor will worry. . . . If I don't paint, sculpt, act, sing, dance, I can criticize others, knowing I could do better.

5. Make your deal. The deal is: "Okay, Creative Force, you take care of the quality, I'll take care of the quantity." Sign your deal and post it.

A word of warning: this is a very powerful exercise; it can do fatal damage to a creative block.

TASKS

1. Read your morning pages! This process is best undertaken with two colored markers, one to highlight insights and another to highlight actions needed. Do not judge your pages or yourself. This is very important. Yes, they will be boring. Yes, they may be painful. Consider them a map. Take them as information, not an indictment.

   Take Stock: Who have you consistently been complaining about? What have you procrastinated on? What blessedly have you allowed yourself to change or accept?

   Take Heart: Many of us notice an alarming tendency toward black-and-white thinking: "He's terrible. He's wonderful. I love him. I hate him. It's a great job. It's a terrible job," and so forth. Don't be thrown by this.

   Acknowledge: The pages have allowed us to vent without self-destruction, to plan without interference, to complain without an audience, to dream without restriction, to know our own minds. Give yourself credit for undertaking them. Give them credit for the changes and growth they have fostered.

2. Visualizing: You have already done work with naming your goal and identifying true north. The following exercise asks you to fully imagine having your goal accomplished. Please spend enough time to fill in the juicy details that would really make the experience wonderful for you.

   Learning is movement from moment to moment.

   J. KRISHNAMURTI

   Name your goal: I am_____

   In the present tense, describe yourself doing it at the height of your powers! This is your ideal scene.

Read this aloud to yourself.

Post this above your work area.

Read this aloud, daily!

For the next week collect actual pictures of yourself and combine them with magazine images to collage your ideal scene described above. Remember, seeing is believing, and the added visual cue of your real self in your ideal scene can make it far more real.

3. Priorities: List for yourself your creative goals for the year. List for yourself your creative goals for the month. List for yourself your creative goals for the week.

4. Creative U-Turns: All of us have taken creative U-turns. Name one of yours. Name three more. Name the one that just kills you.

Forgive yourself. Forgive yourself for all failures of nerve, timing, and initiative. Devise a personalized list of affirmations to help you do better in the future.

Very gently, *very gently*, consider whether any aborted, abandoned, savaged, or sabotaged brain-children can be rescued. Remember, you are not alone. All of us have taken creative U-turns.

Choose one creative U-turn. Retrieve it. Mend it.

Do not take a creative U-turn now. Instead, notice your resistance. Morning pages seeming difficult? Stupid? Pointless? Too obvious? Do them anyway.

What creative dreams are lurching toward possibility? Admit that that they frighten you.

Choose an artist totem. It might be a doll, a stuffed animal, a carved figuring, or a wind-up toy. The point is to choose something you immediately feel a protective fondness toward. Give your totem a place of honor and then honor it by not beating up on your artist child.

CHECK-IN

1. **How many days this week you do your morning pages?** Regarding your U-turns, have you allowed yourself a shift toward compassion, at least on the page?

2. **Did you do your artist date this week?** Have you kept the emphasis on fun? What did you do? How did it feel?

3. **Did you experience any synchronicity this week?** What was it?

4. **Were there any other issues this week that you consider significant for your recovery?** Describe them.

Recovering a Sense of Self-Protection

This week we explore the perils that can ambush us on our creative path. Because creativity is a spiritual issue, many of the perils are spiritual perils. In the essays, tasks, and exercises of this week, we search out the toxic patterns we cling to that block our creative flow.

Dangers of the Trail

CREATIVITY IS GOD ENERGY flowing through us, shaped by us, like light flowing through a crystal prism. When we are clear about who we are and what we are doing, the energy flows freely and we experience no strain. When we resist what that energy might show us or where it might take us, we often experience a shaky, out-of-control feeling. We want to shut down the flow and regain our sense of control. We slam on the psychic brakes.

Every creative person has myriad ways to block creativity. Each of us favors one or two ways particularly toxic to us because they block us so effectively.

For some people, food is a creativity issue. Eating sugar or fats or certain carbohydrates may leave them feeling dulled, hung over, unable to focus—blurry. They use food to block energy and change. As the shaky feeling comes over them that they are going too fast and God knows where, that they are about to fly apart, these people reach for food. A big bowl of ice cream, an evening of junk food, and their system clogs: What was I thinking? What . . .? Oh, never mind. . . .

For some people alcohol is the favored block. For others, drugs. For many, work is the block of choice. Busy, busy, busy, they grab for tasks to numb themselves with. They can't take a half hour's walk. "What a waste of time!" Must-dos

Saying no can be the ultimate self-care.

CLAUDIA BLACK

and multiple projects are drawn to them like flies to a soda can in the sun. They go, "Buzz, buzz, buzz, *swat!*" as they brush aside the stray thought that was the breakthrough insight.

For others, an obsession with painful love places creative choice outside their hands. Reaching for the painful thought, they become instant victims rather than feel their own considerable power. "If only he or she would just love me . . ."

This obsessive thought drowns out the little voice that suggests rearranging the living room, taking a pottery class, trying a new top on that story that's stymied. The minute a creative thought raises its head, it is lopped off by the obsession, which blocks fear and prevents risk. Going out dancing? Redoing the whole play with an inner-city theme? "If only he or she would love me . . ." So much for *West Side Story*.

Sex is the great block for many. A mesmerizing, titillating hypnotic interest slides novel erotic possibilities in front of the real novel. The new sex object becomes the focus for creative approaches.

Now, note carefully that food, work, and sex are all good in themselves. It is the *abuse* of them that makes them creativity issues. Knowing yourself as an artist means acknowledging which of these you abuse when you want to block yourself. If creativity is like a burst of the universe's breath through the straw that is each of us, we pinch that straw whenever we pick up one of our blocks. We shut down our flow. And we do it on purpose.

We begin to sense our real potential and the wide range of possibilities open to us. That scares us. So we'll all reach for blocks to slow our growth. If we are honest with ourselves, we all know which blocks are the toxic ones for us. Clue: this is the block we defend as our right.

Line up the possibilities. Which one makes you angry to even think about giving up? That explosive one is the one that has caused you the most derailment. Examine it. When asked to name our poison, most of us can. Has food sabotaged me? Has workaholism sabotaged me? Has sex or love obsession blocked my creativity?

Mix and match is a common recipe for using blocks: use one, add another, mix in a third, wear yourself out. The object of all of this blocking is to alleviate fear. We turn to our drug of choice to block our creativity whenever we experience the anxiety of our inner emptiness. It is always fear—often disguised but *always* there—that leads us into grabbing for a block.

In the middle of difficulty lies opportunity.

ALBERT EINSTEIN

Usually, we experience the choice to block as a coincidence. She happened to call . . . I felt hungry and there was some ice cream . . . He dropped by with some killer dope. . . . The choice to block always works in the short run and fails in the long run.

The choice to block is a creative U-turn. We turn back on ourselves. Like water forced to a standstill, we turn stagnant. The self-honesty lurking in us all always knows when we choose against our greater good. It marks a little jot on our spiritual blackboard: "Did it again."

It takes grace and courage to admit and surrender our blocking devices. Who wants to? Not while they are still working! Of course, long after they have stopped working, we hope against hope that this time they will work again.

Blocking is essentially an issue of faith. Rather than trust our intuition, our talent, our skill, our desire, we fear where our creator is taking us with this creativity. Rather than paint, write, dance, audition, and see where it takes us, we pick up a block. Blocked, we know who and what we are: unhappy people. Unblocked, we may be something much more threatening—happy. For most of us, happy is terrifying, unfamiliar, out of control, too risky! Is it any wonder we take temporary U-turns?

As we become aware of our blocking devices—food, busyness, alcohol, sex, other drugs—we can feel our U-turns as we make them. The blocks will no longer work effectively. Over time, we will try—perhaps slowly at first and erratically—to ride out the anxiety and see where we emerge. Anxiety is fuel. We can use it to write with, paint with, work with.

Feel: anxious!
Try: using the anxiety!
Feel: I just did it! I didn't block! I used the anxiety and moved ahead!
Oh my God, I am excited!

Workaholism

Workaholism is an addiction, and like all addictions, it blocks creative energy. In fact, it could be argued that the desire to block the fierce flow of creative energy is an underlying reason for addiction. If people are too busy to write morning pages, or too busy to take an artist date, they are probably too busy to hear the voice of authentic creative urges. To return to the concept of a radio set, the workaholic jams the signals with self-induced static.

Only recently recognized as an addiction, workaholism still receives a great deal of support in our society. The phrase *I'm working* has a certain unassailable air of goodness and duty to it. The truth is, we are very often working to avoid ourselves, our spouses, our real feelings.

When we are really honest with ourselves we must admit our lives are all that really belong to us. So it is how we use our lives that determines the kind of men we are.

CESAR CHAVEZ

In creative recovery, it is far easier to get people to do the extra work of the morning pages than it is to get them to do the assigned play of an artist date. Play can make a workaholic very nervous. Fun is scary.

"If I had more time, I'd have more fun," we like to tell ourselves, but this is seldom the truth. To test the validity of this assertion, ask yourself how much time you allot each week to fun: pure, unadulterated, nonproductive fun?

For most blocked creatives, fun is something they avoid almost as assiduously as their creativity. Why? Fun leads to creativity. It leads to rebellion. It leads to feeling our own power, and that is scary. "I may have a small problem with overwork," we like to tell ourselves, "but I am not really a workaholic." Try answering these questions before you are so sure:

The Workaholism Quiz

1. I work outside of office hours: seldom, often, never?
2. I cancel dates with loved ones to do more work: seldom, often, never?
3. I postpone outings until the deadline is over: seldom, often, never?
4. I take work with me on weekends: seldom, often, never?
5. I take work with me on vacations: seldom, often, never?
6. I take vacations: seldom, often, never?
7. My intimates complain I always work: seldom, often, never?
8. I try to do two things at once: seldom, often, never?
9. I allow myself free time between projects: seldom, often, never?
10. I allow myself to achieve closure on tasks: seldom, often, never?
11. I procrastinate in finishing up the last loose ends: seldom, often, never?
12. I set out to do one job and start on three more at the same time: seldom, often, never?
13. I work in the evenings during family time: seldom, often, never?

14. I allow calls to interrupt—and lengthen—my work day: seldom, often, never?
15. I prioritize my day to include an hour of creative work/play: seldom, often, never?
16. I place my creative dreams before my work: seldom, often, never?
17. I fall in with others' plans and fill my free time with their agendas: seldom, often, never?
18. I allow myself down time to do *nothing:* seldom, often, never?
19. I use the word *deadline* to describe and rationalize my work load: seldom, often, never?
20. Going somewhere, even to dinner, with a notebook or my work numbers is something I do: seldom, often, never?

In order to recover our creativity, we must learn to see workaholism as a block instead of a building block. Work abuse creates in our artist a Cinderella Complex. We are always dreaming of the ball and always experiencing the ball and chain.

There is a difference between zestful work toward a cherished goal and workaholism. That difference lies less in the hours than it does in the emotional quality of the hours spent. There is a treadmill quality to workaholism. We depend on our addiction and we resent it. For a workaholic, work is synonymous with worth, and so we are hesitant to jettison any part of it.

In striving to clear the way for our creative flow, we must look at our work habits very clearly. We may not think we overwork until we look at the hours we put in. We may think our work is normal until we compare it with a normal forty-hour week.

One way to achieve clarity about our time expenditures is to keep a daily checklist and record of our time spent. Even an hour of creative work/play can go a long way toward offsetting the sense of workaholic desperation that keeps our dreams at bay.

Because workaholism is a process addiction (an addiction to a behavior rather than a substance), it is difficult to tell when we are indulging in it. An alcoholic gets sober by abstaining from alcohol. A workaholic gets sober by abstaining from *over*work. The trick is to define overwork—and this is where we often lie to ourselves, bargaining to hold on to those abusive behaviors that still serve us.

In order to guard against rationalization, it is very useful to set a *bottom line.* Each person's bottom line is different but should specifically mention those behaviors known to be off-limits. These specific behaviors make for more immediate recovery than a vague, generic resolve to do better.

If you really have no time, you need to make some room. It is more likely, however, that you have the time and are misspending it. Your time log will help you find those areas where you need to create boundaries. *Boundary* is another way to say bottom line. ("Bottom line, I will not _____." That is your boundary. See Setting a Bottom Line in this week's list of tasks.)

As with creative U-turns, recovery from workaholism may require that we enlist the help of our friends. Tell them what you are trying to accomplish. Ask them to remind you gently when you have strayed off your self-care course. (This will backfire if you enlist the help of people who are active workaholics themselves or who are so controlling that they will overcontrol you.) Bear in mind, however, that this is *your* problem. No one can police you into recovery. But in some parts of the country Workaholics Anonymous meetings are springing up, and these may help you enormously.

One very simple but effective way to check your own recovery progress is to post a sign in your work area. Also post this sign wherever you will read it: one on the bathroom mirror and one on the refrigerator, one on the nightstand, one in the car. . . . The sign reads: WORKAHOLISM IS A BLOCK, NOT A BUILDING BLOCK.

Drought

In any creative life there are dry seasons. These droughts appear from nowhere and stretch to the horizon like a Death Valley vista. Life loses its sweetness; our work feels mechanical, empty, forced. We feel we have nothing to say, and we are tempted to say nothing. These are the times when the morning pages are most difficult and most valuable.

During a drought, the mere act of showing up on the page, like the act of walking through a trackless desert, requires one footfall after another to no apparent point. Doubts sidle up to us like sidewinders. "What's the use?" they hiss. Or "What do you expect?" Droughts tell us that they will last forever—and that we will not. A haunting anticipation of our own death, approaching long before we're ready for it, long before we've done anything of value, shimmers ahead of us like a ghastly mirage.

What do we do? We stumble on. How do we do that? We stay on the morning pages. This is not a rule for writers only. (The pages have nothing to do with writing, although they may facilitate it as they do all art forms.) For all creative beings, the morning pages are the lifeline—the trail we explore and the trail home to ourselves.

During a drought, the morning pages seem both painful and foolish. They feel like empty gestures—like making breakfast for the lover we know is leaving us anyhow. Hoping against hope that we will someday be creative again, we go through the motions. Our consciousness is parched. We cannot feel so much as a trickle of grace.

During a drought (during a *doubt*, I just accurately wrote with a slip of the finger), we are fighting with God. We have lost faith—in the Great Creator and in our creative selves. We have some bone to pick, and bones to pick are everywhere. This is the desert of the heart. Looking for a hopeful sign, all we see are the hulking remains of dreams that died along the path.

And yet we write our morning pages because we must.

During a drought, emotions are dried up. Like water, they may exist somewhere underneath, but we have no access to them. A drought is a tearless time of grief. We are between dreams. Too listless to even know our losses, we put one page after another, more from habit than hope.

And yet we write our morning pages because we must.

Droughts are terrible. Droughts hurt. Droughts are long, airless seasons of doubt that make us grow, give us compassion, and blossom as unexpectedly as the desert with sudden flowers.

Droughts do end.

Droughts end because we have kept writing our pages. They end because we have not collapsed to the floor of our despair and refused to move. We have doubted, yes, but we have stumbled on.

In a creative life, droughts are a necessity. The time in the *desert* brings us clarity and charity. When you are in a drought, know that it is to a purpose. And keep writing morning pages.

> *Truly, it is in the darkness that one finds the light, so when we are in sorrow, then this light is nearest of all to us.*
>
> MEISTER ECKHART

> *The unconscious wants truth. It ceases to speak to those who want something else more than truth.*
>
> ADRIENNE RICH

To write is to *right* things. Sooner or later—always later than we like—our pages will bring things right. A path will emerge. An insight will be a landmark that shows the way out of the wilderness. Dancer, sculptor, actor, painter, playwright, poet, performance artist, potter, artists all—the morning pages are both our wilderness and our trail.

Fame

Fame encourages us to believe that if it hasn't happened yet, it won't happen. Of course, *it* is fame. Fame is not the same as success, and in our true souls we know that. We know—and have felt—success at the end of a good day's work. But fame? It is addictive, and it always leaves us hungry.

Fame is a spiritual drug. It is often a by-product of our artistic work, but like nuclear waste, it can be a very dangerous by-product. Fame, the desire to attain it, the desire to hold on to it, can produce the "How am I doing?" syndrome. This question is not "Is the work going well?" This question is "How does it look to them?"

The point of the work *is* the work. Fame interferes with that perception. Instead of acting being about acting, it becomes about being a famous actor. Instead of writing being about writing, it becomes about being recognized, not just published.

We all like credit where credit is due. As artists, we don't always get it. Yet, focusing on fame—on whether we are getting enough—creates a continual feeling of lack. There is never enough of the fame drug. Wanting more will always snap at our heels, discredit our accomplishments, erode our joy at another's accomplishment.

(To test this, read any of the many fan magazines—*People*, for instance—and see if afterward your life somehow feels more shabby, less worthwhile. This is the fame drug at work.)

Real learning comes about when the competitive spirit has ceased.

J. KRISHNAMURTI

Remember, treating yourself like a precious object will make you strong. When you have been toxified by the fame drug, you need to detox by coddling yourself. What's in order here is a great deal of gentleness and some behavior that makes you like yourself. Sending postcards is a great trick. Mail one to yourself that says, "You are doing great . . ." It is very nice to get fan letters from ourselves.

In the long run, fan letters from ourselves—and our creative self—are what we are really after. Fame is really a shortcut for self-approval. Try approving of yourself just as you are—and spoiling yourself rotten with small kid's pleasures.

What we are really scared of is that without fame we won't be loved—as artists or as people. The solution to this fear is concrete, small, loving actions. We must actively, consciously, consistently, and creatively nurture our artist selves.

When the fame drug hits, go to your easel, your typewriter, your camera or clay. Pick up the tools of your work and begin to do just a little creative play.

Soon, very soon, the fame drug should start to lessen its hold. The only cure for the fame drug is creative endeavor. Only when we are being joyfully creative can we release the obsession with others and how they are doing.

Competition

You pick up a magazine—or even your alumni news—and somebody, *somebody you know*, has gone further, faster, toward your dream. Instead of saying, "That proves it can be done," your fear will say, "He or she will succeed *instead* of me."

Competition is another spiritual drug. When we focus on competition we poison our own well, impede our own progress. When we are ogling the accomplishments of others, we take our eye away from our own through line. We ask ourselves the wrong questions, and those wrong questions give us the wrong answers.

"Why do I have such rotten luck? Why did he get his movie/article/play out before I got mine out? Is it because of sexism?" "What's the use? What do I have to offer?" We often ask these questions as we try to talk ourselves out of creating.

Questions like these allow us to ignore more useful questions: "Did I work on my play today? Did I make the deadline to mail it off where it needed to go? Have I done any networking on its behalf?"

These are the real questions, and focusing on them can be hard for us. No wonder it is tempting to take the first emotional drink instead. No wonder so many of us read *People* magazine (or the *New York Times Book Review*, or *Lears,* or *Mirabella,* or *Esquire*) and use them to wallow in a lot of unhealthy envy.

We make excuses for our avoidance, excuses focused on others. "Somebody (else) has probably said it, done it, thought it . . . and better. . . . Besides, they had connections, a rich father, they belong to a sought-after minority, they slept their way to the top . . ."

Competition lies at the root of much creative blockage. As artists, we must go within. We must attend to what it is our inner guidance is nudging us toward. We cannot afford to worry about what is in or out. If it is too early or late for a piece of work, its time will come again.

As artists, we cannot afford to think about who is getting ahead of us and how they don't deserve it. The desire to *be better than* can choke off the simple desire to *be*. As artists we cannot afford this thinking. It leads us away from our own voices and choices and into a defensive game that centers outside of ourselves and our sphere of influence. It asks us to define our own creativity in terms of someone else's.

This compare-and-contrast school of thinking may have its place for critics, but not for artists in the act of creation. Let the critics spot trends. Let reviewers concern themselves with what is in and what is not. Let us concern ourselves first and foremost with what it is within us that is struggling to be born.

When we compete with others, when we focus our creative concerns on the marketplace, we are really jostling with other artists in a creative footrace. This is the sprint mentality. Looking for the short-term win, ignoring the long-term gain, we short-circuit the possibility of a creative life led by our own lights, not the klieg lights of fashion.

> *Only when he no longer knows what he is doing does the painter do good things.*
>
> EDGAR DEGAS

Whenever you are angered about someone else beating you out, remember this: the footrace mentality is *always* the ego's demand to be not just good but also first and best. It is the ego's demand that our work be totally original—as if such a thing were possible. All work is influenced by other work. All people are influenced by other people. No man is an island and no piece of art is a continent unto itself.

When we respond to art we are responding to its resonance in terms of our own experience. We seldom see anew in the sense of finding something utterly unfamiliar. Instead, we see *an old* in a new light.

If the demand to be original still troubles you, remember this: each of us is our own country, an interesting place to visit. It is the accurate mapping out of our own creative interests that invites the term *original*. We are the *origin* of our art, its homeland. Viewed this way, originality is the process of remaining true to ourselves.

The spirit of competition—as opposed to the spirit of creation—often urges us to quickly winnow out whatever doesn't seem like a winning idea. This can be very dangerous. It can interfere with our ability to carry a project to term.

A competitive focus encourages snap judgments: thumbs up or thumbs down. Does this project deserve to live? (No, our ego will say if it is looking for the fail-safe, surefire project that is a winner at a glance and for good.) Many hits are sure things only in retrospect. Until we know better, we call a great many creative swans ugly ducklings. This is an indignity we offer our brainchildren as they rear their heads in our consciousness. We judge them like beauty-pageant contestants. In a glance we may cut them down. We forget that not all babies are born beautiful, and so we abort the lives of awkward or unseemly projects that may be our finest work, out best creative ugly ducklings. An act of art needs time to mature. Judged early, it may be judged incorrectly.

> He who knows others is wise; he who knows himself is enlightened.
>
> LAO-TZU

Never, ever, judge a fledgling piece of work too quickly. Be willing to paint or write badly while your ego yelps resistance. Your bad writing may be the syntactical breakdown necessary for a shift in your style. Your lousy painting may be pointing you in a new direction. Art needs time to incubate, to sprawl a little, to be ungainly and mis-shapen and finally emerge as itself. The ego hates this fact. The ego wants instant gratification and the addictive hit of an acknowledged win.

> I will tell you what I have learned myself. For me, a long five or six mile walk helps. And one must go alone and every day.
>
> BRENDA UELAND

The need to win—now!—is a need to win approval from others. As an antidote, we must learn to approve of ourselves. Showing up for the work is the win that matters.

TASKS

1. The Deadlies: Take a piece of paper and cut seven small strips from it. On each strip write one of the following words: *alcohol, drugs, sex, work, money, food, family/friends.* Fold these strips of paper and place them in an envelope. We call these folded slips *the deadlies.* You'll see why in a minute. Now draw one of the deadlies from the envelope and write five ways in which it has had a negative impact on your life. (If the one you choose seems difficult or inapplicable to you, consider this resistance.) You will do this seven times, each time putting back the previous slip of paper so that you are always drawing from seven possible choices. Yes, you may draw the same deadly repeatedly. Yes, this is

significant. Very often, it is the last impact on the final list of an annoying "Oh no, not again" that yields a break, through denial, into clarity.

2. Touchstones: Make a quick list of things you love, happiness touchstones for you. River rocks worn smooth, willow trees, cornflowers, chicory, real Italian bread, homemade vegetable soup, the Bo Deans' music, black beans and rice, the smell of new-mown grass, blue velvet (the cloth and the song), Aunt Minnie's crumb pie . . .

Post this list where it can console you and remind you of your own personal touchstones. You may want to draw one of the items on your list—or acquire it. If you love blue velvet, get a remnant and use it as a runner on a sideboard or dresser, or tack it to the wall and mount images on it. Play a little.

3. The Awful Truth: Answer the following questions.

Tell the truth. What habit do you have that gets in the way of your creativity?

Tell the truth. What do you think might be a problem? It is.

What do you plan to do about the habit or problem?

What is your payoff in holding on to this block?

If you can't figure out your payoff, ask a trusted friend.

Tell the truth. Which friends make you doubt yourself? (The self-doubt is yours already, but they trigger it.)

Tell the truth. Which friends believe in you and your talent? (The talent is yours, but they make you feel it.)

What is the payoff in keeping your destructive friends? If the answer is, "I like them," the next question is, "Why?"

Which destructive habits do your destructive friends share with your destructive self?

> *How often—even before we began—have we declared a task "impossible"? And how often have we construed a picture of ourselves as being inadequate? . . . A great deal depends upon the thought patterns we choose and on the persistence with which we affirm them.*
>
> PIERO FERRUCCI

> *It's a funny thing about life; if you refuse to accept anything but the best, you very often get it.*
>
> W. SOMERSET MAUGHAM

Which constructive habits do your constructive friends share with your destructive self?

4. Setting a Bottom Line: Working with your answers to the questions above, try setting a bottom line for yourself. Begin with five of your most painful behaviors. You can always add more later.

- If you notice that your evenings are typically gobbled by your boss's extra assignments, then a rule must come into play: no work after six.
- If you wake at six and could write for an hour if you were not interrupted to look for socks and make breakfast and do ironing, the rules might be "No interrupting Mommy before 7:00 A.M."
- If you are working too many jobs and too many hours, you may need to look at your billing. Are you pricing yourself appropriately? Do some footwork. What are others in your field receiving? Raise your prices and lower your work load.

Bottom Line

1. I will no longer work weekends.
2. I will no longer bring work with me on social occasions.
3. I will no longer place my work before my creative commitments. (No more canceling piano lessons or drawing class because of a sudden new deadline from my boss the workaholic.)
4. I will no longer postpone lovemaking to do latenight reading for work.
5. I will no longer accept business calls at home after six.

5. Cherishing:
   1. List five small victories.
   2. List three nurturing actions you took for your artist.
   3. List three actions you could take to comfort your artist.
   4. Make three nice promises to yourself. Keep them.
   5. Do one lovely thing for yourself *each* day this week.

CHECK-IN

1. **How many days this week did you do your morning pages?** Has reading your pages changed your writing? Are you still allowing yourself to write them freely?
2. **Did you do your artist date this week?** Let yourself do an extra one. What did you do? How did it feel?
3. **Did you experience any synchronicity this week?** What was it?
4. **Were there any other issues this week that you consider significant for your recovery?** Describe them.

Recovering a Sense of Autonomy

This week we focus on our artistic autonomy. We examine the ongoing ways in which we must nurture and accept ourselves as artists. We explore the behaviors that can strengthen our spiritual base and, therefore, our creative power. We take a special look at the ways in which success must be handled in order that we not sabotage our freedom.

Acceptance

I AM AN ARTIST. As an artist, I may need a different mix of stability and flow from other people. I may find that a nine-to-five job steadies me and leaves me freer to create. Or I may find that a nine-to-five drains me of energy and leaves me unable to create. I must experiment with what works for me.

An artist's cash flow is typically erratic. No law says we must be broke all the time, but the odds are good we may be broke some of the time. Good work will sometimes not sell. People will buy but not pay promptly. The market may be rotten even when the work is great. I cannot control these factors. Being true to the inner artist often results in work that sells—but not always. I have to free myself from determining my value and the value of my work by my work's market value.

The idea that money validates my credibility is very hard to shake. If money determines real art, then Gauguin was a charlatan. As an artist, I may never have a home that looks like *Town and Country*—or I may. On the other hand, I may have a book of poems, a song, a piece of performance art, a film.

I must learn that as an artist my credibility lies with me, God, and my work. In other words, if I have a poem to write, I need to write that poem—whether it will sell or not.

I need to create what wants to be created. I cannot plan a career to unfold in a sensible direction dictated by cash flow and marketing strategies. Those things are fine; but too much attention to them can stifle the child within, who gets scared and angered when continually put off. Children, as we all know, do not deal well with "Later. Not now."

Since my artist is a child, the natural child within, I must make some concessions to its sense of timing. *Some* concessions does not mean total irresponsibility. What it means is letting the artist have quality time, knowing that if I let it do what it wants to it will cooperate with me in doing what I need to do.

Sometimes I will write badly, draw badly, paint badly, perform badly. I have a right to do that to get to the other side. Creativity is its own reward.

As an artist, I must be very careful to surround myself with people who nurture my artist—not people who try to overly domesticate it for my own good. Certain friendships will kick off my artistic imagination and others will deaden it.

I may be a good cook, a rotten housekeeper, and a strong artist. I am messy, disorganized except as pertains to writing, a demon for creative detail, and not real interested in details like polished shoes and floors.

To a large degree my life is my art, and when it gets dull, so does my work. As an artist, I may poke into what other people think of as dead ends: a punk band that I mysteriously fall for, a piece of gospel music that hooks my inner ear, a piece of red silk I just like and add to a nice outfit, thereby "ruining it."

As an artist, I may frizz my hair or wear weird clothes. I may spend too much money on perfume in a pretty blue bottle even though the perfume stinks because the bottle lets me write about Paris in the thirties.

As an artist, I write whether I think it's any good or not. I shoot movies other people may hate. I sketch bad sketches to say, "I was in this room. I was happy. It was May and I was meeting somebody I wanted to meet."

As an artist, my self-respect comes from doing the work. One performance at a time, one gig at a time, one painting at a time. Two and a half years to make one 90-minute piece of film. Five drafts of one play. Two years working on a musical. Throughout it all, daily, I show up at the morning pages and I write about my ugly curtains, my rotten haircut, my delight in the way the light hit the trees on the morning run.

As an artist, I do not need to be rich but I do need to be richly supported. I cannot allow my emotional and intellectual life to stagnate or the work will show it. My life will show it. My temperament will show it. If I don't create, I get crabby.

As an artist, I can literally die from boredom. I kill myself when I fail to nurture my artist child because I am acting like somebody else's idea of an adult. The more I nurture my artist child, the more adult I am able to appear. Spoiling my artist means it will let me type a business letter. Ignoring my artist means a grinding depression.

There is a connection between self-nurturing and self-respect. If I allow myself to be bullied and cowed by other people's urges for me to be more normal or more nice, I sell myself out. They may like me better, feel more comfortable with my more conventional appearance or behavior, but I will hate myself. Hating myself, I may lash out at myself and others.

If I sabotage my artist, I can well expect an eating binge, a sex binge, a temper binge. Check the relationship between these behaviors for yourself. When we are not creating, artists are not always very normal or very nice—to ourselves or to others.

Creativity is oxygen for our souls. Cutting off our creativity makes us savage. We react like we are being choked. There is a real rage that surfaces when we are interfered with on a level that involves picking lint off of us and fixing us up. When well-meaning parents and friends push marriage or nine-to-five or anything on us that doesn't evolve in a way that allows for our art to continue, we will react as if we are fighting for our lives—we are.

To be an artist is to recognize the particular. To appreciate the peculiar. To allow a sense of play in your relationship to accepted standards. To ask the question "Why?" To be an artist is to risk admitting that much of what is money, property, and prestige strikes you as just a little silly.

To be an artist is to acknowledge the astonishing. It is to allow the wrong piece in a room if we like it. It is to hang on to a weird coat that makes us happy. It is to not keep trying to be something that we aren't.

If you are happier writing than not writing, painting than not painting, singing than not singing, acting than not

The job of the artist is always to deepen the mystery.

FRANCIS BACON

The function of the creative artist consists of making laws, not in following laws already made.

FERRUCCIO BUSONI

What moves men of genius, or rather what inspires their work, is not new ideas, but their obsession with the idea that what has already been said is still not enough.

EUGÈNE DELACROIX

acting, directing than not directing, for God's sake (and I mean that literally) let yourself do it.

To kill your dreams because they are irresponsible is to be irresponsible to yourself. Credibility lies with you and God—not with a vote of your friends and acquaintances.

The creator made us creative. Our creativity is our gift *from* God. Our use of it is our gift *to* God. Accepting this bargain is the beginning of true self-acceptance.

Success

Creativity is a spiritual practice. It is not something that can be perfected, finished, and set aside. It is my experience that we reach plateaus of creative attainment only to have a certain restlessness set in. Yes, we are successful. Yes, we have made it, but . . .

In other words, just when we get there, *there* disappears. Dissatisfied with our accomplishments, however lofty, we are once again confronted with our creative self and its hungers. The questions we have just laid to rest now rear their heads again: what are we going to do . . . *now?*

This unfinished quality, this restless appetite for further exploration, tests us. We are asked to expand in order that we not contract. Evading this commitment—an evasion that tempts us all—leads straight to stagnation, discontent, spiritual discomfort. "Can't I rest?" we wonder. In a word, the answer is no.

As artists, we are spiritual sharks. The ruthless truth is that if we don't keep moving, we sink to the bottom and die. The choice is very simple: we can insist on resting on our laurels, or we can begin anew. The stringent requirement of a sustained creative life is the humility to start again, to begin anew.

It is this willingness to once more be a beginner that distinguishes a creative career.

> *No amount of skillful invention can replace the essential element of imagination.*
>
> EDWARD HOPPER

A friend of mine, a master in his field, finds himself uncomfortably committed years in advance of his availability. He is in an enviable position on a business level, but he finds it increasingly perilous to his artistic health. When the wheel turns and the project committed to three years ago must be executed, can he do it with imagination and his initial enthusiasm? The honest answer is often an uncomfortable *no*. And so, at great financial cost, he has begun cutting back his future commitments, investing in the riskier but more rewarding gain of artistic integrity.

Not all of us, always, can muster such creative courage in the face of fiscal temptation, but we can try. We can at least be willing. As artists, we are travelers. Too heavily encumbered by our worldly dignity, too invested in our stations and positions, we are unable to yield to our spiritual leadings. We insist on a straight and narrow when the Artist's Way is a spiral path. Invested in the outer trappings of a career, we can place that investment above our inner guidance. Deciding to play by the numbers, we lose our commitment to counting ourselves and our own goals worthy.

Creativity is not a business, although it may generate much business. An artist cannot replicate a prior success indefinitely. Those who attempt to work too long with formula, even their own formula, eventually leach themselves of their creative truths. Embedded as we often are in the business milieu of our art, it is tempting to guarantee what we cannot deliver: good work that duplicates the good work that has gone before.

Successful movies generate a business demand for sequels. Successful books generate a demand for further, similar books. Painters pass through popular periods in their work and may be urged to linger there. For potters, composers, choreographers, the problem is the same. As artists, we are asked to repeat ourselves and expand on the market we have built. Sometimes this is possible for us. Other times it's not.

As a successful artist, the trick is to not mortgage the future too heavily. If the house in the Hamptons costs two years of creative misery cranking out a promised project just for cash, that house is an expensive luxury.

This is not to say that editors should stop planning seasons or that studios should scuttle their business bottom line. It *is* to say that the many creatives laboring in fiscal settings should remember to commit themselves not only to projects that smack of the sure thing but also to those riskier projects that call to their creative souls. You don't

> *You are lost the instant you know what the result will be.*
>
> JUAN GRIS

need to overturn a successful career in order to find creative fulfillment. It *is* necessary to overturn each day's schedule slightly to allow for those small adjustments in daily trajectory that, over the long haul, alter the course and the satisfactions of our careers.

This means writing your morning pages. Taking your artist date. "But I run a studio," you say—or whatever other thing it is you must do. "People depend on me." I say, all the more reason to depend on yourself and protect your own creativity.

If we ignore our inner commitment, the cost rapidly becomes apparent in the outer world. A certain lackluster tone, a rote inevitability, evicts creative excitement from our lives and, eventually, our finances. Attempting to insure our finances by playing it safe, we lose our cutting edge. As the promised projects diverge further and further from our inner leanings, a certain deep artistic weariness sets in. We must summon our enthusiasm at gunpoint instead of reveling in each day's creative task.

Artists can and do responsibly meet the demands of their business partnerships. What is more difficult and more critical is for us as artists to continue to meet the inner demand of our own artistic growth. In short, as success comes to us, we must be vigilant. Any success postulated on a permanent artistic plateau dooms us, and it, to failure.

The Zen of Sports

Most blocked creatives are cerebral beings. We think of all the things we want to do but can't. Early in recovery, we next think of all the things we want to do but don't. In order to effect a real recovery, one that lasts, we need to move out of the head and into a body of work. To do this, we must first of all move *into the body.*

No longer conscious of my movement, I discovered a new unity with nature. I had found a new source of power and beauty, a source I never dreamt existed.

ROGER BANNISTER
ON BREAKING THE
FOUR-MINUTE MILE

Again, this is a matter that requires acceptance. Creativity requires action, and part of that action must be physical. It is one of the pitfalls of Westerners adopting Eastern meditation techniques to bliss out and render ourselves high but dysfunctional. We lose our grounding and, with it, our capacity to act in the world. In the pursuit of higher consciousness, we render ourselves unconscious in a new way. Exercise combats this spiritually induced dysfunction.

Returning to the notion of ourselves as spiritual radio sets, we need enough energy to raise a strong signal. This is where walking comes in. What we are after here is a *moving* meditation. This means one where the act of motion puts us into the now and helps us to stop spinning. Twenty minutes a day is sufficient. The object is to stretch your mind more than your body, so there doesn't need to be an emphasis on fitness, although eventual fitness is a likely result.

The goal is to connect to a world outside of us, to lose the obsessive self-focus of self-exploration and, simply, explore. One quickly notes that when the mind is focused on *other*, the self often comes into a far more accurate focus.

It is 6:30 A.M. when the great blue heron stirs from its resting place in the short grasses and rises above the river on huge rhythmic wings. The bird sees Jenny down below. Jenny, down below, sees the bird. The pumping of her legs carries her in an effortless floating stride. Her spirit soars up to the heron and chirps. "Hello, good morning, lovely, isn't it?" At this time, in this place, they are kindred spirits. Both are wild and free and happy in their motion, in the movement of the winds, the clouds, the trees.

It is 4:30 P.M. when Jenny's boss looms in the doorway to her office. The new account is being picky and wants still more changes in her copy. Can she handle that? "Yes," Jenny says. She can because she is still soaring on the glad energy of her morning's run. That heron; the steely blue of it flashing silver as it made that great banking turn . . .

Jenny would not call herself an athlete. She does not run in marathons. She does not run in cheery singles groups. Although her distances have gradually increased and her thighs have gradually decreased, she does not run for fitness. Jenny runs for her soul, not her body. It is the fitness of her spirit that sets the tone of her days, changes their timbre from strained to effortless.

"I run for perspective," says Jenny. When the client picks at her copy, Jenny detaches and soars above her frustration like the great blue heron. It is not that she doesn't care. It is that she has a new perspective—a bird's eye view—on the place of her tribulations in the universe.

> To keep the body in good health is a duty. . . . Otherwise we shall not be able to keep our mind strong and clear.
>
> BUDDHA

Eve Babitz is a novelist—and a swimmer. Tall, blond, and as generously curved as the freeway cloverleaf of her native Los Angeles, Babitz swims in order to direct the traffic flow of her own overcrowded mind. "Swimming," she says, "is a wonderful sport for a writer." Every day, as she swims the aquamarine oblong of her neighborhood pool, her mind dives deep into itself, past the weeds and clutter of its everyday concerns—what editor is late with a check, why the typist persists in making so many errors—and down to a quiet green pool of inspiration. That rhythmic, repetitive action transfers the locus of the brain's energies from the logic to the artist hemisphere. It is there that inspiration bubbles up untrammeled by the constraints of logic.

Martha is a carpenter and a long-distance bicylist. Carpentry challenges her daily to find innovative solutions to construction problems, to untangle the intricacies of a complicated design situation requiring a simple answer to a complicated question. "How can I build in work space without using floor space when I'm done working?" or "Is there some kind of cabinet that could fit in this corner and around on this wall without seeming too modern for my furniture?" Pedaling from her home in the suburbs to her job in the city, Martha encounters her answers to these questions. In much the same way that a red-winged blackbird will suddenly take flight and cross her line of vision, Martha will be pedaling when "louvered doors" will flash as a design solution. Pumping her bicycle rhythmically and repetitively, Martha also pumps the well of her creativity. "It is my time to let my imagination roam and work out problems," Martha says. "Solutions just come. Somehow I am freed to free-associate, and things begin to fall into place."

Here in this body are the sacred rivers: here are the sun and moon as well as all the pilgrimage places . . . I have not encountered another temple as blissful as my own body.

SARAHA

The things that begin to fall into place are not merely work associated. When she bicycles, Martha has a sense not only of her own motion but also of the motion of God through the universe. She remembers riding alone on Route 22 in upstate New York. The sky was an azure bowl. The cornfields were green and gold. The ribbon of black asphalt that Martha rode seemed to her to head straight into the heart of God. "Silence, a blue sky, a black ribbon of highway, God, and the wind. When I ride, especially at dusk and at early morning, I feel God. I am able to meditate more in motion than sitting still. Being alone, having the freedom to go wherever I want, having the wind blow, riding alone in that wind, allows me to center myself I feel God so closely that my spirit sings."

Exercise teaches the rewards of process. It teaches the sense of satisfaction over small tasks well done. Jenny, running, extends herself and learns to tap into an unexpected inner resource. Martha would call that power *God*, but whatever it answers to, exercise seems to call it forth in other circumstances when we mistrust our personal strength. Rather than scotch a creative project when it frustrates us, we learn to move through the difficulty.

"Life *is* a series of hurdles," says Libby, a painter whose sport is horseback riding. "I used to see it as a series of obstacles or roadblocks. Now they are hurdles and challenges. How well am I taking them?" In the daily schooling of her horse, "teaching her to think before she jumps, to pace herself properly," Libby has learned the same skills for her own life.

Part of this learned creative patience has to do with connecting to a sense of universal creativity. "Riding, my rational mind switches off," she says. "I am reduced to feeling, to being a participant. When you ride through a field of grass and little flecks of fluff from the wheat ears float around you, the feeling makes your heart sing. When a rooster tail of snow sparkles in the sun in your wake, that makes your heart sing. These moments of intense feeling have taught me to be aware of other moments in my life as they occur. When I feel that singing feeling with a man and know that I have also felt it in a field of grass and a field of snow, then I know that is really my own capacity to feel that I am celebrating."

It is not only the sense of a communion with nature that creates a singing in the heart. An endorphin-induced natural high is one of the by-products of exercise itself. A runner may feel the same celebratory sense of well-being pounding a dirty city street that Libby finds as she posts rhythmically along a country trail.

"God is in his heaven; all's right with the world" is how Robert Browning characterized this feeling in his long narrative poem *Pippa Passes*. It is no coincidence that Pippa experienced this feeling as she was walking. Not everyone can afford to ride a horse or even a ten-speed bicycle. Many of us must rely on our feet for transportation and for recreation. Like Jenny, we can take up running. Or we might make walking our sport. As an artist, walking offers the added benefit of sensory saturation. Things do not whiz by. We really see them. In a sense, insight follows from sight. We fill the well and later tap it more easily.

Gerry is a confirmed city dweller. His country walks are limited to persuing window boxes and pocket gardens. Gerry has learned that "in cities, people are the scenery." He has also learned to look up, not down, and to admire the frippery and friezes that often grace buildings that look quite, well, pedestrain at street level. As he roves the city canyons, Gerry has found a whole panoply of scenic attractions. There is the orange-marmalade cat that sits in the window above the window box with both pink and red geraniums. There is the copper church roof gone murky green that glistens silver in rainstorms. An ornately inlaid marble foyer can be glimpsed through the doors of one mid-town office building. On another block, someone has sunk a lucky horsehoe in civic concrete. A miniature Statue of

Liberty soars unexpectedly atop a dignified brick facade. Gerry feels at liberty himself, roaming the city streets on tireless feet. This courtyard, that cobbled walkway—Gerry gathers urban visual delights the same way his primordial ancestors gathered this nut, that berry. They gathered food. He gathers food for thought. Exercise, much maligned as mindless activity among certain intellectuals, turns out to be thought-provoking instead.

God bless the roots! Body and soul are one.

THEODORE ROETHKE

As we said before, we learn by going where we have to go. Exercise is often the going that moves us from stagnation to inspiration, from problem to solution, from self-pity to self-respect. We *do* learn by going. We learn we are stronger than we thought. We learn to look at things with a new perspective. We learn to solve our problems by tapping our own inner resources and listening for inspiration, not only from others but from ourselves. Seemingly without effort, our answers come while we swim or stride or ride or run. By definition, this is one of the fruits of exercise: "*exercise:* the act of bringing into play or realizing in action" (*Webster's Ninth*).

Building Your Artist's Altar

Morning pages are meditation, a practice that bring you to your creativity and your creator God. In order to stay easily and happily creative, we need to stay spiritually centered. This is easier to do if we allow ourselves centering rituals. It is important that we devise these ourselves from the elements that feel holy and happy to us.

Many blocked creatives grew up in punitively religious homes. For us to stay happily and easily creative, we need to heal from this, becoming spiritually centered through creative rituals of our own. A spiritual room or even a spiritual corner is an excellent way to do this.

This haven can be a corner of a room, a nook under the stairs, even a window ledge. It is a reminder and an acknowledgment of the fact that our creator unfolds our creativity. Fill it with things that make you happy. Remember that your artist is fed by images. We need to unlearn our old notion that spirituality and sensuality don't mix. An artist's altar should be a sensory experience.

We are meant to celebrate the good things of this earth. Pretty leaves, rocks, candles, sea treasures—all these remind us of our creator.

Small rituals, self-devised, are good for the soul. Burning incense while reading affirmations or writing them, lighting a candle, dancing to drum music, holding a smooth rock and listening to Gregorian chant—all of these tactile, physical techniques reinforce spiritual growth.

Remember, the artist child speaks the language of the soul: music, dance, scent, shells . . . Your artist's altar to the creator should be fun to look at, even silly. Remember how much little kids like gaudy stuff. Your artist is a little kid, so . . .

> *Art does not reproduce the visible; rather, it makes it visible. The moon develops creativity as chemicals develop photographic images.*
>
> NORMA JEAN HARRIS

TASKS

1. Tape your own voice reading the Basic Principles. (See page 17). Choose a favorite essay from this book and tape that as well. Use this tape for meditation.

2. Write out, in longhand, your Artist's Prayer from Week Four. Place it in your wallet.

3. Buy yourself a special creativity notebook. Number pages one through seven. Give one page each to the following categories: health, possessions, leisure, relationships, creativity, career, and spirituality. With no thought as to practicality, list ten wishes in each area. All right, it's a lot. Let yourself dream a little here.

4. Working with the Honest Changes section in Week Four, inventory for yourself the ways you have changed since beginning your recovery.

5. List five ways you will change as you continue.

6. List five ways you plan to nurture yourself in the next six months: courses you will take, supplies you will allow yourself, artist's dates, and vacations just for you.

7. Take out a piece of paper and plan one week's nurturing for yourself. This means one concrete, loving action every single day for one week: please binge!

8. Write and mail an encouraging letter to your inner artist. This sounds silly and feels very, very good to receive. Remember that your artist is a child and loves praise and encouragement and festive plans.

9. Once more, reexamine your God concept. Does your belief system limit or support your creative expansion? Are you open minded about altering your concept of God?

10. List ten examples of personal synchronicity that support the possibility of a nurturing creative force.

CHECK-IN

1. **How many days this week did you do your morning pages?** How was the experience for you? Have you recommended morning pages to anyone else? Why?
2. **Did you do your artist date this week?** (Have you considered scheduling an entire artist's day? Whew!) What did you do? How did it feel?
3. **Did you experience any synchronicity this week?** What was it?
4. **Were there any other issues this week that you consider significant for your recovery?** Describe them.

Recovering a Sense of Faith

In this final week, we acknowledge the inherently mysterious spiritual heart of creativity. We address the fact that creativity requires receptivity and profound trust—capacities we have developed through our work in this course. We set our creative aims and take a special look at last-minute sabotage. We renew our commitment to the use of the tools.

Trusting

CREATIVITY REQUIRES FAITH. FAITH requires that we relinquish control. This is frightening, and we resist it. Our resistance to our creativity is a form of self-destruction. We throw up road-blocks on our own path. Why do we do this? In order to maintain an illusion of control. Depression, like anger and anxiety, is resistance, and it creates dis-ease. This manifests itself as sluggishness, confusion, "I don't know . . ."

The truth is, we do know and we *know* that we know.

Each of us has an inner dream that we can unfold if we will just have the courage to admit what it is. And the faith to trust our own admission. The admitting is often very difficult. A clearing affirmation can often open the channel. One excellent one is "I know the things I know." Another is "I trust my own inner guide." Either of these will eventually yield us a sense of our own direction—which we will often then promptly resist!

This resistance is really very understandable. We are not accustomed to thinking that God's will for us and our

> *Adventures don't begin until you get into the forest. That first step in an act of faith.*
>
> MICKEY HART
> GRATEFUL DEAD DRUMMER

Do not fear mistakes—there are none.

MILES DAVIS

own inner dreams can coincide. Instead, we have bought the message of our culture: this world is a vale of tears and we are meant to be dutiful and then die. The truth is that we are meant to be bountiful and *live*. The universe will always support affirmative action. Our truest dream for ourselves is always God's will for us.

Mickey Hart's hero and mentor, the late, great mythologist Joseph Campbell, wrote, "Follow your bliss and doors will open where there were no doors before." It is the inner commitment to be true to ourselves and follow our dreams that triggers the support of the universe. While we are ambivalent, the universe will seem to us also to be ambivalent and erratic. The flow through our lives will be characterized by spurts of abundance and long spells of drought, when our supply dwindles to a mere trickle.

If we look back at the times when the world seemed to be a capricious and untrustworthy place, we see that we were ourselves ambivalent and conflicted in our goals and behaviors. Once we trigger an internal yes by affirming our truest goals and desires, the universe mirrors that yes and expands it.

There is a path for each of us. When we are on our right path, we have a sure-footedness. We know the next right action—although not necessarily what is just around the bend. By trusting, we *learn* to trust.

Mystery

Creativity—like human life itself—begins in darkness. We need to acknowledge this. All too often, we think only in terms of light: "And then the lightbulb went on and I got it!" It is true that insights may come to us as flashes. It is true that some of these flashes may be blinding. It is, however, also true that such bright ideas are preceded by a gestation period that is interior, murky, and completely necessary.

We speak often about ideas as brainchildren. What we do not realize is that brainchildren, like all babies, should not be dragged from the creative womb prematurely. Ideas, like stalactites and stalagmites, form in the dark inner cave of consciousness. They form in drips and drops, not by squared-off building blocks. We must learn to wait for an idea to hatch. Or, to use a gardening image, we must learn to not pull our ideas up by the roots to see if they are growing.

Mulling on the page is an artless art form. It is fooling around. It is doodling. It is the way that ideas slowly take shape and form until they are ready to help us see the light. All too often, we try to push, pull, outline, and control our ideas instead of letting them grow organically. The creative process is a process of surrender, not control.

Mystery is at the heart of creativity. That, and surprise. All too often, when we say we want to be creative, we mean that we want to be able to be productive. Now, to be creative *is* to be productive—but by cooperating with the creative process, not forcing it.

As creative channels, we need to trust the darkness. We need to learn to gently mull instead of churning away like a little engine on a straight-ahead path. This mulling on the page can be very threatening. "I'll never get any *real* ideas this way!" we fret.

> *The most beautiful thing we can experience is the mysterious.*
>
> ALBERT EINSTEIN
>
> *What shakes the eye but the invisible?*
>
> THEODORE ROETHKE

Hatching an idea is a lot like baking bread. An idea needs to rise. If you poke at it too much at the beginning, if you keep checking on it, it will never rise. A loaf of bread or a cake, baking, must stay for a good long time in the darkness and safety of the oven. Open that oven too soon and the bread collapses—or the cake gets a hole in its middle because all the steam has rushed out of it. Creativity requires a respectful reticence.

The truth is that this is how to raise the best ideas. Let them grow in dark and mystery. Let them form on the roof of our consciousness. Let them hit the page in droplets. Trusting this slow and seemingly random drip, we will be startled one day by the flash of "Oh! That's *it!*"

The Imagination at Play

When we think about creativity, it is all too easy to think *art* with a capital *A*. For our purposes, capital-*A* art is a scarlet letter, branding us as doomed. In order to nurture our creativity, we require a sense of festivity, even humor: "Art. That's somebody my sister used to date."

We are an ambitious society, and it is often difficult for us to cultivate forms of creativity that do not directly serve us and our career goals. Recovery urges our reexamining definitions of creativity and expanding them to include what in the past we called hobbies. The experience of creative living argues that hobbies are in fact essential to the joyful life.

Then, too, there is the hidden benefit that they are also creatively useful. Many hobbies involve a form of artist-brain mulling that leads to enormous creative breakthroughs. When I have screenwriting students stuck at the midpoint of act two, I ask them to please go do their household mending. They usually balk, offended by such a mundane task, but sewing has a nice way of mending up plots. Gardening is another hobby I often assign to creativity students. When someone is panicked halfway across the bridge into a new life, repotting plants into larger and better containers quite literally grounds that person and gives him or her a sense of expansion.

Spiritual benefits accompany the practice of a hobby. There is a release into humility that comes from doing something by rote. As we serve our hobby, we are freed from our ego's demands and allowed the experience of merging with a greater source. This conscious contact frequently affords us the perspectives needed to solve vexing personal or creative conundrums.

It is a paradox of creative recovery that we must get serious about taking ourselves lightly. We must work at learning to play. Creativity must be freed from the narrow parameters of capital *A* art and recognized as having much broader play (that word again).

As we work with our morning pages and artist dates, many forgotten samplings of our own creativity may come to mind.

> *For me a painting is like a story which stimulates the imagination and draws the mind into a place filled with expectation, excitement, wonder and pleasure.*
>
> J. P. HUGHSTON
> PAINTER

- I had forgotten all about those paintings I did in high school. I loved painting those flats in drama tech!
- I suddenly remembered I played Antigone—who could forget her? I don't know if I was any good, but I remember I loved it.
- I'd forgotten all about the skits I wrote when I was ten. I set them all to Ravel's *Bolero* no matter what they were about. I made my brothers and sisters swoon about the living room.
- I used to tap-dance. I know you can't believe it now, but I was something!

As we write, digging ourselves out of denial, our memories, dreams, and creative plans all move to the surface. We discover anew that we are creative beings. The impulse cooks in us all, simmering along all the time—without our knowledge, without our encouragement, even without our approval. It moves beneath the surface of our lives, showing in bright flashes, like a penny, in our stream of thought—like new grass under snow.

We are intended to create. We refurbish a dowdy kitchen, tie bows on a holiday cat, experiment with a better soup. The same child who brewed perfume from a dab of this and a dash of that, half dish soap and part cinnamon, grows up to buy potpourri and to boil a spice pot that says, "Christmas."

As gray, as controlled, as dreamless as we may strive to be, the fire of our dreams will not stay buried. The embers are always there, stirring in our frozen souls like winter leaves. They won't go away. They are sneaky. We make a crazy doodle in a boring meeting. We post a silly card on our office board. We nickname the boss something wicked. Plant twice as many flowers as we need.

Restive in our lives, we yearn for more, we wish, we chafe. We sing in the car, slam down the phone, make lists, clear closets, sort through shelves. We want to do something but we think it needs to be the *right something*, by which we mean *something important*.

We are what's important, and the something that we do can be something festive but small: dead plants go; mismatched socks bite the dust. We are stung by loss, bitten by hope. Working with our morning pages, a new—and gaudy?—life takes form. Who bought that azalea? Why the sudden taste for pink? Is this picture you've tacked up a *you* you're going toward?

Your shoes feel worn. You throw them out. There's a garage sale coming and you are playing host. You buy a first edition, splurge on new sheets. A friend worries once too often about what's come over you and you take your first vacation in years.

> *Play is the exultation of the possible.*
>
> MARTIN BUBER

The clock is ticking and you're hearing the beat. You stop by a museum shop, sign your name on a scuba-diving sheet, and commit yourself to Saturday mornings in the deep end.

You're either losing your mind—or gaining your soul. Life is meant to be an artist date. That's why we were created.

Escape Velocity

My friend Michele has a theory, a theory born of long and entangled romantic experience. In a nutshell, it goes: "When you're going to leave them, *they know*."

This same theory applies to creative recovery. It occurs when you reach what Michele calls *escape velocity*. As she puts it, "There's this time for blast-off, like a NASA space launch, and you're heading for it when *wham*, you draw to you the Test."

"The Test?"

"Yeah. The Test. It's like when you're all set to marry the nice guy, the one who treats you right, and Mr. Poison gets wind of it and phones you up."

"Ah."

"The whole trick is to evade the Test. We all draw to us the one test that's our total nemesis."

A lawyer by trade and a writer by avocation and temperament, Michele is fond of conspiracy theories, which she lays out in sinister detail.

"Think of it. You're all set to go to the Coast on an important business trip, and your husband suddenly needs you, capital *N*, for no real reason. . . . You're all set to leave the bad job, and the boss from hell suddenly gives you your first raise in five years. . . . Don't be fooled. Don't be fooled."

> *One does not discover new lands without consenting to lose sight of the shore for a very long time.*
>
> ANDRÉ GIDE

Listening to Michele talk, it was clear that her years as a trial attorney stood her in good stead as a creative person. She, at least, was no longer fooled. But is it really so sinister as she implied? Do we really draw to us a Test? I thought about everything Michele had told me and I concluded that the answer was yes.

I thought of all the times I'd been fooled. There was the agent who managed to undo done deals but apologized so prettily. . . . There was the editor who asked for rewrite upon rewrite until gruel was all that remained, but who always said I wrote brilliantly and was her brightest star.

A little flattery can go a long way toward deterring our escape velocity. So can a little cash. More sinister than either is the impact a well-placed doubt can have, particularly a "for your own good, just wanting to make sure you've thought about this" doubt—voiced by one of our nearest and dearest.

As recovering creatives, many of us find that every time our career heats up we reach for our nearest Wet Blanket. We blurt out our enthusiasm to our most skeptical friend—in fact, we call him up. If we don't, he calls us. This is the Test.

Our artist is a child, an inner youngster, and when he/she is scared, Mommy is what's called for. Unfortunately, many of us have Wet Blanket mommies and a whole army of Wet Blanket surrogate mommies—those friends who have our second, third, and fourth thoughts for us. The trick is not to let them be that way. How? *Zip the lip. Button up. Keep a lid on it. Don't give away the gold.* Always remember: the first rule of magic is self-containment. You must hold your intention within yourself, stoking it with power. Only then will you be able to manifest what you desire.

In order to achieve escape velocity, we must learn to keep our own counsel, to move silently among doubters, to voice our plans only among our allies, and to name our allies accurately.

Make a list: those friends who will support me. Make another list: those friends who won't. Name your W.B.'s for what they are—Wet Blankets. Wrap yourself in something else—dry ones. Fluffy heated towels. Do not indulge or tolerate *anyone* who throws cold water in your direction. Forget good intentions. Forget they didn't mean it. Remember to count your blessings and your toes. Escape velocity requires the sword of steely intention and the shield of self-determination.

"They will try to get you. Don't forget that," warns Michele. "Set your goals and set your boundaries."

I would add, set your sights and don't let the ogre that looms on the horizon deflect your flight.

TASKS

1. Write down any resistance, angers, and fears you have about going on from here. We all have them.
2. Take a look at your current areas of procrastination. What are the payoffs in your waiting? Locate the hidden fears. Do a list on paper.
3. Sneak a peek at Week One, Core Negative Beliefs (see page 45). Laugh. Yes, the nasty critters are still there. Note your progress. Read yourself the affirmations on page 51. Write some affirmations about your continued creativity as you end the course.
4. Mend any mending.
5. Repot any pinched and languishing plants.
6. Select a God jar. A what? A jar, a box, a vase, a container. Something to put your fears, your resentments, your hopes, your dreams, your worries into.

7. Use your God jar. Start with your fear list from Task I above. When worried, remind yourself it's in the jar—"God's got it." Then take the next action.

8. *Now,* check *how:* Honestly, what would you most like to create? Open-minded, what oddball paths would you dare to try? *Willing,* what appearances are you willing to shed to pursue your dream?

9. List five people you can talk to about your dreams and with whom you feel supported to dream and then plan.

10. Reread this book. Share it with a friend. Remember that the miracle is one artist sharing with another. Trust God. Trust yourself.

Good luck and God bless you!

CHECK-IN

1. **How many days this week did you do your morning pages?** Have you accepted them yet as a permanent spiritual practice? How was the experience for you?

2. **Did you do your artist date this week?** Will you allow yourself these on a permanent basis as well? What did you do? How did it feel?

3. **Did you experience any synchronicity this week?** What was it?

4. **Were there any other issues this week that you consider significant for your recovery?** Describe them.

As a recovering creative, you now have put many hours into your recovery over these three months, changing rapidly as you grew. For your recovery to continue, you require a commitment to further creative plans. The contract on the following page will help you accomplish them.

Creativity Contract

My name is _____. I am a recovering creative person. To further my growth and my joy, I now commit myself to the following self-nurturing plans:

Morning pages have been an important part of my self-nurturing and self-discovery. I, _____, hereby commit myself to continuing to work with them for the next ninety days.

Artist's dates have been integral to my growth in self-love and my deepening joy in living. I, _____, am willing to commit to another ninety days of weekly artist's dates for self-care.

In the course of following the Artist's Way and healing my artist within, I have discovered that I have a number of creative interests. While I hope to develop many of them, my specific commitment for the next ninety days is to allow myself to more fully explore _____.

My concrete commitment to a plan of action is a critical part of nurturing my artist. For the next ninety days, my planned, self-nurturing creative action plan is _____.

I have chosen _____ as my creative colleague and _____ as my creative back-up. I am committed to a weekly phone check-in.

I have made the above commitments and will begin my new commitment on _____.

_____ (signature)

_____ (date)

EPILOGUE

The Artist's Way

IN ENDING THIS BOOK, I yearned for a final flourish, some last fillip of the imagination that would sign the book. This was a small and harmless conceit, I felt—until I remembered the number of times I have enjoyed a painting and been distracted by the outsized artistic signature of its maker. So, no final flourishes here.

The truth is that this book should probably end with an image from another book. As I recall it, and this may be my imagination and not my memory at work, an early edition of Thomas Merton's *Seven Story Mountain* featured a mountain on its book jacket—the seven-story mountain, no doubt.

Maybe it did and maybe it didn't. I read the book many years ago, a precocious twelve-year-old. What I conjure now is a mountain of Himalayan proportions with a path winding upward to its height. That path, a spiral path, is how I think of the Artist's Way. As we pursue climbing it, we circle back on the same views, over and over, at slightly different altitudes. "I've been here before," we think, hitting a spell of drought. And, in a sense, we have been. The road is never straight. Growth is a spiral process, doubling back on itself, reassessing and regrouping. As artists, our progress is often dogged by rough terrain or storms. A fog may obscure the distance we have covered or the progress we have made toward our goal. While the occasional dazzling vista may grace us, it is really best to proceed a step at a time, focusing on the path beneath our feet as much as the heights still before us.

The Artist's Way is a spiritual journey, a pilgrimage home to the self. Like all great journeys it entails dangers of the trail, some of which I have tried to enumerate in this book. Like all pilgrims, those of us on the Artist's Way will often

> *I finally discovered the source of all movement, the unity from which all diversities of movement are born.*
>
> ISADORA DUNCAN

> *Creation is only the projection into form of that which already exists.*
>
> SHRIMAD BHAGAVATAM

> *A painting is never finished—it simply stops in interesting places.*
>
> PAUL GARDNER

be graced by fellow travelers and invisible companions. What I call my marching orders others may sense in themselves as a still, small voice or, even more simply, a hunch. The point is that you will hear something if you listen for it. Keep your soul cocked for guidance.

When Mark Bryan began cornering me into writing this book, he had just seen a Chinese film about Tibet called *The Horse Thief*. It was an indelible film for him, a classic of the Beijing school, a film we have since searched for in Chinese video stores and film archives, to no avail. Mark told me about the film's central image: another mountain, a prayerful journey up that mountain, on bended knee: step, lie prostrate, stand and straighten, another step, lie prostrate . . .

In the film, this journey was the reparation that a thief and his wife had to make for damaging their society by dishonoring themselves through thievery. I have wondered, since then, if the mountain that I see when thinking of the Artist's Way isn't another mountain best climbed in the spirit of reparation—not to others, but to ourselves.

Words for It

I wish I could take language
And fold it like cool, moist rags.
I would lay words on your forehead.
I would wrap words on your wrists.
"There, there," my words would say—
Or something better.
I would ask them to murmur,
"Hush" and "Shh, shhh, it's all right."
I would ask them to hold you all night.
I wish I could take language
And daub and soothe and cool
Where fever blisters and burns,
Where fever turns yourself against you.
I wish I could take language
And heal the words that were the wounds
You have no names for.
J.C.

THE ARTIST'S WAY
QUESTIONS AND ANSWERS

Introduction

ALTHOUGH CREATIVE RECOVERY IS a highly individual process, there are certain recurrent themes and questions that we have encountered over and over in our teaching. In the hopes of answering at least some of your questions directly, we include the most commonly asked questions and answers here.

Questions and Answers

Q: *Is true creativity the possession of a relatively small percentage of the population?*
A: No, absolutely not. We are all creative. Creativity is a natural life force that all can experience in one form or another. Just as blood is part of our physical body and is nothing we must invent, creativity is part of us and we each can tap into the greater creative energies of the universe and pull from that vast, powerful spiritual wellspring to amplify our own individual creativity.

As a culture, we tend to define creativity too narrowly and to think of it in elitist terms, as something belonging to a small chosen tribe of "real artists." But in reality, everything we do requires making creative choices, although we seldom recognize that fact. The ways in which we dress, set up our homes, do our jobs, the movies we see, and even the people we involve ourselves with—these all are expressions of our creativity. It is our erroneous beliefs about creativity, our cultural mythology about artists ("All artists are broke, crazy, promiscuous, self-centered, single, or they have trust funds") that encourage us to leave our dreams unfulfilled. These myths most often involve matters of money, time, and other people's agendas for us. As we clear these blocks away, we can become more creative.

Q. *Can I expect dramatic results to begin occurring right away?*

A. The answer is both yes and no. While dramatic changes will occur within the twelve-week course, much more dramatic changes occur when Artist's Way tools become life tools. The shift over a two- to three-year period can feel like a downright miracle: blocked filmmakers who make one short film, then a second and then a feature; blocked writers who began with essays, reviews, and articles moving into whole books and plays. If the basic tools of morning pages and the artist date are kept carefully in place, you can expect to experience large life shifts.

Q: *What factors keep people from being creative?*

A: Conditioning. Family, friends, and educators may discourage us from pursuing an artist's career. There is the mythology that artists are somehow "different," and this mythology of difference inspires fear. If we have negative perceptions about what an artist is, we will feel less inclined to do the diligent work necessary to become one.

On a societal level, blocked creative energy manifests itself as self-destructive behavior. Many people who are engaged in self-defeating behaviors, such as addicts of alcohol, drugs, sex, or work, are really in the hands of this shadow side of the creative force. As we become more creative, these negative expressions of the creative force often abate.

Q: *How does this book free people to be more creative?*

A: The primary purpose—and effect—of *The Artist's Way* is to put people in touch with the power of their own internal creativity. The book frees people to be more creative in many different ways: First, it helps dismantle negative mythologies about artists. Second, it helps people discover their own creative force, access it, and express it more freely. Third, it provides people with an awareness about their self-destructive behaviors and allow them to see more clearly what the impediments on their individual path might be. Finally, the book helps people identify and celebrate their desires and dreams and make the plans to accomplish them. It teaches people how to support and nurture themselves as well as how to find others who will support them in fulfilling their dreams.

Q: *One of the central themes of* The Artist's Way *is the link between creativity and spirituality. How are they connected?*

A: Creativity is a spiritual force. The force that drives the green fuse through the flower, as Dylan Thomas defined his idea of the life force, is the same urge that drives us toward creation. There is a central will to create that is part of our human heritage and potential. Because creation is always an act of faith, and faith is a spiritual issue, so is creativity. As we strive for our highest selves, our spiritual selves, we cannot help but be more aware, more proactive, and more creative.

Q: *Tell me about the two central exercises in the book—the morning pages and the artist dates.*

A: The morning pages are three pages of stream-of-consciousness longhand morning writing. You should think of them not as "art" but as an active form of meditation for Westerners. In the morning pages we declare to the world—and ourselves—what we like, what we dislike, what we wish, what we hope, what we regret, and what we plan.

By contrast, the artist dates are times for receptivity, preplanned solitary hours of pleasurable activity aimed at nurturning the creative consciousness. Used together, these tools build, in effect, a radio set. The morning pages notify and clarify—they send signals into the verdant void; and the solitude of the artist dates allows for the answer to be received.

The morning pages and artist dates must be experienced in order to be explained, just as reading a book about jogging is not the same as putting on your Nikes and heading out to the running track. Map is not territory, and without reference points from within your own experience, you cannot extrapolate what the morning pages and artist dates can do for you.

Q: The Artist's Way *is a twelve-week program that requires daily commitments. How much time do I need to devote to it each day, and what can I accomplish in these twelve weeks?*

A: It's a daily commitment of a half hour to an hour. One of the most important things we learn during the twelve weeks is to give up our ideas of perfection and to see a new perspective, to change our focus from product to process.

Participants enter the program with certain unstated expectations and preconceived notions of what will happen and what they will get out of it. And often, just as in a great short story, they are profoundly surprised and thrilled to discover something entirely different. Therefore, to predict what someone will learn from this course would undermine the very principle on which it was built. It is experiential, and the results are something to be discovered, not explained.

Q: *What can I do to overcome my self-doubts about being a good artist?*

A: The point is not to *overcome* your self-doubts about being an artist. The point is to *move through* your self-doubts. Many of us believe that "real artists" do not experience self-doubt. In truth, artists are people who have learned to live with doubt and do the work anyway. The exercises in the book will help you dismantle the hypercritical inner Censor and perfectionist. You will learn that part of being fully creative means allowing for an "off" day. Because the Artist's Way focuses on process rather than product, you will learn to value your "mistakes" as part of your learning.

Q: *Why do artists procrastinate, and what is procrastination really about?*

A: Artists procrastinate out of fear, or because they try to wait for the "right mood" in order to work. *The Artist's Way* will teach you how to separate mood from productivity. It will also teach you to value a self-loving enthusiasm over mechanistic discipline.

Q: *How can I expand my ability to derive new ideas?*

A: Learn to miniaturize your critic, your Censor. While you may not fire your critic entirely, you can learn to work around the negative voice. When we use the morning pages and the artist dates—specifically designed to put us in touch with our nonlinear intuitive selves—we expand our ability to derive new ideas. As we lessen the static, the interference caused by old habits and blocks, and become clearer and more able to listen, we become more receptive to creativity and its sometimes subtle arrival in our consciousness.

Q: *What is the most common misconception about creativity?*

A: The most common misconception is that we would have to leave our current lives in order to pursue our dreams. It is easier for us to use our jobs, families, financial situations, time obligations, etc., as a way (or ways) to keep us "safe" from the anxiety caused by stepping out of our comfort zones into the creative process. When we allow ourselves to be thus thwarted, we deny ourselves tremendous joy. The most effective way to center confront blocks is to form creative cluster groups in the lives we're already leading.

Forming a Sacred Circle

When I was a little kid, one of my favorite heroes was Johnny Appleseed. I loved the idea of a vagrant wanderer traveling America, apple blossoms in his wake. It is my hope that this book will also create blossoming, that artists and circles of artists will spring into being. Trusting this to be the case, the following essay is intended for use in establishing your own artists' circle. It is my experience as a teacher that an atmosphere of safety and trust is critical to creative growth. I have found these guidelines to be helpful in establishing that atmosphere.

The Sacred Circle

Art is an act of the soul, not the intellect. When we are dealing with people's dreams—their visions, really—we are in the realm of the sacred. We are involved with forces and energies larger than our own. We are engaged in a sacred transaction of which we know only a little: the shadow, not the shape.

For these reasons, it is mandatory that any gathering of artists be in the spirit of a sacred trust. We invoke the Great Creator when we invoke our own creativity, and that creative force has the power to alter lives, fulfill destinies, answer our dreams.

In our human lives, we are often impatient, ill-tempered, inappropriate. We find it difficult to treat our intimates with the love we really hold for them. Despite this, they bear with us because of the larger, higher level of family that they honor even in our outbursts. This is their commitment.

As artists, we belong to an ancient and holy tribe. We are the carriers of the truth that spirit moves through us all. When we deal with one another, we are dealing not merely with our human personalities but also with the unseen but ever-present throng of ideas, visions, stories, poems, songs, sculptures, art-as-facts that crowd the temple of consciousness waiting their turn to be born.

We are meant to midwife dreams for one another. We cannot labor in place of one another, but we can support the labor that each must undertake to birth his or her art and foster it to maturity.

It is for all these reasons that the Sacred Circle must exist in any place of creation. It is this protective ring, this soul boundary, that enlivens us at our highest level. By drawing and acknowledging the Sacred Circle, we declare principles to be above personalities. We invite a spirit of service to the highest good and a faith in the accomplishment of our own good in the midst of our fellows.

Envy, backbiting, criticism, have no place in our midst, nor do ill temper, hostility, sarcasm, chivvying for position. These attitudes may belong in the world, but they do not belong among us in our place as artists.

Success occurs in clusters. Drawing a Sacred Circle creates a sphere of safety and a center of attraction for our good. By filling this form faithfully, we draw to us the best. We draw the people we need. We attract the gifts we could best employ.

The Sacred Circle is built on respect and trust. The image is of the garden. Each plant has its name and its place. There is no one flower that cancels the need for another. Each bloom has its unique and irreplaceable beauty.

Let our gardening hands be gentle ones. Let us not root up one another's ideas before they have time to bloom. Let us bear with the process of growth, dormancy, cyclicality, fruition, and reseeding. Let us never be hasty to judge, reckless in our urgency to force unnatural growth. Let there be, always, a place for the artist toddler to try, to falter, to fail, to try again. Let us remember that in nature's world every loss has meaning. The same is true for us. Turned to good use, a creative failure may be the compost that nourishes next season's creative success. Remember, we are in this for the long haul, the ripening and harvest, not the quick fix.

Art is an act of the soul: ours is a spiritual community.

I have been a working artist for twenty-five years and for the past fifteen I have taught creative recovery. In that time, I have had ample opportunity to experience firsthand what it means to lack creative support and what it means to find it. Often, it is the difference between success and failure, between hope and despair.

What we are talking about here is the power of breaking isolation. As in any other recovery process, this act is a potent first step. Creative recovery, like any other recovery, may be facilitated by the company of like-minded people. For recovery from something, twelve-step groups seem to work especially well. For recovery to something, creative clusters show remarkable results.

When people ask me what I think is the single most important factor in an artist's sustained productivity, I know I am supposed to say something like, "solitude," or "an independent income," or "childcare." All of these things are good and many people have said so, but what I think is better and more important than any of these things is what I call "a believing mirror."

Put simply, a believing mirror is a friend to your creativity—someone who believes in you and your creativity. As artists, we can consciously build what I call creative clusters—a Sacred Circle of believing mirrors to potentiate each other's growth, to mirror a "yes" to each other's creativity.

In my experience we can benefit greatly from the support of others who share our dreams of living a fuller life. I suggest forming a weekly cluster and going through the exercises in the book together, sharing and comparing each answer. Often someone else's breakthrough insight can trigger one of our own.

Remember, we live in a culture that is toxic to art. A remarkable number of toxic myths about artists flourish. In addition to our purportedly being broke, irresponsible, drug-riddled and crazy, artists are also deemed selfish, out of touch with reality, megalomaniacs, tyrants, depressives and, above all, people who "want to be left alone."

At the very least, we are sure we will be.

Ask budding artists why they are afraid to move deeply into their creativity and they will tell you, "I'm not sure I want to spend the rest of my life alone."

In America, we seem to confuse artists with cowboys. We see artists as self-contained, driven loners who are always riding off into the sunset to do our thing—alone. If you'll pardon the joke, the cowboy analogy is so much bull. Most of us enjoy a little company. One of our great cultural secrets is the fact that artists like other artists.

Think about it for just a second: What did the Impressionists paint? Lunch . . . with each other. What did the Bloomsbury Group write about? Dining out with—and gossiping about—each other. Whom did John Cassavetes make films with? His friends. Why? Because they believed in one another and enjoyed helping each other realize their dreams.

Artists like other artists. We are not supposed to know this. We are encouraged to believe "there is only so much room at the top." Hooey. Water seeks its own level and water rises collectively.

Artists often help each other. We always have, although mythology tells us otherwise. The truth is that when we do, very powerful things happen. I will give a case in point. Film director Martin Scorsese developed, shaped, and fine-tuned the script for *Schindler's List*—then gave the project to his friend Steven Spielberg, feeling the material should be his. This unballyhooed act of creative generosity finally gave Spielberg his shot at an Oscar as "a real director"—even though Scorsese knew it might cost him his own shot, at least this year. And yet, to read about it in the press, these men are pitted against each other, artist versus artist, like athletes from warring nations in our mini-wars, the Olympics. Hooey, again.

Success occurs in clusters.

Until we accept the fact that life itself is founded in mystery, we shall learn nothing.

HENRY MILLER

I learn by going where I have to go.

THEODORE ROETHKE

As artists, we must find those who believe in us, and in whom we believe, and band together for support, encouragement and protection.

I remember sitting in a hotel room twenty years ago with two then-little-known directors, Brian De Palma and Steven Spielberg. Scorsese, then my fiancé, was off in France, and I was being consoled over take-away pizza by his two friends.

Spielberg was talking about a film he longed to make about the UFO phenomenon. There was scant support for the project and Spielberg was discouraged—although the project itself excited him. What to do? De Palma encouraged him to follow his heart and make that piece of art. That movie became *Close Encounters of the Third Kind*.

I tell this story not to drop names, but to make the point that even the most illustrious among our ranks as artists were not always illustrious and won't ever be beyond the fears and doubts that are part of creative territory. These fears and doubts will always, for all of us, be something to move through with a little help from our friends.

We all start out the same way—rich in dreams and nothing more. If we are lucky, we find friends to believe in our dreams with us. When we do, that creative cluster becomes a magnet to attract our good.

I have been teaching *The Artist's Way* for a long time. I've discovered that while I don't believe in a quick fix, rapid and sustained creative gains can be made—especially if people are willing to band together in clusters. When I travel to teach, it is with the goal of leaving creative clusters behind me in each locale so that people can work together to nurture and support each other over the long haul.

In Chicago there is a cluster that has been together for years. The group began with questions like, "Will I be able to write again?" and "I'd like to try to improve, but I'm scared," and "I really want to produce," and "I'd like to write a play."

Years later, the cluster is the same, but the questions are very different. "Who's throwing Ginny's Emmy nomination party?" and "Should Pam do her third play with the same theater company?"

As creative people, we are meant to encourage one another. That was my goal in writing *The Artist's Way* and it is my goal in teaching it. Your goal, it is my hope, is to encourage each other's dreams as well as your own. Creative ideas are brain-*children*. Like all children, they must be birthed and this birthing is both a personal and collective experience.

It was my privilege recently to midwife a book in my own creative cluster. My friend Sonia Choquette, a gifted psychic and teacher, was able to shape her long years of experience into an invaluable tool kit, *The Psychic Pathway*. As her friend, I received her book as nightly installments on my fax machine. I would fax her back, believing in her when she, like all artists, had trouble believing in herself.

Raised, like so many of us, to hide her creative light under a bushel lest her dazzle diminish the light of others, Sonia experienced doubt, fear and deepening faith as she moved past these creative barriers into creative birth.

I know there are those among you who fear undertaking projects that seem to demand many dark nights of the soul. Let me suggest to you that such nights may also be, in the beautiful Spanish words, *noches estrelladas*—star-studded.

Like neighboring constellations, we can serve each other both as guides and as company. In walking your artist's way, my deepest wish for you is the company of fellow lights and the generosity to light each other's ways as we each pass temporarily into darkness.

> *God is glorified in the fruitage of our lives.*
>
> JOEL S. GOLDSMITH

Know this well: Success occurs in clusters and is born in generosity. Let us from constellations of believing mirrors and move into our powers.

Sacred Circle Rules

1. Creativity flourishes in a place of safety and acceptance.
2. Creativity grows among friends, withers among enemies.
3. All creative ideas are children who deserve our protection.
4. All creative success requires creative failure.
5. Fulfilling our creativity is a sacred trust.
6. Violating someone's creativity violates a sacred trust.
7. Creative feedback must support the creative child, never shame it.

8.   Creative feedback must build on strengths, never focus on weaknesses.

9.   Success occurs in clusters and is born in generosity.

10.   The good of another can never block our own.

Above All: God is the source. No human power can deflect our good or create it. We are all conduits for a higher self that would work through us. We are all equally connected to a spiritual source. We do not always know which among us will teach us best. We are all meant to cherish and serve one another. *The Artist's Way* is tribal. The spirit of service yields us our dharma: that right path we dream of following in our best and most fulfilled moments of faith.

An Artist's Prayer

O Great Creator,
We are gathered together in your name
That we may be of greater service to you
And to our fellows.
We offer ourselves to you as instruments.
We open ourselves to your creativity in our lives.
We surrender to you our old ideas.
We welcome your new and more expansive ideas.
We trust that you will lead us.
We trust that it is safe to follow you.
We know you created us and that creativity
Is your nature and our own.
We ask you to unfold our lives
According to your plan, not our low self-worth.
Help us to believe that it is not too late
And that we are not too small or too flawed
To be healed—
By you and through each other—and made whole.
Help us to love one another,
To nurture each other's unfolding,
To encourage each other's growth,
And understand each other's fears.
Help us to know that we are not alone,
That we are loved and lovable.
Help us to create as an act of worship to you.

INDEX

Walking in This World

The Practical Art of Creativity

This book is dedicated to Jeremy P. Tarcher,
editor, publisher, and visionary.
With gratitude for his clarity, wisdom, and wit.
Above all, with gratitude for his friendship.

ACKNOWLEDGMENTS

Sara Carder, for her meticulous care
Carolina Casperson, for her believing eyes
Sonia Choquette, for her visionary optimism
Joel Fotinos, for his faith and vision
Candice Fuhrman, for her grace and acuity
Kelly Groves, for his clarity and enthusiasm
Linda Kahn, for her clear-eyed perception
Bill Lavallee, for his optimism and strength
Emma Lively, for her stubborn faith
Larry Lonergan, for his humor and guidance
Julianna McCarthy, for her artful heart
Robert McDonald, for his inspiration and artistry
Bruce Pomahac, for being a believing mirror
Domenica Cameron-Scorsese, for her love and discernment
Jeremy Tarcher, for his friendship and guidance
Edmund Towle, for his good-humored wisdom
Claire Vaccaro, for her sense of beauty

CONTENTS

INTRODUCTION

IT IS A DIM DECEMBER DAY. Outside my window, down in Riverside Park, an old woman strolls in the weak sunlight, leaning on the arm of her companion. Slowly and carefully they move along the cobbled path. Every so often they pause to take in the antics of a squirrel scampering along a tree branch or a bold blue jay swooping noisily down in front of them to claim a crumb.

One of my favorite ways to talk with friends is to walk with them. I love being engaged with the larger world and with each other. I love having my thought interrupted by the raven sailing in to land on a stone wall. I love the slow drift of autumn leaves, of snowflakes, of apple blossoms—each in season. Walking and talking humanize my life, draw it to an ancient and comforting scale. We live as we move, a step at a time, and there is something in gentle walking that reminds me of how I must live if I am to savor this life that I have been given.

I try to catch every sentence, every word you and I say . . .
ANTON CHEKHOV

Savoring this life becomes an automatic and appropriate response the minute I dispense with velocity and pressure. This earth is beautiful and so are we—if I just take the time to notice. At this time I split my life between New Mexico and New York, between walks in Riverside Park and walks on a dirt road through sagebrush, where we need to be alert for rattlers, to whom the road is an inconvenience, an interruption of their fields of rolling sage and fragrant piñon.

It is on these walks that my best ideas come to me. It is while walking that difficult clarity emerges. It is while walking that I experience a sense of well-being and connection, and it is in walking that I live most prayerfully. In New York I am a cave dweller, walking in the late afternoons, dazzled by the gold beribboned sunsets that bedizen the city skyline. When I can, I walk with friends, noting always how companionable our silences become, how effortlessly deep and true our conversations. It is my hope that the careful, slow structure of this book will allow it to approximate such walks for you. By going slowly, we move quickly through our many layers of defense and denial until we touch the living pulse of creativity within us all. The Great Creator made this world to dazzle and move us. When we slow our tempo to match the natural world's, we do find ourselves dazzled and moved.

Ten years ago I wrote a book called *The Artist's Way,* suggesting that our creative unfolding was a spiritual unfolding and that we could work—and walk—hand in hand with the Great Creator. A decade has passed and the teachings of that book still ring true to me. The two pivotal tools, three pages of longhand morning writing called Morning Pages and a weekly solo adventure called an Artist's Date still serve me—and now a million plus readers—very well. In ten years nothing has changed. The drill remains exactly the same. In addition, another powerful tool, the Weekly Walk, has emerged as pivotal.

> *Time is not a line, but a series of now-points.*
>
> TAISEN DESHIMARU

> *The best thoughts most often come in the morning after waking, while still in bed or while walking.*
>
> LEO TOLSTOY

Nothing brings home the beauty and power of the world that we live in like walking. Moving into our bodies, we embody the truth that as artists we are out to make a "body of work," which means we must encompass more than each day's march. A Weekly Walk helps us to acquire such an overview. It allows us to find both perspective and comfort. As we stretch our legs, we stretch our minds and our souls. St. Augustine, himself a great walker, remarked, "Solvitur ambulando"—"it is solved by walking." The "it" that we solve may be as particular as a bruising romance or as lofty as the conception of a new symphony. Ideas come to us as we walk. We also invite their quieter friend, insight. Walking often moves us past the "what" of our life into the more elusive "why."

Perhaps it would be helpful to give you a sense of what my creative practice is like. It is daily and portable. Its only requirements are paper, pen, and shoes.

I wake up in the morning, reach for a pen and a Morning Pages journal, and I dip my soul into my current life, noting what makes me agitated, what makes me irritable, what finds me excited, what feels like drudgery. I dip my pen to the page with the same methodical devotion that a woman in the high mountains of Tibet scrubs clothes in the stream, scouring them against a rock. It is a ritual, a way to start the day and a way to come clean before myself and God. There's no pretending in Morning Pages. I really am that petty, that fearful, that blind to the miracles all around me. As I write, the light dawns—just as the sun comes up over the mountains—and more is revealed. I see why I am frightened, whom I should call to make amends to, what I need to do in this particular day's march to inch ahead a little. Just as the women washing clothes may pause long enough for that one moment of connection as the sun dazzles the flank of a towering peak, so, too, I get my moments of insight, my glimpses into the why behind the what that I am living. But for the most part, the pages are routine. I do them because I do them. I do them, because they "work." They keep my consciousness scrubbed clean.

Once a week I take some small adventure, an Artist's Date. And I do mean small. I go to the fabric store. I visit the button shop. I sneeze as I enter a dusty secondhand bookstore. I take myself to a pet shop and go to the bird section, where zebra finches, lovebirds, and cockatiels vie for attention under the doleful watching glance of a slow-moving African Gray. If I am lucky, I might visit a rug store and sense a swath of eternity tied down a knot at a time. I might visit a large clock store and hear the rhythmic ticking, steady as a mother's heart.

When I am on an Artist's Date, I stand a little outside the flow of hurried time. I declare an hour off limits from hurried production and I have the chance to marvel at my own "being" produced. I am just one soul amid so many souls, one life led amid a bouquet of lives. When I step aside from pushing time, from racing the clock, even for just one hour, I feel myself drawn to merciful scale. "We are all in this together," I learn. That and, "It is beautiful."

As driven and stressed as anyone I have ever taught, I had to learn to stop running. Walking did not come naturally to me—and it did not come a moment too soon. I was in my mid-forties before I discovered the power of this essential tool. Now, if I can daily but at least once weekly, I take an extended, soul-refreshing walk.

In our busy lives these walks may be sandwiched in by getting off the subway one stop early, leaving the house a few minutes earlier to walk instead of cab short distances. Lunch hours may become walk times, or a walk may be fit into the very late afternoon. How you walk matters less than *that* you walk. Walking allows the insights of your own inner teacher to enter a dialogue with the teacher you encounter in these pages.

> *Ideas come from everywhere.*
> ALFRED HITCHCOCK

Since I wrote *The Artist's Way,* I have heard many stories of the miraculous. Sometimes in a restaurant or on a crowded street someone will stop me and say the sentence, "Your book changed my life." I am glad to have been a conduit, but that is what it is that I have been. I simply wrote down the precepts of divine intervention in our lives the moment we engage our creativity and, through that, engage our Great Creator. What I taught, essentially, is that we are all connected and that as we notice that and surrender to that, we join a long and safe lineage: The Great Creator loves artists and is waiting as a lover waits to respond to our love when we offer it.

What we call God does not matter. That we call on God does. There is an interactive, benevolent, well-wishing something that buoys the sails of our dreams, softens our landings when our parachutes billow closed after a creative flight. This creative something, the Great Creator, takes interest in our creativity, moves naturally and inevitably to support our creativity, recognizing our creative ideas as children of its own making.

Walking in this world, we do not go unpartnered. We do not speak our prayers unheard. There is someone or a something listening with the most tender of hearts. As we open to our inner life, our outer life also shifts. Lives are transformed by a gentle form of listening that is like walking with a cherished friend who listens and then says, "You might want to try X. Oh, look at that great squirrel. . . ."

As artists in tune with the Great Creator, we are coaxed along, cajoled along, coached along. I am not saying that God is Burgess Meredith turning each of us into a Rocky, but that image might not be so far off. God is the Great Artist, and every artist encounters God in the precise form or forms most helpful and necessary to his own creative unfolding. Kindness begins to occur and it occurs as we need it, where we need it, and how we need it. One woman finds a voice teacher. Another finds a source of wonderful yarn. One man gets free editing time on an AVID bank. Another man discovers an art supply store that carries the most beautiful German pencil sharpeners to use on his composing pencils.

> *Our aspirations are our possibilities.*
>
> SAMUEL JOHNSON

Nothing is too small. Nothing is too large. As we practice walking, writing our Morning Pages daily, and venturing into our Artist's Dates weekly, we begin to get a notion of the scope and scale of God—one eye on the sparrow and the other on the vast and starry universe. We are a part of all that, and, by the simple act of reaching out our hand to connect, we become a partnered part of life.

As we go within, we discover that we are not alone there. The loneliness we fear finding in art is actually the loneliness of disconnecting ourselves from our creativity and our creator. As we try our hand literally at the making of something, we do meet our maker. As we try to make more and more, more and more is made of us and through us. "Not I, but the Father doeth the work."

Artists throughout the centuries have talked about inspiration. They have reported the whispers of the divine that came to them when they inclined their ear to listen. Aligning their own creativity with that of their creator, composers exclaimed, "Straight away the ideas flew in on me!" Such ideas can—and do—fly in on all of us. They are the squirrel scampering along the branch. They are the stray pink blossom lighting on a cheekbone. They are the light but definite touch of the unseen world touching our own whenever we are willing to be touched.

Walking in This World is intended as a gentle pilgrimage. We will move issue to issue, walking and talking about the deeper concerns of our souls. I say "souls" because creativity is a spiritual rather than an intellectual endeavor. Creativity is a daily spiritual practice and, like all spiritual paths, it is both mysterious and trackable.

Walking in This World is intended to demystify the obstacles commonly found on the creative path. It addresses issues common not only to creative beginners but to those much further down the creative road. If *The Artist's Way* can safely be said to have launched many travelers on the creative seas, this book is intended to bring to those travelers needed supplies in the form of clarity and encouragement. The creative life is rewarding but difficult. Much of that difficulty is eased by a sense of shared faith and companionship.

> *It is your work in life that is the ultimate seduction.*
>
> PABLO PICASSO

Walking in this world a footfall at a time, we walk accompanied by angels, by and large unseen but not unfelt. As we open ourselves to divine guidance—in the form of our own listening creativity—we are brought to the divine in this world and in our all-too-worldly hearts.

Basic Tools

MANY PEOPLE who have worked with my earlier books *The Artist's Way* and *The Vein of Gold* will have a familiarity with the basic tools of my creative practice. Newcomers will need such a familiarity. Therefore, all readers should take the time to review or learn the three simple tools: Morning Pages, the Artist's Date, and the Weekly Walk. You will be asked to practice them for the duration of this course.

TOOL 1: Morning Pages

Morning Pages are the primary tool of a creative recovery. From my perspective they are the bedrock of a creative life. Three pages stream-of-consciousness writing done before the day "begins," Morning Pages serve to prioritize, clarify, and ground the day's activities. Frequently fragmented, petty, even whining, Morning Pages were once called "brain drain" because they so clearly siphoned off negativity. Anything and everything is fuel for Morning Pages. They hold worries about a lover's tone of voice, the car's peculiar knocking,

> . . . we all need the reassuring and healing messages that treasured rituals provide.
>
> SARAH BAN BREATHNACH

the source of this month's rent money. They hold reservations about a friendship, speculation about a job possibility, a reminder to buy Kitty Litter. They mention, sometimes repeatedly, overeating, undersleeping, overdrinking, and overthinking, that favorite procrastinator's poison artists are fond of.

I have been writing Morning Pages for twenty years now. They have witnessed my life in Chicago, New Mexico, New York, and Los Angeles. They have guided me through book writing, music writing, the death of my father, a divorce, the purchase of a house and a horse. They have directed me to piano lessons, to exercise, to an energetic correspondence with a significant man, to pie baking, to rereading and refurbishing old manuscripts. There is no corner of my life or consciousness that the pages have not swept. They are the daily broom that clears my consciousness and readies it for the day's inflow of fresh thought.

I write my Morning Pages in *The Artist's Way Morning Pages Journal* that I designed for just such use. You might write your Morning Pages in a shiny spiral-bound notebook. Some people write their pages by computer, although I strongly recommend writing them by hand. Even the shape of my writing tells me the shape and clarity of my thoughts. Of course, at times Morning Pages are difficult to write. They feelstilted, boring, hackneyed, repetitive, or just plain depressing. I have learned to write through such resistant patches and to believe that Morning Pages are a part of their cure. I know people who are "too busy" to write Morning Pages. I sympathize, but I doubt their lives will ever become less busy without Morning Pages.

> *We must be willing to get rid of the life we've planned, so as to have the life that is waiting for us.*
>
> JOSEPH CAMPBELL

It is a paradox of my experience that Morning Pages both take time and give time. It is as though by setting our inner movie onto the page, we are freed up to act in our lives. Suddenly, a day is filled with small choice points, tiny windows of time available for our conscious use. It may be as simple as the fact that we wrote down "I should call Elberta" that cues us into calling Elberta when a moment looms free. As we write Morning Pages, we tend to get things "right." Our days become our own. Other people's agendas and priorities no longer run our lives. We care for others, but we now care for ourselves as well.

I like to think of Morning Pages as a withdrawal process but not in the usual sense, where we withdraw from a substance taken away from us. No, instead, we *do* the withdrawing in Morning Pages. We pull ourselves inward to the core of our true values, perceptions, and agendas. This process takes approximately a half hour—about the same time normally set aside for meditation. I have come to think of Morning Pages as a form of meditation, a particularly potent and freeing form for most hyperactive Westerners. Our worries, fantasies, anxieties, hopes, dreams, concerns, and convictions all float freely across the page. The page becomes the screen of our consciousness. Our thoughts are like clouds crossing before the mountain of our observing eye.

When I first began writing Morning Pages, I lived at the foot of Taos Mountain in New Mexico. I was stymied in my life, my art, and my career. One morning I simply got the idea to write Morning Pages, and I have been doing them ever since. A day at a time, a page at a time, my daily three pages have unknotted career, life, and love. They have shown me a path where there was no path, and I follow it now, trusting that if I do, the path will continue. For the duration of work with this book, and, I hope, far longer, I would ask you to write daily Morning Pages. They will lead you to an inner teacher whose profundity will amaze you. Only you can swing open the gate for your teacher to enter. It is my hope you will do so now.

TOOL 2: The Artist's Date

Pivotal to a creative recovery is a second essential tool: the Artist's Date. Grounded in a sense of adventure and autonomy, the Artist's Date is a once-weekly, hour-long solo expedition to explore something festive or interesting to your creative consciousness. If Morning Pages are assigned work, the Artist's Date is assigned play. But do not be misled into skipping it as "less important." The phrase "the play of imagination" has well-earned currency because art *is* made by an imagination at play. The artist who forgets how to play soon enough forgets how to work. The flier into the unknown, the leap of faith onto page, stage, or easel, becomes ever more difficult to take without practice.

> *It's a great relief to me to know that I can actually be creative and be happy at the same time.*
>
> JAMES W. HALL

> *A hunch is creativity trying to tell you something.*
>
> FRANK CAPRA

At bottom, art is an image-using process. We dip into the well of our consciousness to find images and events for our imagination to employ. Unless we are careful, it is easy to over-fish our inner well, to deplete our reservoir of images. Fishing for something to say, do, or draw, we find new ideas more and more elusive. Nothing "hooks" us.

The conscious use of a weekly Artist's Date, and double that, if we are working flat out, replenishes the inner well and creates a sense of well-being. Synchronicity—that uncanny knack of being in the right place at the right time—picks up markedly as we practice Artist's Dates. Just as cabin fever and a sense of personal restless claustrophobia overtakes an invalid who is sick and too long housebound, so, too, an artist without Artist's Dates suffers a sense of constriction. I know this from personal experience, as I have suffered long periods of ill health. Always, when I return to the practice of Artist's Dates, my sense of well-being increases and my work deepens and enlarges.

For the duration of this course, and longer I would hope, you are asked to take your inner artist on a weekly outing. Expect resistance and self-sabotage—as you plan something adventurous and enjoyable, only to catch yourself sabotaging your date. Our inner artist is a volatile and vulnerable creature, needy as the child of divorce. It wants your undivided time and attention at least once a week so that it can tell you its dreams and difficulties. Painful as these may be, is it any wonder we sometimes avoid such contact? Be alert to resisting your resistance.

TOOL 3: Weekly Walks

Most of us spend life on the run, too busy and too hurried to walk anywhere. Beset by problems and difficulties, we feel walking is a frivolous waste of time—our valuable time. "When will I do it?" becomes one more problem, one more question for our busy mind. The truth is that walking holds our solutions.

It was during a time in which my life felt directionless both personally and creatively that I discovered the solace and direction to be found in walking. At the time I owned a 1965 Chevy pickup named Louise. Every afternoon I would load Louise with a half-dozen dogs and point the truck down a dirt road into the sagebrush. A mile into "nowhere," I would park the truck on the roadside and signal to the dogs that they were free to roam—as long as they stayed within hailing distance. Then I would set off walking. I would walk a forty-five-minute loop, south and east toward the foothills, then north and west directly toward Taos Mountain. As I walked, emotions would wash through me. I was grieving a lost marriage and the death of my father, for many years a close creative companion. I would walk and ask for guidance. Clouds would pass in front of the mountain. I would notice the cloud and then notice that I did have a sense of guidance. I knew what to write, how to write it, and that write it I should. A day at a time, a walk at a time, even a simple step at a time, my sad and tangled life began to sort itself. I say sort itself because all I did was "walk through it." I have been walking ever since.

"Walk on it" is good advice, whether the problem is a persnickety plotline or a persistent personality clash. Native Americans pursue vision quests, Aborigines do walkabout. Both of these cultures know that walking clears the head. Too often in our modern culture we mistake the head for the source of all wisdom rather than the manufacturer of malcontent. For the duration of this course, you are asked to take at least one twenty-minute walk a week. You will find that these walks focus your thinking and instigate your breakthroughs. You will contact the

What we have to learn to do, we learn by doing.

ARISTOTLE

"imagic-nation"—that realm of larger thoughts and ideas well known to shamans and spiritual seekers. It is my hope that the habit of walking and the habit of talking to those you love as you walk will both be awakened by this course.

HOW TO USE THE BASIC TOOLS

1. **Set your alarm clock to ring one half hour earlier than usual; get up and do three pages of longhand, stream-of-consciousness writing.** Do not reread these pages or allow anyone else to read them. Ideally, stick these pages in a large manila envelope or set them aside and hide them somewhere. Welcome to Morning Pages. They will change you.

2. **Take yourself on an Artist's Date.** You will do this every week for the duration of this course. A sample Artist's Date: Take yourself to your local children's toy store. In the front of the store, near the cash register, you will find "impulse buys" like stick-'em stars, funny pencils and pens, bubbles, and stickers. Let your artist have a treat or two. You may want gold stars for every day you do get your Morning Pages written—that's seven stars for seven days, we hope. The point of your Artist's Date is more mystery than mastery. Do something that enchants and entices your artist.

3. **Take a Weekly Walk.** Outfit yourself in your most comfortable socks and shoes. Set out for a good twenty-minute ramble. You may choose a park, a country road, or an urban route. Where you walk matters less than that you walk. Go far enough and long enough that you feel both your body and your mind "unkink." You may discover that you like walking very much and that you enjoy doing it more than once weekly. Walks definitely help you to metabolize the content of this course.

Creativity Contract

I, _____, commit my-
self to the regular use of the three basic tools. For the
duration of this course, I will write Morning Pages
daily and will take an Artist's Date and a Weekly Walk
once a week. Additionally, I commit myself to excellent self-care, adequate sleep, good food, and gentle
companionship.

_____ (signature)

_____ (date)

Discovering a Sense of Origin

This week initiates your creative pilgrimage. *You* are the point of origin. You begin where you are, with who you are, at this time, at this place. You may find yourself hopeful, skeptical, excited, resistant, or all of the above. The readings and tasks in week one all aim at pinpointing the "you" you have been evading. When we avoid our creativity, we avoid ourselves. When we meet our creativity, we meet ourselves, and that encounter happens in the moment. The willingness to be ourselves gives us the origin in originality.

Setting Out

You say you want to make art. You want to begin or you want to continue. This is good. We need a more artful world, and that means we need you and the specific contribution that you and you alone can make. But to make it you must start somewhere, and that is often the sticking point.

"It's too late."

"I'm not good enough."

"I'll never be able to pull this off."

We all have our fears, and they feel as real as the chair you are sitting in. Like that chair, they can be slouched into or left behind. Sometimes we need to sit up and ignore the cricks in our back and shoulders and just begin. That's how it is with art. We just need to begin.

Begin where you are, with *who* you are. In order to go where you want to go creatively, you have to start somewhere. And the best place to start is precisely

All serious daring starts from within.

EUDORA WELTY

The realization of the self is only possible if one is productive, if one can give birth to one's own potentialities.

JOHANN WOLFGANG
VON GOETHE

where you are. This is true whether you are a beginning artist or someone with long miles down the track. In fact, seasoned artists can waste time and energy mulling the dignity of their acquired position in the field when the truth is, they still need to just start again.

Writing doesn't really care about where you do it. It cares *that* you do it. The same is true for drawing. I watched a friend of mine waste a solid year because he "couldn't work without a studio." When he did get a studio and went back to work, what he made were a few largish paintings but a great many beautiful miniature charcoal and pencil drawings that he could have done on a TV table had he been so inclined. No, he didn't work—not because he didn't have a studio but because he didn't work.

There is room for art in any life we have—any life, no matter how crowded or overstuffed, no matter how arid or empty. We are the "block" we perceive.

If you are a beginning musician and want to learn piano, sit down at the piano and touch the keys. Great. Tomorrow you can sit down at the piano and touch the keys again. Five minutes a day is better than no minutes a day. Five minutes might lead to ten, just as a tentative embrace leads to something more passionate. Making art is making love with life. We open ourselves to art as to love.

Instead of thinking about conquering an art form, think instead of kissing it hello, wooing it, exploring it in small, enticing steps. How many of us have burned through promising relationships by moving too swiftly? How many of us have burned out in new creative ventures by setting goals too high? Most of us.

Doing any large creative work is like driving coast to coast, New York to Los Angeles. First you must get into the car. You must begin the trip, or you will never get there. Even a night in New Jersey is a night across the Hudson and on your way. A small beginning is exactly that: a beginning. Rather than focus on large jumps—which may strike us as terrifying and unjumpable—we do better to focus on the first small step, and then the next small step after that. "Oh, dear," you might be sniffing, "where's the drama in such baby steps?" Think about that for a minute. When a baby takes its first step, it is *very* dramatic.

Today my mail contained a manila envelope from a friend, a born storyteller who spent years wanting to write and not writing. Last June, on a perfectly ordinary day, Larry did an extraordinary thing for him: He picked up a pen and started writing. I now have a fat sheaf of stories in my hand. All he needed to do was begin. And then begin again the next day.

Often, when we yearn for a more creative life, we cue up the sound track for high drama. With great dissonant chords crashing in our heads, we play out the scenario of leaving those we love and going somewhere lonely and perhaps exotic, where we will be Artists with a capital A. When I hear this plan, I think, *Okay. You do it.* Experience has taught me that my artist performs best when the stakes are lower. When I keep the drama on the page, pages accumulate.

I hate to say this, but making art is a little like dieting. One day you just have to start and what you do that day is the beginning of success or failure. I cannot write an entire book today, but I can write one page. I cannot become an accomplished pianist, but I can put in fifteen minutes of piano time. Today you may not get a one-woman show in SoHo, but you can sketch the battered leather chair with your cocker spaniel sprawled in splendid comfort or you can sketch the curve of your lover's arm. You *can* begin.

Creativity is inspiration coupled with initiative. It is an act of faith and, in that phrase, the word "act" looms as large as the "faith" that it requires.

When we do not act in the direction of our dreams, we are only "dreaming." Dreams have a will-o'-the-wisp quality. Dreams coupled with the firm intention to manifest them take on a steely reality. Our dreams come true when we are true to them. Reality contains the word "real." We begin to "reel" in our dreams when we toss out the baited hook of intention. When we shift our inner statement from "I'd love to" to "I'm going to," we shift out of victim and into adventurer. When we know that we "will," then we couple the power of our will with the power of future events. In this sense, what we "will do" becomes what "will happen." To prove this to ourselves, we need to couple the largeness of our dream with the small, concrete, and do-able "next right thing." As we take the next small step, the bigger steps move a notch closer to us, downsizing as they move. If we keep on taking small enough next steps and therefore keep chipping away and miniaturizing what we like to call "huge" risks, by the time the risk actually gets to our door, it, too, is simply the next right thing, small and do-able and significant but nondramatic. Many of us falter, thinking that in order to begin a creative work we must know precisely how to finish it and, beyond that, to insure its reception in the world. We are, in effect,

> *In dreams begins responsibility.*
> WILLIAM BUTLER YEATS

asking for a guarantee of our success before we have taken the single most important step necessary to insure it. That step is commitment.

When we realize that we want to make something—a book, a play, a sketch, a poem, a painting—we are yearning for the completion of that desire. We hunger to make art the same way we may hunger to make love. It begins as desire, and desire requires that we act upon it if we are to conceive things.

Despite our culture's well-earned reputation for encouraging instant gratification, we are *not* encouraged to act decisively upon our creative desires. We are trained to think about them, doubt them, second-guess them. We are trained, in short, to talk ourselves out of committing art or committing *to* art.

When movie director Martin Ritt told me "Cerebration is the enemy of art," he was urging that as artists we follow that Nike slogan, "Just do it." He wasn't saying that brains were counter to the creative process, but he was urging us to use our brains to actually make art, not think about making art. Thinking is not the enemy, but overthinking is.

If you *conceptualize* launching a project, you begin to understand the issue of overthinking. Think of your project as "the arrow of desire." Imagine yourself eyeing the bull's-eye, pulling back the bow—and then thinking about it. Worrying about it. Considering whether you are aiming exactly right or whether you should be a smidgen higher or lower. Your arm begins to get tired. Then your aim begins to get shaky. If you manage to finally shoot the arrow, it does not sail with confidence and strength. You have that in your vacillation about exactly *how* you should shoot. In short, you have mistaken beginning something with ending something. You have wanted a finality that is earned over time and not won ahead of time as a guarantee. You have denied the process of making art because you are so focused on the product: Will this be a bull's-eye? We forget that intention is what creates direction. If we aim with the eye of our heart—"*That* I desire to do"—then we aim truly and well. "Desire," that much-maligned word, is actually the best guide for our creative compass. Horseback riders who jump the Grand Prix fences of terrifying heights talk of "throwing their heart" over the fence so their horse jumps after it. We must do the same.

> Action is eloquence.
>
> WILLIAM SHAKESPEARE

We have attached so much rigamarole to the notion of being an artist that we fail to ask the simplest and most obvious question: Do I want to make this? If the answer is yes, then begin. Fire the arrow.

We take no step unpartnered. We may feel like the fool from the Tarot deck, stepping heedlessly into blank space, but that is not reality. The Great Creator is an artist and he/she/it is an artist in partnership with other artists. The moment we open ourselves to making art, we simultaneously open ourselves to our maker. We are automatically partnered. Joseph Campbell speaks of encountering "a thousand unseen helping hands." I think of these hands as an invisible web ungirding any creative endeavor. It is like throwing a switch or toppling the first domino—there is a spiritual chain reaction that occurs the moment we act on faith. Something or somebody acts back.

It is when we fire the arrow of desire, when we actually start a project, that we trigger the support for our dream. *We* are what sets things in motion—people and events resonate toward our fiery resolve. Energy attracts energy. Our arrow is the speeding pickup truck that attracts summer dogs to chase it down the road. We generate the energy and excitement. Then others will give chase. "Build it and they will come."

> *Nothing great was ever achieved without enthusiasm.*
>
> RALPH WALDO EMERSON

Creative energy is energy. When we are worrying *about* creating instead of actually creating, we are wasting our creative energy. When we are vacillating, we are letting air out of our tires. Our pickup is not speeding down the road and may never even get out of the driveway. Our project goes flat.

Does this mean we should race off wildly? No, but it does mean that once we have a heart's desire we should act on it. It is that action, that moving out on faith, that moves mountains—and careers.

The book you are holding now is a book that I am writing on Riverside Drive in Manhattan and in my upstairs bedroom in northern New Mexico—also, in the car and in truck stops as I drive cross-country between the two. None of this behavior matches my drama about being a real writer. In that drama, either I have gone to Australia, where I walk the beaches and beg for inspiration, or else I am freezing in a cabin near Yosemite with nothing to do all winter but shiver and write. When we approach creativity that way, it smacks of the creativity firewalk or the creativity bungee jump—definitely terrifying and not something I'd want to try in the next few minutes or without my will made out. It is one of the ironies of the creative life that while drama is a part of what we make, it has almost no place in how we make it. Even those famous artists who suffered famously dramatic lives were remarkably undramatic in their actual work habits. Hemingway wrote five hundred words a day, wife in and wife out. Composer Richard Rodgers wrote a composition every morning, nine to nine thirty. His colleague, Oscar Hammerstein, rose at six and put in banker's hours on his farm in Doylestown, Pennsylvania. Unseduced by glamour or by drama, their output was both steady and prodigious. This argues that we get a lot further creatively by staying put and doing something small and do-able daily in the life we already have.

So much of the difficulty with beginning lies in our perception that we have "so far to go." We have separated art from process into product—"So far to go until it's finished"—when we think like that and we have also separated ourselves from God. When we are afraid to begin, it is always because we are afraid we are alone—tiny, like little Davids facing giant Goliaths. But we are not alone.

God is present everywhere. The act of making art is a direct path to contact with God, and we do not need to travel any geographic or psychic distance to experience the grace of creation in the grace of our own creating.

Goethe told us, "Whatever you think you can do, or believe you can do, begin it, because action has magic, grace and power in it." This was no mere bromide. It was a report on spiritual experience—an experience that each of us can have whenever we surrender to being a beginner, whenever we dismantle our adult's aloof avoidance and actively seek the Great Creator's hand by reaching out our own to start anew.

If we stop watching the movies in our head with the scary sound tracks and start listening to things like "Whistle While You Work" or "Zip-A-Dee-Doo-Dah," we may begin to make a little headway. We need to get into reality. Art is about making art, nothing more dramatic than that. Puccini may have written *Madame Butterfly*, but he still hummed as he walked on a sunny street. He still ate pasta and he still spent enough time with his friends to concoct a plot the village gossip might handily have provided. High art is made by people who have friends and the need to dine on more than inspiration soup.

TASK

What the Hell, You Might As Well

Often we experience a sense of powerlessness because we do not see any direct action that we can take to concretely alter our sense of being stuck, in a particular way. At times like this we'd do well not to be so linear. Sometimes, we need to exercise just a little elbow grease in any creative direction that we can find. If nothing else, taking a small creative action moves us out of the victim position. Suddenly, we realize that we do have choices and options and that our passivity may boil down to a stubborn laziness, a sort of tantrum that says "If I can't make X better right now, then I am not going to do anything." Instead of a tantrum, try doing this instead:

In Heaven an angel is nobody in particular.

GEORGE BERNARD SHAW

Take pen in hand and number down from 1 to 20. List 20 small, creative actions you *could* take. For example:

1. Paint the kitchen windowsill.
2. Hang lace on my bedroom door.
3. Put the primrose into a good pot.
4. Change the downstairs shower curtain.
5. Buy photo albums and put my dog pictures in one.
6. Send my sister the fudge recipe she asked for.
7. Send my sister fudge.
8. Buy red socks.
9. Wear them to church.
10. Make a computer file of poems I love.
11. Send a great poem to each of my friends.
12. Photograph my current life and send the pictures to my grandmother.
13. Designate something a "God Jar," a special incubator for my dreams and hopes.
14. Designate something else a "what the hell!" basket for my resentment, annoyances, and fears.
15. Throw a slumber party and request that each guest bring a good ghost story to tell.
16. Make a pot of soup.
17. Give away every outfit I even mildly dislike.
18. Get a CD player for my car and stock it.
19. Go to a great perfume store and get one great perfume.
20. Take an elderly friend to a good aquarium.

Commitment

Very often, calling it professionalism, we become too busy to make art for art's sake. We are committed to a certain careerist, professional agenda and we tell ourselves that is all we have energy or time for. This is false. When we make the art we love, it *makes* time and energy available to us for our professional pursuits. Why? Because we feel more vital, and that vitality is assertive energy that makes room for its own desires.

Follow your bliss.

JOSEPH CAMPBELL

Change everything, except your loves.

VOLTAIRE

When we say "I will articulate my true values, I will express my essence," that word "will" throws a switch. When we "will," then we "will." In this sense we are predicting our future and shaping it simultaneously. Everything is energy. Ideas are simply organized energy, a sort of mold into which more solidified energy can be poured. A book begins as an idea. So does a social movement. So does a building. We cast our dreams and desires ahead of us, and as we move toward them, their content takes on solidity. We cocreate our lives. This is both our responsibility and our privilege. A symphony moves both through and ahead of a composer. As he moves toward it, it moves toward him. In a sense, as artists, we both pitch a ball of creative energy and catch it.

Commit to make something you love and you will find that the needed supplies come to hand. You must "catch" them when they do. A free studio for recording. Use of an editing bank. A windfall of costumes from your aunt's attic. A church space newly renovated and looking for a worthy cause, like your embryonic theater company. Our creative energy triggers a creative response.

Commit to playing the music you love, and the music of life becomes more lovely. Just as making love can quite literally make love, so, too, making art—a form of the verb "to be"—can quite literally make art out of being. The art of creative living, like the actor's art, is a moment-to-moment receptivity, a harmonious leaning into the unfolding melodic structure of existence such as great string ensemble players use in cocreating chamber music. Those who create for love—like the devotees who practice their spiritual tradition with ardor—give off a certain undefinable something that is attractive, and it attracts to them their good.

When we make art for the sake of making art, we tend eventually to make money. Money is energy, and it follows the path we lay down for it. When we commit that we will do something, the finances that allow us to do it follow. Our committed intention attracts supply. This is spiritual law, if not what we are taught to believe. Money is really a codified form of power. Often we think we need X amount of money to attain Y space, but what we really need is the space itself. Intention creates power, often as money, sometimes as access. Art triggers abundance, but it triggers it in diverse forms. Our cash flow may not immediately increase, but our opportunity flow *will* increase. So will many benevolent coincidences or synchronicities that will enrich our lives and our art if we let them. Receptivity is key, and that key unlocks the treasure chest.

Faith moves mountains, and when we see art as an act of faith, then we begin to see that when we commit to our art, mountains may indeed be moved as a path becomes clear. Committed to the "what," we trigger the "how"—needed money may appear in the form of an unexpected bonus, a timely and lucrative freelance job, a surprise inheritance, matching funds, or even a corporate scholarship. When we invest energy in our dreams, others often invest cash. A gifted young pianist receives an unexpected year's financial backing from an older couple from his hometown who are "betting" on him and his talent. A young actor, similarly marooned in a backwater, is given travel funds to audition

> *How often things occur by mere chance which we dare not even hope for.*
>
> TERENCE

for the conservatory that chooses him and gives him a scholarship. As we commit to our dreams, something benevolent commits back. Supportive coincidence can be counted upon. Artist to artist, we can safely have faith in the Great Creator's interest in our creative pursuits.

Art is a matter of commitment. Commitment is of interest to the Great Creator. When we display the faith necessary to make our art, the Great Creator displays an interest and an active hand in supporting what it is we are doing. We receive supply in all forms.

A composer who works most often on commission for others recorded for himself a small personal work that he thought of as a musical prayer. It is a simple piece of music and a simple, short recording. So simple and so short that the composer looped it four times and considers the resulting twenty-minute version something a person might meditate to—"just something I made for myself, for my own spiritual use."

Staying a few days as a houseguest at another composer's house, he played the brief recording for his friend. It happened to be running when the doorbell rang and a prominent record company executive came to visit. "What's that?" he immediately wanted to know.

"Just a little personal something I laid down to express myself."

"You mean a prayer?"

"Something like that."

"I've just been made the head of a new division on contemporary spiritual music. Do you think you could build an album around that?"

"Yes, I suppose I could."

Out of the tiny recording, a large and beautiful album was born. Out of the album, a new direction for the composer's career was born. He began to work with larger choral groups and to write more music for voice. This new direction was profoundly satisfying.

"I had always loved chorales, and the idea of a modern oratorio expressing our spiritual values was like an answered prayer for me—a prayer I had barely voiced before it was answered."

It may well be that the "self" in self-expression is not only the voice of our finite, individual self but also the voice of the Self, that larger and higher force of which we are both subject and substance. When we express our creativity, we are a conduit for the Great Creator to explore, express, and expand its divine nature and our own. We are like songbirds. When one of us gives voice to our true nature, it is contagious and others soon give tongue as well. There is an infallibility to the law that as we each seek to express what we are longing to say, there is always someone or something that is longing to hear precisely what we have expressed. We do not live or create in isolation. Each of us is part of a greater whole and, as we agree to express ourselves, we agree to express the larger Self that moves through us all.

> *To be what we are, and to become what we are capable of becoming, is the only end of life.*
>
> ROBERT LOUIS STEVENSON

TASK

Express Yourself

Take pen in hand and number from 1 to 10. List 10 positive adjectives used to describe you, for example:

1. Inventive
2. Original
3. Zany
4. Hard-driving
5. Humorous
6. Articulate
7. Innovative
8. Generous
9. Enthusiastic
10. Active

Take pen in hand again and write yourself a personal ad using the terms you listed to create a positive and provocative picture of your uniqueness, for example:

Experience the laser insights of an inventive, humorous, and innovative creative guide.

It is worth noting here that the point of this tool is not self-transformation but self-acceptance. If you are intense, so be it. There are those who love intense. If your irreverent humor offends the hyperserious crowd, it *will* be appreciated elsewhere. When we affirm rather than deny the characteristics often singled out, we begin to have a much more accurate idea of by whom, and where, our traits will be appreciated.

Snow

There is a soft and beautiful snow falling outside my window. The ink-black trees in Riverside Park look like a line drawing of trees. The sky is gray and luminous. It's a day for soup and knitting, if we did that anymore. It is certainly a day for knitting up the soul.

> *The most beautiful thing we can experience is the mysterious.*
>
> ALBERT EINSTEIN

We go pell-mell, most of us, and a day like this, when the snow muffles the drumbeat of that insistent sound track that urges us to achieve, achieve, achieve, can come as a relief—the way a bad cold can force us to bed and to getting current with ourselves.

The snowflakes are more than flurries, less than a storm. They fall each with a particular velocity, feathers from a pillow given a firm celestial shake. Higher realms feel very close in a snowstorm.

As a little girl, my bedroom window overlooked our driveway. The peak of our garage had a floodlight, and when it snowed, I would lie in bed and watch the dancing flakes falling in swirls, sometimes rising in a whirl like a great petticoat. I grew up in Libertyville, Illinois, in a house in the country, yellow wood and field-stone, a kind of overgrown cottage filled with small rooms and odd corners, places for the imagination to play, to stare out the window at the snow.

Genius, in truth, means little more than the faculty of perceiving in an un-habitual way.

WILLIAM JAMES

We all need a window for the imagination. We need a time and a place to stare out the window at the snow. On a day like today, with a great black crow flapping through the dark limbs, it is easy to see how Poe could write his *Raven*, mere blocks from here, staring at the same snow and some dark bird, a century ago. Artists have stared out of windows and into their souls for a very long time. It is something in the staring-out that enables us to do the looking-in. We forget that.

So often we try to gird ourselves to face a harsh and difficult world when we might instead gentle both ourselves and our world just by slowing down.

We worry rather than ruminate. We fret rather than speculate. Even football teams take time-outs, but it is so hard for us, as artists, to do the same. So often we feel there is so much we yearn to do and so little time to do it in. We could take a cue from music here: "Rest" is a musical term for a pause between flurries of notes. Without that tiny pause, the torrent of notes can be overwhelming. Without a rest in our lives, the torrent of our lives can be the same.

Even God rested. Even waves rest. Even business titans close their office doors and play with the secret toys on their desks. Our language of creativity knows this. We talk about "the play of ideas," but we still overwork and underplay and wonder why we feel so drained.

A friend of mine, a glorious musician, works on two music faculties and tours internationally. Sometimes his great voice, an instrument of beauty as large and soaring as a pipe organ, reaches my ear haggard with fatigue. His great strength becomes his great weakness. He forgets to rest.

As artists living with the drone of commerce, we have forgotten that "rest" is a musical term, and that to hear the music of our lives as something other than a propulsive drumbeat, driving us forward as the war drums drove men into bloody battle, we may *need* to rest.

The ego hates to rest. The ego doesn't want to let God, or sleep, mend up the raveled sleeve of care. The ego would like to handle all that itself, thank you. As artists, we must serve our souls, not our egos. Our souls need rest. This is something my artist-mother knew well.

As artists, it serves us to consciously find windows to the world of wonder—we must locate places that open the trapdoor in our imagination and allow the breath of greater worlds to enter our too-claustrophobic lives. You may find the window for your imagination in the upper cranny of your neighborhood library. There, tucked amid the rafters, amid the high and dusty tomes, you may look out an upper window and sense a world of other writers staring over your shoulder with you. Or you might find your imagination climbing aboard a Persian carpet in an Oriental-rug store, where the leaf-by-leaf turning of intricate patterns, like woven stained-glass windows, might transport you to bygone centuries. A clock store might paradoxically help you step beyond time as you stand amid a small forest of chiming and ticking grandfathers and magical cuckoos.

We are the children of our landscape; it dictates behavior and even thought in the measure to which we are responsive to it.

LAWRENCE DURRELL

The most visible joy can only reveal itself to us when we've transformed it, within.

RAINER MARIA RILKE

For Allison, it was always a visit to a grand plant store that gave her imagination room to breathe. Something in the steamy jungle air, the brightly flaming colors, spoke to her of special worlds. Carolina loved antique-clothing stores. She would handle a vintage frock and feel herself transported to a gentler world. For David, the world of vintage model cars lit up the boy explorer that is his inner artist. He loves the sleek lacquered shells resembling beautiful oversized bugs. Just whizzing a model along a showcase lid gives him a thrill. For Edward, model trains and great toy stores—more for himself than his "excuses," his young nephews—light up his imagination.

The imagination is not linear. It needs to step beyond ordinary time and space. This is why the world of vintage movie posters gives Michael a thrill. This is why Lorraine loves to visit the large, multifloored fabric stores downtown in Chicago's Loop and the bigger ones over near Greek Town. "I can make anything I want," she often thrills, and although she may choose a dark navy gabardine for a sensible office dress, she has still fingered a rustling taffeta that she would have worn to a turn-of-the-century tea dance.

For each of us, safety and rest come in myriad and very personal forms. My childhood friend Carolina just sent me a long white antique nightgown that makes me feel cherished. Baking pies makes me feel safe— pie making is a tradition among the women in my family. Making vegetable soup, another family tradition, also soothes and calms my hectic citified, careerified soul. My mother, Dorothy, when overwrought, would retreat to the piano and play the Blue Danube waltz until her soul settled back into three-quarter time.

> *The proper use of imagination is to give beauty to the world . . . the gift of imagination is used to cast over the commonplace workaday world a veil of beauty and make it throb with our esthetic enjoyment.*
>
> Lin Yü-t'ang

Jean, in the throes of an unexpected and overwhelming divorce, found herself agitated and adrenalized, afraid of "going under" financially. She needed more hours in a day to frantically do all that she felt should be done. A wise older friend familiar with Jean's abandoned hobby, doing needle- point, and familiar, too, with the fact that such a meditative activity would help Jean to quietly tap her deeply creative sources, suggested that Jean return to needlepoint. When she did, she returned also to a sense of optimism and perspective. A stitch at a time, she began to mend her heart and her life—slowing down, she speeded herself toward recovery and creativity.

I am typing on a manual typewriter, looking at the snow from a window I have curtained in white lace. The white lace reminds me of my mother's love of snow. Maybe because she grew up in a strict wooden farmhouse surrounded by strictly planted fields and level ground, my mother loved a snowy day. Snow brought magic to such landscape, you couldn't see ten miles to the next red barn and silo. You were back to the enchanted land that must have existed before we cleared the great broad- leaf forests of maple and oak. Before you could see too far and not enough. In the winters my mother sat us down at the dining table and taught us to cut snowflakes from folded paper, stiff and white. We would tape them to the windows to have the delight of snow on winter days that were simply dark and short. Reminding me to rest, the snow reminds me of my mother, resting now, in peace.

Sometimes on Sundays in Manhattan, my musical colleague, Emma Lively, and I attend a tiny church where the music consists of nineteenth-century Protestant hymns with uplifting and reassuring literary images. "God is a rock, a harbor, a haven, a sanctuary, a fortress." Above all, God is a place of rest and safety.

TASK
Do Nothing

This task asks that you do nothing—and that you do it thoroughly for fifteen minutes. Here is how to set your "nothing" up. First of all, cue up a piece of music that is both calming and expansive. Secondly, lie down. Stretch out on your back, fold your arms comfortably, and let your imagination speak to you. Close your eyes and follow your train of thought wherever it leads you—into your past, into your future, into some part of your present that you have not been able, due to busyness, to fully enough inhabit. Listen to the music and to your thoughts gently unspooling and repeat to yourself gently this simple phrase, "I am enough . . . I am enough . . ." Stop striving to be more and appreciate what it is you already are.

CHECK-IN

1. **How many days this week did you do your Morning Pages?** If you skipped a day, why did you skip it? How was the experience of writing them for you? Are you experiencing more clarity? A wider range of emotions? A greater sense of detachment, purpose, and calm? Did anything surprise you? Is there a "repeating" issue asking to be dealt with?
2. **Did you do your Artist's Date this week?** Did you note an improved sense of well-being? What did you do and how did it feel? Remember, Artist's Dates can be difficult and you may need to coax yourself into taking them.
3. **Did you get out on your Weekly Walk?** How did that feel? What emotions or insights surfaced for you? Were you able to walk more than once? What did your walk do for your optimism and sense of perspective?
4. **Were there any other issues this week that felt significant to you in your self-discovery?** Describe them.

Discovering a Sense of Proportion

This week inaugurates an ongoing process of
self-definition. As you redraw the boundaries and
limits within which you have lived, you draw yourself
to a fuller size. Coming into ourselves, we sometimes
encounter resistance from those in our immediate
environment. The readings and tasks of this week aim
at bolstering the sense of a realistic self in the face
of difficulty and even discounting.

Identity

All of us are creative. Some of us get the mirroring to know we are creative, but
few of us get the mirroring to know *how* creative. What most of us get is the worried advice that if we are thinking about a life in the arts, we'd better plan to have
"something to fall back on." Would they tell us that if we expressed an interest in
banking?

It could be argued that as people and as artists, we are what we are—however,
we also become ourselves, *all* of ourselves, by having our largeness mirrored back
to us. I think of a scene from the Disney version of *Cinderella,* when the heroine
sees herself in the dress for the first time and realizes she is a beauty. It's like the
scene when the young hero first puts on his military uniform and becomes who he
is. There is a magical "click" of recognition when the looking glass says back, "Yes,
we are what we dream."

Too often we lack such mirrors and such transforming moments. No magic
wand taps our life to make us into what we dream.

Like Rumpelstiltskin, the artist most frequently has to name himself. "I am an artist"—a filmmaker, a composer, a painter, a sculptor, an actor, a something—something the outer world has yet to acknowledge. Often braced by scanty support, an artist's identity is tied to a stubborn seed of inner knowing, a persistent "unrealistic" certainty in the face of sometimes daunting and difficult odds, sometimes doubting and difficult friends, sometimes dismaying and even arid creative circumstances. The fledgling composer composes, the fledgling writer writes, the fledgling painter paints from an inner imperative.

It is Nature who makes our artists for us, though it may be Art who taught them their right mode of expression.

OSCAR WILDE

An ounce of action is worth a ton of theory.

FRIEDRICH ENGELS

As artists, we are often in the ugly-duckling position. We have been born into families that regard us as "odd"— and we come to regard ourselves that way. (Sometimes our families are supportive, but our culture, as a whole, is not.) Our desire to make things and to make something of ourselves in the arts is often reflected back to us as "Who do you think you are?" I call this "growing up in the fun house," where our soul's aspirations are mirrored back to us in a distorted and distorting fashion that makes them appear egotistical and unrealistic: "Don't get too big for your britches," "Who do you think you are?" We often don't really know the answer to that. We know something along the lines of "I think I might be . . ." When we are surrounded by people who either cannot see us or cannot acknowledge what they see, our image blurs. We begin to feel both a certain self-doubt *and* a certain stubborn inner knowing that we may then dismiss as crazy. Part of us knows we're more than they see; part of us fears we're less than we hope. This inner friction is painful.

As artists, when a shoe doesn't fit us, we may try to walk in it anyway. If we are told that it fits, we may start to use our excellent creative imaginations to imagine that it fits. We may further tell ourselves that our own discomfort at the pinching and the pain of a wrong shoe—and a wrong personal and creative identity—is just our "ego." And, we might add, just our "grandiosity." For many of us, declaring ourselves an artist is a "coming-out" process. "I think I am, I think I might be, I really identify with . . . oh, dear God, I think I am." Like any coming-out process, this is turbulent.

If we have been raised to be "officially talented" in one arena and not in another, we can be deaf and blind to the guidance that tries to nudge us toward an expanded role. "You are so musical," Julius was frequently told—but he couldn't hear it. In Julius's world, his concert pianist brother was musical and so was his operatic younger sister. "I'm just the appreciator," Julius would say. "Everybody needs an audience." A full two decades' worth of musical compliments fell on Julius's deaf ears. He wrote lyrics to "help out" his songwriter friends. When they said "You've really got an ear," he ignored them—despite the mounting evidence that he had something musical that kept slipping into expression. Oddly, it took a trip to foreign soil—to a locale where no one knew his famous family and his musical limitations—for Julius to begin writing music. A summer's European vacation became a musical odyssey.

"I swear there was music in the air. It was everywhere," Julius reported back. Away from his family role and definition, Julius began jotting down his "tunes," humming them into a tape recorder, putting them down in rudimentary fashion on children's notation paper. He didn't call himself a composer, a songwriter, or even a musician, but he did call himself happy. "Maybe I am a little musical," he finally conceded. He has been writing music and slowly learning to make music ever since. At this writing he's just started piano lessons, and when his teacher says "With your gifts you could go far," he no longer argues or turns a deaf ear. He just says thank-you and continues his exploration of unwrapping his newly acknowledged musical gift.

It could be argued that as artists we are less made than born, and often into circumstances that mask our identity. The realization often comes like something from a fairy tale—a glimpse in a cracked mirror of a creature they did not know they were. It is here the phrase "takes one to know one" comes into play. It is often an older artist who says "This is what you are, or what you might be."

All of us need and require accurate Believing Mirrors. Believing Mirrors reflect us as large and competent creatively. They mirror possibility, *not* improbability. They ignore "the odds" against us. These mirrors are held by people large enough and expansive enough spiritually not to be threatened by the size and grandeur of another artist shaking out his sizable wings. When I was twenty-two and a fledgling artist, veteran literary agent Sterling Lord took me on. The same year, William McPherson, who later won a Pulitzer of his own, hired me to write for him at *The Washington Post*. These men saw something, and all artists tell stories like mine of older artists who "mysteriously" gambled on them.

I was born at the age of twelve on a Metro-Goldwyn-Mayer lot.

JUDY GARLAND

As artists, we are often grateful and indebted to those who help us know the things we know. An unhappy violist encounters an older composer who suggests a possible affinity for arranging. An arranging career sprouts wings. A singing teacher tells a young pianist, "Don't sing, play!" A photo-shop owner tells a farmer's wife, "You've got quite an eye. I wonder what you could do with a real camera." The answer is "Be a photographer," and that answer, like the film itself, develops over time when exposed to the right encouragement.

Sometimes our encouragement bubbles up unexpectedly in the passing interest of a neighbor, an art-supply clerk, an elderly aunt. Sometimes we come across a magazine article or book, catch a half hour of talk radio in our area of interest, run across a video or an Internet site specializing in our interest. We also experience a phenomenon that I call "inner support." This is an insistent and private inner knowing that tells us we are meant to be, do, or try something—even when there appears to be no outer support.

Richard Rodgers grew up with a doctor father and a brother who also entered medicine. When his own interests ran straight to the Broadway footlights, his family was supportive but unschooled in how to lend that support. Rodgers remembers going to see Saturday matinees of Jerome Kern musicals and knowing he had to grow up to be a composer—but just how to do that was uncharted territory. He tried "regular" high school, and when that failed to compel his interest, he went to the forerunner of Juilliard, where he was the only declared Broadway-bound composer on the premises.

> *No bird soars too high, if he soars with his own wings.*
>
> WILLIAM BLAKE

"Everyone was very kind," he remembers—his classically oriented classmates regarded him with fondness as well as curiosity. They shared his love of music, but after that and beyond that he was on his own, making his way as best he could through friends of his brothers and schoolmates and a certain lucky break involving a family friend. There was no map and, in later years, he would remark that he found his way by "just doing it." That inner itch to "just do it" is the artist's compass.

Although as artists we make maps, we seldom find them. An artistic career does not resemble the linear step-by-step climb of a banker's career trajectory. Art is not linear, and neither is the artist's life. There are no certain routes. You do not become an novelist by moving from A to B to C. Novelists are made from schoolteachers, journalists, and grandmothers. You do not become a composer by attending music school. That might make you a splendid theoretician, an avid structuralist, a discerning critic, but a composer? That is something made by music itself.

Sometimes, in the throes of an identity shift, we say in despair, "Sometimes I don't know who I am," and we are absolutely right. We are correctly sensing that some part or parts of our self are not yet spoken for—or perhaps not yet listened to. We are far more multiple and rich than most of us assume. We are far larger and more colorful, far more powerful and intricate, far more deep and far more high than we often concede.

This is the way it is with artists. The painter becomes a potter in a fit of pique and boredom, only to discover an unsuspected passion. Like Joshua Logan, the actor becomes a director, the writer steps forward to act. None of it is expected, none of it is predicted, and yet, in cozy retrospect, the tracery of what might be called destiny is often clear. "This is what I am. This is what I am meant to do."

> *Curiosity is one of the permanent and certain characteristics of a vigorous intellect.*
>
> Samuel Johnson

It is one of the mysterious happinesses of the creative life that when we become willing to listen, the "still, small voice" seems to grow louder. The web of life is interconnected and an artist's prayer in Omaha is as clearly heard as the same prayer uttered in Manhattan. "Help me become what I am," we pray—and we do.

Cole Porter was from Indiana, not a hotbed of composers, not a musical Mecca, although it now features a marvelous music school. In his day it featured only his mother's gentrified encouragement. From birth Porter was a citizen of the world—and a worldly citizen at that. He knew because he listened to what he "knew." Art begins in the heart. By listening to our heart's desires and listening to them closely, we are not only led into making the art we dream of making but also into the dream of that art being realized on a meaningful scale. Like the farmer in *Field of Dreams,* we must trust enough to build it—whatever "it" is—and trust that "they" will come.

For each of us the "they" will be different. For one it will be the loving recognition from a spouse or admiring neighbor. For another the scholarship to study abroad. For another the photo published locally. For yet another the chance to perform the Christmas solo. It is a spiritual law that no art blooms without an artist also blossoming. Like the wild rose, we may be spotted by the wayside in Nebraska or drifting with a gracious tendril on the weathered wallpaper of a country home. All art calls forth art. When we say "I am," those around us speak up. Some will say "I always knew you were." Some will say "I am too."

Mystics hear voices. The question "Do you hear voices?" is used to sort the sane from the insane. And yet, as artists, we do hear voices and most insistently when we

Guided by my heritage of a love of beauty and respect for strength—in search of my mother's garden, I found my own.

ALICE WALKER

seek the guidance for our art. We are led. We are prompted. We are urged. We are *called*.

We do experience synchronicity—the fortuitous inter-meshing of an inner need with an unexpected and grace-filled outer circumstance. We are forced—and reinforced—to know our path, and the more willing we are to ask what our true creative identity is, the clearer and more unmistak-able our guidance becomes.

As a young, inexperienced writer, I was working at my babysitting job, when my phone rang and a high school colleague inquired whether I would like to take a job at *The Washington Post,* opening letters. I went for the interview. "I hope you don't think you're a writer," the man who hired me dolefully warned. I responded, "Oh, I am a writer. I hope you don't think I'm a journalist." He hired me and in the end we were both right—I became a first-rate journalist, writing for him and covering arts for *The Post.*

This is not to say that we will always believe our guidance or trust it. It is sim-ply to say that the guidance is there. We are made by the Great Creator and we are intended to be creative ourselves. As we seek to cooperate with that intention, the still, small voice that all spiritual paths speak of becomes an ever more present re-ality. When we "go within," there is someone or something there to meet us and it is *not* mute as to our identity.

"I don't know where I got the strength of character to believe in myself," an artist will say. "It was just blind faith." And yet, faith is not blind. It is farseeing and, even as we claim to stumble in believing darkness, we are led inch by inch and hunch by hunch into what we are becoming—and so is our art.

As artists, we often speak of our creations as our "brainchildren," but we forget that our ideas and dreams impregnate us. We are inhabited by a larger life than we know. As we doubt our own identity, that identity is still guiding us, still nudging us to our rightful path. We may doubt our creative viability but, like children who *will* be born, our dreams and desires nudge us forward. Something larger and finer than we know calls us to be larger and finer than we dare. So we act on faith, de-scend into doubt, and watch in amazement as our dreams carry us forward with a knowing of their own. Sometimes our dreams feel born despite us.

As we dare to make our brainchildren reality, our dreams take on flesh and sinew. Not all dreams will come "true," but there will be truth present in all our dreaming. The Great Creator made us. We are ourselves works of art, and as we work to bring forward the art within us, we express our inner divinity. Perhaps this is why so many artists' stories abound with miraculous coincidence and "inspired" hunches. Art may be the finest form of prayer. Making art is quite literally a path "to our Maker." In the act of creation, the creator reveals himself or itself to us and we, too, are revealed to ourselves as something of the divine spark from which we

Pure logic is the ruin of the spirit.

ANTOINE DE SAINT-EXUPÉRY

ourselves are made. It is this primal fact of connection, artist to artist, Great Creator to us as creator, that the truest sense of our own identity is born. We make art not merely to make our way in the world but also to make something of ourselves, and often the something that we make is a person with an inviolable sense of inner dignity. We have answered yes when our true name was called.

TASK
Identify Your Identity

Take pen in hand and answer the following questions by filling in the blanks as rapidly as you can:

1. When I was a small child, I dreamed of growing up to be _____.
2. In my childhood, my interest in what art was encouraged? _____.
3. In my childhood, my interest in what art was discouraged? _____.
4. If I had had more encouragement, I would have probably tried _____.
5. The teacher who helped me see my gifts was _____.
6. The childhood friend who helped me see my gifts was _____.
7. If I had another life, the art form I would start exploring early is _____.
8. The reason it is too late for me in this lifetime is _____.
9. One action I can take in the direction of my childhood love is _____.
10. I now commit to this dream by _____.

For many of us, questions such as these bring up sadness. Schedule an hour's undivided time and take your adult self on some small walking adventure. Do not be surprised if many feelings and intuitions and insights bubble to the surface during this Artist's Date. For many of us, our artists have been waiting to speak with us for years.

Becoming Larger

One of the pivotal problems in creative growth is the question of accurate self-assessment. How do we know how large we can be if we don't know how large we are? Frightened of being big-headed and egotistical, we seldom ask "Am I being too limited, too small for who I really am?" Expansion can be frightening. Growth can feel foreign, even "wrong."

Most of us know the story of the three blind men who are asked to describe an elephant. One feels the trunk and says, "Ah. It is long and thin and wriggly like a snake."

Genius is mainly an affair of energy.

MATTHEW ARNOLD

It is better to ask some questions than to know all the answers.

JAMES THURBER

Another feels the leg and says, "Ah. It is round and sturdy and a great deal like a tree."

The third blind man feels the elephant's side. He says, "Ah. An elephant is very like a wall. . . ."

The joke, of course, is that the elephant was very like all of these things and that its sum is something larger than any of its parts.

As artists, we are often in that elephant's position—a large and complicated creature poorly known to itself and others. Like Alice after she ate the mushroom, we experience shifts in size as hallucinogenic events. One day we will feel very large and competent. The next day we will feel that yesterday's grander size was just grandiosity and that we are really much smaller and more wobbly than we knew. Changing sizes, we go through growing pains, and many of those pains are the pangs of an identity crisis. We may pray about it only to discover prayer is no help: God himself seems to be forging our new identity. The more we pray for it to go away, the stronger it actually becomes.

At age forty-five, after twenty-five years as a writer of words, I suddenly began to hear melody. Music piped through my system like a small chapel flooded with sound by an outsized organ. I found this scary. After all, I "knew" I was a writer, but a musician? This was "too much" to even dream.

When we change sizes creatively, we begin to wonder, *Oh, dear. Now what kind of animal am I?* And usually we begin to ask people to help us to know. This is where we often get in trouble. Many times our friends will know only the trunk part of us, or maybe even just the tail. In other words, what is mirrored back to us may be only the part of our artist a friend is comfortable with or can easily see.

In this way, quite inadvertently we often get miniaturized. We often get fragmented. We often feel "shattered" as we go through change because we need people who can help us to hold a larger and clearer picture of the whole creative animal we are. And, yes, that animal just might be an elephant. Oh, dear!

Understandably, friends can tend to reinforce the you that they see. They can want to hold on to a you that doesn't threaten them and that gives them a comfortable sense of their own size and importance. It is not that they are competitive precisely, it is just that they are used to thinking of you in a certain way—as a screenwriter, say, not a director—and used to thinking of themselves in relationship to you in a certain way. When you start to get bigger, it can scare both you and your friends. They worry about being abandoned. You worry about being grandiose. It is very hard to say to yourself and to others "Actually, I think I might be an elephant. I think I might be much bigger and grander than I thought. But don't worry, elephants are loyal." More often, we are disloyal to our newly emerging parts. We can allow ourselves to be talked out of our possible creative flights. Like *Dumbo,* we can be made to feel ashamed of our newly discovered, magnificent ears.

> *The beginnings of all things are weak and tender. We must therefore be clear-sighted in beginnings.*
>
> MICHEL DE MONTAIGNE

Some of our friends might tend to want to downsize us again to what we were. They have our second, third, and fourth thoughts for us. Other times, we deliberately call those friends who we know will downsize us to who we were before. "You're a perfectly good playwright. *Why* would you want to try writing a movie?" We want to be grounded by their negativity back into our formerly comfortable size and shape. The problem is, we aren't that size, and we aren't that shape. Not any longer.

The tricky part about changing sizes creatively is that we want to keep our old friends but not our old identity. We can keep those who are willing to see more of the elephant. But some of our old friends may need—at least temporarily—to be declared off limits, those who see only the elephant's tail. Their doubts of our new size are a poison for our emerging elephant. An alternative is to find new friends who can see, recognize, and support what it is we are becoming. "Ah, yes, you're an elephant, come over here."

When I suddenly began writing music, I thought I might be crazy, and so did a lot of my friends. I wasn't any longer the Julia any of us knew. Following the muse was one thing—following music, quite another.

"You write *books,*" one friend actually wailed.

"You have such a gift for melody," a new friend, a composer himself, told me—and thank God he did. It can be difficult to hold our belief in the emerging parts of our creative identity. We even more than our friends may fear that we are acting crazily. A new gift can seem too good to be true. We can have a debilitating attack of modesty, asking, "Who do I think I am?" Our behavior may feel crazy, especially if the new talent was unsuspected for many years.

It's part of our cultural tradition to believe and act as if artists are crazy. Is it any wonder we sometimes feel that way ourselves? At our craziest-looking, we are sometimes our most sane. Michelangelo looked pretty strange, flat on his back, near the ceiling. With sweat, plaster, and paint stinging his eyes, not even he may always have enjoyed the comfortable certitude that he was painting a masterpiece. Strapped to a plank, with an arm tired from painting at a contortionist's angle, he, too, may have wondered, *What am I doing?*

> *If a plant cannot live according to its nature, it dies; and so a man.*
>
> HENRY DAVID THOREAU

> *All aglow in the work.*
>
> VIRGIL

What the hell *are* we doing? Who the hell *are* we, really? That is what we are trying to find out, and asking people is one way to do it. Often, older or more experienced artists can say, "Of course you're an actor!" or "Of course you are a writer." They can smell out our identity because it resonates with their own. They've seen baby elephants in the pupa stage before. We may not know what we are, but they do.

My friends now number many musicians who routinely think of me as "just a musician." One, who worked with me on two musicals, knew me two years before he realized I "also" wrote books. So, when a new gift puts in a sudden appearance, remember: If elephants have long memories, they also have long lives. And in a single life you may inhabit many different arts.

Nelson Mandela has remarked that we do no one any favors "hiding our light" and pretending to be "smaller than we are." And yet, calling it modesty, we often try to play small and even stay small. When the creative power moving through us asks us to expand, we would rather contract, calling it more comfortable—it isn't really. We are spiritual beings, and when our spirit grows larger, so must we. There will be no comfortable resting in yesterday's definition of ourselves. It is spiritual law that as the Great Creator is always exploring, experiencing, and expanding through its creations, we must cooperate or feel the pitch of spiritual dis-ease. We can try to play small, but if the universe has big plans for us, we are better off cooperating than resisting. Creativity is God's true nature and our own. As we surrender to becoming as large as we are meant to be, great events can come to pass for us and countless others. In a sense, the size the Great Creator makes of us is none of our business. We work on art and we are the Great Creator's work of art. Perhaps we shouldn't meddle.

> *Many small maken a great.*
> GEOFFREY CHAUCER

TASK
Size Shifting

Although many of us have accomplished estimable things, although we may hold demanding jobs and have extensive professional résumés, when it comes time to look at our own dreams, we are suddenly struck by a debilitating modesty. Our dreams seem too big and too good to be true. We doubt our ability to accomplish them. Use the following quiz to miniaturize your doubts instead of yourself.

Take pen in hand and finish these phrases as rapidly as you can:

1. If I let myself admit it, I think I have a secret gift for _____.
2. If I weren't afraid, I'd tell myself to try _____.
3. As my own best friend, I would really cheer if I saw myself try _____.
4. The compliment I received that seemed too good to be true was _____.
5. If I acted on that compliment, I would let myself try _____.
6. The best person to cheer me on in my secret identity is _____.
7. The person I should carefully *not* tell my dream is _____.
8. The tiniest realistic step I could take in my dreamed direction is _____.
9. The hugest step I could take in my dreamed-of direction is _____.
10. The step I am able to take that feels about right to me is _____.

Sometimes, we are so overwhelmed by our life events, so swamped by the needs and expectations of others and our own feelings of (over)responsibility, we can feel completely lost, wandering in the dark woods of our own life, as hapless and at risk as Hansel and Gretel. *Where am I?* and *Who am I?* we wonder, anguished and often angry. Creating a wish list helps us remember who we are—and take small, concrete, creative actions to reinforce that identity.

Number a blank sheet of paper from 1 to 20. Writing very quickly, finish the phrase "I wish" twenty times. Your wishes will range from large to small, from simple comforts you yourself can provide to large life desires you can begin to outline for later action. This tool *never fails* to point out some small, do-able steps and, even more important, to locate our position in the compass of our own true desires. A wish list might read:

1. I wish my health were more solid.
2. I wish I had a perfume I actually liked.
3. I wish I could see my daughter.
4. I wish workmen would arrive on time or at least call if they're going to be late.
5. I wish I had a pair of nice slacks for walking.

Very often, each "wish" will suggest some small action. For example:

1. Health more solid—step up walking regime and schedule a doctor's visit. Check results of bone density test.
2. Perfume—get to a good department store and "try" a few.
3. See my daughter—schedule a visit from her formally. Call and "really" invite her. Don't just "miss" her.
4. Workmen—call and say, "Where are you? When are you coming?"
5. Slacks—go looking even if you hate shopping. See if you can find a local seamstress if shops and catalogues yield nothing.

A wish list often reveals that we need to take a concrete action for optimism to return. When we are active on our own behalf, we tend to feel less overwhelmed by the needs and wants of others.

The eyes upturned to Heaven are an act of creation.

VICTOR HUGO

Sometimes to "embody" knowledge we must literally get into our bodies. Take the information you have just gleaned from the above task and one more time walk on it. Allow yourself to walk into a new and larger identity in your imagination. It is often there that we first learn to comfortably inhabit a larger self.

Transformation

Art is not linear. Neither is the artist's life, but we forget that. We try to "plan" our life and "plan" our career—as if we could. We also try to plan our growth. This means transformation catches us by surprise. The notion that we can control our path is pushed on us by advertisements and by books and by experts who promise us we can learn to control the uncontrollable. "Empower yourself," magazine headlines trumpet. Seminars and whole expos promise the same illusory goal. And yet, experience teaches that life, and especially life in the arts, is as much about mystery as it is about mastery. To be successful we must learn to follow not the leader but our

> *But not only medicine, engineering, and painting are arts; living itself is an art.*
>
> ERICH FROMM

own inner leadings, the "inspiration" artists have acknowledged through the centuries. "Something" is telling us to make art. We must trust that something.

Because we cannot see where we are really going, because we do not believe that the universe has any plan for us, any worthy plan we might like, our imagination begins to fly frantically around the cage of our circumstances like a cooped-up bird. We want freedom—and we will get it—but we need to get it gently and with grounding.

"I am already successful," we may tell ourselves—and rightly. We may have spent years and considerable energy getting to the top of our profession, only to be struck by a bout of inner restlessness and the unshakable, unpalatable, and unwelcome conviction that our life no longer fits us and we must try to find a new one. Tempted to "ditch everything," we may fantasize running off to the South of France or the north of Africa. We may say to ourselves, "It would be wonderful never to have to do X again," naming something for which we are well paid and well respected. Our professional niche may be so perfect, so carefully chiseled, and so "right," we do not see how we can make any change at all without totally shattering the life we have so carefully built up.

It is a spiritual law that when we are ready to transform, transformation will come to us. We are all conduits for a great creative energy that seeks expression in us and through us. When we yearn to be different, it is not just our restless ego. It is our accurate response to the creative energy within us that is seeking a new venue for expression. We are all creative and we are, in turn, creations. Just as we get restless to make something new, so, too, our creator may be restless to make something new from us. We are not experiencing a bout of hubris, we are actually experiencing a bout of humility. As we let go of our ego's demands to be totally in charge, we slip gently and quietly into a series of changes that we may set in motion through our own hand but experience as the hand of the Great Creator working through us. As we do as inwardly directed, a direction emerges.

> *Nature never did betray the heart that loved her.*
>
> WILLIAM WORDSWORTH

> *It is only by risking from one hour to another that we live at all.*
>
> WILLIAM JAMES

Think of taking yoga and receive a yoga flyer in your mail. Develop an interest in France and spot the ad for a bicycle vacation just after you've said, "Oh, but France would be fattening." Clarify any wish or dream or goal and experience the uncanny feeling that you have somehow magnetized information, people, and opportunities to flow toward you. The spiritual shorthand for this is the phrase "Take one step toward God and discover that God has taken a thousand steps toward you."

Call it "open-mindedness" or "the willingness to be always a beginner," but receptivity and openness characterize the temperament of all great artists, and as we consciously foster these qualities in ourselves, we are given the chance to grow and transform—not perhaps by large and immediate strokes but by small. And each tiny shift can be accompanied by inner quaking. "What's going on? Who am I? What am I doing?" we may inwardly howl as our known identity shifts.

When we begin to see that we can actually change our life, we often panic. Of course we do—prisoners often panic when they realize they can open the door of their cell and walk out "free." "Free" is terrifying after confinement. That's why we panic. "I have no idea who I am!" we gasp.

Often we are surprised to discover that there even *are* new parts to our identity. If we have surrounded ourselves with only one set of mirrors—academics, for example, or corporate types, they may see and reflect back only the parts of ourselves that they can understand. They may not show us anything like our full nature. It's a little like bird-watching. Many specimens look a lot alike until they start to fly, then you see a flash of scarlet and say, "Oh, my, that wasn't a . . . It was a . . ."

When Michael first entered creativity work, he was a lonely and alienated man. Of course he was. A man of quicksilver intelligence and rapier wit, he was ill matched to the tightly laced academic circles he traveled in. His humor was viewed with suspicion; his levity was not welcome. Self-importance was the order of the day, and self-important people liked to make Michael feel like nothing. Once Michael realized he was something, just not the something they were buying, he began to seek colleagues and pastimes where his personal traits were appreciated. Eventually, he navigated out of an academic career and into a creative one. The author now of three books, he is in demand for his lively and good-humored lecture style.

> It requires a direct dispensation from Heaven to become a walker.
>
> HENRY DAVID THOREAU

When we are changing sizes, we feel large, clear, and powerful one day, tiny and defenseless the next. We feel euphoric and then we feel enraged. This is good. This is healthy. It just doesn't feel that way. Our identified self seems false. It is not "false," just incomplete. We have the reverse of the phantom-limb syndrome, where an amputated arm or leg still itches or pinches where there is no arm or leg. Our itching and pinching may presage the sudden appearance of a new creative limb—an arm or leg of a creative career we hadn't anticipated. No wonder we panic! What are these weird sensations? Why are we suddenly interested by performance poetry, Puccini, oil paints?

We may try several sets of creative hats and shoes looking for those that fit. This is normal, natural, and to be encouraged. It is also very threatening to those who want an artistic career to progress in neat linear increments like an academic or professional career. Would that it could. More often we experience awkward growing pains as we grope toward a new identity role.

DO NOT INSIST ON BEING LINEAR.

To avoid panic, it helps to think of change as experimental and to treat ourselves a little like a science project. You will need to try small doses of new identity and see how it wears. Your best gift to yourself in this time will be humor. You do not need to "make yourself over" wholesale. You just need to give the newly discovered and varied parts of yourself some gentle play. And the key word is gentle. Your panic does not mean you *are* crazy, just that you feel it.

DON'T PANIC ABOUT PANIC.

If you are panicked, tell yourself, "Ah! Good sign: I am getting unstuck."

It is spiritual law that we are in the process of becoming what we *already* are—perfect creations of a perfect creator. This means that at our most awkward and ill at ease, we are still in divine order and moving ever closer to God's intention. Faith in this process, a belief that we can change and still experience the unchanging support of the universe, is critical to any sense of comfort as we grow.

The lilies of the field began as buds. We are asked to trust that just as they had a glorious and safe unfolding, so will we. In the natural world, we see butterflies emerge from awkward yet protective cocoons. We must remind ourselves to trust that sometimes we, too, are being protected in our growth. Our erraticism, our ungainliness, our panic— these, too, are natural to the passage of change. The Great Creator experiences all his creation in the throes of shifting identity. The unfolding saga of life on all levels is one of constant transformation, constant changing of form. When we cooperate with our need and desire to grow, we are cooperating with spiritual law. Even before we "ask," our coming needs are clear. The trajectory of our growth is not as lonely as it feels. We are experiencing universal growing pains, and our loneliness, alienation, desperation, and doubt have been felt by many before us, survived by many before us—and answered many times before by the Great Creator who made—and is making—us all.

It takes a long time to bring excellence to maturity.

PUBLILIUS SYRUS

The bravest are the tenderest— The loving are the daring.

BAYARD TAYLOR

Art, and artful living, is a constant collaboration between what we are made from and what we wish to make of ourselves. As we open ourselves consciously to inspiration and instruction as to our truest current form, we are led not only to creativity but also to comfort.

TASK
Shape Shifting

When we are changing sizes and shapes as an artist, we often are afraid of looking foolish. We want to be "finished." We want to be "good at it." We want to read the review that exclaims, "Well worth the creative risk!" Unfortunately, change—and the risks that go with it—invite feelings of vulnerability. Sometimes, simply blurting out our secret dream is a tremendous relief, so that's what we will try to do here on paper. Finish the following phrases as fast as you can:

1. If it weren't so foolish, I'd love to try _____.
2. If it weren't so expensive, I'd love to own a _____.

3. If I were twenty-one again, I would let myself study _____.
4. If I could take the next five years off, all expenses paid, I'd study _____.
5. If it weren't so nuts, I'd love to try _____.
6. If I gave in to my secret dream, I would let myself _____.
7. If I'd had ideal parents and a perfect childhood, I'd be a _____.
8. The dream I have never told anyone is _____.
9. The artist I admire and think I am a lot like is _____.
10. The artist I secretly look down on because I have more talent is _____.

Now, rather than feel foolish over what you have just admitted, take pen in hand again and write a letter from your adult self to your inner artist. Spend at least fifteen minutes writing to your inner artist about the dreams it has revealed. Find a concrete form in which you can take an action on your inner artist's behalf.

CHECK-IN

1. **How many days this week did you do your Morning Pages?** If you skipped a day, why did you skip it? How was the experience of writing them for you? Are you experiencing more clarity? A wider range of emotions? A greater sense of detachment, purpose, and calm? Did anything surprise you? Is there a "repeating" issue asking to be dealt with?

2. **Did you do your Artist's Date this week?** Did you note an improved sense of well-being? What did you do and how did it feel? Remember, Artist's Dates can be difficult and you may need to coax yourself into taking them.

3. **Did you get out on your Weekly Walk?** How did that feel? What emotion or insights surfaced for you? Were you able to walk more than once? What did your walk do for your optimism and sense of perspective?

4. **Were there any other issues this week that felt significant to you in your self-discovery?** Describe them.

Discovering a Sense of Perspective

No man is an island, and our creative unfolding occurs within a distinct cultural landscape. Cultural mythology permeates our thinking about art and artists. The readings and tasks of this week aim at detoxifying your thinking regarding the arts and your place as an artist in our society. Art is tonic and medicinal for us all. As an artist, you are a cultural healer.

Medicine

We are all artists—some of us are declared, accomplished, and publicly esteemed artists. Others of us are the private kind, making artful homes and artful lives and shying away from the public practice or pursuit of our art. Some of us—officially "not artists" and "without a creative bone in our body"—are artists nonetheless because creativity is in our blood. In our DNA.

There is one and only one label that seems useful to me in discussing ourselves. That label is "creative." I have been teaching for twenty-five years. (And making art for longer than that.) I have never, *ever* encountered a person who was not creative in some form. Most often, people are creative in many forms. It is the excess of creative energy, not the lack of it, that is what makes people feel—and get labeled—"crazy."

Sarah, a book writer now, was known to family and friends for many years as "high-strung," "nervous," "nutty," even crazy. She had "too much energy" and it spilled out in making dramas out of daily life. She was always in a pitched battle with something—everything she experienced seemed to be heightened and adversarial. She wasn't precisely depressed, but she did tend to view life in adversarial terms. She moved from therapist to therapist, antidepressant to antidepressant, and "quick-fix" enthusiasm to "quick-fix" enthusiasm. She tried meditation, energy work, and self-help groups. All helped—sort of. Nothing seemed to really make her more comfortable in her skin or in the world we live in. At long last, Sarah began to work with creativity tools. She did Morning Pages, Artist's Dates, and a wide variety of Artist's Way exercises. Her mood lightened. Her energy steadied, and her optimism did not so much return as to make a first appearance on the stage of her adult life.

Creative projects of all stripe began to sprout wings in Sarah's household. She and her children made masks for Halloween, cookies and cut-out snowflakes for Christmas. By New Year's she had a resolution—to try writing the book she had always dreamed of. Carving out a wedge of time for herself during her kids' after-school playtime, Sarah began writing. Her children fielded phone calls: "Mom's writing." And Mom was writing—not only her book, but the distorted dramatics her life had undergone when she had channeled all her creative energy into interpersonal theatrics instead of writing. With plots and dialogue and high stakes on the page, Sarah's tendency toward personal melodrama settled down. Self-expression began to heal her character issues that years of therapy had not touched. At this writing, Sarah has written five books and published four of them. She is not "crazy" anymore, but she is crazy about her work. As she found a way to channel and express her colorful inner selves, her life took on a gentler yet more vibrant shape and her dreams took on Technicolor clarity.

> *Love is exactly as strong as life.*
>
> JOSEPH CAMPBELL

"When I was little, I always wanted to be a writer," she says now. "It's just that for years I didn't think I really could be and so I abandoned my dream and myself." Finding the courage to dream again, Sarah also found that the parts of herself she had misplaced were alive and well—once they were finally welcome.

I have seen incredible creativity practiced by people in their attempts to avoid their own creativity. A therapist might call those contortions neurosis; I call them "creative knots," as in "I will *not* be creative and so I will be miserable." (In a lot of very creative ways.)

Let's start by getting rid of the nasty labels—"crazy," "grandiose," "flaky," "neurotic." Our true nature is *creative*.

Yes, using our creativity is therapeutic, but that is not because we need to be fixed. What we need is to be expressive. What's inside us is not all nasty and horrid and terrifying, not all shame and secrets and neurosis. Our inner world is a complex, exquisite, and powerful play of colors, lights, and shadows, a cathedral of consciousness as glorious as the natural world itself. This inner wealth is what the artist expresses.

The Great Creator lives within each of us. All of us contain a divine, expressive spark, a creative candle intended to light our path and that of our fellows. We are shiny, not tarnished; large, not small; beautiful, not damaged—although we may be ignorant of our grace, power, and dignity.

The human being, by definition, is a creative being. We are intended to make things and, in the old phrase, to "make something of ourselves." When we lose interest in ourselves and our lives, when we tell ourselves our dreams don't matter or that they are impossible, we are denying our spiritual heritage. When we do this, we become depressed and drained, even physically ill. We become snappish, irritable, high-strung. We call ourselves neurotic—this is not the case. We are not neurotic, we are miserable—miserable because we have stifled our creative selves. Those selves are alive—well—and too large for the cage we have put them in, the cage we call "normal."

> *For good and evil, man is a free creative spirit.*
>
> JOYCE CARY

> *Out of your vulnerabilities will come your strength.*
>
> SIGMUND FREUD

In our culture we are trained to hide ourselves and punished when we show ourselves. So we hide ourselves from others and from ourselves. It is the hiding of our true nature that makes us feel or act crazy.

We are trained to pick at ourselves, to rectify ourselves, to label ourselves. Most of our religions emphasize the notion of original sin. Most—not all—of our therapies center on our wounds and not on our gifts. Some, not all, of our 12-Step recovery can center on our character defects and not our assets.

Most of us carry what I call "word wounds"—descriptions of certain qualities that have been conveyed to us as pejorative. I for example have been called both "intense" and "hyperfocused." In our culture we have demonized creativity. We are scared of it and by it. We tell scary stories about artists and how broke, nuts, crazy, drunk, selfish they are. In our culture we are afraid of our creativity. We think it's some nitroglycerin compound that could blow us all up. Nonsense.

Practicing our creativity is healing. Not because we are sick but because we are essentially well. As we express our intrinsic nature, which is beautiful and specific, particular and original, we experience a healing transformation less in ourselves than in our relationship to the world. We are not at fault. We are not powerless. We are very large, and in expressing this truth, healing occurs. What is healed is the rift between our spiritual stature and our mistaken perception of ourselves as flawed.

Creativity is medicine. It is not dangerous or egotistical. It is life-affirming and essential. The more we use it, the more steadily and readily and easily we use it. The more we ground it and regularly access it, the better off we are. The "healthier" we are. Humor and acceptance enter the picture. Far more than self-scrutiny or self-correction, self-expression may be the key to a much more synthesized and effective sense of self.

Yes, we are sometimes unhappy. But this is not because we are neurotic and need to be "adjusted" to the existing norm. This is because we need to express ourselves—which will then change both us *and* the existing norm. Creative change begins in the heart. When we start within ourselves and move outward, expressing what we love and what we value, life gets better, we feel better, and the world gets healthier too.

> *Most of us are about as eager to be changed as we were to be born, and go through our changes in a similar state of shock.*
>
> JAMES BALDWIN

The tools and process of my book *The Artist's Way* are taught by many therapists. Often, they facilitate Artist's Way groups and report back "miracles of healing." To my eye, the healing is no miracle. The health was always there, waiting to be discovered and expressed as creativity.

I am not interested in debating with people over the reality of mental illness. What I want to focus on is the reality of our considerable mental health. Our society, even our world, might be "sick," but we carry within us the exact medicine to heal it and ourselves.

That medicine is creativity.

TASK

Bless Your Blessings

One of the most medicinal tasks we can undertake is a simple walk. It is difficult to remain mired in negativity and depression when we are "shaking it out" a little.

Walking with an eye to the positive can take a gentle vigilance. As a form of medicine for ourselves, we can consciously turn our thoughts to the ancient practice of practicing gratitude—a footfall at a time. Take yourself out-of-doors and set a goal of a simple twenty-minute walk. Aiming toward the outer world, allow your inner world to fall into a brighter perspective by consciously—and concretely—enumerating your life's blessings. People, events, situations—any of these may be cause for gratitude. As you warm to your task of focusing on the good in your life, both your heart and your step will lighten.

Art Is Therapeutic, Not Therapy

When we are blocked creatively, we often experience ourselves as miserable—and we then wonder, "How neurotic am I?" Thinking that therapy will supply that answer, or at least alleviate our misery, we often turn to therapy only to find that our misery continues unabated. Of course it does. We are miserable not because we are neurotic but because we are creative and not functioning in our creativity. Therapy may help us to "understand" our blocks. We do better to simply get over them. Art is therapeutic. It is *not* therapy. Therapy aims at transformation through understanding. Art aims at transformation more directly. When we make a piece of art about something we don't understand, we come to understand it, or, at least, our relationship to it through our own experience—which is more full-bodied than merely cerebral. In this sense, art "works" therapeutically whether we understand it or not.

> *I am still learning.*
> MICHELANGELO

Therapy aims at disarming emotion, placing wounded emotions "in perspective." Art, on the other hand, uses wounded emotions—or any other fuel handy—not to alter our perception of an existing outer reality but to alter that reality through a reality we express. Handel's complex, ecstatic, exultant, and conflicted feelings and perceptions about God created *The Messiah. The Messiah,* in turn, helps others to understand God differently.

Harper Lee wrote one book, *To Kill a Mockingbird,* in 1960. She lives in Manhattan now and still has no plans to write another. And why should she? With one small and "simple" book, she accomplished a great swath of healing. Anyone reading her work comes away from it more whole, more compassionate, more in touch with the interior life of his own vulnerable, childlike self.

Books, poems, plays, symphonies—they aim at healing the soul. They take human emotions and human concerns and, through the alchemy of art, make us somehow feel better about all of it—and us.

Music produces a kind of pleasure which human nature cannot do without.

CONFUCIUS

The first and the simplest emotion which we discover in the human mind is curiosity.

EDMUND BURKE

Bernice, a Jungian therapist, often sends her patients to music rather than introspection. "Music touches something higher in us," she explains. Music may touch something higher more directly, but all of the arts touch something that is beyond the ordinary machinations of life. It is the overview, this "something higher and more," that makes even the most homespun art somehow therapeutic. Baking a good pie, one feels better for having baked it. The same is true of writing a simple song or even dashing off a quick poem to tell your child she is beloved. When the child calls to say "I got your letter," she is also saying "And it made me feel cherished." Feeling cherished, we feel healed, and, perhaps as much as anything else, the act of making art can be described as the act of cherishing our experience, feelings, and perceptions. This, we are told, is how God regards all of creation. Perhaps it is in this careful attention that we contact the divine spark when we create. Contacting that divine spark is always therapeutic.

Healing is a somewhat automatic by-product of self-expression, not a goal per se. This fact can confuse some people—particularly therapists, who want to "understand" the workings of a process that is both mysterious and spiritual. Intellectually, many doctors and therapists do know that something heals beyond their own skill, but understandably, they want to know what that something is, and control it as part of the healing process that they can administer like a good medicine. Therapy and creative recovery are not mutually exclusive, but they do function differently and come out of two very different sets of assumptions.

We may feel different after making something. We may see something in a different light, but that inner shift of focus comes from expressing what it is we do feel and see rather than striving to feel and see things differently, with more balance and less sting. For an artist—and for the artist in each of us—talking about something may be less useful than painting about it, writing about it, or composing about it. Merely cerebral understanding does not heal. Nor, contrary to many therapeutic models, does the simple expression of emotion, verbally or even physically. Humans are complex, creative beings, and when we create something that expresses our own complexity, we arrive at an inner distillate of clarity through our own *creative* inner process. Many therapists, and many art teachers for that matter, are controlling and intrusive in their premature questioning and direction. They encourage creative clients to cerebrate. This is often the last thing we need. Therapy aims at making us normal. Art aims at expressing our originality. The norm has nothing to do with it.

Enlightened therapies urge us to "accept how we feel." Art teaches us to *express* how we feel and so alchemize it. Art acknowledges that feelings are mutable and that we contain the power to mutate the dross of our wounds into the ore of art. In this sense, art gives us the ability to *always* move out of the victim position. Therapy adjusts us to the world. Art adjusts the world itself.

"Art" is a form of the verb "to be." It is not mere cleverness to point this out. At its core, life is artful and creative, each moment contains choice as much as each brush stroke in a painting, each syllable in a poem, each note in a melodic line. It is because of this, its insistence on choice, choice, choice, that art demolishes the victim position. When bullying life demands of us some injustice: "You want to make something of it?" the artful answer is yes.

When we make something of "it," whatever "it" is, we make something else of it. Art allows us to live freely, even within our restlessness, like Dylan Thomas's green sea singing in its chains. Holocaust victims scratched butterflies on the walls of concentration camps. That assertive creative act spoke plainly: "You cannot kill my spirit." At its core, art is triumphant. At its best, therapy is acquiescent: I accept my influences and accommodate myself to their result. Therapy constructs a self; art presupposes and asserts a self. At bottom, art is rebellious: You cannot name me. I am more than the sum of my parts.

In therapy we seek to examine the impact of those in our life and our resultant wounds and adjustments. We see ourselves in relation to person X or event Y. Our inner workings are understood and understandable in theoretical terms. We deduce why we are what we are. And we often deduce from a flimsy set of stock characters—the nuclear family. Life, even the most impoverished, is far richer than that in its mysterious variables and forces.

Art works in primary colors. We dip our pen, our brush, our hand, directly into the self. "I see it this way," we say. We are the origin of our art. It rises like a river head, asking no one's permission. Art says, "I am." Therapy

> *I hate that aesthetic game of the eye and the mind, played by these connoisseurs, these mandarins who "appreciate" beauty. What is beauty, anyway? There's no such thing. I never "appreciate," any more than I "like." I love or I hate.*
>
> PABLO PICASSO

says, "They were, therefore I am." Therapy may be turbulent, but it is tame compared to art. Therapy may be rewarding, but it makes something of what we *were,* while art makes something of what we *are.* Freud complained, "Whenever I get somewhere, a poet has been there first." Of course. An artist flies direct.

Art is alchemy. It turns the ore of life into gold. Learning to make art rather than drama from a heated imagination is a skill best learned early and practiced fully. If we are to make living art—*and an art of living*—we must be willing to stand knee-deep in the rapids of the human condition, accepting that life, by its nature, is turbulent, powerful, and mysterious. It is the artist's bet that life is better encountered and expressed than diminished and discounted by trying to "fix it" therapeutically. It is the artist's conviction that understanding something intellectually is often far less healing than making something artistically transformative from our shattered selves.

> *Let the world know you as you are, not as you think you should be, because sooner or later, if you are posing, you will forget the pose, and then where are you?*
>
> FANNY BRICE

"Keep the drama on the page, the stage, the canvas, the film," an artist learns. It is there that the monsters and beauties, the jewels and junkyard memorabilia of the imagination, can be sorted, shaped, and transformed into art. Dexterity at living with the dramatic shadow play of the creative mind comes with time. A younger artist may mistake intense emotion for a cue to act in his outer life, not his inner one. When turbulent emotions pinch the raw nerves of the creative psyche, there is a choice: Act on this, or act out on this.

With art as our alchemy, the pain of the lost lover becomes the pang of the love song. The misery of a misplaced sense of direction becomes the frantic, seething chords of a dissonant jazz anthem. "Nothing is wrong, nothing is wasted, nothing is neurotic, nothing is disowned, everything is possible in art" must become the artist's credo.

TASK

You Want to Make Something of It?

Although therapy may have loftier goals, its most common use is to arrive at a different accommodation of our grudges. "They" did "that" and so we feel bad. The aim of most therapy is that we feel less bad. We come to "understand" why "they" may have done "that" and we make our peace with it. Art is more anarchistic.

Art is more aggressive and more assertive than therapy. It is an action, not a reaction. Dipping directly into ourselves as source, we create something new that would not exist without us as its origin. For this reason art is affirming in a way that therapy is not.

Set aside a stack of magazines with pictures. Buy a piece of poster board and some glue. Locate a scissors, tape if you want it, and give yourself a full hour's time. Scan your consciousness for a situation you would like to understand more fully.

Do you have a mesmerizing personal relationship that seems patently destructive yet you cannot end it? Do you have a tyrant boss to whom you are in feudal bondage? Do you have a bond that is so close to someone that you feel joined at the hip? Are you homesick for the wide open spaces of the West but are living in the vertical canyons of Manhattan? Any of these dilemmas make excellent fuel for the task of collaging.

Holding this theme loosely in mind, spend twenty minutes pulling images that attract you and *may* feel connected to your theme. Spend another twenty minutes arranging your images and gluing them in order. Now spend a final twenty minutes writing about what you've found.

What you discover through this process may surprise and intrigue you. A relationship that seems punitive and one-sided may be revealed to be a source of creative fire. A longing for a "greener" life and environment may be overridden by an actual love of urban images and energy. What you find through making a collage may not even address the specific topic you "worked" on. Instead, a far larger and more holistic sense of healing may emerge.

Anger

When we are angry at being overlooked, it is not arrogance and grandiosity. It is a signal that we have changed sizes and must now act larger.

Very often when we feel small and unheard, it is not because we *are* small and unheard but because we are acting small and unheard. We are not intended to be small. Often we are cornered not into being powerless and puny—as we feel—but into being large.

The problem here is our perspective. When we are angry "out of all proportion," that is a very accurate phrase.

> One cool judgment is worth a thousand hasty counsels. The thing to do is supply light and not heat.
>
> WOODROW WILSON

We have lost a sense of our true size and power, and the intensity of our feelings makes us feel "hopping mad," another telling phrase, as our mental image of ourselves becomes—or can become—very cartooned. We experience ourselves as puny and tiny and futile. The size of our anger has dwarfed our perspective and our personality. This is because we do not realize that the power we are perceiving is within us as the power for change. When we are "unspeakably" angry, what we really are is large and unspoken. We are not yet speaking in a way that gives voice and direction to our power. When we feel impotent with rage, we are actually potent with rage—we simply have not yet seen how to effectively use our anger as the fuel that it is.

> *Advice is what we ask for when we already know the answer but wish we didn't.*
>
> ERICA JONG

When we cannot sleep, when we are "eaten alive" by an inequity or slight, the monster that is eating us is our anger over our own displaced power. We are very powerful. That personal power is what we are feeling as a "towering rage," and that artificially externalized wall of rage can make us feel small and puny until we figure out that it is a power within ourselves and not the sheer wall of the "odds" stacked against us. The odds are against us until we are "for" ourselves.

Anger asks us to step up to the plate for ourselves and for others. It points to a path we are trying to avoid. Often we try to act "modest," and that is partially a refusal to be as large, clear, and articulate as we really are. Anger signals us that we are being called to step forward and speak out. We hate this and so we fantasize retreating instead.

Rage at a bully or at a bullying situation is actually a wonderful sign. Once we own it, it is our own rage at allowing ourselves and others to be bullied. If it is our own, we can use it. Yes, this rage feels murderous and distorting, but it is actually a needed corrective. If our rage is that large, so are we.

Our reticence can make us angry. We "know" we should speak up for ourselves but sometimes find we just "cannot."

We do not need to shout, but we do need to act and to speak our truth. A word about that order: Actions do speak louder than words, and so we must take actions that articulate our creative values.

A writer angered by a string of rejections might self-publish—as I did and will always do. A musician frustrated by the "state of the art" in the recording business can more cost-effectively cut a disc, DAT, or a small CD for far less money and energy than indulging in years of therapy to "accept" his feelings of frustration. A proactive creative act is far less expensive than the health problems and life-shortening caused by stewing in feelings of resentment and bitterness—or the even more expensive waste of retreating from the fray entirely.

Luckily for all of us, artists are stubborn. The best-selling author advised by her psychiatrist that she should aim for a secretarial career kept writing (me). The famous filmmaker fired from a documentary project kept making movies (Martin Scorsese). The talented actress cut from Boston University's acting program kept acting (Oscar-winner Geena Davis). The lawyer who "should have" spent his time "on his cases" won the argument that he should write as well (John Grisham). Something inside spoke clearly enough that these artists listened, and a few outer "someones" whispered, or shouted, that they, too, knew who we were. These discerning outer voices affirm our identities and alter our destinies.

Sometimes when we get angry enough at being treated as if we are small, we get brave enough to trust those who think—and say—we might be big. One slight too many and we finally say our true name, but we "swallow" a lot of anger first.

> *I'm not a teacher: only a fellow-traveler of whom you asked the way. I pointed ahead—ahead of myself as well as you.*
>
> GEORGE BERNARD SHAW

> *No man can know where he is going unless he knows exactly where he has been and exactly how he arrived at his present place.*
>
> MAYA ANGELOU

Center stage belongs to those who are willing to move there, some talented and some not. Rather than angrily decrying the behavior and lack of talent of the "arrogant spotlight-grabbers," we need to use our anger to turn our own voltage up a little despite our fears. We need to say our own names as artists. When we do, we feel self-respect. Self-respect comes from the Self. The market will say what it will, but we need to say our own name as artists.

Anger is a call to action. It is challenging and important to let our light shine. It is important to name ourselves rather than wait for someone else to do it, or pretend that we can continue to bear it when we can't. When we complain that others do not take ourselves and our values seriously, we are actually saying that *we* don't. If our aesthetics matter so much to us, we must act on them in a concrete and specific form.

This is why a failed musical comedy means write another song. This is why a bad review of your novel means write a short story, a poem, anything that signals to your inner world that you still believe in yourself. When we fail to endorse ourselves as artists, others also can undercut us. When we endorse and support ourselves as artists—concretely, in some small form—then others may misread us or mishandle us, but they cannot castrate us or our self-respect.

Anger is a profoundly powerful fuel that we can use to make art and to make more artful lives. When we deny our anger or fritter it away in complaints, we are wasting precious fuel and precious clarity. Anger is a searchlight. It shows us our moral terrain and it shows us the damage we feel done to that terrain by others. It shows us, above all, our choices. If something angers us, we can try to "make do" with stuffing our anger or we can "make something of it" in the literal sense of a piece of art.

Anger causes poems, plays, novels, films. Anger causes symphonies and paintings. When we think of our anger as something that should be excised or denied rather than alchemized, we risk neutering ourselves as artists.

> *In the beginning was the Word. Man acts it out. He is the act, not the actor.*
>
> HENRY MILLER

Anger asks us for reservoirs of strength that we often do not know we have. We are galvanized into heroics that we did not feel were a part of our emotional repertoire. We act larger than we feel and end up being larger than we were.

A highly acclaimed classical musician angered by the narrow gauge of highly produced digitalized recordings goes out on a limb to encourage a young and talented musician. *The club is too small, too elite, too canned,* the master musician thinks angrily, and throws the door open a little by lending his prestigious name to a more risky project. Anger has opened his heart and his mind.

> *Everything vanishes around me, and works are born as if out of the void. Ripe, graphic fruits fall off. My hand has become the obedient instrument of a remote will.*
>
> PAUL KLEE

Anger is not comfortable. The focused use of it to create art requires emotional maturity we must often reach for to muster—and yet we can. When we do, our world changes by a jot. Anger sometimes signals not our immaturity but our maturity, our seasoned judgment, and outraged temper into form for the sake of healthy change.

TASK

Use Anger as Fuel

Most of us may feel we "get" angry, but we seldom feel we "are" angry. The tool you are using now is a startling one in this regard: You are probably angrier than you think, and that blocked or unused anger is a powerful source of creative fuel once you are willing to acknowledge it and tap it more directly.

Take pen in hand. Number from 1 to 50. List 50 angering grievances from the historical to the hysterical. Be as petty as possible. You will be astonished at what tiny things "still" anger you. For example:

1. I'm angry the Catholic Church dropped Latin.
2. I'm angry our church uses bad folk songs.
3. I'm angry the candy shop closed.
4. I'm angry my sister is fighting with my brother.

After you have written for a while, you will notice the question popping up: "What can I do about it?" This question pops up like toast. We do not like being victims of so much anger, and so we intuitively look for a positive solution. Jot down the solutions as they come to you. At exercise's end, you will have cleared fifty negatives and come up with a list of do-able positives. Do some of them, using your formerly stuck anger as fuel.

Cartography

The artist is a cartographer; he maps the world. The world within him, and the world as he sees it. Sometimes that world is very strange. Sometimes our maps are rejected—seen as unrealistic or distorted or unlikely. Magellan sailed with maps made largely of conjecture—as artists, we are always conjuring and conjecturing on the shape of what we see and "know."

A great work of art focuses the imagination of a vast audience on a previously inchoate problem. *The Grapes of Wrath* showed us the Depression. *One Flew Over the Cuckoo's Nest* showed us our democratic horror at institutions run amuck. All novels are "novel" because they are seeking to tell us something new. Known or unknown, famous or anonymous, all art is an attempt to map the territory of the heart.

> *Whatever creativity is, it is in part a solution to a problem.*
>
> BRIAN ALDISS

Let me say it again: As artists, we are cartographers. We draw from our own experience, and we *draw* our experience, sketching in the territory we have encountered and others will encounter. The perceptions of a novel or a musical composition may predate their consensus map of consciousness of their own times. For this reason, artists must have courage, even heroism, to state what they see and hear.

Early in his career, Beethoven enjoyed personal and professional favor. His work was widely heard and widely revered. He was hailed as a large creative talent. His life was sunny and his creative vistas expansive. As his life wore on, Beethoven's cultural fortunes shifted. His work was considered less accessible, too abstract and demanding. As his personal battle with hearing loss deepened his isolation, he was plunged into a harrowing, nearly suicidal depression. He was caught on the horns of a dilemma: He was called to write music and his talent as a musician was called into question by the music he wrote. He could not be true to himself and go back to earlier forms. There seemed to be no audience for his musical work except himself and God. Contemplating suicide, Beethoven chose life and, in one famous letter to God, vowed to continue to write music no matter how ill received it was. He would write "for the glory of God alone." The resultant music, too modern and advanced for Beethoven's peers, has come to be considered masterworks centuries later. A visionary and a leader of musical thought and form, Beethoven wrote for our times and not his own.

Thou didst create the night,
but I made the lamp.
Thou didst create clay,
but I made the cup.
Thou didst create the deserts,
mountains and forests,
I produced the orchards,
gardens and groves.
It is I who made the glass out
of stone,
And it is I who turn a poison
into an antidote.

SIR MUHAMMAD IQBAL

Late Beethoven told us more of our century than of his own. As artists, we draw not only consensus reality but the lineaments of approaching reality. This is why Ezra Pound dubbed us "the antennae of the race." This is why our perceptions are so often discounted as "not in reality," when in fact they are a part of a reality that we are not yet in.

George Orwell told us more of the future than *1984*. George Gershwin told us more of the urban—and urbane— revolution than any demographics.

As artists, we explore the territory of the human heart, braving the dark woods to report to our human tribe that a trail can be found, and we will survive. As artists, we are scouts of consciousness, trailblazers for community and culture.

Of necessity, artists report dangers we might wish to ignore. Like the scout who returns to report an unpassable gorge requiring an unforeseen detour, the artist may report perceptions that feel unbearable to others. From Sam Shepard to Samuel Beckett, the artist may encounter and encapsulate the loneliness of missed connections. The heart of darkness *is,* all too often, the human heart. As artists, we must muster self-respect and compassion for the difficulty of our own calling. The great adventure of the creative life lies not only in the territory seen but in the fact that much of what we see has not been seen before. Human stories are as old as the earth, but human consciousness is always the edge of the known world, like fine telescopes focused on deep space. As artists, we routinely step beyond, straining our eyes and vision to discern and record the shapes heaving into birth from darkness.

We function on nerve, daring, stamina, vision, and persistence. Mountains appear where no mountains are known to be. Lakes shine in the light where there are no lakes. The artist does not see as others see. His imagination yokes together disparate images, some fanciful, some frightening, some enlightening. The artist's inner world may resemble a fairy tale—there are ogres, trolls, monsters, witches. Everything is heightened, intensified, dramatized. This pitch of intensity forges art from the raw materials of the imagination. As an artist matures, so does his skill at encompassing such pitched emotion.

Does this mean that we cannibalize our lives? Emphatically, no. It does mean that we own them, shaping and reshaping the acreage of our personal experience into a philosophical habitat that expresses accurately our view of the world.

"Look at it this way," the artist says, and shows the world what his inner world has revealed to him. Franz Kafka was Kafka before we had the term Kafka-esque. George Orwell predated Orwellian. Each of us carries an internal lens through which we view the world. The willingness to reveal what that lens sees is what determines an artist. And an artist must continually open that lens to take in new and wider realities.

Make visible what, without you, might perhaps never have been seen.

ROBERT BRESSON

A woman in her mid-fifties gets up daily to write a song. She has been musically inclined since childhood, but it took her until her forties to muster the emotional courage to express her songs in more than her inner ear.

"I think I am too old for this," she tells me, yet her year's moneys are budgeted to include the expense of cutting a CD of her work. She could be buying expensive clothes or meals out or gifts for her children, but she has learned that what matters most to her is the process of expressing her heart through art.

"If I don't tell my parents' story, who will?" a writer asks me, explaining a decade's diligence on a long family saga.

Come forth into the light of things, Let nature be your teacher.

WILLIAM WORDSWORTH

"My computer class is very exciting," a woman artist tells me. "I am so much less limited now in the ways that I can see. I was defining myself so narrowly as a fine artist."

For each of these artists, the act of making art is the act of revelation. First to themselves and then to the world: "Listen! Look! It looks like this!" they are saying.

Like Audubon sketching his birds, great art is sometimes made by the simple act of witness rendered to the world: "I saw this beautiful thing." Of course, not all of what we see as artists is beautiful, nor do we render it beautifully, yet just as a crude and handmade map gives us a sense of direction, so, too, the mapmaking of art points the human compass straighter toward home.

TASK
Mapping Your Interests

Maps begin as the roughest of sketches, approximately whole continents. We can similarly sketch in our areas of creative interest, working in the loosest terms.

Take pen in hand. Finish the following:

Five topics that interest me are

1.
2.
3.
4.
5.

Five people who interest me are

1.
2.
3.
4.
5.

Five art forms that interest me are

1.
2.
3.
4.
5.

Five projects I could try out are

1.
2.
3.
4.
5.

When we map out our "coulds" instead of our "shoulds," we shift from the realm of probability into the more interesting realm of possibility. When we name and claim an interest, we seem to magnetize that area, drawing to ourselves people, places, and things that speak to our emerging interests.

CHECK-IN

1. **How many days this week did you do your Morning Pages?** If you skipped a day, why did you skip it? How was the experience of writing them for you? Are you experiencing more clarity? A wider range of emotions? A greater sense of detachment, purpose, and calm? Did anything surprise you? Is there a "repeating" issue asking to be dealt with?

2. **Did you do your Artist's Date this week?** Did you note an improved sense of well-being? What did you do and how did you feel? Remember, Artist's Dates can be difficult and you may need to coax yourself into taking them.

3. **Did you get out on your Weekly Walk?** How did that feel? What emotions or insights surfaced for you? Were you able to walk more than once? What did your walk do for your optimism and sense of perspective?

4. **Were there any other issues this week that felt significant to you in your self-discovery?** Describe them.

Discovering a Sense of Adventure

This week you are asked to jettison some of your personal baggage. The essays and tasks are aimed at helping you claim a greater sense of freedom. You will be asked to consciously experiment with open-mindedness. You will dismantle many unconscious mechanisms that may have impeded your artistic expression. You will focus on self-acceptance as a route to self-expression.

Adventure

Too often, we think we know what we love. It is more accurate to admit we know only some of what we love, and that the "sum" of what we love can grow larger. This requires an open mind.

An hour's adventure in a nineteenth-century photography exhibit may do more to spark your visual artist than six months in a sensible computer-graphics program. A visit to the zoo may mean more to your creative animal than a virtuous visit to an art supply store.

Humans are by nature adventurous. Watch a toddler expand his territory a wobbly step at a time. Watch a teenager test curfew. Watch an eighty-year-old grandmother sign up for an art tour of Russia. The soul thrives on adventure. Deprived of adventure, our optimism fails us. Adventure is a nutrient, not a frivolity. When we ignore our need for adventure, we ignore our very nature. Often we do exactly that, calling it "adulthood" or "discipline." When we are too adult and too disciplined, our impish, childlike innovator yearns to rebel. Too often, that rebellion takes the form of a stubborn,

> *To die will be an awfully big adventure.*
>
> SIR JAMES M. BARRIE

self-involved crankiness rather than an exuberant and expansive risk. Risks, we tell ourselves, are too risky. When we avoid risk, we court depression.

Depression is emotional quicksand. Once we get stuck, it's hard to pull free. Our struggles exhaust us and depress us further. It is easier to avoid depression than overcome it, and, yes, we avoid it by taking risks. If we remember that we need to court, woo, and romance our creative selves, we begin to have a notion of what sort of risk best serves us.

Adele lives in Manhattan. On her good days she loves the vigor of the city. She finds the rich red tones of the buildings on her Upper West Side street adult and invigorating. She loves the window boxes and the glimpses of richly painted rooms beyond. On her bad days Adele feels trapped by the city. She is a westerner at heart and she longs for wide-open spaces and wide horizons. The city feels claustrophobic. "Tame." And so, on her worst days, Adele calls the Claremont Riding Academy, reserves a horse, and goes riding.

Claremont is not the wide-open spaces, but it does have horses and the stench of horse sweat and it is somehow so daring—three stories of horses wedged into a Manhattan brownstone—that it feels anarchistic and rebellious even to crack open the door and step into the hidden world of horseflesh and leather. And so, when Adele feels too dull and too domesticated, she gets on a horse and feels like she's sitting a lot taller in the saddle, living in a world of risk and adventure.

Caroline, a hothouse flower, needs to have a taste of luxury when her world feels too much like a treadmill. She has taught herself that few things lift her spirits more rapidly than a visit to a really good florist shop, where beauty in all its delicacy and daring can be found intertwined amid wicker baskets and faux vertigris vases. Although she seldom spends much—settling on a truly shocking color of Gerber daisy can give her tiny kitchen a transfusion of color—Caroline always feels her money and time is well spent when she buys herself not merely a bouquet but the optimistic sense that this earth is, or can be, a garden of earthly delights.

> It's like driving a car at night. You never see further than your headlights, but you can make the whole trip that way.
>
> E. L. DOCTOROW

Adam, a mild-mannered writer, gets his sense of worthy risk by taking himself to travel stores. He cannot always up and leave his job, but he can take daring mental vacations. He sometimes buys a guidebook, *Most-Used Egyptian Phrases*, and learns a few key words to get him to and from a pyramid. Other times he plans a trip he actually can take, *A Pocket Guide to Day Trips in the Greater Boston*

Area. What is pivotal to him is not so much leaving life as he knows it as knowing that he could.

"Most of the time my life is fine, but I need to know that I have psychic permission to get away from it all," Adam explains. A stop in a sports store to look at a new model cross-training shoe, a pamphlet from the bike store about a bicycle vacation in France, these imaginary risks add a needed risk to Adam's Mr. Nice Guy persona. "And I love Indiana Jones movies," he adds.

The creative imagination is a will-o'-the-wisp. Wooed best by enticement and not by aggressive assault, the imagination responds to being coaxed and cajoled. Just as in romance, too serious, too fast, and the fun fizzles out. We need to flirt with an interest, approach it with a sidelong glance. Children's books might be a better first date with a new interest than enrolling in a master's program. If you want to write a novel about an automotive inventor and need to know how an automobile engine works, a good children's book may tell you just what you need to know, while a scholarly tome on the laws of physical dynamics may tell you just enough to squelch your budding interest entirely. More is very nice as something to look forward to and not so nice as part of the phrase "More than I could handle or absorb." Adventures should be manageable, not overwhelming.

It is not so much that the creative imagination is shallow; rather, it is selective. Dumping a huge load of facts into your imagination can stall its gears rather than start them humming. A biographer sifts the truth from a quarry full of facts. A poet or novelist intuits a quarry full of truth from a single fact. Too many facts, too fast, and the artistic attic gets both stuffy and overstuffed. The imagination feels stifled, not stimulated. Creative heights are best reached when we are not overburdened by an overly intellectual freight of facts.

It is one of the paradoxes of the sustained creative life that the more lightly we take ourselves, the more serious work we will probably be able to do. The more we bear down on ourselves, the more constricted we will feel, and the more vulnerable we will be to creative injury.

> *To create, you must empty yourself of every artistic thought.*
>
> GILBERT
> (OF GILBERT AND GEORGE)

Very often, consummate artists are consummate enthusiasts. Director Mike Nichols breeds Arabian horses. Coppola grows great grapes. Novelist John Nichols is an avid bird-watcher. Sculptor Kevin Cannon plays formidable jazz guitar. They have taken a cue from the Great Creator and developed a playful appetite for life itself.

If you play softball once a week, it's a little easier to handle the curve ball of a vicious review. If you let yourself bake an apple pie or two, it's a little harder to think the artist's life, or life in general, is so rotten. If you go salsa dancing once a week, or even once a month, it's a little harder to think that the purpose of your art is to make you rich and famous, and that if it hasn't, it's worthless and so are you.

In light of all this, I am not sure where we got the idea that in order to be "real" artists we had to do things perfectly. The minute we see that word "perfect" (and I think critics are the ones who drag it in the door), spontaneity goes out the window. We get so sure that we can't be a great composer that we never let ourselves write our kids a goofy lullaby or play improvisational noodles at the piano. We're so respectful of "great" art that we always, chronically, sell ourselves short. We're so worried about whether we can play in the "big leagues" that we refuse to let ourselves play at all.

Here's what I like about God: Trees are crooked, mountains are lumpy, a lot of his creatures are funny-looking, and he made it all anyway. He didn't let the aardvark convince him he had no business designing creatures. He didn't make a puffer fish and get discouraged. No, the maker made things—and still does.

European film directors often enjoy creative careers, during which their films mature from the manifestos of angry young men to the rueful wisdom of great works by creative masters. Is an afternoon siesta the secret? Is their *vita* just a little more *dolce?* We've taken espresso to our American hearts, but we haven't quite taken to the "break" in our coffee breaks. Worried about playing the fool, we forget how to simply play. We try to make our creativity linear and goal oriented. We want our "work" to lead somewhere. We forget that diversions do more than merely divert us.

> An original is a creation motivated by desire.
>
> MAN RAY

How did all this sternness get in here? We let it in. We dragged it in. We even begged it to please come in. And why? Our own natural antic and animal high spirits scare us silly. There are few things more fun than exercising our talents, and since most of us keep them on a pretty tight leash, we are scared that if we let them off, we will need a lion tamer.

As little kids, we might fool around rhapsodically on the piano. We might improvise for hours, pouring out our hearts and our adolescent angst. We play so much and so often that people might say we're good, have a talent, could even have a career—"if we're serious enough about it." Then what happens? We get serious.

We begin to "practice," not play. We begin to seek perfection like the Holy Grail. We begin to compete. We go to school, music school, and to master classes, and to intensives and . . . and we may end up with quite a hot career. Meanwhile, some of our ardor cools. Music becomes something we "master." We become musical acrobats capable of flying across the keys with amazing ease, performing astounding stunts—but we have forgotten the sheer thrill of flying.

Anything worth doing is worth doing badly.

How we hate *that* idea. We know it as beginners but forget it as we advance. Trial-and-error becomes beneath our dignity. Of course it does. It pulls the rug out from underneath our seriousness. We don't really have a nice big block to stand behind while we "figure things out." What's to figure out? God was humble enough to just doodle, to just noodle, to fool around—why are we so serious?

When making art becomes about making a career, it has the same deadening impact as when making love becomes about making a baby. Rather than enjoy the process, we become focused on the result, everything else is just foreplay. There's a rush to get it over with and move on to the main thrust of things, our Brilliant Career.

> 'Tis an ill cook that cannot lick his own fingers.
>
> WILLIAM SHAKESPEARE

Focused on career goals—prosperity, security, celebrity—we remove ourselves from the sensuality of process. The delight of a first published poem becomes First Published, not "Nice paper. Like how they laid it out." The exciting event becomes "I wonder how it will be received" instead of "What do *I* think of it?"

It becomes about perfection and other people's perception, not the joy of creation, the play of ideas.

When our art boils down to a calculated career move, we ourselves tend to become hard-boiled and calculated. Not bad traits for the hero of a detective novel, but we might need one to detect any fun in our lives.

The creative imagination leaps crag to crag and does not chug up the mountain like an automated chairlift. If we treat the creative self like a young and curious animal, we will get the right idea. A young animal pokes its curious nose here and there. Our creative animal must be allowed the same freedom. Nothing—or something—may come to your sortie into reading about the Norman Conquest, and the "something" that might come may be nothing like the "something" you first envisioned. You *could* start out with an interest in Robin Hood, only to find yourself writing the diary of Maid Marian. The greater your appetite for adventure, the more adventuresome the creative elements at hand when you turn to working on something. It does not take much to spark the imagination, but just what will do it is always the question, and the answers can be very queer indeed. Georgia O'Keeffe wrote home: "I got half-a-dozen paintings from that shattered plate." Someone else may simply have gotten a cleaning job. Do not be too hasty to name your soul's delights.

Sticks and stones, marbles and peacock feathers, a smooth gray river rock—what we take to heart is what speaks to us uniquely. As artists, we are like beachcombers, walking the tide line, pocketing the oddments washed ashore—some small stray thing will tell us a story to tell the world. There is a reason we call art a "calling"—but we do have to answer the call. Intuition speaks to us as impulse. We must learn to explore, not repress, our intuition. Intuition is key to creative unfolding.

> *There is not a sprig of grass that shoots uninteresting to me.*
>
> THOMAS JEFFERSON

> *All are needed by each one: Nothing is fair or good alone.*
>
> RALPH WALDO EMERSON

"I wanted to learn more about the city," Kenton remembers. "After all, I lived there, but I didn't know much about it. I didn't really know how old things were. I didn't know which parts of town were built first. I didn't know significant historical turning points. I was occupying the great new job in the great new town and I was kind of lonely—but lonely for a sense of roots as well."

On impulse, Kenton began browsing the architecture section of his new neighborhood's swank Barnes and Noble. He found a book on Victorian architecture and realized his neighborhood was filled with vintage homes that were only passing for modern. Detecting here a new cornice, there a portico, Kenton began to feel there was a lot more to his neighborhood than met the eye. He next went to a secondhand bookstore and there found a shelf of "local authors." Amid the texts was a how-to-renovate guide that he picked up for fifty cents. A free Saturday afternoon found him showing up for a lecture at the neighborhood library, "Our Historic District and What We Don't Know About It." At the lecture, Kenton found himself picking up a flyer for a neighborhood garden tour. On that garden tour, thinking, *What am I doing here?* Kenton met two pieces of destiny. He got an idea for a photojournalism essay he would place with a local underground paper and he met a very interesting young woman—who is now his fiancée.

Opening to our intuition *is* like opening to a new love affair. Our first adventure may be a coffee date that feels a little stiff but has a few memorable possibilities. Our second flyer may be a little more bold—say, a kiss good-bye on the cheek.

Our third venture may mark the beginning of a budding passion, an interest that we can't quite shake, that companions us through our days. An intuitive leading is a lead we must follow. "Destiny" arrives as a humble lunch, not a fanfare.

TASK

Draw Yourself to Scale

An adventure does not need to be large or intense to be adventurous and nutritious for our artist. Arguably, most of us lead lives with too much adventure in it. The nightly news and daily headlines are packed with extremes of all sorts. For this reason, this tool, the "adventuring tool," is a gentle one. We all have adventurous lives, but we must see them to know it.

Go to an office supply or art supply shop. Acquire a small blank notebook suitable for sketching. Carry this notebook with you and carry, too, a sketching pencil or pen so that you can begin to capture the many small adventures of life as you actually live it.

When you enter the adventure of each moment by sketching the office where you are waiting for the doctor, sketching the bus stop where the bus is taking "forever," sketching the coffee mug while your friend is powdering her nose, you begin to gain a sense of yourself as leading a life that is crammed with interesting character and characters the moment you take the time to focus. You do not need to sketch well to enjoy sketching.

The summer I was twenty-one, I carried such a sketchbook with me all over New York. I still have the awkward sketch that I made waiting in what was to become my first literary agent's office. I have a drawing of the gawky plant and hard-to-sit-on chair. One glance at the sketch and I am "back there," alive to the great adventure of launching what was to become my literary career. A few pages later in the same sketchbook, I have a drawing of my friend Nick Cariello. "You make me look too old," he complained as I sketched him—he has since aged into and through the Nick I saw as I drew him.

> *To me every hour of the light and dark is a miracle.*
>
> WALT WHITMAN

So much of the adventure of the life we lead rushes past us in a blur. Velocity is the culprit. Velocity and pressure. A sketchbook freezes time. It is an instantaneous form of meditation focusing us on the worth of every passing moment. So often the great adventure of life lies between the lines, in how we felt at a certain time and at a certain place. This tool will help you to remember and savor the passing parade.

The Verb "To Be"

It is all too easy to think of art as something we aspire to, an ideal by which to measure our efforts and find them falling woefully short. Well, that is one way to think of art, and God knows we have bludgeoned ourselves with it pretty thoroughly. Our concepts of "great art" and "great artists" are often less something we aspire to than something we use to denigrate our own effort. We might want to try thinking about art a little differently.

Catherine was a highly acclaimed young singer. She had a very pure and very "scopey" operatic voice. She responded like a Maserati to direction and could corner on a dime, making her a director's favorite. She had been to the finest conservatory in America, studied with the most rigorous and respected teachers, won competitions and fine notices. She seemed set for a career in the world of opera, except for just one thing: Broadway was what made her heart sing. Like *Madame Butterfly* suffering the pangs of unrequited love, Catherine sang opera but dreamed Broadway—until her health broke down.

> *The time of the singing of birds is come.*
>
> SONG OF SOLOMON

"I just didn't have the heart to sing one more tragic aria. I may have the gift for it, but I wanted to return it unopened. Opera was heavy lifting for me, not vocally but emotionally. I was being groomed for a career I didn't want and I was going along with the agenda. As a result, my heart was broken and so was my health."

Fortunately, Catherine encountered a wise older woman who asked her what she wanted in life, to be admired or to be happy? Catherine saw that her motives for pursuing an operatic career were based in a snobbery she herself did not respect. Screwing up her courage, Catherine admitted her heart's desire. "I deviated from being a diva and became a happy hoofer instead." Turning her ambitions and her talents toward Broadway, Catherine has been working steadily ever since. She laughs, "If the shoe fits, you're supposed to wear it—even if it's tap."

"Art" is less about what we could be and more about what we are than we normally acknowledge. When we are fixated on getting better, we miss what it is we already are—and this is dangerous because we—as we are—are the origin of our art. "We" are what makes our art original. If we are always striving to be something more and something different, we dilute the power of what it is we actually are. Doing that, we dilute our art.

A musician with a profound gift for melody decides that dissonance and minimalism are preferable to his flowing musicality. A sculptor who prefers small-format work feels that without a towering and aggressive masterwork he is diminutive in talent. A filmmaker born to cinema verité admires the drawing-room comedy he will never be able to perfect. An artist whose line drawings make people weep with their stunning simplicity decides that only oil painting is high art.

Arthur Kretchmer, a great editor, once remarked to me, "What is it about writers? If something is easy for them, they don't respect it. Instead, they find their métier and kick it in the teeth."

Sometimes as artists, we practice a self-rejecting aesthetic that is like what adolescents do in terms of their physicality. This is a self-loathing that sets in and says whatever we are, it is not as good or as beautiful as whatever it is the other one has. If we are small, dark, and exotic, we want to be tall and bland and blond. If we are a Nordic goddess, we wish our eyes were brown and not cobalt and that our skin looked like a sultry Gauguin. In other words, whatever we are is not what we wish ourselves to be. Comedians yearn for drama; dramatic actors crave comedy. Born short-story writers lust for the National Book Award for their novels; natural novelists scream for the stage. Not that we can't do more than one thing, but one of the things we should let ourselves do is what comes naturally and easily. So why don't we?

> Be ye lamps unto yourselves.
> Be your own reliance.
> Hold to the truth within
>   yourselves
> As to the only lamp.
>
> BUDDHA

Art is not programmatic. We cannot "improve" ourselves into great artists by doing creative sit-ups. Great artists are actually the greatest amateurs—from the Latin verb *amare*, "to love." They have learned to wriggle out of the seriousness of rigid categorization and allow themselves to pursue the Pied Piper of delight. Picasso is a fine case in point. He found beauty in a tin can, in a rusted coiled spring, in a junkyard. Delighted with his roadside finds, he delighted the world by assembling great art out of his simple love of found objects. What a loss if he had said instead, "Pablo, get a grip! You are the maestro! No tin cans for you. Think Guernica! Think serious!"

No surprise that it was Picasso himself who remarked, "We are all born children. The trick is how to remain one." Mozart, we are told, remained one. Why do we get so damn adult?

If we stop trying to improve ourselves and start trying to delight ourselves, we get further as artists. If we lean into what we love instead of soldiering toward what we "should," our pace quickens, our energy rises, optimism sets in. What we love is nutritious for us. If you are crazy about Schubert, play a little Schubert. Your Liszt will be less listless. If you are wild about yellow right now for no apparent reason, paint something yellow and call that closet the sunroom. Instead of resisting yourself, try finding yourself irresistible. Try out the idea that you might be onto something when you catch sight of an amaryllis in the florist's window and think, *Oh, I'd love to have that.*

> *It is the addition of strangeness to beauty that constitutes the romantic character of art.*
>
> WALTER PATER

Children learn at a prodigious rate. If you watch a child learning, you see that he will move from interest to interest, hungrily grazing among multiple appetites: the blocks, the crayons, the Legos, this way and that, experimenting. When we set to structure a curriculum for our artist, we forget that the artist within is childlike and cantankerous. Enticement works better than entrapment. Curiosity gets us further than curriculum. Serious art requires serious play—and play, by definition, is anarchic, naughty.

To be an artist you must learn to let yourself be. Stop getting better. Start appreciating what you are. Do something that simply delights you for no apparent reason. Give in to a little temptation, poke into a strange doorway, buy the weird scrap of silk in a color you never wear. Make it an altar cloth, set your geranium on it, frame it—try letting yourself be that nasty, derogatory little word, "arty." Drop the rock. A lot of great artists work in their pajamas. Ernest Hemingway and Oscar Hammerstein both worked standing up because they liked that.

Sometimes we get a lot further in our art and in our lives when we let ourselves do a little of what comes easily and naturally. If you like to draw horses, stop drawing chairs. If you would love to take ballet, do it and let modern jazz be someone else's winter sport. If you have a deep love for Broadway, tell Chopin you'll be back.

Painting your kitchen is creative. Putting bells on your kid's school shoes is creative. Restructuring the office is creative. Getting the bad stuff tossed from the closet is creative. None of that's going to blow up Western civilization, and it *is* going to cheer us up, our world up, and, by the tiny overflow joie de vivre, help Western civilization by one tiny jot. It is self-expression, not self-scrutiny and "correction," that brings healing and happiness. Bells on the shoelaces, sonnets in the schools. These are not so far apart. Writing a novel and doing something novel on a Saturday afternoon are *both* creative leaps—one large and one small, but each is grounded in the right to express creative choice.

Very often a little friendly and easy art can send us back up those other slithery slopes with a bit more humor and optimism.

> *Today isn't any other day, you know.*
>
> LEWIS CARROLL

Artists of all stripe tend to equate difficulty with virtue and ease with slumming. We do not lean into our ease and enjoy the ride of our gift. Instead, we make firm resolves to work on our areas of difficulty. We call this improving ourselves—okay, sometimes we do improve a wobbly area, but if we do not practice the joy of using our talents where they fall easily, we rob ourselves of self-expression. The "self" has a few things it "selfishly" enjoys—and it is dangerous, as an artist, to ignore these natural affections and predilections.

This is not to say you have to "give up" high art. Instead, I am saying to try "Hi, Art!" like you are waving to someone friendly out the window of your pickup truck.

TASK
Allow Yourself to Be

Seriousness is the enemy of spontaneity. What we "should" love and what we do love are often two different things. Allow yourself to admit to some of your more anarchistic forbidden pleasures. (Many French romantic liaisons last longer than marriages. Why? Because they are officially a "forbidden delight.")

Take pen in hand and finish this phrase 10 times:

Secretly, I would love to _____.

You have just cast the net of dreams and scooped from your subconscious some secret and hidden desires. Take pen in hand again and for fifteen minutes allow yourself to fully inhabit one of your secret desires. How does it feel to be doing it? Where are you when you do it? Who cheers you on? What surprises you? Make this mental movie as vivid as possible. Be sure to flesh out your supporting cast and color in your setting. Initiative often begins in the imagination. As Stella Merrill

Mann summarizes it, "Ask, believe, receive." Give yourself the initial gift of conceptualizing a fully inhabited secret desire.

Invention vs. Convention

As artists, we are innovators. We experiment and explore. We make things new—at the very least, we make things anew. Every painting edges us forward a hair in skill and experience, even if we are in a workshop class that copies an old master. Every time a pianist tackles Franck or Beethoven, interprets Debussy—there is still some personal nuance that the artist brings to the work. A new staging of an old ballet, the millionth high school production of *Romeo and Juliet*—each expression of art breathes new breath into the work and into the world. Even when we are doing something that "has been done," we bring to bear fresh creative energy. And when we deliberately explore and extend our creative territory, we innovate even further and even more.

> *It is the first part of intelligence to recognize our precarious estate in life, and the first part of courage to be not at all abashed before the fact.*
>
> ROBERT LOUIS STEVENSON

> *You never know what is enough unless you know what is more than enough.*
>
> WILLIAM BLAKE

Some people are innovators by temperament and trade. Other people are conservers. As artists, we are most often innovators. Those who work with our work—agents, managers, publishers, gallery owners, curators, producers—are most often conservers. As innovators, we must not be *so* innovative that we burn our bridges, but we must not allow our conservers to be so conservative that we spend entire careers shoring up the bridges we have already built. Conservers focus not on the forward-moving edge but on the known territory of "how it's done" and "the way it is in the business" and "what will sell." They tell us not how to skin the creative cat a new way but how the cat has already been skinned. They talk about "what works" rather than "what *could* work." They say things like "That's not how the business runs."

Conservers want artists to believe that "how it is done" is how it has to be done. They often talk about the odds against accomplishment of an artistic dream. They often come up with the numbers that "prove" the impossible odds stacked against us. They often forget what we as artists know—the odds are not impossible. They never are and they never will be. They may look impossible. They may sound impossible, but those are largely scare tactics. The phrase "scared out of our wits" is a very precise phrase. As artists, when we allow conservers to terrorize us, we *are* being scared out of our wits—wits being those innovative and inventive smarts that allow us to figure out, always, one more way to skin a cat.

As an artist and an innovator, we must always ask, "How *can* we?" We must always look for, and find, still *another* way to skin the cat, publish the book, shoot the film, stage the play—as artists, we are practitioners not of how it *is* done, but of how it *could* be done. We are charged with finding not the problems but the solutions. As artists, we are concerned with making things, while conservers are often concerned with making do with the world as they find it.

When Jean met and married Gordon, she was a working artist with a lively and varied career. Painting, sculpture, and photography were her favorite pursuits. She moved nimbly among the three, making a brisk and interesting career for herself. "You've got to specialize—you've got to market yourself," Gordon solemnly advised her. "You can't just chase whatever whim catches your fancy. It's not good business."

Impressed and intimidated by her husband's "expertise," Jean shaped her career to his wishes instead of to her own. For the decade that their marriage lasted, she largely did as she was told, focusing as her husband told her she should. Instead of flourishing, she felt her career growing "successful"—but stagnant and stale. Depression set in before divorce. When her husband abruptly left her, claiming *he* felt stifled, Jean found herself suddenly free. After a few months of dizzy disorientation, she began exploring a variety of creative interests.

"I'd been defining myself so narrowly, as just a painter. I've got all sorts of creative skills I love using." Long a "closet techie," Jean explored new computer skills, studied layout and newsletters. To her delight, people loved paying her to do exactly that. A lively design business was born.

As artists, we are more like inventors than we are like those who mass-produce the inventions. We may do both, of course, and often do, but we are at heart those who make what others may make more of. We create a painting that may later become a greeting card, a poster, or a calendar piece, but the kernel of invention remains with us. We try to see if an idea "flies." Like the Wright brothers, we make the gadget that then becomes the staple of the industry. As artists, we are interested in what can be done rather than how it can't be done.

Any profound view of the world is mysticism.

ALBERT SCHWEITZER

Some agents, some managers, some producers and dealers and curators, are themselves innovators and creators. They bring to our work their own inventive daring—most do not. As conservers, they are oriented toward what has sold rather than what could sell. They look more often for the downside than the upside. They may additionally be looking most often for the known sale and the proven return and where they can make the most financial reward in the short term rather than thinking of the long-term creative rewards of making a superior work and trusting the market to respond to that.

As artists, we know very well that something can "not be done," only until someone does it. Some artist, somewhere, decides to shove the fence back a little and extend his or her and all of our range. *Showboat* brought serious concerns to musical theater. *Oklahoma!* and *Carousel* brought "real" stories and characters and plays that could stand in their own right as dramatic material. The musical was no longer defined merely as boy-meets-girl—from Rodgers and Hammerstein on out, it tackled real issues and ideas. They had moved the fence, buying everyone more creative acreage.

> *Trifles make perfection—and perfection is no trifle.*
>
> MICHELANGELO

As examples like these make pointedly clear, as artists, we must listen most carefully to our inner guidance and secondarily to our outer advisers. This isn't just spiritual law—trusting the still, small voice to guide us—it's good business practice as well. The interaction of commerce and creativity is a tricky dance, and we as artists must lead it. Show a new direction in your painting to a dealer who is being asked for more of last year's series and you may hear a worried and dispiriting "Mmmm." Do not be fooled. He cannot see what you as an artist may sense, that your direction is the new direction the market will soon be following. For an artist willing to have a learning curve, all directions lead to somewhere worthy.

"Nothing succeeds like success" is a truism for a life in the arts. The problem lies in parsing out what constitutes a success—and for an artist that may be making something new and challenging rather than repeating a known success. It may be having a body of work that is personally respectable, following not merely the market but our own very changing interests. I have been told "short stories don't sell" and then found yes, they did. I have been told "memory plays don't work" and won prizes for the same play. I have been told "never use first person for a novel" and published the same novel to good reviews, good reception, and personal satisfaction.

The business of art is a machine, but an artist is the live, animating spark that runs it. That spark can be extinguished by too much "realism" and too much "I know you don't want to hear this, but . . ." Well-meaning advisers can advise us straight into a creative slump, straight into a fallow period, straight into a wall of inner resistance. They forget that they cannot sell what we do not make and so often urge us to make what they know they can sell, forgetting that if they deaden our spirits too often and too much, the work will deaden as well and there will be nothing to sell.

As artists, we have a form of inner power the advisers can never extinguish or ultimately thwart. And this is always the key.

It is the question of "odds" that always baffles conservers when they deal with artists. Conservers like to think they know the odds. They like to think they know what sells—and they do know until another artist invents another memorable and unpredictable something and thus creates a market for that. As artists, we are first and foremost the origins of our work. Since each of us is one-of-a-kind, the market, for all its supposed predictability, is actually vulnerable to falling in love with any of us at any time.

I say this and I know this because I believe and know creativity to be a spiritual issue. "Faith moves mountains"— Christ told us that, and he may have meant that literally.

We speak of the Great Creator, we speak of Christ but seldom make the connection that the spiritual laws he taught are actually the spiritual laws related to creativity. "Knock and it shall be opened." "Ask and you shall receive"—these are not mere spiritual bromide, they are spiritual laws as they relate to manifestation.

> *I find that I have painted my life—things happening in my life—without knowing.*
>
> GEORGIA O'KEEFFE

- Ask
- Believe
- Receive

As artists, we routinely ask for inspiration. We need to learn from Christ's example that we can also ask for the material manifestation of our visions to come to us as money, support, opportunity. Our faith, which is a request coupled with an expectation of its successful fulfillment, is no different from the faith of a navigator setting out to prove the world is round. Creative dreams come to us as visions that we are charged with fulfilling. When we allow the Great Creator to do this to us, through us, then we are aligning ourselves with the spiritual power necessary to negate the "odds."

TASK
Strike Up a Dialogue

In addition to the outer conservers that we encounter in a creative career, we all also carry an inner conserver, who functions as a gatekeeper on our more expansive impulses. The best creative careers are built by a fruitful inner dialogue between our inner innovator and our inner conserver. It is a practical skill that can be practiced. Take pen in hand and allow your two sides to strike up a dialogue. It might look like this:

INNOVATOR

*I'd love to go back to school
full-time. I've been shut up
in my painting studio a decade
and I'm lonely and bored.*

CONSERVER

*You make your living from the
work you do in that studio. You
can't just quit.*

INNOVATOR

Well, I'd like to, that's for sure.

CONSERVER

*What about a once-a-week class?
You'd have time to do that and,
if you pick the right one, it's
a lot of stimulus.*

INNOVATOR

*That's a good idea and less of
a radical free fall. Thank you.*

All successful creative careers are built upon dialogues like the one above. As we both move forward and solidify where we've been, "solid" careers take shape. They are like gardens that require patient nurturance, where no one plant runs wild.

We all have angels guiding us . . . What will bring their help? Asking. Giving thanks.

SOPHY BURNHAM

CHECK-IN

1. **How many days this week did you do your Morning Pages?** If you skipped a day, why did you skip it? How was the experience of writing them for you? Are you experiencing more clarity? A wider range of emotions? A greater sense of detachment, purpose, and calm? Did anything surprise you? Is there a "repeating" issue asking to be dealt with?

2. **Did you do your Artist's Date this week?** Did you note an improved sense of well-being? What did you do and how did it feel? Remember, Artist's Dates can be difficult and you may need to coax yourself into taking them.

3. **Did you get out on your Weekly Walk?** How did that feel? What emotions or insights surfaced for you? Were you able to walk more than once? What did your walk do for your optimism and sense of perspective?

4. **Were there any other issues this week that felt significant to you in your self-discovery?** Describe them.

Discovering a Sense of Personal Territory

Saying yes to our creative selves may involve saying no to our significant others. This week focuses on boundaries. The essays and tasks aim at helping us to define our creative identities as opposed to our many other roles. Expect to feel heightened emotions as energy rebounds into your own court.

Sexuality vs. Caretaking

As artists, our sexual energy and our creative energy are very closely intertwined. This is why we have love songs. Love sonnets. Torch songs. And the phrase "Carrying a torch," because as unrequited lovers we still carry a bright enough spark to speak of being "shot down in flames."

When someone who ignites our creative imagination crosses our path, that person is a "fuse lighter." Our creative engine kicks over. We suddenly have things to say and long for new ways to say them. We say them in paint, in dance, in poetry, in plasticine sculpture. We suddenly "come alive to the possibility." We are galvanized. People ask, "Are you in love?"

In a sense, we are in love—and we are also in love with our own artist, who is suddenly mirrored back to us as exciting and adventurous, powerful, perhaps even dangerous. We experience more energy. We burn the candle at both ends, staying up late to work on a project. Getting up early to grab an hour at the easel, like a stolen bout of lovemaking on the way to work.

Creative energy and sexual energy are both our personal energy. Our use of them is private, and to pretend otherwise is debilitating and abusive. In point of fact, the two energies are so closely intertwined, they may be experienced as nearly identical. We conceive children and we conceive creative projects. Both energies are sacred.

They spring from the same source, our inner core. Our creative energy, like our sexual energy, must not be squandered. And yet, we are often asked to do just that.

As artists, we must be alert to what people ask us for and reward us for being. Our partners and friends do condition us into behaviors quite unconsciously. We must be alert to what they reward us for with their thanks and reciprocity. And to what ways they are withholding and manipulative in their lack of approval and generosity. These things condition us, and they are also the conditions in which our art will or will not be made.

> *It is only with the heart that one can see rightly; what is essential is invisible to the eye.*
>
> ANTOINE DE SAINT-EXUPÉRY

Festivity breeds creativity. Rigidity breeds despair. When our high spirits are straitjacketed in the name of virtue or discipline, the vital and youthful spark in us that enjoys adventure and is game for invention begins to flicker like a flame in a draft.

> *Be it life or death, we crave only reality.*
>
> HENRY DAVID THOREAU

Creativity responds to nourishment and warmth. If we are forbidden to be childlike—told perhaps that it is "childish" or "selfish"—if we are urged to be too sensible, we react as gifted students do to an authoritarian teacher—we refuse to learn and grow. Our considerable energy is channeled into resistance and over time solidifies into a hard-to-penetrate shell of feigned indifference.

The universe is alive with energy. It is fertile, abundant, even raucous—so are we. Most of us are high spirited, humorous, even pranksterish with the least encouragement. What is lacking for so many of us is precisely the least encouragement. We buy in to the notion that life is dreary and difficult and something to be soldiered through. We tell ourselves, "Oh, well, what did I expect?"

The truth is that as children, many of us expected much more. We had dreams and desires and inklings of delight and full-blown passions. We practiced ballet in the living room, we sang wildly, we loved the goo of finger painting. We loved, period—and love is a passionate and energizing force. In order for our creativity to flourish, we must reclaim our right both to love and to be loved. We must become a little nuts about ourselves, about our notions, whimsies, and ambitions. Instead of chiding ourselves or allowing ourselves to be chided into an "adult" solemnity, we must regain our right to be goofy, earthy, even silly. In lovemaking we speak of "foreplay," and we must allow ourselves to play at the things we love. This means that if our partner is restrictive, we must get a little clever at daring to be ourselves in private. Instead of yanking on our bootlaces and asking ourselves to get better, we need to loosen up the shoelaces, take off the shoes, and wiggle our feet in the green grass of earth.

Creativity is sensual, and so are we. As we celebrate rather than repress our passion, we are rewarded by more passion, and that is the fuel for art.

If our romantic partner insists on always using us to process with, never taking us out to something simply fun, we will begin to feel snappish and hostile. The same is true of our creative partnerships. We may be caring, we may be acute, we may be an invaluable sounding board, but that's not romance, and that's not creative collaboration either. Nurturing is a part of a partnership—overnurturing is the usurping of your creative energy for someone else's agendas.

When we are asked to overcaretake, to "mother" or "father" our friends or lovers or colleagues, our artist reacts with depression and also with rage. Both as artists and as people, such demands can make us feel curiously desexualized, as if we are truly being neutered, castrated, and used.

A woman writer married to an omnivorously needy partner was astounded to discover that after her divorce, both her creative energy and her sexual energy came springing back to life like a lioness waking up after years of medication and depression from living in a too-small zoo cage. As she sharply realized, creative and sexual energy are connected. Dampen our creative ardor and our sexual selves dampen as well. Dampen our sexual selves by demanding we overnurture and parentalize ourselves, and our creativity suffers.

It is no coincidence that artistic annals are filled with the tales of incendiary romantic intrigues, yielding blazing creative work. Our muses *are* fuse lighters, and the blaze they ignite may be passionate, creative, or both. Does this mean we must sexualize all our relationships or creative collaborations? Emphatically, *no.* But it *does* mean that we must be alert to avoid those bonds and entanglements that neuter our exuberance, hence our sexuality and creativity. If someone refuses to share our humor, we are cast as grim parents to their infantile demands. Artists can marry, but they must marry well. And, I would argue, there must be *merriment* in their marriage for their work to continue to flourish. And if the work is dead, the relationship will soon follow suit. If our energy must always be all-nurturing or stern, our creative keyboard is stuck on middle C.

In artist-to-artist relationships, *both* artists need to be nurtured and seen. Neither partner should be neutered or neutralized by excessive caretaking. Agendas cannot replace adventures.

> *I cannot understand; I love.*
> ALFRED, LORD TENNYSON

If a man wants to be mothered, he will not respond with enthusiasm to your sexy new dress—*or* your new song. Similarly, a woman artist might demand an all-caretaking daddy from her spouse, saying her "artist child" needs pampering.

Neither sex is immune to creative castration by relationships that drain creative reservoirs without the tenderness to refill them.

Sexuality can be sublimated in the name of art, but it need not be. Damaging sexual entanglements *do* damage our creativity, but enlivening ones nurture and spark it.

Married to a narcissistic and greedy actress, Daniel felt increasingly drained, and his work life withered. Later, involved with a woman artist who found both him and his work attractive, Daniel's creative life rebounded robustly with plays, novels, films—all the creative brainchildren of a happy coupling.

> *The aim, if reached or not, makes great the life; Try to be Shakespeare, leave the rest to fate.*
>
> ROBERT BROWNING

Our mythology around artists and sexuality tends to dwell on the negative, on the promiscuity of artists, on their self-destructive sexual binging. Far more pernicious is the subtle leeching of creativity and sexuality through overcaretaking, and far less often mentioned is the happy blossoming artists may experience when settled in a relationship that is alive to their creative and sexual energies.

If there is an art to romance, it can equally be said that there must be romance to art.

TASK

Putting a Tiger Back in Your Tank

When we are in love, we find our partners fascinating and ourselves with them. When we are in a creative recovery, we find *ourselves* fascinating. We fall in love with our own ideas, insights, inspirations, and impulses. We are interested by what we have to say and think. We feel alive, alert, and vibrant—and, if we don't feel that way, we know it and resent it. Admitting those who leave us cold, we warm to our own interests.

Take pen in hand and finish the following phrases as rapidly as you can:

1. Among my friends, a "fuse lighter" who makes me feel creative and powerful is _____.
2. Among my friends, a "wet blanket" who drains and dampens me is _____.

3. Historically, a relationship that left me depleted from overcaretaking was
   _____.

4. Realistically, a current relationship that leaves me feeling neutered is
   _____.

5. My most reciprocal, mutually nurturing creative friendship is with
   _____.

Once you have sorted through your acquaintances and intimates for those who allow you to be fiery, ask yourself the same question: "Do I allow myself to have passion?" Take pen in hand and write yourself a love letter. Be as specific and as affectionate as you can imagine.

Stop Being "Nice," Be Honest

"Charity begins at home" is not a bromide. It is a direction. It means start with being nice to yourself, your authentic self, then try being nice to everyone else. When we place ourselves too low in the pecking order, we feel henpecked and, yes, we feel peckish. We neglect our work or do it distractedly. Soon our work may develop a querulous tone, sour and dyspeptic, like ourselves. When we undervalue ourselves, we literally bury ourselves in lives not our own. Meeting the expectations of others, we may misplace our own values.

> *When you are content to be simply yourself and don't compare or compete, everybody will respect you.*
>
> LAO-TZU

Value systems are as individual as fingerprints. Each of us has a set of priorities that may be baffling to others but absolutely necessary to ourselves. Violating our true selves, we soon feel worthless and undeserving. This in turn prevents our acting on our own behalf, and so we suffer further.

When I was a young single mother, I felt guilty because I craved time away from my daughter. I wanted silence. I needed to hear my own thoughts. I also needed to take my own soul by the hand occasionally and not have to worry about keeping my daughter's tiny hand clutched. Whatever dreams I harbored had better take the back burner, I lectured myself—although I never stopped writing—and so I tried putting my dreams on the back burner, where they proceeded to boil—and so did my temper. Domenica was a delightful child. I began to find her not so delightful. I was snappish, irritable, and guilty. Yearning for more writing time, a luxury of my premotherhood years, I felt cornered and trapped. Wasn't my child more important than my brainchildren? I lectured myself. I could see no way out.

"Take a night off," an older woman friend, an actress, advised me. "Take care of your artist. That will make you a much better mother. You need to get in reality here. Society tells you motherhood comes first, but—with you—it doesn't. If you're honest about that and put your artist first, you might be quite a good mother. Lie to yourself about it—and did you know most child abuse comes from too much togetherness?"

> *That which we understand we can't blame.*
>
> JOHANN WOLFGANG
> VON GOETHE

We get our lives wrong because we get our questions wrong. We get our questions wrong because we have been raised in a culture that is punishing to the forms of freedom necessary for artists to flourish. These freedoms are the ones that allow us to be a little less nice so that we can be a little more genuine. Richard Rodgers needed piano time and took it every morning—*then* he was a devoted father—only then.

I had not known that too much "nice" caused child abuse, but I could believe it. Taking my friend's radical advice, I began getting up an hour earlier to write Morning Pages while my daughter slept. I also began a practice of taking Artist's Dates, getting me and my creative consciousness a few of the sort of festive adventures that I had been devising—and resenting—for my daughter. I was rewarded with this self-care by a movie idea—I wrote a script and sold it to Paramount.

What was even more "paramount" was this: I found that my mother had been quite right to post over her kitchen sink a small poem I had always dismissed as doggerel. It read:

> *If your nose is held to the grindstone rough*
> *and you hold it down there long enough*
> *soon you'll say there's no such thing*
> *as brooks that babble and birds that sing.*
> *Three things will all your world compose—*
> *just you, the grindstone, and your darned old nose.*

I've taught for twenty-five years. I've had a great many students worry that they were selfish. It is my considered opinion that most creative people are actually too selfless. Instead of asking "Julia, am I selfish?" they should ask, "Julia, am I selfish enough?" "Selfish enough" gives us the self for self-expression.

As artists, when we are too nice for too long, we stop being nice at all. "I just need to get to the goddamn piano," we say correctly, or "I haven't written in days and it's driving me crazy," correctly, or "If I don't get to the easel, these kids are gonna walk the plank." Our slowly stoked fires of resentment—caused by too many yesses where a timely no would have been more honest and given us time and space to work—begin to set our tempers to a simmer and then to a boil. If we persist in still being nice, we get to cook ourselves an ulcer or develop high blood pressure. For an artist, being too virtuous is no virtue at all. It is destructive and counterproductive. Have I mentioned that it is no fun?

> *Jump.*
>
> JOSEPH CAMPBELL
>
> *I love those who yearn for the impossible.*
>
> JOHANN WOLFGANG
> VON GOETHE

A sustained artistic career is made of two variables—talent and character. By "character" I do not mean the good or bad kind, I simply mean the character or tone of a personality, its exact nature. Great talent linked to an erratic character will yield an erratic career—bursts of promise subverted, flashes of glorious clarity and brilliance lost or muddled by the "flaw" in the stone of resolve. A sustained creative career requires discipline—the courage to evict what does not serve the goal of excellence. This is what it means to have character.

"What does not serve" varies person to person. For one it may be an overly dramatic friend. For another, too many high-octane dinner parties full of boast-and-toast talk. Whatever ungrounds an artist ungrounds his or her work. Whatever ungrounds an artist must be curtailed, avoided, or indulged in with care. As artists, we learn this from bitter experience. A virtuoso concert violinist learns that even a single scotch the night before playing certain works costs in terms of the necessary manual dexterity to safely undertake musical flight. Indulgence has a price. Airline pilots know the same thing as does the FAA. Pilots are checked for abuse of alcohol and other substances. If they overindulge, lives are endangered. For an artist, the life of his work is endangered. Self-indulgence spells self-endangerment. Our large self falls prey to our petty vices. It is enlightened self-interest to be selfish enough to be self-protective. Being self-protective may not seem "nice." We may say no to invitations that do not serve us.

As an artist, being nice is not nearly as important as being authentic. When we are what we truly are and say what we truly mean, we stop shouldering the

Did you know that secret? The awful thing is that beauty is mysterious.

FYODOR DOSTOYEVSKY

responsibility for everyone else's shortfalls and become accountable to ourselves. When we do, astonishing shifts occur. We become aligned with our true higher power, and creative grace flows freely.

When we stop playing God, God can play through us. When I stopped rescuing my blocked writer-boyfriend, I moved from writing articles and short stories to writing books. That's how much energy he had consumed. When a composer dropped his high-maintenance girlfriend, he finally finished an album that had simmered a decade. An officially "burned-out" woman painter stopped volunteering her time to the all-consuming neighborhood environmental group and found she suddenly had time to both paint and teach, solidly increasing both her productivity and her income. Her volunteerism had long felt involuntary. Willing to seem less saintly, she felt herself far more free.

Teaching those around us what our priorities are—and remembering them ourselves—makes for harmonious relationships. Clarifying ourselves to others brings honest connections that are grounded in mutual respect. Honesty starts with us. Identifying those who habitually abuse our time and energies is pivotal, but identifying them is only step one. Avoiding them is step two, and this is where a lot of us stumble. It is as if we doubt we have a right to tranquility, respect, and good humor. Shouldn't we really suffer? Shouldn't we find it more spiritual not to upset the status quo? Artificial acceptance of people and circumstances we resent makes us ill tempered. A little honest self-love does wonders for our personality, and for our art.

"But, Julia," I've heard people wail, "are you saying we should be selfish?"

Personally, I prefer selfish to simmering, cranky, hostile, and long-suffering. And is it really selfish to take time to have a self? You need a self for self-expression—and you need a self for a lot of other things as well. If the unexamined life is not worth living, the unlived life is not worth examining, or painting, or sculpting, or acting.

Too often, the rich world that feeds career-making work gives way to a hothouse world, and later works that feel recycled. For artists at every level, the necessity for nutritive inflow remains. Ironically, that inflow may be impeded by success itself, with the multiple demands made on our creative time.

A man at the very top of his art form professionally found himself so overbooked and so overburdened with advising others and lending his prestigious name to worthy causes that his life was no longer his own. The prestigious institutions with which he had aligned himself seemed to possess omnivorous appetites. Each request was "reasonable," each cause was "worthy." What he was was exhausted, burned-out, and baffled. "I'm at the top," he told me, "where I was always supposed to get, but I don't like it very much." Of course not. He had no time for his personal art, the beloved vehicle that had taken him to the top.

Knowing what you can not do is more important than knowing what you can do. In fact, that's good taste.

LUCILLE BALL

To live well is to work well, to show a good activity.

THOMAS AQUINAS

It is impossible to say yes to ourselves and our art until we learn to say no to others. People do not mean us harm, but they do harm us when they ask for more than we can give. When we go ahead and give it to them, we are harming ourselves as well.

"I knew I should have said no," we wail—until we start to actually do it. No, we cannot take on the one extra student. No, we cannot take on the one more committee. No, we cannot allow ourselves to be used—or we stop being useful.

Virtue—and the false virtue of being too virtuous—is very tempting. The problem with worthy causes is that they are worthy.

"You cannot be healthy and popular all at the same time," an accomplished older actress once warned me. "People want what they want and if you don't give it to them, they will get angry."

True enough, but our artist also wants what it wants and if we don't give it to our artist, our very core gets angry. If we think of the part of our self that creates as being like a vibrant and gifted inner youngster, we begin to imagine how dispirited a series of "Not now, be nice, just be a good sport and wait until later" dismissiveness on our part can make it.

When we start saying "Can't, because I am working," our life starts to work again. We start to feel our artist begin to trust us again and to ante up more ideas. Again, think of the artist as being quite young. What does a child do if disciplined too rigidly? It sulks. It lapses into silence. It acts out—our artist can be fairly depended upon to do some or all of these behaviors when we insist on being "nice" instead of honest.

It is never too late to start over. It is never past the point of no return for our artist to recover. We can heap years, decades, a lifetime of insult upon our artist and it is so resilient, so powerful, and so stubborn that it will come back to life when we give it the smallest opportunity. Instead of being coaxed into one more overextension of our energies in the name of helping others, we can help ourselves by coaxing our artist out with the promise of some protected time to be listened to, talked with, and interacted with. If we actively love our artist, our artist will love us in return. Lovers tell secrets and share dreams. Lovers meet no matter how adverse the circumstances, sneaking off for a rendezvous. As we woo our artist with our focused attention and private time, it will reward us with art.

TASK
Be Nice to Yourself (There's a Self in Self-Expression)

Many of us work too hard on being selfless. We forget that we actually need a self for self-expression. Take pen in hand and do a little archaeology—dig through your "shoulds" until you arrive at some "coulds." Complete the following sentences with 5 wishes. Write rapidly to evade your inner censor.

If it weren't so selfish, I'd love to try . . .

   1.
   2.
   3.
   4.
   5.

If it weren't so expensive, I'd love to try . . .

   1.
   2.
   3.
   4.
   5.

If it weren't so frivolous, I'd love to own . . .

   1.
   2.
   3.

4.

5.

If it weren't so scary, I'd love to tell . . .

1.

2.

3.

4.

5.

If I had five other lives, I'd love to be . . .

1.

2.

3.

4.

5.

These lists are powerful dreams. They may manifest in your life rapidly and un-expectedly. For this reason, you may want to put these lists into your God Jar for safekeeping. Do not be surprised if "parts" of your "other" lives begin to show up in the life you've actually got.

Energy Debts

All actions require creative energy. We seldom acknowledge this. As artists, we must learn to think of our energy the way a person thinks about money—am I spending my energy wisely here, investing in this person, this situation, this use of my time? As a rule, artists are temperamentally generous, even spendthrift. This natural inclination must be consciously monitored. An artist must return enough to the inner well to feel a sense of well-being.

> *Whatever is worth doing at all is worth doing well.*
> LORD CHESTERFIELD

A phone call with a tedious creative colleague is draining. What is getting drained is our creative bank account. A phone call or conversation in which our feedback is asked, used, and unacknowledged is like coaching someone on their stock market investments and not getting a thank-you for their big win. Conversely, a phone call that feels reciprocal is a win-win for both parties. You aren't just a site where someone is downloading information. You are a partner in a genuine dialogue that expands you both. I have a musician friend whose conversations are so rewarding, they send me racing to the page to write. Something in our give-and-take just plain gives.

As people and as artists, we crave to be seen for who and what we really are. If we are in relationships where the dividends we need are never extended back to us, that is a bad investment. Too many of those, and we bankrupt our creative stores. We must ask not only "Do I love this person?" but "Is this relationship self-loving?" Any relationship that risks your artist's identity is not.

A creative person is intended to be fed and supported by both divine and human sources, but none of those needed nutrients can reach us if we have turned ourselves into a food source for others, allowing them to dine freely on our time, our talents and our reserves. If we give someone who is without scruples and needy full access to our time and attention, it is like giving them our creative checkbook. They will spend us willy-nilly, and when we turn to use our own reserves, we will find them missing.

> *The art of being wise is the art of knowing what to overlook.*
>
> WILLIAM JAMES

Creativity expands in an atmosphere encouraging to it, and constricts self-protectively in an atmosphere that is cynical or hostile. This is why artists can have a difficult time accessing their best work in academia. This is why our close friends must be safe and smart, but not so smart-aleck that our creative child is afraid to speak up. When we lose our voice or our energy creatively, it is not some mysterious malady. It can usually be traced directly to an encounter in which our energy was abused.

If someone squanders our time by refusing to be pinned down as to when rehearsals or writing sessions or deadlines can be accomplished, we are put on hold. We cannot invest in other directions because we are always aware that we might be "suddenly" called on to invest when the erratic person is available. If we put our life and our planning on hold to accommodate another, too often we will feel tapped out because we cannot really claim any time and energy as safely and positively as our own. We are "on call." It is like having the door to your creative house unlocked and not knowing when someone will enter.

Think of your energy as money. Does this person tie up too much of your time and energy for you to invest it elsewhere? Is he the human equivalent of an investment you cannot liquidate when you need to? If so, he is then not only expensive in himself, he is also costing you finding and making other more emotionally and creatively remunerative relationships.

Our creative energy is our divine inheritance. If people insist on squandering it and we cooperate, we will find ourselves creatively bankrupt, drained of goodwill and good feelings, short-tempered and short-fused. If our energy is squandered on their poor judgment, our continuing to invest in them robs us of the power to effectively invest elsewhere or in ourselves.

As artists, we must husband our energy as carefully as our money. We must spend it along lines that are personally and creatively rewarding. We must invest it wisely in people and projects that return our investment with measurable satisfaction, growth, and achievement.

Every exit is an entry somewhere else.

TOM STOPPARD

Just as we expect and demand a fair return on our investments, we have a right to expect and receive a fair return on our investments of energy—both personally and professionally. Does this mean that we will never—or should never—extend ourselves in generosity toward our friends, family, and work? No. But it does mean that we must be alert to when and where our investment of energy is valued in return.

We must also be clear that "valued in return" may involve—and must involve— a return that is in some way compatible with what we extend. If a great apple pie is extended as a sign of love, "Could I have the recipe?" is not acknowledgment. It is ignoring the key ingredient—the love in the recipe. Similarly, if intellectual acuity is extended to a friend or a spouse or a colleague, that true ingredient must be acknowledged as well.

As an artist with thirty-five years of experience, I am the equivalent of the senior partner at a law firm. That is not ego, it is simply the level of my practice. While I may gladly undertake a "let's parse this out" political discussion on a close friend's creative career, I cannot undertake a regime of lunches involving creative counseling. I would come home both too fat and too thin, overnourished and undernurtured.

As artists, all of us need to invest wisely in ourselves and in others. We deserve recognition and respect and acknowledgment for the actual worth of our investments of time, talent, and keen observation.

I am closer to the work than to anything on earth. That's the marriage.

LOUISE NEVELSON

In our personal friendships, we require peers who see and acknowledge the skills we bring to the table. It is perfectly fine to talk with friends about our career situations and our fiscal dilemmas, but if those friends are giving us advice from their own considerable professional acuity and attainment, that should get some small nod from us, as ours hopefully does from them. This reciprocity of respect may be largely tacit, but it must be there or we may feel slighted or used.

Artists routinely apprentice and even adopt younger artists, but if you examine such arrangements closely, there is a reciprocal flow of energy from elder to younger, younger to elder. The apprentice helps, not merely helps himself. Such relationships can be controversial but mutually catalytic. Georgia O'Keeffe was both benefactor to—and benefitted by—her young protégé Juan Hamilton. Musical mentorships are commonplace. Aaron Copland helped Bernstein, who helped Copland. "Part of what I think we teach younger artists is professionalism," explains one master musician.

For the elder artists who teach and mentor, the rewards are real, but the demands can be unrealistic. In their desire to give, they may expend more than they can refund to themselves. A student who thoughtlessly misses lessons and expects and demands rescheduling can tip the balance from possible to impossible in a teacher's busy schedule.

If our teaching or mentoring feels thankless, we are either overextended or unthanked or both. As older, established artists, the company we keep may very well be underlings, and sometimes people help themselves to our help. When we are unhappy in a relationship, when we "blow things out of proportion," it is because the proportions within the relationship, and perhaps in our life as a whole, are somehow skewed. We are not crazy, but something is. We feel drained because we *are* drained. If the person who emptied the tank cannot help to fill it, well then, we must fill it elsewhere—and put a little red flag next to the person's name in our consciousness. When overtaxed by a friend, we must ask, Is this an understandable, rare situation—a death in the family, a job loss—that requires our marshaling extra help, or is this person habitually taxing, habitually dramatic and accident prone, a chronic abuser of our time and attention, a chronic undernurturer, or in between?

As artists, we have antennae sensitive to the thoughts and feelings of those around us. We can be chilled by indifference, hurt by lack of consideration, and we can be exhausted and diminished if we are in the company of those who talk down to us or treat us subtly like the identified patient: "Oh, you and your crazy ideas." As artists, we *need* our crazy ideas, and we need those who don't think they're too crazy. Symphonies and screenplays begin as crazy ideas. So do novels and nocturnes, bronzes and ballets.

Writers must write. Piano players must play pianos. Painters must paint and singers must sing. We can use our creative energy in the support of others, but if our artist gets lost in the transaction, if our aid and support is treated as generic cheerleading, if we are not acknowledged and nurtured in return in a way that fits our actual personal needs, then we are being inadvertently battered.

Alan sold a book and was required to do a substantial rewrite in order to bring the book fully into form. Rather than appreciating the pressure he was under, Alan's wife chose this "quiet time. You're just rewriting" to invite her extended family for a large and noisy visit. Wanting to be a good sport, wanting not to seem like a prima donna, Alan struggled with his growing anger as loud voices and interruptions cost him time and focus. Finally, exasperated and hurt, Alan rented a room in a nearby motel and retreated there with his computer and his unfinished book. It wasn't that he didn't love his wife and her family, it was that they were unable to see that he was at the glass-mountain phase of a project—the heart-breakingly hard make-it-or-break-it period when an artist knows he just may not be quite good enough to bring to bear the excellence he knows he is required to.

One of the most difficult things that happens to an artist is the sorrow that occurs when misperceived in the public arena. This makes it doubly important that in our private arena our artist be acknowledged and respected. I am not saying that we should swoon around the house—or march around the house—wearing the air "I am a great artist." What I am saying is that if you are a writer and someone doesn't respect your writing time, she is not respecting you. If you are a pianist and someone doesn't respect your need to practice, he is not respecting your personal and professional priorities.

Some people batter us often and for agendas of their own. Other people, excellent ones, may bruise us as they racket through a set of terrifying personal rapids.

> *There are so many selves in everybody and to explore and exploit just one is wrong, dead wrong, for the creative person.*
>
> JAMES DICKEY

> *The world is made up of stories, not of atoms.*
>
> MURIEL RUKEYSER

Learning to decipher which is which takes practice. As artists, we must practice generosity not only toward others but also toward ourselves.

Early in a creative career, sainthood isn't too common. But as we become revered and respected for our work, we can develop a weakness for being revered and respected. Our Achilles' heel can be the compliment that makes us feel that we alone can properly mentor a talented youngster. This seemingly harmless form of hubris actually undercuts our own usefulness to the young artists we tutor. Yes, yes, it's wonderful to be a wonderful teacher, a generous friend, but it's healthier to be ourselves, active artists acting on our own behalf. "You cannot transmit what you haven't got," 12-Step programs warn, and unless we make room for art, we resent making room for everything else. And some people—the gifted but needy student or colleague—always ask us to make too much room for them. And we cooperate!

Rather than speak our mind to someone else, we turn up the voice-over in our own head. This is that chiding voice that says "Now, now. Be nice. Be reasonable. Be whatever is convenient for everyone else."

Ours is a culture that tells us "bigger is always better" and that "more" is better too. As artists, big is not always better and more is sometimes less. As artists, when we overdiversify, we also grow diffused. The name we have worked so hard to make means less as it is stretched too thin—along with our energies—in the name of being a "good sport," a "good guy," a "mensch." As artists, we know all too well how a helping hand at a timely intersection can move us up the ladder. Is it any wonder that as we first feel the rush of success, we often rush to help too many others? Directors may overcommit to "executive-producing" to help younger directors. They become a creative umbrella for less developed talents and often fail to see when that umbrella is so big that it puts their own work into the shade. Committing to help others, we may undercommit to ourselves. Instead of investing our energies wisely in husbanding what we have gained and making a modest expansion, we "go for broke"—a telling phrase—and in the end we break our own hearts by being overtired, overextended, and bankrupt of our own creative energies. When we "energy-debt" to others, the worst debt we incur is to ourselves.

> *Creativity is really the structuring of magic.*
>
> ANN KENT RUSH

Without sufficient containment for our own temperaments to thrive, without physical and psychic walls to shield us from the demands and dramas of others, we become overstressed. Our nerves short-circuit and our ideas lash like live wires—

we are filled with energy, but it's not grounded and usable. Our art suffers and so do we. When we begin to set boundaries—no calls after eleven, no calls before eight, no work on Saturdays, and no on-demand makeup lessons for missed classes—we begin to experience a sense of faith. Why? Because we feel safe. It is hard to have faith in the future when we have no charity for ourselves in the present. When we ourselves feel like the food source, it is hard to find food for thought.

We cannot chronically and repeatedly make up the shortfalls of our colleagues without exhausting ourselves and our resources. We cannot chronically and repeatedly allow others to spend our time and our energy foolishly without discovering eventually that we have been robbed of our creative lives—and given the burglars the keys. We cannot take on "difficult" people and situations to prove our heroism and realistically expect to be either heroic or triumphant in the long run. Saving the day too often means that at the end of the day we have nothing left for ourselves, our own lives, loves, and passions. What we have is a life squandered and not cherished, misspent and not invested.

Life is denied by lack of attention, whether it be to cleaning windows or trying to write a masterpiece.

NADIA BOULANGER

When we insist on playing God by trying to be all-powerful and all-understanding and all-giving and all things to all people, God can work no miracles in our own lives, because we never allow the time or space to let a divine hand enter our affairs. While it is true the divine source is an inexhaustible flow, as humans we are finite. We do tire, and we tire most easily from tiresome people.

TASK
Invest in Yourself Energetically

Sometimes, it takes a little sleuthing to actually see our self-destructive patterns. We are so enculturated to "not be selfish" that we may have difficulty setting aside the demands and expectations of others. Our own artist may be so concerned with helping to caretake other artists, we may find our stores of optimism depleted. When we reach for our inner resources, we find that our inner well has run dry, quite simply tapped too many times to help others.

Set aside a solid half hour's writing time. You are going to write—and receive—a letter from your artist's best friend suggesting that you make a few simple changes.

The writer of your letter intends nothing but good and has been watching you and how you lead your life for a long time. There will be some simple suggestions—"Get more sleep"—and some complicated suggestions—"See less of Annie."

Some of the ideas are going to be surprisingly do-able—"Take a life-drawing class"—and others will require some thought—"You need new friends." Allow your letter writer to say whatever is needed to bring you to reality in ways that you chronically sell yourself short. At the end of a half hour, read your letter carefully and place it in your God Jar. If you have carefully selected a "believing mirror," you may additionally wish to share the letter with that friend.

I am what is around me.

WALLACE STEVENS

CHECK-IN

1. **How many days this week did you do your Morning Pages?** If you skipped a day, why did you skip it? How was the experience of writing them for you? Are you experiencing more clarity? A wider range of emotions? A greater sense of detachment, purpose, and calm? Did anything surprise you? Is there a "repeating" issue asking to be dealt with?

2. **Did you do your Artist's Date this week?** Did you note an improved sense of well-being? What did you do and how did it feel? Remember, Artist's Dates can be difficult and you may need to coax yourself into taking them.

3. **Did you get out on your Weekly Walk?** How did that feel? What emotions or insights surfaced for you? Were you able to walk more than once? What did your walk do for your optimism and sense of perspective?

4. **Were there any other issues this week that felt significant to you in your self-discovery?** Describe them.

Discovering a Sense of Boundaries

Creativity requires vigilant self-nurturing. The damaging impact of toxic inflow must be countered and neutralized. This week's readings and tasks focus on helping us to interact with the world in ways that minimize negativity and maximize productive stimulation.

Containment

My favorite Tarot card is the Magician. I think of it as the artist's card. He stands alone, holding one arm aloft, summoning the power of the heavens. He has no audience. His power—and our own—lies in our connection, personal and private, to the divine. As artists, we may perform in public, we may publish or show in public, but we must invoke and rehearse and practice and incubate and first execute within a circle of safety and privacy—or else.

Or else what?

Making a piece of art requires two very different forms of intelligence—the largeness of vision to conceptualize a project and the precision and specificity to bring that project fully and carefully to focused form. Often a project will reveal itself in large swaths very rapidly—like a series of lightning strikes. An artist will see clearly and quickly the large thing she is going to build. Then, years may follow as she labors to bring in what it is she saw. During those years, focus can be lost or diffused by distracting and destructive influences.

When you are conceptualizing something large, sketching in the lineaments of a book or play, a picky and inappropriate question can derail your process, sometimes catastrophically. If you say, "I have started to write a new novel" and the per-

An essential portion of any artist's labor is not creation so much as invocation.

LEWIS HYDE

Art is not a pastime but a priesthood.

JEAN COCTEAU

son across the table asks, "What's your closer?" that can be a very destructive question. You may not know that yet—nor should you. Material needs time to evolve and find its own feet. As you live with a piece, writing it and "finding" it, it will tell you the answers to those questions—however, if you overplot a piece of work first, trying to dictate its shape, you can run into the same problem a parent might have deciding at a child's birth that he should be a mathematician, doctor, lawyer, or opera singer—the child may not agree. Given a long enough creative childhood—and enough privacy—your project will reveal itself eventually to you as its parent. But a protective parent we must learn to be.

As artists, we must be very careful to protect ourselves and our work from premature questions and assumptions. It is not appropriate to describe our work in a few short sentences, watching the look of interest turn into one of "I'll pass" on the listener's face. Talk uses creative power. Talk dilutes our feelings and passions. Not always, but usually. It is only talk with the right person and at the right time that is useful.

As artists, we must learn to practice containment. Our ideas are valuable. Sharing them with someone who is not discerning is like being talked out of a precious stone—you knew it was a diamond until someone tossed it aside. Most of us do not have the self-worth to yell, "Hey, that's the Hope diamond you just discussed!" But it might have been.

In order for persons or projects to grow, they require a safe container. Both a person and a project need a roof over their head. Both a person and a project need walls for privacy. Just as it is uncomfortable to have people enter your home when it is in chaotic disarray ("Oh, my Lord! What is my red lace bra doing on the piano?!"), it creates embarrassment and discomfort to show a project too early to too many people. What's worse, it's risky. Projects are brainchildren. They deserve our protection.

As the world of commerce has overrun the world of art, artists in all fields are routinely asked to "pitch" their work, or "write up a quick proposal." Any seasoned editor will tell you that a book proposal seldom bears much resemblance to the final book. An honest editor or studio executive will tell you that a great pitch does not often deliver a great book or a great film. This is no mystery. The energy that belonged in making the book or film was wasted and diffused by the "selling" of an idea that wasn't yet in solid form.

Just as we wouldn't wake the baby so that the party guests could all coo and chortle and loom at her, we don't want to trot our projects out like performing seals. We all know the horror stories about toddlers who were told "Sing, darling!" Well, projects prematurely exposed to scrutiny tend also to develop a certain sullenness about growing up. We call our projects "brainchildren," and that word can be instructive. Just as it is traumatic to talented youngsters to trot them out and demand they perform for the dinner guests, with later psychotherapy and stage fright as a result, so, too, our projects can develop mysterious tics and phobias if they are prematurely auditioned and critiqued.

Writers' conferences are dark with the stories of books that miscarried by being read too soon and by the wrong eyes. "I showed an early draft to a friend who was a blocked writer. The comments were so negative, I never got the book back on track."

As a young writer, I, too, made the mistake of showing an early draft of a novel to a friend who wanted to write but wasn't writing. "Nothing happens in this novel," my friend complained, meaning no murder, no mayhem, no bloodcurdling drama of the kind she longed to write. The drama in my book was psychological—as I am sure was the writer's block that sent the novel straight to a bottom desk drawer, where it lived out the rest of its days despite an encouraging note from the one other reader I had sent it to, a New York editor who liked it.

Before we became so modern, many marriages began with meeting a friend of a friend. People vouched for the person they felt you might find interesting. And people vouched for you. In the arts, we need to be alert to the need for such checks and balances. If someone says to you, as to me, "So-and-so could help you with your musical," then you'd better find out if they have ever had any actual success helping anyone with a musical, or if they are an "expert" with nothing to share but their largely unworkable theories.

> *Always the wish that you may find patience enough in yourself to endure, and simplicity enough to believe; that you may acquire more and more confidence in that which is difficult, and in your solitude among others.*
>
> RAINER MARIA RILKE

As artists, we are open-minded but we need not be gullible. Many of the people purporting to be able to help us shape our craft have very little experience with crafting something themselves. What we are looking for is people who have done what we want to do—not someone who has watched others do it. It feels different to be in the cockpit at Cape Canaveral than it does to watch from the ground. A great writer like Tom Wolfe may be able to accurately convey the experience, or damn nearly, but many "experts" in your art may not have enough knowledge of creative liftoff to safely teach you how to withstand its rigors.

It is experience that teaches what a tremor means and what it does not. As artists, we must find people who can share actual experience rather than a sanitized, dramatized, glorified, or press-filtered version. When "help" is volunteered, we must be certain it is timely and actually helpful. We must ask ourselves always, "Am I opening myself or my art to early and improper input, input that is ungrounded or inappropriate?" Another way to put it is: "Do they really know more about what I am doing than I do?"

The sacred circle of privacy is like the seal on a bell jar. It keeps the contents fresh. It keeps germs from getting in. It's unpleasant to say friends can be germs— but they certainly can be. They can "spoil" a batch of paintings or a perfectly good play by their few ill-considered or even malicious remarks.

> *All in all, the creative act is not performed by the artist alone; the spectator brings the work in contact with the external world.*
>
> MARCEL DUCHAMP

Cooking images are very apt and very clear: "Too many cooks spoil the broth" being a homelier way of saying "Practice containment." Keep your creative ingredients your own.

You do not want people prematurely tasting your project and making worried little murmurs. You do not want their ingredients added before you have done what you want with the ingredients you yourself chose.

You may not have added your spice yet when they say "Terribly flat." Instead of catching on, *Oops, this applesauce needs cinnamon,* you may think, *Oh, dear, bad applesauce,* and toss the whole batch out.

One of the most useful creative laws I know is this: "The first rule of magic is containment."

TASK
Practicing Containment

Most blocked creatives are blocked not by a lack of talent but by a lack of containment. Rather than practice discernment and discretion in whom we choose to show a project to, we throw open the doors and welcome comments from all corners. If we look closely at why we have abandoned certain projects and dreams, we can often find the offender—the ruthless commentator that caused us to lose heart.

TASK
Rescue and Recall

Entire novels, movies, and musicals have been rescued, resuscitated, and restored through this simple reclamation tool. One best-selling nonfiction book owes its publication to this too. You might want to try it.

Take pen in hand and answer these questions as quickly as you can. That will give you the information with minimal pain; the information will give you back your power.

1. Have you ever spoiled a creative project by indiscriminate input too early?
2. What was the project?
3. What was the input?
4. What about that input especially confused or threw you?
5. How long did it take you to realize what had happened to you and your project?
6. Have you looked at the project again?
7. Can you commit to looking at the project again?
8. Choose a friend to whom you can commit that you will reexamine your project.
9. Reexamine your project. (Do this process as gently as you can.)
10. Call your friend and debrief your findings.

If you do not already own a God Jar, select or designate one now. A God Jar is a container for your sacred hopes and dreams. It might be a ginger jar, a cookie tin, a Chinese porcelain vase. My God Jar is Chinese porcelain and features two intertwining dragons, the symbols for creativity in Chinese lore. Into your God Jar should go the name and description of anything you are trying to incubate or protect. The play I am hatching goes into the God

A miracle is an event which creates faith. That is the purpose and nature of miracles.

GEORGE BERNARD SHAW

Jar—not into group discussion. The difficulty I am having in my rewrite also goes into the God Jar, as do my hopes for a successful resolution.

In addition to a physical God Jar, it also helps to select one person as a personal "believing mirror." A believing mirror is a carefully chosen individual who helps a project's growth by believing in it even in embryonic stages. A believing mirror ideally practices a form of shared containment. The seed of an idea is protected and incubated by the warmth of their shared belief. Another way to think of a believing mirror is the old expression "secret sharer." It is a form of containment to select a trustworthy companion for our dreams and to confide their shape there only. Most of us need to talk to someone, sometime, about our creative aspirations. The right person to talk to is a believing mirror.

Inflow

Ours is a stimulating world—often an overstimulating one. We have cell phones, car phones, radios, televisions, and the constant barrage of media in all forms. Beyond this, we have our families, our friends, our jobs, and our other pursuits—all potential sources of stress and sensory overload. As our phones shrill, we, too, become shrill and rung out.

> *It always comes down to the same necessity; go deep enough and there is a bedrock of truth, however hard.*
>
> MAY SARTON

"I can't hear myself think," we sometimes say, and we are not lying about that. If "still waters run deep," the noisy rapids of our lives make it hard to be anything but shallow. Our deeper selves are muffled, overtaxed, and overextended. Our sensibilities are stripped of their fine tuning. We become numb to our own responses and reactions. Life is "too much" for many of us.

The act of making art requires sensitivity, and when we cultivate sufficient sensitivity for our art, we often find that the tumult of life takes a very high toll on our psyches. We become overwrought and overtired. Our energies are drained not by coping with our output of creative energy but from coping with the ceaseless inflow of distractions and distresses that bid for our time, attention, and emotional involvement. As artists, we are great listeners, and as the volume is pitched too high, our inner ear and our inner work suffers.

When a creative artist is fatigued, it is often from too much inflow, *not* too much outflow. When we are making something, we are listening to an inner voice that has many things to tell us—if we will listen. It is hard to listen amid chatter. It is hard to listen amid chaos. It is hard to listen amid the static of ungrounded and demanding energy.

Contrary to mythology about us, artists are generous, often overly generous. We listen to others deeply, sometimes too deeply for our own good. We are susceptible to their hurt feelings and their pouting when we withdraw, and so sometimes we do listen to them even as our creative energy ebbs out of our own life and into theirs. This creates exhaustion, irritation, and, finally, rage.

It's not that we are unwilling to share our time and attention. It is that people must give us the courtesy of listening accurately to our needs about when and how we can do it. We may have huge energy stores, but they are *our* energy stores and we have the right to determine along what lines we want our energies to flow. For this reason, we may need to draw more boundaries than many people, and those who love us must be conscious that unless they can respect this, they are not a friend at all.

And when is there time to remember, to sift, to weigh, to estimate, to total?

TILLIE OLSEN

As artists, our inflow level must be kept manageable and we must "train" our friends and families and colleagues at work when and how we need our space, both physical and psychic. This may mean no calls in the morning before eleven. Or voice-mail calls returned every day after three. It may mean "Patience. No contact on demand."

For many artists, expressing is almost a matter of emptying themselves to let inspiration move through them. We do not want to be in our human personalities and concerns when we are in the midst of creating. This is why busy executives have secretaries—to monitor their inflow and keep it from becoming overwhelming to their creative process. As artists, we may need this same protective shield and have to erect it ourselves.

Virginia Woolf said all artists need a room of their own—I think that room may be at Starbucks, or in the basement, or in the bathroom, sitting on the floor. It may be the words "Not now."

An artist requires solitude and quiet—which is different from solemnity and isolation. Artists require respect for their thoughts and their process, but that respect must start with us. An artist needs to be treated well—but often we are the ones who must begin that treatment, and one way we do it is by carefully setting our own valve on how much inflow is allowed to come into us. When we are embedded in family life, or in a sea of students, this can be difficult. If our phone rings constantly, we can't hear ourselves think. When something "gets to us," that is often quite literal because it *gets* to us. We want to "be reasonable." We want to not "fly off the handle." But it can be too much to handle the building up of something yearning to be expressed (inner pressure) and the nudging to conform (outer pressure) to what a "normal" person might act like. Creativity is a process of birth. Labor pain is not a time for manners.

Labor is intense and it is intimate. The whole psyche is turned inward to cooperate with what is being born. Similarly, when I write a book, I am listening to what I must write. When I am writing music, I am following a melody line that I must hear in my head. That takes attention. Attention requires focus. If we have friends and colleagues who, when we don't take their calls, do not get that we're busy, that is a form of abuse to us as artists. "Are you working?" must be asked and answered truthfully. Why? Because when we create, we are psychically very open. We can be flooded by energies. Creative energy—and psychic energy—can flow in many directions. When our friends interrupt our creative time to ask us to problem-solve for them, they are often inadvertently squandering our creative energies. They are deflecting our creative energy into flow lines that will illuminate their work and their lives and not our own. When people simply call and download in great detail, our creative energy gets depleted by trying to solve their problems. "So, don't do it," you might say. Easier said than done.

> *Living in process is being open to insight and encounter. Creativity is becoming intensively absorbed in the process and giving it form.*
>
> SUSAN SMITH

Creative work is often invisible to other people. If they see you typing, they may know you're writing. If they hear the piano picking out a tune, they may realize music is afoot, but even the threat of interruption may strike them as bearable.

"This will take just a minute," they say without realizing that they are breaking the thread of your concentration and that finding the thread again may be very, very hard.

It is difficult enough to make a piece of art without the added burden of being available while you are doing it. For many very creative people it is hard to muster the self-worth to say "I will get back to you" or "I cannot talk now." As simple as such boundaries sound in the telling, you need only listen for a few minutes to the perceived "selfishness" of a creative parent to recognize that we have a culture where on-tap and on-demand attention are equated with love, and deferred gratification is equated with coldness.

"My father wrote first thing in the morning," the daughter of a famed creator recalls with scarcely banked fury. "Only afterward was he available to be a parent. . . ."

Perhaps, because much creative work is done in the home, the necessity of boundaries is more resented than, say, a banker father's work hours away from the house. Perhaps, too, there is a certain sibling rivalry as "brainchildren" are perceived as competition for parental or espousal attention.

Just a tender sense of my own inner process, that holds something of my connection with the divine.

PERCY BYSSHE SHELLEY

Love the moment, and the energy of that moment will spread beyond all boundaries.

CORITA KENT

A hardworking portrait artist whose commissioned work required long studio hours and great discipline to meet client deadlines like birthdays and Christmas ruefully recalled that "studio time was considered fair game. My friends would call from their office, unaware that they were, in effect, interrupting me at my office—and I had no secretary to deflect the calls."

For many of us, turning the phone off is an option we have never considered. TV and radio are also automatic—almost a form of civic duty. We "have to" be informed. Silence can be very threatening, but it is a threat worth trying in half-hour increments. Practice turning everything off—for one half hour—and tuning into yourself. A half hour is time enough for a bath, a letter, a bit of reading, a manicure, some meditation. It is just long enough to hear yourself think or catch a cat-nap. What you do with your half hour matters less than the fact that it is *yours*. Setting even such small boundaries is a huge step toward self-care—which leads to the self in self-expression.

TASK

A Room of Your Own

For most of us, privacy takes a little planning. We love our friends, our family, and our art. In order to be alone together, "just the two of us," you and your art—you may need to sneak off like illicit lovers, or plan a weekend away like a married couple trying to keep the zing of romance in their relationship. Take pen in hand and list 10 ways and places you can have privacy with your art. For example:

1. I could get up an hour early.
2. I could stay up an hour late.
3. I could take my artist to Starbucks for a writing date.
4. I could borrow the key to a friend's apartment and go do my art there.
5. I could take a sketchbook or notebook and go sit in the back of a church.
6. I could take a train ride.
7. I could find a quiet reading room at a library.
8. I could arrange with friends to hide out and house-sit while they're out of town.
9. I could go home to my family; it could drive me to the page, the easel, the sketchbook.
10. I could plan and execute a tiny vacation. Even a day and a half of solitude could reorder my thoughts and priorities.

Day Jobs

If we do not limit our inflow, we become swamped by the life demands of others. If we practice too much solitude, we risk being flooded by stagnation and a moody narcissism as our life and our art become emptied of all but the big question "How am I doing?" What we are after is a balance, enough containment and autonomy to make our art, enough involvement and immersion in community to have someone and something to make art for.

> *And beyond even self-doubt no writer can justify ruthlessness for the sake of his work, because being human to the fullest possible extent is what his work demands of him.*
>
> MAY SARTON

Raymond Chandler sold insurance. T. S. Eliot worked in a bank. Virginia Woolf ran a printing press with her husband, Leonard. What gives us the idea that people with "day jobs" can't be real artists? Very often our day jobs feed our consciousness. They bring us people and ideas, stories and subjects, opportunities as much as obstacles. A day job is not something to "outgrow." It is something to consider, especially if your art feels stale. You may have cannibalized your own creative stores and need to restore them with contact from new sources. As artists, we need life, or our art is lifeless.

Art thrives on life. Life feeds it, enriches it, enlarges it. Cloistering ourselves away from life in the name of being artists causes us to run the risk of producing art that is arid, artless, and, yes, heartless.

For most artists, there is something risky about too much unstructured time, too much freedom to make nothing but art. We talk about self-expression, but we must develop a self to express. A self is developed not only alone, but in community. Community functions like resistance in weight-training—the contact with others makes us stronger and more defined. Day jobs help not only to pay the rent but also to build stamina and structure. Artists need both stamina and structure.

Often, a day job provides both. A novel can be a vast savannah in which I wander alone—a musical may mean six years sailing across uncharted seas. Navigators needed the stars to structure their voyages. We artists, too, need other points of reference to stay on course.

Chekhov advised young actors: "If you want to work on your art, work on yourself." He did not mean "Contemplate yourself." He meant we ought to do those things that develop in us creative sinew. A day job can do that. So can some committed community service. So can taking the time to practice the art of listening to something other than our own concerns. A day job requires that skill.

Although we might like to think of ourselves as more rarified, artists are people, and people *do* need people. And things. And hobbies. And, yes, fun. If you strip your life down to get serious about your art, you will find that you get serious, period. If all you think about is your Art with a capital A, then it's always there, twitching and heaving like a space alien having its death throes in the middle of your stark, serene, and artsy loft. You begin to wonder how you will ever lift that thing or even get it out of the house for a walk. Your serious career begins to become your serious problem, which you can talk about, seriously, to other "serious" artists and, perhaps, to an endlessly empathetic therapist who understands how sensitive you are. None of this will get much art done.

The concept "I am a serious full-time artist" can get a little dreary—like one of those oversized New York artist lofts does in a chill winter light. What do you fill

> *If we had to say what writing is, we would define it essentially as an act of courage.*
> CYNTHIA OZICK

> *A clay pot sitting in the sun will always be a clay pot. It has to go though the white heat of the furnace to become porcelain.*
> MILDRED WITTE STOUVEN

a space like that, a concept like that, with? Lofts are supposed to be empty to be chic. And if you start emptying your life of normal human pursuits so it looks like a "serious" artist's life "should," pretty soon you've got the same problem as that drafty acre of chic industrial space: groovy, but do you really want to live there? Doesn't all that empty hipness make you want to visit your aunt Rachel's homey, overstuffed three rooms, where there is a lot of bric-a-brac and comforting clutter and food in the refrigerator?

In our cash-conscious culture, we have a mythology that says you must be a full-time artist to be a real artist. We hear this to mean "no day jobs." The actual truth is we are all full-time artists. Art is a matter of consciousness.

> *It is the soul's duty to be loyal to its own desires. It must abandon itself to its master passion.*
>
> REBECCA WEST

A friend of mine gets cranky when he is separated too long from his piano. He also gets cranky when he is closeted too long with his piano. Our love affair with our art is like any other love affair—it needs separation as much as it needs togetherness.

Our life is supposed to be our life and our art is supposed to be something we do *in* it and with it. Our life must be larger than our art. It must be the container that holds it.

Life is not linear. Our Artist's Way is a long and winding road, and we travel it best in the company of others, engaged not in the inner movie of the ego but in the outer-directed attention that fills the well with images and stocks the imagination with stories. Rather than yearning to be "full-time artists," we might aspire to being full-time humans. When we do, art is the overflow of a heart filled with life.

That day job may not be a millstone after all. It might be a life-support system.

TASK

Commune with Your Community

We have a great deal of "artist-as-loner mythology." It is as false as our mythology regarding the American West. Cowboys didn't settle the West. Families did. Communities did. Similarly, art is made by artists who know and love other artists and other people. When we think about who and what we love, we get ideas about who and what we would love to make. When we think about what my aunt Bernice would enjoy seeing, we begin to see in a new way, more focused and particular. Modern life is restless. We often move from city to city and in moving we lose touch with parts of ourselves and whole communities. We encompass a great many "chosen losses," and to make it up to ourselves, we must also learn to encompass "chosen gains." Ritual and regularity are a part of how we commit to community.

Take pen in hand and answer the following questions:

1. A daily ritual I could take in community is _____.
2. A community paper I could read is _____.
3. A community store I could support is _____.
4. A community concern I could support is _____.
5. A community service I could volunteer is _____.

Sometimes our commitment is as small as a daily cup of coffee in the same coffee shop. Our community reading might be the local underground paper or a networking paper in our field, let us say *Back Stage* for actors or *The Village Voice Literary Supplement* for writers. We might buy our Christmas and birthday presents at the local independent children's bookstore. We might join a cleanup crew on "park day" or spend one hour a week reading to the elderly. None of these community commitments requires training, and they all offer

> *While you are upon earth, enjoy the good things that are here.*
>
> JOHN SELDEN

us an anchor in the changing seas of life. All of us need a good dose of daily sweetness—the goodwill we put into life and the good cheer we draw from cherished familiar faces. Artists may need community and companionship more, not less, than other people. Our projects can take a long time to incubate, develop, and mature. In the meanwhile, we need a life and life needs us.

CHECK-IN

1. How many days this week did you do your Morning Pages? If you skipped a day, why did you skip it? How was the experience of writing them for you? Are you experiencing more clarity? A wider range of emotions? A greater sense of detachment, purpose, and calm? Did anything surprise you? Is there a "repeating" issue asking to be dealt with?

2. **Did you do your Artist's Date this week?** Did you note an improved sense of well-being? What did you do and how did it feel? Remember, Artist's Dates can be difficult and you may need to coax yourself into taking them.

3. **Did you get out on your Weekly Walk?** How did that feel? What emotions or insights surfaced for you? Were you able to walk more than once? What did your walk do for your optimism and sense of perspective?

4. **Were there any other issues this week that felt significant to you in your self-discovery?** Describe them.

Discovering a Sense of Momentum

Creativity thrives on small, do-able actions. This week dismantles procrastination as a major creative block. The readings and tasks aim at a sense of personal accountability and accomplishment. The key to a creative life is sustained, consistent, positive action. This is possible for all of us.

Easy Does It, But Do It: Flow

Most artists get blocked not because they have too few ideas but because they have too many. Our competing ideas create a sort of logjam—and that is why we feel stuck. When we think about a project, we think, *I could try this and this and this and maybe I could try this and this and this and, oh, I could try that and then and what if and oh, dear!*

When we get to the *Oh, dear!* the mental gears either clutch up and freeze, leaving them stuck and immobilized, or they start to whir frantically, like a bike pedal when the chain has slipped. Is it any wonder we get confused and frightened? Sometimes, our friends unintentionally panic us, even our closest friends. I remember a testy, difficult lunch with my beloved friend and frequent director, John Newland. I had just started work on a new musical—songs and concepts felt like they were being dumped down a chimney into the top of my head—a little like Santa Claus gone berserk and just pouring the presents willy-nilly from the rooftop. John innocently asked, "What's your act one closer?" I didn't know. I had so many ideas, I couldn't even read the menu much less plot the show's proper build.

"Don't ask me that!" I wailed. "I don't know!" I snapped.

"It's just *me,*" John chided, "your old *friend.* Why are you so angry?"

I was angry because I was overwhelmed, I was overwhelmed because I had so many ideas about what I *could* do that I was panicked.

Whenever you feel stymied, stuck, or frantic, remind yourself, this is the result of having too many good ideas—even if it feels like you have no good ideas at all.

The trick is to establish a gentle flow, to keep that gentle flow trickling forward. This keeps the dammed-up ideas from bursting through and flooding you. It keeps the pressure from becoming so great, it clogs your mental system and shuts down your flow, leaving you even more tense, like an overfilled balloon.

Remember, creativity is not fickle, finite, or limited. There are always ideas. Good ideas. Workable ideas, brave and revolutionary ideas. Calm and serviceable ideas. The trick is to gently access them and allow them to flow. In other words, it's time for that 12-Step adage "Easy does it," because the truth is, easy *does* do it, and frantic, forced, and frenetic does not.

> *The season is changeable, fitful, and maddening as I am myself these days that are cloaked with too many demands and engagements.*
>
> MAY SARTON

> *It is in the knowledge of the genuine conditions of our lives that we must draw our strength to live and our reasons for living.*
>
> SIMONE DE BEAUVOIR

You must take some small step or the ideas will remain jammed up and the creative pressure behind the jam will continue to escalate. When it does, it will often manifest as attacks of self-doubt and self-loathing. "I am so stupid!" you might wail, when the actual problem is "I am so smart!"

What you are trying to do is move energy out of you. That is what starts the logjam gently moving. That is why you cannot achieve calm by listening to talk radio or watching TV—or listening to your friends' helpful suggestions for that matter. You want to quiet your mind by gently siphoning off its overflow, not adding to it.

In our culture, we are trained to deal with anxiety by always putting more in. A drink, a shopping spree, a rendezvous with Häagen-Dazs—we tend to medicate our anxieties, not listen to them. The trick is to flow more out, not add more in.

This is where you can serve others and yourself. Instead of zoning out with the news, write your elderly uncle a letter. The operative word is "write." Do not call to talk. You do not want to tip the balance further by adding in more. You need to release thoughts. Think of a balloon that's too full. If you let air out, it zips ahead.

If you blow more air in, things pop. When you feel tense and stuck, your life is like that too-taut, overfilled balloon. You are stretched too tight. This is why you cannot let in the well-meaning words of friends. This is why the chatter of a neighbor drives you suddenly so crazy. This is why you are a hair trigger. You are too full of creative energy and you need to gently siphon some off. Take a walk and remind yourself:

1. I do have good ideas.
2. I have many good ideas.
3. Slowly and gently, one at a time, I can execute them.

People become addicted to talk therapy because it does temporarily siphon energy off. People become addicted to overmedicating because it wins them momentary relief from their too-full state. So does overexercising. What is needed is to make forward motion creatively. The truer the dream, the more creative pressure it has, and the more important it is to begin with small actions to keep them from getting frozen up. Don't just talk. *Do.* You need to express yourself in some concrete, small way.

If your head is awhirl and you "cannot think straight," then start by straightening something up. Fold your laundry. Sort your drawers. Go through your closet and hang things more neatly. Straighten your bed. Go get the lemon Pledge and dust and shine your bookcase and your dresser—often, when we are engaged in such small, homely tasks, a sense of being "at home" will steal over us. When we take the time to husband the details of our lives, we may encounter a sense of grace. In 12-Step slang, "God" has often been said to stand for "Good Orderly Direction." Often, in making a sense of order, we encounter a direction we can valuably express ourselves in.

A letter, a memo, a stack of valentine's cards. This will prime the pump. In my creative practice, I write daily. Every day. Three pages in the morning. Almost always some more writing follows later in the day. When I began writing music, I at first binged on it and wore myself out. Then I was afraid to start again, and pressure built up. When I learned that it, too, yielded to the "a little daily keeps it flowing" technique, I slowed way down, and my productivity speeded way up.

You need to claim the events of your life to make yourself yours. When you truly possess all you have been and done, which may take some time, you are fierce with reality.

Flonda Scott Maxwell

No matter how stupid and overwhelmed you may feel in the face of the complexities and terrors of change, the problem is not—not *ever*—that you are stupid. It is simply that your excellent mind is working overtime and so you need to calm it down. Instead of discounting your anxiety or labeling your anxiety, use it as creative fuel.

TASK

Easy Does It, But Do *Do It*

A close friend of mine accuses me of practicing the Martha Stewart school of creativity. A man who lives with his wife and servants, he has all but forgotten the sense of well-being that comes from doing one small something to sort our world and our own place in it. Most of us have many small areas where we could benefit from a little housekeeping. Take pen in hand and list five areas that you could neaten up. Choose one area and execute a little cleanliness-is-next-to-godliness energy—does this experiment put you in touch with a greater sense of benevolence?

A few examples of possible chores:

1. Polish my shoes.
2. Clear the surface of my desk.
3. Straighten out my bookshelves.
4. Sort my receipts into good order.
5. Throw out old magazines.

What we are after with this task is the experience of using stuck energy in a productive way, however small. Once we realize that our sense of being stymied by the outer world can actually be altered by simple and small actions on our own part, we begin to have more faith in the benevolence of the universe itself. In other words, if God is in the details, we had better be there ourselves!

Breakthroughs

One of the difficulties with the creative life is that when we have creative breakthroughs, they may look and even be experienced as breakdowns. Our normal, ordinary way of seeing ourselves and the world suddenly goes on tilt, and as it does, a new way of seeing and looking at things comes toward us. Sometimes this "new vision" can seem almost hallucinogenic in its persuasive shifting of perspective. What seemed certain now seems uncertain. What seemed out of the question now seems possible, even probable. It is as though we have had a strobe light sweep across our experience and freeze into bas relief a certain previously unquestioned assumption.

> *Life ought to be a struggle of desire toward adventures whose nobility will fertilize the soul.*
>
> DAME REBECCA WEST

> *Courage—fear that has said its prayers.*
>
> DOROTHY BERNARD

Creativity is grounded not in dreamy vagueness but in piercing clarity. We "see" a piece of work and then we work to shape it. We "envision" a new direction and then we move toward it. The creative journey is characterized not by a muzzy and hazy retreat from reality but by the continual sorting and reordering and structuring of reality into new forms and new relationships. As artists, we "see things differently." In part, this is because we are looking.

When we are willing to look—and willing to see what we see—we open ourselves to losing comfortable assumptions about the nature of "things." Those things may be creative—we paint a chair at skewed angles because that seems more "chair" to us suddenly—and this new viewing may apply to our human relationships as well. Suddenly and unexpectedly, we may apprehend them in a new and startling light. Sometimes such breakthroughs are frightening. When they are, we might call them "strobe-light clarity."

We might realize equally, "This relationship is going nowhere" or "My God, I am going to marry this man." Suddenly, our future has different casting than we imagined. We got a clear glimpse of ourselves solo or in an unexpected coupling. Such glimpses, a kind of "flash forward to your future," can be very disorienting. We "see" the shape of things to come, but that doesn't mean they are "there" yet. The bad relationship still needs to finish falling apart. The new relationship needs to finish coming together. We "know" what's going to happen, but we cannot force time to match our perceptions—and we ourselves actually need time to become grounded and able to handle the change we have foreseen.

When strobe-light clarity hits an area of our life or our work, we suddenly see the outlines of that arena with startling and heightened drama. "Why, I could paint this way!" we gasp, or "My God, she has no intention of ever standing on her own two feet. I am not helping her, I am enabling her!" When strobe-light clarity hits, it is harsh but distorted. We get a quick and terrifying glimpse of an unfamiliar truth that has the same disorienting effect as a strobe light flashed across the dance floor—everything jerks into new positions without our seeing the transitions. It can be tempting—in the flash of strobe-light clarity—to dismiss our former work or our former understanding as false. It is not false. It is simply outmoded. The way we used to paint was fine for then. And our friend may well have been authentically helped and is now only trying to create a wrong dependency. Strobe-light clarity is so sudden and so sharp that it is discontinuous. It is something we catch out of the corner of our eye: "What was that?!"

When we have such dramatic breakthroughs in our creative and personal reality, we must take care to integrate and absorb their meaning before acting on them. It is not that all of our prior understandings are inauthentic. It is more that they were incomplete. Our new insight offers a corrective to our prior understanding but it is a corrective that needs to be lived with a little before we act on it.

> *The great thing about getting older is that you don't lose all the other ages you've been.*
>
> MADELEINE L'ENGLE

Strobe-light clarity is the creative equivalent of "This relationship is over." That may well be, but we do not need to move all of our belongings into the street. We can take a beat and assess our future options. When we decide, *I am bored with this art form as I have practiced it,* we are posing a question—"What next?"—that the universe is already in the process of answering. Creativity is always an interactive dance between our inner world and our outer world. Opportunity does not knock only as soon as we are willing to hear it. Arguably, it has been knocking for some time, and we have turned a deaf ear, a blind eye, to what our accepted consciousness had screened out and now is open to receiving.

Sudden breakthroughs *can* feel like breakdowns. It is helpful to think of them not as "breaking down" but as "breaking up." Think of your consciousness like a frozen river that breaks up in spring from a solid sheet to many floes. This is what is happening to your creative consciousness—what was solid is becoming fluid, new forms and new structures are becoming possible. New growth is afoot.

Instead of being unable "to see the forest for the trees," we suddenly see both the forest and the trees. *My God, I could include photographic snippets in my painting surfaces,* we think. We have shifted our mental furniture, repainted the old bureau a beautiful robin's-egg blue and given ourselves a whole new vista and venue.

The narrator should be first person and a male, we suddenly "know." And we "know," too, that it doesn't matter that we are female and writing this character.

Memoirs of a Geisha is a brilliantly conceived and executed first-person narrative of an Oriental woman—written entirely by an Occidental man.

When we get a flash of strobe-light clarity, walls fall away. We see suddenly that we "can" do what we "couldn't" a moment before. We have a "flash" of invention and, like glimpsing the bright underfeathers of a bird, we suddenly realize our creative life is not colorless and lackluster, as we thought.

"I didn't realize what I was doing," we may gasp when we see that behind our own back and through our own hand, the Great Creator has orchestrated something new and original that we had no idea we were making. "Why, if I string all those heartbreak poems together, I have got the spine of a great performance piece. What a great idea!"

Strobe-light clarity is like a glimpse of yourself in a new and for-once-flattering mirror. It's like catching a glimpse of an attractive stranger and then going, "My God, I am that stylish woman." We look so different, so impossibly possible to ourselves that we are caught off guard. Our age falls away and we are abruptly young at heart, caught by the throat with the sudden emotion that says "This is real. . . . " We suddenly get just a glimmer of where we are heading and that new growth is possible, even impending at our advanced age—whatever it is.

Strobe-light clarity tells us this new growth will be terrifying. There is a "monster movie" drama to a sudden flash of insight. "Oh, dear God! What was that?!" we gasp. Seen so quickly and sharply, the most normal things can appear frightening. So it is with our new growth. The thought *I have got to go back to grad school* can be as scary as an ax murderer looming at us from the corner. As the light of reality grows around this sudden thought, the ax murderer begins to look more like a teacher and less like someone who is out to dismember our known reality. When you are in the grips of a sudden and startling flash of clarity, move slowly and gently with yourself so that you do not bolt in terror, tripping on the furniture of your consciousness.

Breakthroughs are not breakdowns. They just feel that way. Remember, you, too, are breakable. Be gentle with yourself while you grow accustomed to your new mental and emotional terrain.

> *Life was meant to be lived and curiosity must be kept alive. One must never, for whatever reason, turn his* [sic] *back on life.*
>
> ELEANOR ROOSEVELT

> *We are not human beings trying to be spiritual. We are spiritual beings trying to be human.*
>
> JACQUELYN SMALL

TASK
Geography

As a child, my favorite subject in school was geography. I loved the images of foreign cultures that startled my eyes—baskets and balls of rubber balanced atop heads; the plane dipping low over the head of the falls; hidden in the jungle highlands; the long, slender wands used by Egyptian healer priests to trace the body's energy meridians; the art and artifacts of other ages called across time and distance.

Begin by considering the following questions.

1.   What culture other than your own speaks to you?
2.   What age other than the one we're in resonates with your sensibilities?
3.   What foreign cuisine feels like home to your palate?
4.   What exotic smells give you a sense of expansion and well-being?
5.   What spiritual tradition intrigues you beyond your own?
6.   What music from another culture plucks your heartstrings?
7.   In another age, what physical age do you see yourself being?
8.   In another culture and time, what is your sex?
9.   Do you enjoy period movies? Or movies, period?
10. If you were to write a film, what age and time, what place and predicament, would you choose to explore?

Now, collect a large and colorful stash of magazines and, if possible, catalogues. Find a good photo of yourself and place it in the center of a large sheet of posterboard. Working rapidly, select images from your magazines and catalogues and use them to establish your leading character—you—in an imaginary world filled with beloved objects and interests.

Finish Something

As artists, we often complain about our inability to begin. *If only I had the nerve to start X*—a novel, a short story, the rewrite on our play, the photo series we're "thinking" of. I would like to suggest that you start somewhere else—start with finishing something.

There must be some obscure law of physics that revs into action when artists finish something. And that something can be reorganizing the medicine cabinet, cleaning out the glove compartment, or taping your cherished road maps back into usable companions. The moment we finish something, we get a sort of celestial pat—sometimes even a shove—a small booster rocket of energy to be applied elsewhere.

How can you begin your thesis if you can't finish your mending? How can you fill out your grad school applications if your shower curtain is stained and torn, half on and half off its rings, while the new curtain waits expectantly folded on the toilet tank?

My favorite thing is to go where I've never been.

DIANE ARBUS

It is good to have an end to journey towards; but it is the journey that matters in the end.

URSULA K. LE GUIN

Most of us have households and studios filled with half-done projects: sorting the photos of our portfolio, a project half in albums, half in shoe boxes; realphabetizing the business Rolodex—another project half done; organizing the consecutive drafts of your last play, yet another "when I get back to it" agenda—the list goes on. No wonder we drag our feet at the thought of starting something else. We've had too many false starts, too many half-finished, halfhearted projects.

Christian, a young composer, had great enthusiasm and a great many projects. He was always racing ahead on some new musical theme, going full steam until something else caught his eye and that something became the focus of a new burst of energy. Christian was the kind of young artist often called "promising," but he was too fragmented to deliver on that promise.

"Clean up your arranging room," an older composer advised him. "Make systems. Put everything in order and give every scrap of work its proper place."

Although he felt that he was wasting time and energy that he could be using on writing music, Christian grudgingly complied. As he began to assemble three-ring binders and put all of the work on each project carefully into place, a curious thing happened: self-respect began to rear its noble head.

I certainly have done a lot of work, Christian caught himself thinking. He saw that several projects were very near completion and that he had been denying himself the satisfaction of a job well done. Predictably, he almost did the same avoidant behavior on organizing the room itself. He worked on it until it was two-thirds done and then he stopped.

No one needs to know that you've shut the world out and are meditating as you stroll down the street. Twenty minutes to a half-hour every day is a good amount of time to restore a sense of serenity.

SARAH BAN BREATHNACH

"How's that arranging room coming?" his friend, the savvy older composer, asked him. Christian confessed that he had stopped before finishing his clean-up.

"It's much better," he said defensively. "I know where almost everything is and you wouldn't believe how much work I have done, really. I had no idea how many projects I had come so far on."

"Finish that room. Get every last bit of it in order. You are close to the reward but not there yet. Finish it and see what happens."

Grudgingly, working under half steam, almost laughing at how he lollygagged and dawdled, Christian finally finished the clean-up of his little room. There was a place for everything. Every project stood squarely in place, sorted and simple to see. Christian felt a buzz of new energy. It felt like optimism but a bit more focused than optimism. It took him a while to name this new emotional component, but when he did he saw it was something different from inspiration, something more solid and firm than hope.

"I felt determination," Christian recalls. Many things that had seemed vague and illusory now seemed squarely within his grasp. A project at a time, moving folder to folder, Christian began completing work. Within a month of arranging his arranging room, Christian had multiple projects in final form, able to be moved to the next step, submitted for grants and competitions.

"I suddenly showed something more than 'promise,'"Christian relates. "I had actual finished projects. I wasn't just 'talented' anymore. I was something much better—productive."

There seems to be an unwritten spiritual law that if we want our good to increase, we must focus on appreciating and husbanding the good that we already experience. This can be done by writing gratitude lists enumerating the many things in our current life that are fruitful and rewarding. On a concrete level, it can be done by the careful husbanding of what we have. This means that buttons get sewn on, hems get tacked up, smudges get scrubbed off doorjambs. We make the very best of exactly what we have and we find that almost behind our back the Great Creator redoubles and reinforces our efforts and makes something even better. This is where the old adage "God helps those who help themselves" can be tested and found to be true.

A body in motion remains in motion, and nowhere is this law more true than in creative endeavors. When we want to grease the creative wheels, we do very well to muster a little elbow grease elsewhere. Mend the trousers. Hang the curtains. I do not know why hemming the droopy pant leg gives you the juice to get to the easel, but it does. I cannot tell you what it is about detoxing the mud

In order to carry out great enterprises, one must live as if one will never have to die.

MARQUIS DE VAUVENARGUES

closet that makes you see more clearly how to end a short story—or start one—but it does.

Finishing almost anything—sorting your CD collection, pumping up a bike tire, matching and mating your socks—creates both order and an inner order: "Now, start something," finishing something says.

TASK
Learning to Navigate the Learning Curve

This is an exercise in encouragement. Faced with doing something new, we often forget we have successfully done many "somethings" old. Take pen in hand and list 10 things you have learned to do despite your doubt they could be mastered.

For example:

1. Spanikopita—I can actually make it and it's good.
2. Spanish—I can actually speak it well enough to communicate more than "How are you?"
3. The backstroke—I didn't drown, and now I like it.
4. How to change oil
5. How to operate my new computer
6. Calculus—another calculated risk I succeeded at
7. Ear training—yes, I *can* notate simple melodies more and more accurately.
8. Reading at open mic—I can speak into the microphone and hold my own most of the time.
9. I did learn how to work Photoshop on my computer.
10. I am able to give my dog heartworm pills without losing my hand.

Skills can be learned, and we can learn that the learning curve always involves excitement, discouragement, dismay, misery, and, eventually, mastery.

CHECK-IN

1. **How many days this week did you do your Morning Pages?** If you skipped a day, why did you skip it? How was the experience of writing them for you? Are you experiencing more clarity? A wider range of emotions? A greater sense of detachment, purpose, and calm? Did anything surprise you? Is there a "repeating" issue asking to be dealt with?

2. **Did you do your Artist's Date this week?** Did you note an improved sense of well-being? What did you do and how did you feel? Remember, Artist's Dates can be difficult and you may need to coax yourself into taking them.

3. **Did you get out on your Weekly Walk?** How did that feel? What emotions or insights surfaced for you? Were you able to walk more than once? What did your walk do for your optimism and sense of perspective?

4. **Were there any other issues this week that felt significant to you in your self-discovery?** Describe them.

Discovering a Sense of Discernment

This week poses a challenge: Are we actually able to go the distance? To answer in the affirmative, we must learn to keep certain demons at bay, most notably success, "the unseen enemy." The readings and tasks of this week aim at naming and declawing the creative monsters that lurk at higher altitudes. Anger is a frequent companion of this week's explorations. As we unmask our villains, we often feel a sense of betrayal and grief. This is replaced by a sense of safety as we name our true supporters more accurately.

Making Art, Not "Making It"

In the study of overeating, it has been discovered that certain foods are "trigger foods"—the first bite leads to the craving for more, more, and more. For many artists, fame is a trigger food, or can be. When fame is sought for itself, we always will want more, more, and more. When it occurs as the by-product of our work—which it does and often will—then it is more easily metabolized. But we must stay focused on *what* we are doing, not *how*.

When we are in the midst of making something, in the actual creative act, we know we are who and what we are because we forget our public reception for a minute. We become the art itself instead of the artist who makes it. In the actual moment of making art, we are blessedly anonymous. Even when done in public, the act of making art is a private act. Creativity is always between us and our creative energy, us and the creative power working through us. When we are able to stay clearly and cleanly focused on that, then we are able to do very well.

We can always make art. What we cannot always do is make it in the venues we might choose or even in the field that we consider our rightful playing field. Actors who are not acting tend to forget that they can still learn a monologue, still try their hand at writing a one-person show, still try learning piano, watercolor, or clay. When we insist that we will express our creativity in only one field, or even in one corner of one field, we lose sight of two things: our versatility and our opportunity. We tend to isolate and to brood, resentful over not being appreciated, resentful over not being chosen when we can actually make choices of our own that put our creative power, if not our "career," squarely back in our own hands.

> *Creative minds have always been known to survive any kind of bad training.*
>
> ANNA FREUD

> *We flood our minds with words! They mesmerize and manipulate us, masking the truth even when it's set down squarely in front of us. To discover the underlying reality, I've learned to listen only to the action.*
>
> JUDITH M. KNOWLTON

It is difficult to be depressed and in action at the same time. Actors forget that the key word is "act." Waiting to be chosen by an agent, waiting to be cast in a part, waiting to be well reviewed, they forget they can put on a show by reading at an open mic, recording monologues on a home video, throwing a benefit for their church group, going to old-age homes and performing. In a word, they can *act*.

Musicians can learn a new music, whether or not it can be seen as applicable to their particular métier. They can remember that the term is "play music," not "work at their career." Broadway melodies are enjoyable to play on the violin. The Beatles can be a welcome change from Bach. If we are really serious about our art, then we need to be serious about making it—not about being perceived as "a serious artist."

Self-respect lies in the writing and the playing, not in the reviews. Not even in the mental review of what has been done. Or how it was perceived in the public eye.

That phrase "the public eye" tells us the danger of focusing on "How am I doing?" instead of "What am I doing?" What exactly is the public eye? And why does it seem to always be closed or winking during our solos?

When making art becomes about making a career and making a profit—not that we don't enjoy those as benefits—then making our art is someone else's responsibility, not our own. We need a "lucky break," we say. We fall into talking about the way it is "in the business," and the odds against us, and the next thing that happens is that we feel powerless and depressed and mad—mad because we're not "making it" fast enough. And we don't mean art.

Clarence was a talented musician, so talented that "big things" had always been predicted for him. He played for "big names" on "big albums" and was always on the verge of his "big break." A chronic dissatisfaction that "it"—the really big break—hadn't happened yet kept Clarence from ever noticing and enjoying the many marvelous and exciting things that did happen. He had played with Bob Dylan and other idols of his. He had appeared on David Letterman's show and toured Europe with a red-hot band. His life looked glamorous from the outside but felt glamourless on the inside. He didn't play music for the joy of it. He played it to impress a producer or to rack up another Grammy nomination.

There has to be more to making art than this, Clarence caught himself thinking, and it was at this point that he saw the flyer calling for parents' help with the school music pageant. No one had contacted him directly. He was too big a fish for that. Looking at the little flyer, Clarence thought, *This might be fun. And the kids would be happy if I got involved.*

Clarence did get involved. Very involved. He had an extensive and expensive home studio where he could record tracks. The "little music pageant" began to have some very glossy and professional musical help. Next Clarence enlisted his wife—talented both as a costume designer and as a fine backup singer. Soon the entire house was filled with lively children's music and draped with brightly colored costumes.

"It's like Santa's workshop over here," Clarence told his friends, laughing. Laughter became a regular guest in the household as Clarence was relieved of his "serious focus" on his "serious career." Never before had the little school had such a sophisticated and happy production. There were even videotapes of the kids' star turns as they sang out to Clarence's professional music tracks.

"I think they got a lot out of it," Clarence said with satisfaction, "and I know I did."

Using his art artfully in the service of his family, community, and friends, Clarence reconnected to the joy that had made him an artist in the first place. He again came in contact with the generous part of himself that spilled out into music and self-expression. His art became about making something instead of about "making it." He now makes time every year for the children's music pageant. It gave him back the gift of giving by putting the "heart" back into his art.

> *Those who lose dreaming are lost.*
>
> AUSTRALIAN ABORIGINAL
> PROVERB

Focused on success as a business goal, we often lose sight of success in terms of our personal spiritual well-being. We focus "out there" rather than on our own inner experience. Doing that, we can become lost.

"I always knew I was supposed to make good," says Joy. "Everyone was betting on me."

Joy had been a performer since childhood, when her parents first pushed her center stage. A talented actress with good comedic skills, she quickly got regularly cast in her small midwestern city, and when she made the "big move" out to Hollywood, she found regular casting there as well. She worked more than any of her friends and "really had very little to complain about" except for the fact that she just wasn't happy.

Entering a creativity recovery, she began writing Morning Pages and, as she did, began to wonder how much of her center-stage personality was really her own idea. "You're a born actress," her mother had always told her—but was she? Acting got her a lot of attention but brought little satisfaction.

As her self-exploration progressed, Joy noticed she really loved writing. Writing was what her serious "brilliant" sister did for a living, and it had always been off limits for her. She was the family cut-up and "star." Telling herself she was "just exploring," Joy began to let herself write. As she did, she found that she felt more comfortable in her own skin, more at home with herself creatively. She continued to work as an actor, but her writing held more and more of her attention. After a solid bout of urging from her best friend, she tried her hand at a monologue. It flew from her pen. She tried another. Then another. Then another. Before six months had passed, she had enough monologues for a one-woman show and the same best friend volunteered to direct it.

> *One of the marks of an intelligent person is to be able to distinguish what is worth doing and what isn't and to be able to set priorities.*
>
> ANNE WILSON SCHAEF

"I was terrified, stepping forward as a writer," Joy recalls, but her friend printed flyers, found a good venue, and was convinced that Joy's actor was just the midwife to her real talent as a writer.

"I didn't give up my actress, but I stopped acting as though acting were all of me," Joy remembers. Her one-woman show was a modest hit. Her friend next suggested she try a one-act play.

"With friends like you, who needs an agent?" Joy complained, but she set pen to page, and page to stage soon followed. It is several years later now, and Joy enjoys her success as a "hot" young playwright. She enjoys the process of making her art and finds "making it" a happy coincidence, not her goal.

"Once I let go of my idea that making art was about making it, meaning fame, I began to make the art I wanted to make and that gave me something that looks an awful lot like the life I always wanted to have."

When we surrender to becoming what we are meant to be instead of trying to convince the world of who we think we are, we find our proper creative shoes and can walk in them comfortably. Not surprisingly, they sometimes take us far. Moving comfortably and at a less driven pace, we also enjoy the journey, finding pleasure in our companions and our "view" each step of the way.

TASK
Make Something for Someone Else, Not to Be Somebody

When we are focused on making a career in the arts, we often forget that our artful nature is a gift we can bring to the personal as well as the professional realm. We write for a living but do not take the time to write letters to our friends. We draw for a living but use our artistic skills only on paid commissions. Hobbies are out the window as "too frivolous," and as we focus seriously on our art, we become very serious indeed.

They do not know that ideas come slowly, and that the more clear, tranquil and unstimulated you are, the slower the ideas come, but the better they are.

BRENDA UELAND

Take pen in hand, number from 1 to 5. List 5 people to whom you feel closely connected. Next to each name, devise one creative project you could undertake to show them your love and gratitude for their friendship. Select one project and execute it. For example:

1. My daughter—write out memories of raising her.
2. My sister—write out "artist" stories of her courage.
3. Carolina—draw her as a child and now as a friend.
4. Emma—make a photo album of our creative adventures.
5. Connie—make an "arts and crafts" recipe box for her.

We don't need to devote years, months, days, or even hours to a connection project, but it is often true that art made from the heart leads us to more and more art. As we free ourselves from our "get serious" mold, we often encounter new energies and new interests. When art becomes a part of our greater life, we often discover greater life in our art.

Velocity and Vulnerability

Any sudden change in velocity creates vulnerability for an artist. Two things come at us—opportunity and diversion or, more bluntly, useful things and opportunities to be used. When your life changes speed, it is often difficult to discern what is a genuine opportunity and what, on closer inspection, is an opportunity for someone else at your expense.

As our success and visibility as artists rise, so does the flow of two often difficult to distinguish things: opportunities and diversions. It is no coincidence that in Chinese the hexagram for "opportunity" and "crisis" are the same. As we become brighter and stronger as artists, others are attracted by that clarity and glow. Some of them will help us on our way, while others will try to help themselves, diverting our creative light to their own path. Those who actually offer us invitations and work in alignment with our true values and goals are opportunities to be cherished, and colleagues to bond with. Those who covertly present their own agendas in the disguise of a lucky break for us are opportunists, not opportunities. They represent a creative crisis in the making. They are what I call "piggybackers," and they must be identified and weeded out of our creative garden.

Piggybackers have a project they want to attach to your name, fame, reputation, and energy, and they seldom say "You could really help me," which would give you a chance to think about it on a clear level. Instead, they say, "I could really help you . . ." and they present their agenda cloaked in ways that make it look as though it could be compatible with your own. Maybe it is. Maybe it isn't.

When a piggybacker wants a share of your creative trough, he can be *very* persuasive. Flattery can flatten your will to resist. This is dangerous. Just as weeds and flowers can look a lot alike, a piggybacker can often successfully pose as something nicer. Weeds are greedy, and choke out

Success can make you go one of two ways. It can make you a prima donna, or it can smooth the edges, take away the insecurities, let the nice things come out.

BARBARA WALTERS

It is distraction, not meditation, that becomes habitual; interruption, not continuity; spasmodic, not constant toil.

TILLIE OLSEN

the garden by claiming too much territory. A piggybacker will do the same—and often, that is how you know them. Piggybackers often use flowery phrases: "I got this wonderful opportunity and I immediately thought of you, you're so wonderful, so gifted, so talented, so blah-blah-blah . . . ."

Piggybackers do not really care what your actual goal is. They care about harnessing your time, energy, and expertise to pursue goals of their own.

Piggybackers may have goals and agendas quite different from your own—although they are loath to reveal it. They may send you something fairly repellent to your values and yet insist you have huge swaths of common ground and that, therefore, you should endorse it. It is my experience that every time you are "generous" against your better judgment, you end up embarrassed.

Piggybackers like to offer you an opportunity and then, once you have signed on, try to run off with the project. Your "opportunity" gets trampled under their opportunism. In their race to win—and win big—artistic values get lost.

Arthur scored a substantial success with a best-selling book. For the first time in his adult life, he had money, recognition, and a seemingly assured future. Agents were eager to represent him, and publishing companies were eager to bid on his next project. Everyone was betting that Arthur would go on to bigger and better things—including Arthur himself. He had a winning personality and he was on a winning streak. It seemed nothing was beyond his reach—until he began to grab for all of it at once, telling himself that each opportunity was too good to pass up.

First, there was the infomercial. "It will sell who you already are and tell people who you are becoming." The filmmaker was persuasive and Arthur parted with 25,000 of his newly earned dollars, telling himself what the filmmaker told him, that it was "an investment in his future."

Next, there was the decision to join a prestigious think tank. All it took to "get in" was another $25,000. Most of the people involved had corporate sponsors, but since Arthur was really his own corporation . . . After listening to how much the prestigious credential would help him look more solid, Arthur was "in" again.

After a short while, it began to look like the line formed to the right. Everyone had a wonderful opportunity for Arthur to help himself and help them in the bargain. He really needed a high-powered and well-paid assistant. "They" really needed a better office than just a room in the house. "It"—the new big book—deserved a glossy,

What I am actually saying is that we each need to let our intuition guide us, and then be willing to follow that guidance directly and fearlessly.

SHAKTI GAWAIN

professionally designed proposal to "properly package" Arthur's good ideas. And, too, where was the Arthur Web site? Someone of his stature needed a "presence on the Web" to tell interested consumers who and what he was.

And what was that?

Arthur found himself overcommitted, overtired, overworked, and underpaid. His money and name underwrote a great many opportunities that simply didn't pan out in his real favor.

"I'd have done a lot better to buy nothing, bank my money, and wait for all of the furor around my 'fame' to die down." Instead, Arthur found himself struggling to meet his mortgage on his newly bought designer bachelor pad, meet the credit card payments on his newly acquired designer suits, and, as to getting any real writing done, he lacked the focus even to try. Ironically, his success had cost him everything that helped him make a success of himself in the first place—solitude, mulling time, the space and concentration necessary to forge some genuinely original thinking. Now Arthur fit the mold. He looked like many another Armani-clad huckster and he sounded the same—frantic and desperate to score.

As artistic visibility increases, so does artistic vulnerability. Velocity creates porosity—things and people whiz past our defenses and, if they breach our walls—"This will take only a minute"—they can create havoc. Their "minute" can take a great deal of time to detox from. It may cost us hours from our writing or our practice time. Like any other human being, we need time to metabolize our lives, our gains, and our losses. Blinded by our celebrity—we look like a shiny nickel to a lot of people—they can ignore our humanity. They attack our boundaries rather than understand them.

To have realized your dream makes you feel lost.

ORIANA FALLACI

Three times in the last three decades I have unwisely involved myself with creative people and projects about whom I had reservations. In each case, the human flaw I had suspected resulted in a flawed project as well. Piggybackers are after the glory of the "win" more than the good of the project. In their rush for success they may rush a project and, like hothouse tomatoes forced to grow too fast, such projects emerge cardboard and tasteless—attractive enough looking but not succulent or nourishing—nowhere nearly as creatively tasty as the real thing.

A creative name and reputation has weight and width. If we lend our name and reputation to ventures of questionable merit, we lose both our credibility and our chances of continuing to gain ground ourselves.

No matter what level we make our art on—community theater to Broadway, small town open mic to major poetry venues—the question "Is this an opportunity or an opportunity to be used?" must be asked.

We all want to be generous. We all want to find colleagues. We all want to work. We must be alert to the caliber not only of our own work but of those whom we align ourselves with.

As an artist, some risks are worth taking and some risks are not. This is not snobbery. This is not exclusivity. This is discretion, discernment, and accountability to ourselves and our gifts.

The phrase "more trouble than it is worth" is something to ask about any venture. Some difficult and daring things are worth expenditure, worth the risk. Lesser projects and troublesome collaborators are creative quicksand—we get stuck and go down with them. As artists, we must learn to stick to our art and not sticky situations.

As artists, we are open in a way that differs from many people's, so we are very vulnerable at being caught off guard. Inspiration can be caught out of the corner of the eye and on the fly, and so can opportunity, but this openness to creative possibility can also make us open to creative exploitation. Caught off center and off guard, we might agree to help someone do something that takes us far from our own work and priorities. Anytime your career shifts gears into something faster, think of what happens when you are driving a car: The shift from fifty-five to sixty-five is often the difference between seeing and enjoying the scenery and whizzing past things, saying, "Was that a gas station I just passed or a convenience store? Did I miss the exit?"

I don't want to get to the end of my life and find that I just lived the length of it. I want to have lived the width of it as well.

DIANE ACKERMAN

As artists, we easily miss the exit or get off at the wrong interchange. If you have someone else deflecting your attention, it is even easier. Think of trying to read the turnpike signs at a complicated interchange when someone is chatting in your ear about things not of bearing to the matter at hand: "How do we get there?" As artists, the "there" we are trying to get to is the work we can respect ourselves for and hopefully be respected for. The fame and hoopla are diversions, and after an expensive one, if someone—say, your agent or manager—is constantly calling you with opportunities that may serve them but not you, you will lose your focus, stop seeing clearly, and miss your opportunity to take a route through your own career that you like.

Opportunity knocks with a Christmas-morning feeling. There is often, for me, a hushed sense of awe as an opportunity slides into place: "Oh, this is so neat!" Sometimes we go just a little numb, as in "Pinch me. Can this be real?" Opportunists, by contrast, have more of a pressured feeling of last-minute shopping, the kind of impulse buy where you know you shouldn't but you do.

The simplest way to put it may be this: Facts are sober. Reassurances are not. Facts are what we are after in sorting the difference between an opportunist and an opportunity. Facts are "Well, let's see, I've worked on five Broadway shows and three national tours." Hype is "I have lots of experience working with singers." ("Lots," like what?)

When we are embarrassed by our own lack of credentials, when we feel lucky to be getting any help at all with our dreams, we may forget that we have a right to prices and accountability. As we begin to ask about both, either our sense of ease or our sense of unease will continue to grow. Discernment is a combination of gut instinct and a little careful reportorial work. We don't want to be told "There, there, don't you worry." We want to be told "I've done this six times and I've got three good friends I could call if I get in trouble."

> Since you are like no other being ever created since the beginning of time, you are incomparable.
>
> BRENDA UELAND

As artists, we must be alert not only to our lucky breaks but also to our unlucky choices. We must learn when and how—pull the plug on people and ventures that do not serve our authentic goals and aspirations. All too often, the "big chance" offered us by another may be a big chance to be used.

TASK

Slow Down and Feel Strong

Speed creates an illusion of invincibility. We hurry through our days numbing ourselves to the deeper flow of our lives. We feel shallow and push ourselves to live harder when what we need is to live more deeply and quietly. A potent mantra for calming down is to repeat to yourself the phrase "There are no emergencies." If there are no emergencies in your life, what situation could you allow to unfold more gently?

Take pen in hand. Number from 1 to 5. List 5 areas in your life where you feel a sense of haste and pressure. Ask yourself if your sense of urgency is misplaced. Often we simply have anxiety about something unfolding naturally. We want to force our own growth like hothouse plants rather than allow situations—and ourselves—to ripen.

Turn again to your list of 5 haste-makes-waste areas. Can you reset your time line in each area so that you live more gracefully with ambiguity? One of the most common slogans in 12-Step work is "Easy does it." Too often, we hear this phrase to mean "Oh, calm down." The phrase

> *It is the creative potential itself in human beings that is the image of God.*
>
> MARY DALY

means much more than that. It is the distillate of a vast network of spiritual wisdom that has learned that "Easy does it" actually means "Easy accomplishes it."

No person, place, or situation benefits from our harried pushing forward. Everything and everyone benefits from our slowing down—letting go and letting God—so that a natural pace and progression can be discovered.

A phrase from the drug culture, "Speed kills," warns us of the danger of too much velocity. We are vulnerable and exquisite creatures, complex mechanisms intended to move at a human and humane pace. We elect that pace every time we slow down to gather—and feel—our strength.

Creative Saboteurs

Most environments have some undesirable elements—mosquito season in the hot, wet South. Winter chills diving far below zero in the cold, ice-locked winter in Minnesota. Even idyllic environments have their hostile elements and, as artists, we need to know and name the elements in our environment that are clear and present dangers of the trail. In the Southwest, where I live half of every year, I have learned to walk with an eye peeled for rattlesnakes and even the stray tarantula. As an artist, I must pay equal heed to the psychologically dangerous denizens of my environment. I call these characters "creative saboteurs," and the appearance of any of them—just like the sighting of a baby rattler on an evening's stroll—can focus our attention on survival and off the beauty of whatever it was we were making. A creative saboteur doesn't always rattle before it strikes, so we do need a measure of self-protective alertness.

Because all environments have some negative elements, it is a fantasy to think we can completely escape creative saboteurs. I have found it more useful to take the same approach I take toward the more dangerous high-desert dwellers—know them, name them, and avoid them. A creative saboteur is not a friendly animal, and no matter how innocent it may try to appear, its very presence means you must be alert to impeding damage to you and your dreams.

Don't let them tame you!

ISADORA DUNCAN

Grace does not pressure—but offers.

JOHN BOWEN COBURN

A playful name for a creative saboteur allows us to retain a sense of our own power. "Why, it's just a Wet Blanket Matador," we can say to ourselves when hit with the dampening impact of their uninvited and often ill-considered opinions and advice. The following is a typical exchange with a Wet Blanket Matador:

ARTIST: *I'm so excited. I think I've finally cracked the top of act two.*
WET BLANKET MATADOR: *Well, I'm sure it'll shift once you get it on its feet anyway. Structure really can't be determined solely by the playwright. It's also in the playing. Theater is a collaborative art, after all, blah-blah-blah . . . .*

This character will use an energetic wet blanket to deflect, dampen, and confuse your creative thrust.

As the artist/playwright, an exchange like this can dampen your enthusiasm. We are usually too well mannered to respond "Of course it's a collaborative art, but you have to have something to collaborate on, dim bulb."

Wet Blanket Matadors like to employ an air of sad superiority, as if they have seen you and your like come and go countless times before. Their tone is that of a worried camp counselor listening to an ill-advised twelve-year-old planning a picnic amid grizzlies. Wet Blanket Matadors will typically tell you, "Oh, no! South!" the minute that you say, "I've decided to go north." Their contrariness is comic once you catch on to their ability to *never* co-sign your perceptions. Successfully identified, a Wet Blanket Matador becomes less a saboteur than an occasion for comic relief.

Now let's look at a related character: the Amateur Expert. Like the Wet Blanket Matador, this citizen dwells in negativity but bolsters his opinions with the company of facts and figures that may have no relevance whatsoever to the actual success of your progress. Long on theory, short on experience, an Amateur Expert can give you a million reasons why something *won't* work but no functional advice to help something work. Amateur Experts are trivia freaks—they resemble fan club presidents in that they know what shampoo Rita Hayworth preferred but are unable to recognize a Hayworth in the making.

Both the Wet Blanket Matador and the Amateur Expert bludgeon creatives by their presumed superiority. They just "know" they "know better" than we do. . . . This persona is intended to deflect such pointed questions as "Exactly what have *you* ever done anyway?"

The next destructive character knows worse and cannot wait to tell us. Like a malaria-bearing mosquito, the Bad-News Fairy delivers a sting and a lingering malady. Rather than speak from her personal negativity, she carries—and delivers—the negativity of others. This is a typical exchange:

> ARTIST: *I've just finished my new operetta and I'm pretty damn excited.*
> BAD-NEWS FAIRY: *Of course, you know that operetta funding has just been cut by a million percent and, as my close friend Nigel Nix told me just yesterday, operettas as an art form are really of no interest to anyone anymore, especially him and Percy Pursestrings, who controls all funding you might be interested in.*

Notice that this saboteur always washes his hands. It's never *his* nasty little bacteria that are causing your creative cold. It's someone else's he just "happens" to pass on to you.

No roundup of creative saboteurs would be complete without mentioning that art snobs come in two primary colors: Very Important People and Very Serious People. VIPs like their clothes labeled and their art the same way. When they meet you, they want to check out your creative passport to make sure your skills have been stamped in all the right places. For them it's not that you can play the piano, but that you got into Juilliard. It's not that you can paint but that the Whitney owns one of your paintings. Forget that you're a writer, do you have an A-list agent or mere talent? These

> *The thing that makes you exceptional, if you are at all, is inevitably that which must also make you lonely.*
>
> LORRAINE HANSBERRY

people are about who's who and not what's what. If you're Beethoven, you'd better be able to prove it. Contact with a VIP normally leaves an artist feeling very unimportant.

Now let's look at their close cousins, Very Serious People. The exchange here has to do with the notion that *you* are a mere artist, while *they* are a lover of *ART.* Your work, whatever it is, pales by comparison to the "great works" they ultimately know. To hear them tell it—and they will—art is a matter of life and death. And, of course, dead artists fare better than the living at "making the art" of *their* informed perceptions. Like oenophiles who horde vintage wines but won't drink it, the very serious art crowd can't be bothered with mere enjoyment and appreciation. What they "know" is "no."

As artists, we are often, far more often, more insecure than grandiose. We are stubborn as crabgrass, yes, but we are just as easily stepped on. Yes, we spring back—but sometimes only after years of discouragement. As we move our art into public venues, what we need is to find a few friends who encourage us by mirroring our competency—that, and the inner resolve to post a few signs that say "Keep off the grass."

Surviving a creative saboteur is like surviving a snakebite. It can be done and it makes a good story afterward. However, the first step—as with any snakebite—is to name and contain the poison. We cannot afford our own or anyone else's denial. We have been bitten. We have been poisoned. Damage has been done and the delicate and fine nerve endings of our art are badly hurt. Step one is to get away so that you are not bitten again. Do not stand stock-still in astonishment, poking the snake to see if it might want to bite again. Snakes bite. They bite once and they do bite again. If you think you have been bitten, assume you have been bitten and jump back. Don't listen to people who want you to "find the lesson" in your experience. There will be plenty of time for that afterward. For right now, put distance between you and the snake.

> *Integrity is so perishable in the summer months of success.*
>
> VANESSA REDGRAVE

> *In solitude we give passionate attention to our lives, to our memories, to the details around us.*
>
> VIRGINIA WOOLF

Do not engage with the people who want to talk with you about how rare this particular kind of poisonous snake is. Do not start to feel that the odds of your having been bitten make any difference in the fact that you have been bitten. Later on, after you have a few weeks' recuperation, you can enjoy lunch with someone who says, "Oh, he's always a viper and he bit me too," but such talk is for later, not right now.

First administer first aid. That means you acknowledge you have been bitten, don't pretend you have not, and reach for the antidote. The antidote is someone who supports you before, during, and after your creative injuries. This is a friend who doesn't say anything much besides "That's awful" and "What can I do to help?"

The answer to "What can I do to help?" is very straightforward: "Love me." That, and "Help me to forgive myself for having gotten fooled, hurt, bitten. Help me to let myself off the hook and not blame me for someone else's bad behavior. Help me to stop calling myself stupid. Tell me, accidents happen. There are snakes out here. Why, any one of us could have run into a nasty creature like you did."

It is spiritual law that if we cannot always avoid injury, we can always later turn it to good use. The silver lining of surviving snakebite is the compassion that it brings to bear both toward ourselves and later toward others. There will always be creative saboteurs. Their bite will always sting and, as we learn to identify them and avoid them, we can share our experience, strength, and hope with others: Creative saboteurs hurt us, but they can be survived.

TASK
Perform an Exorcism

Creativity is a spiritual issue and that means we can invoke forces to cast out our demons. A spiritual-creativity injury is an excellent opportunity for a spiritual ritual of your own devising. Here are two of my favorites. They are both powerful and playful, a potent combination:

> *The beginning of compunction is the beginning of a new life.*
> GEORGE ELIOT

1. Exorcize a creative demon: Reflect on your injury and make a creativity monster embodying all the nasty elements of your tormentor. Making this monster is cathartic, but destroying it is more so. Burn it, bury it, abandon it in the wilderness twenty miles from your house, throw it over the gorge bridge, and send it downriver. Get rid of it. One student made a "word monster" using all the controlling rules of grammar and usage. She wrote more freely later.

2. Create a creativity totem: Make a being that embodies all the spiritual forces you would like to muster to your support. This can be a doll, a sculpture, a painted image, a piece of music, even a collage. Place it prominently and protectively in your environment. It is the act of making art that heals the broken creative heart.

CHECK-IN

1. **How many days this week did you do your Morning Pages?** If you skipped a day, why did you skip it? How was the experience of writing them for you? Are you experiencing more clarity? A wider range of emotions? A greater sense of detachment, purpose and calm? Did anything surprise you? Is there a "repeating" issue asking to be dealt with?

2. **Did you do your Artist's Date this week?** Did you note an improved sense of well-being? What did you do and how did you feel? Remember, Artist's Dates can be difficult and you may need to coax yourself into taking them.

3. **Did you get out on your Weekly Walk?** How did that feel? What emotions or insights surfaced for you? Were you able to walk more than once? What did your walk do for your optimism and sense of perspective?

4. **Were there any other issues this week that felt significant to you in your self-discovery?** Describe them.

Discovering a Sense of Resiliency

This week dismantles the myth of artist as superhero. No artist is immune to negative emotions. The key to surviving such emotions is accepting them as necessary, a known and expectable part of the creative trail. The readings and tasks of this week invite a sense of compassion for the difficulties of our elected creative journey. As the week focuses on the inner trials faced by artists, it assures us that while the dark night of the soul comes to all of us, by accepting this we are able to move through it.

Worry

It is valuable to think of creative artists as being like skittish racehorses, nervous until they are out the gate and actually running.

In my experience, no artist is ever immune to or beyond apprehension in many forms. Successful artists have learned to identify and deal successfully with these close-sibling emotions. It helps to make a few important distinctions, distill a few working definitions. Here they are:

Panic is an escalating sense of terror that can feel as if we are being flooded and immobilized by the glare of change. Panic is what you feel on the way to the altar or to the theater on opening night, or to the airport for a book tour. It is rooted in "I know where I want to go, but how am I going to get there?"

Worry has an anxious and unfocused quality. It skitters subject to subject, fixating first on one thing, then on another. Like a noisy vacuum cleaner, its chief func-

I think these difficult times have helped me to understand better than before how infinitely rich and beautiful life is in every way and that so many things that one goes around worrying about are of no importance whatsoever.

ISAK DINESEN

Any disaster you can survive is an improvement in your character, your stature, and your life. What a privilege!

JOSEPH CAMPBELL

tion is to distract us from what we really are afraid of. Worry is a kind of emotional anteater poking into *all* corners for trouble.

Fear is not obsessive like worry and not escalating like panic. Fear is more reality based. It asks us to check something out. Unpleasant as it is, fear is our ally. Ignore it and the fear escalates. A sense of loneliness joins its clamor. At its root, fear is based in a sense of isolation. We feel like David facing Goliath with no help from his cronies and a concern that this time, his trusty slingshot might not work.

The more active—and even more negative—your imagination is, the more it is a sign of creative energy. Think of yourself as a racehorse—all that agitated animation as you prance from paddock to track bodes well for your ability to actually run.

In both my teaching and collaborative experience, I have often found that the most "fearful" and "neurotic" people are actually those with the best imaginations. They have simply channeled their imaginations down the routes of their cultural conditioning. The News at Five is never the good news, and so when they play the possible movie of their future they routinely screen the one with danger and dire outcomes. They do the same with creative projects.

Worry is the imagination's negative stepsister. Instead of making things, we make trouble. Culturally, we are trained to worry.

We are trained to prepare for any negative possibility. The news tutors us daily in the many possible catastrophes available to us all. Is it any wonder that our imaginations routinely turn to worry? We do not hear about the many old people who make it safely home; we hear of the grandmother who did not. On the brink of opening a play, we therefore expect critical snipers, not raves. One reason Morning Pages work so well for artists is that they give a way to siphon off worry at the very beginning of our creative day. Similarly, the spot-check inventory of blasting through our blocks by the naming, claiming, and dumping of any worries, angers, and fears related to a project can also get an artist out the starting gate effectively.

Fears for our own safety and the safety of others, the sudden suspicion of brain tumors and neurological disorders, the "realization" that we are going blind or deaf, any and all of these worrisome symptoms indicate we are on the brink of a large creative *breakthrough*, not breakdown, although the resemblance between the two can feel striking.

Poised to shoot a feature film, I found myself abruptly plagued by the "conviction" that a sniper was about to shoot me in the eye. Where this phobia came from, I don't know, but it plagued me on the city streets. That it arrived on the brink of my shooting a film, I consider no coincidence. Also, noncoincidentally, once the camera was running, my sniper ran away.

Authors leave on book tours, huffing on their inhalers. Filmmakers populate the ER, suddenly beset by hives. Pianists know the terror of imminent arthritic crippling. Dancers develop club feet, stubbing their "en pointe" toes walking to the bathroom. We survive these maladies and the success that they presage more easily if we remember not to worry about worry.

After thirty-five years in the arts and twenty-five years of teaching creative unblocking, I sometimes think of myself as a creative dowsing rod. I will meet someone and my radar will start to twitch. Creative energy is clear and palpable energy, disguised perhaps as neurosis or fretfulness, but real and usable energy nonetheless. I feel a little like a tracker—the bent twig of someone's undue anxiety tells me that person has an active imagination that needs to be focused and channeled and that when it is we will have quite a flowering.

One of my daughter's high school friends was a hyperactive teenager with bright, avid eyes and a restless energy that jogged him foot to foot as he exclaimed, "Look at that! Look at that!" his attention darting here, then there. Nothing escaped his worried attention. He literally looked for trouble.

That boy needs a camera, I thought, and gave him one for his high school graduation present. It's ten years later and he's a filmmaker. No surprise to me. His worrisome intensity lacked only the right channel.

When we focus our imaginations to inhabit the positive, the same creative energy that was worry can become something else. I have written poems, songs, entire plays with "anxiety." When worry strikes, remind yourself your gift for worry and negativity is merely a sure sign of your considerable creative powers. It is the proof of the creative potential you have for making your life better, not worse.

As performers, we *must* learn, and the rest of us *can* learn: We can learn to throw the switch that channels our energy out of worry and into invention. If we are to ex-

> *Ideas have come from the strangest places.*
>
> JOYCE CAROL OATES

pand our lives, we must be open to positive possibilities and outcomes as well as negative ones. By learning to embrace our worried energy, we are able to translate it from fear into fuel. "Just use it, just use it," an accomplished actress chants to herself when the worried willies strike. This is a learned process.

In my experience, artists never completely outgrow worry. We simply become more adroit at recognizing it as misplaced creative energy.

I have sat in the back of movie theaters with accomplished directors who suffered attacks of asthma and nausea as their movies were screened for preview audiences. As a playwright, I have watched in horror as my leading lady stood heaving like a carthorse, hyperventilating in the wings before stepping onstage to perform brilliantly.

It is palpable nonsense to believe that "real artists" are somehow beyond fear, and yet that is the version of "real artists" so often sold to us by the press. We learn of an artist's nerviness—"Steven acquired his first camera at age seven"—but we seldom hear of an artist's nerves. It is for this reason that I like to tell the stories I was privy to in my twenties, when I was married to young Martin Scorsese, who was friends with young Steven Spielberg, George Lucas, Brian DePalma, and Francis Ford Coppola. From my privileged position as wife and insider, I witnessed fits of nerves and bouts of insecurity suffered through with the help of friends. Because all of the men in our intimate circle matured into very famous artists, these stories are quite valuable—not because they drop names but because they drop information. They tell us in no uncertain terms that great artists suffer great fears like the rest of us. They do not make art without fear but despite fear.

> *The really great writers are people like Emily Brontë who sit in a room and write out of their limited experience and unlimited imagination.*
>
> JAMES A. MICHENER

They are not worry free but they are free to both worry and create. They are not superhuman and we need not expect ourselves to be so either. We need not disqualify ourselves from trying to make art by saying "Since it's so terrifying for me, I must not be supposed to do it."

Let me say it again: Some of the most terrified people I ever met are some of the greatest American artists. They have achieved their careers by walking through their fears, not by running away from them. The very active imaginations that led them into jittery terrors are the same imaginations that have allowed them to thrill us, enthrall us, and enchant us. Your own worries may similarly be the pilot fish that accompany your great talent. They are certainly no reason not to swim deeper into the waters of your own creative consciousness.

TASK
Let the "Reel" Be an Ideal

Our imagination is skilled at inhabiting the negative. We must train it to inhabit the positive. On the brink of a creative breakthrough, we often rehearse our bad reviews—or, at least, our bad day. We imagine how foolish we will look ever to have hoped to have our dreams. We are adroit at picturing our creative downfalls.

Fortunately, success sometimes comes to us whether we can imagine it or not. Still, it comes to us more easily and stays more comfortably if it feels like a welcome guest, something looked forward to with anticipation, not apprehension. This tool is an exercise in optimism, and that word "exercise" is well chosen. Some of us may have to strain to constructively imagine our ideal day. But let's try it.

Take pen in hand. Set aside at least one half hour for writing freely. Imagine yourself at the beginning of your ideal day, a day in which all of your dreams have come true and you are living smack in the middle of your own glorious accomplishments. How does it feel? How good can you imagine feeling? Moment by moment, hour by hour, happening by happening, and person by person, give yourself the pleasure in your own mind's eye of the precise day you would like to have. For example:

> *One word frees us of all the weight and pain of life: That word is love.*
>
> SOPHOCLES

"I wake up early, just as a beautiful morning light spills into the room and focuses on the wall where I have hung the covers of my best original cast albums for my Broadway shows. My bedroom has a fireplace and my row of Oscars and Tony awards balance happily on the mantel. I slip from bed so as not to wake my beloved, who is happily still asleep. It is a big day, day one of rehearsals for a new show. Casting has gone well. The director is superb. Everyone is eager and excited to be at work, and so am I. I have worked with many of these people before. We have a loyal, constructive, and brilliantly talented core group of talent that was working in what they call "Broadway reborn," as the melodic songs of our work echo the best of Rodgers and Hammerstein. . . ."

Let your imagination be a real "ham." Spare no expense and consider nothing too frivolous. Do you have telegrams of congratulations wreathing your makeup mirror? Did somebody send you two dozen roses, and a dozen fresh bagels for breakfast? When the phone rings with great news, who is calling to say "That's great!" Is it your favorite sister or the president? This is your day and you have it exactly as you want.

> *There's only one corner of the universe you can be certain of improving and that's your own self.*
>
> ALDOUS HUXLEY

Allow yourself to inhabit your absolute ideal from morning until nightfall. Include your family and friends, your pets, time for a nap or high tea. Enjoy scones and excellent reviews. Accept a lucrative and prestigious film deal. Make arrangements to tithe a percentage of your megaprofits to charity. Stretch your mind and your emotional boundaries to encompass the very best day you can imagine and allow yourself a sense of peace, calm, and self-respect for a job well done.

Fear

If you'll pardon the levity, most of us are afraid of fear. We think it's a bad thing. We *know* it's a scary thing. We're afraid of becoming afraid, scared of becoming scared. We know all too well how our fears can escalate into terror, and how our terror can either translate into frantic action or into paralyzing inertia. Because so many of our experiences with fear have been negative, we fail to see fear as positive or useful. It is both. Let me repeat: Fear is positive and useful. Fear says things like "I'm afraid that second movement is boring, and you might want to look at shifting a little of the harmony" or "I'm afraid my characters talk too much at the top of act two without the stakes being clear" or "I'm afraid there's something wrong with the bridge on my viola and I need to get it checked" or "I'm afraid I've overdosed on vermilion in this series and need my eye to fall in love with something else."

Fear is a blip on the radar screen of our consciousness. Fear tells us "Check this out." It is something we catch out of the corner of our eye. It enters our thoughts the way a dark shadow looms across a doorway. "Is someone there?" we may gasp. Yes, someone is there. Often it is a perception spoken by a part of ourselves that we have neglected and failed to attend. The punctilious part of ourselves may be correctly afraid that we *should* have written out the bass parts fully and not done the shorthand of "everything in treble clef, it's okay." It's *not* okay with the part of ourselves that believes, like the Boy Scouts, in being prepared. "I'm afraid I won't look professional enough," this fearful part insists. And it could be right. Fear asks that we check something for clarity. Fear requires action, not assurance.

As creative beings, we are intricate mechanisms. We have fine-tuned sensing mechanisms that extend beyond the ordinary realm of five senses. Sometimes we feel something large and good is about to happen. We wake up with a sense of anticipation and openness—spiritual attitudes we cultivate through Morning Pages and Artist's Dates. At other times, that very same openness brings to us a sense of foreboding. If we have bought into the currently popular spiritual position that fear is somehow "bad" or even "unspiritual," we will try to dismiss our fear without exploring its message.

> *I did not wish to take a cabin passage, but rather to go before the mast and on the deck of the world, for there I could best see the moonlight amid the mountains. I do not wish to go below now.*
>
> HENRY DAVID THOREAU

"Don't feel that way," we will tell our fearful selves. "What's wrong with you?" By focusing on ourselves as the probable source of anything "wrong," we blind ourselves to the possibility that there might, in fact, be someone or something wrong in our environment.

Edward, a playwright, was committed to a large production of his newest and best play. The producer was all smiles and good vibes, all sunny promises and projections—yet Edward kept fighting a pit-of-the-stomach sense of apprehension in the man's presence.

"Stop it, Edward. What is this? Do you have some neurotic fear of success?" Edward's self-attacks were merciless as his fears continued to mount. "I am afraid this producer is too good to be true," Edward's instincts told him—in the form of bouts of insomnia and a few telling dreams about children's games in which the producer refused to play by the rules. As the dates for preproduction moved closer, Edward felt his fears rising further.

"It's all handled," the producer assured him, but Edward could not be assured. Beating himself up for "groundless fears," Edward finally picked up the phone and asked a few people a few questions. He learned that his producer wasn't producing anything. The venue was not locked down. Ads had not been placed. Deal memos for refreshments and concessions had not been finalized.

Every man feels instinctively that all the beautiful sentiments in the world weigh less than a single lovely action.

JAMES RUSSELL LOWELL

How many cares one loses when one decides not to be something but to be someone.

COCO CHANEL

"I am so glad you called," a few people told Edward, "I need to be able to plan my schedule and, without a firm commitment on your side, I can't really do it."

Edward's producer was not productive. Edward's fears were not groundless, but well founded. The exploratory actions that Edward took—finally—on his own behalf taught him that he was traveling in company he could not afford. A few more phone calls and Edward learned that his producer's actions and attitudes had left a trail of burned bridges. Edward could not afford to have his name linked with a bad apple. He was involved with an opportunist, not an opportunity. Reluctantly but appropriately, Edward pulled the plug and disassociated himself from his trouble-making friend.

"I am so relieved you did that," a friend phoned to say.

"I didn't know how to tell you," another caller said.

"I hear you might be looking for a new producer and I would love to work with you," a third caller proposed.

Edward and his new producer worked rapidly and effectively. Edward experienced none of the mysterious fears and misgivings he had previously. His fear had truly been a messenger, and the message had been "Edward, you can do better and treat yourself better. You are right, here, to fear the worst."

When fear enters our lives, it is like a mouse scurrying across the floor of our creative consciousness. *Did I actually see something there, or was it a trick of the light?* we wonder. We get still and listen. Do we hear a faint rustling? Is that a tap of a twig on the window? A genuine problem of the arc of act two—or is it . . . there it is again. This time we turn on the overhead light. We gently move the furniture away from the wall. Striving to still our hammering heart, we focus the flashlight of our consciousness into the dark and neglected corners, where we see, "Oh. I *do* have a mouse." Or "I have a dust ball the size of a healthy rat. I need to vacuum in here." In short, respected as a messenger, fear asks us to take a more accurate reading of our true perceptions to listen to *all* parts of our consciousness with care. As a rule of thumb, fear is *never* groundless. There is almost always some grounding action we can take in response to our fears.

Often we are so quick to label our fears neurotic or ill based or paranoid that we do not ask what signal our fear is really sending.

When you feel afraid, tell yourself, "This is good, not bad. This is heightened energy available for productive use. This is *not* something to medicate—or meditate—away. This is something to accept and explore." Ask yourself:

1. What signal is my fear sending me?
2. What affectionate name can I give to this messenger part of myself?
3. What grounded action can I take to respond to this fear?

Many fears are based on a simple lack of accurate information. Rather than take a small exploratory action in a needed direction—say, finding a new voice teacher or signing up for a computer class—we allow our fears to be the bogeyman who keep us from entering the gates to our dreams. "I'm afraid my voice may not be strong enough" translates into "Strengthen your voice." Each of us has fears that are particular to our own needs. When we listen to our fears with tenderness and care, when we accept them as messengers rather than as terrorists, we can begin to understand and respond to the unmet need that sends them forward. When we employ humor and tenderness to our fearful selves, they will often stop shaking long enough to deliver a needed message.

TASK
Admit Your Fears and Open the Door to Help

Very often the most damaging aspect of our fears is the sense of isolation and secrecy that they breed in us. We are afraid and we are afraid to admit we are afraid. Closeted alone with our fears, we forget that we are never alone, that we are accompanied at all times by a benevolent higher power who has sympathy and solutions for our problems.

Take pen in hand. The tool you are now asked to learn is extremely powerful and positive. It can be used in all times of emotional duress and it can be applied to any and all problems, personal or professional. This tool is affirmative prayer, and it works by singling out each negative situation and "claiming" divine attention and intervention upon our behalf. Let us say the problem is fear-born procrastination on entering a creative project. The prayer might go something like this:

> *Lord I disbelieve—help thou my unbelief.*
>
> E. M. FORSTER

"I am guided carefully and expertly exactly on how to begin work on my new project. I am shown carefully and clearly each step to take. I am supported fully and happily in taking each step into fruitful work on this new project. I intuitively and accurately know exactly how to begin and what to do to begin correctly."

In writing out affirmative prayers, it is important that we do not ask for help, we affirm that we are receiving it. Affirmative prayer is not a prayer of petition. It is a prayer of recognition and acceptance of the divine help that is at hand. Very often the action of writing an affirmative prayer clears away fear from our lens of perception. We suddenly see that we *are* guided, that divine mind is answering our request for help and support. We often intuitively know the right action to take and feel within ourselves the power to take that action. Fear becomes a cue for prayer and a deepened sense of our spiritual creative companionship.

Once you have written out your affirmative prayer, choose the most personally powerful and resonant phrase in it to use as a mantra while you walk. Perhaps you wrote "My fearful self is clearly guided." You can distill that still further to "I am clearly guided," and you can walk with that reassuring thought until it begins to take on emotional weight.

Restlessness

For an artist, a bout with restlessness is best met with curiosity—not with the conclusion that your true cranky character is surging to the fore. Irritability is the flag waved by restlessness. Restlessness means you are on the march creatively. The problem is, you may not know where.

> *Nothing is so perfectly amusing as a total change of ideas.*
>
> Laurence Sterne

Restlessness is full of switchbacks, like a mountain trail. We feel one thing. Then another. We reverse ourselves. *I am full of energy and I have no energy*, we think. *I have no energy and I am full of energy*, we reverse the thought. We are a country of contradictions. North looks good and then south. Nothing feels right. Everything feels wrong. Nothing is right, but then, nothing is really wrong either. We are out of sorts. Under the weather—but the weather is fine except for our own emotional weather, which is stormy. We are volatile and changeable. Of course we are, we are restless. We cannot depend on ourselves to set a course—fortunately, we don't have to.

"Inspiration enters through the window of irrelevance," artist M. C. Richards has observed—many artists will tell you the same thing. It is as though the making of certain pieces of art on certain themes lie in our destiny, just below our conscious mind, where we feel that we are choosing. How our life and work will unfold. One clue at a time. A happenstance at a time, destiny and our destined work reveals itself to us. One day, often quite abruptly, clarity comes and we say, "Ah-hah! That's why . . ."

If you talk to enough artists, you will learn that lucky breaks and chance meetings are run-of-the-mill elements, stock characters that show up when our restlessness reaches unbearable levels. It is as though our restlessness calls to the very heavens for "something" to happen. And something—or many somethings—does. This is why, as uncomfortable as it is, as unpleasant, even unbearable—restlessness is a good omen. If you visit the reptile house at the zoo as a storm is coming on, you will see the creatures slithering in agitated anticipation. They know a change is on the way. Being alert to the possibility of change opens our ears and eyes to receive psychic signals more often and more quickly. Irritated, restless, ready for change, we snap, "Goddammit! What is it?" when destiny knocks. But destiny does knock, and it can be colorful and expansive if we will allow it to be. When we are restless and our lives feel colorless, it is a clue and a cue that they are about to become colorful—if we cooperate. Prayers, and especially creative prayers, are answered, but answered in ways we may not anticipate or appreciate. Again, this is why artists speak that spiritual-sounding word—inspiration. That is not some gauzy bromide, it is our actual experience. As artists, we *are* irrationally, intuitively, and insistently inspired. Sir Arthur Sullivan attended a traveling exhibition of Japanese art and returned home to write *The Mikado*.

> *Make friends with the angels, who though invisible are always with you. . . . Often invoke them, constantly praise them, and make good use of their help and assistance in all your temporal and spiritual affairs.*
>
> ST. FRANCIS DE SALES

About ten years ago I was living in Manhattan and I underwent an intense and nasty bout of cabin fever. I blamed it on the city. "This damn island," I groused, "it's like a giant cruise ship going through choppy seas with all of us shut up in our tiny cabins. I hate it. I want out. Out somewhere!" I started walking a lot.

Walking near the Morgan Library on Madison Avenue, I noticed a small corner bookshop with a neatly lettered sign, THE COMPLETE TRAVELLER. On "impulse," I

382 THE COMPLETE ARTIST'S WAY

opened the door. *This is stupid, Julia,* my rational side flicked on the voice-over. *Your commitments are going to keep you right here, so this is just an excursion in idiotic fantasy.* That's when I noticed the shelf full of old and battered books about explorers. I pulled one down. The thick, creamy pages were dusty with age. They stuck together a little, even gave off a faint powder to the touch. Thinking, what the hell! I bought it—my father had loved boats and the sea.

The moment we indulge our affections, the earth is metamorphosed; there is no winter and no night; all tragedies, all ennuis, vanish,— all duties even.

RALPH WALDO EMERSON

Several months later, out on book tour, I was perched in Los Angeles on a cliff overlooking the Pacific, staring vaguely out the window toward—Australia? Hawaii? Somewhere. Suddenly, I remembered the book, tucked in my suitcase on another whim. Looking out the window at the vast flat sea, a few palm fronds dancing in and out of my sight line, I opened the book. That book opened an inner door. Suddenly, I heard music—a lot of music, wave on wave stepping ashore complete with lyrics. I grabbed a notebook and a pen, I grabbed my tiny toy keyboard, another traveling afterthought, and began notating what I heard.

My hotel, the old Art Deco "musicians" hotel, the Shangri-la, was a scant block or two from a mall where I found an electronics store and I bought a cheap tape recorder. The music was spilling through so fast, I needed to catch it on tape lest I miss some of it on the page. I heard soprano arias, booming bass parts, a large chorale—and I think I heard it all because in a fit of pique and irritability I went into a small travel store. That store was like Alice's doorway into Wonderland. An entire musical awaited my entry.

This story may not convince you that anything magic was afoot. You may not want to picture some invisible being giving me a quick shove—I don't blame you. And yet, it is my experience that when we are willing to be irrational and intuitive— even when we despise those words—we are rewarded by promptings, callings, that come to us from some mysterious and deft sources that guide and encourage us toward what might best be called destiny.

"I don't see why I should stick my head in this antiques store," we can catch ourselves grousing. And yet, opening an old photo album, some inner leaf turns within us and the notion for a novella rears its head.

When we insist on routine, when we insist on linearity, destiny will still knock, but it may have to work harder to get our attention. In my experience, destiny is willing to work very hard indeed—we are the ones who turn a blind eye, a deaf ear. We mire ourselves in a nasty mood and in our preconceptions about how change must come to us. We think, *It will have to be A or B or C.* In fact, when it does come, it is often, as my friend actress Julianna McCarthy ruefully notes, "H. Heliotrope."

Inner malcontent actually triggers outer change—if we are willing to listen to our malcontent with an open mind and listen to what will feel like a wave of irrational promptings. Those oddball, harebrained, nonlinear, and screwball itches, hunches, and urges are the path through the briar patch. Follow your strange creative cravings and you will be led into change a step at a time. I cannot prove this to you, nor would I. This is an experiment you must do for yourself and with yourself. You will never trust an unseen and benevolent partnering from higher realms unless you experience it for

> *We are never so ridiculous through what we are as through what we pretend to be.*
>
> FRANÇOIS, DUC DE LA ROCHEFOUCAULD

yourself. As someone who is by nature exhaustingly skeptical—and equally exhaustingly open-minded and experimental—I am speaking from my idiosyncratic experience—and the experience of watching two decades of artists as they experimented and recorded the result.

"This is so stupid. What am I doing here?" we may ask ourselves when, on a whim, we have gone to an adult education class on the kooky subject of origami.

Yet, our lives are as intricately folded, as cleverly made, and as particular as that ancient pursuit. When we acknowledge the right of mystery to intercept and direct us, we acknowledge the larger issue that life is a spiritual dance and that our unseen partner has steps to teach us if we will allow ourselves to be led. The next time you are restless, remind yourself it is the universe asking "Shall we dance?"

TASK
Find the "Rest" in Restlessness

In writing out a piece of music, a composer uses a "rest" to indicate a tiny, nearly imperceptible pause that is sometimes necessary before plunging ahead into the sea of notes.

Sometimes, and particularly when we are restless, it is a good idea to take a rest and allow our inner leadings to bubble up to the surface unimpeded. Certain

These are only hints and
guesses,
Hints followed by guesses, and
the rest
Is prayer, observance, discipline,
thought and action.

T. S. ELIOT

Every autobiography is
concerned with two characters,
a Don Quixote, the Ego, and
a Sancho Panza, the Self.

W. H. AUDEN

atmospheres can create a sense of rest in us and, while we are all individual, here are a few restful places to try a five-minute breather:

1. **The back of a church or synagogue:** There is often a calm humility that comes from just a few minutes tucked in a pew, even for the nonreligious. We breathe in "faith."

2. **A large plant store or greenhouse:** There is a sense of "other realms" that is palpable in visiting a green space. Plants do have a secret life and they will share it.

3. **A forest:** Even if you live in the city and your forest is in a park, you will sense a different rhythm if you allow it.

4. **A carpet store for fine Oriental rugs:** There is a sense of the sacred in the intricate patterns and handmade excellence. The very amount of time required to make a beautiful rug reminds us of the beauty of our own life's tapestry.

5. **A travel store:** The reminder that ours is a rich and various world filled with adventures can often, oddly, calm a restless heart. An imaginary junket down a jungle river, a trek through the Scottish Highlands, a bicycle trip through France—all of these are options for us, and knowing that we have such spirited options can be strangely calming.

Insecurity

I am trying to learn to play the piano. I have a friend who plays the piano as one who can leap across peaks in the thinnest atmosphere with no fear of falling. He is nimble and daring and may not even feel a need for nerve, he is so nervy. I would love to play like that.

Today I made the mistake of looking up the mountain and seeing that the peak was still far above me and wrapped in mysterious clouds. I saw that the way up to it was a treacherous climb of switchbacks and crevasses. I knew I would fall. I knew

I would fall. I knew it was all danger, all failure. In short, I compared myself to my gifted friend.

At the root of comparison is something a little nastier: insecurity. Instead of saying "I wish I were better than *I* am," we say, "I wish I were as good as *he* is." In one fell swoop we negate our work and our originality. No two players play alike, and there is that word, play. As artists, we do better focused on the play of learning than on the work of getting ahead. Centered on our own creative trajectory, each small gain is an encouragement. Each slight increment of mastery holds the sweet promise that the days of awkward repetition and frustrating blunders do lead somewhere after all. When we compete and compare instead of strive to emulate and empathize with other artists, we greet their skills with hostility and our own lesser skills with dismay. When we embrace the idea that all artists at all levels are still learning, still struggling, still evolving, growing, and grappling with their craft simply at a different altitude, we are encouraged by another's mastery to know: "It can be done." We need such encouragement. Our talent may be large, but our struggles may be large as well.

This morning, trying to play "When the Saints Go Marching In," I started crying in anger and frustration. Why didn't I learn this in fourth grade like everyone else? Where was I then?

As artists, most of us contain a highly evolved and sharp-clawed inner perfectionist. This perfectionist has nothing to do with having standards and everything to do with self-punishing, self-flagellating, and self-defeating premature judgments regarding our potential. The root word of "potential" is "potency," or "power." Just as the eagle's fledgling is less formidable than the eventual eagle, so, too, our embryonic steps in a new art form fail to accurately convey our later creative flight.

> *Authority poisons everybody who takes authority on himself.*
> VLADIMIR ILYICH LENIN

My music room is a geranium red and my piano is a small Chickoring upright. Gold gilt letters declare "Established in 1823." The piano may know far more than I. It has one sticky key, D above middle C, but with my lame and halting progress, that hardly matters. I type better than I play and I type with two fingers. And yet, I have written seventeen books and numerous plays and screenplays. So, too, my primitive piano skills have allowed me to pick out beautiful melodies. The trick is, *allowed* me.

Grace is available to us always, at any stage of the creative journey. As beginners, we need the grace to begin. As apprentice artists, we need the grace to continue.

As accomplished artists, we need the grace to again accomplish what it is we can. At all levels of creative endeavor, the Great Creator is present and partnering us.

"We are brought along like fighters," remarks the estimable actress Julianna McCarthy. She means that the Great Creator always gives us strength enough and support enough and guidance enough to meet the precise creative challenges at hand. We may be overwhelmed, but God is not. If we fail at Plan A, God has an endless supply of Plan Bs. There is always not only a fallback position, but also a net. That net is having the faith to try again.

When we say that making art is an act of faith and that as we make art we pursue a spiritual path, we are not talking loosely. There is grace in our every artistic encounter. Miracles do happen. We do not plan them. We hope for them and then we are open to the creator's mentoring hand in improving our suggestions. What looks difficult or impossible to us does not appear difficult or impossible to the Great Creator. As we set our egos aside and allow that creative power to work through us, miracles are routinely accomplished— seemingly by our own hand. Creative energy is like electricity. It will flow whether we allow it to or not. As we open our circuitry to conscious collaboration with higher forces, we are shaped by the energy that moves through us into the artists we dream we can become. The minute we relinquish the notion that our creative dreams are centered in the ego, the minute we begin to see them as spiritual adventures, we allow the Great Creator to shape us as only it can and will.

> *There is certainly no absolute standard of beauty. That precisely is what makes its pursuit so interesting.*
>
> JOHN KENNETH GALBRAITH

When I move a step at a time, I can edge up the mountain. If I go slowly and gently, playing "Twinkle, Twinkle, Little Star," I can even be proud to have edged up a ledge and I can say, "Wow, I am doing it." It takes vigilance to be gentle. It is easier to wail at myself, "Oh, my God, you will never learn."

We do not know how to ask ourselves for real growth. We do not know how to realistically dig in. We make our new art a mountain we cannot climb instead of trying our luck with a small incline and then a steeper one and then a slightly steeper one. Instead of being inspired by those creative climbers who hop crag to crag, we are discouraged.

I love the piano. How I play it can break my heart. That I play at all, at age fifty-four, when it is like going on a blind date and suffering through my insecurity, thrills me, and is a miracle.

TASK
Exactly the Way I Am

At the root of most insecurity is the conviction that we must somehow be better—or other—than what we are in order to be acceptable. We want to play better than so-and-so—or at least as well as so-and-so. Lost in all of this improvement and striving for perfection is the idea that there is a great deal to like about ourselves exactly the way we already are.

> *There are as many kinds of beauty as there are habitual ways of seeking happiness.*
>
> CHARLES BAUDELAIRE

Take pen in hand. Number from 1 to 50. List 50 specific and positive things that you like and approve about yourself exactly the way you are. These likable traits can be physical, mental, spiritual, personal, or even professional. For a glimpse at their possible diversity, consider these examples:

1. My handsome hands
2. The shape of my nose
3. The general use of grammar
4. The shape of my feet
5. My Spanish accent
6. My knowledge of American history
7. My knowledge of twentieth-century art
8. My pie-baking ability
9. My choice in walking shoes
10. My consistencies of letters to friends

So often we are focused on what we would like to change—and change for the better—that we fail to celebrate what is wonderfully enjoyable exactly the way it is. We are often far closer to our own ideal—and ideals—than we dare recognize. Self-esteem is an active choice, not a sudden given. We can choose to actively esteem our many positive traits. By counting our blessings we can come to see that we are blessed and that we need not compare ourselves to anyone.

Self-Pity

Yesterday, wading through the rewrite of a play, I stepped into the black hole I call self-pity. I went down, sputtering, "But! This is silly! I have so much to be grateful for! Burble!"

The fact that I have been a writer for thirty years has done very little to armor me against a solid attack of self-pity. The fact that I have gotten through hard rewrites before, and will doubtless do so again, doesn't really matter. I am like any other artist—happy when I am working freely and unhappy when the work becomes too much like work. I write both because I love to write and because I have to write. I am called, and if I don't answer, the calling just gets louder until I do answer or I have a bout of self-pity because I "have" to answer.

At root, self-pity is a stalling device. It is a temper tantrum, a self-inflicted drama that has little to do, ever, with the facts. Self-pity isn't very interested in facts. What it likes is "stories." As Serah, the noted singer, likes to remark, "Facts are sober. Stories are emotion." Self-pity thrives on stories that go "Poor innocent me and terrible, mean them . . ." Self-pity likes to make us feel the world is an adversarial place and that the odds are stacked against us. Self-pity likes to point out the way we are never truly appreciated, valued, cherished. What self-pity really wants is a cheering section and a fan club. It wouldn't hurt, either, to have a few good designer suits to lounge around in, Camille-like, while our worried lovers hover and offer us sips of something cool. Self-pity is not interested in our getting over it. Self-pity is interested in our "getting over." Struck by a bout of self-pity, we want an appreciative audience for our suffering, not a bout of self-improvement.

> *Any coward can fight a battle when he's sure of winning, but give me the man who has pluck to fight when he's sure of losing.*
>
> GEORGE ELIOT

Self-pity is not interested in our spiritual status. It turns a deaf ear to our peppy affirmations. For an artist, self-pity constitutes a chronic and formidable creative block. Self-pity has one job and one job only: It intends to stop us in our tracks. If self-pity can just keep us mired in what's-the-use, we will not have to do anything to find out. I am pretty sure that self-pity was a party guest in the Garden at Gethsemane. It was that satanic little voice that whispered "You can still wriggle out of this. They aren't going to appreciate you anyway."

"They aren't going to appreciate you" is often a trigger for self-pity. Please note that "they" (by which we often mean critics or even that more vague creature, "the public") has little or nothing to do with our own self-respect.

Self-pity focuses our attention on how we are perceived rather than on what we are perceiving. It takes us out of our creative power and tells us that we are powerless, we will never "make it." Even if we already have, self-pity isn't interested in realistic self-assessment. It is interested in stalling us. For an artist, focusing on the odds "against making it" is like sipping a poisonous drink. It weakens us. When we focus on the impossibility of the outer world and its megalithic proportions, how small and weak and helpless and thwarted we all are, well then, we feel "what's the use," and the world doesn't get much better than that, does it?

Beauty is as relative as light and dark.

Paul Klee

Self-pity never asks "Well, what do you think of what you're doing, how you're living, what you are making?" That question might lead us to shake things up a little in some interesting directions. Self-pity doesn't want us to shake things up. It wants to shake us up, like one of those old-fashioned double-whammy martinis that puts you straight on the floor with its punch.

Self-pity wants you on the floor—and the floor feels like the floor even when it is the floor of a creative penthouse. All artists get attacks of self-pity, and we get them with our Oscars leering down from the mantel. We get them with our National Book Award glinting in the lovely golden light pouring through our study window. We get them—we get them—because if we don't watch out, we are about to do something big.

Self-pity is a scraggly red robin. It means that once we get over it, we are going to spring into action. Self-pity—as all of us know—is different from the vague gray numbness of garden-variety depression. Self-pity has an edge to it like a shard of glass. We can use that shard of glass to cut, not ourselves, but our sense of hopelessness, into ribbons. In other words, used properly, a good dose of self-pity is a jump start for creative action. "What's the use?" converts quickly into "What's next?"

If you don't medicate it with a walloping pitcher of martinis, an ill-considered love affair, a bout of overwork or overeating, a solid attack of self-pity is the signal that you are about to either make yourself sick or make yourself healthy. The healthy part of us cannot stomach self-pity and so it will be goaded into action. Oddly, that action may *not* be taken down the lash and laid across our creative back. The action may be something that starts with compassion: "Of course you are *hurt*. Your work was unfairly received. Cry a little."

Although self-pity *appears* to be grounded in the lack of appreciation from others, it is *actually* grounded in our *own* discounting of our self and our struggles. A few tears of sorrow over work ill used, a moment of surrender to our genuine fatigue and heartbreak—a little actual grief can very quickly take the claws out of self-pity's hold on us. When we say "Of course you feel bad," then we are on the brink of something a little interesting. We begin to raise the question "If this makes me feel so bad, what can I change?"

"I am tired of being talked down to by the academic poets," we wail, and then we start exploring master's programs. Someone points out publicly that we have a tendency toward something unforgivable in our painting—romantic blue washes, for example, and we think, *I'll show them romance! I'll show them shimmering light!* and we dig in, perfect our technique, and get even "more so" of the quality of question. We persist and persist and our fatal artistic "flaw" is often revealed to be our own strength. This was true of the hyperexpressivity of violinist Nadja Salerno-Sonnenberg. This was true of Hemingway's stripped and soldierly prose.

The answer to "What can I change?" often surprises us. We might get a stubborn "Nothing! I love that piece and I think I will play it more!" We might get "I am bored by this curriculum and I want to include a lot more." We might get "What I'd really like to get done is ____." In other words, the question "What can I change?" snaps us back onto our own creative spine. Now we are asking the questions that only we have the answers to: What do we respect? What do we like? What do we want to do more of? We spring into action on that.

Of course, most of this self-pity springing into action is often accomplished after a nap. Have I said that self-pity is often born of fatigue? It lays us flat because we may need to be there for a while. There is something about being horizontal—without the benefit of drink or drug—that allows the imagination to do a little lucid daydreaming. We get up from our bed of pain thinking, *I could try that.* And we do.

TASK
Take a Little Pity on Yourself

Most of the time when we are struck down by a bout of self-pity, it is because we feel underappreciated. The truth is, sometimes we *are* underappreciated. The efforts we make and the effort we expend seems to go unnoticed by everyone but us. It is as though we had a tiny, built-in resentment collector, an inner gauge that processes reality by tiny little clicks that say "You see? Not appreciated again."

We cannot make others appreciate us, but we can take the time, care, and attention to appreciate ourselves. "That was really nice of you," we can say. Or "How thoughtful!" One of the Toughlove spiritual laws advises, "Other people's opinions of me are none of my business." A more positive counterpoint might be phrased "My own opinion of me is all that matters."

Take pen in hand. Writing rapidly to avoid your inner censor, complete the following sentences valuing yourself:

1. It was generous of me to_____.
2. It was thoughtful of me to_____.
3. It was nice that I_____.
4. I was a good friend when I_____.
5. I was sensitive when I_____.
6. I did a good job when I_____.
7. I was very professional about_____.
8. I went beyond the call of duty when I_____.
9. I deserve a thank-you for_____.
10. I should get an Oscar for_____.

Self-appreciation takes practice, and it is the only reliable antidote to self-pity.

Doubt

Doubt is a signal of the creative process. It is a signal that you are doing something right—not that you are doing something wrong or crazy or stupid. The sickening chasm of fear that doubt triggers to yawn open beneath you is not a huge abyss into which you are going to tumble, spiraling downward like you are falling through the circles of hell. No, doubt is most often a signal you are doing something and doing it right.

Beauty is one of the rare things that do not lead to doubt of God.

JEAN ANOUILH

Creativity is a spiritual issue, and although we seldom look at this squarely, the creative life features the same spiritual obstacles as any other spiritual path. The phrase "dark night of the soul" has gained common usage, and we think of it as it applies to the harrowing periods of doubt and drought that may come to someone on their spiritual quest.

Spiritual seekers of all stripe endure its painful ravages, whether they are Trappist monks like Thomas Merton or young Lord Buddha. What we don't talk about often is the fact that artists, too, are spiritual seekers, and we frequently suffer the dark night of the soul regarding our creative calling. Even worse, we often suffer it publicly.

To be an artist of depth, one cultivates a level of sensitivity that is acute. Performing artists, for example, listen with an ear cocked to the spiritual questions posed by a great piece of music or a great part onstage, and they open themselves to receive the energies required to manifest those questions creatively. Tackling these towering creative pinnacles, they are like tender birds who have learned to perch on skyscrapers as well as on trees. They still have all the acute sensitivity they have ever had, and they have also adapted enough to live in the fiercely competitive winds of high-altitude performance—but this does not mean it is easy. Artists facing an Olympian role *are* like athletes—highly trained, highly strung, and highly susceptible to injury, physical and psychic.

As I write, a gifted friend of mine is limping home after an extended tour. He is a musician of prodigious gifts, able to scale pieces whose heights and depths,

> It is not because angels are holier than men or devils that makes them angels, but because they do not expect holiness from one another, but from God only.
>
> WILLIAM BLAKE

whose creative cliffs, switchbacks, and drop-offs require the skills of a virtuoso. He has them. He uses them. And he doubts them. Doubt is a dangerous thing as you are leaping crag to crag above the artistic abyss. A well-placed doubt can send you tumbling—he recalls an entire Japanese tour bedeviled by troubling memory strain due to jet lag. He did not falter but feared he would, and carried that fear as a handicap, leaping ledge to ledge musically. This type of anxiety sends an artist to a place of darkness and terror that is difficult for most people to imagine.

In a sense, how we do as performers is none of our business. It is God's business how we do, and as we "suit up" and "show up," we are like monks doing matins—we fill a form and the form is larger than ourselves. Very often the beauty of a trained voice lifted in song can lift an untrained heart to a new altitude in connection to something or someone larger than our self. A great concert is an initiatory tribal experience. We touch the largeness of life through the largeness of the performer. Garland singing of yearning and love allows each of us to touch those feelings of yearning and love. The "somewhere over the rainbow" is a place located in the human heart, and art—and artists—allow us to access it.

Babies are necessary to grownups. A new baby is like the beginning of all things— wonder, hope, a dream of possibilities.

EDA J. LE SHAN

Last night I had dinner with three young classical musicians, rising stars with phosphorescent talent. The dinner table should have floated like something from a hokey séance. There was that much creative power and light seated there, ordering pasta with pesto and arugula salad, fettuccine livornese and penne vodka.

"Do your teachers prepare you for doubt?" I asked them.

The young talents flickered like fireflies. The question alone created a certain shimmer of unease. One was headed to Japan on a tour with the Met, and was frightened by the prospect.

"Not really," one violinist said.

"We're told to just ignore it, I think," said a violist.

"Critics are often jealous," sniffed a second violinist defensively. She had not yet suffered a critical savaging, but she "had heard."

Under their cosmopolitan chic, these young artists were still novices hoping to get through on a wing and a prayer.

No, they were not prepared.

"Do not pick up the first doubt," creative elder Julianna McCarthy warns me, the voice of six decades of experience on the stage, laying down the dictum.

For an artist, the first doubt is like the first drink for a sober alcoholic: We cannot afford to romance it. The first doubt leads to the second. The second leads to the third, and in no time you are staggering, hurting yourself on the sharp edges of the furniture.

One of the reasons artists need to talk to and hear from other artists is that the press is not a trustworthy mechanism for relaying information about the creative life. In the press, artists are either anguished or heroic, they are not what they must be—adroit, like spiritual samurai—to remain balanced amid turbulent doubts.

When a doubt moves at an artist, the artist must learn how to step aside and let the charge pass by. An artist cannot afford to be deeply pierced by doubt and finish the tour.

For an artist, doubt is both part of the territory and an ever-present danger. Doubt is the twister in Kansas. Doubt is the sickening temperature drop and unseasonable storm at twelve thousand feet. Doubt is the earthquake of the heart, the forest fire of self-criticism that threatens to take down everything in its blistering path. In other words, doubt is both normal and deadly, like coral snakes in Florida. Doubt is not to be toyed with.

There is a difference between doubt and self-appraisal. Doubt likes to come to the door disguised in the worthy suit of self-appraisal, "Maybe you should work on your . . ." Like a suitor, you should consider, but under that respectable overcoat is the dagger of despair: "Maybe you really are rotten at this." Doubt should not be allowed to enter—and it *will* try, at three A.M., in a strange city, with a polite knock, like a serial killer asking to share coffee while you phone the police.

> When it is not necessary to change, it is necessary not to change.
>
> LUCIUS CARY,
> LORD FALKLAND

The annals of art are dark with the destruction wrought by this satanic saboteur. Symphonies have been tossed into the fire; novels, too, have been burned at the stake. Stradivari routinely smashed violins far better than those of his rival makers. "Feel the feelings but don't act on them. This, too, shall pass," artists need other artists to tell them.

As the cool light of day reveals, doubt and self-appraisal are not the same thing. It takes practice, but an artist can learn the difference. Self-appraisal has a certain steadiness of character. It knocks in daylight and poses a simple question, and if you don't listen, it goes away. Then it comes back, knocks again gently, and poses the same question. Gently. As something for you to consider. To think about. To look at changing. "Maybe it's time to get a new bow." Self-appraisal has an opinion, a thought for your consideration. It has an idea to hand you, not an indictment. It doesn't whisper at midnight when you are alone and exhausted. Doubt is what does that.

Doubt is the one who likes to separate its victim from the herd, get the lamb off always and then call in its cronies. Doubt strikes you when *you* are alone, but doubt itself travels in packs. Along with doubt come its nasty friends: despair, self-loathing, feelings of foolishness and humiliation. When doubt attacks, it's always with the same lot of lower companions like the bad boys in an Italian gangster movie. An artist needs to learn to spot these characters and see them as lowlife bullies and not as Boy Scouts bravely bearing the truth.

Doubt comes to the door in darkness, pretending to be alone and in need of your compassionate ear. But if you let him in, he'll bring his friends, and doubt can be very persuasive getting in.

Doubt is a great seducer. "I just want you to think about this," it whispers. Out come the artist's ears. Out comes the dagger. "Maybe you didn't and don't have enough talent after all. . . ." Feel the sharp piercing? It might be your creative lung collapsing around the blade.

The changes in our life must come from the impossibility to live otherwise than according to the demands of our conscience.

LEO TOLSTOY

No, as artists, we need lucid self-appraisal, not shadowy and sinister doubt. Self-appraisal is best practiced in broad daylight in the comfort of your own home and among very trusted friends.

All artists suffer doubts. Great directors watch from the back of screening rooms and have to breathe their hyperventilated doubt into brown paper bags. Brilliant actresses suffer stage fright as painful as rickets. Doubt is a part of the territory as an artist. Surviving doubt, learning to discern what is emotional terrorism and what is a proper, suggested course adjustment, is something an artist becomes more skilled at over time—and often only with the help of his creative elders who have suffered doubt themselves.

In a convent or monastery, a suffering novice can speak to a spiritual director. "Doubt is normal," they are softly told. "Why, without doubt, why would we need faith?" When, as artists, we suffer doubt, we do well to seek compassionate counseling. "Doubt? It comes with the territory, kid," director John Newland used to growl at me tenderly.

Art is a spiritual practice. Doubt is normal. We need faith to survive it and we also need charity. When doubt attacks, we must be vigilantly self-loving. We must not open the door to the stranger who hands us the bottle of scotch, the pills, and the gun. Keep the chain on the door, politely or not so politely defer taking the doubt that is offered. Sleep with the light on if you need to. Call a friend in the middle of the night. Find an old comedy on television. Travel with a beloved children's book like a Harry Potter volume or *The Little Engine That Could*. Your artist does not need to be scared by things that go bump in the night. The dark night of the soul comes to all artists. When it comes to you, know that it is simply a tricky part of the trail and that you will see better in the morning.

TASK
Doubt Your Doubts

Imagination is more important than knowledge.

ALBERT EINSTEIN

All artists experience doubt. Experienced artists learn to weather doubt without succumbing to self-sabotage. When doubt darkens the heart, it is wise to think of this gloom not as "reality" but as passing weather, like a badly overcast few days. During bouts of doubt, our judgments will not be accurate and should not be acted upon. Like a nasty cold snap, doubt is something to be survived, and so we should aim for actions that are warm, loving, nondramatic, and non-self-destructive. Rather than working on self-improvement, focus instead on self-care. Try to be actively selfish on your own behalf.

TASK
The Self in Self-Expression

Take pen in hand and list 10 small ways in which you could be *selfish*, that might make it easier for you later to be *selfless*. For example:

1. I could let myself call my long-distance friend, Laura.
2. I could let myself subscribe to *Western Horseman*.
3. I could let myself buy a pair of parakeets for my studio.
4. I could let myself get a new easel.
5. I could let myself declare "me" off limits after seven, one night a week, and use that time and space to write.
6. I could let myself turn my phone off during my art hours.
7. I could let myself take a portrait seminar and get some expert tips.
8. I could let myself shoot a roll of black and white just because I'm crazy about it.
9. I could let myself make a weekly writing date to get me off the dime on my thesis.
10. I could let myself get that new recording I'm curious about.

If you have difficulty thinking of 10 small ways to be creatively selfish, finish this sentence 10 times:

If I weren't so selfish, I'd _____.

CHECK-IN

1. **How many days this week did you do your Morning Pages?** If you skipped a day, why did you skip it? How was the experience of writing them for you? Are you experiencing more clarity? A wider range of emotions? A greater sense of detachment, purpose and calm? Did anything surprise you? Is there a "repeating" issue asking to be dealt with?

2. **Did you do your Artist's Date this week?** Did you note an improved sense of well-being? What did you do and how did you feel? Remember, Artist's Dates can be difficult and you may need to coax yourself into taking them.

3. **Did you get out on your Weekly Walk?** How did that feel? What emotions or insights surfaced for you? Were you able to walk more than once? What did your walk do for your optimism and sense of perspective?

4. **Were there any other issues this week that felt significant to you in your self-discovery?** Describe them.

Discovering a Sense of Camaraderie

Despite our Lone Ranger mythology, the artist's life is not lived in isolation. This week focuses your attention on the caliber of your friendships and creative collaborations. Loyalty and longevity, integrity and ingenuity, grace and generosity—all of these attributes are necessary traits for healthy creative exchange. The readings and tasks of this week aim at the difficult art of sorting our personal relationships.

Keep the Drama on the Stage

Artists are dramatic.

Art is dramatic. When artists are not making artistic dramas, they tend to make personal ones. Feeling off center, they demand center stage. Feeling on tilt, they tilt at an imaginary windmill.

"This relationship is in trouble," they announce. "Why, it's got all sorts of problems."

Or "I'm sure it's nothing serious, but it's possible I'm going deaf. Did you hear what I said?"

All of us are creative, but those of us who are for a living had better learn to create with the same quotidian grace as our cousin who works at the bank, our father who administers his department at the university, or our neighbor who manages the hardware store. When we make our creative work and our creative lives too special and too dramatic, we uproot those lives from a sense of community and continuity—and that's exactly what we like to do whenever we get too nervous. Nervous, we create dramas to make ourselves more nervous.

We announce, "I've been thinking about *your* character, and I'm not so sure I should trust it. What do you think about that, wife?"

To the skilled ear, there is a predictively reactive tone to these sudden besetting dilemmas. Reality need not apply, the relationship is probably fine. Deafness would not drown out a compliment, and your character is less a question than the character you're dealing with: a nervous artist.

A friend of mine is a world-class musician who develops health problems on the cusp of every major concert tour. Health fears are his Achilles' heel. Mysterious maladies always arrive as his departure date nears. Another friend of mine, a fine writer, loses all humor and sense of personal perspective every time a writing deadline looms. His marriage is always "over" or, at least, on the rocks, until he settles down to write. People like these should furnish seat belts for those riding shotgun in their lives. You would think that *someone* would have the nerve to say "Oh, just stop it." As artists, we should say it ourselves, but drama gives us an excuse to not make art and so artistic anorexia is addictive. We get an adrenalized anxiety from not making art. We can binge on this chemical roller-coaster when work is due.

> Compassion is the antitioxin of the soul: where there is compassion even the most poisonous impulses remain relatively harmless.
>
> ERIC HOFFER

> Her great merit is finding out mine—there is nothing so amiable as discernment.
>
> LORD BYRON

Artists love making art the way lovers love making love, and just as lovers become snappish when they need to go to bed and make love, artists become snappish when they need to make art. Artistic anorexia, the avoidance of the pleasure of the creative, is a pernicious addiction that strikes most artists sometimes and always takes us by surprise. Instead of making art, we make trouble—and we make it because we are bingeing emotionally on *not* making art. We need to get to the piano and practice. We need to do our vocal exercises. We need to show up at the easel or the page. We need to go full steam ahead, and when we don't, we tend to blow off steam by venting inappropriately about any number of imaginary ills. Our aches and pains become the world's pain in the neck. Goddammit, art is a serious business, and you had better believe we will raise hell if anyone gets too festive in our vicinity.

"You just don't understand," we start snapping at people who do understand all too well. John Barrymore's performance as the imperious theatrical impresario in *Twentieth Century* should be required viewing for all artists prone to occasional bouts of self-importance. The *art* is what's important. We are intended to serve our art, not treat our friends and family as servants. The arrogant-artist archetype doubtless has its twisted roots somewhere in low self-esteem and posturing out of a need to disguise our vulnerabilities. If we have too much ego invested in our work and not enough ego strength coming from the rest of our lives, it's easy to act out the arrogant-artist archetype.

At root, we have lost our sense of humor and, as a result, our sense of scale. When we take ourselves too seriously and demand that others do the same, we inadvertently tighten our creative muscles and strain our own performance. Touring artists should probably carry a backpack of comedies. If we remember—or watch—*That's Entertainment*, we may loosen up, lighten up, and deliver the caliber of work we aspire to. There is a bumper sticker that reads "Angels fly because they take themselves lightly."

It is one of the paradoxes of a creative career that our careers take off once we loosen our fearful, ego-ridden grip. A sense of humor is attractive. It indicates a sense of scale. As an artist, a sense of scale is what gives our work proportion, perspective, and personality. As artists, we want to avoid being "over the top." The best way to do this is to avoid being top-heavy— that is, big-headed because we feel so small. As a rule of thumb, artists should repeat this mantra: Sudden problems in my life usually indicate a need to work on my art. Lest this sound like artist bashing, let me simply admit that I

> *Man is an over-complicated organism. If he is doomed to extinction he will die out for want of simplicity.*
>
> EZRA POUND

have bashed myself against the rocks of my creative imagination countless times before arriving at this conclusion.

A book deadline is not a NASA launch. A concert date is not a countdown for nuclear testing. As one cellist jokes, "I could be getting hit by a bus right now. Instead, I'm walking onstage to play a Brahms sextet." High profile and high pressure do not need to be synonymous. But the temptation to make them that way is enormous, particularly if we are feeling slightly off our game.

Our dogs should bite when they sense this senselessness drama coming on. My dog, Tiger Lily, a gold-and-white cocker spaniel, has learned to roll her eyes and pout eloquently whenever my humor evaporates. Tiger Lily's Westie sidekick, Charlotte, smells a rat whenever the household mood darkens unnecessarily. She has a small purple toy, Ratty, suitable for such occasions. When too much drama sets in, she presents Ratty at the offender's feet, with the strong, yipped suggestion that a game of catch might get us a lot further than whatever the hell game *this* is.

It is probably not an accident that the verbs *exorcise* and *exercise* are so similarly spelled. Most of the time when an artist is engaging in drama instead of art, he needs to move out of his head and into his body—if not into his body of work. A brisk walk up a steep hill, a few forced laps in the pool, and reality threatens to set in—the reality that the only drama in our very nice life is the one that we're creating ourselves. With our fine imaginations, artists can be drama addicts. We can also become physically addicted to our adrenalized anxiety in place of authentic creation. Too much drama is not fun, but it gives us something to do instead of making art. Until we break the code on this avoidance, we *believe* our dramatic scenarios.

"I know I should paint," we wail, "but does he love me?"

"All right, I should get to the piano, but I'm not certain I get enough respect from my peers."

"I'll get to the typewriter and work on the book as soon as I fire off a letter about my goddamn tennis shoes not holding up."

"I'll pick up the viola and practice *after* I know where my musical career is going."

As artists, we can be con artists—not that we con others, we usually don't. But we do con ourselves. We con ourselves into thinking that our dramatic dilemmas mean more than our art, and that indulging in drama will ever-satisfy our creative impulses.

If we can just convince ourselves to indulge in a little terrifying doubt—about our talent, about our lovability, about our competencies, creative and otherwise, then we can usually manage to stall ourselves in our creative tracks and *really* give ourselves something to worry about. If we can stage a nice, nasty drama, we can often subvert or sabotage our genuine creative growth.

> *What annoyances are more painful than those of which we cannot complain?*
>
> MARQUIS DE CUSTINE

What a relief! How much easier to worry about boy/girl dilemmas than whether or not our book has the proper art, our rehearsal has been sufficient to move the music into our hands and hearts, our mastery of our new photographic equipment has actually sharpened the focus of our work.

Artists are dramatic. Channeled into our work, drama is fine, but artists risk being addicted to emotional drama. We can display an alarming predilection standing at the edge of the cliff, looking straight down, while asking gullible friends, "Will

I fall?" or "Shall I jump?" "Why would anyone want to do that?" you may ask. The answer is that it gives us something to do instead of making art.

Art is the itch we have to scratch, but we're the only ones who can scratch it. And if we refuse to scratch the surface of our own dramatic resistance, if we refuse to allow ourselves the dignity of genuine creative risk, then you will know us by how close to the cliff we are standing.

TASK

Keeping a "Ta-dah!" List

Facts are the opposite of drama. If you have been working with Morning Pages, you have probably become more and more accurate at generating grounded to-do lists that spell out the priorities of the day as revealed in the pages. In order to have a firm sense of self-respect as artists, we need to employ a second daily list. That list is the "ta-dah!" list, as in the bow well taken after a successful recital. "Ta-dah!"

Rather than always focusing on what is left to do, we need to give ourselves a hand for what we've already done. Your ta-dah list is a nightly bow to personal applause for the many small creative actions taken in the course of a day. A ta-dah list might read:

> *In our era, the road to holiness necessarily passes through the world of action.*
>
> DAG HAMMARSKJÖLD

1. Did my Morning Pages
2. Dropped Carolina a note
3. Put in 15 minutes at the piano
4. Repotted the geraniums
5. Read the essay in *The Atlantic* related to my thesis
6. Threw together a pot of soup
7. Inputted the bills to my computer home management program
8. Talked to Bruce—instant emotional restoration
9. Worked on actual writing of the thesis for one hour
10. Scheduled the dog at the groomer
11. Hemmed my droopy skirt
12. Ordered thesis-related book from amazon.com

13. Picked paint for kitchen windowsill
14. Tuned into the classical station for *Opera Hour*
15. Did the dark laundry

A ta-dah list can easily escalate to double this length. Often our days are far busier and more productive than we realize. Additionally, a ta-dah list may function as a subtle goad—"I'll love writing it down," we think as we tackle a creative something we've been avoiding. If to-do lists live out our priorities, ta-dah lists recognize our accomplishments. Ta-dah!—I did work on my art today. Creative lives are made of minutes—and minute amounts of work *do* add up.

The Good of Getting Better

As artists, we are not interested merely in expressing ourselves; that realm may belong to therapy. We are interested in expressing ourselves more and more accurately, more and more beautifully. This brings us squarely to the issue of craft, to our need for accurate assessment by others and ourselves.

> *In the greatest confusion there is still an open channel to the soul. It may be difficult to find because by midlife it is overgrown, and some of the wildest thickets that surround it grow out of what we describe as our education. But the channel is always there, and it is our business to keep it open, to have access to the deepest part of ourselves.*
>
> SAUL BELLOW

Accurate and useful are most often found in the company of the grounded combination of personal experience and excellence. It is for this reason that artists have always apprenticed other artists. A great music teacher certainly shapes and colors the playing of her students—they become at once more fully themselves and somehow also recognizably "hers." It is, in part, a matter of shared technique, but it is also a matter of shared musical values. A great teacher both attracts and produces great students. It is a sort of spiritual lineage or, to cast it in the terms of the market, a "brand name." A great conservatory with great teachers puts a recognizable "stamp" onto its artists.

Sometimes, teachers and students seem to intersect by divine planning more than by set curriculum. This was the case for Emma and her teacher.

The great violin and viola teacher Joyce Robbins retired to southern California after a long teaching career in New York. A gifted viola player spending an unexpected year in California found Robbins and embarked on a course of study that changed her playing and perception of playing. She learned to hear.

"I just missed studying with this great teacher in the East. She had retired to California the year I enrolled. I never expected to go to California, but when I did I had to look her up. It was a three-and-a-half-hour round-trip commute to study with her, and I really got to know the California freeway system. On the other hand, I learned how actually to listen to myself as I played. I began to play more softly, with less stridency, and to listen to the actual sound I was making rather than just focusing on the technique of how I was making it. As a result, I began to sound much better. In the time since, whenever I hear a viola student with a particularly full and gentle sound, I wonder if he hasn't studied with my teacher and learned some of the same gift of hearing that she passed to me."

Yet, artists are everywhere and fine arts conservatories are not. A brilliant young painter in South Milwaukee may not have the familial or community support to study other than locally—and locally may offer some very fine teachers, or it may offer teachers whose own work is underschooled, underdeveloped, and unduly influenced by the supposed sophistication of a few powerful arts publications.

Try to discover your true, honest, untheoretical self.

BRENDA UELAND

Wanting to bloom where we are planted, we may seek out local teachers and either get lucky or experience an inner certainty that they are cramped in their creative calling and that they in turn can cramp us. Not wanting to be egotistical, many students stay too long at the fair, studying with teachers whom they have outgrown, often experiencing an uncomfortable creative constriction that manifests as teacher-student tension, even competition, that cannot often be directly addressed. How do we say "You see, I think I have outgrown you"? Often we say it best by simply thanking our mentor for time and talent given—then moving on.

Just as an excellent teacher can strengthen and clarify an artist, a bad teacher can damage, muffle, and muddy an artist. It is the impact of poor teachers that has blocked or battered many artists into at first healthy and later self-defeating hermeticism. Declaring themselves above, beyond, or outside the market, they court two possibilities, and usually encounter a mixture of both. Freed from outer influences, they may incubate and develop a strikingly original style. That's the good part. Freed from outer influences, they may also hit an artificially low ceiling, having taken their work as far as they can without further input.

Art, in some ways, is like any other skill—we enjoy doing it. Then we enjoy doing it well; then we enjoy doing it better. The refusal to allow ourselves the tools and techniques to move from "well" to "better," often calling it sort of faux purity, has nothing pure about it. We have allowed our pride and fear to taint our creative process. Yes, our inner creator may be childlike, but we have allowed ourselves to cross the line to *childish*. Defensive and defended, we have shied away from authentic growth.

> *I will tell you what I have learned myself. For me, a long five- or six-mile walk helps. And one must go alone and every day.*
>
> BRENDA UELAND

A talented regional string player may struggle for years with self-perceived flaws, only to finally encounter an expert teacher who says, "You outgrew that instrument years ago, it's crippling you—get rid of it!" Not a perception likely to be jumped to by the artist alone.

Art, as remarked, is a form of the verb "to be" and, as artists, our spiritual and intellectual perceptions often lead and goad our need for increased technique. We can see it but we can't paint it. We can hear it but we can't play it. We need help. We can get help—or we can give up, discouraged by the gap between our inner standards and our own ability to meet them. Writer Tillie Olsen warns correctly of the danger of "the knife of perfectionism in art." If we keep its blade constantly at our creative throat, we fail to progress because we so stifle our learning process. A teacher is a guide through creative pitfalls such as these.

Each of us learns in our own way and at our own pace, and yet *someone's* excellent method will have something to offer us if we are willing to offer ourselves the opportunity to learn.

Authentic growth, however, is the goal, and that will not occur if we enroll ourselves in classes and curriculums that are themselves stagnant, stifling, or simply inadequate and ill advised. What we are after is excellence, and it can be found, but we must look for it, not only in ourselves, as we have been, but also in others. We must be neither blinded nor dazzled by brand-name credentials—blinded to the possibility that they might mean something valid or too dazzled by what they *might* mean to see that in this particular practitioner they mean very little. In other words, we must be open to finding our teachers and open to being teachable—while simultaneously holding an awareness of our equally valid, genuine perceptions and skills that must be protected.

It is an often repeated spiritual axiom that "when the student is ready, the teacher appears." Over the years, I have heard many stories of miraculous intersections and meetings. The divine mind knows no distance, and so a student's prayer in Omaha is heard as loudly and clearly as a student's prayer in Manhattan. When we ask to be led, we are led. When we ask to be guided, we are guided. When we ask to be taught, we are taught. A young sculptor working in a small midwestern industrial city prays for guidance and is led to a renowned sculptor working ten miles away in the very same off-the-beaten-path locale. A talented actor in a tiny New Mexico town intersects with a retired Hollywood director, who helps secure him a scholarship at a famed acting conservatory. Guidance and generosity are always closer at hand than we may think. It always falls to us to be open to receiving guidance and to pray for the willingness and openness to know it when it arrives.

> *The best career advice to give the young is, find out what you like doing best and get someone to pay you for doing it.*
>
> KATHERINE WHILEHAEN

It is spiritual law that the good of our projects and our growth as artists must rest in divine hands and not merely human ones. While we are led to and drawn from teacher to teacher, opportunity to opportunity, the Great Creator remains the ultimate source of all of our creative good. It is easy to forget this and make our agent or our manager or our current teacher the source of our "good." When we place our reliance on an undergirding of divine assistance, we are able to hear our cues clearly, thank those who step forward to aid us, release those who seem to impede us, and keep unfolding as artists with the faith that the Great Artist knows precisely what is best for us and can help us find our path, no matter how lost, distanced, or removed we may sometimes feel from our dream. In the heart of God, all things are close at hand, and this means our creative help, support, and success. As we ask, believe, and are open to receive, we are gently led.

TASK
Becoming Teachable

Take pen in hand. List 5 personal situations that are, for you, lingering resentments, sore spots, and sources of self-pity regarding a lack of effective mentoring. For example:

1. My parents both got sick and I never got to Stanford for my poetry master's.
2. My viola was so difficult to play that I damaged my technique by compensating and am still undoing my bad habits.
3. My family had no idea what to do with a writer in their midst. They wanted me to be a lawyer. I had *no* literary support.
4. My hometown had never heard of modern dance. By the time I realized what it was, I was already in my twenties and on a career path as a physical therapist.
5. My very talented older sister got all the creative encouragement as a musician. I had to do the dishes while she serenaded on guitar.

These grievances are real, and you can't change them. You can, however, ask some pointed questions and take some nurturing actions. For example:

1. Would I still like a poetry master's? There are many fine nonresidential programs for older students.
2. As to that viola technique, if you're not in a music program, there are still often excellent teachers who make themselves available for private lessons. The right teacher can undo the wrong learning quite quickly.

Address each of your historic grievances, looking for a present-tense action that creatively soothes your injured artist. Take those actions. Even the smallest can lessen self-pity's sting.

Before, During, and After Friends

One of the trickiest issues in a creative life is the issue of private support and encouragement for our creative leaps—no matter how they are received. As artists, we do not need private adulation, but we do need before, during, and after friends, those people who love and accept us no matter what our current creative shape and size. We need friends who understand that a creative success may bring an onslaught of pressures nearly as devastating as a creative failure.

Friends must be found who understand how to cohabit with our varied creative needs. Sometimes, we are the lonely larva; sometimes, the beautiful butterfly. Our needs and necessities vary with where we are and how we are doing in our creative process.

It helps us to become conscious of our needs first of all for ourselves and then to share our insights with those we know we can trust. Too often, we try either to "go it alone" creatively or we do not ask for what it is we need in ways that can be acted on or understood. When our creative well is low from having worked a long time on a hard project, we need to be enough of a friend to ourselves to take a refreshing Artist's Date to fill the well back up with images and adventure. When a deadline looms and we are dead on our feet from overwork, it can be very hard to take such breaks. Instead, we tend to want to flog ourselves forward, and both the work and ourselves suffer. In such times, a call to a friend might say, "Pray that I can get out of the house to see *Harry Potter*."

In 12-Step programs, participants learn the "sandwich" call. When they are about to do something difficult, they call a friend, do the difficult thing, and then call the friend back and report "Mission accomplished." There are stages of creative work when we can get so painfully stymied that a "sandwich" call is great first aid. We can call and say, "I can't get into my studio and I have work stacking up. I am going to go in for one half hour and just clean my brushes." We can call and say, "I am going to do the fixes on two pages and then call you to say I have." We can say, "I am going to read the first twenty-five pages of the manuscript to see what I think." Or "I'm going to rough out the choreography for the first movement."

All who joy would win Must share it,—Happiness was born a twin.

LORD BYRON

Most of us have friends who are willing and ready to help us if we will just tell them how. In my early sobriety, I sold a script to Paramount and I was so terrified of rewriting it that my friend Jupiter used to come to my house, sit in my rocker, and read for an hour a day while I took my quaking self to the typewriter. An hour a day is a lot more work than no hours a day, and, as friends learn that small donations of time and support are more useful to us than grand gestures, they begin to know the cue lines: "Hook for half an hour and call me back." Or "Try to read the first twenty pages and call me back." Very often, we need help only to get a toe in the water. Once we are in, we can swim. Our help can be a phone call, a writing date where we both show up at Starbucks and scribble for an hour, a faxed check-in, an e-mail saying "I did it." The electronic age has allowed us to make our creative community far-flung. We can also "tame" a coffee-shop owner and faithfully eat a grilled cheese and work an hour in a back booth every day. For years, Dori's Bakery in Taos was like a zoo, full of writers, each of us with our table, nodding to each other and Dori as we sat down to toil. Our friends will help us if we let them know how. Often, all we need is a little welcome company.

An artist in the midst of making a large creative jump—a concert tour, a book signing, a one-person show—is a vulnerable and sometimes volatile creature. And there are those who will attack and exploit that vulnerability and those who will protect and support it. An artist who is suddenly "hot" often gets burned. Without the solid anchoring of tried-and-true friends who stay the course, how is an artist to sort opportunity from opportunists, management from manipulation? Snipers are snipers, creatively as in life. They will hide and shoot. Some colleagues are snipers. Unfortunately, some friends are. Some families are. Often unconsciously jealous and resentful, they greet our good fortune with a chilly reception. A conversation with them can leave us feeling dismayed and dispirited.

> *Transport of the mails, transport of the human voice, transport of flickering pictures—in this century as in others our highest accomplishments still have the single aim of bringing men together.*
>
> ANTOINE DE SAINT-EXUPÉRY

Sometimes, it's sarcastic teasing: "So, how does it feel to be flavor of the week?" Sometimes, it's freelance spiritual advice: "Better watch out that you don't get too big for yourself." Sometimes, it's simple guilt: "I had a feeling this was coming, that you'd be too busy for me once you started on this project. It must be great to be so in demand." A friend of mine, a veteran actress, joked: "I don't know why we're so busy trying to get to the top; what's waiting at the top is envy and resentment." Yes, among other things, and it can be hard to find willing ears for some of our odd, success-driven adventures. I remember thinking, *Who can I call to say Sammy Davis, Jr., invited me to his house, and then told me I was a great dancer?* (I'm not sure my mother *was* the right choice.) The simple fact of your new life can sound like bragging and name dropping, even to yourself. We must find people who can see our vulnerability in such passages and neither encourage it to become terror nor discount it.

As artists, we need people who can see us for who we are—as big as we are and as small as we are, as competent and powerful as we are, and as terrified and as tiny as we sometimes feel. As artists, we need people who believe in us and are able to see our large selves, and people who are able to be gentle and compassionate with our smaller selves. I have a very small and cherished list of people whom I *could* call with a creative terror in the middle of the night. Ed, Jim, Bill, Bob, Julie, Emma, Bruce. I'm not saying I *do* call them to announce at two A.M., "I can't write. I've never been able to write. I've fooled the world and they're finding out at dawn," but if I had to call them, they would understand. Similarly, I hold a willing place on their midnight call sheet. None of us wants to be suicidally depressed at four A.M., but all of us sometimes are, and knowing that we *could* call often calls off the demons. Take a moment to make your midnight madness medical team. Sometimes, it is difficult to find people who can feel equally at home with both our largest and smallest selves.

> *Know that if you have a kind of cultured know-it-all in yourself who takes pleasure in pointing out what is not good, in discriminating, reasoning, and comparing, you are bound under a knave. I wish you could be delivered.*
>
> BRENDA UELAND

For this reason, it is tremendously important to accurately distinguish who among our friends can accommodate each size. If you call a friend who loves "little" you with big news, you may meet an upsetting silence followed by a tepid "Gee, that's great!" that sounds like you've just said your exotic blood disease was now in remission. Call a friend who loves "big" you when you're feeling small, and you may feel as welcomed as a malaria-bearing mosquito. This is especially true if you are surrounded by people who are out of touch or shaky in their own creativity; they may never be able to see your need for validation and support as an artist. To them you're the lucky one, so what's the problem? This attitude may trigger you into your own caretaking, where you join them in neglecting your artist. A young novelist with a best seller gave all his earnings to his friends' worthy causes, "just to put everyone back in the same boat," struggling to keep their heads above water. A recording artist with a hit began frantically producing projects for needy newcomers. When people are judgmental or withholding around our success, we unconsciously try to buy them off—peace at any price, even if it's a piece of ourselves.

Consciously or not, the withholding of approval and appreciation is a powerful manipulation that moves us off our personal perspective and into pleasing others. This can be very expensive. When people are afraid of being artistically diminished themselves, they may never be able to do anything but diminish you. What we want to find are people who are able to be generous to us and to our artist.

We must learn to avoid those who blackmail us by pointing at our abandoning them when we are pulling our energies in and gathering them for a creative jump. We must find those who can both help ground us and help nurture us as we leap.

A public appearance as an artist is best handled with a very clear understanding of the wallop the spotlight packs. Friends who see the glory but not its gory cost are the friends we may not be able to afford. Just as caffeine or an alcoholic drink can hit us hard on an empty stomach, so, too, the glare of the spotlight can throw us off center unless we are well fed spiritually, both before and after. Friends who see our success but do not see its stressors can tend to actually ask us to care for them just at those moments when we ourselves need care. This is why we need before, during, and after friends. We need those who can help us leap and help us land, help us celebrate and help us mourn. Some friends can do only one. Some friends can do only the other. We must find those generous enough in temperament and emotional range to do both.

> *If the book is good, is about something that you know, and is truly written, and reading it over you see that this is so, you can let the boys yip and the noise will have that pleasant sound coyotes make on a very cold night when they are out in the snow and you are in your own cabin that you have built or paid for with your work.*
>
> ERNEST HEMINGWAY

It might be your aunt Bernice. It may be your little sister. It may be the doorman at your building or your best friend from grade school. All of us need a private cheering section when we undergo a public creative jump. We need those selected family members and friends who can provide us with the nutrients of love and creative support. If people see you only as the swan, that publicly graceful creature, and do not know about the feet churning beneath the water, then they are not the friends you truly need.

And yet, just as a swan is supported by water, which is see-through and ephemeral but "there," so, too, are we supported by higher forces that are unseen and ephemeral but "there." Our sincere prayers are answered. Furthermore, if we are lonely and beg for a little more in the way of human support, that support does show up.

Living lately in Manhattan, far from my nest in New Mexico, I have been craving before, during, and after friends, the day-in and day-out kind that I knew in New Mexico. To my shock and relief, I have been contacted by exactly that kind of person. An actor friend of mine from twenty-five years ago has turned up. A beloved teacher from thirty-five years ago. Another from fifteen years ago and a horseback riding girlfriend from further back than that. These friends knew me as young and wild as wistful and a lot of the ways that I still am when I get a chance to be. Today my mail contained notes from two of these recently re-met friends. My voice-mail had a message from my grammar school best girl-friend. All of these "miracle" reunions happened directly following a rather desperate prayer on my part, "Dear God, send me my real friends. I am too lonely with just you and me and good intentions."

> *With thee conversing I forget all time.*
>
> JOHN MILTON

Most of us are too lonely with just God and good intentions and no one knows this better than God. Instead of feeling so piercingly lonely, you might want to try, as I did, to pick up the phone and do some detective work. It took me three phone calls to find Sr. Julia Clare Greene, my high school writing teacher, but when I did and we talked on the phone, she did what a writer was bound to do: She wrote me. Now I have her picture and note tacked above my writing table, and it reminds me that I may have as many friends as I am willing to be friend to.

TASK
There's a Somebody I'm Longing to Meet

Take heart and some heart steps. There are those who will tell you we should be "too mature" to need a cheering section. That's stingy advice, and it's not founded in artistic reality. We both need a cheering section and need to *be* a cheering section.

Invent an imaginary supporter. Take a sheet of paper and write a want ad that expresses exactly what you would really like in a creative colleague. You may already know such a person. If not, your "ad" will help you recognize a possible candidate when he appears:

WANTED

A creative colleague with genuine enthusiasm and generosity for me and my work. Someone to share my hopes, dreams, and disappointments with, who will spoil me a little, cheer for me a lot, and believe in me when I can't believe in myself. Someone who can say—and mean—"That's beautiful, and so are you."

Catcher's Mitt

As artists, we need to focus on process, not on product, and yet, we also need a catcher's mitt—somewhere or someplace where the ball we're pitching is aimed. In order to keep our art moving successfully on its true course, we need the right catcher's mitt. That is how we learn to throw the ball across the plate. Ideally, we want someone with enough range to catch a pitch that goes a little wild, someone with enough enthusiasm to yelp out, "Put it here!"

A compliment is something like a kiss through a veil.

VICTOR HUGO

It is not what we learn in conversation that enriches us. It is the elation that comes of swift contact with tingling currents of thought.

AGNES REPPLIER

We make art to communicate not only to ourselves but also to the world. Someone or something must represent that world, and it must be the *right* someone or something. We must become smart about this.

The great writer Italo Calvino phrased it "The ears call forth the story." This is another way of saying that proper receptivity to our art helps to catalyze that art. "Oh, that's beautiful!" or "I love your phrasing" can be water to our creative garden. An eager "Tell me more about that" or "Show me that again" can bring our artist into blossom just as chill inattention or indifference can nip its growth or stunt it. So, too, skewed and premature criticism can cause it to compensate like a pine in a prevailing wind, and twist in an unnatural direction.

Early work is most often called forward by warmth. "That's going to be great!" You may remember the fairy tale about the bet between the wind and the sun as to who could make a traveler drop his cloak. The wind blew. The traveler, our artist, clutched his cloak. The sun shone gently, warmly, and pleasantly. Our artist took his coat off in the sun.

As a writer, your best catcher's mitt might not be an editor—it might be an avid, word-loving personal friend. Some of the best writing has been aimed to a specific someone—Rilke's *Letters to a Young Poet* was not generic. He didn't write them to "young people everywhere" but to one young mind and heart of interest to him. We can call such a person a muse, but we don't have to. You might like words like fuse lighter, spark, catalyst. It's someone whose particular intelligence lights your own. It is because of this alchemical attraction between souls that artists have always nurtured and encouraged other artists, and often championed their work. Haydn was nicknamed "Papa" because he was a catcher's mitt for Mozart.

At the end of his middle period, frustrated by his growing deafness—and the deafness of others to the music only he could seem to hear—Beethoven, in despair, made God his catcher's mitt and went on to write some of his most glorious music. Still, the story is a lonely one.

God can be the catcher's mitt for us as well, just as Christianity probably caught on because many people needed God in a human form in the same way many of us as artists need our catcher's mitt in a human form.

It is romantic nonsense to believe that we can, or do, make art in a vacuum. It is only a half-truth to say we make it to please ourselves. Even there we are pleasing a certain receptive aspect in ourselves, a sort of internal embodiment of our ideal viewer, reader, or listener. I wrote *The Dark Room* to read to my friend Ellen Longo in installments. She was an avid reader and accountant. I wrote *Popcorn: Hollywood Stories* to make my first husband laugh at my version of the world we both survived.

Great art lies not in the generic but in the specific. It lies not in "More or less"—as we lamely conclude a thought to a bored listener—but in "Exactly like this!" as we excitedly show or tell someone perceptive. A tepid ear, a hurried glance, a lack of real focus—these can chill and even destroy an early work and a fragile worker. Yes, artists are resilient, but we are also like tender shoots. Our thoughts and our ideas must be welcomed or, like shy suitors, they get discouraged and go away.

> *War talk by men who have been in a war is always interesting; whereas moon talk by a poet who has not been in the moon is likely to be dull.*
>
> MARK TWAIN

Does this mean we want constant adulation and approval? Oh, probably. Does this mean we hate criticism and have no rigor, no discipline, no need for improvement? Emphatically, no. What it does mean is that our catcher's mitt must be receptive to our efforts, to our warm-up pitches and our looping fouls as well as to our sizzling fast balls and snaking curves that catch just the tiniest corner of the plate. Our catcher's mitt fields our creative energies, is open to all of them, and has faith in our artist's arm—wild, tired, serviceable, blistering. In other words, our catcher's mitt must be generous—which does not mean nondiscerning.

One of my best catcher's mitts is my friend Ed. When I tell him the writing is a little ragged, he says, "I'm sure it is, but it will tighten up later. It's great you're getting something down." When I tell him I am having a writing day that feels like I am suffering from rheumatism of the writing faculty, he says, "Everybody gets stiff once in a while. It can take a while to warm up. I am sure it's not as bad as you think it is, and you'll probably be limber again pretty soon." When I tell him, "I have so much work to do, I cannot believe it," he says, "True, but you've gotten through long rewrites before, and if you just keep chipping at it, you'll do fine."

Perhaps Ed's gentle coaching comes from the fact that he, too, writes. Perhaps it comes from his years as a senior partner in a law firm, coaching hot young lawyers through pretrial jitters. Maybe it is his long years as a slow long-distance runner that have taught him the value of just logging the miles and not trying to sprint all the time. Maybe I am just lucky and Ed is very compassionate. Whatever the case, I need him. He is like the friend who turns up at the twenty-two-mile marker and gently runs me across the marathon finish line. I know Ed is a superb catcher's mitt because I have also had the other kind.

> *How many are silenced, because in order to get to their art they would have to scream?*
>
> ANN CLARK

I have made the mistake of giving a rough draft of a book to one of my most fastidious and hypercritical friends. I have been told: "This book lacks your usual ease and poise. These essays are really heavy lifting and not very personable."

What do you say to that? "It's a rough draft, you idiot! There's a reason we call them 'rough'!"

I have also given rough drafts of my books to friends who are too nondiscerning. "I don't see how you could change a thing in this book. It's just perfect. Nothing seemed too long or too unfocused to me. I could always figure out what you meant and I just love the way you write anything. I could probably read the phone book if you wrote it. . . ."

Reviews like that from personal friends leave me pretty terrified that I *have* written the phone book. If the praise feels too syrupy, I get the terrible feeling that I will be like the wasp who gets her legs stuck in the sugary jam at a picnic—a good wallow until you want and need some liftoff. No, too much sugar from a catcher's mitt is not what we are really after.

What we want in a great catcher is what you see with a great catcher. Someone avidly crouched near home plate. Somebody slapping his mitt a little eagerly and saying, "Put it here."

TASK
Catch Yourself a Catcher's Mitt

The part of us that creates is youthful and vulnerable. It needs an atmosphere that is friendly and even playful, certainly compassionate, so that it can expand, experiment, and express itself. In many ways, a catcher's mitt is like a spiritual sidekick. Even the Lone Ranger wasn't really alone on all his great adventures. He had Tonto at his side.

> *I believe . . . that every human mind feels pleasure in doing good to another.*
>
> THOMAS JEFFERSON

Often, when we think about periods where we have been particularly happy, we will discover that we had an unacknowledged sidekick, a creative companion who cheered us on by taking a lively interest in our adventures.

Take pen in hand and do a little digging to discover some of your earlier companions and just what qualities they had that let you sparkle.

1. As a child, did you have a catcher's mitt for your creative efforts?
2. Who was your very best catcher's mitt? Mine was my friend Lynnie.
3. What did he bring to you that created joy and excitement in your artist?
4. Do you know such a person now?
5. Could that person be your catcher's mitt?
6. As a child, did you have a larger-than-life creative hero in your favored art? (Someone you just plain liked and identified with, not someone so intimidating, your artist would hide.)
7. What did your artist like in that artist?
8. What would that artist like in your artist?
9. Write a letter to your childhood catcher's mitt or your childhood creative hero.
10. Write a letter back to you.

CHECK-IN

1. **How many days this week did you do your Morning Pages?** If you skipped a day, why did you skip it? How was the experience of writing them for you? Are you experiencing more clarity? A wider range of emotions? A

greater sense of detachment, purpose, and calm? Did anything surprise you? Is there a "repeating" issue asking to be dealt with?

2. **Did you do your Artist's Date this week?** Did you note an improved sense of well-being? What did you do and how did you feel? Remember, Artist's Dates can be difficult and you may need to coax yourself into taking them.

3. **Did you get out on your Weekly Walk?** How did that feel? What emotions or insights surfaced for you? Were you able to walk more than once? What did your walk do for your optimism and sense of perspective?

4. **Were there any other issues this week that felt significant to you in your self-discovery?** Describe them.

Discovering a Sense of Authenticity

In the end, an artist's life is grounded in integrity and the willingness to witness our version of truth. There are no set markets that assure us of safe passage. This week focuses on personal responsibility for our creative caliber and direction. Self-respect lies in the doing, not in the done. For this reason, our personal resiliency is a key to our creative longevity. Defeat is transformed into experience by our willingness to start anew. The readings and tasks of this week ask us to practice a beginner's mind, opening ourselves to renewed endeavors despite setbacks.

Encouragement

Artists are people whose "real" job, no matter what their paying job, is the pursuit of excellence by listening carefully and well to what is trying to be born through them.

Artists are not fragile, but we are delicate. We are subject to the weather conditions in our life. Just as a long gray winter spent indoors can cause depression, so, too, a period where our creative life is led without the sunshine of encouragement can cause a season of despair. We do not notice the darkening at first. We just "don't feel much" like working. If we do work, there will be forced and dreary drudgery to our time at the piano, the easel, the page. We will feel like it's a long hill we are climbing and may even, mistakenly, glance up and say, "Oh, dear, so far to go. I'll never get there."

Why should we all use our creative power . . . ? Because there is nothing that makes people so generous, joyful, lively, bold and compassionate, so indifferent to fighting and the accumulation of objects and money.

BRENDA UELAND

We will discover the nature of our particular genius when we stop trying to conform to our own or to other people's models, learn to be ourselves, and allow our natural channel to open.

SHAKTI GAWAIN

As artists, we routinely tap an inner well, and that well is fed by our spiritual condition. When we have kept our spirit carefully nurtured, the creative water seems to flow easily. When our spirit is dried out with unacknowledged discouragement, our inner well runs dry.

The antidote to depression is laughter, and this is where we are blessed if some of our friends have a good, bleak sense of humor. Sometimes, we can make a phone call that says "I am torn between suicide and doing my fingernails." Or "I am torn between making a gratitude list and leaping off my tenth-story window ledge."

The uncomfortable fact remains that there is always one positive thing we could do—and, damnably, there *is* always some positive something—even though we may still not have the heart to do it. We have to admit that our discouragement is, as one wag puts it, "a dirty job, but one that we have volunteered for, dammit."

There are some impeccably tried-and-true cheer-er-uppers that most of us are loath to try. It is, for example, very difficult to bake a pie and remain suicidal. It is very difficult to send out postcards without admiring ourselves, just a little, for our pluck and valor, even if our card says "Dear God, I am having a terrible time and wish you were here to do it with me." It is very hard to be depressed and watch a vintage comedy. It is hard to be depressed and make vegetable soup. Making almost anything can keep us from making trouble and, since most of us intuitively know this, we may take to our bed, giving our discouragement full rein to mug us. If we are in a 12-Step program, the dire complaints of a newcomer can lighten most despair. There is something very edifying about hearing someone share a truly catastrophic story when what we are worried about is something as elusive as "inspiration." Reading the hard knocks story of a literary great can cheer up most writers. Knowing that Rodgers and Hammerstein went penthouse to penthouse playing the piano and singing—to no good avail—to raise money for *Oklahoma!* can make the doldrums of "I don't feel like writing a song" seem laughably self-indulgent. Then, too, there is something wonderful to be said about just giving in to the full five-hanky storm of life that has a certain cheery effect. Finally, and this can work wonders, there is the possibility of calling someone truly boring. As they launch into breathtaking detail on something you could not care less about, the idea of going back to doing a little creative work can actually seem attractive. That and repeating the following:

All artists get discouraged. All artists have deep inner wells of self-pity into which we periodically dive. All artists are doing better than someone else and worse than someone else. All artists are doing better today than they have in the past and worse than they will in the future. All artists specialize in self-doubt. It is how we hone the creative imagination. . . .

We cannot control everything and everybody in our creative environment. We cannot leap across the dinner table and muzzle the fellow guest who casually observes, "At your age, you must be facing the fact that many of your dreams won't come true." We cannot—or, at least, we do not—hire hit men to take him out for murdering our hope, but that is what an offhand remark can do, especially if we are not alert to flag it as it passes. And we seldom are. "Let it go," we may say, only to have it go underground. When it does, it's poison.

As artists, we don't want to be petty, but the truth is, we *need* to be. If we try to "let go of" a creative slight, we very often simply bury it. There, tucked neatly into our subconscious, it can do its slow and poisonous work. Too embarrassed to repeat to a friend the "tiny" comment that hurt you on your way out the door from an audition, it becomes harder to audition next time. Why? Because we have been discouraged.

"Courage" comes from the root *coeur*, heart. It is easy to tell if you have been discouraged if you check the emotional timbre of your heart. If you feel vaguely blue, a little cross, a bit grumpy, odds are you are "disheartened," meaning discouraged.

It is well worth it to sleuth a bit, to assume there is a cause for your discomfort instead of saying "I'm crazy. What's the matter with me?" Very often, "What's the matter?" is an ignored injury, however slight.

A friend asks to look at your video—and then doesn't. Weeks tick past and your filmmaker thinks, *Oh, what's the use?* You write an essay and send it to a colleague and no sound comes back to let you know that the penny dropped in the well has landed. You record a CD and out it goes to your

> *Discontent and disorder [are] signs of energy and hope, not of despair.*
>
> DAME CICELY VERONICA WEDGWOOD

family, where it falls, evidently, on deaf ears. You have "dragged home the invisible bone," the trophy of all your hard work lies on the floor unnoticed and unapplauded.

"No big deal," says your adult self. But your artist? Your artist has the character traits of a terrier puppy. It was proud to have made that bone and dragged it home, defending it against other dogs and managing to lay it at master's feet. So, how about a pat on the head? Like it or not, whether we hate the Disney description or not, artists *do* need pats on the head. We *do* need encouragement. We *do* need praise and we *do* need comfort. It does not matter how accomplished we are; it is a daunting and damaging thing to have our work ignored.

"I meant to" and "whoops" add up to discouragement. We "should be" more mature—but we really shouldn't. What we should be is alert to the damage of discouragement and clever about addressing it directly. If no one else is cheering us on, we must cheer ourselves on with tokens of our esteem for work well done. We must care for our manuscripts well, not leave them in shabby stacks where we spill coffee over them. We must set Artist's Dates and celebrate our finishing a new story or finally laying to rest the portrait for the grumpy client from hell who could not be pleased, although the portrait was pleasing to everyone else who saw it. We must actively seek out friends who do not shame us around our discouragement and friends who can celebrate with us any small victory. In short, discouragement comes from an experience of stinginess—on the part of a critic, a colleague, a friend, our family. Encouragement just as clearly comes from an experience of generosity. Ideally, from others and ourselves.

> *My business is not to remake myself,*
> *But make the absolute best of what God made.*
>
> ROBERT BROWNING

At its root, discouragement is a decision in favor of stinginess. We are voting that the universe has done its last nice thing for us and that we have come to the bottom of Santa's bag of toys. No one will ever be spontaneously nice to us again—and we certainly aren't going to point the way by mustering any authentic and healing compassion for ourselves either.

We know how to stay discouraged when we are discouraged. We know how to choose our best negative friend to call. Most of us have a secret number emblazoned in our consciousness under the heading "Dial this number for pain and rejection." Most of us know how, if we are really feeling bad, we can feel just a little worse by calling it.

Jennifer has an excellent candidate for the worst person you could possibly call. He is a romantic ex. Someone who still owes her a great deal of money and who manages to ask for one whopping favor every time they speak. Superb at reporting the health and longevity of his stellar romantic involvements, where he is truly appreciated, this ex is skilled at remarks like "I heard you were in a terrible relationship—is that true?" Jennifer experiences the temptation to call this ex as a sign that the devil is alive and well and knows exactly where she lives. And yet, and still, Jennifer can fight calling this man the way a newly sober alcoholic can fight taking the first drink. It just doesn't seem possible to stay away from the pain and rejection that such a call can inevitably bring. Not when it's a clear-cut choice between encouraging herself and reaching for Mr. Poison.

All of us have some version of Jennifer's dilemma. We face the choice of thinking, *Actually, I'm doing pretty well and should really respect myself for my progress*, or, as we so often choose to think, *I am a spineless wonder, incapable of mustering the integrity, resolve, and inspiration necessary to address a postcard.* We all have people who think we are rather nice and doing pretty well and we all have other people who think—as we do often—that we could do better and be better if we would just listen to them. . . .

For most of us, the idea that we can listen to ourselves, trust ourselves, and value ourselves is a radical leap of faith. The idea that we can tell ourselves "Hey, you are doing pretty well and so much better than you did last year" amounts to a revolution. The possibility that we can trust ourselves, our decisions, and our painstaking progress, that this trust might be enough, even admirable, requires that we muster a soupçon of optimism. Optimism about ourselves and our chances is an elected attitude. We can choose to believe the best and not the worst, but to do that we must become conscious of our own negative voice-over and decide to change our mental sound track.

> *Just trust yourself, then you will know how to live.*
>
> JOHANN WOLFGANG
> VON GOETHE

Optimism is critical to our spiritual health. Is our creative glass half full or half empty? Have we wasted a decade or two not getting where we would like, or are we strong and seasoned and facing another couple of decades where our age and maturity and sheer experience may allow us to actualize areas beyond our grasp when we were younger? It's a matter of perception—and faith.

The good news and the bad news is that artists are like plants that can thrive or wither with only a few simple variables. It is hard to kill an artist, but it is very easy to discourage one. All that it requires is a certain withholding quality, and that can cast a spell over a very fine piece of work.

We all know people who tell us our dreams are foolish, pie in the sky, whimsy, and that we should be grateful for what recognition we have won and settle for a lower creative ceiling than our high-flying dreams require. (Those people have settled themselves and are uncomfortable with anyone willing to continue with substantial risks.) Fortunately, we also know people who do not bother to think about the odds or age or anything but the work at hand. Those people are the ones we must consciously choose to listen to. It is to those people that we must take our creative cuts and bruises for poulticing.

> *Perhaps loving something is the only starting place there is for making your life your own.*
>
> ALICE KOLLER

If we are to "take heart" and go on with our work, then we must take our heart seriously. We must listen to its pains and we must bring to it its joys. A heart does not need to be told "Oh, toughen up." It needs you to plan a tiny cheering ceremony and execute it. That done, you will find "the heart"—the courage—to work again and well.

TASK
Taking Heart

If we are to "take heart" and encourage ourselves, we must first find our heart. Our truth lies in what we love, and as we remind ourselves that we have loved and do love, we find our way unerringly back to the place from which accomplishment is possible.

In horseback riding circles, fine riders will talk of "throwing my heart over a fence" and then "jumping after it." What they are talking about is the courage to commit, to be full-hearted. When we are discouraged, we are literally divorced from our hearts. We forget how large our hearts are and how daring. When we trust our hearts, we trust ourselves. The following exercise, taught so beautifully by Oscar Hammerstein as *My Favorite Things*, is a lesson that all of us can teach ourselves whenever the going gets tough.

Take pen in hand, number from 1 to 50, and list 50 specific and particular things your heart loves. For example:

1. Red-winged blackbirds
2. Raspberry pie

3. Lemon curd
4. Beatrix Potter drawings
5. My daughter Domenica's bangs and sooty eyelashes
6. West Highland terriers
7. Plaid ribbons
8. Homemade rice pudding
9. Lily oil
10. The tassels on field corn
11. William Hamilton cartoons
12. Making this list

It's almost impossible to make a list of heart loves without concluding we live in a rich, savory, and enjoyable world where—if we will just "take heart"—things are bound to work out well.

Sometimes, we meet with creative encouragement that we savor, cherish, and act upon. Sometimes, however, we meet with creative encouragement that we discount and disown. Take pen in hand. Number from 1 to 10. List 10 examples of creative encouragement that you acted on *or* ignored. Next to those you acted on, note the action taken. Next to those you discounted, note an action that *could* be taken.

Integrity

What if we experiment with the idea that creativity is a spiritual and not an intellectual transaction? Not so long ago, cathedrals were built for the honor and glory of God. Art and artistry were routinely put to the service of higher realms. Higher realms were routinely credited for the worldly successes of creators.

Brahms exclaimed, "Straightaway the ideas flow in upon me, directly from God!"

"The music of this opera (*Madame Butterfly*) was dictated to me by God; I was merely instrumental in putting it on paper and communicating it to the public," Puccini confided.

> *Two things make a story. The net and the air that falls through the net.*
>
> PABLO NERUDA

If these men, masters at their art, could bow to mystery rather than their own mastery, might there be something medicinal for us in what they say? What if creativity itself is, as our creative ancestors teach us, actually a *spiritual experience*, a way to touch the divine and allow it to touch us? What if we reclaim the making of art as our birthright? Not some frippery on the edge of our serious business of making money. What if we remember and insist that art is central and dignified and important to the human experience?

We are an expression of the Great Creator, and we in turn are intended to create. It is not mere ego but our divine birthright to create. We carry creativity within us as surely as we carry our blood, and, in expressing it, we express our full humanity, which is far more than material. When we fail to answer this calling, when we turn it aside and listen to voices that deflect us, we are not in alignment with our own nature, nor with what might be called our destiny.

When we are headed in the right direction creatively, we feel a sense of satisfaction in each day's journey. We might not be moving as fast as we wish, but we are moving in the right direction and we do know it. At day's end, we can tote up our ta-dah list and say, "I placed three important phone calls. I reached out to check information that I needed. I jotted notes and got a few good paragraphs down."

Conversely, when we are not moving in the right direction, we experience a sense of unease. We have a growing sense of being off the beam. Something isn't sitting right with us. We feel stagnant or else stalemated. Sometimes, when we are moving in a wrong direction and events pick up velocity, we experience an alarming sense of being out of control. Something is "off," we know it and it is getting more and more "off." This is the time to step on the brakes. When we skid to a halt and the spinning stops, we can say, "I was headed straight for the cliff and I didn't have to go over."

Most of us experience the presence of what I often call "my beeper." I will get a "flash" that something is not quite right. If I ignore it, I will get another flash. My beeper will beep until I pay attention to it, checking in on the ominous feeling I am trying to ignore. Recently, my beeper went off that something I had written was not quite right. "Oh, it's bound to be fine," I tried to reassure myself.

> *"I have no name:*
> *"I am but two days old."*
> *What shall I call thee?*
> *"I happy am,*
> *"Joy is my name."*
> *Sweet joy befall thee!*
>
> WILLIAM BLAKE

> *Where there is great love there are always miracles.*
>
> WILLA CATHER

"How bad can it be? I wrote it. Everybody—three editors—read it. What's my problem?" When my beeper persisted and no amount of "It's fine" felt fine, I finally called back the questionable text right as the presses were ready to roll. Was it fine? Absolutely not. An immediate, thorough, page one, start-it-all-over rewrite was what was called for. I gladly rewrote the offending piece and felt I had had a very close call indeed.

And so, a sense of rightness will most usually mean all's well. A sense of wrongness will also usually mean something is wrong. Listening to such gut feelings is always worth the time and trouble it takes. When we let God be God and work through us, we experience both a sense of serenity and excitement. We experience integrity—which comes from the root word "integer," meaning "whole," unfragmented by doubt or discomfort. When we experience a sense of oneness with God, ourselves, and our fellows, we can safely know we are in our integrity.

If this language sounds "serious" and "spiritual," so is the matter at hand. "Know thyself," the Greeks inscribed above their temple door. As artists, we must take this to heart, working to express our inner imperatives and not just filling the form provided by the marketplace. Settling for convention over authentic self-expression, we are falling, in the biblical phrase, for false gods. In the long run, this works out no better for us as artists than it did for those worshiping the golden calf. The "market" is the golden calf. When we worship it, we deaden our souls, risking, over time, our attunement to the work that would move through us. Commerce has its place, but that place is not first.

You will often hear an artist say, "Ah, they had only a shoestring, so I didn't get my going rate, but it was really enjoyable to work on that film." Or "I *love* helping a new composer get something properly recorded, so I brought in a few of my friends and we really did a nice job." Or "They needed some publicity shots for their dance company, and I just loved helping them out. I mean, what's much more fun than shooting a batch of little ballerinas? And that troupe is first rate."

> *If you don't tell the truth about yourself, you cannot tell it about other people.*
>
> VIRGINIA WOOLF

As artists, we have a different kind of accountability than many people. What pays us and pays off in the long run is really the caliber of our work.

As artists, we have an inner Geiger counter and it ticks loud and clear when we are near pay dirt—first-rate, high-caliber ore that means we are working at the top of our form. Because this device is an inner one, it isn't easily fooled by the prestige of a certain venue or the lack of prestige of another. What it detects is quality. It knows the real thing when it is near it. This is what "accountability" is for an artist, the blunt assessment: Is it any good? Fame, money, prestige—none of them can fool this inner meter of excellence. It boils down to the simple fact that artists respect good art—and we respect ourselves when we make it.

The great musician Stephane Grappelli remarked: "A great improviser is like a priest, talking only to his God." In a sense, all artists are like priests as they listen for the voice of inspiration, aspire to excellence, and hold themselves accountable to that high ideal more than to any boss or paycheck. When we violate our creative ideals, we violate our artistic conscience—and we become very uncomfortable.

Whenever we indulge in what might be called "paint by numbers" art, we are engaging in cynicism and skepticism. We are on a subtle level out to "fool" people. We are looking down at our audience and saying "If I just feed them what they are used to getting, I can fool them." Does this mean that we must always and willfully break the mold? No, a first act that is twice the normal length is too long for an audience to sit through comfortably—or perhaps at all. On the other hand, a first act that breaks arbitrarily because "it has to" is not an act that is listening to "where it wants to break" and finding the shape that is authentic for it as a piece of art.

> I honestly think in order to be a writer, you have to learn to be reverent.
>
> ANNE LAMOTT

As artists, we are always engaged in a delicate balancing act. We both know how things "are done" and we must strive to listen accurately to see if that's how our particular piece of art wants to be done. If we ignore all convention, then our rebellion is probably just as destructive and willful as if we blindly follow all rules, cynically calculating that if we "do it right," we can get away with something less than good because it's "done the way they always do it."

This is how skeptics are born. It also promotes a nasty hybrid of blade-runner artist—adapted to such a poisonous environment and promoting an ill-considered, self-aggrandizing myth that *their* adaptation is "normal," and that any "real" artist should be able to survive anything. Nonsense. Artists such as these like to appear on late-night talk shows, telling war stories and focusing as much on their corporate derring-do, the *Star Wars* of the studios and super-agents, than their art. Promoted in the press, and self-promoting, these artificially inflated *artistes* may intimidate genuine artists of a quieter stripe.

In cultures where creativity is embedded in the warp and woof of daily life, shyer souls may practice their creativity with more impunity. In this country, the artist is an endangered species. Grants are diminishing. Public appreciation is also more difficult to find. Too much power has gone into the hands of too few—reviewers stand in for viewers.

Fearing this process, fearing their capacity to survive it, many gifted artists allow discouragement to darken their creative landscape. Of course they do. They may lurk too long in the shadows because they lack support—the before, during, and after friends—to help them tolerate their turns center stage. Many public art situations are toxic to artists themselves. We learn to deal with them, but we do not do it easily. Just as the body must develop antibodies, so in our current culture must the artist's soul. Not everyone can do this. Many excellent artists cannot.

> *If you don't risk anything, you risk even more.*
>
> ERICA JONG

In my twenty-five years of teaching, working to unblock damaged artists, it is my experience that it is not that artists lack quality but that, as a culture, we lack sufficient quality of *character* to nurture and appreciate the artists among us. Until we fiercely advocate and nurture ourselves, we feel stifled. Until more of our reticent artists make more art, we risk continuing to believe the assessments of those who critique but do not create. The quality of our artists is not the true issue. The quality of our critical climate is. We do not have genuine receptivity to the arts.

In light of these facts, many superb artists are not stamped with sufficient critical approval and so they may doubt the very caliber of their art. Making art takes courage—and, although our Lone Ranger, artist-as-loner mythology would tell us otherwise, it requires support.

The people who snort about there being a lack of quality in amateur art have not seen enough diamonds in the rough. They like to buy their art at Tiffany's stamped with a brand name and someone else's approval. They haven't had the courage to walk through church and hear a beautiful, if untutored, soprano, and commit cash on the barrel for her education. They have not been in a school hallway or on a sidewalk and seen a student sketch that caught them by the throat with its unexpected virtuosity—and inquired enough to know how they could help and support that young artist. It takes courage and heart to make art, and it takes courage and heart to support art makers. A celebrated pianist who hails from a small midwestern town always cites the generosity of an older couple from his home city who staked him a no-strings-attached year's rent in New York when he was trying to make his way. This couple had the wisdom to serve the art in the artist, to see the unpolished stone and help it find its setting. In our culture, their discernment and commitment are unusual.

Our culture diminishes both art and artists. Art is secular now, mere ornament, where once it was central to civilized life. Artists are seen as dispensable or, at best, marginal types, gifted perhaps, but mere filigree.

Good art is a form of prayer. It's a way to say what is not sayable.

FREDERICH BUSCH

The imagination has resources and intimations we don't even know about.

CYNTHIA OZICK

Artists are everywhere, and if we do not see them—or see ourselves as perhaps being them—it is because as a culture we have bunkered our artistic soul in the safe citadel of cynicism. We co-sign the assessment of critics who are chic and "critical" but creatively impotent. Quality is not the issue, care is. When I teach that we are all creative and I say that we should all use that creativity to express ourselves, I am sometimes greeted by derisive skeptics who snort, "Don't you think you might be unblocking an awful lot of bad art?"

Let's be real: There is already a lot of art in the world that isn't exhilarating in its excellence. In fact, those who hang back from "inflicting their art" on the world seem to often be those who create more beautifully.

As an artist who teaches, I have far more often been humbled by the superior quality of someone's unblocked work than shamed by the quality of newly unblocked work. It is often ego strength and not the strength of the art itself that determines how far forward an artist is willing to put himself. We have made such a spotlight-riddled, harrowing public spectacle of the arts in this country that many people with enormous talent quite sensibly choose to live outside the limelight.

In our current cultural climate, we have too much acid in the soil of our creative garden. The limelight is acting like lime itself—poisoning the communal root system and support so necessary for arts and artists to flourish. Our critics are likely overly aggressive gardeners, busily weeding and heaping on the acid chemicals, unskilled in encouraging the tender green shoots that hold promise to bloom.

In our culture, we must consciously build safe hatcheries for our art. We must find people and establish places that allow us to flourish. We must become creative about being creative.

As creatives, we must learn to carefully and consciously put our money where our mouth is. We must learn to take the authentic risk of bettering ourselves. Setting aside a genuine hour a day to work on the play will get us further in the long run than telling ourselves we will write the play after we redecorate the apartment—which is why we are taking one more time-consuming freelance job so we can have the right computer table so then we can "really" write. Dreams become reality when we start to treat them as if they are real. When we stop postponing and evading them, and when we can answer "Today, I worked on my dream" with a grounded specific.

Creativity isn't something vague that we are going to do. It is something real that we actually *do* do. It is the refusal to sell ourselves short by shortchanging our artists with empty talk—or empty paychecks. We may have to work at a day job and that day job may give us structure and support, but it is a dangerous lie to tell ourselves that our paycheck from our advertising agency will ever give us the same satisfaction as writing the play we have dreamed about since grammar school.

Often, when we are afraid to try to make what we really want to make, we will say, "I can't make that." The truth is, we could, but we are frightened to try: Not trying, we do not really know whether we could or couldn't make our heart's desire. Very often when we say "I couldn't do that," we are again embracing an ideal of false independence, eschewing spiritual help. We are embracing an idea of God as a withholding God whose intentions for us are counter to our own dreams. Believing, even unconsciously, in such a toxic God, we do not see the Great Creator as a cocreator, a partner, in our dreams. Rather, we see God as a barrier, a withholding parent who denies our dreams. Most often, we are who denies them.

It is at this point that we must muster our integrity and be honest about what it is we really want. We must take the leap—or even the small hop—of faith that moves us slightly toward our true dream. This honest motion on our part is what triggers support for our authenticity—instead of support for a false self we can no longer comfortably inhabit.

"But what about the odds?" You may catch yourself grasping at straws. Odds are a favored guise of false gods. Odds are the denial of miracles. Odds are faith in being faithless, faith in being hopeless, faith in being stuck where we are, isolated from any power that might overcome the odds.

Surprise is where creativity comes in.

RAY BRADBURY

As we commit to our real dreams, we commit to ourselves. As we commit to ourselves, we also commit to trusting the power that created us. We are then aligning ourselves not with false gods but with the true power of the universe, the Great Creator through whose power all dreams are possible.

TASK

Pat Yourself on the Back

You have already accomplished many worthy things. It is a good idea to have ready at hand a list of 25 things you are proud of. This list is where you value your own character and put down in black and white some of the things you have done right. It is important in writing this list to place on it what you are actually proud of, not what you "should" be proud of. There should be at least one entry that makes you grin at the memory, perhaps an episode where you stood up to a bully or managed to think of the exact right comeback at the actual moment of attack.

Take pen in hand and list 25 specific things you are proud of. Do not be surprised by a positive leading to more positives, for example:

1. I am proud I taught Domenica how to ride a horse.
2. I am proud I took her to Sunday pony rides when she was a toddler.
3. I am proud I let her ride double with me to get her balance.
4. I am proud I signed her up for lessons and stood on the sidelines, watching.
5. I am proud I stuck up for Carolina in religion class.
6. I am proud I told the nun that Christian Scientists were as good as Catholics.
7. I am proud I brought my mother wagon loads of wild violets for her garden.
8. I am proud I tried to save the tomato worm by taping it back together.
9. I am proud I picked Tiger Lily from all the puppies at the pound.
10. I am proud I still write Morning Pages even when I am not teaching.

A list such as this one goes a long way toward establishing a beachhead of integrity.

Getting Back on the Horse

We are intended to make something of ourselves. When we feel supported by others, this is a festive feeling. There is a sense of community and a sense of shared purpose and humor—like we're the creative equivalent of a quilting bee or a barn raising. The collective group energy feels firm and exhilarating and fine. We don't wobble because there are helping hands to steady our ladder as we try to climb. Surrounded by support, making something—and something of ourselves—is easy. This is why the great summer music camps like Tanglewood and Aspen and Marlboro matter. This is why painting institutes and writing retreats are so valued. All of us need such support. We don't always have this luxury.

Sometimes, support fails us. Instead of help, we meet hindrance.

Sometimes, we suffer a horrifying creative injury. Our bones may not be broken, but our confidence is. An actress is emotionally disemboweled by a director who makes Hannibal Lecter look like an amateur. A pianist is reviewed by a critic who thinks "beat" is a musical term meaning "to club."

Creative cataclysms like these are common. They are the dangers of the trail. Artists are sensitive animals, and we do get spooked. Certainly, the sensitive horse of our talent gets spooked, and we may get pitched right off it. "I am never trying *that* again!" we vow—meaning the novel; the finger-twisting, heart-shredding concerto; that torture rack, the stage. And the longer we don't try "it" again, the more we convince ourselves we could *never* try "it" again. We say, "It hurt me once, and . . ."

> *Try again. Fail again. Fail better.*
>
> SAMUEL BECKETT

> *Style begins when you seek and discover your strengths, then bank on them for all they're worth.*
>
> SARAH BAN BREATHNACH

There is one and only one cure for a creative injury, and that cure is to make something. If we do not make some small something, our injured yet active imagination will make an even bigger deal out of what happened to us.

Sometimes, the only comfort we can find is naming ourselves. If no one else will pronounce us "artist," then we must say our name to ourselves—and the only way to say it is through art. The bandage must fit the wound. If your musical has been trounced, write some music. If your painting has been pounced on, paint something, even a kitchen chair. If your poetry has had its feet broken, walk to an open mic and read something. A famous director I know well, always conscious that critical reception might curtail his chances to do large-budget works, would remind himself on sleepless nights, "If I can't shoot 35, I can shoot 16, if I can't shoot 16, I can shoot Super 8. If I can't shoot Super 8, I can draw, I can sketch. . . ." In other words, he knew his medicine for his creative losses, however huge and catastrophic, lay in the phrase "I can—and will—create."

> *The way to find your true self is by recklessness and freedom.*
>
> BRENDA UELAND

We *are* intended to make something of ourselves, and sometimes that "making" has to be done without palpable support. We feel defeated and deflated by our interpersonal relationships. We feel like people have let us down, and often they truly have. Even more discouraging, we feel we have let ourselves down—we feel we "haven't been smart enough." And sometimes, we've done that too. As artists, we have off nights and off years. It is part of the territory. It is arguably a *necessary* part of the territory.

During my twenties, it seemed that everything I touched turned to gold. I was an award-winning journalist first—scooping *The Washington Post* and getting written up in *Time*. Next, I married a great love, Martin Scorsese, and worked side by side with him, contributing writing to his films. I became a popular newspaper columnist and had a winning streak as a screenwriter, selling a trio of films to Paramount and writing a successful television movie starring Don Johnson as Elvis. These were heady times.

Enter my thirties. First, a terrible divorce. Then I made a feature film but had my sound track stolen. I dubbed the film and released it in Europe to good reviews, but there was no American release, no "payoff" for three years of work. I wrote novels but didn't get them published. I wrote plays that won prizes but not productions.

Enter my forties. *The Artist's Way* was published. A dozen more books followed throughout the decade. The novels I had written finally saw print. My plays were produced. Instead of the pangs of failure and anonymity, I now learned the dangers of success. The best word for my forties might be "rigorous."

Throughout all of this time, I steadily, on a daily basis, kept writing. I kept working with the tools of creative recovery and even survival for myself and others. I knew from experience that a creative career took faith. In short, no loss of "time" when I was out of favor, no up or down when I was in vogue, ever went without later providing its usefulness. Everything—and I do mean everything—is fuel for the creative fire.

As a teacher and as an artist, I experience creative growth as characterized by periods where creative syntax and confidence shatters. We write "badly" because we are no longer writing as we were and not yet writing as we will. In our culture, there is little understanding of the growth process of an artist—which is often conducted in a very public arena. For the very public artists, for filmmakers and novelists in particular, there is little room for the work made during necessary periods of creative flux. Concert musicians report the same dilemma—a style matures idiosyncratically and spasmodically, moving not from beauty straight to beauty but from beauty through something different to more beauty. Few reviewers value the "something different" stage.

> *You aim for what you want and if you don't get it, you don't get it, but if you don't aim, you don't get anything.*
>
> FRANCINE PROSE

> *Art is our chief means of breaking bread with the dead.*
>
> W. H. AUDEN

Art is made from talent and character. Adversity strengthens our character and can strengthen our art as well. It creates empathy and compassion for the adversity of others. This deepens our heart and our art. Adversity is educational, and like many educations, it is terribly hard to recover from without help. That help, in human or nonhuman form, as coincidence, as timely call, as "impulse" to do something off your beaten path, is a guidance and support we can rely on—but act on it we must. We are not so much rescued as joined.

When I first met veteran director John Newland, we were both living in a tiny mountain town. He was there in official retirement from a long and illustrious career—a retirement that lasted about four minutes before he was directing high school plays, community theater, college acting classes, anything that let his skills and experience have some play, however restricted. For myself, I was in what might best be called a "battered" period. I had taken a few creative tumbles—most notably around discouragement on my musical work—and I was reluctant to get back on the horse. After all, falls hurt, and wasn't I getting a little old for them?

Feeling more than a little sorry for myself, I met up with Newland. I had gone to see an evening of high school monologues he had directed—my daughter was in his cast. I watched from a rickety seat in the tiny auditorium as student after student presented tough and edgy work, daring for our little town, daring for anywhere. I was used to community theater being more tame.

Who the hell did this? I wondered. Someone was putting up some great work. At evening's end, I was pointed to a tall, handsome man with a face like a ravaged cathedral and a shock of snow-white hair to top his alpine height.

"John Newland," he said, shaking my hand. "You've got a talented kid. I hear you're talented yourself, so let's eat some lunch and talk about things."

I met Newland for lunch and found his optimism to be the best thing on the menu. My age? "You're just a kid. I've got forty years on you and I'm still working." My discouragement? "Let me read that musical of yours. I'll bet it's good. We'll put it on." My worry about my career? "You've got another forty years to go, so buck up and let's do something."

We did do something. We put up my musical *Avalon,* and into that small auditorium three thousand miles from New York walked the woman who would become my musical collaborator. She "happened" to be playing chamber music in the same auditorium. A classical violist, she brought a small herd of her classical friends to hear *Avalon* on Newland's and my opening night.

What a good composer, she was thinking even as I sat curled up in the back row, wondering if I would live through the experience of hearing my music performed for the first time. She introduced herself that evening and she reintroduced herself when I moved in next door to her in New York, by "chance," four months later. Within months we were happily collaborating—not, I believe, because I was smart enough to figure out my career but because I was willing to get back on the horse and know it when John Newland rescued me and then she did. It is my observation, after many years of teaching, that such "timely" rescues are par for the course. When an artist sends up a despairing prayer, the Great Creator does hear and answer it.

As artists, when human powers fail us, we must turn to the Great Creator for help. We must "surrender" our sense of isolation and despair and open ourselves to the spiritual help we frequently experience as an unexpected inner strength. Let me be clear about one thing: Artists at all levels experience adversity—some of us quite publicly, some of us in painful privacy. One way or another—bad colleagues, bad reviews—we fall off the horse.

> Creative minds have always been known to survive any kind of bad training.
>
> ANNA FREUD

It is a spiritual law that no loss is without meaning in all of creation. And so, the bitter defection of our creative colleagues who say "Thanks" and then try to shove us off the ladder (failing to mention our contributions at press conferences, claiming credit for our ideas in staff meetings) is actually, somehow, a boon to us. Yes, the shove hurts—and the treachery and the disillusionment. But we more often than not land in a pile of straw. We find our fall mysteriously cushioned. "Angels" appear. Sometimes, we sense them internally, as inspiration, the minute we ask "What's next?" and not "Why me?"

Because creativity is a spiritual issue, injuries to that creativity are spiritual wounds. In my experience, an artist's anguished prayers are *always* answered by the Great Creator. Even as we sob to the fates, and rightly, "I cannot go on," we are going on, and we are going on with spiritual assistance. Something is stirring that means we are already going on. We are gaining ground, first as awareness, and next as action. Creativity is a spiritual practice, and like all spiritual practices, it contains the tool of self-inventory.

We want colleagues of both talent and character. To find them, we must forge brighter our own talent and character. Very often, the people who do betray us and our values are those whom we have felt a vague stirring of unease about and then dismissed that as paranoia. Our gift is that in the future we will hear our forebodings as spiritual telegrams and not as neurosis.

Sometimes, remarkably often, creative angels show up externally. (In the theater world, the term "angel" is actually used.) As our villains slink from the scene of the crime, our heroes and stagehands step forward to try to put up a new and better show. "What if you try this?" a friend asks. Instantly, we see a path—or, at least, a next right step—if only we will take it.

> *I have a sense of these buried lives striving to come out through me to express themselves.*
>
> MARGE PIERCY

As artists, when we are sold down the river, we must look to see in what ways we are selling ourselves short. Yes, the others have been bastards—that is real and irrefutable and painful. What is often more painful is seeing our participation; usually the spot where we shrank back from trusting ourselves is the very point that turned the tide against us. This does not make other people's foul play our fault. It does not mean they shouldn't have acted differently and better—what it does mean is that we will act differently and better in the future. That is the part we can change.

But the way to change this is not through berating ourselves for our stupidity. It is not by trying to make their flaws our fault. It is not by claiming we "drove them to it" somehow. It is by treating ourselves kindly, listening to ourselves gently. It is by telling compassionate people and forces exactly how hurt we are and admitting we need help that we heal. Call your aunt Bernice and tell her that a critic broke your heart. Write a letter to Oscar Hammerstein II, who endured a decade of failures after the success of *Showboat,* and tell him you're on a losing streak, does he have any thoughts. Call the college teacher who thinks you're a huge success no matter how you feel right now. Call yourself home to that part of you that *is* strong enough to continue. That is when the help comes—it bubbles up within us and it enters as lightly as wind stirring a curtain. There will always be help. What we are charged with in "making something of ourselves" is making ourselves willing to listen for that help and to accept it in forms we don't expect. Then act we must.

As artists, we are engaged *always* in a collaborative process with the Great Creator. Stakes that seem impossibly high to us, casting that feels all wrong—these, when we ask for spiritual guidance, may be revealed to be necessary to the plot, important to the growth and maturation of our own creative process. As artists, it is important to remember that all breaks are lucky because bones are often strongest at the broken places. Art is healing, and artists heal.

> *Think of yourself as an incandescent power, illuminated perhaps and forever talked to by God and his* [sic] *messengers.*
>
> BRENDA UELAND

As artists, the Great Creator *will* help us if we help ourselves. How do we find this creative help? We find the creator by creating.

As artists, we do not control our creative world, but we control a lot more of it than we care to admit. We evade knowing how much we do control because it is more comfortable and comforting to coast on the spit of our career resentments than to experience the terrifying vulnerability of trying yet again to bring our work into the world.

Most artists feel and respond like spurned lovers to the thought of really committing to their work. Like a brokenhearted bachelor or shy spinster whose tender dreams were abused, we refuse to be vulnerable again. We "know" how it's worked out before. We "fear" how it may work out again, and so we do not even make a coffee date with our creative dreams to see if this time might be different.

Turned down by a callow agent, we say, "Oh, they're all like that." But are they? Blasted by a cynical gallery owner or a bitter dramaturge, we conclude, "I'll never get into a gallery" or "My work will never be accepted." All too often we don't try again—fearing more damage to our broken creative hearts. We know too well that in our heart of hearts, our creative dreams do not die any more than our romantic ones, and we are frightened by the whispers of these dreams—the undead plays, novels, and paintings that we have shoved into our creative closets, where they live with the muttering ghosts of our broken dreams.

As artists, we are dreamers, and what we fear is the nightmare of our work being shunned, mishandled, or ill perceived. Fearing this, we allow our discouragement to globalize from one person to "they," from a single tough review to "always," from a stinging rejection to "they'll never." We elect a defensive cerebral cynicism.

We begin talking about how "they" will never appreciate our work. We feel alone and abandoned, and we are—not because "they" have abandoned us but because we have. We have given up not only on ourselves but also on God. We have said, "What's the use?" instead of "What's next?" Rather than risk the vulnerability of moving out again on faith, we have hidden our dreams and our hopes under what we call "realism about the market." We have said, "Oh, they're all like that" rather than allow ourselves the terror of discovering they might not be.

> *"Healing," Papa would tell me, "is not a science, but the intuitive art of wooing Nature."*
>
> W. H. AUDEN

Artists, like gifted horses injured at the fence, may shy away from trying the fence again. And yet, a gifted horse can and must be rehabilitated. As artists, we are both the horse and rider of our talent. When we are thrown, we cannot let that throw us. It's part of the territory.

Get back on the horse.

TASK
Ouch! Let Me Make It Better

Creative injuries tend to be secret injuries. "It shouldn't bother me so much," we say. Or "I just seemed to lose interest after that." We deny to others and to ourselves the devastating impact a creative upset can have on us. We fall down from the horse, and rather than get back on, we tell ourselves we have lost interest in riding.

Unmourned creative injuries create scar tissue. We "toughen up," but the wound festers underneath. "I'm just not interested," we say, when we are *very* interested indeed—just injured.

The following exercise is one in compassion and forgiveness. We deserve compassion for the pain we suffered due to our creative injury. We deserve forgiveness because we have allowed ourselves to be stopped, stalled, or stymied and we usually judge ourselves harshly for that.

Take pen in hand and again number from 1 to 10. List 10 creative injuries or disappointments you have not allowed yourself to grieve, get through, or get over. Be very careful to be gentle with yourself. This is an extremely vulnerable and volatile process.

Rationality squeezes out much that is rich and juicy and fascinating.

ANNE LAMOTT

Always be a first-rate version of yourself, instead of a second-rate version of somebody else.

JUDY GARLAND

As you review your injury list, look for a very small and very gentle step you can take to move your artist back toward the arena where the injury occurred. But the steps must be very small and very gentle. Let us say, for example, that you wrote a novel and received some encouraging and some discouraging agents' letters in response to your manuscript. A first step might be rereading the positive letters and the first twenty-five pages of your manuscript. Allow yourself to go slowly and carefully. If you put up a play and received some savage reviews, you might be avoiding theater entirely. Get yourself a set of theater tickets. In other words, coax your artist out to play, then put your artist straight back to work.

CHECK-IN

1. **How many days this week did you do your Morning Pages?** If you skipped a day, why did you skip it? How was the experience of writing them for you? Are you experiencing more clarity? A wider range of emotions? A greater sense of detachment, purpose, and calm? Did anything surprise you? Is there a "repeating" issue asking to be dealt with?

2. **Did you do your Artist's Date this week?** Did you note an improved sense of well-being? What did you do and how did you feel? Remember, Artist's Dates can be difficult and you may need to coax yourself into taking them.

3. **Did you get out on your Weekly Walk?** How did that feel? What emotions or insights surfaced for you? Were you able to walk more than once? What did your walk do for your optimism and sense of perspective?

4. **Were there any other issues this week that felt significant to you in your self-discovery?** Describe them.

Discovering a Sense of Dignity

The key to a successful creative life is the commitment to make things and in so doing make something better of ourselves and our world. Creativity is an act of faith. As artists, we are sourced in the Great Creator, meaning that our funding of strength and power is limitless. This week focuses on the survival of those difficulties encountered at the highest creative peaks. Our graceful ability to encompass difficulty rests in our ability to be faithful. The reading and tasks of this week aim at acquainting the creative practitioner with the survival tools necessary for the successful accomplishment of a sustained creative life.

The Glass Mountain

Today, with charming Currier and Ives snowmen lurching to life under tiny hands in Riverside Park below, I grapple with the icy slopes of depression. *My* mood is the glass mountain of fairy tale lore: I slither down every time I try to clamber up.

"It's the holidays," a friend of mine called to advise gravely—secure that her depression, her heightened sense of nasty odds, held common ground with mine.

I don't think so.

Today's depression and doubt is par for the course at the stage I am in on a new project, this one a musical. I've got the jigsaw puzzle laid out on the floor and I can see a corner here, a corner there, but the big hole in the middle is exactly replicated by my own anxiety: Will I ever find the real substance of this piece? Trying to land a project—a book, a play, a song cycle—is like trying to land a big fish; as

There is only one journey. Going inside yourself.

RAINER MARIA RILKE

Your hand concentrates for you. I don't know why it should be so.

DAME REBECCA WEST

in Hemingway's *Old Man and the Sea,* the world boils down to that fish and me, and I am worried it will get away. As artists, we are often laboring to land big fish against big odds. What's worse, our fish are often invisible fish to the eyes of others, who see us as Daddy, as Mommy, as professor, as girlfriend or boyfriend, and not as someone engaged in a heroic struggle to drag something huge from the archetypal creative sea.

We want to pass for regular citizens. We do not want to turn our phones off or hide in the darkest corners of libraries, writing longhand. And yet, painting, writing, sculpting, and composing does take yards of quiet, uninterrupted time. How to manage this without seeming arrogant or standoffish? People come up with different solutions. My phone is off, but my voice-mail explains my writing hours and when a caller can expect a call back. Novelist John Nichols writes midnight to dawn, an eccentric practice, but it keeps him from snapping people's heads off—"I'm writing!"—when they call him during the day.

So reluctant are we to make a big deal of our work that we may make too small a deal of it. We do not communicate clearly the swaths of silence and solitude we sometimes crave. We fit our work into the crannies of life, and that's good a lot of the time. It lets us have a life, and that life enriches our art. But we do not talk often about sneaking out of our marital bed and stealing down the hall to write, to paint two to four in the night. We do not talk about running away to write our crime novel, holing up in a fleabag motel, on a stolen weekend from our marriage and law practice.

A pianist preparing for a concert tour may be teaching—and teaching well—but he's preparing for a concert tour, wrestling down huge reams of music with his bare hands, even if he continues to teach his conservatory class load. A novelist listening to a book tell its tale may be listening to his children as well, but that book is always talking too, sometimes in whispers, and he *must* keep an inner ear cocked. A playwright cantilevering a new play from page to stage is worried about that brainchild finding its legs, and so listens like a new mother with ears in the night while "real" children, miffed and pouting, complain to their friends, "Mommy's writing."

Sometimes, mommies and daddies—no matter how we love our children—do need to write. Unexpressed art rises inside an artist until it reaches a level of restlessness and longing that must be addressed by making art—nothing else will scratch the itch. Nothing else is "wrong," although it may seem to be.

"What's wrong, Mommy?" our children wonder, sensing our distance and distraction. We have to fight not to snap their heads off if we are mulling a plot line.

"Nothing, Mommy needs to write."

"What's wrong, darling?" asks our significant other.

"Nothing, I just need to paint."

The year I taught film at Northwestern University and at Chicago Filmmakers while also teaching the Artist's Way privately and some classes of the Right to Write, I really needed to write. Teaching was taking too much of my time and focus and my family was taking the rest. I arranged for a brief getaway to Taos, and as I was waiting to board the plane a man's voice began speaking in my head. I grabbed for pen and notebook and began taking dictation. The writing was so welled up in me that it was the fast-paced flood, imperious and imperative: I must get it down. I wrote on the plane ride from Chicago to Albuquerque. I wrote on the bus ride from Albuquerque to Taos. I settled into my motel, still writing, and woke up to days of writing breakfast until dinner, ensconced at the outdoor table at Dori's Café, where they were used to writers. Every night I would get a plaintive call from my family, "When are you coming home?"

"Not yet," I would answer. "I have to ride this out." I stayed in Taos for most of the month and most of a first draft of the novel. I reluctantly went home and began retreating to a corner coffee shop, where I hid in a back booth and wrote the rest. It was several months before I was back to my family in the role they preferred me in: "Mommy" and "wife." I had simply built up too large a debt to my writer not to give it absolute first place for a while. This experience taught me to be careful, to always honor my writer a little more fully. It is easier for a family to adjust to a daily writing schedule than it is for them to adjust to a season of abandonment. It is also easier for them to learn to batten down the hatches and make do during the glass-mountain phase of finishing a book than it is for them to live through that phase being conducted a thousand miles away with only phone calls of reassurance. Every project has a glass-mountain phase, a period when nothing is going well enough because the work is simply so hard. Families and friends learn to know and weather this. They do if we give them an explanation and a chance.

> *Freedom means choosing your burden.*
>
> HEPHZIBAH MENUHIN

We work so hard at "normal" because we've heard so much about artists being crazy. We have heard too many stories of Jackson or Anne Sexton, too many of Sylvia, and Zelda, and fragile Scott. Our reluctance to be *that* kind of person has made us practiced liars—some lies are necessary and self-protective. Women know this. As an experienced artist, I carry my work like a secret pregnancy. I am *always* aware of inner life and the need to protect it. My apology if this metaphor seems gender linked. The creative men I have known and lived with often cast their creative projects as secret military campaigns, an equally gender-linked phrase, calling for secrecy, strategy, and protection.

Trained as we are to be mommies and daddies, and teachers and bankers, lawyers and judges, and so many responsible things, sickened as we are by the woeful tales of artists as irresponsible monsters, we may have difficulty mustering sufficient responsibility to our art and our artists, to protect them during the occasional, necessary times of hard climbing as a large project finally lurches into form—or does not. This delicate and treacherous stage, the glass mountain of creative doubt, is a slippery slope we face alone. It is on its icy flank that we must find small footholds, edging our way upward from concept to actual conception—a difficult birth, as pivotal as conquering our creative Everest—or nearly. "I hear it! I hear it! But I can't get it into my hands," a pianist friend once wailed to me. "I hear it, I hear it! But I haven't got it all on the pages," I have wailed back when a large wave of music knocked me sideways and I struggled to write notes fast enough as I went under.

> It's only when we truly know and understand that we have a limited time on earth—and that we have no way of knowing when our time is up—that we will begin to live each day to the fullest, as if it was the only one we had.
>
> ELISABETH KÜBLER-ROSS

As artists, we don't talk a lot about the quotidian anxiety of creation, at its worst during the glass-mountain phase, but difficult enough all the time. By and large, for most of us, the need to make art, the cost of making that art, and the higher cost of not making it is not something we lightly air. Our glass mountain is *our* glass mountain, and, like most fairy tales, it is invisible to others but very real to us. Art is a vocation, a calling, and if no one hears the call as loudly as we do, that doesn't mean it isn't there, that doesn't mean we don't hear it, and that doesn't mean we don't need to answer when it calls.

Over time, family and friends become more and more adroit at recognizing the symptoms of our creative calling. "Do you need to write?" or "Do you need to get to the piano?" they may begin to ask us. Most of us have drawn to ourselves partners who do love our artist—especially once they are assured that our artist has no desire to leave them. A novelist's wife knows that no meal will ever be as satisfying as a good round at the page. Sandwiches and slices of pie have a way of appearing at the edge of our writing table, where they are gratefully devoured. There is doubtless a special niche in heaven for those who have helped us to birth our creative children. Mere book dedications seem inadequate thanks compared to the gratitude we feel when we are well understood, a gratitude matched only by the terror we may feel when we are misunderstood, as artists sometimes are by those who mistake our need to make things for a need to make something special—and elite—out of ourselves.

When I was young, I had a very good friend, Nick Cariello, who was very political. He invited me to visit his other good friends, who were even more political than he was. I remember a long, winey evening of talk, angry talk, about how artists were just like everyone else. They should not be considered special. They should take out the trash just like the rest of society.

> *We are the hero of our own story.*
>
> MARY McCARTHY

"Yes, we can do our turn at that," I said. "But if you make an artist carry trash eighteen hours a day, an artist will still have to make art. It's our calling." And it is our calling. And so, we do carry the trash. But we carry, also, our stories, our symphonies, our dance, and our dreams. We carry them in daily life, and, every so often, up the glass mountain that is our Everest.

TASK
Scaling the Glass Mountain

Take pen in hand and answer the following questions as rapidly as possible:

1. Do you have a project edging into the glass-mountain phase?
2. Can you protect your work schedule a little more rigorously than usual?
3. How can you steal extra solitude, even a half hour a day?
4. Can you manage an escape from family, friends, and telephones?
5. Have you made friends with Starbucks, the back room at the library, a back booth at Wendy's, writing in your car?

Perhaps too much of everything is as bad as too little.

EDNA FERBER

You may have in your vicinity a spiritual center where you can take a personal creative retreat and share communal meals. Many nuns, priests, and monks are great support during periods of creative doubt. Many convents and monasteries offer hermitage space to gather steam so that projects can be finalized. The sisters at Wisdom House in Litchfield, Connecticut, artists themselves, have long taught Artist's Way courses, and when staying on their grounds I have often walked my way into the quiet necessary to find renewed faith to finish projects.

Landing

In order to make our art, we expand and contract. Expand and contract: big ideas and the minute, painstaking work of getting them down in finer and finer detail. As we concentrate like this, we are first big and then single-pointed. In the heat of the creative moment, our thought—or flow—is hot, thick, dense, fast, and light, like good ink. We are skywriting for a path.

Our creative size has a tidal aspect—we ebb and we flow. Or, if you would, we expand and contract, altering sizes and shapes like one of those luminous mysteries of the sea, the jellyfish, which closely resembles a parachute. When we are at the height of a creative flight and trying to land, we, too, resemble a beautiful, full-bellied parachute trying to touch earth. Lovely? Yes. But safe? Not necessarily. Completing a draft of a novel may spark thoughts of suicide rather than celebration. Creative post partum can be unexpected and *deep.*

Parachutes often land with a lurch. Our creative flights may land the same way. Our chute collapses around us and we stumble around blindly. Or the chute stays somewhat open and we tumble across the field, dragged along by our leftover velocity. In other words, a creative landing may leave us a little bruised, battered, and suddenly claustrophobic as our creative chute collapses and our normal life threatens to smother us.

When we are making things, we sometimes get very, very big. Or simply very, very free. In the height of the creative moment, we are not constricted and downsized by our daily rigamarole—our age, our family tensions, our feelings of being a cog in the wheel. It is hard to come back to our normal size after such a heady expansion—and often, we don't, at first.

Creative flight is exactly that—flight. We get a higher than bird's-eye view of our life and our dreams and often many other things as well. We "see" the big picture, and such a vision can leave our ordinary perception shattered. We are staggered by the magnitude of what we have seen, and our own size feels foreign.

As we try to land back in our own life, we may shoot past our real size and feel like someone very small. This is why astronauts undergo debriefing, and why veteran artists, over time, learn specific skills to help themselves reacclimate to their lives and families. Finishing a long project is also a little like driving cross-country—when you get home, you may need to hide out and sleep for a couple of days before seeing your friends—otherwise, reentry can be bumpy. This is normal, just scary. It is hallucinogenic, like *Alice's Adventures in Wonderland:* I was so big and now I am so small. Or our life may feel like Mother Hubbard's—we feel pinched and can't quite wedge ourselves back into the shoe we normally walk in. It's not so much that our head is too big but that it's still full of very big ideas.

The creative world is full of cherished and hoary stories of what artists act like and look like when they visit the ethers in creative flight. In the pitch of taking down the music for my first musical, I put a silk smock dress on and wore it backward—perhaps for days—without noticing. Seized by an idea that we fight to land, who has time to think about clothes, to worry about looking normal? A famous novelist I know often forgets to put in his teeth.

Comfort is the key during creative flight. Everything else goes by the board. And then the flight ends, and you think, *Oh, I should wash my hair, call my brother, sweep the kitchen, or clean and pitch from drawers.* Intuitively, we try to ground ourselves by a sudden binge of cleaning, scrubbing, cooking, calling friends. Reentry is a volatile process. We become seasoned only after time, learning to send up flares to show our progress: I am still in the chute and hope to emerge next week.

As a sober alcoholic, I am wary of anything too high and too fast. Euphoric is more of a memory than a sought-after state. And yet, when I do get a sudden rush of voltage, I find it a little thrilling as well as daunting. I know it is dangerous and I must remember that I will need to land carefully.

We do not land with grace, perhaps, but we can learn to land more and more safely. We can learn to let the intense energy of our fever-pitched work ebb from

> *O world invisible, we view thee,*
> *O world intangible, we touch thee,*
> *O world unknowable, we know thee.*
>
> FRANCIS THOMPSON

*Learn the craft of knowing
how to open your heart and to
turn on your creativity. There's
a light inside of you.*

JUDITH JAMISON

*A little of what you fancy does
you good.*

MARIE LLOYD

us more gently as we practice. Does a bath work? Cleaning? Calling a certain very old friend—that can be truly grounding.

Above all, we can remind ourselves: The ground does exist, and we find our feet again.

"I try not to talk with anybody for a couple of days," a seasoned novelist explains. "I know that when I have finished a big piece of work I am a little weird and so I try to give myself enough space to be weird in private." I might make a pot of soup. I might read a bad detective novel. I might take my dog out for some really long walks. Eventually, I start to feel normal again. I notice I need to scrub the floor or vacuum the car. I realize my running shoes are getting worn out and I think maybe I can handle going to town and getting a new pair. I might even put that off a day until I can't stand not going. The point is that a big piece of writing is a little like a big storm. It leaves you shaken and disoriented and things need time to settle down. You don't want to talk with your friends and sound like you just went through an alien abduction. You want to wait until you can ask how their kids are and if the movie at the art house is worth getting over to see. In other words, you don't want to reenter the world until the world has more in it than you and your capital-A Art. For me, that's a few days' transition, and when I try to skip it, I act pretty strange and people do notice. I like to let the dust settle now.

TASK
What Makes You Feel Grounded?

Take pen in hand and list 10 activities that always make you feel more grounded, for example:

1. Making soup
2. Vacuuming
3. Changing my sheets
4. Doing the laundry
5. Baking a pie
6. Watching those horse-training videos

7. Waxing the car
8. Cleaning the refrigerator
9. Calling my best friend from grade school
10. Cleaning my office and paying bills

The regular use of this tool is one of the most confirming rituals possible in a creative life. Like the daily ta-dah list, this tool helps to put a sense of grounded celebration into our creative life. It does this because it emphasizes life itself. While we may "live for our work," our life is, and must be, larger than our work. By allowing the dailiness of life to step forward again, we become, in a sense, our own parents, saying "Welcome home" after each of our creative flights. A student-turned-colleague adds the writing of congratulatory postcards to herself as a regular part of this routine. "Good work!" the postcard exclaims. She has postcards on successfully completing arranging assignments, recording assignments, and musical workshops. As her jumps get larger and more public, her private practice of self-congratulations grows even more important. Our work feels not only good, but better, when we place it within the comforting confines of our ongoing routines and relationships.

What you are after is a grounded sense of connection to your life and relationships before, during, and after creative flight.

Age and Time

There is a remarkable book of flower photographs by Irving Penn, who made his initial mark as the signature photographer of *Vogue,* photographing models at the height of their youthful bloom. His lens captured Suzy Parker, as glorious as a hothouse orchid, a woman as trained to a forced and topiary beauty as a single perfect bloom forced to perfection. Perhaps, as a reaction to this hybrid, highly bred haute couture, Penn turned his camera to the world of flowers in bud, in bloom, and past prime in ripening and glorious decay.

Penn's shots are remarkable. We admire the buds in all their nascent glory. We admire the vibrancy and potency of blooms at their perfect prime. But the revelation of the book is the beauty of the flowers as they pass from ripeness to gentle decay, falling from perfection to what Penn

> *And the day came when the risk [it took] to remain tight in the bud was more painful than the risk it took to blossom.*
>
> ANAÏS NIN

reveals as a different perfection. There is a poignancy and power to beauty nearly spent. It holds the remnant of what it was, and its fading grandeur reminds us that we die to bloom again. We are "gone to seed, according to plan."

Oh, if only we took our sense of aging from the natural world. If only we watched the mentoring and grave care and leadership and wit of older animals mentoring the young.

I worked with director John Newland during his seventies and eighties. A tall, snowy-haired man with a gloriously ravaged face and a hawk eye for cant and shenanigans, he was far more daring than the younger directors who have supplanted him in his field. Like Miles Davis, he had learned "Do not fear mistakes. There are none." He cut shabby scenes with a merciless glee. He allowed a full range of rage and daring—in fact, he demanded it. He knew the full range of the human keyboard. He expected all octaves to be accounted for and wasn't satisfied when they were not.

> I wish that life should not be cheap, but sacred,
> I wish the days to be as centuries, loaded, fragrant.
>
> RALPH WALDO EMERSON

Yes, youth passes behind us, but we are blind so often to what we are gaining and to the beauty of what we become as artists. There is not a note of silvery sound or a hair turned silver that isn't perfect and beautiful. It is difficult not to rage at the passing of physical beauty and strength, the exquisite daring and dexterity we once possessed, the turn of a phrase or a haunch as perfect as a ripe peach, as gleaming and golden as the hard-won golden apple—of course we miss these things.

But we gain in beauty. We gain in tenderness. We gain in longing and desire and in satiation if we get the chance—not merely or only exquisitely in our sexual and our physical selves but our creative selves as well.

At fifty-four, I am still willing to learn. I am willing to entertain the idea that everyone who is learning something they care about—whether it is the piano, as with me, or the emotional weather of someone they are newly involved with—anyone who is learning will feel this treacherous mix of vulnerability and frustration, of hope and discouragement. There is an exciting element of self-respect: You are trying.

I think that one of the benefits of doing something "at my age" is that I have lived long enough not to think that "hard" means wrong or even un-do-able. It may just mean hard. And, too, I no longer think my hard is worse than someone else's hard. I think all beginners have high hopes and dash themselves against their own expectations and dreams like waves against a cliff until they get it: over and over, like a wave, yes, but perhaps, a gentler one. Water *does* wear away rock. Practice *will* make if not "perfect," then "better." Take me and the piano.

Clearly, it is mind and muscle and heart that must be trained. All of them must learn patience, the virtue I hate, and repetition, the idea God had the sense to use daily. Ah, yes, the sun rises and the piano waits. I simply need to tell myself, make a routine, not a special occasion, out of this. Appreciate the players leaping up on the craggy heights, but don't be discouraged by them. They show you what players can do and what a piano can do. And even that word "piano" means "softly."

I also worked, during his seventies and eighties, with veteran actor Max Showalter. At eighty-two, he traveled to Taos to teach at a creativity camp that I was leading. He commandeered the piano and held a hundred of us spellbound for several hours as he replayed his seven decades in show business and his eight decades of life. "You have to be positive. They have to know life is good—every scrap of it," Max told me. He lived every scrap of his life fully—he husbanded a great and glorious half-acre of garden when I first knew him in Hollywood in the 1970s and thirty years later he had another glorious half-acre transplanted to Connecticut. In both gardens, we took pictures of each other and of our visions of life. Max caught a photo of me as a budding young woman and, in our last photo together, my hair has glints of silver in the gold. We talked on that visit of the garden of talent he was also husbanding, working with his good friends at the Goodspeed Theatre and in community projects to shepherd young talent into his old trooper's version of the theater: "A place of promise where we all can get bigger than life. *NO!* As big as life allows us and that's plenty."

> *It is the soul's duty to be loyal to its own desires. It must abandon itself to its master passion.*
>
> DAME REBECCA WEST

TASK

The Communion of All Saints

Have you considered asking your creative saints, those artists you admire who have passed over, for help? This personal practice, far from being heretical, honors the fact that art making is a spiritual lineage. Our artistic ancestors *are* sources of inspiration, not only in the survival of their work but in the survival of their creative spirit. By involving them directly, we correctly honor their contributions to our lives, and this practice often yields great creative fruit. Do you have any resistance to this process?

As a culture, we are quite primitive and arrogant in our refusal to honor and acknowledge the inflow and imprint of our ancestors.

> Consider this: what if "original sin" is denying instead of celebrating your originality? Each of us possesses an exquisite, extraordinary gift: the opportunity to give expression to Divinity on earth through our everyday lives. When we choose to honor this priceless gift, we participate in the re-creation of the world.
>
> SARAH BAN BREATHNACH

Experiment: Select one creative elder who has passed on. Ask for help and input on a problem you are facing. Writing very rapidly, transcribe what you hear. Haydn may tell you to use proper files for your musical compositions and organize your workroom.

A young composer became accustomed to an extra sense of guidance in daily affairs—"Stop in this music shop," "Call your old professor," etc. As these leadings palpably paid off in creative terms, the notion of asking for inspiration from creative ancestors seemed, if not reasonable, interesting. Schooled rigorously in the classics, with at least a rudimentary notion of each composer's supposed temperament and life situation, our young composer began asking for specific help. Doing so, she reported that she found Haydn strict and very smart, she found Mozart goofy but inspirational, she found Beethoven kind, focused, and passionate, and that her own compositions were improving enormously. By asking to be inspired, she felt she was.

One day in her Morning Pages, she wondered if such inspiration was just her "imagination." Immediately, she heard, "There are a lot of souls over here who are very interested in what we did, and very interested in what you're doing. We like to help when we can."

Service

In centuries past, art was made for the honor and glory of God. Viewed in this light, a career in the arts was a career of service, not egotism. There is a cue there for us.

The dedication of our work to a higher cause than our own self-promotion frees the work from preciousness. It becomes not about how good we are but about how good we can be in selfless service to something larger than ourselves. Sometimes we can dedicate a book to a person whom we wish to reach. Rilke's classic letters to a young poet tapped his own inner reservoirs of wisdom and generosity.

As artists, we are the bearers of gifts, spiritual endowments that come to us gratis and ask only to be used. A gift for music asks that we give voice to it. A fine photographer's eye asks that we focus it. We are responsible to our gifts for the use of our gifts, and this is a form of accountability too.

> *But if you have nothing at all to create, then perhaps you create yourself.*
>
> CARL JUNG

Some of the best playwriting—Shakespeare's included—was done with an eye to making wonderful roles to serve the talents of friends. Anytime we elect to serve, we open the doors for higher inspiration. We may target a piece of work to someone or something that we feel is worthy; this elected humility removes the tightening that occurs when our work is all about us and our brilliant careers. We may be brilliant in passing but we will no longer be straining for brilliance. Asking to be of service, and to be open to the proper inspiration to serve through our work, we then become teachable, and when we are teachable, our work always improves.

When our work is made only in the service of our hope for fame or recognition, it is hampered by our self-consciousness as we wonder, *How am I doing?* When we are able to work without such self-consciousness, we are able to work more freely and more fully. Our ego steps aside and is no longer a constrictive valve narrowing our creative flows and focus. We think less about "us" and more about "it," the work itself.

I remember sitting under whispering trees at a music park, listening as a brilliant pianist lashed through a blistering performance as dramatic as the incoming storm. I was seated between two grown men who listened to the cascading notes as enraptured as small children, their faces lit with Christmas radiance. Magic was afoot, or, perhaps better, at hand. Later I learned that the musical magician we had so admired had played all evening uphill, against an inner critic that cited that missed chord, this muffled mordent. With a monk's devotion, he had played anyway—such nights are an artist's Gethsemane, a night to be endured only on faith.

"I have to remind myself there is something larger than me and my skill, something more important than my ego's perception," the pianist confided to me. That something is in art itself, the creative power that moves through us, healing and transforming those who encounter it.

"It was like watching Magic Johnson play," one of the men whispered to me on that bench. It was an accurate remark. That word "magic" again, and consummate skill. On Magic Johnson's off nights, he still "hits" more than others. His sailing long ball swooshes still have spooky ease. This is often true for artists. Our "best" nights to others may internally feel our worst. Our perceptions must not be allowed to capsize our professionalism. Novelists with long literary careers report ruefully the great reviews on the books they like least, and the tepid receptions to the works they most cherish. In a sense, the reception of our work by ourselves as well as others is none of our business. Our job is to do it. We work, and the work works through us.

Actors talk ruefully of having terrible nights with rapturous reception, and tepid response to the nights they felt themselves most connected. In a sense, a singer is merely the vehicle for a song, and the song is merely a vehicle for music itself. No matter how accomplished and acclaimed we may become as artists, there is always, at core, this essential anonymity: We are in service of something larger than ourselves.

We have very strange notions about art in our culture. We have made it a cult of the individual rather than what it has always been, a human aspiration aimed at communicating and community. We "commune" through art, both with the forces of inspiration when we work and with other humans who encounter us and those forces through our work. To commune is to attune with an open heart, something impossible if we are thinking only of ourselves.

Manhattan abounds in musicians and music schools. Some of the very best of each are to be found in the vertical canyons of this tiny and overcrowded island. One of the finest music teachers in Manhattan teaches with the greatest amount of innovation—and out of a spirit of service.

"Beginning piano books are just terrible," he says. "Some of the very best students hate to use them. They just don't respond to the music in them and so they become bored." Boredom, of course, is the enemy of learning, and so this music teacher has composed a whole series of beginning music lessons with music he wrote himself and fairy tales to match. Who wouldn't want to learn the waltz that was danced when Sleeping Beauty was awakened with a kiss? Who wouldn't want to play the song a mighty organ played when it fell in love with a gifted young student? Piece by piece, lesson by lesson, seeking only to serve his gifted and disenchanted students, this master teacher has built a curriculum that is lively, innovative, and eminently playable.

"Here, let me write something out for you," he will say, and draw the lines of a staff and make handwritten music paper. "Wouldn't it be fun to learn this?" And the big black notes march across the page, crooked and enticing.

Setting aside all ego and snobbery, setting aside how music "should" be taught, this great teacher teaches from a spirit of love and service. Is it any wonder that his students develop a love of music that serves them very well?

As artists, we are intended to be conduits for inspiration. There are high thoughts and high intentions and higher realms that can speak to us and through us if we allow it. When our ego and our ego-driven fears are given a central place as regards our art, we have rolled a large boulder into our own way, and our career cannot unfold unimpeded because it must divide to make its way with unnatural intensity and velocity around the boulder settled in the stream of our good. On rivers and in the rivers of creative flow, such rapids are treacherous. We are far better served by being of service.

Contemplating a piece of work, we do better to think *Whom is this work for? Whom will it serve?* rather than *How will it serve me?* Once we find a path for our work to be of service—even if that path is merely to create a wonderful role for a friend—then our work goes smoothly forward. It is not about "us" anymore. We have retired as self-conscious creator and aligned ourselves again with all of creation, a worker among workers, a friend among friends. When we do so, our work is less buffered by our own harsh fears. Our fears are set aside every time we simply ask again, "How can I make this work more serviceable?"

> *To believe your own thought, to believe that what is true for you in your private heart is true for all men—that is genius.*
>
> RALPH WALDO EMERSON

Director Steven Spielberg once remarked to an interviewer that he hoped at heaven's gate, God might say to him, "Steven, thanks for listening." This listening for inspiration, this willingness to align our creative will with a sense of higher guidance, is not contrary to a career but a better and more grounded way to establish one. A career solely grounded in the idea of self-advancement is not grounded enough in the advancement of ideas. For all their estimable craft, artists who fail to deepen their goals and their ideas find that their careers run into a certain shallow sameness over time.

Chekhov advised actors, "If you want to work on your career, work on yourself." It might equally be advised, if you want to work on yourself, work to make your career of service to something larger than yourself. Dedicate yourself to something or someone other than yourself. This expansion will make you larger both as a person and as an artist.

We used to routinely call God "the creator." We had a consciousness that our own creativity was a divine gift, an opening for God to work through us. When we enshrined ourselves and our individuality rather than our shared humanity at the center of our consciousness—a shift for which therapy may be thanked for a great deal of useless narcissism and also an unpleasant conviction that art was about compensating—we lost our proper understanding of art as service. We disenfranchised ourselves from our birthright as creators and we lost the understanding that art was an act of the soul and not of the ego. Whenever we take art back to the realm of the sacred, whenever we make it an act of service in any form, if only to such an idea as beauty or truth or humanity, but perhaps better when it is more personably serviceable, we again experience the ease of creative flow and the lessening of our creative doubts. When we ask to "listen," we create works worthy of being heard and we ourselves hear the heartbeat of our common humanity, which is grounded in divinity.

> *Whatever you can do or dream you can, begin it;*
> *Boldness has genius, power and magic in it.*
>
> JOHANN WOLFGANG
> VON GOETHE

We may make a piece of art to promote planetary understanding. We may make beautiful music for the glory and service of music itself. We may write a play for alcoholic women to take heart. We might paint to express gratitude to our creator for the beauty of Queen Anne's lace. When we make our art in a spirit of service, it lightens the burden of our ego. It makes for clarity of focus, purity of intent, and follows a spiritual law that might be simply stated as "Form follows function." When the "form" of our work is open to higher consciousness, its function is raised as well.

Art moves through us. It is colored by our individuality, but we are not precisely its origin. Or, to put it differently, a piece of art may originate with us, but we originate somewhere larger ourselves. We are, each of us, more than we seem, more than the sum of our merely human components. There is a divine spark

animating each of us, and that divine spark also animates our art. When we ask to be of service in our art, we fling open a window in our creative studio. Through that opening, the greater world of inspiration can enter us. A painter friend of mine talks about art needing a "hole for the imagination."
I think I might phrase it as "When we dedicate a piece of art to something larger than our ego, that something larger becomes a felt presence." A great painting, poem, or piece of music carries that indefinable something more. We sense it and, although we try to name it and define it, it eludes definition and containment. There is a breath of the divine that blows through us as artists and blows through our art as well. Walk into a cathedral and you will sense something larger than the artisans. Our hired hands, as artists, also hold a hand with a higher hand. Take Bach, hired to write music so that his church would have something to play once a week at service—that word again. What Bach wrote was more than merely serviceable. Inspired by a spirit of service, he wrote the cantatas, the "little songs," that we love and cherish centuries later.

> *The gift turned inward, unable to be given, becomes a heavy burden, even sometimes a kind of poison. It is as though the flow of life were backed up.*
>
> MAY SARTON

Arguably, we are all in service to an artist greater than our own. Life itself works through us. We are the carriers of dreams and desires that may have originated generations earlier. Music runs in families. So does a gift for drama and for words. When we elect to make art from a spirit of service to a larger whole, we are really simply becoming truthful. We are all part of a larger whole and, in acknowledging that truthfully, we move a notch closer to humility, to a simple and sheer plainness that allows the beauty of the grand design to be seen through us. If beauty is truth and truth beauty—and I believe that this is so—then our acknowledgment of our place in a larger scheme of things strikes a first true note from which more beauty follows.

TASK
Beauty Is Truth and Truth, Beauty

Each of us carries an inner capacity for awe. One of us will be wonderstruck by a musical sequence. Another of us is rendered humble and serene by the sight of a butterfly's wing. Each one of these gateways to the divine is there waiting for us to use it to make contact. There are some things that simply make us happy, some things that we plainly and for no apparent reason love. For this reason, we say, "God is in the details." Each of us experiences the touch of the Great Creator when we allow ourselves to touch upon something that we love.

Because the part of us that creates is youthful and innocent, an ideal place to collect "artist toys" is a good children's bookstore. Go to one now. If dinosaurs are your love, get a dinosaur book. If dogs make you happy, find a book of the dog. Make it a point that your bedside table contains at least one book on a topic that simply delights you. Delight opens the door for the Great Creator to touch us with a sense of well-being. You may love zebra finches or just plain zebras. Let yourself celebrate what you love and that you are the person who loves it. As you connect to the childlike part of you that loves and enjoys the material world, you are connecting to the sense Aristotle had when he remarked, "In all things of nature there is something of the marvelous."

Allow yourself to marvel.

> *Only the heart knows how to find what is precious.*
>
> FYODOR DOSTOYEVSKY

EPILOGUE

I WOULD LIKE TO END this book on a grace note: that is to say, I would like to acknowledge the place of grace in the making of art and artists. It is a great grace that we are born creative beings. It is a great grace that we access that creativity. Although you may language it differently, all creators feel the hand of the Great Creator touching them through their work. Art is a spiritual practice. We may not, and need not, do it perfectly. But we do need to do it. It is my belief that the making of art makes us more fully human. In becoming more fully human, we become more fully divine, touching in our finite way the infinite spark within each of us. Focused on our art, we connect to the artful heart of all life. The creative pulse that moves through us moves through all of creation. It could be argued that creativity is a form of prayer, a form of thankfulness and recognition of all we have to be thankful for, walking in this world.

INDEX

Finding Water

The Art of Perseverance

CONTENTS

ACKNOWLEDGMENTS

Elizabeth Cameron, for her commitment
Sara Carder, for her care
Carolina Casperson, for her daring
Jane Cecil, for her grace
Sonia Choquette, for her vision
Judy Collins, for her generosity
Tim Farrington, for his fortitude
Joel Fotinos, for his faith
Natalie Goldberg, for her resilience
Bernice Hill, for her sagacity
Jack Hofsiss, for his leadership
Tracy Jamar, for her grit
Linda Kahn, for her clarity
Bill Lavallee, for his strength
Laura Leddy, for her prayers
Emma Lively, for her perseverance
Larry Lonergan, for his guidance
Julianna McCarthy, for her inspiration
Robert McDonald, for his art
Bruce Pomahac, for his belief
Susan Raihofer, for her insight
Domenica Cameron-Scorsese, for her loyalty
Jeremy Tarcher, for his wisdom
Edmund Towle, for his friendship
Claire Vaccaro, for her eye
Rosemary Welden, for her enthusiasm
Elizabeth Winick, for her shepherding

To the artists who have gone before me,
leaving a trail of hope and perseverance

PROLOGUE

IT IS MIDDAY, midweek, midwinter. A light snow is falling. Under its spell, Manhattan is hushed. There is a Currier and Ives aspect to the cityscape. Wreathed in scarves and bundled into coats, New Yorkers plunge through the streets, grinning like children at the weather. Snowfall always brings the city quiet—that, and a sense of expectancy.

The lightest frosting of snow and Central Park becomes a fairyland garlanded in lace. Under the soft gray sky miracles seem possible—as when an eagle suddenly appears, lifting off amid the park's pine trees with an audible beating of wings. In Native American culture, sighting the great bird signals that great good is about to happen.

> *We never know the worth of water till the well is dry.*
>
> ENGLISH PROVERB

I am ready for good omens. Entering a new book, I want to believe that what I write will prove to be useful, blessed. Walking in the park, when the great bird soared near me, I felt a quick sense of wonder. "That is an *eagle,*" I thought. "And this is *New York.*" (For many years I lived in New Mexico, where the spotting of an eagle, while rare, was still to be expected.) This is the third time in five years that I have sighted an eagle in New York. Egged on by my own skepticism that the birds really could exist in Manhattan, I have done the research and learned that eagles do live in Central Park, released there deliberately by the Forest Service. Even knowing this, they seem miraculous to me. And so, yes, I believe the bird to be a great good omen. I believe this new book to be blessed and I am grateful for the encouragement.

I am fifty-eight years old. I have been a writer since I turned eighteen. That makes forty years at my craft. I have written plays, novels, short stories, songs, poetry, reviews, and journalism. I have had lean years and fat years. With twenty books to my credit, I have written long enough and often enough to deserve the badge "writer." I have become accustomed to the twin horsemen of a writing career: the desire to write and the fear that this time I will not be able to pull it off.

Over the years, writing has become easier, a daily routine. But there are many days when my stint at the page still takes all of the courage I can muster. "Please,

God, send me ideas," I pray. Then I listen and type out what I hear. "Inspiration" is really as simple as the act of listening and being willing to trust that still, small voice. Some days I am willing to trust. Others, I am not. On those days, I must pray again. "Please, God, send me the willingness to just listen and write." And then I must listen and then I must write.

Over the years, I have learned that there is a flow of ideas that we as artists can tap into. The flow of creativity is a constant. We are the ones who are fickle or fearful. I have learned that my creative condition and my spiritual condition are one and the same. Making art is an act of faith, a movement toward expansion. When I am stymied in my work, I am stymied in my spiritual condition. When I am self-conscious as an artist, I am spiritually constricted. I need to pray to lose my self-centered fears. I need to ask for selflessness, to be a conduit, a channel for ideas to move through. At a time like this, I again post a sign at my writing station, "Okay, God, you take care of the quality. I will take care of the quantity." In other words, it is time to resign as the self-conscious author. It is time to let Something or Somebody write through me. How the ego hates this humbling proposition! And yet, great art is born of great humility.

> *What do you know better than your own secrets?*
>
> RAYMOND CARVER

> *I never know when I sit down, just what I am going to write. I make no plan; it just comes, and I don't know where it comes from.*
>
> D. H. LAWRENCE

"The music of this opera [*Madama Butterfly*] was dictated to me by God. I was merely instrumental in putting it on paper and communicating it to the public," declared Giacomo Puccini.

"Straightaway the ideas flow in upon me, directly from God," stated Johannes Brahms.

These men were not proselytizing. They were simply reporting their creative experience. Artists work with one ear cocked to the Divine, although they may call it by another name. As the virtuoso violinist Stéphane Grappelli assured us, "Great improvisers are like priests. They are thinking only of their god."

The grace to be an acolyte, a servant of art, is the best prayer that an artist can offer. The grace to be again—one more time—a beginner is the most useful position an artist can take. Rather than being full of ourselves and our accomplishments, we are better served by emptying ourselves of our honors. "Show me what it is you want from me," is a serviceable prayer. (And the prayer can be uttered to God, to the Muse or even to Art itself.) Every great piece of art contains a whiff of transcendence. A Pollock or a Rothko has a transparency to it. Looking at the work, we catch a glimpse of the artist's soul. "Show me what it is you want from me," they clearly prayed to *Something*. Their art is a record of the answer they received.

But very often what God wants for us is not quite what we had planned. Our egos may tug us one direction while our souls yank us in another. I remember walking one day through the New Mexican sage fields, plotting the novel that I intended to write next, when suddenly I was directed to write a small prayer book about gratitude. "Not me! Not that!" I wanted to protest. The guidance was clear and implacable. How was it possible to write such a book without seeming to be a pious poseur? And yet, how was it possible not to write such a book when it was what was asking to be written, nudging at my hands and heart like a collie dog wanting to be stroked? No, the directive was not to be ignored, and so I did write that book. The novel I planned on came later.

There is a divine plan of goodness for us and our work, but we must go along with the plan in order that it may transpire. Careers do not unfold in an orderly manner. They do not proceed A to B to C. They zig and then they zag. We must tack with them. We must be willing to be made what it is God is making us. For our own comfort, we must be willing to surrender to a power greater than ourselves. At the moment, my career as a public speaker is flourishing. I am an intensely private person who approaches all public engagements with dread, and yet, the invitations keep rolling in and there is rent to pay. So I am, for a while at least, a public speaker. Similarly, there have been years when I was rendered a journalist, a screenwriter, a teacher—never quite what I chose. I had to believe that something wiser than I was choosing for me. Investing too heavily in a single artistic identity—Screenwriter! Playwright! Novelist!—and insisting on living out that identity can put us into conflict with the flow of our destiny. We do better to roll with the punches and to repeat to ourselves the simple prayer, "Thy will be done." We are often rendered something better than what we might imagine.

According to Joseph Campbell, it is possible to see the tracery of destiny in a life. He believed that once a person reached middle age, it was possible to see the contours of fate, the firm nudges we had received that sent us down this life path and not that. Campbell believed that there was a plan for each of us— and I believe the same thing. I believe there is an overarching *Something* that cares for us with great tenderness. It is

The material itself dictates how it should be written.

WILLIAM FAULKNER

this *Something* that we seek to contact when we work at making conscious contact with a Higher Power. It is this *Something* that guards us and guides us, tutors us and mentors us, moving us always toward our good if we will but cooperate.

How do we cooperate? There are a few basic tools that move us into conscious contact with our Creator. The use of these tools is simple and practical. We do not need to search in obscure corners for a pathway to our Maker. The road is broad and clearly lit. God meets us more than halfway if we undertake the simplest of motions toward Him. As we work to become more of the all that we can be, we come into contact with a benevolent guiding force. Some of us will call that force "God." Others will call it "the Universe," "the Higher Power," "Spirit," "the Tao," "the Force," or even, "the Muse." It does not matter what we call it. What does matter is that we experience it—and we will.

When we move toward our own creativity, we move toward our Creator. When we seek to become more spiritual, we find ourselves becoming more creative. Our creativity and our spirituality are so closely interconnected they are in effect one and the same thing. Speaking of God, we often use the terms "Maker" or "Creator" without recognizing that those are the terms for "artist." God is the Great Artist. We are creations and we are intended, in turn, to be creative ourselves.

The Basics

Being an artist means: not numbering and counting, but ripening like a tree, which doesn't force its sap, and stands confidently in the storms of spring, not afraid that afterwards summer may not come.

—Rainer Maria Rilke

I HAVE WRITTEN about creativity many times and in writing about it again I find it necessary to repeat myself. Some things are simply too important to be skipped over. I have been teaching for twenty-five years. In those years, I have discovered that certain pivotal tools *always* work to enrich and enlarge our lives. Because the tools work consistently, it is always worth reteaching them. In my own creative practice, I use many of them year in and year out. If you are already familiar with some of these concepts, I hope you will enjoy this review and use it to renew your practice. If the ideas are new to you, what follows should be sufficient to give you a firm grounding.

This book is structured as a twelve-week course with an alternating series of exploratory essays and matching tools, "Divining Rods." Their aim is to help us to discover the living waters of creativity flowing through our often busy and difficult lives. The essays will trace my daily personal process of "finding water." The tools, many of them perennial favorites of mine, function like dowsing wands to point the way to further spiritual growth.

Morning Pages

In order to find our creativity—or, for that matter, our spirituality—we must begin with where we are. The Great Creator meets us exactly where we are standing—in "the Now"—but sometimes we do not know where that is. We may have moved through our lives unconsciously for a while, perhaps for a great while, and so we must find and take up a tool that tells us where we are and how we actually

A single day is enough to make us a little larger or, another time, a little smaller.

PAUL KLEE

Every moment of one's existence one is growing into more or retreating into less. One is always living a little more or dying a little bit.

NORMAN MAILER

An ounce of action is worth a ton of theory.

FRIEDRICH ENGEL

feel about that. This is the beginning of honesty, and honesty is the first step toward greater creativity.

So, where exactly are we? And how do we really feel? The tool that best helps us find our spiritual bearings is called Morning Pages. I have used them myself for more than two decades. I have written about them many times and I write about them again now because they are the bedrock on which a spiritual awakening can be based.

What, exactly, are Morning Pages and why should we undertake them? Morning Pages are three pages of longhand stream of consciousness that locate us precisely in the here and now. They are written first thing upon awakening and they tell us—and the Universe— what we like, what we don't like, what we wish we had more of, what we wish we had less of, what we wish, period. Our wishes, our unspoken dreams, are the voice of our soul. By letting our soul speak first thing in the morning, we align ourselves with the Great Creator. Over the years, I have come to consider Morning Pages to be a valid form of meditation, perhaps a form uniquely suited to hyperactive Westerners.

Morning Pages catch us as close as possible to our waking mind, before all of our well-meaning defenses are in place. They catch us when we are vulnerable and open. They catch us at our most honest and fragile when we are, perhaps, a bit discouraged, a bit daunted by the day ahead. Pages seldom sound polished or positive. In fact, Morning Pages may seem, at first, to be nothing but a series of gripes, a list of grievances about our discomforts, both psychological and physical. For this reason I sometimes dub Morning Pages "Brain Drain." Here is how they might sound:

"I am awake and I am tired. I feel stuck but I don't know quite where, and I don't know how to get out of it, either. These sheets feel positively gritty. I need to change my bed . . ."

"I forgot to call my sister back yesterday. I wonder if her marriage is going to last. I forgot to buy kitty litter. The car has a funny knock. I need to remember to start on my receipts. I don't want it to be a big emergency like last year. Dear Lord, I hate the IRS."

Griping, whining, kvetching, complaining—Morning Pages help us to siphon off our negativity. We see the cloud of resentment that hangs over us as we begin our day. We learn exactly what we resent. We learn exactly what strikes us as unpleasant or undoable. Without Morning Pages, we may only notice such things on a subliminal level. We don't like something but we don't quite register that fact. It may strike us as too petty, as somehow beneath our dignity. "Toughen up," we might tell ourselves. We may urge ourselves to be more grown up. But such urgings seldom work. Instead, we go through our day accompanied by a constant drip, drip, drip of subtle negativity. This dispiriting sound track is so omnipresent we may not even realize that it is there.

When we first undertake Morning Pages, we are often astounded by the number of things we feel bad about. We may worry that by admitting our negative feelings we are encouraging them. This is far from the case. Jungians call it "meeting the Shadow." I call it meeting the Shadow and asking it for a cup of coffee. When we ventilate the negative, we make room for the positive.

> *Take care of each moment and you will take care of all time.*
>
> BUDDHA

> *Originality does not consist in saying what no one has ever said before, but in saying exactly what you think yourself.*
>
> JAMES STEPHENS

Writing Morning Pages, we lay our negative sound track onto the page. We get it out of our head and on its way to being out of our life. We register it with the Universe instead of just suffering through it unconsciously. For example, you may write, "I hated the way John treated me in that meeting yesterday. He stole credit for my ideas."

There it is in black and white. You are facing something unpleasant that previously you may not have dared to look at squarely. Caught with our guard down first thing in the morning, there is nothing vague about our feelings. We know what is going on and we have our opinions about it. Moving the pen across the page, we discover that we are not the victim of circumstances. We have choices as to how we respond. Morning Pages show us our options. You may "get" that you are being used and that you yourself have been complicit. Just facing the facts, you may experience a substantial shift in your self-worth. When you are in a meeting with John later that same day, you may find yourself being suddenly assertive. "Thank you, John, for bringing up *my* idea about restructuring. Let me elaborate a little on what I had in mind. . . ."

Morning Pages are like a spiritual chiropractor. They put us back on our spiritual spine. They help us to correct our course. We learn to stand up for ourselves if we are being trod upon. We learn to hold our tongue if we have been too hot-headed. Perhaps for the first time, we experience a sense of balance. This is exciting, as we sense that we are becoming more truly ourselves.

Morning Pages are simple and yet profound. To our joy, we discover there is a wisdom inherent in the process itself. We speak to God through our Pages and God speaks back to us in the form of heightened intuitions and inklings. The "still, small voice" gets amplified so that we can easily hear it. We are all adjusted in the precise direction that we need to grow. As we become more honest with God about our dissatisfactions, God is able to do something about them. God works through us to work on us. Increasingly, we take positive actions in our own behalf.

Morning Pages are tough-love friends. They single out the patterns that are defeating us. "I drank too much last night," we write. Then another day, "Drunk again last night." And another, "I am too hung over to move." The Pages urge us to take responsible actions: "I have to do something about my drinking." And then, "I wonder if I should try Alcoholics Anonymous. I could."

The typewriter separated me from a deeper intimacy with poetry, and my hand brought me closer to that intimacy again.

PABLO NERUDA

Morning Pages make us more graceful, but that grace is very practical. We feel the nudge to our consciousness when we are off course, and we act upon it. If we don't, the Pages will bring up that lack of action and nag us about it until we are willing to take action. Subtle and pedestrian seeming, Morning Pages actually make for radical changes. We learn where we are off kilter and just what we might want to do about it. Pages initiate change and they also walk us through that change. We do get sober. We do lose weight. We do taper off of codependent relationships.

But Morning Pages are not all bad news. Sometimes an insight comes to us as we write. We have a sudden breakthrough to clarity. "I get it! Why didn't I see that before?" We abruptly see exactly how we have been sabotaging ourselves. And we see how we can stop. Sometimes we get the glimmer of a new idea, a change in direction that we could take. We get the notion, "I could try it this way instead of that way." Sometimes Morning Pages will suggest a brand-new creative project. We will find ourselves entertaining a course of behavior that had never crossed our consciousness before. If Morning Pages put us in touch with the flow of good new ideas, they also give us the boat to rest in as we ride that flow. Morning Pages make us feel secure—secure enough to take risks.

I had been writing Morning Pages for fifteen years when suddenly the notion that I should try writing music appeared. I was forty-five years old, certain that I was not musical, and yet inclined, too, to trust the Pages after so many years writing them. "What shall I do next?" I asked in Pages. "You will be writing radiant songs," the Pages advised me. "Wouldn't it be fun to write a musical about Merlin?"

I was incredulous. "Oh, c'mon," I thought. "If I were the least bit musical, surely I would have known it by now." I had been raised as the nonmusical member of a very musical family. My piano lessons had lasted precisely six weeks—long enough for me and everyone else to get discouraged. And yet, the Pages persisted: "You will be writing radiant songs."

Sure enough, within a month, having shown no prior musical inclinations, I was suddenly writing songs. Conditioned to believe I was untalented musically, Pages made me open to the possibility that I could be wrong. It is now ten years since I began writing music and I have written three full-length musicals and two albums of children's songs. I now write music as easily as I write prose—and nearly as often. I think of this late blossoming of my musical talent as a fruit of Morning Pages. The lesson I take from it is that we may all be far larger and more gifted than we suspect. If we will but listen to Morning Pages and trust them, we will be led to unfold in miraculous ways.

"I was a lawyer until I began doing Morning Pages," a very successful Broadway actor recently told me. A day at a time, a step at a time, the Morning Pages led him out of his unhappiness as a lawyer and into a flourishing theatrical career. To see him onstage is to feel, "Now *there* is a born actor," but he was not a born actor. He was a "made" actor and Morning Pages are what made the making possible.

"Julia, I was drinking in the outback until I started doing Morning Pages. Now I am a sober Hollywood screenwriter," another practitioner told me. Her Pages mentored her into sobriety, and her sobriety mentored her into a new career.

A Chicagoan in her midfifties who had always dreamed of a playwriting career undertook Morning Pages with fear and trepidation. She longed to write but she feared writing. The Pages proved to be a gently greased slide into her own creativity. She is now an award-winning playwright.

> *You can't sit around thinking.*
> *You have to sit around writing.*
>
> DAVID LONG
>
> *Action is character.*
>
> F. SCOTT FITZGERALD

Of course, not all practitioners report a change in career, but many report a deepened satisfaction in the career that they are in. ("I am much better in the courtroom," a lawyer recently confided to me.) The Pages help many of us to do our work better and to greater personal satisfaction. Stated simply, Morning Pages put us in touch with our need for change. Some of us need more radical change than others. Morning Pages adjust us to the degree that we need adjusting. When we write to our Creator precisely how we are and how we feel, the response back is specifically customized to our needs. Writing Morning Pages, we are forging a one-to-one, personal relationship to the Great Creator. There is great particularity in the ways that we are guided.

I've always had a very comfortable relationship with No. 2 pencils.

WILLIAM STYRON

Start with three pages of longhand morning writing that says exactly where you are. Do this every morning. "Good morning. I am tired. I didn't sleep enough. I dreamed about drowning. I was Japanese . . ." Every morning, no matter how you feel, tell your Pages how you feel. Let your Pages become a morning habit. Something that you do first thing, a sort of Morning Report, a signing in. Very soon you will feel a shift, a sense of relief that you are telling someone, even if that someone is "the Universe," the whole truth.

Morning Pages are the bedrock tool of a creative recovery. I have done Pages now for more than twenty years. In those years, I have probably not missed more than twenty days. Every day I tell the page how I am doing. Every day, the page tells me back that I am making the tiniest soupçon of progress. "At least I am writing Pages . . ." Year in, year out, the Pages nudge me forward ever so slightly. They may suggest I do a musical or try my hand at a novel again. They may suggest I paint my bedroom or make a commitment to a daily walk. They may tell me I need rest and more water.

In creativity, as in running, you have to start where you are. Let us say you are twenty pounds overweight and haven't written in fifteen years. Well, then, your first flyer at contacting help might read, "I am twenty pounds overweight. I haven't written in fifteen years."

Think of what you're doing as putting out your coordinates. Imagine yourself on a life raft bobbing in a vast sea. You want the big boat to save you, but it must know precisely where you are in order to effect a rescue. And so, you do not want to be vague. What you write in your Morning Pages gives the Universe precise information about exactly where you can be found. You want the Universe to help you, and, in order to help you, it needs an accurate account of where you are. So be specific. "I stopped writing fifteen years ago when my novel didn't sell and I thought, 'Oh, what's the use . . .' I still think, 'Oh, what's the use,' if I am honest."

Be trivial, be petty, whine, grump, groan, and complain. Morning Pages siphon off a haze of negativity through which we normally face our day. The negativity goes onto the page instead of just wafting around us as we make our way through our daily lives. "These pages are boring," you might complain. Write them anyway.

> *There is no enlightenment outside of daily life.*
>
> THICH NHAT HANH

Sometimes we try too hard to have something to say. We feel desperate but we don't want to act desperate. We want to pose a little—even on the page. Posing gets us nowhere. We do better to just come clean. It can take getting used to, this nakedness on the page. We want to say, "I haven't written in a while," leaving it vague. We want to say, "I'm a little overweight." But it does us far more good to be accurate. That gives the Universe somewhere concrete to meet us.

> *When every blessed thing you have is made of silver, or of gold, you long for simple pewter.*
>
> W. S. GILBERT

It can be hard at first being naked on the page. We want to pretend we are in better shape than we really feel ourselves to be. We want to pretend we have momentous things to say when the truth may be that we yearn to say something but we don't know what. The truth is that we may feel trivial, like an also-ran. We can put this on the page. We can say, "I really have nothing much to say and so I am going to practice saying nothing much."

Little by little what we have to say and who we have to say it to will become clear to us. The truth, the whole truth, is a gradual process. We want to feel we are clearly defined but often we are not. Often we are vague and muddy around the edges. Often we have been making do with half-truths for a very long time. And so, when we first start writing, our writing is vague. We say, "I don't think I may like X" when what we mean is, "I absolutely hate X."

It is a good idea to have compassion for ourselves when we are starting out. It can take us a while to get our wheels to lurch free from the mud. It can be difficult to write: "I long to write and I am not writing." Just saying it makes the stakes higher. Who am I if I long to write and I am not writing? Am I a pretender? An also-ran? A coward?

*I'd rather have written Cheers
than anything I've written.*

KURT VONNEGUT

*As I write I create myself
again and again*

JOY HARJO

When we first start writing our way out of the muck, we will be tempted to such flash judgments. These judgments are what have kept us so mired for so long. We call ourselves "cowards" instead of extending sympathy to ourselves. "Of course you're scared. Writing really matters to you." That is the compassionate overview that Morning Pages tend to bring.

As we make the commitment to undertaking three pages a day of longhand, we begin to sense that something is committing back. We might call that something the "Universe." We might call it "the Great Creator" or "God." It doesn't matter what we call it. We can feel it. We begin to contact a sense of wisdom not commonly our own. We start to take a longer and less apocalyptic view of our life. We begin to get an overview and the first gentle crumbs of progress are made. This can be very exciting and very humbling.

"You may not be writing what you long to write yet, but at least you are writing your Pages," we may tell ourselves. "You may still be twenty pounds overweight but yesterday you had yogurt instead of French toast and that's a step in the right direction."

Morning Pages are a gentle mentor. They help us make small course corrections rather than dramatic pronouncements. Because they are done one day at a time, they encourage us to live one day at a time. It is a rare day in which a tiny forward step cannot be taken. It is the job of Morning Pages to notice and encourage such small steps.

Our thoughts move across our mind; our hand moves across the page. It is very simple and very centering. We are simply writing down what meditators call our "cloud thoughts." We write down whatever it occurs to us to write, strictly stream of consciousness. Instead of sitting there "doing nothing" for twenty minutes, we are sitting there "doing something" for twenty minutes. This can appeal to our work ethic. Morning Pages are frequently called "positively addicting."

Morning Pages are a simple, doable, and very positive practice. They invite change and they parse out change in small, digestible increments. Over any considerable period of time, "the Pages" function like a loyal, tough-love friend. If there is an issue we are avoiding they will broach it to us—and over and over until we do something about it. "Julia, I was perfectly happy drunk," I have been told. "Then I started doing Morning Pages . . ."

Whether we are drunk in the outback or something less dramatic, Morning Pages will nudge us to make a change, until we do make a change and as we make that change the Pages will walk us through it. Above all else, Morning Pages are loyal. Unlike Manhattan psychiatrists, they do not take two weeks off every August. Instead, they are always there for us, steady and dependable. It's worth a try.

I cannot prove to you that Morning Pages will create a sense of magic in your life, but I can ask you to experiment. Try the pages for a few weeks. Try them for twelve weeks if you can. (That's the period of time required to "groove" a new habit.) Once you become accustomed to them, you may find them indispensable. I have many students who have now been doing Morning Pages for a decade or longer. Do I need to say that they do them because they work?

> *The true object of all human life is play.*
>
> G. K. CHESTERTON

> *The first mistake of art is to assume that it is serious.*
>
> LESTER BANKS

Divining Rod

Set aside an early-morning hour—although you may not need all of it. (Most people report that Morning Pages take them a half an hour to forty-five minutes.) Take your hand to the page and write three pages of stream of consciousness writing. Remember that nothing is too small or trivial to be included. You may find yourself grumpy or "boring." That's fine.

Morning Pages are not intended to be dramatic. They seldom sound good. That's all right. They are not intended to be "real writing." Expect them to be fragmented and to skitter topic to topic. Relax. Explore your own mind with curiosity, not judgment. There is no wrong way to do Morning Pages. Simply write down whatever comes to mind and do that for three pages. As a rule, I do suggest you use standard eight-and-one-half-by-eleven pages. If you use little pages, you will tend to edit your thoughts to fit the small format. Remember, your pages are for your eyes only. They are not to be shared with any audience other than your own consciousness. Do Morning Pages every day and be alert for the shifts that they will lead you to.

Artist Dates

Today it is too warm for snow. The sky is a soft, silvery gray and a fine, light sleet is falling. New Yorkers venture out armed with umbrellas or turning their faces to the fresh, gentle mist. The weather is damp but not unpleasant. Suddenly we are on the cusp of spring. Central Park is the first place to show it. If you look closely, daffodils and hyacinths are pushing their buds upward through yesterday's snow.

This morning I walked two dogs in Central Park. I had my own dog, a naughty cocker spaniel named Tiger Lily, and my collaborator's dog, a sweet West Highland terrier named Charlotte. The dogs plunged through mud puddles and strained at their leashes in pursuit of squirrels. By walk's end, their coats were soaked and they came back inside "wet and wild," flinging themselves onto the Oriental carpets, rolling and twisting to dry their coats.

The dogs enjoy a walk in any weather. They need their daily dose of adventure in order to be happy. All I need to say is, "Leashes!" for them to leap in the air, cavorting. "Hold still!" I have to beg in order to fasten the snaps to their collars. No matter how many times we walk the same route, it is never routine to them. There is always some fresh sight, some new smell for them to revel in. Ever obstreperous, Tiger Lily barks at children and lunges at passing Great Danes. Ever amiable, Charlotte greets children and dogs alike with a wriggle of glad expectancy. Surely we can all be friends . . .

Have a variety of interests. . . . These interests relax the mind and lessen the tension on the nervous system. People with many interests live, not only longest, but happiest.

GEORGE MATTHEW ALLEN

There is no such thing as a missed day of dog walking. Even in the thickest snow or the fiercest cold we venture out. Each day's weather lends its flavor to the walk. It is the combination of routine and adventure that makes the walks so edifying. An adventure that can be counted on, that is a wonderful thing.

In seeking to nurture our creativity, we, too, need adventures that can be counted on. I call them "Artist Dates." As the name suggests, we are out to romance or woo our artist. We do so by taking a weekly solo expedition to do something that is just plain fun. As with any date, the planning is a part of the adventure. The anticipation is a large part of what makes it special. All week long we can look forward to our romantic rendezvous.

I live in Manhattan, a Mecca for artist dates. My apartment is on the Upper West Side, walking distance from The American Museum of Natural History. Up the great stairs and into the dim, cavernous halls I often take myself. I skip the special exhibits and go straight for the museum's staples. I love the dioramas, staged tableaux of wild animals captured in what appear to be their natural habitats. There are dozens of different types of gazelles. There are looming Alaskan brown bears, so huge they dwarf a grizzly. There are mountain goats and bighorn sheep. There are bison and water buffalo. Hippopotami wallow right before my eyes. Great apes cavort amid the tree tops.

I suppose the squeamish might see too much death in all the mounted scenarios. To me, it is all about the diversity of life. It is easy, encountering so many diverse creatures, to feel one has encountered the Great Creator. It is easy, seeing the care taken to twist a horn just so, to sketch in a finely tapering stripe, to believe we, too, are cared for. Clearly the Creator has its eye not only on the sparrow, but also on us.

A multitude of small delights constitute happiness.

CHARLES BAUDELAIRE

Each day comes bearing its own gifts. Untie the ribbons.

RUTH ANN SCHABACKER

The intuition that we are connected to a power greater than ourselves is one of the first fruits of Artist Dates. There is a sense of wonder that enters our lives the moment we slow down enough to give it access. We do not need to be admiring the natural world to feel our own spiritual nature coming awake.

Across the park from The American Museum of Natural History, perched high on Fifth Avenue, is the grand and glorious Metropolitan Museum of Art. An Artist Date there might begin with a visit to Asian Art. What could be more inspiring than the benign gaze of Buddha carved in stone centuries earlier and gazing at us still with perfect equanimity? A quiet steals over the senses. The timeless stone statues are unsigned, yet the artists live on in their work. As with the great cathedrals, the anonymity of the creators is part of what makes the hymn of praise so ecstatic. On an Artist Date, we sense the ecstasy of creation. We appreciate both the artist and the art.

But an artist date need not involve high art. Manhattan contains a fabric district and few dates are as satisfying as a visit to one of the huge commercial fabric stores. Is it velvet you are after? Here is crimson, burnt umber, regal purple. Perhaps you are looking for a heathery tweed? There it is, bolt on bolt of it, in all its misty glory.

Now here is a fine pinstripe, there a natty herringbone. There seems to be no end to the diversity and the possibility of creation. "This has a fine hand," the aging salesman remarks, appreciatively stroking a smooth cashmere. Coats can be made and kilts. Sleek business suits. Drop-dead gorgeous chiffon dinner gowns. A suit for a college graduation. A Christening robe. Something for every occasion. From wedding gown to bathrobe, the imagination can conjure almost anything and it is in this act of conjuring that a sense of play is born. Artist Dates fill us with exuberance. We see that we are not caught by the narrow confines of life as we have known it. No, the possibilities are endless. Just look at that taffeta . . .

Artist Dates bring us optimism. They awaken in us a sense of potential: our own and our world's. They help us to know that we are not alone. Rather, we sense that we are partnered by a large—and playful—*Something*. It is possible, we see, to make more of our life than we have made of it to date. Life is an adventure, not an ordeal, we start to intuit.

> *I want to be able to live without a crowded calendar. I want to be able to read a book without feeling guilty, or go to a concert when I like.*
>
> GOLDA MEIR

> *The aim of life is to live, and to live means to be aware, joyously, drunkenly, serenely, divinely aware.*
>
> HENRY MILLER

Artist Dates bring us a sense of enchantment. There is magic afoot and we encounter it more easily. On an Artist Date, we set our inner dial to "receive" and what we receive is often guidance and a heightened sense of well-being. We feel that we are in harmony, that there is a harmonic higher than our own that partners us at all turns. Agnosticism starts to fade as we encounter a spiritual experience. I do not ask you to believe any of this. I ask you to experiment and record for yourself the result.

An Artist Date is an adventure, a lark, a flier into the unknown. It asks you to have fun and to preplan that fun. For this reason, Artist Dates are notoriously hard to execute. Just try planning an adventure for yourself and watch your killjoy side fly into action. You are suddenly too busy to do anything so frivolous as have fun. Identify this resistance as a fear of intimacy—intimacy with your self.

It helps to think of the Artist Date as being analogous to the quality time a divorced parent spends with a child. Just as that parent will want to drag along the new significant other, so, too, we will want to bring a friend along. We will go to almost any length to keep from spending time alone with ourselves. Like the divorced parent, we are afraid of what we may hear if we actually give our inner creative young-ster some time and attention and a chance to speak to us. It can be frightening to become intimate with ourselves, especially if we haven't been for some time. Expect to hear the unexpected.

"I want to go to a photo exhibit," may come bubbling up when you have de-cided on a "worthy" lecture on computers. "I hate it here," may be the response when you take your inner artist to a very serious new drama. You can be pretty sure you will be caught off guard by something and that that something will give you food for thought.

Many times it is on an Artist Date that a recovering artist first experiences the recognizable presence of God— Good Orderly Direction. For some reason, Artist Dates tend to kick up our level of synchronicity, those experi-ences in which the hand of God or the finger of the Uni-verse feels palpably present. Sometimes, opening the door the tiniest crack to our inner artist leads to large and signif-icant breakthroughs.

> *Art is so wonderfully irrational, exuberantly pointless, but necessary all the same. Pointless and yet necessary, that's hard for a Puritan to understand.*
>
> GÜNTER GRASS

Artist Dates tend to build on themselves. You have an in-terest in France and so you go to see a movie in French with subtitles. The next week, you attend a class on French cui-sine. Three months later, you have signed up for French les-

> *One must be a living man and a posthumous artist.*
>
> JEAN COCTEAU

sons at the local YMCA and you are contemplating taking a bicycle vacation through France. All you did was start to scratch a little itch . . .

Artist Dates connect us to a larger and more fascinating world than our normal beaten path. They remind us that we have many choices and that we make those choices daily. It is hard, when practicing Artist Dates, to feel convincingly trapped in a life we don't like. We become aware that we have the power to change many things: an apartment, a neighborhood, even a city. Doing Artist Dates, we begin to feel ourselves being led. We begin to have the novel feeling that we can even trust that leading. Ours is a fabulous world, far wealthier and more varied than we have allowed. It is on Artist Dates that we first begin to experience the world's abun-dance. It is often on an Artist Date that a recovering artist first learns to hear and to trust hunches. Hunches are often the way that the Universe leads us, and we need to be willing to follow such leadings a step at a time. "Follow your bliss," Joseph

Campbell advised his students. For me, an Artist Date to a Rand McNally map and globe store led to a decade's worth of writing on Magellan, the great explorer.

Often, when we are working full tilt, we are tempted to skip Artist Dates because things "are going so well." The truth is that when we are working full out, we should be doubling our Artist Dates because we are drawing heavily upon the inner well of images from which we make our art. Artist Dates replenish the inner well. They give us stocks to draw on. They make us wealthy.

> *One ought, every day at least, to hear a little song, read a good poem, see a fine picture, and if it were possible, to speak a few reasonable words.*
>
> JOHANN WOLFGANG
> VON GOETHE

> *Being an artist means ceasing to take seriously that very serious person we are when we are not an artist.*
>
> JOSÉ ORTEGA Y GASSET

Think of it like building a CB radio. When you are doing Morning Pages, you have the dial set to "send" and you are broadcasting, "This is what I like. This is what I don't like. This is what I want more of . . ." When the dial is moved over to Artist Date, you have suddenly switched to receive. You begin to be able to hear the Guidance coming back at you. Your radio kit is now fully functional. Because Morning Pages look like work and Artist Dates look like play, it is often much more difficult to do an Artist Date than it is to undertake the Pages. This is America. We understand "work." What we are baffled by is "play"—as in, "the play of ideas," a very literal phrase. It is difficult for us to do something that seems frivolous. We do not see how Artist Dates "work." We need to experiment with them despite our skepticism. Even the tiniest of Artist Dates will yield results.

Artist Dates are like yeast. It only takes a smidgen to create a large chain reaction.

Divining Rod

Once a week, take yourself on a festive, solo expedition. Take the term "Artist Date" literally. It is half "artist" and half "date." Plan your date ahead of time and expect some resistance in trying to accomplish it. Expect, too, that your intimates may want to go with you. They are not allowed. It is your date with you, yourself, alone. You are out to "woo" your own creative consciousness. That is the "date" part of Artist Date. Think mystery rather than mastery. A date should expand your horizons by exploring territory a little bit outside of your usual realm.

An Artist Date is an adventure. It does not have to be "cultural." You may find yourself making a sortie to a new restaurant or stopping in at a hardware store or an art supply shop. Your Artist Date doesn't need to be big and threatening and expensive. It merely needs to entice you. A free flea market might be a better date for you than an evening at the theater. What you are after is the play of ideas—with the emphasis on the word "play."

Walks

It is a bright and sunny day. Spring is again in the air. Coats are left unbuttoned, heads uncovered. It is a good day for stretching the legs and New Yorkers, always great walkers, take to the streets in droves. This past winter was the coldest on record in fifty years. By way of contrast, this mid-forties day feels positively balmy. People are daft with the sunshine and fresh breezes. They run an extra errand on their lunch hour. It is good to be out and about.

I'm not a teacher: only a fellow traveler of whom you've asked the way. I pointed ahead—ahead of myself as well as you.

GEORGE BERNARD SHAW

For those of us working to increase our creativity, it is always good to be out and about, especially on our feet. Walking, the simplest of tools, is among the most profound. It makes us larger than we are. When we walk, we wake up our consciousness. We enliven our senses. We arrive at a sense of well-being. We experience "conscious contact" with a power greater than ourselves. That still, small voice is automatically amplified a footfall at a time. *"Solvitur ambulando,"* St. Augustine is said to have remarked. "It is solved by walking."

No matter what the "it" is, walking helps to unravel it. We may walk out stale from a day caught up with office politics. At first we walk rehearsing the day in our mind: "And then he said . . . and then I should have said . . ." But before long, our consciousness drops the bone we are worrying. Our negativity simply cannot stay

No man can know where he is going unless he knows exactly where he has been and exactly how he arrived at his present place.

MAYA ANGELOU

Happiness walks on busy feet.

KITTE TURMELL

Belief consists in accepting the affirmations of the soul; unbelief, in denying them.

RALPH WALDO EMERSON

in place as our body moves. Despite ourselves, despite our many heartfelt worries, there comes a creeping feeling of optimism. We notice the daffodils at the green grocer's and the large black buckets of pussy willows. We think about buying a pot of tulips. We settle, instead, on fragrant hyacinths. Yes, spring is afoot—a telling phrase. No coincidence, there is a "spring" to our stride.

Sometimes we walk out with a tangled personal situation that needs sorting. We have noticed something that needs attending to and then all during our busy day we have ignored it, shoving it beneath the rug of our consciousness. "But what about . . . ?" our problem nudges us despite our refusal to engage it. "What about . . . ?" it badgers.

When we walk out, the sorting process begins. We do not "solve" our dilemma. Instead, it keeps us company as we walk. It vies for our attention and then it fades away as the details of our walk begin to engross us. We notice the tortoiseshell cat perched on the windowsill. We notice the sign for a new needlepoint shop. We see that an optimistic someone has already planted a window box, then we laugh, realizing when right up upon it that the blooms are fake.

"But what about . . . ?" swims to our consciousness again. The pesky problem is still unsolved. We turn our attention to look at it but it sinks back down. Instead, we notice the mother and child just ahead of us. The mother pushes a stroller with little brother. The child pushes a matching stroller holding "dolly." Both of them step delicately over a mud puddle left over from yesterday's wet weather.

"I could try—" the thought comes suddenly to mind. It is, if not the perfect solution, at least a good possibility. Walking has turned the key.

Spiritual seekers have always walked. There are pilgrimages to Canterbury, to Mecca, to Jerusalem. There are pilgrimages around Kailas, the sacred Tibetan mountain. Aborigines go on Walkabout. Native Americans set out on Vision Quests. There is something in walking that tunes us to a higher key. Each footfall moves us up a step. We do not come home the same as we set out.

In order to be effective, a walk doesn't need to be long. A scant twenty minutes is usually enough to shift our consciousness to a broader and more expansive place. An hour's walk is a luxury. Taken once a week, a goodly walk puts the events of the week into perspective. It shows us an overview. It gives us valuable detachment. And, yes, it gives us words.

Walking is not just for writers but it is especially wonderful for them. Walking starts the writing engine humming. Dante is said to have been a walker. The British Lake Poets were great walkers. (It is no accident that poetry is divided into "feet.") The esteemed writing teacher Brenda Ueland swore by walks, for both herself and her students. She exclaimed, "I will tell you what I have learned for myself. For me, a long five- or six-mile walk helps and one must go alone and every day."

When we walk by ourselves, we find ourselves companioned. We set out alone but soon sense that the Divine is close at hand. It comes as intuition, as insight, as sudden conclusion. The shape of our life comes clear to us as we walk. We take note of the many causes for optimism. Without shame or scolding, walking puts a gentle end to self-involvement. Almost without noticing it, we become engaged with a world larger than ourselves and our concerns. A blue jay hops to a stone wall. A squirrel scampers along a tree branch. Our consciousness follows, entertained. We walk out with our pressing problems, but walking soon invites us to take a longer view. With little effort on our part, we find we attain a wiser perspective. As casual as a walk may seem, profound wisdom can be its byproduct.

> *The only real voyage of discovery consists not in seeking new landscapes, but in having new eyes.*
>
> MARCEL PROUST

> *Solitude is as needful to the imagination as society is wholesome for the character.*
>
> JAMES RUSSELL LOWELL

Statesman Søren Kierkegaard phrased it this way, "Above all, do not lose your desire to walk: every day I walk myself into a state of well-being and away from every illness; I have walked myself into my best thoughts, and I know of no thought so burdensome that one cannot walk away from it. . . ."

Walking makes us more whole. It mends the body/mind split by promoting the release of endorphins, tiny neural messengers of optimism. After a brisk walk, we feel a sense of well-being. Walking integrates our experience and grounds our perspective. It is an exercise in heightened and intensified spiritual listening. We may walk out with our own will set on certain agendas, but as we walk our will is tempered. As movement teacher Gabrielle Roth sees it, "If you just set people in motion, they'll heal themselves." A footfall at a time, our soul is tutored in divine timing. Walking back in, we may still want what we want, but we also come to see how our dreams and desires fit into a larger whole.

Walking makes us rightsized. We sense that we are far larger than we may sometimes feel and yet that there is a *Something* far larger than we ourselves are. We sense that *Something* holds us in benevolent regard. We sense that benevolence as we walk.

"It's just something I have to walk through," we often say, talking about hard times. What we don't realize is that all of life is something we have to walk through. As we take the phrase literally, we can begin to get help with our many difficult problems and dilemmas. Because it is such a simple tool and so readily available to all of us, we do not tend to think of "walking" as a sophisticated problem-solving stratagem.

And yet it is.

We carry wisdom in our bodies. We carry memories and we carry, too, the medicine for what ails us. We can walk our way to sanity. We can walk our way to clarity. Baffled and confused, we can walk our way to knowing the "next right step."

In difficult times, many of us intuitively start walking. We may walk our way through a divorce, a breakup, or a job change. We may walk our way out of one identity and into another, newer and better-suited to us. Answers come to us while we walk—sometimes the answers come to us before the questions. We just get an itch to start walking and when we do, we then begin to get a sense of why.

Karen is in the middle of a nasty breakup. For the better part of a decade she was joined at the hip to Jim—this despite her friends' comments that the relationship did not seem healthy to them. "I lost myself in Jim," Karen describes it. "I gave up so many things to be with him. There were so many things I expected him to be for me. I do not remember who I am without him, and yet I must be somebody."

Seeds of discouragement will not grow in the thankful heart.

ANONYMOUS

It is impossible to walk rapidly and be unhappy.

MOTHER TERESA

If we have listening ears, God speaks to us in our own language, whatever that language is.

MAHATMA GANDHI

Striving to remember who she is, Karen has taken to walking. A fragment at a time, she finds pieces of herself come swimming back to her as she walks. "Today I started thinking about my acting career. I just let that go glimmering about four years ago."

Things that go glimmering away can also come glimmering back to us.

"I didn't get into the Actor's Studio, and I was so ashamed and embarrassed that I quit. Now I realize that many people audition over and over to get in there."

With every footfall, Karen comes more surely into possession of the parts of her that have been missing. By the time she has walked a mile, she is speculating what other audition pieces she could try.

The dark night of the soul is often illuminated by a good brisk walk. Ideas come to us as we walk and so does inspiration. Even if we can't go five or six miles, even if we can't go alone and we can't go every day, walking "works." We walk out with a problem and we come home, if not with a solution, at least with a different angle on what it is that has troubled us.

Right now, I am walking to romance a book idea. I want to write a book, and I want to write a book I would like to read. This means that I must ask myself, "What is it that truly interests me at this time?" In order to ask myself the question, I must get out of my head and into my body.

My body knows things that my head doesn't know yet. We speak of having a "body of knowledge" and this is a literal term. Our body embodies knowledge. We "know things in our bones." We "feel things in our marrow." And the best way to access this corporeal wisdom is to walk.

> *As soon as you trust yourself, you will know how to live.*
>
> JOHANN WOLFGANG VON GOETHE

> *I sing the body electric.*
>
> WALT WHITMAN

Divining Rod

Once a week, take yourself out for a goodly walk. Twenty minutes is enough but an hour serves you even better. Stretch your legs and stretch your mind. Enjoy the sights and relish a new crop of insights. If it fits within your schedule, you may want to walk more than once a week. Many students report that they enjoy a couple of short twenty-minute walks and a weekly longish one. Expect that your walks will calm turbulent emotions and give you the time and space to "process" life as it occurs to you. Many students report that as they walk they feel a conscious contact with something spiritual that feels both larger and benevolent. You may well experience yourself as being "guided."

Creativity Contract

I, _____ , commit myself to the regular use of the three basic tools. For the duration of this course, I will write Morning Pages daily and will take an Artist's Date and a Weekly Walk once a week. Additionally, I commit myself to excellent self-care, adequate sleep, good food, and gentle companionship.

_____ (signature)

_____ (date)

Uncovering a Sense of Optimism

This week inaugurates your creative journey. Hopes high, you set out. Some of you may feel giddy anticipation. Others of you may harbor lingering skepticism. No matter what your cache of secret feelings, now is the time for optimism. The tools you will use have worked for others and they will work for you, as well. You will become more free. You will become both larger and more strong. You cannot work on your creativity without discovering a sense of play. Your imagination will take flight. You will discover creative endurance. Great goodness lies ahead of you as you tap an internal spring. Focus on the positive and begin.

Being a Beginner

It's Monday, the ides of March. The week opens with spring weather, a high in the fifties. People wear their winter coats flung open like capes. There are runners out in their shirtsleeves. Just inside the entrance to the park, there is a scattering of purple crocuses, the first spring flowers. Intoxicated by the gentle wind, the dogs sniff the earth with increased urgency. They are excited by the change in seasons. The sun unlocks smells long frozen by winter.

It is a time for beginnings. At noon today I have my piano lesson. In piano, I am an absolute beginner. I take two lessons a week and I slowly, very slowly, edge my

Even the lowliest, provided he is whole, ca be happy, and in his own way, perfect.

JOHANN WOLFGANG
von GOETHE

way forward. My teacher, Chaim Freiberg, is a tall and handsome man, kind with a graceful humor. He comes to our lessons laden with strong coffee and homemade treats. He shares a sip of coffee, a bite of some Israeli delicacy he has made for his lunch. "Are we ready?" he will ask, always starting the lesson on a personal note.

"Let us try it together," he will say as he scoots his chair next to my piano bench and makes a rich-sounding duet from my simple melody. The duets are encouraging.

Most folks are about as happy as they make up their minds to be.

ABRAHAM LINCOLN

"You are doing very well," he tells me, although to my eye, I am probably his oldest and slowest student. "Let's try it again, and that's an 'A,' " he will gently correct me.

I have been taking piano for two years now. I have a small repertoire that I can play by heart and every week I edge a bit further into new territory. Most of the piano literature is simplified classics. I will pick out a theme by Brahms or Debussy, a beautiful melody line lifted from a larger work.

"Now let's try it again," Mr. Freiberg will urge me. When I stumble, he is all patience. "This note should be just a little longer," he will say.

"You play it once so I can hear it," I will ask. My ear is still better than my eye. When he plays the theme it sounds wonderful.

Mr. Freiberg is a composer as well as a teacher. When he wants me to master a new progression, he will write a piece of music incorporating the lesson that I need. His handwritten music is sketched out on blank paper. The notes are large and clumsy. I sometimes think this makes them easier for me to find. "Lullaby for Julia" is a haunting melody with its roots, like Mr. Freiberg's himself, in Israeli culture. I play the piece and cannot believe it hasn't been played for generations. But no. It is new, freshly minted, just for me. Who could resist such a teacher?

I was fifty-four years old when I finally began taking piano lessons. All through my forties I had bought the excuse that I was too old to start something new. Then one day it occurred to me that I would age whether I knew piano or not and that I might respect myself more as the world's oldest novice than as someone who stayed blocked and yearning. I began to search for a teacher, someone who could accommodate an older student who was trying to learn just for the sake of learning not with an agenda of becoming an accomplished pianist. When I found Mr. Freiberg's ad, it mentioned that he loved Broadway as well as the classics. I did, too, and so I thought we might be a match. So far, we have proven to be just that.

"You're doing very well," Mr. Freiberg tells me. "I think you may go far." I want to believe him. Like any youngster, I hero-worship my teacher.

We are never too old to be young at heart. Being young at heart means simply being willing to be a beginner. I have a special satchel that I carry my music papers in. I keep the satchel in a particular corner near the piano. Nothing else is allowed to take its place there. I am like a kindergartener with her first school bag.

> *To win one's joy through struggle is better than to yield to melancholy.*
>
> ANDRÉ GIDE

> *Happiness sneaks in through a door you didn't know you left open.*
>
> JOHN BARRYMORE

It took courage to allow myself to pursue something that I loved. I had to allow myself the luxury of learning. I had to focus on process and not on finished product. I could not think about the distance I had to travel before I could call myself a pianist. I had to remember that I was learning to play the piano and that the word "play" was operative here.

To begin at all, I had to resign from competition. I had to stop comparing myself to my idols. My brother Christopher is a virtuoso keyboard player. I am friends with a magnificent classical pianist named Robert McDonald. When those men touch a piano it unlocks its mysteries for them. When I touch a key, it is all terra incognita.

The word "piano" means soft, and softly is how the instrument has entered my life. I can now play pieces that baffled me a year ago. Once in a while, during a lesson, I will catch myself thinking, "Oh, my God! I am actually playing this piece!" Mr. Freiberg is very low key. Sometimes on the days when I try the hardest and when my fingers are spaghetti, he will pull out some new trick, gently turning my attention to a new piece of music that he has written, something that he thinks I just might be able to master.

"We will call this one 'Variations,' " he might say and then patiently sketch in the sheet music for five variations on a simple melodic theme. "What do you think of this?" he might ask. His music always has a soothing structure. It is built to be learned from and so one progression interlocks with the next so that the piece as a whole has a pleasing, organic quality.

"I like it," I always say and I always do like it. I have a book that holds some twenty-five of his original compositions. We always begin the lesson by playing through his homemade music before we go on to more formal books.

"Today was a very good lesson," Mr. Freiberg will sometimes tell me. I have noticed how often my "good" lessons come on the days when I had the most resistance, when I felt myself to be the most rusty. As a writer, I have learned that good writing and good moods do not necessarily go together. On some of my worst days, the best work emerges. It is evidently the same with music, and this is a lesson that I tell myself to remember.

I try to show up for my lessons without an expectation of great improvement. I try to love the process that I am in: learning to play the piano. It is the learning more than the piano that matters, I tell myself. I think of my friend Julianna McCarthy. At age seventy-seven, she has recently undertaken a Master's in poetry. "How is it going?" I ask her. She deadpans back, "It's going." When something is "going," we feel the flow. We are swept up by the current of life. What, I ask myself, could be better? Nothing comes to mind.

Divining Rod

Most of us have something we know we wish to do but find ourselves procrastinating about. For me, it was piano. For you, as for me, it might be a round of lessons—beginning modern dance, life drawing, acting, Italian. It might also be a deferred personal project like a play, novel, or nonfiction book. We tell ourselves we are "too old" to undertake our fancy and, in telling ourselves this, we rob ourselves of the opportunity to be a beginner. Being a beginner is very rewarding. It brings both excitement and self-respect.

Take pen in hand. Write about your deferred dream. Choose something enticing about which you have been procrastinating. On the page, allow yourself to imagine yourself actually doing what you long to do. How does it feel? What changes do you need to make to accommodate this new growth?

After you have written for enough time to fully explore your imaginary start, move from the visionary to the practical. Do the footwork necessary to begin. If piano lessons are your goal, start looking for a teacher. Muster the courage to make phone calls. Allow yourself to explore in your own behalf. For today, all you need is the grace to begin beginning. Think—and start—very small.

Encouragement

Winter is back. Small biting flakes pour from the sky. The forecast is for snow mixed with sleet and that is exactly what we are getting. It is a good day to stay inside, but that is not what's on the agenda. Today is lunch with Bruce Pomahac, a special occasion. For the sake of seeing Bruce, I will brave the weather and head downtown. With luck I will find a cab and the cab will drive sanely. Luck is with us. We find a cab. Dodging through traffic, wipers working furiously, we wind our way down to the corner of Twenty-ninth Street and Eighth Avenue. This is the site of Birrichino's, the Italian restaurant where we rendezvous.

To fill the hour and leave no crevice . . . that is happiness.
RALPH WALDO EMERSON

The only true happiness comes from squandering ourselves for a purpose.
WILLIAM COWPER

For the better part of three years now, my musical collaborator Emma Lively and I have met with Bruce once a week for lunch. It is much more than just a shared meal. It is a time of shared dreams and aspirations. All artists need coconspirators to cheer them on in their endeavors. Bruce is such a coconspirator for us. A sparkling man with a crisp wit and ready laugh, a composer himself, he is a source of experience, strength, and hope for us. He is the music director for the Rodgers and Hammerstein Organization, which means all productions of their work must be cleared through him. It is a large and demanding job. It is also work that he loves. For us, Bruce is the keeper of the flame, not only of Rodgers and Hammerstein's work but of our own. He is a treasure trove of Broadway stories. From his vantage point, he has seen it all.

As we struggle to persevere writing our own musicals, he is always ready with a quick word of encouragement, encouragement grounded in his long years of experience. Such encouragement is priceless for any artist. Today in particular we need a dose of Bruce's astringent optimism. Three weeks ago, we put up a staged reading of *The Medium at Large*, a musical we have been working on for four years. The reading was a "backers' audition," intended to entice investors into bankrolling our work. The cast was stellar, all Broadway veterans. Despite short rehearsal time, the two performances were just short of spectacular. We hoped for someone to step forward with a checkbook.

"That was one of the two best readings I have attended in all my years in the business," Bruce assured us in the aftermath. The show had played both days to jammed houses. Backers came and went, pausing to congratulate us on their way out. Our hopes were high. For months all of our attention had been focused on "pulling it off," and now we had. We were pleased with the work we had done, more than pleased with the work our director, cast, and musical director had done. There was nothing to fault. There were no "what if's," no "if only's." We had done ourselves proud. Shouldn't that create interest?

"Now what do we do?" we wondered in the wake of the showcase.

"Now you wait for the phone to ring," we were told. After months of action on the show's behalf, this sudden halt was terrifying. There was no more going to the piano to tinker with a song. There was no more going to the computer to tinker with a scene. There was no more tinkering, period. The die was cast.

Backers would like the show or they would not. It would or would not be up their alley. One producer e-mailed us that while she had liked our show, it was not as serious as the shows she was interested in backing. Our show was a romantic ghost comedy: "Sex can be very nice/with a good poltergeist . . ." Her current shows concerned women in Bosnia and the threat of nuclear war. No, we were not a match, but she had enjoyed the show. We tried to take her e-mail in good humor, but our humor was wearing a little thin. Could we have done so much work for nothing?

> *The best things are nearest: breath in your nostrils, light in your eyes, flowers at your feet, duties at your hand, the path of God just before you. Then do not grasp at the stars, but do life's plain, common work as it comes, certain that daily duties and daily bread are the sweetest things of life.*
>
> ROBERT LOUIS STEVENSON

A backer's audition costs about $15,000, what with renting a theater, paying a director and a musical director, paying actors a stipend, printing promotional materials and programs. If someone steps forward to go ahead with the show, it is clearly money well spent. If no one steps forward, it is money spent, period. And the money spent was hard-earned.

In the face of ominous-seeming quiet, Emma and I tried to count our blessings instead of the costs. We told ourselves: we learned our show is strong; we learned the music really plays; we learned the pacing is good; we learned the book of the show is funny . . .

We practiced our optimism like a mantra but in the days following our backers' audition, Emma and I fought with depression. When the showcase was over it was so *over*. Our phone wasn't ringing. Our e-mail was silent. So many people had seemed to enjoy the show so much, surely there must be *some* interest, we told our-selves. But silence reigned.

Needing reassurance, we phoned Bruce who gently reminded us that *Oklahoma!* fell on deaf ears when Rodgers and Hammerstein auditioned it on what is often called "the penthouse circuit." Hat in hand, they played the show through fifty times without getting a dime's backing. And they were Rodgers and Hammerstein! (At the time, Rodgers was the veteran of a long and successful collaboration with Lorenz Hart. Hammerstein was the veteran of a fruitful relationship with Jerome Kern.) As a combination, Rodgers and Hammerstein, they were a new entity, but surely *someone* should have been able to hear their potential. But no one did. Why should our luck be any better? Perhaps we had just joined the club.

"You're in the same boat now with everybody else," Bruce assured us.

It did help to hear that the odds were not stacked against us in particular. It did help to hear we were part of a time-honored tradition, that getting backing for a show was always difficult. There was something refreshing about looking the difficulties squarely in the face. Knowing the worst, we felt better. There is an old wives' tale that states that from conception to completion the average length of time for a musical to ges-tate is seven years. By that standard, Emma and I were right on schedule, just past the halfway mark and looking to stay the distance. But how did people do that? How did they keep their optimism and their courage intact? We needed help.

"You're lucky you've got other projects," Bruce told us. His hint was spoken as a true artist. He was reminding us that the joy had to lie in the process and not in the product. Doing the work was the best cure for the difficulty of doing the work.

And so, we decided to do what we knew how to do and went back to work on another show, *Magellan*. The minute we were back at the piano in creative waters, our anxiety eased. Focused on our work, we forgot our recent disappointment. All that mattered was getting *Magellan* right, and we had our work cut out for us there.

And then a director called—a Tony Award–winning director.

He wondered if he could submit the script of *The Medium* to the Goodspeed Opera House, a seedbed for new musicals. Could he? *Could he?* We said he could. We knew the direc-tor's work and were excited by it. It was wonderful that he liked the show that he had seen. "He liked it! He liked it!" Emma and I exclaimed to ourselves over and over again.

Genius does what it must, talent does what it can.

EDWARD BULWER-LYTTON

So we weren't so crazy after all. The show had played as well as we thought it had. Here was the proof. We readied a packet of materials for the director to submit.

No sooner had the director called than we got a tiny nibble from a producer. Then another tiny nibble. One producer wanted a synopsis of the script. Another producer wanted a reading copy and a demo CD to show to her partner. No one was saying, "Count me in," but there was at least a glimmering of interest.

> *If we go down into ourselves, we find that we possess exactly what we desire.*
>
> SIMONE WEIL

"Just hang in there," Bruce told us now over lunch. "You are at the point where so many people get discouraged. It's good that you've got more than one project to work on. The waiting is hard. It's a tough business, a tough business." Bruce paused to break off a crust of Italian bread. His sympathy was hard-edged. His very presence constantly reminded us that we had to be in the business for the long haul.

Outside the restaurant window, the storm continued to rage. The snow and sleet were now egged on by a nasty wind. Bruce, Emma, and I all ordered steaming bowls of split pea soup. I got a side order of homemade sausages.

"What do we do now?" I asked Bruce, although I thought I knew the answer.

"You keep the faith," he answered. "You keep the faith." With that he ladled up a sip of soup. I tried my own. It was hot and good. Suddenly the storm seemed less threatening. The day seemed less bleak. Thanks to Bruce, our optimism rallied. Perhaps we could keep the faith. Perhaps our backers' audition had not been in vain.

Divining Rod

Take pen in hand and make a list of people you can go to for encouragement. These people are your "believing mirrors." They may not be artists themselves and they need not be. What they must be is optimistic, believers in the essential goodness of life. You are a part of what they believe in. They reflect back to you your competency and potential. They are on your side and bring to your discussions a sense of optimism and hope. You owe it to yourself to be in regular contact with these individuals. Some of the names on your list may be people with whom you have fallen out of contact. Pick up the telephone. Drop them a call or a line. Tag base with your believing mirrors. You may wish to tell them that you have undertaken work with this book and that they can expect to be hearing from you more regularly.

Focusing

Last night, I taught down in SoHo. The students handed me index cards, recording just what they had done for their Artist Date this week. "I went to see the Chuck Close exhibit at the Met." "I went to a trim store in the fabric district." "I went to my very first yoga class." The Manhattan revealed through their index cards is rich and varied. "I went to a samurai movie." "I went to a children's magic show without a child to accompany me." "I went to the Twenty-eighth Street flower market." "I went to see *The Producers*." Teaching a class in Manhattan gives me the flavor of Manhattan, a glimpse of the many lives it is possible to lead here.

But I am living one life in particular, and that life must be fully inhabited for me to thrive as an artist. Sometimes, it is difficult for me to commit to my Manhattan life. I miss New Mexico with its purple folded mountains, its vast savannahs of silvery-green sage. I miss the scent of pinion on the wind. I miss the canyons populated by fir trees.

> *A musician must make music, an artist must paint, a poet must write, if he is to be at peace with himself. What a man can be, he must be.*
>
> ABRAHAM MASLOW

> *The thing about performance, even if it's only an illusion, is that it is a celebration of the fact that we do contain within ourselves infinite possibilities.*
>
> DANIEL DAY-LEWIS

In Manhattan, the canyons are made from concrete. They are beautiful, but I must train myself to see their beauty. Last night on the way down to class, the cab passed through Greenwich Village. It was snowing and from the taxi window, I spotted a crowded flower stand at a corner Korean grocer's. Through the silvery snow, the flowers flared bright with unexpected intensity.

"Look how beautiful," my companion breathed. And beautiful it was—if I took the time to see it. I had to force myself to focus. I had to take myself by the nape of the neck and give myself a mental shake. "There! Look at that!"

As an artist, I must take the time to see. My artist's eye must be schooled in the particular. It is not healthy for me as an artist to be tuned to the inner movie, always watching the "what if, if only I had's" as they unspool on the inner screen. ("What if I'd kept my ranch in New Mexico?" "If only I still had my horses.")

"What if" and "if only" are poison for any artist. They throw us into the past. They dull our lens on the passing world. And it is in the passing world that inspiration lies in wait for us. For an artist to be vital, for the work to hold up, there must be primacy given to the here and now. I know this but lately must work to practice it. If I live in the "then" instead of in the "now," the art dries up. My writing loses its snap and vigor. It becomes vague and generic. I do not see the bucket of jonquils, flaring like struck gold through the wet city night.

> No bird soars too high if he soars with his own wings.
>
> WILLIAM BLAKE

Lately, the inner movie has been compelling me. I have felt an undertow pulling me out of my daily life and into a twilight world of fears and regrets. I have had trouble holding on to my optimism. I have felt myself slipping away from the life I have now and into a half world of the life I might have had, if only . . . If only I had chosen differently . . . If only I had chosen better . . .

I worry that this is the knife edge of depression beginning. It frightens me as I feel my mind starting to skip toward the cliffedge. My family has a history of depression. My father was hospitalized many times for manic depression. My mother was hospitalized for depression, period. They were fragile, gifted people and I sometimes feel that my legacy from them is both their fragility and their gifts. I must work to husband my own optimism. I must cling to the small and positive: walking the dogs, putting words to the page, taking time at the keys. I must not entertain the large and overwhelming. For me that is romancing trouble.

A veteran myself of three breakdowns, I have had to learn to live each day very carefully. I must write. I must walk. I must pray. I must content myself with small amounts of progress. Above all, I must not binge on drama and despair. That was what I did during my black, drinking twenties. Now I am a sober alcoholic. My sobriety and my sanity require daily maintenance. For me, self-pity is the rim of the glass. I cannot afford to think, "Poor me, poor me." It leads to "Pour me a drink."

Divining Rod

We can choose to focus on the positive or on the negative. We can choose to see the beautiful or the ugly. We speak of "training our eyes" on something and that is a literal phrase. Our eyes can be trained to focus on those areas of life that reward us with grace and beauty.

Take pen in hand. Number from one to five. Make a list of five beautiful things you have recently spotted. For example, the little white dog coming into your building. The Harlequin Great Dane going out. The stargazer lilies at the Korean grocer's. The golden yellow gingko tree midway down your block. The crescent moon rising over the skyline. Each day yields beauties enough for a short list. You may wish to make writing this list a nightly practice.

Grounding

It is a starry night. Even in Manhattan where the lights from skyscrapers compete with the sky, the stars tonight are clearly visible, drawing the earth to scale. In Manhattan, my apartment is one set of lights amid millions. In the galaxy, Manhattan is just a sprinkling of lights on something known as planet Earth. It is all a matter of perspective. Seated at my writing desk, looking out at the glittering lights, I strive for a sense of optimism, a feeling that as small as I am, what I am doing still matters in the scheme of things.

> *Boredom is not an end-product. It is comparatively rather an early stage in life and art.*
>
> F. SCOTT FITZGERALD

Optimism is partially the happy accident of psychodynamics and partially a trained response. Some people seem to be born optimists. The rest of us need to work at it a little. One way I work at my optimism is by talking with my friend Larry Lonergan. Larry is a spiritualist medium. He lives with one foot in this world and one foot in the next. It is from Spirit and a carefully maintained spiritual practice that Larry garners his optimistic bent. When I need to feel better, I dial Larry's number for a dose of optimism. His is a farseeing perspective. He always holds the long view.

"You are on the verge," Larry told me just this afternoon. "There are many things pending. You just need to keep the faith while things unfold." Unfortunately, Spirit is vague about timing. "They say it will be 'soon' but they do not tell me what 'soon' means," Larry said ruefully. He sounded a little guilty that the other side wasn't more forthcoming. Still, "soon" means something. It is the encouragement I need today.

What "soon" means to me is to keep on trying. Don't quit right before the miracle. Show up at the page. Show up at the keys. Bite the bullet and focus. I have *Magellan,* the opera I am working on that needs more attention. I need to listen to it and flesh it out with more music where it is needed. If I go to the keys, music will come to meet me there. I simply must be willing to go to the keys.

I cannot give up just because the going is tough right now. "Soon" there will be more interest. I must be ready to receive that interest by having kept the faith myself. This means I must buck the tide of discouragement. I must see my fifty-eight years as years of valuable experience, not merely "age." This perspective can be tricky to maintain.

Ours is a youth-oriented culture. We are trained by television and the media to focus on those who are young. Our pop stars are youngsters. Their fortunes are immense and their futures bright. We do not read much or hear much about life in the arts for older people. We do not have many role models for doing what we must do—and that is persevere.

> *Babies are necessary to grownups. A new baby is like the beginning of all things— wonder, hope, a dream of possibilities . . . Babies are almost the only remaining link with nature, with the natural world of living things from which we spring.*
>
> EDA J. LESHAN

I am friends with a pianist who is midstride on what promises to be a long and brilliant career. Now in his fifties, he finds the traveling side of touring more grueling than it once was. He still tours and tours widely, but he husbands his energies more carefully than he did in his twenties, thirties, and forties. When jet lag strikes, he tells himself, "This is just chemical. You don't really hate your life." As a mature artist, long accustomed to the public eye, he has learned to talk to himself in private. Feeling overwhelmed or beset, he lectures himself, "Don't be a hothead. Don't overreact. Is this really worth your getting upset about it?" What he is telling himself, in many forms, is "Consider the big picture. Take the longer view." When I speak with him, he tells me to do the same thing.

If we have some spiritual underpinnings, it is easier to take the longer view. Meditation gives us the sense of something larger and other than ourselves. My pianist friend both runs and swims, two forms of active meditation. He also puts in long hours at the keyboard, hours when he is connected to higher realms. Myself,

I walk for Guidance. Additionally, Morning Pages give me a connection to the divine and a connection, too, to what might be called "divine intention," a sort of overarching benevolence that I count on when the going gets rough.

One thing that I didn't anticipate when I was younger is how often the going gets rough. As an older artist, I tend to work on larger projects, projects that require years rather than months or weeks to germinate and come to fruition. There is no instant feedback loop. Nothing that says to me often and loudly, "You are doing fine." In order to have that sense of reassurance, I need to work at a spiritual practice—my Morning Pages, my Artist Dates, and my walks—and I must listen also to my friends. I call Bruce or I call my friend the pianist. I can piggyback on their faith when my own faith wears thin. And my faith does wear thin.

With the best of intentions and the most diligent of practices, it still wears thin. Fatigue can make it hard to have faith. Too much busyness can make it hard to have faith. Too much or too little solitude can impact faith. For that matter, so can a bout of hunger or overwork, anything carried to an extreme. Faith thrives on routine. Look at any monastery and you will see that. Faith keeps on keeping on.

Right now, my sister Libby is my walking exemplar of faith. She is an animal portrait artist and she has been suffering for nearly a year from an injured painting arm. The injury occurred when she was shied into by a startled horse. The horse was frightened by the sight of a large standard poodle wearing a snow-white ruff because he himself had been injured. My sister doesn't blame the horse for being spooked or the poodle for looking spooky, but she estimates that a thousand pounds of pressure was suddenly thrown onto her arm. Blinded by fear, the horse charged directly into her, catching her arm at a skew angle.

Great art is the outward expression of an inner life in the artist, and this inner life will result in his personal vision of the world. No amount of skillful invention can replace the essential element of imagination.

EDWARD HOPPER

"I thought my arm was broken," she recalls. "It hurt so badly." She had it x-rayed immediately. An injury to her painting arm, after all, was an injury to her livelihood. The elbow seemed to be the center of trouble. She was put on ibuprofen and sent to physical therapy. A year of treatment followed and none of it truly helped. Whenever she painted for more than a few minutes, her arm would start to throb. She tried working with a sling. She tried bracing her arm. There were days when she could barely hold a brush.

Because her income depended on her ability to paint, there were many days when she fought panic. "I tell myself it's one day at a time," she would phone and tell me then. I could hear the anxiety eddying in her voice. "So I'll paint just a little today and then I'll let the arm rest."

Finally, on the advice of an older friend, she went to a chiropractor who told her it was not her elbow that was injured at all but her shoulder where the pain originated. The shoulder was dislocated. It had "separated" from its proper position. The chiropractor manipulated the shoulder back into alignment, which helped considerably—but not enough. A rotator cuff may be torn. Libby is now waiting for the results of a belated MRI. "I am good for about a half hour now," she says.

It is art that makes life, makes interest, makes importance . . . And I know of no substitute whatever for the force and beauty of its process.

HENRY JAMES

Accustomed to long days at the easel, a half hour seems barely enough time to get started, and yet she has managed to keep painting at the altered pace. She works on her commissions daily, a tiny piece at a time, but work she does and the commissions, somehow, get finished, although her daily fear is that they won't.

Suddenly saddled with abundant free time and nothing but nerves to fill it with, she has also turned to the page and begun writing a book. "I had to do something with my creative energy or it was going to turn in on me," she says. "I don't know what will come of the book but at least I have done something productive."

The doing of something productive regardless of the outcome is an act of faith. The doing of a small something when a large something is too much for us is perhaps especially an act of faith. Faith means going forward by whatever means we can.

"Just do the next right thing," twelve-step programs advise their members. Their advice is good advice for the artist. For the alcoholic, sobriety is achieved one day at a time. For the artist, so is a creative career. My sister edges forward on a portrait today. That is all she can do and all that she needs to do. The slogan "Easy does it" applies as much to her as it does to someone battling the bottle a day at a time.

A new moon is rising. It is a thin sliver of hopefulness. They say the new moon blesses beginnings. I believe that. From her studio window in Racine, Wisconsin, my sister spies the moon. It washes her hay field with silver. That same moon rises over Manhattan. I see it above the roofs of brownstones. I call my sister.

"Just keep on keeping on," I tell both my sister and myself as I face the blank page and she faces the blank easel. As the sickle moon peers in her studio window, my sister readies a canvas for the start of a new portrait. She keeps the faith.

Divining Rod

The smallest and gentlest acts keep us grounded. As we husband our lives with care and attention, we are rewarded with feelings of peace and accomplishment. What actions keep you grounded? Morning Pages may be one such action—as is making your bed. Making a nightly list of daily beauties may help to ground you—as does regularly opening all of your mail. It may help you to pick up scattered clothes or to do your mending. You may get grounded, as I do, by a phone call to your sister or another believing mirror. Doing all the dishes and leaving yourself nightly with a clean sink may be yet another source of grounding and self-esteem. Some people love to vacuum. Take pen in hand and list five homely actions that are grounding for you. Execute one of them.

Possibilities

Right now, although snow still blankets the ground of Central Park, golden crocuses have joined the purple ones in popping into bloom. Sheltered by a stone wall, the particolored flowers push upward through the snow. "Welcome to the Park," they seem to say. "Welcome to spring."

Twenty feet further on, a forsythia bush flares brightly, bursting into bud. Despite the chill air, green-gold rosettes garland its branches. Very soon there will be yellow blossoms, the golden bushes lighting the park like bonfires, signaling "spring." Even now, four plump-breasted robins hop

Art is the sex of the imagination.

GEORGE JEAN NATHAN

No one should drive a hard bargain with an artist.

LUDWIG VAN BEETHOVEN

through the snow, picking for tidbits beneath the frozen crust. Robins, too, mean spring, despite the appearance of winter.

Today I am bundled into an oversized coat. With my layer upon layer, I am a little too warm—and I look like someone out of *Doctor Zhivago*. I have the two dogs with me, straining at their leashes, and they, too, are bundled into coats. While I admire the early flowers, Tiger Lily plunges in pursuit of a robin. I laugh and tell myself she is a perfect artist's dog, always chasing something that is just out of reach—a possibility.

This morning, I spent my own time chasing an opera. I hear the music to *Magellan* in my head and I see the production of it in my mind's eye. Yet I must labor to bring what I see and what I hear into concrete notes on a page. I have been sketching in *Magellan* for nearly six years now, adding this sprig of melody, this scrap of lyric. Magellan's journey was large and grand. I am striving to make something to match it but I must work a little at a time, always laboring to bring into form something just beyond my reach. I am like Tiger Lily, leaping after that elusive bird. One day, I will catch it. At the least, I will certainly try.

As artists, we must learn to try. We must learn to act affirmatively. We must learn to act as though spring is at hand—because it is. We are the spring that we are waiting for. Wherever creativity is afoot, so is a blossoming. All creative acts are acts of initiative. Whether we are playing a concerto, perfecting a plié, scribing a novel or sketching a sketch, we start with nothing—"the verdant void"—and impregnate it with our own creative spark. Art is born, but not without labor on our part.

In order to make art, we must be willing to labor. We must be willing to reach inside and draw forth what we find there. On an inner plane, we are all connected to a larger whole. This is what is meant by inspiration, this connection to something greater than ourselves. But it begins with where we are and what we are. It begins with possibility.

> *An artist is someone who turns his coat inside out and falls in love with the color of the lining.*
>
> JEANNE TARDIVEAU

Honesty is the starting off point of possibility. Honesty begins with specificity. I am typing at a small Chinese lacquer desk, looking north out a large window to a view of Manhattan. I am on the eleventh floor and my view overlooks the tops of many town houses. If I edge to the left of my desk, I can look out across Central Park. I can see across the reservoir rimmed by cherry trees that will soon be a pale pink froth as the season turns. For tonight, though, the park looms dark. Yesterday's snow has melted. Now I am left with ink-black branches. Soon they will be leafy green, but not yet. For tonight, the trees resemble line drawings of trees.

Looking due north out my writing window, I stare across the tops of town houses and into the flanks of two large skyscrapers. The skyscrapers feature large, square windows. I can watch the blue-gray flickering light of television streaming from many of them. On my desk, I keep a pair of birding binoculars. I could train them on my neighbors if I were so inclined. I do not do it. Spying on a neighbor raises the possibility that a neighbor could be spying on me. That is a thought I prefer to avoid— but it is possible. Entertaining the possible is the province of art. It is the possible that sets the creative engine humming.

There are only two ways to live your life. One is as though nothing is a miracle. The other is as though everything is a miracle.

ALBERT EINSTEIN

"It is possible," the artist thinks, "that I can write a play."

"It is possible I can make a sculpture."

"It is possible I can make a film."

Out of the notion, "I can" comes the next thought: "I think I will." The impulse is playful. It doesn't consider the odds. It is an impulse born of pure faith. The artist has a vision and that vision includes the successful completion of the art he has in mind. An artist is like a lover who cannot pause to entertain the possibility of being spurned. He must press his suit. His whole impulse is to love.

Like the crocus that pushes into spring willy-nilly, the artist also pushes forward into growth. The crocus lies beneath the snow waiting for the slightest touch of warmth to spring forth. Like the crocus, the artist does not pause to ask if his work is timely or welcome. Critical reception will perhaps be chilly like an unseasonal snow but, like the crocus, the artist survives.

Divining Rod

Very often we are our own wet blanket. We do not allow ourselves to see and to seize our opportunities. The following exercise is designed to catch you off guard and allow you to see your "coulds" rather than your "shoulds."

Take pen in hand and number from one to ten. Use the phrase, "I could try _____" and fill in the blank with whatever comes to mind. For example, "I could try writing poems again" or "I could try practicing Italian every night for half an hour." Write very rapidly and do not concern yourself with the practicality of your responses.

CHECK-IN

1. **How many days this week did you do your Morning Pages?** If you skipped a day, why did you skip it? How was the experience of writing them for you? Are you experiencing more clarity? A wider range of emotions? A greater sense of detachment, purpose, and calm? Did anything surprise you? Is there a "repeating" issue asking to be dealt with?

2. **Did you do your Artist Date this week?** Did you note an improved sense of well-being? What did you do and how did it feel? Remember, Artist Dates can be difficult and you may need to coax yourself into taking them.

3. **Did you get out on your Weekly Walk?** How did that feel? What emotions or insights surfaced for you? Were you able to walk more than once? What did your walk do for your optimism and sense of perspective?

4. **Were there any other issues this week that felt significant to you in your self-discovery?** Describe them.

Uncovering a Sense of Reality

As you explore your inner world, your outer world will come more sharply into focus. As you face your imagined barriers, you will encounter real ones, as well. This week's work will help you to become more grounded and farseeing. As you seek your own internal support, as well as the support of friends, your creativity will become more steady. As you undertake small actions on your own behalf—watering the garden, as it were—larger actions will seem more possible. A sense of your own power will return to you.

Claustrophobia

A fierce wind rattles the windows. The sky is a glowering gray. The clouds move across the heavens in fast forward. It is bitter cold again, a day to stay inside. It is a day that invites claustrophobia.

> *Action may not always bring happiness, but there is no happiness without action.*
>
> WILLIAM JAMES

So much of an artist's career hinges on the sense that we are going somewhere, that we are not just trapped by the four walls of wherever we are. For creative sanity, I must believe that if I just do the next right thing, a path will unfold for me. I must believe there is a divine plan for me and my work.

As an artist, I must believe in higher forces, sources of inspiration, movements of destiny. I must believe in something larger and wiser than myself. Some artists believe in God. Others believe in Art. No matter what we call it, a belief in it is necessary for our sheer artistic survival.

If I believe my writing is leading me somewhere—somewhere beyond what I can see—then I can endure the cabin fever of a day like today. If there is enough of a sense of adventure in the work itself then I do not need to plunge into the outdoors seeking the feeling of an adventure. And so, I must turn to the page. I must find my adventure within my own creative consciousness. I must keep the drama to the page.

Today I received a phone call from a young writer. It was the third call I've had from her in so many days. Each day, she has called in with some new misadventure. Her friends are misbehaving. Life itself seems to be misbehaving. Things have not been going her way, and she blames the stress in her life for her not settling down to work. I know how she feels, but I am also growing suspicious.

Trouble is only opportunity in workclothes.

HENRY J. KAISER

Artists love drama and when we do not create it on the page or on the stage, we often create it in our lives. It is my suspicion that the young writer's life will stay stressful and dramatic until she decides to go back to work. Once she is working, the drama will settle down.

"But you don't understand," I can hear her wailing at me.

I understand all too clearly. How many valuable writing hours have I myself wasted on drama? Focused on things that were out of my control, I failed to use the power that I did have, the power to create. It is the voice of my own experience that says to me that when too many people start behaving too badly, I probably am just not working hard enough. Over the years, I have ruefully noticed that when I am on track in my writing, everyone seems to behave much better.

We hear so often that the artist's temperament is restless, irritable, and discontented. All of that is very true—when we are not working. Let us get in a good day at the page or the easel and we are suddenly sunny and user-friendly. It is the blocked artist who is such a study in malcontent. Artists have an itch that nothing can scratch except work.

"But I can't work. I am too upset," the young writer tells me. I know how she feels but I also know that if she would just start working, her life would settle down and with it her emotions. "You don't understand how they are treating me," the young writer insists. "They're really acting terrible."

What I understand is that she is not working and that she is prickly. Most of the time her friends behave very well. Most of the time she is able to allow them to behave as they need to. It is only when she is not working that her friends develop mysterious ticks and flaws. It is only when she is not working that her normally very nice boyfriend suddenly becomes the monster. It is when her mind is not on her work that it is so closely focused on the workings of everyone else's personality. Her own personality is what is on tilt, but she can't see that.

"You think everything comes down to work," she accuses me.

"I think a lot does."

"You'd be upset, too," the young writer tells me.

I listen to her and I believe her. Drama is contagious. Already I am wanting her friends to shape up and fly right. I am wanting her life to become easier. Listening to her woes, I am becoming upset. I want to "fix" things for her. It takes me a moment to realize that nothing probably needs fixing.

> *It is not irritating to be where one is. It is only irritating to think one would like to be somewhere else.*
>
> JOHN CAGE

Everything will fall into perspective if she simply gets to the page. In the meanwhile, I can simply get to the page. Clad in a pair of red plaid pajamas, I settle in at my writing desk. The day is claustrophobic but the adventure of writing is not.

Divining Rod

Often we are restless, irritable, and discontent because we are not cherishing the life we have. Any life—and I mean any—has some things in it that are well worth noticing and appreciating.

Take pen in hand. Number from one to ten. List ten things that you can cherish in the life you've actually got. An example might be, "I cherish my good views from this apartment," or "I cherish my proximity to good walking trails," or "I cherish the amount of sunlight I get in my bedroom." What you cherish may surprise you. (You might not cherish what you think you "should.") Allow yourself to be as whimsical as the Spirit moves you to be.

Inhabiting the Present

The day is cold and crisp. The flowers in Central Park shiver in the chill. We are back to winter again although now we are nearing April and such throwbacks are increasingly rare. A wicked wind nips at the windows. I am suffering a throwback of my own right now. I have received a writing packet from my sister Libby. The packet is an excerpt from the book she is writing. It details her first trip to Europe two decades ago. She includes many letters that she sent to me then and I realize now, reading, that she was writing to me when my daughter, Domenica, was still just a seven-year-old. The past tears at my heart.

Art is not to be taught in academies. It is what one looks at, not what one listens to, that makes the artist. The real schools should be the streets.

OSCAR WILDE

Man is always more than he can know of himself; consequently his accomplishments, time and again, will come as a surprise to him.

GOLO MANN

Scanning the letters, I see my daughter when she reached just to my hip pocket. I remember our catch phrase for when we needed to cross a street or go somewhere else that was dangerous: "On your mother's hip," I would tell her. In the letters, my sister is in Italy. She sees many beautiful brown-eyed children and their chocolate eyes remind her of Domenica. As she writes to me, I am living still in the Hollywood Hills. I own a silken black horse named Jazz. I am young and wild. The me that Libby writes to still exists, caught now in the body of a fifty-eight-year-old woman. Oh, the past was sweet.

I am on dangerous ground. My mind wants to gild my memories. It wants to present the past in soft focus, as muzzy and sentimental as a greeting card. It doesn't want to remember the long days spent drinking, the dangerous twilight rides, jumping my horse while drunk. My mind wants to remember chilled white wine and elegant dinner parties, not the scotch, neat, burning its way into my system every morning. No, I cannot afford to romance my past. It does not serve me. To stay emotionally sober, I must focus the lens of my perceptions clearly on the now. This is what serves me both as a person and as an artist.

In order to function well as an artist, I must love the present. I must function in the present, savoring the sweet that is to be found there. I must put the Hollywood Hills far behind me. I live on a different coast in a different time. I must be able to look out my writing-room window and cherish the current view: red brick town houses, roof gardens, the backs of apartment buildings with their fire escapes clinging to their flanks. Pigeons flock along the roof lines but far above them I must note the highsoaring sea gulls—Manhattan is a seaport, after all. And what's this? A shuffling at my feet. I must smile at the dogs coming in to disturb my work, reminding me that we have yet to go to the park today. "What about us?" the dogs insist. "Forget the past."

Every man feels instinctively that all the beautiful sentiments in the world weigh less than a single lovely action.

JAMES RUSSELL LOWELL

The present is complicated enough. Putting aside my sister's book, I must be able to field the phone call from my daughter, now twenty-nine. She hopes she is not interrupting my writing. With excitement, she tells me that she has been offered a parttime job training horses and that she thinks she may take it, needing something positive to do besides wait for the next audition. My daughter, an actress-writer-director, now lives near the Hollywood Hills. She rides a mustang through the high canyons. She traces the very trails I used to ride with Jazz.

Divining Rod

We need to fall in love with ourselves. One of the best ways to do this is to view yourself as a character, one you are fascinated by. If you observe yourself closely enough, you are very interesting. Think of the Brontës' novels about "ordinary" people. With this tool, you will become your own biographer.

Take pen in hand. Set aside about a half hour's writing time. You are going to write about yourself in the third person. Do not write, "I am fifty-six years old and I live in New York." Instead, write, "She/he is fifty-six years old and lives in New York." Sketch in your life and your surroundings exactly as they are just now. Talk about what you love and what you hate. Talk about what you want more of and what you want less of. Place yourself smack in the middle of life and describe that life in succulent detail. "She lives in a spacious apartment high above the city. Once an eagle came to roost on her eleventh-story balcony . . ."

Staying in Training

In ten days, I am leaving for Paris. I will be there for one week and in order to prepare myself, I am studying French, which I haven't spoken in nearly forty years. Every day, for an hour, Emma and I park ourselves on matching leather couches and scowl intently as we repeat the cues from an audiolingual learning program. "*Bonjour, Madame. Bonjour, Monsieur.*" We learn how to ask directions to our hotel, how to accept a dinner date, how to order wine and beer. I keep waiting for the part of the program where the speaker orders a Perrier or a coffee. Instead, I am tutored in how to dicker about prices. "*Onze euros? C'est trop cher.*" Emma and I have yet to do our French today. With luck, we will get to it in late afternoon, settled in on our couches as the sun sets outside the window. With luck, the lesson will seem sweet to me. Making art has taught me that the tiniest smidgen of progress is something to be savored.

> There are as many kinds of beauty as there are habitual ways of seeking happiness.
>
> CHARLES BAUDELAIRE

> Beauty is an ecstasy; it is as simple as hunger.
>
> W. SOMERSET MAUGHAM

As an artist, I must cherish each tiny bit of track as I am able to lay it down. Two pages further on the book? Very good. Two phone calls made on behalf of the musical? Also good. I must scan the horizon for the next right thing and do that thing, however tiny it may seem. A career must be husbanded. Care must be taken. Every day must bring some small bit of progress. How would an artist with any self-worth act? Act that way. Tonight I am traveling to the East Village to hear two singers do a cabaret. The singers, a male and female duo, are friends of mine and I want to support them. They are both Broadway stars and the evening's work will not advance them a notch, but it has allowed them to fill their days with something productive, something done for sheer love. He is about to do a show at Lincoln Center. She is about to head off to Europe as the lead in a new musical. The evening's program, romantic duets, will showcase sides of themselves that are not currently at play. I will make the trek to hear them sing so they will know I am voting in favor of their dreams.

It is all too easy as an artist to allow the shape of our career to be dictated to us by others. We can so easily wait to be chosen. Such passivity invites despair. To remain healthy and vital, artists must stay proactive in their own behalf. Writers must write for the love of writing and not merely, or only, to fulfill a book contract. Actors must consciously choose ways to keep acting when they are not winning auditions. Singers must find ways to sing in between Broadway parts.

Artists are very much like athletes. As an artist, I must be alert to keeping myself in effective training. Like a creative triathlete, I must take care to be well-rounded. I must take stock of my talents and take the time and care to try to use them fully. This is what my musical friends are doing. This is what I myself must do.

Just at the moment, I am writing nonfiction. It is a very particular kind of writing and to do it I must be alert in very precise ways. I must constantly tune into my environment in a very grounded and factual way. Nonfiction writing requires the "grit" of facts. Specificity in all forms is very helpful but it also produces a kind of emotional myopia. As a balance, I am also listening to opera, which is headier and more romantic and expansive. Opera allows my dreamer to step front and center. On a day when I allow myself to move between the two forms, I feel more balanced. Too much nonfiction and I feel I have my nose to the grindstone. Too much opera and I fear that I will simply drift away from life as I know it. Mixing the two, taking small steps forward in each, I find harmony, even optimism.

It's late afternoon. A nippy wind tugs at the windows. There is a window in the living room that can be kept shut only when tied with a ribbon. Even at that, the cold air leaks in and the ribbon flutters in the draft. It is sunset. Time to begin the day's French. Emma and I settle in to concentrate. *"Bonsoir, Madame."* The window creaks open. The phone shrills. It is my sister Libby with very good news about her injured arm. Her MRI has given her a fresh diagnosis. "I am doing the happy dance," she says. "What is wrong with me is just bursitis, not a torn rotator cuff. It can and will be fixed."

"Très bien, Libby," I tell her. She will soon be back to more hours at the easel.

"Très bien," she replies, laughing.

> *If poetry is like an orgasm, an academic can be likened to someone who studies the passion stains on the bedsheets.*
>
> IRVING LAYTON

> *Art is an experience, not the formulation of a problem.*
>
> LINDSAY ANDERSON

> *Art for art's sake . . . It is the best evidence we can have of our dignity.*
>
> E. M. FORSTER

Divining Rod

It is all too easy as an artist to bewail the "odds stacked against us." It is harder—but necessary—to improve those odds by taking small actions in our own behalf. This is the power of perseverance, what I call "laying track." No matter how trapped we may feel by large cultural crosscurrents, there is always some small something that we can do in favor of our artist.

Take pen in hand. Number from one to five and list five small actions you could take on your own behalf. Any small action will suffice. For example, in preparation for my French trip, I can "Work with French tapes one hour daily." I can "Buy a small French-English dictionary." I can "Buy a guide-book to Paris." Such small actions can add up to a large sense of optimism. From your list, take one forward-moving action.

Perfectionism

Were I called on to define very briefly the term art, I should call it "the reproduction of what the senses perceive in nature through the veil of the soul."

EDGAR ALLAN POE

Art is a private thing. The artist makes it for himself.

TRISTAN TZARA

We have been graced with another spring day. The sky is a luminous blue. The breeze is fresh. The forsythia in the park edge closer to full bloom. The dogs are ecstatic. So many smells. So much adventure. It does not take much to make them happy.

I am a more difficult case. I would be happy, if only . . . Regret still plucks at my sleeve. I must work to muster optimism. What is the "next right thing"? I ask myself. Ah, yes.

Today is a teaching day for me, which means that I begin the day by reviewing the lesson that I will be teaching tonight. This week's work centers on perfectionism and the crippling impact it can have on our creativity. As always, reviewing the work, I see that I have not really grown beyond the lesson at hand. Creativity is a spiral path;

we pass through the same issues over and over again at slightly differing altitudes. I have written twenty books, some more easily than others. My own perfectionism is not banished, just disguised. Now I call it "having standards."

I recently threw away two hundred pages of work, judging it simply "not good enough." Perhaps with more patience, the work could have been improved. Perhaps with more self-forgiveness, the work could have been seen as promising. But perfectionism is not patient, not self-forgiving. It is self-castigating. It is loveless. It allows the critic in us to have ascendancy and the final say. My critic has been ruling the roost lately.

At the moment, I grapple with my critic on a daily basis. It makes it difficult to write. Because he is such a permanent fixture in my creative pantheon, I have named my critic. He is called "Nigel." In my mind's eye, he is a gay man with impossibly high aesthetic standards. My work is never good enough for Nigel. He is always ready with a red pencil. According to Nigel, who has never been known to say anything nice, it is the critic's job to be critical.

An artist must be a reactionary. He has to stand out against the tenor of the age and not go flopping along.

EVELYN WAUGH

The artist is extremely lucky who is presented with the worst possible ordeal which will not actually kill him. At that point he is in business.

JOHN BARRYMORE

"A critic is critical," Nigel assures me. He wants to get his hands on all of my work—and the sooner the better, in his opinion, if not mine. Perhaps all creators have their Nigels. Perhaps everyone's Nigel feels they don't quite measure up.

Like my Nigel, everyone's critic has doubts, second thoughts, third thoughts. The critic analyzes everything to the point of extinction. Everything must always be groomed and manicured. Everything must measure up to some mysterious and elusive standard.

The critic lacks generosity. It's in a hurry to reach final draft, polished form. It does not want to wait and see where a thought is going. Forget first drafts. Forget the charming roundabout. It prefers dull declarative sentences. The critic loves logic and it fears inspiration.

I sometimes think of the critic as a character left over from caveman times, times concerned with sheer survival. The critic hunches at the edge of the clearing and watches for dangerous intruders. If we send in an original thought, that thought is often shooed away. To the critic, an original thought may appear disturbing, even dangerous. It wants to see what it has seen before. It has seen a cow but it has never seen a zebra. Don't try to tell it that a zebra might be interesting. Those stripes don't look like such a good idea. Get those zebras out of here! Give us some nice, docile cows for our creative clearing. That's more to the critic's liking.

To the critic, ease feels foreign—and suspicious. Work should be work, shouldn't it? Surely nothing can simply flow? Damn the colloquial! Every thought, each sentence, must be carefully weighed. Nothing can begin without knowing the ending. There is no room for exploration, for ambiguity. The critic is a nervous man. The critic likes known routes.

> *The artistic temperament is a disease that affects amateurs.*
>
> G. K. CHESTERTON

The critic believes in product, not process. Do not try to simply rough something in. Forget sketching. That's not good enough. The critic does not like us to have the joy of creation. It is interested in fixing things, not in creating things. It insists there must always be something to fix.

I have recently been rereading Dorothea Brande's excellent book, *Becoming a Writer.* She carefully distinguishes between two functions of the writer, the creative impulse and the critical one. She believes these two functions must be taught to work independently. It is her belief that the critic can be trained to stand aside, that we can learn to write freely and then to invite our critic in for the second draft process when its discernment may prove valuable.

In order to train the two separate functions, she recommends a practice of early morning writing. (She does not call this practice "Morning Pages" and I knew nothing of her theories when I myself devised Morning Pages as a creative practice.) Like mine, her morning writing cannot be done "wrong." The critic's vote does not count. From this the critic learns that it must sometimes stand aside, that it will not be allowed to strangle the embryonic art as it struggles to emerge.

I do believe that Morning Pages can train the critic to stand aside. I believe that our critic can be trained and tamed—just not permanently. I myself have enjoyed long periods where Nigel was largely silent and I was free to do my first-draft work. Such periods are blissful. Such periods have always been interrupted, however, because the critic is patient. It is cunning, baffling, and powerful. It is never permanently paralyzed. It will wait until we are tired, until we let down our guard. It will wait until it senses some weakness and then it will one more time insist that it should have the upper hand. "I am not so sure this is any good," the critic will weigh in. It seems only reasonable to consider the doubt that it raises. And that first doubt leads to another and another.

My friend Julianna McCarthy, a consummate actress, asserts that for artists it is lethal to pick up the first doubt. The critic will tempt us to drink of this poison. The critic likes us crippled and dependent. It likes to hoard its power and lord it over us. Rarely does the critic offer us constructive criticism. The critic is a black-and-white thinker. Our work isn't flawed or improvable. It is terrible. Condemnation is the critic's stock in trade.

> *The first prerogative of an artist in any medium is to make a fool of himself.*
>
> PAULINE KAEL

I am thinking now of the last time I taught perfectionism—or rather, how to avoid it. I was greeted at the start of the class by a nervous young woman. She wanted just a moment for a word with me. She looked tormented.

> *Everyone needs to work. Even a lion cannot sleep, expecting a deer to enter his mouth.*
>
> HITOPADESHA

"I think I may have done something really wrong," she told me. "I am a jazz pianist. For my Artist Date this week, I decided to take myself to a jam session. I got there and when I heard the first man play, I thought, 'This is impossible. He's so good. I will never be as good as he is.' I just sat slumped in my chair, defeated. I suppose I could have tried to get up and play something but I really felt like, 'Oh, what's the use?' I just slunk home. What was the matter with me, do you think?"

"I think you suffered a bout of perfectionism," I told her. "You took your critic with you on that date."

"Yes, I suppose I did."

"I think you listened to your critic and raised the jumps too high too fast."

"I think maybe I did." Just having the diagnosis gave the young woman relief.

Perfectionism doesn't believe in practice shots. It doesn't believe in improvement. Perfectionism has never heard that anything worth doing is worth doing badly—and that if we allow ourselves to do something badly we might in time become quite good at it. Perfectionism measures our beginner's work against the finished work of masters. Perfectionism thrives on comparison and competition. It doesn't know how to say, "Good try," or "Job well done." The critic does not believe in creative glee—or any glee at all, for that matter. No, perfectionism is a serious matter.

As artists, we must learn to be alert whenever things become too serious. When we stop being able to laugh we often stop being able to create. Our perfectionist takes center stage, the critic cracks the whip and sends our artist cowering. The larger our perfectionist looms, the smaller our talent seems to become. It is our perfectionist that needs to be miniaturized. A little laughter goes a long way toward drawing things to scale.

> *An artist is a man of action.*
>
> JOSEPH CONRAD

When I become too serious, my pets come to my rescue. At my most morose, Charlotte will nudge at me insisting that now is the perfect time for a game of toss the ratty. My dogs do not believe in perfectionism. Out and about on a spring day, they do not criticize themselves. They do not say, "Look at those extra pounds the winter put on you." Tugging at their leashes, they chase squirrels they will never catch, and they do so with enthusiasm. My dogs know a thing or two about the art of being happy. I watch them and learn.

Divining Rod

All of us carry an Inner Censor. The censor is in charge of keeping us small. Negative and critical, it is always at our creative throat. As we become more accomplished, our critic becomes ever more sly and skillful in its attack. Let us say you are a writer. At first, the critic will attack you for being unpublished. After you do publish, your critic will tell you you are a one-book author. After many books, the critic will say you are repeating yourself and are a has-been.

As you become increasingly distinguished, your critic's attack will become more subtle and subversive. Artists do not seem to outgrow their critics, but we can learn to evade them. For many of us, it helps to name and describe our Censor. This transforms it from the voice of authority into a cartoon character. I have my Nigel but students have had censors as diverse as Bruce the shark from *Jaws* and "Sister Mary Priss, a thin-lipped ruler-toting dictator who always finds fault with what I do."

Take pen in hand. Identify, name, and describe your Censor. What does it look like? What does it sound like? Is its voice cruel or bullying? What does it say? Where did this voice come from? Sometimes it is as recognizable as a parent or a negative grammar-school teacher. Sometimes our critic seems to come from out of nowhere but it is still convincing in its attack.

Whether you can "really" draw or not, sketch your critic in action. Search through magazines until you find an image that sums up your critic. Clip it and mount it. By reducing your critic to a cartoon character, you lessen its power.

Taking Action

This morning there was a light haze over Manhattan. The air was damp and balmy but it was not clear. The day was torn between rain and shine. It could have gone either way. For me, the weather perfectly mirrored my inner dilemma. Wanting to move ahead but uncertain as to just how, I myself have not been clear. When I am not clear, I am frustrated. Recently, I have been frustrated a lot.

Aggravated, I have tried to treat myself with tenderness. I have tried to remind myself that I have been here before, in creative limbo, and that sooner or later something shifts. Eventually, always, there is a break in the weather and a way to move ahead. It is all a matter of having patience, I told myself—but today I was not patient. I was socked in, on the verge of turbulence, just like the day itself.

At ten a.m., I took a cab south. I was meeting with my collaborator Emma and director Randall Myler. We were set to rendezvous at The Big Cup to brainstorm ways in which we could go further with our musical *The Medium at Large*.

The Big Cup was a Chelsea coffee bar. It featured gay men, loud music, and strong coffee as well as scones, muffins, cookies, brownies, and croissants. While rock music pounded over the sound system, morning diners pore over the day's paper or check their e-mails. Emma and I settled in with coffee with almond syrup and a chai latte.

> *Inspiration follows aspiration.*
> RABINDRANATH TAGORE

"How are you doing?" Emma asked me.

"How are *you* doing?" I asked her back.

We were frustrated and we felt we had run out of ways to go forward. We were hoping that Randy would have some ideas. So much of the trick with a creative career is maintaining optimism and forward motion. So much consists of doing the next right thing, however tiny. Often we get discouraged because we are unable, left to our own devices, to see a next right step. Discouragement acts as blinders. This is where friends come in handy. This is where brainstorming matters.

Friends often have ideas that we may not have entertained. Sometimes it helps to talk to someone who is not in our field and doesn't know the rules that we, sometimes unconsciously, are playing by. "Have you tried . . .?" someone will ask and it will be something so simple that it—simply—hadn't occurred to us. There are many different ways to skin the cat and some of those ways are going to be outside of our peripheral vision. A good friend can be like borrowing a radar dish—suddenly we are scooping up all sorts of signals where before there were none.

Dressed in an oversized plaid shirt and blue jeans, Randy arrived. He is a director and directors are nothing if not direct. Propped forward on his chair to be heard above the din, he was full of suggestions. "Have you tried . . .?" he asked and, "Did you think of . . .?" Very often, the answer was, "No." Emma and I talked with him for an hour, taking copious notes.

From Randy's perspective, we were far from stuck high and dry. There were all sorts of tiny ways to go forward. If we were willing—and we were—there were any number of things that we could do. And there was something to be said, too, for patience. Randy himself once incubated a musical for nineteen years. Our four on *The Medium* was nothing to him. We barely had our feet wet, but if we wanted to get them wet further . . . We left The Big Cup buzzed on caffeine and buoyed up by Randy's enthusiasm.

It will never rain roses. When we want to have more roses, we must plant more roses.

GEORGE ELIOT

No great discovery was ever made without a bold guess.

ISAAC NEWTON

I would not say that the weather had cleared by the time we took our cab back north, but I myself felt clearer. I could see some usable track ahead. There was a playwriting contest Emma and I could enter. There was another director we could call. There was a theater out on Long Island that might be perfect for a small production. There was a producer that we could tag base with . . .

One more time, Emma and I were back to small, doable actions. We were able to see the shape of the day. We would get on the phone and make the calls that seemed intimidating but necessary. We would ready a packet for submission . . .

Late in the afternoon, we walked in the park. The morning's haze had given way to a clear, steady light. The park was filled with joggers and strollers. Dog owners lolled along the reservoir path. We noted that white crocuses had joined the purple and the gold. We saw that several forsythia bushes were actually blooming. On a sheltered hillside, jonquils were budding. Soon they would be open. We had entered the playwriting contest. We had called the producer. We were waiting for a call back from the director. We had checked out the theater on the Internet. By the time we got to the park, we were ready to celebrate a day well done.

> *The shortest answer is doing.*
> ENGLISH PROVERB

"It's amazing," Emma said to me, "what a difference it makes to be able to take an action. It is the difference between optimism and despair."

A squirrel skittered along a stone wall. Tiger Lily, my cocker spaniel, took off after it. Emma and I laughed with delight. We were having the same fun, chasing our brilliant careers.

Divining Rod

This tool asks you to engage the help of a friend. You may wish to choose someone from your previous list of encouraging friends. What you are after is a really good brainstorming session. You want your friend's input on the next steps that you might take regarding your art. For your self, this will be an exercise in open-mindedness. It is astonishingly easy to dismiss our friends' input as too naïve to be really workable. Don't be so sure. Friends are often cannier than we think, and they may suggest directions that are far more promising than the tried-and-true routes we are so discouraged by. Do not dismiss this tool until you have tried it. Now is the time to practice assertiveness on your artist's behalf.

You will need to call a friend and set a formal date. Explain to your friend that you are meeting on behalf of your artist. A dinner date or a coffee date is ideal. You will need time enough to settle in and really explore. In preparation for your date, you might wish to jot down a list of the actions that you have taken and those you think it is possible to take. These you can share with your friend to start the ball rolling.

You may also wish to set out your goals related to your project. As our friends may be quick to point out, sometimes our goals are too farsighted. (We may ultimately want to see our show on Broadway while our more tangible, reachable goal might better be to secure a good workshop production.) Use your friend to help you generate a doable list of next steps. Remember it is fair game to ask your friend for spiritual help as well an intellectual input. It is quite legitimate to say, "Can you put my project in your prayers?" Even our most secular-minded friends may display the surprising willingness to be a spiritual support for our dreams. "I'm not so long on prayers, but I could send you good vibes," one friend of mine phrased it.

CHECK-IN

1. **How many days this week did you do your Morning Pages?** If you skipped a day, why did you skip it? How was the experience of writing them for you? Are you experiencing more clarity? A wider range of emotions? A greater sense of detachment, purpose, and calm? Did anything surprise you? Is there a "repeating" issue asking to be dealt with?
2. **Did you do your Artist Date this week?** Did you note an improved sense of well-being? What did you do and how did it feel? Remember, Artist Dates can be difficult and you may need to coax yourself into taking them.
3. **Did you get out on your Weekly Walk?** How did that feel? What emotions or insights surfaced for you? Were you able to walk more than once? What did your walk do for your optimism and sense of perspective?
4. **Were there any other issues this week that felt significant to you in your self-discovery?** Describe them.

Uncovering a Sense of Support

Critical to any creative journey is a sense of creative support. You must practice discernment, weeding out that which does not serve and watering the shoots you want to foster. This week's tasks invite you to consciously interact with those who are positive on your behalf. Reaching out to others for their belief, you will also reach within and steady your personal confidence. If you had the faith, what might you try? This week's explorations will lead you into knowing your own mind.

Friends to the Work

Early this morning my phone rang. It was a fellow writer checking in. We have made a plan to piggyback on each other's energy for a while. She is having a hard time writing a book proposal. I am having a hard time writing, period. Her last proposal didn't sell and she is discouraged. Stymied, she goes to the page and comes up dry. She is struggling with a stubborn block. I struggle with blocks myself, and so I am a willing conspirator to help dismantle hers.

> *Good friends, good books and a sleepy conscience: this is the ideal life.*
>
> MARK TWAIN

I love the idea for her new proposal and am convinced it will sell quickly and well. She needs only to finish up her first draft and then do some quick fixes to the top of the proposal, adding in more anecdotes to make it more reader-friendly. Crippled by fear and discouragement, she has found it impossible to do this work, work normally well within her range.

A survivor of similar blocks, I am a compassionate witness to her creative struggle. Her check-in call helps send me to the page. We are both in this together—"this" being a life in the arts.

There is a lot of mythology around the artist as a loner. As my friend novelist Tim Farrington ruefully phrases it, "The lonely genius stereotype, the semiautistic gifted person slaving passionately away in noble isolation." Well put, Tim, and complete hooey. The artist's life need not be isolated and lonely—we are just tutored to believe that it is. And such tutoring can be a self-fulfilling prophecy. An artist who needs help and support may be loath to ask for them. After all, aren't "real" artists beyond such needs? In a word, no.

> The worst solitude is to be destitute of sincere friendship.
>
> FRANCIS BACON

> Work and love—these are the basics. Without them there is neurosis.
>
> THEODOR REIK

We're fed a great deal of romance surrounding the lonely lot of the artist. We picture the garret from *La Bohème,* see the lone, starving artist, struggling with depression, struggling with sheer eccentricity. *We are trained to see artists in this way.* Over a recent weekend, teaching in San Francisco, I asked for a show of hands from all the people who believed an artist's life would be lonely. In a room filled with two hundred people, nearly two hundred hands went up. Believing this, we can try to live it out—a prospect that makes for a great deal of pain. Who wants to try writing a novel if the act is going to cost us all our friends? And so novels go untried and artists go on blocked.

The truth is that creativity occurs in clusters. Consider Paris in the twenties and the cluster that built up around Gertrude Stein's hospitality. Consider the Bloomsbury Group convening for Thursday night cocktails and inadvertently launching a movement. It can be argued that successful art is built on successful friendships. It can certainly be said that friends are what enable an artist to go the distance. Let me give you a case in point.

I recently attended the book signing of a red-hot New York writer. She had three novels out to rave reviews from the normally dyspeptic *New York Times.* She had a play opening in Moscow and another in New York. Her career was sizzling. After her well-attended signing, I was invited to dinner with her friends. We filled a long sixteen-person trestle table in a trendy East Side bistro—included were the members of not one but two writers' groups that the red-hot writer attended—and had attended for all the years she was shaping her sizzle-worthy work.

"I owe it all to you," she called down the table at one point. Her friends hooted derisively in response, but on questioning did admit to having read certain pivotal drafts and offering notes. They had been for her "believing mirrors," mirroring back her competency and her talent. They had cheered her on, step by step, draft by draft. They had offered suggestions, reservations, encouragement, advice.

Am I suggesting that we should make art by committee? Hardly. Remember that the writer still had to write her drafts solo, but she did so with the support of her friends. Draft by draft they cheered her onward, signaling "Yes!" as the work came into focus. They believed in it. They believed in her. She, in turn, could believe in their belief when her own belief felt shaky. They formed a cheering section to hurrah her over the finish line. With their support, she made it.

I recently had my own experience with the power of friends to keep a project on track. I wrote a novel, a slender romantic novel, a love story about two misfits who lived in Manhattan. When I finished my first draft, I sent it to an editor and two friends. The editor was someone with whom I had worked repeatedly on non-fiction. The friends were people who had been reading my work in rough to polished form for nearly twenty years.

"Good start, keep moving," my friends signaled back. "This book is a really good time." They loved the little book even in seed form. The editor, by way of contrast, had grave problems with the central premise—and a lot of problems with the rest of it, too. Her notes cut me to the core—where my friends stood waiting to cheer me on.

"She's off. She just doesn't get it. Maybe she's never had a dysfunctional relationship," they opined. "Just keep at it. The book is delightful."

"Are you sure?"

"Oh, Julia, don't give up on it because of one person's opinion."

And so, egged on by my friends, I set aside the editor's notes and went back to work. A second, third, fourth, fifth draft flushed out the first. The book began to make the rounds of professional readers, as well as my friends. Other editors loved it. On impulse, I sent the finished book back to editor number one.

"Now I get it!" she exclaimed. "It's terrific. I guess the lesson here is never to send me an early draft!"

I didn't say to her, "How can you be so blithe about your change of heart? I could have committed suicide over your first notes!"

For me, the lesson was the value of friendship—and the unique value of friends to my work. I knew that without my friends' help I would have abandoned the novel. I would have taken the editor's notes too closely to heart and given up on my book, telling myself, perhaps, that I had delusions of grandeur thinking I could pull off a romantic comedy. Arguably, I wouldn't even have seen this as self-destructive, just "realistic." (Today, thanks to my perseverance, the novel is pubished by St. Martin's Press.)

Friendship is one of the most tangible things in a world which offers fewer and fewer supports.

KENNETH BRANAGH

Ruefully, I thought back to an earlier novel I had scuttled, not yet trusting the power of friends. I had again sent the book to two friends and one editor. The editor wrote back, "Divide the number of roses and sunsets by two and publish!" I thought the note was sarcastic and, despite my friends' pleas that they liked the book and that roses and sunsets *could* be cut, I put the novel in a bottom drawer where it lived out its days.

Too many people miss the silver lining because they're expecting the gold.

MAURICE SETTER

You might be thinking from all of this that I am a hypersensitive writer. I think that I am. But I think that most artists are hypersensitive—or, in the word of famed writing teacher Natalie Goldberg, *delicate*. It's not that we can't take criticism, but that we often cannot take it in a balanced way. This is where friends come in.

Friends help us to weigh the positive against the negative. They help us to know when we have been savaged and when we just *feel* like we have been savaged. They help us to sort out when criticism has a point and when it is pointless. They help us to tell the difference between being bludgeoned and *feeling* bludgeoned. These are distinctions it is difficult to come to on your own.

I call it those people in whom we trust completely and with good reason "before, during, and after" friends. They are our true benefactors, our believing mirrors, mirroring back to ourselves our strengths and possibilities. It takes a while for a person to earn a place on this bench. They must prove themselves, over time, to be not only softhearted but also hardheaded. They must be tough-minded without being nasty. They must be user-friendly without being mushy. To be a believing mirror, they must, like a good mirror, have a clean, clear surface that allows them to mirror back without distortion what they are asked to reflect upon. There is nothing of more benefit to a career than a set of good believing mirrors. I know this from hard-won experience.

Not all work will be inspired. Not all work will point in the right direction. Friends who know our work, our body of work, will be quick to notice when a new direction is struck. They make good sounding boards to discuss the validity of the direction we are trying, whether we are moving fruitfully forward into new terrain or have simply gone off on a tangent. Over time, friends will form opinions as to our vein of gold, that area of the creative field we may work most successfully. "Try another mystery," they may urge or, "I love it when you write romantic comedy."

Writing is not the only art form that benefits from friendly vision. "I see you've been really working on your backgrounds," a portrait painter might be told. "I like what you did in the second movement," a choreographer might hear. Ideally, a friendly viewer takes to mind both where the work has already been and where it might be trying to go. There is a sense both of history and of possibility. Sometimes a friend to our work will actively seek to open doors on our behalf.

Friends may not know better than we the direction work needs to take, but they may know at least as well. When I was working on my poetry album, *This Earth,* with composer Tim Wheater, he urged me to focus on political poems, not romantic ones. The resulting album won *Publishers Weekly*'s "best original score." I doubt a more confessional album would have succeeded so well.

> *I figure if I have my health, can pay the rent and I have my friends, I call it "content."*
>
> LAUREN BACALL
>
> *Always be a little kinder than necessary.*
>
> SIR JAMES M. BARRIE

Friends may be able to tell us when we are working badly and when our critic is simply working overtime. A straightforward, "It sounds fine to me," may be the indicator we are on the right track and not, as our fears told us, meandering blindly. Unfortunately our own Inner Critic is not a trustworthy guide as to the caliber of our work. Sometimes—rarely—our critic will let the second-rate work slip past. More often, our critic will mercilessly attack work that does not deserve such attack. This is where the validating support of friends comes into play.

"This work is rubbish," our critic may announce.

"I'm not so sure about that. It seems sound to me," a friend may opine.

Listening to our friendly viewers over a hyperactive Inner Critic is a learned skill. All too often, it is fear that prevents an artist from stepping onto center stage. The shy creator may be comfortable creating but uncomfortable with the resultant spotlight. Here, too, is where the championship of our friends is pivotal. As artists, we need to have those who can root for us as we gather ourselves to take some terrifying leap of artistic faith. We may call such a friend to say, "I am afraid to send off my article but I am going to go mail it now." We may phone back to say, "I just mailed it." In 12-step lingo, this is known as a "sandwich call." Something difficult sandwiched in between our supports.

Belief is contagious and sometimes when we cannot believe in ourselves we can at least believe in the belief of others. "Maybe I'm not so bad," we might think. "Maybe I should take another stab at it." And then we do.

Divining Rod

You have made a list of encouraging friends. You are now asked to put that list into further action. By phone, e-mail, or letter, contact your believing mirrors. Catch them up on where you are on your projects. Be specific about the areas where you feel you need help. You have brainstormed in depth with one of them and now you are scanning your web of friends for further help and guidance.

Do not be surprised by the loving input you may receive. Our friends can be quite wise regarding the proper care and maintenance of our artist. Very often, when we are driven in our art, we fail to take loving actions toward ourselves. We neglect to celebrate the many small victories as they pass. Let us say you have just finished a draft of a project and you are now focused on the work—and future drafts—that remain to be done. A friend may very well suggest that you celebrate the work you have already accomplished. Schedule a dinner to do precisely that.

Allow your friends to be friendly. As you are more open with them about your hopes, dreams, and disappointments, they are able to be more supportive to you in your process. For you, the challenge is adequate selfdisclosure. Try trusting your friends rather than playing the Lone Ranger. This flies in the face of our cultural mythology that tells us artists are loners. We need not be loners. (Successful artists seldom are.) Remember that success occurs in clusters and is born of generosity. Allow your friends the chance to be generous.

Discouragement

As artists, we do not often marinate ourselves in self-satisfaction. We do not often think, "This is the greatest"—although it might be. It takes constant vigilance not to slip into negativity, or simple apathy. It takes courage to believe over any given period of time that we are getting better and not sliding into decline. To keep on keeping on takes energy and commitment, two variables we may need to borrow. Novelist Tim Farrington describes a day's work as "pushing the boulder uphill." For many an artist, on many a day, he is quite right.

Often, it is tenacity, not talent, that rules the day. Aided by our friends' support, we are able to be tenacious, to try one more round of submissions, to knock on one more gallery door. William Kennedy's novel *Ironweed* underwent fifty submissions before hitting pay dirt—and this book went on to receive the National Book Award!

> There is nothing on this earth more to be prized than true friendship.
>
> THOMAS AQUINAS

> There is no wilderness like a life without friends; friendship multiplies blessings and minimizes misfortunes; it is a unique remedy against adversity, and it soothes the soul.
>
> BALTASAR GRACIAN

For most artists, discouragement is the private hell we do not talk about. In my case, for example, I am discouraged on two fronts right now. The first front is *Avalon,* the musical I've worked on for seven years. It is currently sitting in limbo. In my manager's words, it is generating "respectful interest" but no real takers. The second disheartening front is my novel, which keeps getting "almost" bought. It is difficult, living through "almosts." How many more times can I bear to hear that "the editorial side loved the book but it didn't make it past sales and marketing"? It does no good to muster defenses like, "Editors are loving it." Until we have a "yes," we have a "no." And "no's" are difficult to live with. I try to practice that art. Every day I read the poems of Ernest Holmes. I pray not to be cynical. I pray not to close my heart.

Tomorrow, *Avalon* may find a producer. Tomorrow, my novel may find a publisher. For today, the assignment is to stay faithful, to keep on acting as if, to put words to the page despite their difficulty, to maintain optimism despite pessimism, to keep on keeping on. For this, I need help. I have learned to ask for it.

"Any good word yet?" Larry Lonergan asks when I talk with him. In the face of my discouragement, he stubbornly insists that good news is coming. He believes that the novel will sell and that *Avalon* will find a home. On the days when my belief wobbles, I piggyback my belief onto his. Faced with his faith, I find my own.

I do not sabotage myself. I keep on stubbornly working. So much of keeping on is just keeping on.

He who sees a need and waits to be asked for help is as unkind as if he had refused it.

DANTE ALIGHIERI

It's late afternoon. I have just talked with my friend the struggling writer. She reported in that she had managed to complete a page of work and that the proposal again seemed to be edging forward. "Thank you so much," she told me. "It was possible to write knowing I was going to talk with you later."

"I got some work done today, too," I told her. "And I may have pages that I can salvage from the two hundred pages I pitched out. That would be a miracle." Together we laughed. The real miracle was the relief of one artist sharing with another. We were in the writers' boat together.

Divining Rod

This tool requires a little legwork and a little footwork. You may wish to take yourself to your local bookstore or else let your fingers do the walking and go to Barnes and Noble or amazon.com. You are looking for a biography or an autobiography that details the artist's life. You are on the look out for experience, strength, and hope. You want to hear from the horse's mouth exactly how disappointments have been survived. It helps to know that the greats have had hard times too and that your own hard times merely make you part of the club.

In writing musicals, I look to books about Rodgers and Hammerstein. Their success is laudable but very hard won. Rodgers once faced such discouragement that he almost quit the music business to become a lingerie salesman. Hammerstein survived more than a decade's bitter disappointment between his early success with Jerome Kern and his later success with Rodgers. Sometimes, when I am most bitterly disappointed, I will take myself to the page and ask, "What would Oscar Hammerstein tell me?" Then I listen for whatever guidance seems to come through. Very often I receive wisdom that does not seem to be my own or the product of my own imaginings. I am always told to persevere.

Take pen in hand. Number from one to five and select five mentors from among the deceased. Focusing on one of them, ask for any help and input that they might have for you at the current time. Sit quietly and listen to hear what guidance comes to you. Write out what you "hear." Very often you will find that there is a wisdom available to you that does not seem to be your own.

Joining Humanity

Spring has gone back into hiding. Today the day is cold, drab, and gray. The park is emptier than it has been. The streets seem emptier, too, as if people are staying indoors and applying themselves to the task at hand. For me, the task at hand is an ordinary day of work. I have gotten a phone call from my friend the writer and she has said she will be working a short day, but work she will. Already it feels comfortable, our routine of checking in with each other. It makes the workday more doable, makes it something shared between friends.

It is the ego's dicey proposition that as artists we should always be "special" and different. The ego likes to be set apart. It likes to look down its nose at the rest of humanity. Such isolation is actually damaging. It is like the reverse of the Midas touch turning everything golden into a problem. Let us say we have fear—as all humans do—the ego would have us having "artistic fear" which sounds like a specialized something that perhaps only an expert, and an expensive expert at that, could help us cope with.

If we have plain old ordinary fear then we are within reach of a solution. Fear has been with humankind for millennia and we do know what to do about it—pray about it, talk about it, feel the fear, and do it anyway. "Artistic" fear, on the other hand, sounds somehow nastier and more vir-

I know what things are good: friendship and work and conversation.

RUPERT BROOKE

ulent, like it just might not yield to ordinary solutions—and yet it does, the moment we become humble enough to try ordinary solutions.

It is only by courting humility that we stand a chance as artists. When we choose to join the human condition rather than set ourselves apart from it, we begin at once to experience relief. If we stop calling our writer's block "writer's block" and begin using words like "resistance" and "procrastination" we are suddenly no longer in rarefied territory.

One of the greatest disservices we can do to ourselves as artists is to make our work too special and too different from everybody else's work. To the degree to which we can normalize our day, we have a chance to be both productive and happy. Let us say, as is often the case, we are resistant to getting down to work. We have a choice. We can buy into our resistance—Writer's block! Painter's block!— or we can simply say, "I don't feel like working today, and I'll bet an awful lot of other people are in the same boat."

The minute we identify with the rest of humankind, we are on the right track. The minute we set ourselves apart, we are in trouble. When we start thinking that as artists we are very different from other people, we start to feel marginalized and hopeless. When we realize that we are probably in pretty much the same boat as everyone else, we begin to edge toward solution. Our shared humanity is the solution. Our "specialness" is the problem.

> *If a man write a better book, preach a better sermon, or make a better mouse-trap than his neighbor, tho' he build his house in the woods, the world will make a beaten path to his door.*
>
> RALPH WALDO EMERSON

"It's hard, starting a novel" can be normalized into "It's hard starting any new project." "How will I ever meet this portrait deadline?" becomes "How will I ever meet this work deadline?" The fact of being a novelist or a portrait artist matters less than the all-too-human thought "I am not sure I can pull it off this time." All workers face this fear. It's normal.

"I am having trouble starting, please stick me in the prayer pot," we may ask our friends, reducing our resistance from a gigantic block into something more manageable.

"My critic is going bananas, please pray for me to get a little break," we may ask, reducing our critic from a godly authority figure into a mere annoyance.

Any time our work process becomes something we can share with our "normal" friends, we are on the road to health. Everyone may not experience writer's block, but everyone has experience with resistance. When we stop insisting on being special, an "artist," we can begin to solicit commonsense solutions, which our friends may have plenty to offer. All we need to do is ask for help.

The human being does not exist who has not procrastinated. Many human beings have devised stratagems to deal with their procrastination. Suddenly, we can avail ourselves of their help. We don't need to talk to another writer to be understood. "I know I should, but I just can't make myself" is something anyone can understand. Suddenly starting on the novel is just a chore, no more glorified than cleaning out the broom closet. You'll feel better once you've made a stab at it. Which you can, with a little help from your friends.

"Work for a half an hour and call me back to say you've started," a friend may suggest who spends her days editing tiresome legal briefs and knows a thing or two about procrastination.

"Schedule yourself a treat or a bribe," another friend weighs in. "Work first. Bribe second. I always allow myself a half hour of reading the tabloids after scrubbing the bathrooms."

"Take a sheet of paper and list all of your angers and resentments about the project," a third friend interjects. "That really helped me when my boss gave me an impossible assignment." Suddenly we are on the road to recovery. Our creative dilemma has become a human dilemma.

All human beings are creative. The more we can accept and welcome that fact, the more normal our own creativity can become. If it is "normal," then it can be shared with everyone. If it can be shared with everyone, then there is lots of help available to us when we get discouraged. Our friends will understand.

> *Friendship is a strong and habitual inclination in two persons to promote the good and happiness in one another.*
>
> EUSTACE BUDGELL

The ego doesn't like the proposition that artwork is like any other work. The ego likes mysterious and self-serving hokum like, "Artwork requires inspiration." Hooey. As any honest artist will tell you, inspiration is far more often a by-product of work than its cause.

We don't feel inspired, far from it, but we begin anyway and something in the act of beginning seems to jump-start a flow of ideas. In cozy retrospect, we can call such ideas "inspiration," but as they occur they are far more workaday. One thing seems to lead to another and another, and before we know it an "inspired" day's work has transpired. The only genuinely inspired part of that day was the very beginning when we decided to accept the Nike slogan, "Just do it."

Outside my writing-room window, the gray day edges toward charcoal. Night is settling in. Tonight there is no showy sunset, no final flourish to the day. It is simply another day finished, another day's work done and that, too, is good. A quick check-in call to my friend the writer reveals that she, too, has again had a productive day. Tonight she goes to her writers' group, pages in hand. It feels good to be turning out proposal pages again, to be one more time moving forward. "I am just so glad to be working," she says, laughing. It feels good to be a worker among workers, a friend amid friends. We will write again tomorrow.

> *Without wearing any mask we are conscious of, we have a special face for each friend.*
>
> OLIVER WENDELL HOLMES

Divining Rod

You are asked to turn one more time to your list of encouraging friends. You are about to use this list again but a little differently. You are now to choose one name from among your supporters and to call that friend not to talk about your creative troubles but to listen to the details of his or her everyday life. This is an exercise in turnaround and it will serve you well. Henry Miller advised young artists to develop an interest in people and that interest is what you are working at now. Tell your friend, "I was just missing you, and I realized I wanted to know much more about how your life was actually going."

Listening to our friends as well as speaking to them of our own lives is very grounding. The more we know of what they are up to, the more we can feel that despite the essential isolation of the creative path, we are living a life in community. We can think, "I may be writing right now, but Ed is at his law firm and Sonia is still seeing clients. Libby is feeding her horses right about now, and Larry is heading out on his daily constitutional." Knowing our friends' schedules gives us a sense of companionship as we face the page or the easel. The bottom line is that we make art about the human condition and our lives must be rich with experience in order for our art to remain vital.

Sobriety

For about a month now, I have been working with a young writer on the film adaptation of one of my novels. Every day we rendezvous by phone and put in an hour's work on the script. Little by little, we chip away at the problems and work our way toward a solution. We are on draft three now, and with each draft the movie comes more into focus. There is nothing very mysterious about making the movie better. All it takes is our focused time and attention. Nothing could be simpler. Nothing could be more rewarding. And yet, each day, when it is time for the work phone call, it is tempting to just get on the phone and socialize. We laugh about our resistance, but it is hard, settling in to work. The ego doesn't like punching in and doing work on a schedule. The ego likes more mystery and hokum.

The idea that the biggest secret of making art might just be making some art is a conclusion the ego works very hard to avoid. The ego wants us to be "in the mood" to make art at the very least. And yet, as any working artist will honestly tell you, waiting for the mood is a huge time waster. We are married to our art and just as the first caress can lead to interest between a long married couple, the first lick of work can lead to an appetite for work. In other words, mood more often follows action than instigates it.

How the ego wants it to be different!

The ego doesn't like the proposition that there is one divine mind working through all things and available to each of us. No, according to the ego, we each have a limited store of creativity. We each tap—or don't tap—our creative potential and there's no use praying for more creativity because we're

> I regard the theater as a serious business, one that makes or should make man more human, which is to say, less alone.
>
> ARTHUR MILLER

not going to get it. And who can believe that God is interested in our art anyhow? The ego discounts and discards the actual spiritual experience of countless artists.

Artists know that when we are working at our best something larger than ourselves is working through us. We are a conduit, a channel for a greater creativity than our own limited resources. In fact, we are tapped into an infinite flow of creative ideas, ideas that come through us but are not really our own. How the ego hates this proposition. You mean we can ask for more creativity? Yes. You mean we can count on a greater flow of creativity? Yes. You mean all of us actually are creative and can be still more creative? Yes.

> *Those thinkers who cannot believe in any gods often assert that the love of humanity would be in itself sufficient for them; and so, perhaps, it would, if they had it.*
>
> G. K. CHESTERTON

> *Problems are messages.*
>
> SHAKTI GAWAIN

The ego doesn't like this. It is far too democratic and egalitarian for the ego to stomach. The ego loves competition, not camaraderie. What the ego has in mind is a small tribe of "real" artists who are "special" and "different." If we listen to the ego, we become dangerously marginalized. Our art becomes more difficult for us to make because we are too busy trying to make ourselves into artists. We become focused on "How am I doing?" rather than "What am I doing?" Our attention strays from process to product—and we, as much as our work, become the product we are producing. "Do I look like a real artist?" we wonder.

The ego loves to keep us wondering. The ego likes uncertainty because wherever there is uncertainty there is grounds for obsession, particularly self-obsession, the ego's favorite plaything. The ego wants us to think about being an artist rather than simply be one. The ego doesn't want art to boil down to the very basic question of process.

If we accept the premise that all human beings are creative, then it becomes "normal" behavior to be creative. If it is normal to be creative, then we can expect our friends to support and encourage it—and not just our officially "creative" friends, either.

As we demythologize creativity, we exorcise a great many demons. We have no need for the demon of feeling special and different, isolated and alone. If creativity is normal, then it can be committed right in the heart of our family and friends—which is where creativity needs to be committed. I wrote my first novel in an upstairs bedroom at my parents' house. My parents were hospitalized, I was doing stand-in duty as parent-in-residence, and in the hours when my sisters and brothers didn't need me, I wrote a novel.

"I'm going to go upstairs and write for a while," became as normal a sentence as, "I'm going to go downstairs and tackle some of the laundry." My novel was simply one more job I had set for myself. I cooked meals, did laundry, helped kids with their homework, and I wrote. Just as I couldn't let the laundry pile up, or the dishes pile up, I couldn't let the writing pile up, either. A certain regular amount of writing was required.

Making writing part of normal life instead of something special and apart from it served me very well. I didn't have the language for it then, but my writing life was "sober." By "sober" I mean nondramatic. When I actually did get physically clean and sober, in 1978, one of the first areas my new friends helped me to address was the issue of emotional sobriety in my work life. Work needed to be daily and doable, I was told. "One day at a time" and "Easy does it" were slogans I could actually apply to my writing. Desperate to find sanity and a sober life, I did as I was told.

I learned to write daily, one day at a time, one page at a time. I learned to set a sober quota on work—for me, three pages daily—and to consider my workday "done" when my quota was fulfilled. As directed, I posted a sign in my work area, "Okay, God, you take care of the quality; I'll take care of the quantity." The sign was intended to keep me from bingeing on negative emotions. There was no point, I was taught, in indulging in emotional benders related to work. Work was something to be normalized. My ego was best kept out of it.

If I were writing a screenplay, my quota was three script pages a day. If it were a novel, three novel pages a day. Eventually nonfiction books yielded to the same three-page-a-day formula. Three pages were long enough to feel I had done *something* and short enough to allow room to do something more or else—visit with friends, for example, or take in a movie.

Because it was not allowed to take over my whole life, work allowed me to have a life. My only job was three pages a day. If I did them first thing in the morning, then I had the whole rest of the day to fill with preoccupations other than myself.

I learned, in the early years of sober writing, to make the sandwich calls that said, "I'm going to write for a while now," and then, "I've finished writing for the day." It wasn't always to another writer that I called in my work commitment. Sometimes it was to an actor or a singer or a "nonartistic" friend. Friends of all stripes could be friends to my work. Work was nothing glorified. It was one more chore. I went to work at my typewriter the same way my friend Jackie went to work at her dress shop. I showed up. I ignored my resistance. I did my *pages*. When my pages were through for the day, so was my identity as a self-conscious writer. For the remainder of the day, I was a girlfriend, a mother, a sister—many different roles beside "artist."

> *When a woman tells the truth, she is creating the possibility for more truth around her.*
>
> ADRIENNE RICH

Freed from the weight of my entire identity, writing became something I did more lightly. Writing itself became easier, less tortured, less self-important. I became a woman who wrote, not a woman writer. As my identity as a writer became a garment worn more loosely, I discovered I had many other identities that I could inhabit with greater ease. My friendship base broadened. I could be friends with a lawyer and a kindergarten teacher. I could be friends with a painter and a housewife. You didn't have to be an artist to be my friend. I didn't have to *act like* an artist to be your friend. What we had in common was our shared identity as *human beings.* This was special enough for me.

It remains special enough for me. Now that I am an older artist, I find I must consciously fight the temptation to *pose* as an artist. With a substantial résumé to point to, I must work harder to take myself lightly. The rules of creation remain exactly the same and I do well when I adhere to them. Three pages a day. Keep it simple and keep it doable. When it's done, it's done.

> *Love the moment, and the energy of that moment will spread beyond all boundaries.*
>
> CORITA KENT

Working at my work a day at a time, I have written twenty books now plus a great deal of music and a number of plays and screenplays. It has all been accomplished by the "easy does it" method. I try to be a conduit and a channel. I try not to be self-conscious, not to be worried about how "I" am doing. For three pages daily, I "listen" and write down what I "hear." In a sense, I cannot take credit for what I accomplish. My productivity has really been born of cooperation. This cooperation is what I can model for artists younger than myself. I "show up" for work. They can do the same.

"We got through it!" exclaimed the young writer when I worked with her today. Indeed, we had finished another draft. Our movie is starting to have flesh on the page. The characters are behaving like characters. The scenes are unfurling like scenes. This is exciting—exciting enough that I am tempted to binge on the work. Fortunately, I know better. I am going to Paris for eight days and while I am gone, the young writer will have time to write certain scenes we now know are missing. When I get back, we will go through the draft process again, working again a little at a time. We will do *un peu,* as they say in Paris—or they do if I remember any of my high school French.

Divining Rod

Most of us accomplish too little because we are expecting to accomplish too much. Daunted by the size of the task we wish to accomplish, we freeze up. We are defeated before we begin. And so, we do not begin. For example, we want to write a novel but see it as an enormous expenditure of time that we just don't have. "I'd love to," we say, "but—" It is only when a creative career is broken down into daily increments that it becomes doable.

A novel, after all, is written one page at a time. If we set a daily quota of three pages, that means we will have ninety pages in a month, 180 pages in two months, 270 pages in three months and in a scant four months we will have 360 pages—the length of a modest novel.

Books are not the only art form that lends itself to a gentle quota. Piano can be learned in a scant twenty to thirty minutes a day. That same half hour can be spent at the easel. Or at the barre. Although we love them and even crave them, we do not really need vast savannahs of time to work at our art. What we need is the willingness to work at our art in the time that we have actually got.

Take pen in hand. Explore the following questions. What art form could you begin practicing if you actually tried "easy does it" as a work practice? What art form do you tell yourself you have no time for? Is it really true? When in your day can you find twenty minutes to spare for working on your art? How do you kill time—TV? The phone?—and can you stop doing that? What is your artistic goal and what is a daily, workable amount that you can reasonably expect from yourself? Can that amount be lessened? What amount of work can you accomplish daily without drama? That is your sober quota.

The Best Kind of Friends

Who would have thought Paris would be about people and not about things? What could be more striking than the Eiffel Tower ablaze each night with dazzling lights, the glittering Seine rippling through the city? What could be more enticing than the roadside stands selling freshly made crepes, the corner cafés with their café crème and chocolat chaud? All true, but for me, Paris was a city of friendships.

She became for me an island of light, fun, wisdom, where I could run with my discoveries and torments and hopes at any time of day and find welcome.

MAY SARTON

Although April in Paris is a time of budding trees and brilliant gardens, the sights to be seen in Paris are often not out and about in the streets but in the carefully lit rooms of galleries, most especially in the Musée d'Orsay which houses a brilliant collection of Impressionist paintings. There we have a record of friendships celebrated and talents generously nurtured by well-chosen friends. Gauguin and Van Gogh, Picasso and Matisse—these artists brought out the best in each other and were wise enough to know it. Their work cross-pollinated each other's. Their friendship made it possible for each of them to go the distance. What did the Impressionists most love to paint? Lunch with each other.

Ah, duty is an icy shadow.

AUGUSTA EVANS

One of the reasons our society has become such a mess is that we're isolated from each other.

MAGGIE KUHN

Part of husbanding our talent lies in finding those who are generous enough to reflect us back as talented. Creativity flourishes in an atmosphere of acceptance. As we learn to number friends to our work among our friends, that work can strengthen and bloom. It could be argued that friendship is often the determining factor between a career that flourishes and one that languishes. We are responsible for choosing our friends.

During my twenties, I was married to young filmmaker Martin Scorsese. He numbered among his friends George Lucas, Steven Spielberg, Brian De Palma, and Francis Coppola. Not one of those men was yet famous. All were upwardly mobile and generous in their support of one another's emerging talents. They screened early cuts of their films for comments and input. I remember a sequence of *New York, New York* being reversed and revamped at George Lucas's suggestion. As each member of this creative cluster percolated upward, they continued to pool their resources. It was routine for one director to suggest to another a talented young actor he had found. Scorsese suggested De Niro to Coppola for *The Godfather: Part II*. Every one benefited from one another's generosity. And no one was famous to begin with—although all would become so with one another's help.

It helps to remember that the famous do not begin as the famous, they merely begin as the gifted and interesting. All of us have friends we can call both gifted and interesting. We require even more of certain friends—that they be gifted and interesting and *generous*—generous enough to reflect us back as also gifted and interesting. This is what makes a mere friend into a "believing mirror."

For many of us, believing mirrors can take a little getting used to. Often, we have grown up surrounded by fun-house mirrors that reflected our dreams to us as egotistical, grandiose, even preposterous. It takes generosity not to diminish the dream of another. True believing mirrors are always generous.

How do we know if we have encountered a true believing mirror? There is a feeling of excitement and possibility. There may be a positive comment that we can cherish and replay. ("Why girls, this song could win you an Oscar," remarked one believing mirror on first hearing a melody of mine and Emma's. We were thrilled.) There will be no hint of cynicism, no suggestion that your dream is *crazy*. There will be the ring of sincerity and blessed optimism.

Believing mirrors are believers, first of all, in the basic good of life. Setting aside chic skepticism, they are upbeat and encouraging. They believe in the college try. What's more, they believe in trying again. They are realists. They expect good things, but they know good things take work. They assume you will do the work because your dreams are good and worthy. They will help you if they can.

Remember, Ginger Rogers did everything Fred Astaire did, but she did it backwards and in high heels.

FAITH WHITTLESEY

Life was meant to be lived, and curiosity must be kept alive. One must never, for whatever reason, turn his back on life.

ELEANOR ROOSEVELT

What they cannot know is exactly how much help they already are giving us simply by existing. One positive friend may be all that it takes for us to keep on keeping on. Let me give you a case in point.

In 1946, Tennessee Williams was ill and believed he might be dying. With death-bed courage, he wrote a letter to Carson McCullers, whom he greatly admired. "I wanted to meet her before I died," he later wrote, and so he invited her to Nantucket, where he was summering. "This tall girl came down the gangplank, wearing a baseball cap and slacks." Their friendship was forged.

The summer unfurled with long conversations, long swims in the ocean, long writing sessions at opposite ends of a kitchen table where he worked on *Summer and Smoke* and she worked on the theatrical adaptation of *The Member of the Wedding*. For both writers, the friendship was catalytic and timely, offering each rich encouragement from a respected source. Williams did not die. Instead, he staged a renaissance. McCullers offered him friendship and "spuds Carson," which were baked potatoes with olives, onions, and cheese in them. He thrived on both.

For Williams and McCullers, their pairing was the timely meeting of a believing mirror. Their relationship refreshed and rejuvenated them. McCullers later referred to the summer as one of "sun and friendship." Both the sun and the friendship were sorely needed.

Williams and McCullers had each won early critical acclaim followed by years of sharper criticism that both took too much to heart. In sharing with each other, they were able to alleviate the wounds left by the critical establishment and return to an appreciation of the work itself, the sheer joy and self-respect to be found in doing it. Over and over, in his correspondence with others, Williams would draw the focus back to what McCullers had "produced." An appreciation of the heroism of artistic production against all odds—that is the gift of a true believing mirror. I have enjoyed that gift for some years now.

From the first time I met the little girl, until her death recently, a period of a little over seventy years, we were friends.

Mrs. Mary E. Ackley

I have been friends for twenty years with Sonia Choquette. Often, when I am despondent over my work, when Larry has not been able to convince me of my merits, it is Sonia whom I will call. She believes in me and believes in the ultimate success of my body of work. "Look at all you've done over the past year," she will urge me. "You've written a novel, you've written a prayer book, you've worked on an opera. Why, you're doing better than you think."

One needs something to believe in, something for which one can have wholehearted enthusiasm.

Hannah Senesh

It is a function of believing mirrors to focus us always on the positive, on the bottom line of our "doing better than you think." Sonia will remind me that I *am* writing when my critic is telling me I am not writing well. Sonia will raise the possibility that perhaps what I am writing threatens the critic, and that is why it is so vituperative right now. It is not that a believing mirror ignores negativity, it is more that a believing mirror considers the negative but still votes on the side of the positive.

A rejected novel "just needs to find the right people." A delayed musical is "just waiting for the climate in the market to be right." Both of these views are forward-looking, refusing to be discouraged. More than almost anything else, a believing mirror is stubborn. It is loyal and it is farseeing. A believing mirror conveys dignity. It says, "Look at all you've done."

A believing mirror focuses on our process as an artist. It finds dignity in the fact of making art, not in the fact of having made it as an artist—although a believing mirror always allows that it believes we will do that, too. A believing mirror does not believe in a capricious and withholding universe. It believes in rewards for work well done. "You've done too much good work for it to come to nothing," a believing mirror will say.

Creativity is an act of faith and believing mirrors give us faith in our faith. *Catch-22* was submitted twenty-two times before it was accepted as a novel for publication. It took powerful faith to continue the submission process. "Powerful faith" is a gift of believing mirrors. For a writer, a literary agent may be a believing mirror. For an artist, a dealer. But there are many nonprofessional relationships that nurture our self-belief. Friends, spouses, siblings, parents—any of these may be a source of believing eyes.

There is something healthy at the heart of every artist, something that welcomes the "ah hah" of inspiration in whatever form it comes. Take the odd-couple pairing of Irving Berlin and Cole Porter, united by their mutual appreciation of each other's genius and by no other circumstance. Berlin came from the ghetto and extreme poverty. Porter came from privilege. Berlin was a conventionally married man. Porter was a celebrated homosexual living in a marriage of convenience. Even their melodic approaches could not have been more different, and yet the men admired each other and struck up a lively and enduring correspondence. To the outside world, their alliance was unlikely. As believing mirrors, they saw and mirrored back to each other the talent both worked to cultivate.

There is a purity to the connection between believing mirrors, an ability to see past the differences to the divine spark within. It is this ability to see past appearances that marks many of the more famous artistic alliances. At a pivotal point in their fledgling careers, Fitzgerald and Hemingway forged a friendship of believing mirrors. Talk about an attraction of opposites! Fitzgerald was delicate and self-destructive. Hemingway was full of bravado and machismo. What they had in common was admiration for each other's work. Fitzgerald brought Hemingway to Scribner's and helped him get paying career legs under him. Hemingway urged Fitzgerald to trust his imagination and write freely. "For Christ's sake, write and don't worry about what the boys say, whether it will be a masterpiece or what."

I'm not going to limit myself just because people won't accept the fact that I can do something else.

DOLLY PARTON

A seeker went to ask a sage for guidance on the Sufi way. The sage counseled, "If you have never trodden the path of love, go away and fall in love. Then come back and see us."

JAMI

There can be a bottom-line tough-mindedness to believing mirrors, a tendency to focus on the use of talent and to ignore the rest. In my relationship with novelist Tim Farrington, many daily details are exchanged but the bottom-line question is always, "Are you writing?" As Farrington has phrased it to me, "Writing rights all." And so, I can talk to him about my fears, my misgivings, and my doubts, and he will always bring it back to the question of my talents and whether I am using them.

Assumed in a believing-mirror relationship is the fact that it is God's will for us to use our talents. This in itself is radical. We have often been raised with a false sense of modesty. We have been taught it is better, somehow more spiritual, to be small not large. We have been tutored to hamper our own creative flight with doubts as to whether such flight is seemly. A believing mirror wants us to soar. To them, our bigger self is our true self, the self to aspire to.

Pivotal to self-expression is the idea that there is a benevolent, interested Universe that wants us to expand. Without such belief, we may buy into our self-doubt and by doing so sharply limit what we are able to attain. We may think, "Wouldn't it be lovely" and then automatically dampen our enthusiasm with "That could never happen"—but perhaps it could. It is the function of a believing mirror to keep us focused on the "Perhaps it could."

For a believing mirror, nothing is too good to be true. Spiritually grounded even if not conventionally religious, a believing mirror focuses on the divine spark of genius within us all. Because that divine spark is godly in origin, anything is possible. When we are connected to the Divine within us, nothing is beyond our reach.

Elmer Green, known to the world as the father of biofeedback, speaks of the existence of what he calls "lifetrons." Tiny energy units galvanized by intention, lifetrons set up a flow of benign coincidence. It is my contention that when we set up an alliance of believing mirrors, we catalyze lifetrons into service on our behalf. Christ spoke of this when he said, "Whenever two or more are gathered together in my name, there I am in the midst."

There is a sacred quality to an alliance of believing mirrors. We are dedicated to seeing each other as pure spiritual potential. Our human personalities, our foibles and flaws, are somehow overlooked. We are focused on the big picture of what is right with ourselves rather than on the smaller and more limiting picture of what is wrong. A believing mirror sees our shortcomings as mere stumbling blocks not the behemoths they sometimes appear to ourselves.

Today I spoke to a believing mirror about the fear and doubt I experienced on a current creative project. When I wound down, my friend said, "So. This is just the period on this project when you will have to be patient." Note the optimism in this diagnosis. "The period" (it will end) "on this project" (one of many you've done) "when you will have to be patient" (as you assuredly have the emotional maturity to be). I got off the phone and turned back to the project with renewed calm and determination. Surely I was patient enough to do just a little more.

The renewed determination to "do just a little more" characterizes a believing-mirror exchange. Because they are certain we are going to succeed eventually, believing mirrors are in no panicked haste. They remind us to simply take the next right step, faithfully believing that everything is unfolding exactly as it should. If you tell a believing mirror of a sudden and dramatic breakthrough, they may act as if there is nothing either sudden or dramatic about it. To them, it is simply the continued unfurling of something right and proper.

The idea of your dream as "something right and proper" is yet another earmark of a believing mirror's faith. They want you to succeed, so every circumstance that reinforces your success is seen as natural and good. Believing mirrors do not worry you will get too big for your britches. They may worry about whether or not your britches are big enough for you. Theirs is a refreshing perspective.

In Paris, the city of friendship, it is still possible to go to a café called Deux Magots and enjoy a hot chocolate where Hemingway and Fitzgerald met each other over drinks. It is possible to go to a bookstore called Shakespeare and Company and celebrate the friendship that James Joyce enjoyed with its proprietor. It is possible, buying Parisian postcards, to celebrate your own circle of believing mirrors, each of whom deserves a note. Writing those notes, it is possible to feel both gratitude and hope.

Divining Rod

Picasso credited Matisse with catalyzing some his own most inspired work. Friends who are friends to our work are often such catalysts. Believing mirrors point us in new, promising, and fruitful directions. For this they deserve our appreciation and thanks.

Take pen in hand. Go to the page and recall there, in specific detail, the ways in which your believing mirrors have helped you to persevere. (As a jog to memory, it may help to go project by project.) It is easy for me to say that my friends Sonia and Larry are responsible for my having the courage to continue working on my musical *The Medium at Large.* It is to my literary agent Susan Raihofer that I owe a vote of thanks for her ongoing belief in my novel *Mozart's Ghost. The Artist's Way* I owe to the belief and support of Mark Bryan. Tim Wheater is the person whom I thank for my play *Love in the DMZ.*

Survey your own list of believing mirrors and recall the precise ways in which their optimism and strength have become your own. It is time for a timely thank-you. A phone call, a postcard, a brief letter—any of these are ways to contact and nurture our believing mirrors. Take time now to make a connection of gratitude. Your believing mirrors may turn your thanks aside, saying, "Oh, c'mon, it's nothing," but we know that it is not.

Believing Mirrors in Action

> *A friend is one before whom I may think out loud.*
>
> RALPH WALDO EMERSON

Paris is six hours ahead of New York and so, coming back to New York, I found myself in the grips of jet lag. It was bad enough as I walked the dogs in the park, each leaden step an insult to the balmy spring day. It was far worse when I sat myself down to write. Seated at the computer, jet lag bore a remarkable resemblance to writer's block. Fortunately, my phone rang.

"How is your writing going?" my friend Rhonda wanted to know. I told her that my writing felt painfully cramped and stilted. "It has for days," I added dramatically.

"Oh, I remember when it felt that way on your last project," she chortled. "Then before you knew it that project was sailing along and then it was finished. I'm sure it will be the same on this project."

I did not ask Rhonda where she got her insane optimism. I knew the answer to that. Rhonda is a friend to my work and has been for many years now. A determined optimist, she expects the best both of me and of the Universe. *Of course* I will be able to write through what she might call this "resistant patch." A believing mirror does not expect creation to be without difficulty but it does expect for that difficulty to be mastered. No, no self-pity around Rhonda.

So next, I complained by e-mail to Tim Farrington that I was in the "slog, slog, slog" section of working on a new book. He shot back briskly, "Slog, slog, slog stage of a new book is great you know." I wanted to slug him. Then he added, "Ignore that Inner Critic; they never let up." I wanted to say, "Some days it's easier to ignore the Inner Critic than other days," but I knew he already knew that.

Still feeling sorry for myself, I called my friend Natalie Goldberg, the famous writing teacher.

"I had a bad writing day," I whined to her.

"Well, you know that goes with the territory," she shot back. "You have to be in it for the whole enchilada, the bad writing days and the good."

Something in what Natalie said surrendered me. Yes, of course. How could I forget that bad writing days just came with the territory? I was in it for the long haul, and the long haul was what my friends expected of me. That was why Rhonda could be almost gleeful reminding me of bad writing spells from the past. That was why Tim Farrington could assure me I was actually in a great stage. That was why Natalie could listen to my whining and cheerily remind me that it came with the territory, that I had signed on for the whole enchilada.

I was shopping for drama and not finding any among my friends. Larry and Sonia were both stubbornly optimistic. I was wanting a bad writing day to mean "throw in the towel." They were reminding me it just meant my hat was in the ring. Annoying as I found it when no one would cosign my drama, my believing mirrors were functioning perfectly, refusing to let me derail myself too far. A bad writing day, even a whole string of bad writing days, was nothing to get myself wound up about. If Tim Farrington could tell me the Inner Critic never lets up, that was the voice of his experience speaking and he wasn't talking about quitting the writing game. Clearly, instead of licking my wounds, I just needed to toughen up a little. One more time, I needed to get emotionally sober.

Owing perhaps to jet lag, a genuine biochemical event, I was on a "dry drunk," an emotional bender that closely resembled the real thing. Unless I wanted to court a breakdown—or a drink—I needed to snap out of it. A good glimpse of myself in a believing mirror showed me how distorted my thinking was. Tempted to more drama by beating myself up, I reminded myself that all of us undergo bouts of distorted thinking. No one, and certainly not me, is immune. We need our believing mirrors for timely rescue. We *all* need our believing mirrors.

If artists are not essentially self-destructive by nature, we do tend to binges of relentless self-criticism and it is during such periods that we must rely on the more temperate judgment of our believing mirrors. In my own case, I have found that my Inner Critic's most scathing comments are often reserved for what will later appear to be my strongest work. When I was writing my recent book *Walking in This World,* my critic worked overtime to assure me how terribly I was writing, what a rotten job I was doing trying to marshal my ideas onto the page. Bedeviled and beset, working uphill all the way, I finally gave a stack of the essays over to be read by a believing mirror.

"I think this writing is good, actually very strong," the diagnosis came back, puzzled. "Tell me again exactly what you think is wrong with this."

Of course, there was no way to say *exactly* what I felt was wrong with the work. My critic wasn't armed with a rational attack. It had stuck with vague, impossible to fix pejoratives, words like "weak."

"I just thought it was weak or something."

"No, I don't think so. I actually think the essays are strong."

> The greatest good you can do for another is not just to share your riches, but to reveal to him his own.
>
> BENJAMIN DISRAELI

When I showed the same stack of essays to a second believing mirror and once again met with praise not pans, I began to get a little bit excited. Maybe my critic was so active not because the work was bad but because the work was good. My believing mirrors thought it was and they had a track record of accuracy.

Believing mirrors are not flatterers. They know too well that we are counting on them for objectivity. Some of my believing mirrors are very tough critics. I know that to pass muster with them, I must really be able to pass muster. Believing mirrors do not always come back 100 percent in our court. A believing mirror may say, "Mmmm. There was something a little wobbly in the second half." They may say, "Your voice seemed muffled somehow. Did you say what you really meant?" Or, "I felt you were evading an issue here." Such reservations, spoken with our best interests at heart, mean, "Back to the drawing board, something's not right here."

This afternoon, my phone rang. It was Ed Towle, one of my oldest friends and one of my most trusted readers. He was calling from his car in L.A. He was trapped in traffic and found himself wondering how my writing was going.

"I'm trapped in traffic, too," I laughed. "I have so many ideas right now, and I'm not getting them on the page in any order."

"It's a first draft for Christ sake. You're not supposed to have any order. You're not supposed to know how it fits together because it doesn't yet. That's for later."

Ed is himself one of the finest writers I know. It is encouraging to me that he doesn't believe in an overplotted linear first draft. Talking to him, I begin to relax. I start to think, "Oh, yes, my books always start out as a mess. It always takes multiple drafts to put them in shape."

The word "always" is comforting. I have written before, it reminds me, and I will write again. Writing is a messy process and that's equal parts "mess" and "process." When I relax into my known writing history, I begin to loosen up. This book is no worse or harder than any other book. It's just worse and harder because it's the current book.

I have been friends with Ed Towle for twenty-five years. We started reading each other's writing just after we graduated from Georgetown. Ed was one of the earliest readers of *The Artist's Way* and his comments helped shape that and future books. "Perhaps," I think, "I should trust him now. He tells me to keep on keeping on."

"Trust" is one of the key elements in finding a believing mirror. We need to trust the sensibility of the friend we are dealing with. We cannot feel they're talking through their hat. We cannot feel they are just humoring us. Such humoring is not what we need. We need friends who are tough-minded enough to tell us what they see.

It is nine p.m. on Holy Saturday night. That makes it three a.m. in Paris, already Easter, and my constitution is by now somewhere mid-Atlantic. My body clock might be reading midnight. Rather than trying to write more tonight, I am going to make an early night of it. My little cocker spaniel, as if sensing this, has already made a nest for herself at the foot of my bed. I have a fine collection of tabloids, reading guaranteed to put me to sleep. Last night, happily, I dreamed I was writing a novel.

> *Love, and do as you will.*
> ST. AUGUSTINE OF HIPPO

Divining Rod

Our friends are not always available to us. Sometimes we will be struck by doubt or despair and find that we must act in our own behalf to muster the courage to continue. We may be in a foreign country or simply in a different time zone. Our friends may be temporarily caught up in their own busy affairs. It is at times like this that we most need a note of encouragement—even if we have to write it ourselves.

Take pen in hand. Write yourself a letter of encouragement, singling out the many things that you have done well. Give yourself the respect of a job well done—even if your work has not yet met with worldly acceptance. Be specific in your praise. Give yourself the review that you wish that would receive. For example, upon receiving a rejection letter, you might counter that news with "Dear Julia: Your novel *Mozart's Ghost* is a delightful—and very inventive—confection. Your characters are clear and warmly drawn. Your dialogue sparkles . . ." Post this letter where you can read and enjoy it.

CHECK-IN

1. **How many days this week did you do your Morning Pages?** If you skipped a day, why did you skip it? How was the experience of writing them for you? Are you experiencing more clarity? A wider range of emotions? A greater sense of detachment, purpose, and calm? Did anything surprise you? Is there a "repeating" issue asking to be dealt with?

2. **Did you do your Artist Date this week?** Did you note an improved sense of well-being? What did you do and how did it feel? Remember, Artist Dates can be difficult and you may need to coax yourself into taking them.

3. **Did you get out on your Weekly Walk?** How did that feel? What emotions or insights surfaced for you? Were you able to walk more than once? What did your walk do for your optimism and sense of perspective?

4. **Were there any other issues this week that felt significant to you in your self-discovery?** Describe them.

Uncovering a Sense of Balance

Pivotal to any creative journey is the ability to resist the cliff's edge of drama. All of us are tempted to binge on negativity. It is the careful husbanding of optimism that allows us to move productively forward. This week's spiritual toolkit is aimed at dismantling the hobgoblins of fear and distrust that poison your well. You will align yourself with a Higher Power that extends itself in benevolent ways on your behalf. Sketchbook in hand, you will practice being in the now, where there is always sufficient safety for you to experience balance.

The Rim of the Glass

I am back from Paris but my body has not yet joined me in New York. I am still on Paris time and that throws me off kilter. Awake in the night, I find myself replaying a laundry list of fears. I pray. I write. I go back to bed. I do not like it, the lying awake, the negativity. One more time, it reminds me too strongly of the drinking days, of the many early mornings when I woke up shaking, fighting off despair and self-loathing. "I am not drinking," I remind myself. "I haven't had a drink in many years, and I do not need to have one now. I am just scared." I wish I could place a phone call to one of my close friends, but it's late and they are sleeping. Awake and restless, I turn to the keys. The familiar tapping of the keys is comforting.

I have mentioned that I am close friends with Larry Lonergan. He sees humor and divine timing where I see catastrophe. When I am in trouble, I frequently go see Larry to see what it is *Spirit* has to say about my dilemma. And Spirit, as told to me by Larry, is often blunt.

"You're wearing yourself out," he said to me today. "There's nothing wrong with you except your attitude. Are you getting out at all? Spirit thinks you're keeping your nose too close to the grindstone. Are you?" (I was.)

Over the years, Larry has batted close to a thousand. He will say, "You're going to write a short book before the longer one and the idea will come to you shortly."

When unhappy, one doubts everything; when happy, one doubts nothing.

JOSEPH ROUX

I may wail, "But, Larry, I have no ideas" only to have an idea strike me, an idea for a short book, that I *will* write before tackling the longer book. Over the years, I've learned to trust Larry's input. He does not always say what I want him to say, but what he does say tends to hold up in my experience. Sometimes what he says seems uncanny to me.

"An idea is going to come sailing in on you from out of the blue," he once said. "It looks like a romantic comedy. Have you been thinking about writing a comedy lately?"

It would have done no good to say, "Larry, all that's on my mind is tragedy." Walking in Central Park, admiring a plump robin, an idea came—and an idea for romantic comedy at that.

Sometimes I almost feel I am cheating, being able to number both Larry and Sonia Choquette among my friends. I feel like I have two guardrails up that help me to keep my car on the road. When my own headlights fail me, theirs kick in. They light up enough of the road that I am able to keep driving ahead.

"I'm worried about money," I wail.

"Your money's fine. You're just scared by being off your writing routine," I hear back. (Sonia is fond of telling me I thrive on routine. Which I do.)

As I am grappling with writing this book on the importance of persevering faith and enduring friendships, I turn to my friends for the faith and support to do it. I write to my friend Tim Farrington that I am toiling through a tough first draft and that I hate slogging. Tim fires a writerly letter back.

"I think you're supposed to hate slogging. I thought that's what slogging was all about. I'll pray for a day of optimism and joyful productivity for you soon . . . you'll find your groove. . . . I know it sounds Pollyanna-ish but you're in God's hands and the Spirit will move when it moves. Our job is to show up, and you're doing your job. The rest is God's, it actually really truly is. . . . Just be you at the keyboard, in the hands of God. Wait, listen, love the silence, and eventually the silence will sing for you, as it always has and always will."

"Eventually the silence will sing for you . . ." How lucky I am to have a friend who can believe this and articulate it for me. I am lucky in my friendships, but I am also careful in them. I avoid people who are too negative because I have my own well-known-to-me negativity to deal with. I know all too well how a negative day can become a negative week if I am not careful. I must be vigilant at maintaining optimism. I must be skilled at titrating my energy so that there is "enough" belief to see me through.

> *Make a virtue of necessity.*
> GEOFFREY CHAUCER

And so, I seek out people who are optimistic, self-starting, and farseeing. I seek out people who are experienced in the difficulty of trusting themselves and who have learned to do it against the odds. As professional seers, both Sonia and Larry had to learn to live with being "different" from their fellows. Both had to learn how to keep their own counsel when what they saw—how much they saw—differed from consensus reality.

As an artist, I, too, must be able to see into the future. I must be able to cast an idea forward and see it fleshed out and standing on its own, a real creation. A book, a film, or a play begins as a notion, a blueprint, and that blueprint must be held in mind for the book to gather weight. As the writer, a book must be "real" for me before it can be real for anyone else. If I hold a book as "real," then I can find others who can also see it. It takes a special sort of constructive imagination to be able to look at the bare bones of a creative project and see it in the mind's eye as fully clothed. This special skill is what I have looked for over the years as I have slowly and carefully collected my believing mirrors.

It is five a.m. I am still awake and lonely, still on Paris time. Frightened, I am writing to muster courage. Comfortless, I try to write of what comforts me. What comforts me are my friends. It is still too early to call them. They live in earlier time zones and are still abed. I lie in bed deliberately counting my blessings. I know I am meant to place my dependency on God, but God can seem distant. "God speaks to me through people," I was taught when I was newly sober. Seeking to be emotionally sober now, two and a half decades later, God still speaks to me through people. I need to hear Sonia's familiar voice although I know that what she will say to me is, "You're fine. Jet lag is just a biochemical event. It will pass."

"It will pass," that is a touchstone of emotional sobriety. "It will pass," I tell myself. That done, I mercifully drift to sleep.

Divining Rod

Bedtime is a time of hobgoblins and convincing, although groundless, fears. Many of us grew up with the comforting words of a childhood prayer that ran, "Now I lay me down to sleep. I pray the Lord my soul to keep. And if I die before I wake, I pray the Lord my soul to take." Older and more sophisticated now, we often consider ourselves to be beyond such prayers—but are we? The night can make children of us all.

Take pen in hand. You are to write yourself a simple bedtime prayer. What gentle well wishes do you tell your frightened soul? You might try something along the lines of, "Dear God, I am going to sleep now and I need your help. I ask you to turn my troublesome day to good account. Please give me peaceful slumber and the blessing of feeling your presence. Guard and guide me while I sleep. Allow me to wake with a clear idea of your will for me. May I do your will always . . ."

Faith

I have accepted fear as a part of life—specifically the fear of change . . . I have gone ahead despite the pounding in the heart that says: turn back . . .

ERICA JONG

The flowering trees along Columbus Avenue are packed with blossoms, white and pink. They are like oversized wands of cotton candy poking into the air. Walking back from my piano lesson this afternoon, I passed a street vendor doing a brisk business in sunglasses. Clearly spring is here and, judging by the vendors' wares, New York's notorious summer is lurking, just waiting to pounce. I was told as much today. When I came up in the elevator, I shared it with a woman and her large wooly dog.

"I am afraid it's too hot for him already," the dog owner confided in me. "He is bred to retrieve birds in the extreme cold. He's not bred to withstand heat." She sounded worried. The weather outside was barely balmy, not at all hot. Still, her big dog did look winded. He sat on the elevator floor and gently huffed.

"Maybe he will get a chance to get used to it a little by little," I suggested. That was how I myself planned to adjust to New York's legendary summer heat.

"Maybe." The dog owner sounded doubtful, as though my optimism were wildly out of line with reality as she knew it. Like her dog, she had a soulful, doleful gaze. I couldn't wait to slip out on my floor. Vigilant about my own negativity, I wanted to cling to my optimism. I could choose to project impending doom or impending happiness. My vote went to happiness.

Optimism is an elected attitude, a form of emotional courage. It is a habit that can and must be learned if we are to survive as artists. So often, "things" look so bleak. The book doesn't sell. The play is not produced. The audition goes brilliantly but the part goes to someone else. In order to survive such disappointments, we must master optimism, not as a form of denial but as a deeply rooted faith that we are somehow partnered in ways that we cannot see. We must look for the silver lining, knowing that there *always* is one.

For everything you have missed, you have gained something else.

RALPH WALDO EMERSON

As artists, we must cultivate faith. We must learn to see beyond appearances. We must trust that there is something larger and more benevolent than the apparent odds stacked against us. For the sake of sheer survival, we artists must learn to have a deep and abiding belief in our own work and its worthiness, despite the world's apparent acceptance or rejection. As artists, we have a vocation. There is Something that "calls" to us to work. In answering that call and making art, we keep our side of the bargain. Our efforts will be rewarded, although not perhaps in the ways that we had planned.

As artists, we must be in it for the long haul, not just the showy seasons of success. As artists, we are subject to cycles of acceptance. There will be bleak seasons and fruitful seasons. There will be successes and there will be failures. We cannot control the reception of our work. We must find our dignity in the doing. We must learn to say that our work, even if unsung, does count for something.

There is dignity in the act of making art, no matter how that art is received. Much of the best work I have ever written has never been published or produced. Faith tells me that there must be some reason for that that I cannot yet see. I cling to my faith and turn aside bitterness. I work although my work has come to "nothing." I have whole novels that haven't yet sold. I have fine plays that have seen no productions. My artist's faith tells me to keep on writing, that there must be a way, and a reason, to keep on keeping on. Faith allows for a career to take detours. Faith allows for a career to even grind to an apparent outward halt. Faith takes, always, the longer view. It divorces our creative practice from its current reception.

As artists, we must be resilient. Delicate as we are, we must also be stalwart. We must take our cue from the natural world and vow to be like the perennial flowers, stubbornly reappearing season after season. There is some simple dignity that lies in the labor of doing the art for art's sake and not for the glory and acclaim that we hope will accrue. I am a writer and writers write. Every day that I write, I am keeping my side of the bargain.

There are many days when I do not "feel" like writing. These are the days when I tell myself I have nothing to say, the days when I want to say, "Oh, what's the use" and count my thwarted art as the reason I do not go on. "Why try? It will come to nothing anyway," I catch myself thinking.

On those days I write anyway. Such thinking is the rim of the glass of despair. Despair is the poisonous drink an artist cannot afford to even sip. In order to go forward on these days, I must be willing to be small, not large. I must be willing to write from a spirit of service, to write simply because writers write. It does no good to demand to always be brilliant. That demand is an instant prescription for writer's block. No, in order to write, I must be willing to write badly and to have the faith that if I go forward "writing badly," some purpose is still be being served.

> *A prudent man will think more important to him what fate has conceded him, than what it has denied.*
>
> BALTASAR GRACIAN

We are creations and we are intended, in turn, to be creative ourselves. Like the fruit trees, we are intended to blossom. The trees put forth their froth whether there will be admiring eyes or not. So, too, we are intended to flower in our art even if our art does not meet with a welcoming reception. We must make art for the sheer sake of making art. That is being true to our nature. That is being true to our path.

Divining Rod

Most of us focus not on what we have done and have accomplished but upon those things we have yet to do. Most of us can make a quick list of dreams that are yet to be fulfilled. And yet, we have done many things well and in order for us to have true self-worth we must value the worthy things that we have done.

Take pen in hand. Number from one to ten. List ten things which you have accomplished already that you are proud of. My list includes teaching my daughter to horseback ride, learning to play the piano, studying French, studying Italian, completing a children's album, and designing a beautiful apartment. Your own list will reflect your own values. You may wish to praise yourself for more than ten accomplishments. When I am teaching a class, I sometimes ask students to enumerate fifty.

Keep It Simple

It is a shiny bright new-penny day. The sky is cloudless, clear blue from horizon to horizon. Spring is leaping tree to tree in Central Park. Joggers are out in happy throngs. Young parents, singly and in pairs, push baby carriages along the cinder paths. The weather is so intoxicating it announces firmly, "Winter is truly over." Two nights ago, driving home from SoHo in a taxi, I passed a church with a gloriously blooming magnolia tree gracing its gate. Even as I type this, the tree beneath my writing window is bursting into leaf.

This morning I got a call from the blocked writer. She was due to start again at the top of her proposal and make some fixes. She said she knew what she had to write but she was hoping to find some inspiration before she could start. She thought she would do some reading to see if other people had been brilliant before her, if something in what they wrote might not spark something in her.

Greed's worst point is its ingratitude.

SENECA

Be a good animal, true to your instincts.

D. H. LAWRENCE

"I thought I would read some really great writers to see if I can get inspired," she said. My stomach sank as I listened to her plan. "What I need to do is come up with something really interesting," she continued. "The beginning of this proposal has to be brilliant, really fascinating." With stakes like that, no wonder she was blocked!

Gently, I told her I thought she might get more blocked shopping for brilliance, that she might do better simply to be willing to write—badly if necessary—and then see what comes of that. Very often our "bad" writing contains the seeds of our "good" writing within it. We resign from being perfect and, when we do, perfection steals in unawares. The trick lies in losing our self-consciousness. There are stratagems that help with that, chief among them trying to be of service.

"Have you ever tried to write from a spirit of service?" I asked her.

"I have trouble with the whole idea of spirituality," she answered with a trace of petulant rebellion. After a beat, she added, "But at this point I am desperate enough to try anything."

I suggested she post the little sign I had been taught to use, "Okay, God, you take care of the quality, I will take care of the quantity." From the silence on the line, I could practically hear her thinking, "How corny." Politely, she got off the call.

In order to be unblocked, I am willing to be corny. I have learned through hard experience that my artist needs to be babied. It needs a sense of safety. (Successful nursery rhymes are nothing if not corny.) I might wish it were different, but the part of me that creates is young and vulnerable. To ensure my productivity, I must be protective of this inner innocent. This means I need to keep things very simple.

I cannot control the outer world, but I can control the inner world I create in. That world can be Utopian in its simplicity. As in kindergarten, the rules must be gentle and fair. Such innocence serves me well. It has and does keep me productive. Hence, the posting of corny signs. Hence, the setting of very modest quotas. I do not want my artist getting discouraged, not when I can prevent it.

As an artist, I do best when reaching for humility. I must be willing to be just a worker among workers, just an artist among artists. Competition has no place in this scenario. Competition creates stress. Stress creates constriction and constriction creates block. Think of your artist as an emotional youngster. For that youngster, it's scary to be the center of attention. The glare of the spotlight can create the paralysis of block.

To function freely as an artist, I must take the focus off of winning, off of being the brightest and the best. I must give up such ego-driven notions as being "fascinating" and "brilliant." (Those judgments are for critics to make in due time, not in my own beleaguered mind.) I need a safe, critic-free arena in which to do my work. Then, with the ground rules in place, I must gently go forward. Simpleminded as it sounds, I must simply write—a word at a time, a sentence at a time, a paragraph

What we call fate does not come into us from the outside, but emerges from us.

RAINER MARIA RILKE

and a page at a time. My quota must be daily and doable. Just a little, done daily, adds up to quite a lot. What we produce can always be improved, but produce we must. "Easy does it" and the corny slogan about taking care of the quantity and not the quality allow us to produce.

For me, it is good to talk with the blocked writer because in her I hear my own temptation to block. There is always a good reason why she cannot write just yet. Listening, I hear my own temptation to indulge in drama and realize my own need to keep the drama on the page. Sharing my "tricks," reminds me to use the tricks I have found. My Morning Pages are one stratagem I use daily to keep me from indulging in drama. In my pages, I write about my fears and then I make a short list of what it is I might be able to do about those fears. For example, on any given day, I can panic about money OR I can write—which earns money. My daily list always includes "write." When I am writing, my money seems oddly able to take care of itself.

So many things are out of our control, but making art *is* in our control. There is always a small and doable creative something we can do if we are willing to move ahead without a guarantee. We may not be able to work at our art on the level that we wish we could, but we can always do something.

The ghosts you chase you never catch.

JOHN MALKOVICH

One drink is too many for me and a thousand not enough.

BRENDAN BEHAN

I cannot guarantee how an editor will respond to my work, but I can write daily. An actor cannot guarantee winning an audition, but he can always work on a new monologue that will put him one leg up on a future audition. A singer can work on scales. A songwriter may not be able to get a record deal but he can write another song. In other words, we can always make things for love. Extending ourselves in love toward our art nurtures feelings of dignity. When we commit ourselves to the process of art and not to the need to produce a saleable product, we begin to experience the joy of creation.

The bright day draws toward a close. The setting sun gilds the newly emerging leaves. The whole world seems lit by optimism. On the phone with my friend the blocked writer, I get the great good news that she decided not to start by reading but instead to try actually writing. She has posted my corny sign. To her great satisfaction, she managed two full pages and once again has a sense of where she needs to aim tomorrow. Telling me of her victory over her block, her voice is calm and centered. Just for today, the drama stayed on the page. There might be a God after all.

Divining Rod

All of us have need of a calm oasis that speaks to us of beauty and serenity. For some of us, this will be a spot in nature, perhaps a grove of pine trees or a meandering stream. For those of us who live in the city, the spot of beauty may be man-made—a church or synagogue that feels far removed from the city's hustle and bustle.

Set aside a half hour's time and take yourself to a spot that speaks to your spirit. You may wish to take a notebook or simply to sit quietly, allowing your thoughts and impressions to bubble up unimpeded. A towering tree may evoke a sense of dignity and wisdom. A stained-glass window can evoke a sense of awe. Allow yourself to feel the transcendent feelings that come upon you. Enjoy a sense of communion with a power greater than yourself. You may find yourself experiencing insights about how your life could be more fully your own. When you leave your place of beauty, you will take with you a renewed sense of optimism and potential.

No Regrets

Last night I went to a sophisticated New York dinner party, the kind of party that is so sophisticated you want to slash your wrists after it. The dinner-table conversation was rife with hot gossip, the "inside scoop" on the publishing world and how crooked and rigged and rotten it was. I listened with a tightening feeling in my chest. I was trying to write this book and if I gave a moment's thought to how futile it all was, I would be on the brink of suicide.

Alcohol doesn't console, it doesn't fill up anyone's psychological gaps, all it replaces is the lack of God.

MARGUERITE DURAS

Wishing for a lighthearted and soignée persona, I instead sat at the dinner table numb with escalating terror. Names piled on names, each one fancier and shinier than the last. Brittle laughter echoed all around me. I felt dumbstruck, like a hayseed. I cursed my naive Midwestern roots.

How would I ever be able to keep up a conversation with these "real" New York-ers? What was there to say to people who put their faith in *The New York Times* and in who you knew? My books, dubbed "self-help" and mentioning God, are of the type *The New York Times* chooses not to review, and yet my publishing experience has to date been positive. Was that just a crazy fluke? It certainly didn't make for chic story-telling.

The party wore on. More names were dropped. Forget being just a "famous" writer. These writers were so famous they had famous editors. Imagine having Jacque-line Onassis on the other end of the editorial phone! By comparison, my whole career had been made around the edges, without the imprimatur of the powers that be. I didn't know anybody "important." What I knew, all I knew, was how to write—and that often felt in question to me.

For me to survive as a writer, there had better be a God, something larger and more powerful than *The New York Times*. Without such a God, I am lost. My career is hope-less, my dreams are futile, and I am helpless against the odds. With such a God, I just might have a chance. I need to carefully hoard my optimism. I need to side with Oscar Hammerstein who called cynicism the cause of grief and grief the enemy of his art. "Anything that kills my enthusiasm is the enemy," he declared. As an artist, I need to believe I have a chance. As artists we all need to believe we have a chance—because we do. I believe that the Great Creator loves other artists and is active on our behalf to find us a break. I believe this not only because I have to believe this, but also because it is my experience.

It is a risky, block-inducing business, thinking about the odds stacked against us, the people we should have known, the times we should have been more astute polit-ically. When we compare ourselves to others, there will always be someone who is do-ing better than we are. There will always be someone who is more successful, who has played his or her cards "right" while we have bungled ours. When we compare our-selves to others, there will always be people who are one "up" to our one "down." When we meet them, we feel discouraged. When we feel discouraged, we shut down.

> *Drunkenness is temporary suicide.*
>
> BERTRAND RUSSELL

> *Drunkenness is nothing but voluntary madness.*
>
> SENECA

> *The main motive for "nonattachment" is a desire to escape from the pain of living, and above all from love, which, sexual or nonsexual, is hard work.*
>
> GEORGE ORWELL

Shut down, we "block" and our productivity dwindles. Yes, the business of comparison is a dangerous business. Sitting at that dinner, although I certainly knew better, I was busily drawing comparisons. In those comparisons, I came up woefully short.

As artists, we do much better trying to keep things simple. We do better to compare ourselves solely to ourselves. Self-inventory is useful, while self-flagellation is not. Without calling our whole identity into question, there are inquiries that we can fruitfully ask. How am I developing as an artist? Am I doing the work necessary for me to mature? Did I work today? Yes? Well, that's good. Working today is what gives us currency and self-respect. It is what cannot be taken away from us. There is dignity in work. Not working is what makes an artist crazy. An artist who is not working can get into all sorts of trouble. Trouble even worse than a New York dinner party.

> *I did not find you outside, oh Lord, because I made the mistake of seeking outside You who were within.*
>
> ST. AUGUSTINE OF HIPPO

> *God does not die when we cease to believe in a personal deity, but we die on the day when our lives cease to be illuminated by the steady radiance, renewed daily, of a wonder, the source of which is beyond all reason.*
>
> DAG HAMMARSKJÖLD

There are always reasons not to work. There are always other things vying for our attention. Then, too, there is the attractive and seductive notion that if we don't work now, later it will be easier, we will somehow be more "in the mood." We will enjoy blessed confidence and joie de vivre. In my experience, that magical "later" never comes. Work is called "work" for a reason. It may be good, it may be rewarding, but it is often hard. And besides, "mood" is a dangerous friend.

Sometimes when my writing is the hardest, it turns out to be the best. Sometimes, when my writing is the easiest, it has just that flaw, it's too easy. I didn't examine what I was saying closely enough. On rereading, it strikes me as glib or at least not careful enough. If writing must be one thing, it must be filled with care. We must tell the truth. How else to earn our reader's respect? On my hardest days, there is still some precarious good being eked out. I have tried and that trying counts for something. Compared to not trying, it counts for a lot.

Yesterday I got a phone call from an old and beloved colleague who is not working. Did I realize, the colleague wanted to know, how very much money we could have made if I had just decided a few things differently a decade or so ago? Why, so-and-so was raking in a fortune. We had just left money sitting on the table. If only I would have listened to him more carefully I would be much, much more solvent. . . . Who wouldn't like to be more solvent? Why couldn't I have been smarter? My colleague had just been thinking about it all, he said. He sounded sad and angry. In fact, he sounded just this side of bitter and discouraged.

I listened to his thoughts and found myself thinking about the way I needed to believe that we are guided at all times, and that we do the best we can by the light we have to see by. If God is all powerful, and I believe that God is, then there is no such thing as an irreparable mistake. If I ask for guidance and my course needs correcting, I will get the guidance necessary to correct my course. There is no need for harsh recriminations. There is no need to count back over the past looking for wrong turns. The decisions of a decade ago must be seen as the best decisions we could have made at the time. In any case, a decade past is a decade past and there is no changing things. Today can perhaps be done better but the past cannot be undone. If my colleague had been working on something constructive and forward-looking, I think he would have known that. Not working, he was scratching at the past, raking it over and over again, like a dog rubbing raw its own hide.

Greater happiness comes with simplicity than with complexity.

BUDDHA

The reward of a thing well done is to have done it.

RALPH WALDO EMERSON

In order for us to go forward, we must live in the now. We must take the day that we have been given and make of it what we can. We cannot change the past. We can only regret it, and such dwelling leaches optimism from the day at hand. It is one more way to be blocked and a sadly effective one—if only . . . If only things were different, but they're not!

Talking with my sad colleague, I feel myself one more time on the slippery slope. The past is seductive. I must struggle to keep it in its place. It is too easy for the mind to seize upon some golden moment and to believe the great lie that since then everything has been ashes. "What's the use?" and "Why try?" are what come of such distorted thinking. It takes vigilance to keep from gilding the past. Each day, I must find something to love in the day at hand.

Today the temperature has climbed to the mideighties and New Yorkers are muttering in the streets. Walking back from piano, I heard the couple behind me, "It's a shame we don't get a real spring. We're slipping right past spring and into summer." For a moment, I joined them in their despair. I had a New York summer coming up after all, and it might be really hard. Then, catching myself, I snapped out of it. The day was glorious, albeit a little warm. The dreaded summer was still not at hand. The trees were barely leafing yet and there were jonquils blooming at their feet. We were, in fact, having spring.

Divining Rod

When we focus on the beauty of the now, we are able to let go of regrets about the then. When the adventure of each day's passage is celebrated, it reinforces our sense that we are in the right time and place. In other words, rather than gilding the past, we must make an attempt to gild the present. Few things do this as effectively as sketching.

Buy yourself a blank notebook. My favorite size is about five-by-seven. I like the kind with black leather covers that can easily be located at an art's supply store. Notebook in hand, proceed through an ordinary day—but take the time to do a little sketching. You may have to wait at a doctor's office. Sketch the waiting room. You may take yourself out for a cappuccino. Draw the café. If you are meeting a friend for drinks, ask if you can try a quick line drawing. Many of us find that although we are not "real" artists, we have a charming talent for the amateur sketch. Allow yourself to carry your notebook with you as a companion. You are seeking to become enchanted with yourself as a character. As you illustrate your life, you also illuminate it. There is more of interest than you at first realized.

CHECK-IN

1. **How many days this week did you do your Morning Pages?** If you skipped a day, why did you skip it? How was the experience of writing them for you? Are you experiencing more clarity? A wider range of emotions? A greater sense of detachment, purpose, and calm? Did anything surprise you? Is there a "repeating" issue asking to be dealt with?

2. **Did you do your Artist Date this week?** Did you note an improved sense of well-being? What did you do and how did it feel? Remember, Artist Dates can be difficult and you may need to coax yourself into taking them.

3. **Did you get out on your Weekly Walk?** How did that feel? What emotions or insights surfaced for you? Were you able to walk more than once? What did your walk do for your optimism and sense of perspective?

4. **Were there any other issues this week that felt significant to you in your self-discovery?** Describe them.

Uncovering a Sense of Autonomy

Essential to any creative unfolding is a sense of self-direction. We are the "origin" in "original." The tasks of this week will help you to specify exactly who and where you are, locating the powerful currents that trace through your life. Listing your loves will allow you to move closer to them. Listing your fears will allow you to move beyond them. God lives in the details, the concrete, knowable facts of your life. As you explore your psyche and its place in your environment, your compass will become ever more accurate in pointing you true north.

The Doctor's Advice

Today was an untidy day with a doctor's appointment smack in the middle of my writing time. I took a cab down to the appointment—sixty blocks south through busy streets—while spring enticingly hovered in the air. I found the address and dodged my way through some yellow tape where a sidewalk was being repaired. I rode up in the elevator. I made it to the appointment with minutes to spare. The reading material offered in the waiting room featured an article on Google. If I were to search myself on the web, I might find a portrait of a wild-haired, highly strung woman with the caption, "She would rather be writing."

Happiness is when what you think, what you say, and what you do are in harmony.

MAHATMA GANDHI

"You seem overwhelmed," I was greeted. The doctor surveyed me gravely. I did feel overwhelmed. I wanted to be at home, sticking to my simple grid, not out and about in the city. I needed to be at my desk, putting words to the page. Whenever I am not writing enough, I feel overwhelmed. And appointments like the one I was keeping take large nasty bites out of the time I have earmarked for writing.

I find that it is not the circumstances in which we are placed, but the spirit in which we face them, that constitutes our comfort.

ELIZABETH T. KING

"I am not writing enough," I complained tersely. "It makes me tense." The doctor eyed me and I eyed the doctor. I did not want to be there.

"Maybe you should rent a cabin in the country and go away for the summer and write," I was advised, somberly. "Country places aren't that expensive," he added, perhaps seeing dollar signs flash before my eyes.

What? Was the doctor crazy? I pictured myself in the country, somewhere in the middle of nowhere with nothing to do but stare at the page. Wasn't that the greased slide to writer's block? Wasn't I really better off staying right where I was and doing just what I was doing?

I didn't want to rent a cabin in the country. I wanted to write right where I was, smack in the middle of New York City. I wanted to write about the excitement of the flower district, the garment district, the antique district. I wanted to write about exactly where I was planted, in the rich soil of a bustling metropolis. I wanted to write, period. I had a lust to simply lay some track, to put some words to my experience, to try to achieve an optimistic balance by putting things onto the page. My daily quota of three pages felt skimpy. It was just enough to keep me grounded, but barely. The rest of my life seemed suddenly to be wildly out of whack and I knew from experience that if I could just write through it steadily enough, life would calm back down. "Keep the drama on the page," I lectured myself. But drama seemed to follow me everywhere, even to the doctor's.

For the past several days, my phone messages, lengthy and dramatic, have been from people who are not functioning in their art. "Call me," they say, but to call them is to invite their drama to spill over into my life.

I must be serene in the place where I am planted. At the moment, that is right in the middle of Manhattan. It is hard listening to their messages, listening to the endless variety of things that can be put before work. I say before "work" but what I mean is before emotional sobriety, the simple grid of a positive life lived one day at a time. Such a life must be free of frenzy, free of the frantic rushing here and there that cannibalizes tranquility. To be emotionally sober, I must set my own gentle pace. I try to do that but lately I have felt jostled and pressed. The "world" has been too much with me.

Yesterday I went to dinner with a fancy lady writer, and she advised me at some length of the many things in the city of which I really ought to be availing myself. "When would I find time to write?" I caught myself thinking. There are many things that give me pleasure, but there are few things that give me as much pleasure as the joy of making something. No, for me I must cling to my grid and keep things very, very simple. I tell myself this almost as a mantra. Despite myself, despite all that I "know," I feel myself spiraling into drama and despair. "Just keep it simple," I tell myself daily in my Morning Pages. Go to the keys. Go to the typewriter. Go for a walk. Edge forward a little. Guard yourself against despair. Try to sleep. If you do find yourself lying awake at night, count your blessings and not your fears. The first blessing is that you are sober, if not emotionally, at least physically. Do not sip at the glass of despair.

Acceptance makes any event put on a new face.

HENRY S. HASKINS

That which does not kill me makes me stronger.

FRIEDRICH NIETZSCHE

Man needs difficulties; they are necessary for health.

CARL JUNG

Divining Rod

When you begin to slide into despair, it is because you have lost your sense of grounding. Therefore, the tool to apply is one of gentle well-being. Put simply, your need is to count your blessings. Gratitude is a homely but effective antidote to despair.

Take pen in hand. Number from one to twenty-five. Begin with the big things. In my case, I start with, "I am sober today." And then, "I have my health." And then, onward to, "I have a safe place to live," and "My rent is paid." From the large, move to the small, "I like my bed. It is very comfortable." "I love my flannel sheets. They are cozy." You may find as many people as objects on your list. "I am grateful for my friendship with Sonia."

"I am grateful for my rapport with my daughter." Area by area, survey your life and look at the sheer number of positives that you have. Yes, today you may have had a rejection letter on your novel, but you did go forward on some new writing. You did write your Morning Pages. Grief and loss come to all of us but gratitude lists help us to keep things in proportion. The half-empty glass is actually half full. It is all a matter of perception.

The Abyss

Another night of insomnia has worked its wicked magic. If sleep mends the raveled sleeve of care, the lack of sleep creates cares. I tell myself that all is well, but my mind does not believe this. Exhausted, fairly staggering with fatigue, it lurches from worry to worry. I tell myself not to project. I tell myself to live one day at a time, but my mind doesn't listen to my advice. It evades the careful fences I have set up for it. Instead I am rehearsing my catastrophic future. In that future, I wander homeless through Manhattan's maze.

I know that these imaginings are both negative and dramatic. I know that they probably will not come to pass, but I also know that when I had my first and worst nervous breakdown, I did wander alone through the streets of London. The police scooped me up and took me to a locked ward. I barely knew my name.

Human life begins on the far side of despair.

JEAN-PAUL SARTRE

What happened once could happen again, I fear. Yes, I fear. That is the task my mind has set for itself, the endless surveying of worst-possible scenarios. Despite myself, I am romancing trouble. Despite myself, I stray near the edge of the cliff.

Right now I am not long on resilience. I am not long on faith. I am standing on the edge of a great chasm. That chasm I call "the abyss." The Devil lives in that chasm, and if I stand too close to the edge of the cliff, he gets his hands around my ankles. For a week now he has had a very good grip, and I have been struggling not to be pulled down. I have been filled with fear and with anxiety.

The Devil always comes at me through despair. The Devil talks about the odds stacked against me and how foolish I have been. The Devil likes to say, "What's the use? Game over." The Devil comes at me as anxiety and the thing I cannot fix. The Devil comes at me, above all, as a drink. The Devil wants me to think that if I just have a drink, everything will be better, at least more bearable. There is nothing that taking a drink is going to make better. The Devil tells me I am about to lose "everything" and I think that perhaps I am. The Devil would certainly like to paralyze me with fear so that losing things becomes more likely.

As I have felt myself sliding toward the cliff, I have reached out to find help, hands to hold on to, a tree to grasp. I have, a little at a time, found what I was looking for. I talked with my friend Bernice, a wise Jungian therapist, who told me to inch my way back gently, to work my emotional recovery the same way I did when I was struggling to get sober the first time. That means being willing to try working just the slogans of sobriety—"One day at a time," "Live and let live," "Let go and let God," "Easy does it." Just now, writing this little essay, talking about the abyss, I am working "Easy does it." I am trying to write something small, something centered in the day that I am in. What has me so frightened, I wonder?

I think the abyss began yawning open for me when I read a new book about Bill Wilson, the cofounder of AA. In that book, Bill was revealed to be a depressive womanizer who begged for a drink on his deathbed. Reading these things, I felt shaken. Would I still be craving a drink as I lay dying? Would there be no respite? No grace? I called friends to talk about it, and they said, "So? He was human." They sloughed off my concerns. I felt that I was dealing with more than, "So he was human." I was dealing with a fear that the center would not hold.

"Do you think you had him on a pedestal?" I was asked. I didn't think so.

"Everyone who taught me sobriety is dead," one woman told me.

I didn't find it comforting to think about that. I have been scared enough thinking about the age of the people I love, most of them in their seventies. As my mind rehearses its negative scripts, I mentally attend funerals. So many of my closest friends are so old!

"Just for today, they are still with you," I tell myself. Just for today you can phone them and hear their voices. Just for today, you are all still in this together. You are not alone.

> *Change is not made without inconvenience, even from worse to better.*
>
> SAMUEL JOHNSON

Divining Rod

When large fears overrun us, we must turn to tiny yet revolutionary actions. We must, despite our fears, "Whistle a happy tune." When tragedy seems to loom from all corners, it is a good time for comedy. "This too shall pass" applies to our despair but sometimes we must practice a little creative distraction to allow time to pass. Therefore, I am suggesting to you what has been suggested to me: when the chips are down, rent a comedy. When the chips are very down, rent five of them. Stage your own minifilm festival. In 12-step parlance, this is called "acting as if." A little laughter can go a long way toward lightening the heart.

Bringing Up Baby, It Happened One Night, The Philadelphia Story, The Princess Bride, Damn Yankees, Splash. These titles and many more serve as worthy distractions from our existential angst. (Now is not the time to rent *The Razor's Edge* or *Leaving Las Vegas*.) When you feel yourself to be in critical condition, you must treat yourself as gently as you would a sick friend.

Flagellating ourselves is not virtue. It is self-obsession. What we are in need of in our darkest times, is the magic of a little self-forgetting. It is not the moment to pore over the ills of the world. It is not time to get serious about becoming a better person. You are already a fine person, you have just lost the perspective that tells you so. Be gentle with yourself. Now is not a time for inventory and self-searching. Those activities are better left to when you are more balanced. And you will again be balanced. Allow laughter to lead the way.

Going Back to Basics

I have just set up a typewriter in the corner of my bedroom. I have moved the computer to one side and I tell myself that someday I might get back to using it, but not now. For right now, I want to get back to basics, and basics for me are the comforting clicks of a typewriter trotting forward and the slow and steady accumulation of pages.

I am trying to take Bernice's sound advice and back myself away from the cliff. To end the emotional bender of terror, I must set myself a gentle and familiar routine. In order to feel sane and steady, I must keep things sane and steady. I must set a mental discipline not to imagine the worst, not to let my mind go skittering toward the cliff. "One day at a time," I tell myself and for today I have a roof over my head and work to do. I am not homeless. I am not broke and desperate. I may be near a breakdown again but I am not having one yet. And the "yet" may never come. I cannot afford drama. I need clarity and gentleness and I need, as experience has taught me, to keep things very basic.

Creatively, I am a creature of habit. My daily habits form the grid that I must cling to right now. I need to do a few simple things and to keep doing them. I do my Morning Pages. I take my Artist Dates. I walk. Whenever I fall off my simple grid, it is quite a tumble. Whenever I pick up the first doubt and allow that doubt to spiral me deep into despair, I need my basics to get me emotionally sober again. And so, I needed to get a typewriter and I needed to roll a piece of paper into the machine. I needed to have the tactile reassurance of a book unfolding, and unfolding a page at a time in an old-fashioned and orderly way. One day at a time, one page at a time. This is what I can live with.

Reflect upon your present blessings, of which every man has many; not on your past misfortunes, of which all men have some.

CHARLES DICKENS

What you really value is what you miss, not what you have.

JORGE LUIS BORGES

I feel hopelessly old-fashioned. I have been trying to write on a computer but that has not worked for me. It is too modern, too confusing. One press of a button and I can zoom anywhere in the manuscript. I found myself pushing buttons and then wandering, lost, in the maze of words that I found. Just as my mind skittered from fear to fear, the computer skittered from essay to essay. Surely someone knows how to use this machine correctly and it is an advantage to them, but not to me. The computer only mirrors and amplifies my own confusion.

It was comforting today when I found a store that still sells typewriters and Mark, the man who helped me, listened to my panic for a moment before asking gently, "Are you a writer?" I confessed that I was. "We have writers all over the city," he assured me. "There are a lot of people who can't work on a computer." He named a writer I greatly admired. She was a long-standing client. I do not know if she works on a Selectric, like I do, but I do know that she calls in and gets Mark, who hears her anxiety about having an old familiar machine and he gets her one.

My friend Natalie Goldberg writes longhand. My friend Ed Towle uses speck-led books. I write my Morning Pages longhand but when it is time for me to think book, I want the horse and carriage of a typewriter. (It occurs to me that a part of a typewriter is called "the carriage." I think that name is no coincidence.) With the safety of my typewriter set up in the corner of my room, I feel my terror starting to ebb away.

Every form of addiction is bad, no matter whether the narcotic be alcohol or morphine or idealism.

CARL JUNG

This afternoon I talked once again with my friend Bernice. One more time, she listened to my fears and then she reiterated to me, "You are still on an emotional binge. The anxiety is like a drink. Your system is drunk with anxiety. You need to do tiny things to move yourself back from the chasm." I needed to wash my hair. I needed to clean my room. I needed to fold clothes, straighten sheets. I needed small, concrete actions in the life that I actually have, not in the terrible life that I imagine as coming toward me. So, what are the facts? Facts, unlike fears, are sober. These are the facts:

Any coward can fight a battle when he's sure of winning, but give me a man who has plucked to fight when he is sure of losing.

GEORGE ELIOT

I am sitting at a window facing north. The tree below my window is coming into leaf. The leaves are tender and bright, unfolding daily like tiny flags. Since last I wrote a book, I have moved from my old quiet apartment on Riverside Drive to a new apartment more in the midst of things. It's being in the midst of things that is tricky for me. The world feels too much with me. I get overwhelmed and I want someplace safe and quiet in which to dream and work. New York does not feel safe and it does not feel quiet. It is many other things: vibrant, chock-full of life, bristling and bustling with excitement. But no, not quiet. I must seek quiet out here. I can do that one day at a time.

Just at the moment, I am balanced on a knife edge. I am trying to find my sea legs again and I am needing to be very gentle to find them. I tell myself that I will be all right, that it is just a matter of going forward a day at a time, doing the small and doable things that will lead me one more time to a feeling of stability.

Today I was in the Greek diner on the corner of my block. An old woman was there with her companion. She edged her way forward with a cane. "I am eighty-eight," she said, to no one in particular. Her face was fine and alive. In my building, down on the eighth floor, lives a ninety-two-year-old who always puts on fresh makeup and wears her scarves tied just so. The idea of growing older in New York scares me. The city seems so overwhelming, and how much more so to a senior citizen? What courage it takes to live here! But I do live here, and I will live here for the foreseeable future. That future looms large and frightening to me. "God does not give us more than we can handle," I am told but I wonder if God doesn't overestimate me just a little. Or perhaps, and this is likely, I underestimate God.

Divining Rod

When we are at our bleakest, we often "know" better. On my blackest days, I can remember my sunny days. It is just that I doubt that I will ever get back to them. At times like this, continuity and consistency are the keys to winning through. Tiny positive actions yield large results. And so we must look to the small and the doable rather than to the large and seemingly unfixable.

Sticking to our grid of positive actions adds to our shaky self-esteem. There is power to be found in perseverance. As 12-steppers say, "Don't quit five minutes before the miracle." And so, we write Morning Pages rather than abandoning them. We force ourselves to undertake the levity of a small Artist Date. We make ourselves go for walks. Rather than trying to act big and strong, we allow ourselves to be small and convalescent.

Take pen in hand. Write a letter to God, taking care to be as small as you actually are. This is the time to write a letter that says, "Dear God. I need help to get my hair washed and get out of my pajamas. Please help me to clean up and get dressed and make my bed." Such an honest letter to God builds intimacy. We are no longer posing. By asking God to meet us exactly where we are, we are practicing compassion toward ourselves. Compassion, like humor, begins our healing.

Focusing on the Positive

The tree beneath my writing window is now nearly fully in leaf. The leaves are bright green, fresh, filled with life. I live on the eleventh floor of an apartment building and the tree reaches nearly as high. I do not recognize its type. Its leaves

To attempt the destruction of our passions is the height of folly. What a noble aim is that of the zealot who tortures himself like a madman in order to desire nothing, love nothing, feel nothing, and who, if he succeed, would end up a complete monster!

DENIS DIDEROT

Art is too serious to be taken seriously.

AD REINHARDT

Surely all art is the result of one's having been in danger, of having gone through an experience all the way to the end, where no-one can go any further.

RAINER MARIA RILKE

are four-pointed and from a slight distance they are spatulate, like a maple's leaves. What matters to me about the tree is its very existence here in the heart of Manhattan.

When I need to dream, I look at that tree. Its leaves dance lightly in the evening breeze. A grackle hops limb to limb in its upper branches. The tree is a blessing, a gift from nature, a gentle wink from God: Yes, even amidst this concrete, I am still here. I need God to be here.

My friend Bernice tells me that in times of despair we cut ourselves off from God. God, she says, reaches us through small positive actions. If you want to find God, she suggests trying something concrete and affirmative. God might be found in brushing the dog. God might be found in scrubbing the sink. God might be found in doing a load of laundry. And, in my case, God might be found in typing.

"God does not live in the abstract," Bernice tells me. As a writer, I believe God lives in the tap-tapping of my typewriter keys, in the tiny bell that sounds when I reach the end of a line. God may live also in stacks of snowy white paper. I have a friend who swears God lives in her cleaning supplies. When she has a crisis of faith, she cleans house. When I have a crisis of faith, I go to the page.

Tonight I am at the page and it is calming to me. I reach for words and my reaching is a tiny prayer. "Find me here, God," I am praying. As if on cue, my little dog Tiger Lily lets out a long and gentle sigh. She is curled serenely on the end of my bed. Her breathing is deep and rhythmic. Animals breathe naturally as we are taught to breathe by meditators. Perhaps this is why it is so calming to touch the muzzle of a cab horse, to smell its hay-sweet breath. The horses queue up at the southern end of Central Park. As taxis whirl past them, honking and rushed, the horses stand drowsily, waiting for the cluck of the reins. We, too, need to wait and rest, alert to the cluck of our God. God knows and loves our animal selves.

A friend of mine says that she meditates by stroking Kellie, her cat. "I know it isn't formal. I know it isn't how most people do it, but I swear that for me it works,"

April says. When she strokes her cat, she reaches the spiritual realms of a larger world. "God brought us together," April says of her pet, a rescue cat. "We were meant to be."

Every night, in a monastery, the monks make prayerful rounds. There is the same feeling of Godly duty in the dog-walking rounds of my neighbors. Each night, between nine and eleven, the owners come out with their dogs. In my building alone, there are two gay little Westies, a silky golden retriever, a fine brindled boxer, a giant chocolate brown Chesapeake Bay retriever, and above all Rovie, a squat dark-coated pit bull who has three people walking her each in their turn.

If Tiger Lily knows I am her servant, she wisely does not let on. Instead she flatters me with a wild greeting whenever I come in the door. "Thank God you're home," says her bounding leap as she does a quick spin in the air. Bernice is right, I think; God is in the concrete facts of our life. The leap of a young dog is a joyous prayer.

> *One does not become enlightened by imagining figures of light, but by making the darkness conscious.*
>
> CARL JUNG

Divining Rod

When joy is elusive, we must actively seek it out. We must put ourselves with people and things that bring us delight. Sometimes, when we are at our most depressed, it can be difficult to even recall the joys in life. It is for this reason, that one more time we must take pen in hand. Turning to the page, number from one to fifty. Now list fifty things which you love.

For example: raspberries, kittens, red-winged black-birds, brown-eyed Susans, hazelnut lattes, kalamata olives, oil paints, *The New Yorker*, fall leaves, blackberries, West Highland terriers, fantail goldfish, good tweed cloth, parakeets, African violets, New York pizza, real whipped cream, calico cats, window boxes, gargoyles, stained-glass windows . . .

Using your list of fifty items as a resource list, plan a week in which you allow your self to be near what you love. You may take yourself to an aquarium store to visit goldfish. You might buy yourself a pint of raspberries or a hazelnut latte. On your walk, you might keep a special eye turned for good window boxes or calico cats. An African violet is not an expensive purchase and it repays the expenditure with lasting beauty. As your list will quickly show you, there are many small ways in which we can fill our lives with those things that bring us happiness.

The Bagel Scrap

It is a cool gray day. There is a light breeze that holds a trace of moisture. It looks like we are going to have a rain. The red-brick town houses below my writing-room window are somber. Earlier in the day, I saw an optimistic sunbather stretching out a towel on a rooftop but then the day turned damp and the sunbather got discouraged. Now the roof is empty. A few pigeons perch on its cornice. A few more wheel in flight heading toward the park.

He who fights with monsters might take care lest he become a monster. And if you gaze for long into an abyss, the abyss gazes also into you.

FRIEDRICH NIETZSCHE

This morning, on our way into the park, Tiger Lily snatched up a scrap of bagel. There was no getting it away from her. She was fierce in holding on. She gripped that bagel as tightly as an old man chaws a cigar. She had exactly what she wanted. On her turn in the park there was no chasing squirrels, no mock attacks on passing dogs. She had one thought only, that bagel, and everything else passed her by in a blur.

When we have an obsessive fear, we hold on to it like Tiger Lily and her bagel. We cling to the thought with a diehard intensity, nothing can pry us loose. It is a mantra we repeat to ourselves, "I am afraid that X is going to happen." Afraid of X, we fail to notice Y. We are fixated and, in our fixation, we feel trapped.

We are never trapped. There are always choices. We do have freedom of will and movement and we can exercise them. We can find a small way to move forward and pry open the jaws of our trap. It is a question of being open-minded, but when our mind is trained on the bagel scrap, nothing can help us. This is when we must learn to let go and let God. But how do we do that?

For me, this is where the tool of walking comes into play. It is difficult to walk and keep our mind trained on the bagel scrap of fear. We may start off, like Tiger Lily, focused on our obsession, but soon enough other thoughts will start to nudge loose our grip. We see the cat in the window, calico and plump. We see the pair of matched pugs coming toward us, the Korean grocer's buckets full of gently budding pussy willows. The window dressing has been changed in the thrift shop. Tiny things catch our attention and tiny changes begin to happen along our neural pathways. We have something to chew over besides our bagel. In a moment of distraction, we drop the scrap.

We cannot change anything until we accept it. Condemnation does not liberate, it oppresses.

CARL JUNG

Talent develops in quiet places, character in the full current of human life.

JOHANN WOLFGANG VON GOETHE

What happens when we drop the scrap? We may have a moment of free-floating panic. We may dive wildly to our feet looking for another scrap to hold on to. Freedom is disorienting. What do we do when we have so many choices? This is where the walk helps us out again. If we just start moving, a footfall at a time, a footfall at a time we will be led. First we notice the calico cat. Then we think perhaps we would like to have a cat. If not a cat, something else plump and comforting. A needlepoint pillow, for example. It does not purr but it does sit on your lap. Little by little, as we walk, we can identify what it is that we are missing. For me, in the city, it is often "nature." If I get to the park, that yearning begins to be soothed. Walking out, I hear what it is I am missing.

So much of being sane and happy begins with the doing of things that are sane and happy. This means that we must train ourselves to think small rather than large. We become frightened because we have "big decisions" to make. But big decisions can be made gently, a small step at a time. But again, notice that word in there— "step." Walking leads us a step at a time. Walking gives us a gentle path. We are talked to as we walk. We hear guidance. It comes from within us and from the world around us. Walking is a potent form of prayer. "Guide me, show me," we pray as we walk, and as we walk we are guided and we are shown.

Walking in the park today, Tiger Lily got distracted and dropped her scrap of bagel. Suddenly she was straining at the leash, happily in pursuit of a provocative squirrel. Suddenly she was yapping, tugging at the lead. She desperately wanted to intimidate a black-and-white Jack Russell terrier named Hannah.

"She was born in Ireland," Hannah's owner cheerily reported.

"She's beautiful."

"I think so."

"Hannah is a rough-coated Jack," Hannah's owner volunteered.

"Tiger is a cocker spaniel with a tail," I reported back.

Not needing names or formal introductions, the two dogs crouched in play.

Tiger Lily, a blond-and-white beauty herself, leapt and pirouetted at leash end. She was all dramatic posturing, all bravura and show. "Just let me at her," her body language seemed to say. I loosened the leash. With nothing to fight against, Tiger Lily suddenly wagged her tail. She stepped forward and sniffed Hannah's nose. No longer clutching her bagel scrap, she found herself making a friend.

> *Against the assault of laughter, nothing can stand.*
>
> MARK TWAIN

> *We do not see things as they are. We see them as we are.*
>
> THE TALMUD

Divining Rod

The task I propose now requires a little bit of planning and extra soupçon of effort. I am asking you not only to take a walk but to take a walk at an unusual time for you. Break your routine and enjoy the sense of adventure it immediately brings to you. Allow yourself at least one half hour.

You might want to get up early and get out to explore your neighborhood while your neighbors are still sleeping in. You might want to take a leisurely after-dinner stroll while your neighbors are tucked safely indoors. By venturing out at an odd time, you will experience a more vivid focus. You might catch the morning light streaming through the park. You might spot the crescent moon just as it clears the skyline, a snowy-white sickle against a cobalt sky. One more time, you are being urged to experience yourself as a character. Your thoughts and perceptions are interesting. What do you notice that is new and interesting to you in your habitual habitat?

CHECK-IN

1. **How many days this week did you do your Morning Pages?** If you skipped a day, why did you skip it? How was the experience of writing them for you? Are you experiencing more clarity? A wider range of emotions? A greater sense of detachment, purpose, and calm? Did anything surprise you? Is there a "repeating" issue asking to be dealt with?

2. **Did you do your Artist Date this week?** Did you note an improved sense of well-being? What did you do and how did it feel? Remember, Artist Dates can be difficult and you may need to coax yourself into taking them.

3. **Did you get out on your Weekly Walk?** How did that feel? What emotions or insights surfaced for you? Were you able to walk more than once? What did your walk do for your optimism and sense of perspective?

4. **Were there any other issues this week that felt significant to you in your self-discovery?** Describe them.

Uncovering a Sense of Resolve

All creativity requires grounded action. There is nothing airy-fairy about the artist's world. It requires good husbandry. Making art requires that we put our shoulder to the wheel. Action is the key to success. In this week's tasks, you will focus on small actions that lead to a larger unfolding. Just as a bucket is filled a drop at a time, so too a creative life develops by the smallest acts. One more time, you will invite the Great Creator's aid on your behalf. You may experience a sense of heightened autonomy as you undertake long-postponed endeavors.

Savoring

It is a beautiful day, clear, cool, and sunny, but I find myself caught in self-questioning, missing the day at hand. It is so easy to become caught in the mind, in the weighing of invisible variables: Should I have? Was I right to? Am I doing the right thing? We become like Prufrock, wondering if we dare to wear our trousers rolled. I am determined to "have" the day.

Birds sing after a storm; why shouldn't people feel as free to delight in whatever remains to them?

Rose Fitzgerald Kennedy

Life unfurls a day at a time. It is full of situations that will resolve themselves if we give them enough time and give God a chance to get his hand in. The trick is not to panic. The trick is not to overreact. Life unfolds one day at a time, and we must let it. This is the discipline I have set for myself.

My phone rang earlier today and it was a friend of mine calling in, frantic. She outlined the "jumps" ahead of her in the month and it was several jumps too many and all of them hard. I suggested she might want to try simplifying things a little. My advice fell on two deaf ears. She was much too busy to think about having the day she was having. She was far ahead in the days that were coming up. Jumping ahead, she was wild with anxiety.

The wildest colts can make the best horses.

PLUTARCH

Ride the horse in the direction that it's going.

WERNER ERHARD

It is so easy to rush ahead into fear and panic. It is so easy to miss the beauty that awaits us in the here and now. The tiniest things can bring joy. Just this morning, as I walked my dog in the park, I came upon a family taking a photograph. We were in the part of the park where cherry blossoms make a pink canopy overhead, some boughs hanging down so far they nearly touch the ground. As I passed, a mother had urged her child to stay balanced on a tree stump. He balanced gingerly, arms out to the side to keep things steady. "Now how about a smile," the mother urged. Sure enough a brave three-cornered smile lit the child's face and there he was, a buoyant six-year-old caught forever in a soft pink cloud. "What a great photo," I called out.

So much of life is like taking a photograph. We must pause to catch the moment and savor our delight. Savoring the moment is a learned art, and it is an art that must be practiced to be perfected. The mother must notice the pink blossoms and think to bring her camera. Her child is growing up, growing up daily, and the seasons of his life will come only once. This spring Sunday is worth capturing.

This week my daughter came in from California for a brief visit. For two days in a row, we ate lunch together in the tiny Greek diner on the corner of my block. Then we strolled arm in arm through the neighborhood. Three blocks up and one block over we came upon Claremont Riding Academy. It is an old brownstone filled with horses. When my daughter was four, she took riding lessons there. Now she is much older, old enough to have a four-year-old herself, and we stood hip to hip watching a lesson together, recalling the past. My daughter patted my hand.

"You were a little bit littler," I told her as we watched the young rider urge her mount around the arena.

"I don't think my feet quite reached the stirrups," my daughter recalled.

"I am so glad I taught you to ride," I told her. That was something I had done right.

"It's one of my great joys," she whispered back, her voice throaty with emotion. The young rider cued a trot, posting up and down.

I thought of a photograph that I cherish of my daughter and me. She is two years old and I am thirty-one. She is atop a small spotted pony. I walk beside her, guiding her mount. She wears a brave tricornered smile just like the little boy's in the park. In both photos, the one I cherish and the one I saw taken, there is a poignant mixture of safety and excitement. I think it is always a mixture of safety and excitement that we are after.

As an artist, it does me good to have the safety of the Morning Pages that I write daily. There is a steadiness to the Pages. They "mother" me. It also does me good to take an Artist Date, a small soupçon of adventure, a tiny act of daring, like piloting a pony or balancing on the stump of a tree. I do not need a big adventure, just the smallest something will do. When I manage it, I feel my heart tug upward, making its own tricornered smile.

Divining Rod

A friend of mine is a very fine novelist. She fills her books with small details that are garnered on her daily walks. She is always alert for some telling detail, a freshly seen "something" that will bring the reader pleasure. No matter where we live, no matter how drab our surroundings, there is always magic to be seen. I live eleven stories up overlooking a city landscape and yet my apartment is on the flight path for large birds headed to the park. If I am alert, I can see a hawk, a heron, a flock of Canadian geese. Outside my window is a rusting fire escape. On rainy days, it is hung with silvery drops. On dry days, it is the frequent landing spot for a matched pair of blue jays.

Take pen in hand. Number from one to five. Pretend you are a novelist and that your own neighborhood is the setting for your current book. List five delights of your own locale. You might want to single out the Greek diner or the newsstand. You might mention the stands of chicory poking up near the mailboxes. Allow yourself to see your world as an interested stranger might see it.

Feelings Aren't Facts

He is well paid that is well satisfied.

WILLIAM SHAKESPEARE

Everything has its wonders, even darkness and silence, and I learn, whatever state I may be in, therein to be content.

HELEN KELLER

It is balmy today and glorious. The fruit trees in Central Park are in full and joyous bloom. Tiny pink petals float through the air. Families are out, kites in tow, and the adults are childlike themselves, running the kites back and forth. "Daddy, give me a turn!" The daffodils and jonquils are spent now. Dandelions already laze across the grass. Friends are out in pairs, ambling through the park. At the gate on West Eighty-sixth Street, I bump into a happily married couple I know who love to run together. They are dressed in brief shorts and shirts. Their smiles are contagious. "How are you doing?" the wife wants to know. "Everything good?" In the face of their sunny optimism, it seems niggardly to confess the truth.

And what is the truth? I have been having a hard time of it. I have been washed over by fear and anxiety. I have been having trouble sleeping and the city, New York, New York, has seemed huge to me and frightening. I have had what might be called a negative week. I have had the companionship of Nigel, my Inner Critic, who has busily told me that I am a foolish woman and that my dreams will come to naught. When I talked with my older friend Bernice, she accurately said I was on an emotional binge, what I call a "dry drunk." I have felt that way, not sober enough, unable to see the beauty and hope all around me, instead caught up in feelings of despair.

"Feelings aren't facts," I have lectured myself. Again and again my Morning Pages have urged me to keep things simple. I now dread going to bed, knowing that I will lie awake while my fears parade past me dressed in their most ghoulish and convincing garb. Negativity seems to cling to me these days like a cloud of cheap perfume. "Just don't drink," I remind myself. "You can live through another breakdown if you just don't drink." Each day passed sober is a small victory. Each day edges me slightly back from the abyss. At the corner newsstand, I try to not glance at the day's dire headlines. Must all the news be bad news? It seems that way.

I am not sophisticated enough to take in cynicism and shrug it off. I do not know how to be hip. I do not know how to be "with-it." At times, I think I am simply not grown up enough. I do not know how to listen to bad news and bounce back brightly. I tell a woman that I am frightened that I am one more time sliding toward a breakdown, and she replies, "This city has driven many people to madness." What am I to say to that? "Thanks a lot"? It is as though she has just given me a small but decisive shove toward what I think of as the brink.

Bernice tells me that the way back into sober thinking is through thinking small. "Get tiny," she advises. "Find small actions and take them. God lives in the concrete actions not in the abstract. Wash your hair."

And so I wash my hair, which does look better and clean and glossy. I clean the top of my bedroom bureau. I make my bed. Each small action restores a sense of optimism and with optimism comes hope. I hope I will turn the corner soon and be back to having a sense of equilibrium. I hope I will begin to see the many small beauties that fill my world. I hope I will be able to shake off the drama of comments that come floating my way. I need a way to just edge through the afternoon. I am, after all, here. Here is where I need to find some beauty. Here is where I need to find some faith. I live a block from Central Park. It has beauty. And there are many other things that have beauty as well if I am just willing, as Bernice says, to get tiny, not large. A block up Columbus Avenue from my apartment there is a good plant store. It is filled with beauty. Out on a brief Artist Date this week, I stopped in the plant store. I bought a bouquet of sweet williams and a small potted African violet. I have the violet set up on my dining-room table. Its delicate tissue paper blooms are vibrant and deep. Its velvety dark green leaves are covered with the softest fur. The plant is beautiful.

> *I'm grateful for computers and photocopiers. I appreciate where we've come from.*
>
> JULIAN SIMON

"Write a poem to your little plant," Bernice tells me. "Put a festive cloth over your computer." She is urging me to get playful.

When I get playful, I have again a childlike faith and that faith tells me that I can edge ahead. "Think little, get little, be little," I urge myself. Big things are accomplished by many, many tiny strokes. If you cannot right now take in the big picture, try taking in the little picture. Try to just do the next right thing. And what is the next right thing?

So many memories come flooding back to me. As I lie in bed, not sleeping, I have a hit parade of thoughts that all turn toward the dramatic. I remember being sick before and how very frightened it made me. If I am to avoid becoming sick again, I need to cling to the simplest of thoughts, "Just don't drink, just don't kill yourself from despair." One more time I just need to put in time, to go forward a crumb at a time. I have been here before and survived it. I will be able to survive this, too. My humor will return and with humor will come strength.

Gardens start with seeds. Seeds are tiny and look like nothing much. And yet, it is from seeds that we get blooms and from blooms that we get hope. Hope is what tells us that if we just keep going a day at a time we will be led. Hope is what tells us that there is always a tiny something that is possible, some place for God to meet us.

> *He who is contented is rich.*
>
> LAO-TSU

Divining Rod

Spiritual seekers speak of the "dark night of the soul." It is an inexplicable period of black despondency that steals over us for no apparent reason. I am in one now. Prone to breakdowns, I tend to experience dark nights as a regular, if unwelcome, occurrence. Over the years, grappling with both my alcoholism and my depressions, I have had to learn many self-protective measures. I have a need for all of them. And for friends like Bernice who can gently remind me how to use them.

It is a truism of 12-step programs to say, "You cannot think your way into right action but you can act your way in to right thinking." Faced with despair, small actions do hold the antidote. We can train ourselves to act in our own behalf.

Take pen in hand. Number from one to ten. List ten small actions that you could take which would make you feel better. For example, "I could get a good haircut." Or, "I could polish my shoes." Or, "I could sort my receipt pot." Or, "I could clean my refrigerator." If you are depressed, most of these small tasks will still seem beyond your reach. Choose the smallest and least threatening and execute that.

Rain

Today is a wet, gray day. The rooftops of the brownstones beneath my writing window are slick and wet, shiny silver and black. Today there are no intrepid sunbathers. Everyone is tucked indoors waiting for the storm to pass. Even the birds are in hiding, nestled under the brownstones' eaves, tucked away in high tree branches. No one wants to get wet—or any wetter than they are. It is a day of limited adventures.

Despite the wet, I will head over to Central Park. The dogs will like it there, once they get over their initial squeamishness at the weather. We will make a loop near the reservoir, underneath the fragrant pink trees. There is much to be said for dailiness, for braving the elements in the name of "routine." Life is made of small sweetnesses, and they come to us when we are willing to be little, instead of big.

What do I mean by being willing to be little? I mean that on a gray day we count the beauty of the raindrops hanging from the fire escape railing. We listen for the song of birds even though those birds are out of sight. A gray day is a good day to polish a pair of shoes, to put new laces in your sneakers, to run a damp cloth along the window ledges cleaning up the grime. On a gray day, we are like children and perhaps it is a good day to act like them.

In a tall bookcase just off of my writing room, I keep a row of children's books. I have books on fish, on Africa, on trains and, today's book, a book on birds. Written to perhaps a twelve-year-old's level, these books are just the kind you might use in grammar school to give a report. With the rain slicking the windows, I turn the pages slowly. I learn that the smallest bird weighs only 0.5 ounces while the largest bird weighs 275 pounds.

Curled in a large leather reading chair with a lamp lit against the afternoon gloom, I learn that birds have hollow bones supported by interior struts. A pigeon's skeleton is so light, it weighs only one-twentieth of the weight of the bird. In order to assure a pigeon of a quick escape from danger, the wing muscles are very

My crown is called content, a crown that seldom kings enjoy.

WILLIAM SHAKESPEARE

I am not an adventurer by choice but by fate.

VINCENT VAN GOGH

Do you not see how necessary a world of pains and troubles is to school an intelligence and make it a soul?

JOHN KEATS

powerful, counting for a full third of the bird's weight. Strong wing muscles enable the pigeon to take off rapidly and to accelerate swiftly to a speed of up to fifty miles per hour. The pigeon is built for daring escapes from danger.

By way of contrast, the peregrine falcon embodies danger. Able to dive at the rate of 175 miles per hour, it bags its quarry by knocking it to the ground with the force of its impact and slashing it with its talons. The northern reaches of Central Park make an urban home for the peregrine falcon. Birders haunt the park, tramping through forested areas and creeping up to wetlands. They carry binoculars and often a Sibley field guide. They speak in excited whispers, jotting down their sightings of the day. To my eye, the birders themselves are an exotic species.

The silvery day is starting to lighten. The gray mist shrouding tall buildings is starting to thin. While water drops still cling to the fire escape railings, no new droplets are forming. We have had the rain we are going to have and by late afternoon, the day may begin to clear and brighten. The dogs are eager now to get outdoors to the park.

> *Every time a child says, "I don't believe in fairies," there's a fairy somewhere that falls down dead.*
>
> SIR JAMES M. BARRIE

Sometimes we must play the sleuth with ourselves, asking ourselves what makes us eager. We must follow our noses and allow ourselves to pursue curiosities. We must edge our way toward the wetlands, careful not to startle the birds that we seek. It is good to sneak up on an enthusiasm. Let us say we have an interest in Paris, as I recently did. We might begin by searching the Internet to find a guidebook on Paris. We might order the book. Next, we might try our hand at language. Prior to our Parisian trip, Emma and I studied French with the Pimsleur Method. We queued up CD's and listened carefully, responding to the cues that said, "Where is the hotel?" and "I would like to eat dinner with you at nine." Although there were a disconcerting number of ways to order wine, I practiced my lessons faithfully. Eventually, thankfully, I learned how to decline a glass of wine. As a sober alcoholic I was interested in being able to say "No." And say "No" I did all through the journey that was our next step. *"Non, merci, merci bien,"* I managed to say, declining red wine, white, and pink.

Before our trip, still anticipating it, we began learning foods we would encounter. We learned that hot chocolate was *chocolat chaud*. We learned that a ham and cheese crepe was *jambon et fromage*. It was thrilling once we made it to Paris, to put our newly won knowledge to the test. I ordered a crepe from a stand at the flank of the Eiffel Tower. In a cozy bistro I ordered a raspberry soufflé and declined the dessert crepe made with Grand Marnier. Each morning, for breakfast, I would order a *café crème*. That, and a *pain chocolat*. It was delicious being a beginner in the language, making my way a syllable at a time. It was nearly forty years since I had studied French in high school. After all that time, stray phrases would come swimming back.

The afternoon has cleared. I have taken "the girls" out to the park. The weather reminds me of Paris, luminous and soft, lightly misting. As I pass the benches lining the westward walk, I hear a dog owner calling to his dog, *"Fifi. Ici. Ici, Fifi."* Fifi, a cream-colored dog with a sweet face, crosses obediently to her owner's side. *"Bonjour,"* I say as I lead my charges from the park.

> *Beauty is truth, truth beauty.*
>
> JOHN KEATS

> *He must pull out his own eyes and see no creature, before he can say, he sees no God; he must be no man, and quench his reasonable soul, before he can say to himself, there is no God.*
>
> JOHN DONNE

Divining Rod

We speak of having a "childlike wonder" without realizing the cue that is contained in the phrase. It actually gives directions for an action plan. To awaken our sense of wonder—a necessary ingredient in all creativity—we must be willing to be childlike. We have heard this before in spiritual matters. Christ told us that in order to have faith we must "become as little children." Since creativity is a matter of faith, becoming childlike can help us in our creative endeavors. We must learn to explore with openness and curiosity. What better place to do this than a children's bookstore?

Set aside one full hour. Take yourself to a good children's bookstore. Allow yourself the delicious luxury of browsing. Chances are that many books will pique your interest. There are books on cars, trains, and butterflies. There are books on birds, reptiles, and dinosaurs. There are books on Indians and books on India. Do not be too adult to be enticed. What is more fun than a picture book on dogs or cats or horses? Or maybe you want to know how an automobile engine works?

A children's book on Magellan set me off on a year's worth of writing about the great mariner. As scholars will tell you, Magellan is a very adult subject but the children's books on his adventure fired my imagination more than the worthy biographies that bore his name.

Remember that too much information can dampen the imagination. You can always explore a topic at more depth if you wish, but children's books are an ideal place for starting off.

The Stubbornness of Dreams

A friend of mine is suffering from a depression. She worked for a long time to manifest a dream and the dream seems to have gone glimmering. She is at a loss as to the next action to take. She feels adrift without her dream to moor her. Who is she if she doesn't have a dream?

"I admire people who don't give up," she says. "I admire people who keep on going despite the odds." Her gentle voice is sorrowful.

"Maybe you just need to resolve to be one of those people," I tell her. I am telling her what I tell myself: Act your way into right thinking.

"I'd like to be," she says. She sounds weary, small and sad.

"Just do the simple things," I tell her. "Set up a gentle grid and stick to it. Go back to basics." I urge her to write Morning Pages, to take Artist Dates, to go for walks. I tell her that optimism will come seeping back—this is what I have been telling myself and I do believe it. I am in a black period, a bleak time, but I believe that such time will pass. I tell my friend exactly what it is I myself most need to hear.

Dreams come to us from a divine source. If we follow them, they lead us back to a divine source. When we work toward our dreams, we are working toward our God. In reaching for guidance about our dreams, we are reaching toward God. Our dreams are not futile. They do not spring from our egos. They have their roots in our souls. My friend is right to fear the destruction of her dream. Dreams must be guarded like children. Like children, they must be nurtured and soothed.

As an artist, it can be very difficult to sort through destructive criticism. When we receive feedback that is vague or simply way off the mark, it can be hard to have the resilience necessary to spring back. In my friend's case, the "no's" she has been receiving around her dream are particularly frustrating because she knows that the work she has done is good. She has had support and encouragement from two estimable authorities—people who, unfortunately, are not in the position to offer concrete help. "Your show is good," they have told her. "Keep on keeping on."

What my friend needs is the gift of healing. Her beleaguered heart must find some way to mend. I have said to her that she should try walking. Walking has a way of drawing pain to scale. Walking has a way of giving us perspective. My friend laughs. She does walk. Walking has made her dreams feel only more painfully real.

"I walked all the way home from Times Square," my friend countered. "The more I walked, the stronger became my dream."

"Well, then. I guess you can't give up," I tell her.

A step at a time we are led forward and sometimes those steps are literal. On the strength of her dream, my friend must one more time take action. Praying for guidance, she was told to push forward. To be an artist, one needs a good dose of stubbornness. We need a mulish side that refuses to be bullied or cowed. "I will win out," some obstinate voice in us must be insisting. "There has to be a way," is the mantra we must chant.

Many times, success comes through unseen doorways. When conventional routes have been exhausted, success steps forward wearing an eccentric cloak. How many times do breaks come to us through sources as unlikely as "my dentist's cousin"? How often do we find that we are led through a maze of lucky breaks and coincidence? Embracing her dream again, my friend is about to step into the maze. "Dear God, show me," must be her prayer.

Another friend of mine is a minister. He warns against depending on one source for our well-being. "God has a thousand ways to meet you," he says. "Do not look for someone else to give your dream permission to go forward," he warns. "When you make one person or place the source of your lucky break, you are

> *Art is only a means to life, to the life more abundant. . . . In becoming an end, it defeats itself.*
>
> HENRY MILLER

> *Every production of an artist should be the expression of an adventure of his soul.*
>
> W. SOMERSET MAUGHAM

denying the power of God who can work from many corners." Trust God and look for leadings, he advises.

The world of publishing is filled with stories of best-selling authors who became that way by first publishing themselves. A publisher I know laughs ruefully over these stories. "There's more than a grain of truth in them," he says. "Very often a book will be turned down 'everywhere' only to have the author self-publish, driving his book from store to store and ending up with a whopping success."

To be an artist, we must be willing to be Don Quixote, to tilt at a few windmills, to look foolish to others and even to ourselves. Every artist carries within him an Inner Dreamer. The dreamer might be called "the Believer," the part of us that is willing to go forward on faith. Every artist carries, too, an Inner Censor, the skeptical part that might be called "the Devil," the part that tells us the game is over, that we might as well quit.

> *If a man does not keep pace with his companions, perhaps it is because he hears a different drummer. Let him step to the music which he hears, however measured or far away.*
>
> HENRY DAVID THOREAU

The Devil is clever and it comes at us from many quarters. It always asks us to deny the power of God. One of the chief forms the Devil takes is an urge on our part toward self-sufficiency. We count on ourselves and stop counting on a Higher Power. We feel that we ought to be able to figure things out and when we cannot, we conclude that we are phonies, has-beens, crazy. The Devil finds our Achilles' heel and comes at us through that. Let us say we are worried about money. The Devil will tell us that we will soon be homeless. Let us say we are worried about prestige. The Devil will rehearse for us our future bad reviews. Say we are an expert at some area of knowledge. The Devil will tell us that all our expertise matters nothing. It will say we have no answers when our answers lie right before us but we are too blind with fear to see them and pick them up. For me, the Devil is a form of drunkenness. I have alcoholism not alcoholwasm. The Devil comes at me saying, "What's the use? Poor me. Poor me. Pour me a drink."

Help is all around us. Help is at every hand. Help is just waiting to meet and greet us. We are the ones who insist there is no help. Our hearts are closed to the many gentle forms of help that are offered to our suffering souls. What we are after, all that we need, is a sip of water. Our challenge is finding water when we are in a spiritual drought. We need the gentle draught of encouragement, the water of spiritual truth. "There is a God," we need to hear. "You are cared for," we need to believe.

Divining Rod

You have already practiced writing a humble letter to God, perhaps more than one. You have experienced the grace that comes from spiritual candor. There is something very healing in telling God exactly where it hurts and why. It is a relief to get our despondency off our chest. The exercise I am now asking you to undertake requires some further open-mindedness. I am asking you to imagine an answered prayer.

Set aside an hour's quiet time. Take pen in hand and write God a letter about anything and everything that is currently bothering you. Write for as long as a half hour, then stop. Now take your pen to page a second time. This time listen for an answer and write a letter from God back to you. In your fondest hopes and dreams, what compassionate response does God have to your yearnings? Allow your imagination to guide you. Comfort and soothe yourself as you wish that God would. Listen to your deepest intuitions about the solutions and perspectives that God has to offer. There is a wise being within you that deserves to be listened to. The "still, small voice" does speak to us all.

CHECK-IN

1. **How many days this week did you do your Morning Pages?** If you skipped a day, why did you skip it? How was the experience of writing them for you? Are you experiencing more clarity? A wider range of emotions? A greater sense of detachment, purpose, and calm? Did anything surprise you? Is there a "repeating" issue asking to be dealt with?

2. **Did you do your Artist Date this week?** Did you note an improved sense of well-being? What did you do and how did it feel? Remember, Artist Dates can be difficult and you may need to coax yourself into taking them.

What is art: It is the response of man's creative Soul to the call of the Real.

RABINDRANATH TAGORE

The artist's object is to make things not as nature makes them, but as she would make them.

RAPHAEL

3. **Did you get out on your Weekly Walk?** How did that feel? What emotions or insights surfaced for you? Were you able to walk more than once? What did your walk do for your optimism and sense of perspective?

4. **Were there any other issues this week that felt significant to you in your self-discovery?** Describe them.

Uncovering a Sense of Resilience

Most of us have little sense of our true strength. The essays and tasks of this week ask you to focus on your personal resiliency. By focusing on your available resources, you will see that you do indeed have sufficient fuel for your journey. Your spiritual well will not run dry if you take the time and care to replenish it by self-loving actions. At midpoint in the course, your spiritual connection to the Great Creator both deepens and becomes ever more personal, revealing to you perhaps previously unsuspected inner strength.

Support

This morning, I paid a visit to Therese, an older woman who lives in a snug apartment a few blocks south. Therese radiates a sharp, incisive intelligence. She is nobody's fool.

"The problem so many of us have is self-sufficiency," Therese said. "We fall into depending on ourselves instead of God and then we wonder why we feel so alone. We cut ourselves off and then we feel isolated. You know, we really are not alone."

Therese knows whereof she speaks. She is herself a walking example of what can be done with the power of God. A low-bottom alcoholic, she has been restored to sobriety and sanity. Once a helpless drunk, she now helps others.

> *Our real blessings often appear to us in the shape of pains, losses, and disappointments.*
>
> JOSEPH ADDISON

"I am having a hard time writing," I tell Therese. "Words are not coming to me easily. I feel inarticulate."

"Sometimes it is good to be inarticulate," Therese answers back. "When we are dealing with deeper layers of the psyche, we don't always have a line of glib chatter. Occasionally, being struck speechless is good."

"But I make my living with words," I protest, even though I can feel the truth of what Therese has said to me. I find myself wondering what it would be like to be wordless for a while, simply living, existing in the flow of life like a satiny gray river rock, washed over by the flow.

> Two things make a story. The net and the air that falls through the net.
>
> PABLO NERUDA

"You are filled with self-centered fears," Therese tells me. One more time her blunt words seem to accurately name the precise condition I have found myself facing.

I am filled with self-centered fears. I am worried about drinking, about running out of money, ending up homeless, wandering the streets like the many lost souls I see on my rounds in Manhattan. Fight it as I will, my imagination has snagged on the negative. I have a recurrent dream, one in which my daughter is four years old and I am wandering the streets of New York with no place for us to live. It is nighttime and there is no place safe for us to rest.

"It's just a nightmare," I tell myself. "It's just a dream."

And yet I am afraid that the dream will become a reality. I know that I can make it one by simply picking up a drink and allowing the drink to lead the way.

Therese is talking again. "You need to share how you are feeling," she says. "You need to let it out."

"Therese," I tell her. "I am supposed to have answers. I am twenty-eight years without a drink. People look to me for answers—and today I have none. I need help."

"You need support," Therese rephrases it.

Once again, her words accurately name an inner state I lacked words for. I am shaken to the core and I need to feel a sense of divine guidance. I have been craving the help and security of other people. They say that alcoholism is the disease of isolation. I certainly have it. One more time, I need to reach out.

Divining Rod

At our most alone feeling, most of us still number several friends and supporters on whom we could count. Miserable and despondent, we nonetheless have more resources for help than we are able at the moment to see or access. When our despair tells us that we are isolated and without help, cut off from God and from all human understanding, the truth is that most of us do have friends who understand us—if we give them the chance. It is a lie of the mind that we are alone and friendless. We do have allies. The trick to identifying such allies lies in making a list of our resources when we are not sad and beset. Try your hand at this now.

You have already made a list of five people who are encouraging to you and your art. Turn to that list again and see if there are any among them who could be counted upon for more generalized emotional support. In all likelihood, you will find several. Choose one. When you have made your selection, call, write, or e-mail your friend. Explain that you are reaching out, that you are not always so needy but just at the moment you could use some cheering up. Allow yourself to express some vulnerability, to reveal a peek behind the upbeat surface you work so hard to maintain.

When your friend responds to your contact, take time to check in with yourself about exactly how their response makes you feel. You are in a sorting process, seeking to find friends with whom you can be small as well as large. Some of our friends prefer us only when we are doing well. Others, those with broader emotional keyboards, are able to take us in in whatever condition we come to them. (Be alert to avoid in the future those friends who are shaming to you about your feelings of vulnerability. We may "know" better but be unable to "do" better at being upbeat.) You are looking for friends who can take you just as you are.

"You sound tired," such a friend might say to you. "Are you sure you aren't a little under the weather? Maybe you should ease up a little bit." Support for our human selves can go a long way toward easing our panicked sense of isolation. Friends, above all, are friendly. They do not shame us or urge us back to the treadmill when we are suffering from burnout. Friends encourage us to be flexible and kind toward ourselves. They are friends not only to the work but to the worker. Allow yourself to experience their support.

Discernment

The day today is bright but chill, very, very chill. The wind from the west is sharp and needling. People walk clutching their coats and jackets. What happened to spring? Wasn't it just a day or so ago that we were rushing forward into summer? This new, colder weather seems like a betrayal.

Think before you speak is criticism's motto; speak before you think is creation's.

E. M. FORSTER

Give what you have. To someone else it may be better than you dare to think.

HENRY WADSWORTH LONGFELLOW

When you cease to make a contribution, you begin to die.

ELEANOR ROOSEVELT

Out in the park, pale, pink cherry blossoms shiver in the breeze. A flowering plum looks nearly purple with the cold. Still, it is a pretty day and a few landscape artists have set up easels under the bouffant cherry trees. One painter balances her water in a small green cup. She is working in watercolor and she is painting a miniature, each delicate stroke following on the next.

This afternoon, I got a letter from Rhonda. She was writing to say she had received a copy of my latest book and she was enjoying it. Her letter came on pretty stationery. Her writing added more whimsical hearts and flowers. She was looking forward, she said, to our summer's walks. Rhonda is used to my returning to New Mexico every spring. I am used to it, too, and her letter caused me to wince with sorrow.

"Oh, dear," I think to myself. "No walking with Rhonda. No long hikes up El Salto Road past the buffalo and llamas." No, this summer will be more domesticated. My strolls will be around the perimeter of the reservoir and sometimes south to Central Park's small lake, the rowing pond. If I am lucky, and if I go at odd hours, the park will not be too crowded and there will be flora and fauna to spot.

If I am lucky, I will be able to muster optimism. I will be able to stick to my gentle grid of walks. This summer is an experiment, an attempt to forestall danger. Last summer in New Mexico I was struck suddenly and savagely fragile. A breakdown loomed. Far from doctors, diagnosed by telephone, the only solution was to take strong doses of medication and make the long drive back to Manhattan and to relative safety. In Manhattan, doctors are at hand. Friends are nearby who have seen me through rough patches before. In New Mexico, there is only beauty and fear. No, this year is not a year for New Mexico. It is a year to make the most of the wildness and beauty I can find in Manhattan.

Just yesterday, Emma reported that she had spotted something big. "I don't think it was an eagle, but it was very, very large. Its head was brown, not white, and it had thick feathers fluffing out its legs."

To my ear, it sounded worth a jaunt to the park to try spotting this creature. It could be a peregrine falcon or some species of hawk. I could take my birding binoculars and hope for a good glimpse of it. It is not the same as a day's jaunt on the Rio Grande with eagles soaring overhead. It is a tamer, smaller adventure, but it will do.

As I work to bring myself back into balance, I must turn to the tiny things I can do each day to muster a sense of optimism. I wake and curl in a large leather chair to write Morning Pages. I say my prayers. I read some of Ernest Holmes's writings. I go to the computer and work. After I work, I take myself on a small adventure.

With Tiger Lily by my side and the birding binoculars around my neck, I head over to the park. I am looking for Emma's large bird. What I find, instead, are a plethora of robins and one beautiful red-winged blackbird. Later in the day, back at my computer, I glance out the window just in time to catch sight of a heron flying past. My late father loved herons, and I have two Audubon prints of herons framed in my living room. Spotting the high-flying bird, headed to Central Park and the small lake where it makes its home, seems auspicious to me. I am ready to see good omens.

> *If I can stop one heart from breaking, I shall not live in vain.*
>
> EMILY DICKINSON

On a roof garden across the avenue from my building, two large fake owls stand sentinel. They are there to ward off pigeons, their stiff silhouettes signaling, "Danger. Enemy territory." The pigeons give the garden a wide berth.

As artists, we, too, must learn who and what to give a wide berth. We must steer clear, if we can, of people who dampen our enthusiasms, who cut short our flights of fancy. Like the sharp-taloned owl, a sharp tongue goaded by cynicism can quickly tear our optimism to shreds. We are resilient but delicate. We must be alert.

As artists, we must be vigilant. We cannot control everyone around us, but we can learn whose company is good for us and whose company causes us to shrivel and shrink. As we work to set new boundaries, we will provoke some anger and some resentment. When we say "Hands off!" there will be those who take a quick final pinch.

It is the perilous truth that many of the people who talk to us as artists do not know how to talk to us as artists. They mean well but even their well-meaning does not undo the damage they inflict, almost in passing. In America, we are taught how to take things apart, not how to build them. In our school system we learn how to criticize, not construct. As a result, people know how to weigh in with what is wrong but without balancing it with comments about what is right. The artist, hearing only the criticism, begins to shut down. Valid points may be made, but they are made over the artist's nearly dead body. "Oh, what's the use?" A certain sullen stubbornness may set in, "I am not changing anything." Here again is where friends can help us to parse out the criticism that is tough but useful.

In my experience, artists do want valid criticism. We feel a sense of excitement and a willingness to work when a piece of criticism hits the mark and we intuitively feel it will make our work better. Instead of "Ouch!" we register, "Ah ha!" and the creative wheels start to turn as our engine kicks over and we begin "fixing" something—almost whether we want to or not. Sometimes, however, it can take a friend's translation to help us hear criticism accurately. "Maybe he's really saying X," the friend might suggest, giving us a slightly more neutral way to view a set of remarks. Equally, a friend might say, "Oh, Julia, he's way off the mark, just ignore him," which is easier said than done but is possible to do with the help of your friends.

> He does good to himself who does good to his friend.
>
> ERASMUS

When I was a young writer, I lived in an apartment behind the Washington Zoo. Every morning as I woke up and every night as twilight fell, I would hear the roar of wild animals vying to be heard over the sound of traffic. There were lions and tigers and bears—many, many bears. And so it happened that I wrote my early short stories to an exotic accompaniment. The animals were always present, an odd, primal sound track eclipsing the hubbub of the city. They were at once comforting and terrifying.

Judy Bachrach was my best girlfriend in those days, and she was both comforting and terrifying, too. Another young writer, she had firm opinions about all I wrote.

We both wrote for *The Washington Post*. She was that exalted creature, a staff writer. I was a lowly copy aide who freelanced for the paper on the side. Judy was tall and willowy with a striking resemblance to young Lauren Bacall. She was my primary cheerleader and hardest critic. "You can't publish this one," she said of one short story, "it will ruin your career."

The fact that I had no *career* at the time did not faze Judy. She believed in me and my work and my future career was a certainty to her. She—and I—must protect it, she felt. I put the short story in a bottom drawer. I never did publish it. I went on to write other stories, stories that could pass muster with Judy and not damage my career. All of us need our Judy's, friends vigilant enough to tell us when the work wobbles, which it sometimes will. These friends are our sentinel owls and we can use them to protect our creative gardens.

The bravest sight in the world is to see a great man struggling against adversity.

SENECA

Talk that does not end in any kind of action is better suppressed altogether.

THOMAS CARLYLE

Divining Rod

My friend Julianna McCarthy has taught me a parlor game that I believe all artists should learn to play. The game is called "Who Would You Take to the War?" It asks you to survey your friendships and assess them in terms to their health to your well-being and goals. Most of us, looking over our friendships, will discover that we do not have too many friends whom we could take to the war but that we do have some.

A friend that I would take to the war would need to be someone who is able to keep his head and objectivity when the going gets tough. I have such a friend in my believing mirror Ed Towle. Shrewd and longsighted, he keeps his emotions at bay while he parses out the best course of action. I can depend on him both for humor and for realism. If I tell him an emotional story, he puts it in the framework of the "big picture." Ed is a friend I could take to the war.

I could not take my friend Felice to the war. She is prone to drama. She would encourage me to overreact to the first signs of trouble. Felice would encourage my own fears to step too far forward. No, Felice could not be depended upon to keep her head.

My friend Julianna, the inventor of the game, is someone I could take to war. Hardheaded and yet compassionate, she always has an eye on the bottom line, drawing things to scale. If I call her with a manufactured misery, she will snap, "You're doing fine, given that you should have been dead years ago." She is referring of course to my alcoholism and the fact that every day sober is a win. And yet, if I phone her with a legitimate misery, Julianna is quick with compassion. She says, "Life is hard and what you're going through is hard." Her empathy always makes me feel better.

Take pen in hand. Survey your friendships for those people whom you could take to the war. List their names and the qualities that would make them invaluable. This is an exercise in discernment.

Healing

The sun is playing peekaboo. When it is out, the day is warm. When it is hiding behind a cloud, the day is cool. Kids are out in shirtsleeves and shorts on their skateboards. Adults clutch their thin jackets closer to their bodies. The fur on a fluffy collie ruffles in the wind. At the entrance to the park, mock orange is now blooming. The maple trees are coming into leaf. The flowering fruit trees, apple and plum and cherry, are white, purple, and pink according to their nature. Spring is at hand, advancing daily, but the warm weather is still fractious.

This afternoon, I talked on the phone with Bernice who lives in Boulder, Colorado. "It's snowing very hard here," she said. "Of course that is good because we've

I have learned more about love, selflessness, and human understanding in this great adventure in the world of AIDS than I ever did in the cut-throat, competitive world in which I spent my life.

ANTHONY PERKINS

suffered a drought. There's an inch on the ground here but in the mountains it is really building up."

Bernice and I talk on the phone once weekly. I depend on Bernice for her wisdom and her humor. She listens to my life and offers wisdom from a decade further on the path.

Today, I told Bernice that I still was feeling shaky, that New York was feeling overwhelming to me, and that I was longing to be in New Mexico, where the long vistas draw things to scale. I needed a reality check. Wasn't I just as close to a breakdown here as I had been last year in New Mexico?

"No. And you're sounding better than you have been," Bernice responded. "But you're not out of the woods yet. I think you are grieving. I believe your losses around your art have rattled you to the core. For a while, you need to keep a very narrow focus. Remember what I've told you. You need to get tiny."

"Get tiny" is good advice for how to inch forward. In 12-step lingo, we are told to "do the next right thing." When we suffer a loss around our art, we need to find some small positive action by which we can go ahead. Discouraged as I am about *The Medium at Large,* I might still listen through that show to remind myself that it is good, no matter how its reception might feel. Sometimes the action is an action in the outer world—mail the poem off one more time. Sometimes, however, the action needs to be in our inner world. We may need to write a nursery rhyme to comfort our inner creative youngster. We may need to do a piece of doggerel to help us get to the other side.

> *Beauty is as relative as light and dark.*
>
> PAUL KLEE

> *If you don't believe in God, all you have to believe in is decency . . . Decency is very good. Better decent than indecent. But I don't think it's enough.*
>
> HAROLD MACMILLAN

When I suffered a bad review in the Sunday *New York Times*—the only bad review I got on an otherwise well-liked book, *The Dark Room*—I had to write a scrap of poetry to get myself out of the doldrums. And so I wrote a poem at my wrongheaded reviewer:

This little poem goes out to Bill Kent
Who must feel awful the way that he spent
His time critiquing Carl Jung
Instead of on the book I'd done.

Writing the little poem gave me a naughty sense of power. It made me feel that one more time I had an impish sense of play. It is a sense of play that tells us we have things in healthy perspective. It is when life feels deadly earnest that we blow things out of all proportion. With the rim of the glass looming, I have to watch that tendency right now. I sometimes think that self-pity is the dominant, distinguishing characteristic of my alcoholism. If my periodic depressions are biochemical events, they must be fought with every tool I have at hand, both medically and spiritually. But when I am teetering on the brink, the temptations to self-pity seem fiendishly persuasive.

We artists are indestructible; even in a prison or in a concentration camp, I would be almighty in my own world of art, even if I had to paint my pictures with my wet tongue on the dusty floor of my cell.

PABLO PICASSO

This afternoon, I was interviewed by a woman from a large Canadian magazine. "How does it feel," she wanted to know, "to be pigeonholed as a 'Self-Help' writer?" The question went straight to one of my worst creative fears, that I would always be known first and foremost as a teacher and that the level of my craft as an artist would never be allowed to shine. I told the woman frankly that I couldn't afford to think about how I was perceived. "That's a drink for me," I explained. "All I need to do is start thinking about how I am not appreciated and never will be and it becomes, 'Poor me, poor me, pour me a drink.' "

I explained to the woman that my need to stay sober was actually my greatest teacher. All of the stratagems I have learned to apply to the artist's life come straight out of the toolkits I have acquired to maintain my sobriety. When Bernice says, "Get tiny," I hear, "Oh, yes, one day at a time." When Bernice urges me to make small lists and execute them, I think, "Ah, yes, just do the next right thing. Follow first things first."

At the moment, I am shaky. I have no "I" to write from. My ego feels shattered and with it my prose style. I look at older books that I have written and I wonder at the writing style and the wisdom contained within them. "Where did that wisdom go?" I wonder. "What happened to my syntax?"

It is a Friday night in Manhattan. Couples stroll Columbus Avenue, arm in arm. The Chase Bank on the corner is doing a brisk ATM business and nowhere, in any of the faces that I see, do I see a trace of my lost syntax. People are busy. People are happy and my missing syntax is my own sad little secret. I leave the young lovers to the street below and I come upstairs to write. Bernice has estimated that it will take me several weeks longer before I will be back in my stride and writing well. She thinks, as do I, that I need the benefit of a simple routine, a dull and daily life, for my psyche to settle back down again. For my part, I long to burrow into my routine. If it cannot be a summer of long walks in Taos, let it be a summer of long walks in Manhattan. I need to stretch my legs and my imagination. I need to find healing and health.

> *If sex and creativity are often seen by dictators as subversive activities, it's because they lead to the knowledge that you own your own body (and with it your own voice), and that's the most revolutionary insight of all.*
>
> ERICA JONG

Divining Rod

The monasteries of the great world religions run on ritualized schedules. The gong sounds and the monks are called to worship. Their days are fruitfully divided according to regular activities. In our own more secular lives, we are the ones who must set in place our rituals and our rounds. Morning Pages give us a way to begin our days. A midday walk finds our souls stretching as well as our bodies. Winding down to bedtime, it is healing to have a regular evening ritual. In this way, we can begin our day and end our day with a spiritual contact.

Some students have found that simply listing the five beauties of the day places them in a mood of gratitude and receptivity. Just before sleep, they often feel a sense of conscious contact with the Divine. It is in this mood of openness and acceptance that I ask you to undertake an experiment.

Take pen in hand. Remembering that God is the Great Listener, write a simple prayer. (You have done this before when you were feeling shaky. Now try it on a "regular" night.) You might tell God about the day that you have just had. You might revisit your dreams or disappointments. You might ask for guidance, to be awoken the next day with a clear sense of God's will for you. Some evening prayers are prayers of gratitude. Some are prayers of petition. It matters less what you say than that you say it. The evening prayer is a time for candor. Think of this interval as being like a nightly chat between fond lovers. Show God your secret heart.

Soldiering On

It is May Day. The weather is cooperating, sunny and breezy and seventy degrees. In the park, picnickers abound. In the pinetum, a pine grove just off the Great Lawn, there are two picnic tables laden with cakes and sodas and a bevy of young children weaving a merry dance with the streamers from a maypole held aloft by a quickly tiring adult.

Patience is the companion of wisdom.

ST. AUGUSTINE OF HIPPO

At Turtle Pond, the turtles have emerged from their winter's hibernation below the ice-locked pond. The pond is a shimmering surface broken only by the wake of paddling ducks. The turtles bask on rocks and logs, soaking up the sun's warmth after their long winter's chill. On the dock that juts out into the water, parents stand with their young offspring, peering through the railings.

"See, there's a turtle!" they say, pointing to the shell of a lounging turtle. The turtles look like so many silvery river rocks. They are hard to see against the shore.

"I see one," a triumphant and precocious five-year-old trumpets. He points to where a slow-moving turtle is lurching into the water.

"Yes, well, there are lots of them," his father advises. "Can you see the rest?"

"No." Now the child's voice is petulant. "I want ice cream."

A vendor has set up shop nearby, poised for just such an eventuality. The vendor's wagon offers pretzels, hot dogs, "Froze-ade" and, yes, ice cream.

"Want a pretzel?" The father is trying to dodge a sugar high.

"No, I want ice cream."

"What kind of ice cream do you have?"

The vendor waves a hand at a large sign which enumerates a dozen or more ice-cream treats.

"I see." The parent sounds testy now. A sugar high lies ahead. The child stands on one foot. Is it bathroom time as well?

"What kind do you want? Orange? Rainbow? Vanilla?"

"Rainbow." The child points a stubby finger at the rainbow pop.

And so, rainbow it is. The child grabs eagerly at the garish concoction, a swirled mass of pink, orange, lime green, and white.

"Is it good? Are you happy?" The parent sounds a little beleaguered. I flash a look at his left hand: no ring. Another divorced father, trying to make the best of his weekend visitation rights. Seeing his child once a week is far from perfect, but he is making do the best he can.

> *Hasten slowly and you will soon reach your destination.*
>
> MILAREPA
>
> *In art the best is good enough.*
>
> JOHANN WOLFGANG VON GOETHE

Also making do the best he can is the German shepherd who now paddles toward us, front paws striding the ground, back paws hitched aloft in a bicycle contraption. German shepherds are prone to hip problems and clearly this dog's owner was unwilling to put his dog down.

"Here we go. This way, Max," the owner urges, backpedaling in his running gear to keep pace with his dog. Max trots briskly ahead. He is used to the contraption that makes his life possible.

The divorced father and Max's owner have in common a rugged resilience. They both work to make the best of a difficult situation. They both refuse to be counted out by the hand fate has dealt them. They both reach inward and discover there some steadying reserves.

By breaking our life down into daily bites, we all have far more strength than we may realize. It is possible to make the best of a difficult situation "one day at a time." It is a discipline that we must set for ourselves, the narrowing of life's scope to a manageable amount.

Just for today, we are able to do the best we can with our child. Just for today, we can get our dog out for an outing. Just for today, we can soldier on.

As an artist, soldiering on is often what is called for. We may not be able to see any opening, any sure path for our work to follow. "What's the use?" our Inner Critic may hiss. "It's all going to come to nothing anyhow." The hiss of the Inner Critic is the voice of the Devil. It urges us always to despair, to seeing not the progress we have made but the far distance we have yet to travel. "It's hopeless," the Inner Critic announces, dismissing our dreams with a swoop of one hand.

But it is not hopeless. If we are willing to soldier on, there are bright days ahead of us as well as dark. If we muster the courage to continue, there is hope that we might succeed. We need to focus on the possible positive. We need to count on ourselves and on a benevolent larger power that wishes us well. How do we do that?

As we acquire more knowledge, things do not become more comprehensible, but more mysterious.

ALBERT SCHWEITZER

Writing Morning Pages moves us past the negative chatter of our own minds. We put the chatter on the page and emerge inwardly into a quiet oasis. "Easy does it," we tell ourselves and listen with an inner ear cocked to see what may bubble up in the form of guidance. Quite often, the guidance that comes to us is firm, quiet, and gentle. Just for today, we may have no answer to the larger questions of life but we will have answers to many of the smaller ones.

Divining Rod

In times of sorrow and malcontent, walking lends us a sense of overview and perspective. Although we may walk out with our own problems, we quickly encounter the world. We may walk out feeling alone and trapped but we soon sense that we are all in this together—"this" being the shared soup of human experience. The tool I ask you to use next requires you to reach for a larger perspective.

Take pen to page and allow your fingers to do a little walking. Number from one to five. List five circumstances in which you did not get what you wanted, where you felt thwarted and denied. Looking over your list, search out the silver lining that came from each denial. There is always some good that comes from sorrow, some grace that comes from difficulty, some opportunity that comes when one door closes and another opens. You may want to ask a blunt question on the page. "What possible good could come of this?" Ask the question and then listen for the answer. It will often surprise you. In searching for some good that came from my terrible breakdowns, I saw that I had been rendered more compassionate. My breakdowns had given me empathy for the fears and terrors of others.

Having rounded up your disappointments onto the page, having searched for the unexpected blessing that they held, I now ask you to take a longish walk, holding loosely in mind what you have discovered. Allow yourself time enough to slow down and allow the world to speak to you again of its beauties and its glories. What you are after here is a sense of tranquillity. As you walk, you may find your melancholy tinged by acceptance.

CHECK-IN

1. **How many days this week did you do your Morning Pages?** If you skipped a day, why did you skip it? How was the experience of writing them for you? Are you experiencing more clarity? A wider range of emotions? A greater sense of detachment, purpose, and calm? Did anything surprise you? Is there a "repeating" issue asking to be dealt with?

   Teach yourself to work in uncertainty.

   BERNARD MALAMUD

2. **Did you do your Artist Date this week?** Did you note an improved sense of well-being? What did you do and how did it feel? Remember, Artist Dates can be difficult and you may need to coax yourself into taking them.

   Nobody, not even the poet, holds the secret of the world.

   FEDERICO GARCÍA LORCA

3. **Did you get out on your Weekly Walk?** How did that feel? What emotions or insights surfaced for you? Were you able to walk more than once? What did your walk do for your optimism and sense of perspective?

4. **Were there any other issues this week that felt significant to you in your self-discovery?** Describe them.

Uncovering a Sense of Truth

Each of us bears within us an inner compass, a sort of spiritual dowsing wand. When our actions match our values, this compass points true north. This week you are asked to focus on personal grounding. As you plan and execute rituals that both soothe and enliven you, your compass will become more steady. Reaching out to others is another means by which we gauge our own position. As we extend ourselves in empathy toward our friends, we experience ourselves as generous and compassionate.

Change

This morning, though a chill, gray and drizzly day, Tiger Lily and Charlotte went for their annual physicals at Westside Veterinary Clinic. The clinic is a cheerless place with heavily barred windows. It could stand in as a methadone clinic. There is the same air of desperation. In the waiting room, a small Havanese dog yapped repeatedly from the depths of a Louis Vuitton carrying case. A sprightly looking Lhasa apso sat chipper and alert on the lap of its weeping owner.

"He's doing much, much better," the owner managed to gasp between mournful sniffles. "But he's fifteen years old. How old are your dogs?"

Artistic growth is, more than it is anything else, a refining of the sense of truthfulness. The stupid believe that to be truthful is easy; only the artist, the great artist, knows how difficult it is.

WILLA CATHER

"Tiger Lily is five," I indicated the cocker spaniel who was eyeing the little Lhasa aggressively. "Charlotte is four," I nodded toward the Westie.

"Oh, well then. They're young," sniffled the Lhasa's owner.

In the examining room with the kindly lady veterinarian, Charlotte was seized by a bout of shivers. She stood on the silver, metallic examining table and shook with fear. Tiger Lily by way of contrast, snarled and lunged. She was having none of it, the gentle poking and prodding. The nurse handed me a muzzle and asked me to slip it on. "Perhaps she won't bite you," she said doubtfully. I managed to slide the muzzle into place and with a quick yank by the nurse, it was secured. Tiger Lily has never had a bad vet experience so just why she becomes so aggressive is a very good question. The lady veterinarian explained her view.

> *If you don't tell the truth about yourself, you cannot tell it about other people*
>
> VIRGINIA WOOLF

"We have dogs who have had multiple operations begging to come inside for a treat as they walk past," she said, with a chuckle. "And then we have dogs like Tiger Lily who have once had a shot and have learned from that they want never to come back."

The vet found all the stances endearing. She could empathize with Charlotte's trembling and with Tiger Lily's fit of rage.

As artists, when we encounter change, we often react as the dogs do. No matter that the change is "for our own good," change is still change and it is hard for us.

This morning my phone rang and it was a young writer-director on the brink of signing a deal. "I just don't trust them," she complained of her newly acquired partners. "And I can't tell if my red flags are accurate, my stuff or just the process. I guess the bottom line is that I am about to be in business with some possibly questionable characters but the good news is, I am about to be in business."

When we strive to undertake a creative partnership, cold feet abound. We find ourselves questioning our prospective partners and our own ability to size them up. What we are dealing with, of course, is the question of control. When we have no partners, we are squarely blocked. We may be frustrated by that, but we do not feel out of control. We feel safe and even a little smug: we always knew the odds were stacked against us.

When the odds start to shift, when the dominoes are falling in the right direction, we can suddenly feel out of control. Where before we knew how we felt—frustrated—now we feel something worse—vulnerable. And we hate to feel vulnerable. Once more our dreams have been nudged awake. Once more our dreams have the capacity to break our hearts.

No matter that the change we are undergoing is a change for the positive. Like Tiger Lily, we snap and bite. Like Charlotte, we quiver and shake. As we are moved forward, we yearn for the safety of where we have been. We become paranoid, seeing shadows every place. Our new benefactors seem like predators.

"You know how well I take good news," the young writer-director jokes to me.

"I think you need to do some daily things," I say. "You need to cling to whatever aspects of your old life you are able to."

"I could write Morning Pages, I suppose. I could have lunch with an old friend."

"That sounds like a very good start."

Truth is such a rare thing, it is delightful to tell it.

EMILY DICKINSON

When we are rickety, Morning Pages lend us stability. They miniaturize the terrors that we are walking through. They bring life back down to the possible: Exactly what can we do, today?

Taken in a daily bite, most change, however extreme, can be metabolized. Our Pages give us time and place to get used to change. "I am afraid," we write and then, a few sentences on, "I need to remember to buy kitty litter."

When we remember that we have a daily life, we begin to find our grounding. The kitty litter must still be bought whether or not we suddenly have a million-dollar deal. That upstairs toilet needs to be repaired and that is a matter of some urgency. Morning Pages tell us to call the plumber.

It is our job, faced with impending change, to continue to husband the life that we have got. It is our job to buy the kitty litter, call the plumber, keep our hand moving across the page.

"Maybe they are not such monsters," the Morning Pages might suggest, pausing to consider our friend's potential colleagues again once she has vented a little. "Maybe they are doing the best they can and trying as hard as they know how."

Morning Pages allow us to take a longer view. They give us the ballast necessary to stay balanced. Coupled with a longish walk, Morning Pages give us much needed detachment. The Pages raise an issue and the walk helps to resolve it. We might walk out thinking, "Good Lord, I do not trust these people," only to think, after walking on it, "Perhaps I should try trusting a little, perhaps I am the one at fault."

By the time I was paying the vet bill, Tiger Lily was happily chewing on a small dog treat. Her nerves had calmed down. She was no longer in enemy territory. So, too, when we give ourselves the benefit of time to adjust, we may find the world is not the hostile place we take it to be.

Divining Rod

When we are fatigued or overstressed from too much change, we frequently view the world as a hostile place. We brace ourselves for the shock of impending doom. We gird ourselves against the worst. But what if the best is about to happen? What if, despite our fears, we are being handed a resounding success? Are we ready to face that eventuality as well?

Change for the better is still change, and so we need to ready ourselves for the good that comes our way as well as the bad. As always, it is the grounding of our lives with regular routines that makes it possible to handle any eventuality. Morning Pages are one such grounding rod. Walks are another. Artist Dates are a third. In times of sudden or extreme change, however, we may require additional measures to yield us a sense of safety.

We "sense" change like animals and sometimes the most comforting rituals we can undertake are those that speak to our animal natures. My collaborator Emma Lively gets manicures whenever her nerves become too much for her to handle. You can be certain that on the day when we have a critical backer's audition, she will find time to nip out for new nail polish. My friend Sonia, a six-sensory person, works to stay in touch with her other five senses. She favors long hot soaks. For myself, I make a huge pot of homemade vegetable soup. My friend Linda bakes bread.

Take pen to page. List five rituals that are sensory and can move you to a sense of safety and expansion. For example, you may want to burn a stick of savory incense. You may light a scented candle. You may buy fresh flowers. When you are stressed, you need to woo yourself a little. It might be the night for a nice dinner out—or the night for a nice dinner in. Allow yourself the touch of luxury: good bath salts, a new hairbrush, a fresh change of sheets. The psyche speaks in symbols. Tell yourself symbolically that you will be fine.

The Eyes Have It

This afternoon I went to the eye doctor. My doctor is a kind and amiable man who chatted to me about his dozen trips to Paris and his love for that city and the French people. "You could go for a month and not begin to scratch all there is to do there. Did you get up to Sacre Coeur? I love the side streets filled with artists and the many houses where famous artists have lived."

> *Change alone is unchanging.*
> HERACLITIS

> *If we want everything to remain as it is, it will become necessary for everything to change.*
> GIUSEPPE TOMASI DI LAMPEDUSA

"Yes. I got to Sacre Coeur," I murmured. The doctor was talking as he worked and I was now squinting uneasily at an eye chart that was still blurred. What did Paris have to do with my eyes?

"Number one or number two—which one is clearer?" he asked.

"Number two, I guess."

"Ah, yes." He sounded satisfied as though his hunch were being ratified. "Now, try it again. Number one or number two?"

"This time number one."

"Ah, really." Did he sound dismayed?

"Yes." I was not about to be distracted.

"We stayed last time not far from the Trocadero. Did you get over there?" Now he was affixing a reading chart. I could read it all.

"Yes, but not for long." We were still on the Trocadero.

"The gardens are magnificent." He sounded wistful.

"Yes. They are." I had loved the gardens.

"April in Paris. Flowers abloom." The doctor sighed.

"Yes." I sighed too. It had been beautiful.

"Which is clearer now? Number one or number two?"

"Number two." The doctor was fine-tuning things now. As he revealed his enthusiasms to me, my doctor swam suddenly into focus, no longer just a technician.

I have a friend, April, who is open to all whom she meets. In the Greek diner, she knows the name of the owner's wife and the ages of their children. On the street, she greets the homeless man by name. "We're both human beings. We both see each other and recognize each other. Why not know each other's names?" she asks.

Henry Miller advised artists to take an interest in life. By all accounts a lively man, as outgoing as April, he remained open to the end of his long life to new people and new experiences. They were the stuff of his art. He set a fine example.

As artists, we run a risk of staleness if we close ourselves off to fresh experience. Each day must remain an exploratory expedition. We must remain tourists on our home terrain. We must hold on to a sense of adventure. To do this, we must keep our curiosity alive and gently feed it. Walking, the world moves toward us at a manageable rate. We are able to take in the new flowers at the green grocer's, the fresh plantings in a window box. We are able to see that a Turkish restaurant has displaced the pricey French one two blocks from home. We are able to see and admire a silky long-haired lady dachshund who eddies at her owner's feet while she buys a tabloid from the corner newsstand.

Wisdom lies neither in fixity nor in change, but in the dialectic between the two.

OCTAVIO PAZ

Walking, a city becomes a series of linked neighborhoods, each one a manageable size when taken by itself. Every few blocks, there must be a corner deli, a dry cleaner, a frame shop, a copy shop, a shoe repair shop, a florist's. Each neighborhood has the same human needs. There must be a grocery store, a butcher's shop, perhaps a corner stand selling fresh fruits and vegetables. Each neighborhood must be central to itself, self-sufficient, a tiny world.

While he was testing my distance vision, my eye doctor talked about the neighborhoods he and his wife had explored in Paris. "There is a tiny little book of walking tours. We got through perhaps half of them," he said.

Clicking the proper lenses into a contraption that balanced on my nose, the doctor continued. He had been to Paris perhaps a dozen times, starting back in the sixties. He believed the French to be hospitable to women, most especially to attractive women. They were hospitable, too, to anyone who tried to speak their language.

"Well, we tried," I told the doctor. "We spoke French whenever we could, but so many of them spoke English!"

"Ah, yes. That's true," the doctor allowed.

I noticed the doctor's age then—middle-aged, perhaps five years younger than myself. His eyes were bright behind tiny glasses. His beard was chic. I imagined him in Paris, ordering a croissant and a chocolat chaud. No wonder he loved to go.

"My wife won't go back there," he suddenly volunteered. "She doesn't like their attitude about Iraq and she's afraid, too, of terrorists. My wife is a very determined woman. She has her views." He sounded doleful and slightly henpecked.

Remembering his wife and her attitudes, the doctor abruptly became all business. "I am altering your prescription slightly in both eyes," he said. "You will call me if you have any trouble." I promised that I would.

Leaving the eye doctor, I blink for a moment in the bright afternoon's sun. Talking about Paris, I have suddenly "seen" the man who has served me for several years in dutiful anonymity. My eye doctor suddenly has an "I" to speak from. I am sorry that his wife hates Paris. I hope they will be able to work it out.

> *You must be the change you wish to see in the world.*
>
> MAHATMA GANDHI

> *If you compare yourself with others, you may become vain or bitter, for always there will be greater and lesser persons than yourself.*
>
> MAX EHRMANN

Divining Rod

Most of us lead lives of hurried contacts. We rush forward pell-mell and do not take the time necessary to savor life and its occupants. Faces are familiar to us but names go unmentioned. Our regular waiter at the diner goes nameless. We are too busy to "get into it." And yet, getting into it is what we crave and deny ourselves.

Take pen in hand. List five people with whom you have regular yet anonymous contact. On a New York corner there may be a news vendor and a fruit vendor where you make daily purchases without breaking a stranger's careful decorum. In the suburbs, you may go routinely to the same car wash. Your dental hygienist may be another friendly yet nameless face. Your server at Starbucks might be the same every morning. Survey your regular rounds and make a list of those you see but do not let yourself "know."

From your list of anonymous contacts, select one to explore slightly further. Introduce yourself to your corner vendor. Ask that waiter his name. The next time you are riding an elevator with a familiar but nameless face, break the silence and give your own name. Say, "I see you all the time. I thought I might introduce myself." Do the same at the office water cooler. Extend yourself—and your world—by just a bit.

Connecting

The day is cool, breezy, and sunny. On the loop around the reservoir, the cherry blossoms are just past their height. Pink petals are carried on the breeze. Pink petals make a thick carpet underfoot. Soon, the blossoms will be gone and the pink confetti we walk through will turn to brown. Just for today, however, the footing is festive. Just for today the runners tread a pink cloud. Spirits are high. Everyone senses that the beauty of the day is fleeting. There are quicksilver smiles and shouted out comments: "Isn't it something?" Yes, it is something.

Jealousy is all the fun you think they had.

ERICA JONG

Laboring along the north loop, an oversized Akita trudges after its owner. His coat is moth-eaten, half winter, half summer, shed out in spots, deeply furred in others. Another week of warmish weather, another week of grooming from master, and he will be sleek and summer-fit. Just for today, his dignified face looks disgruntled, as if he is saying, "Imagine. A dog of my dignity looking like this!"

In a cordoned-off area just at the water's northernmost tip, a small forest of soon-to-be-planted trees stand with their roots bound in burlap. High in the branches of one of them, keeping an eye on us all, perches a peregrine falcon, motionless except for the alert swivel of its head. Nothing escapes its notice, certainly not Emma and me, two blond women with small, fancy dogs in tow.

"What do you think?" Emma asks. "Do we look like a case of dogs matching their owners?"

"I suppose we do," I answer. Emma's platinum do matches her Westie's crest of bangs. My Veronica Lake waves match my cocker spaniel's silky ears.

Rounding the reservoir's tip, heading back south, we come upon another set of cherry trees, this one creating a pink tunnel, arching over a well-worn trail. The boughs of the trees sweep nearly to the ground.

"I must remember to bring out my camera," Emma says.

"Yes. The blossoms will be gone soon."

This year I am not going back to my beloved New Mexico for the summer. I will not witness the short-lived glory of wild roses flushing pink along El Salto Road, perfuming the air with their heady scent. This summer my flora and fauna will be more domesticated than the bison and llamas I spot back home in Taos. I have seen buffalo as moth-eaten as this morning's Akita. I have seen eagles standing sentinel like this morning's falcon.

"Do not compare. Enjoy." I abjure myself. Although it is less wild than the beauties I am accustomed to, there is great beauty to be found in Central Park. There are, for example, London plane trees, great dappled citizens with wide-spreading boughs.

"Bloom where you are planted," I lecture myself. I must work to open my eyes to the beauty all around me. It takes discipline to find the glory hidden in these concrete canyons. When a snowy dove dives past my writing-room window, its flight declares, "Beauty is everywhere."

As artists, we must be alert. We must savor the glory of each passing moment. We must notice the parade that passes us by. At the corner newsstand, the vendor is a flirt. He has a flashing smile and a wink for the women who stop to buy today's *New York Post*.

At the Greek diner on the corner, George, the kindly waiter, has a saint's compassion for us all. "Menu tonight?" he asks, not wanting to insult the regulars who know what they will eat. "Water? Coffee? Iced tea?" George doesn't want your thirst to go unslaked. When you tell him, "Spanakopita," he acts delighted, as if you have made the wisest of choices—and perhaps you have. The spinach filling is light and fluffy. The Greek salad that comes on the side is tangy and crisp. George serves you deftly, alert to your every need.

> To cure jealousy is to see it for what it is, a dissatisfaction with self.
>
> JOAN DIDION

> The ideal has many names and beauty is but one of them.
>
> W. SOMERSET MAUGHAM

"I got sober in that coffee shop," declares a friend of mine. "I lived there my first year because I couldn't cook without thinking of drinking. I knew everyone in the place and they knew me. I was this young and crazy somebody. They nursed me through my early sobriety. They really did."

Just beneath the surface of New York there is kindness and caring. Just beyond the bustle of the crowd, there is time enough to connect. As artists—and as people—we must connect. We must take the extra beat necessary to notice that the newsstand vendor is flirting again and deserves a smile. A silky, long-haired Yorkshire terrier sniffs inquisitively at your ankles while the vendor makes change.

"Beautiful dog," you take time to murmur. The owner preens, "I think so." There is a flash of connection, another fine filament in the web of connections that holds us all.

Divining Rod

Our lives are far-flung. Friends and relatives live in distant cities. We make contact by phone and e-mail but it is not the same as living close at hand. How can we draw closer? How can we make more connection? Ben, a young musician, who recently studied for a year in France, now lives in Manhattan. He has a small digital camera and he keeps in contact with his French friends by sending them New York images over the Internet. His friends are grateful and intrigued. One of them is so enticed, she is planning a trip to see his life firsthand.

The postcard is a more old-fashioned way to say, "I was here but I was thinking of you there." Using either a digital photo or a postcard, contact one of your distant beloved. Remember that "seeing is believing." Find an image that speaks to you of your life and one that you believe will speak to them. Take the time and trouble to assure them of your ongoing connection. In reaching out to others, we remind ourselves that we, too, are beloved and missed.

Keeping On

Steadily and loudly since nine a.m. there has been hammering coming from the apartment above me. The hammer blows are rhythmic and dull except when they crescendo. They crescendo often.

Life in Manhattan is a series of accommodations. At night, walking the dogs, you must weave between people busily talking on cell phones. On trash days, you must pick your way past plastic bags filled with garbage. Now, when the high level of noise is a pollutant, you must remember, "People have a right to renovate," and they don't mean to be noisy, they just are.

My writing-room window looks out across five rows of brownstones. I see when my neighbors take to their rooftops hoping to catch a few rays. I see when someone goes all the way to the roof just to smoke a cigarette unperturbed. On a day like today, a dull, gray day, there is no one either sunbathing or smoking. Today is one of those just-to-be-gotten-through days. Even the vendor at the corner newsstand, normally an inveterate flirt, is subdued. Today is a day just for keeping on.

So often in a creative career, the magic that is required is quite simply the courage to go on. Singers must sing their scales. Actors must learn their monologues. Writers like myself must spend time at the keys. We would like a break in the weather. We would like a break, period, but the breaks, if they come, will not come today. Today is about keeping on.

Surprise is where creativity comes in.

RAY BRADBURY

Art attracts us only by what it reveals of our most secret self.

JEAN-LUC GODARD

It is very important not to become hard. The artist must always have one skin too few in comparison to other people, so you feel the slightest wind.

SHUSHA GUPPY

Divining Rod

Sometimes we need credit for a job well done, even if there is no one at hand to offer us their praise. We must learn to praise ourselves, to take pride in our abilities to keep on keeping on.

Take pen in hand. List five things at which you have persevered.

Fear of Success

Yesterday I got a phone call from the young writer-director. The news was good, but still difficult. It looked as though a script of hers had made it through a series of hurdles and was now okayed for a September shoot. "It actually looks like I have a go picture," said the quavering voice over the telephone. There was no elation.

"It's good your picture is a go."

"Yes. I suppose so." The doubt in her voice asked, "Is it?"

We are used to soldiering on. We are accustomed to doing our work against the odds and against the tide. When the tide turns, when the odds are suddenly in our favor, we need to find our sea legs. We have become comfortable, sitting on the sidelines, critiquing the game. Now, suddenly, we are being asked to play it. The pitch is coming across the plate and it is our turn at bat.

In making the transition from bystander to player, it helps if we take with us some of our daily routines. Morning Pages will still serve us very well. They have been useful lo these many months at fielding our complaints, let them do service now at fielding our fears. Chief among these fears, of course, is "What if I am not any good?" "What if I have fooled everybody?" "What if I am an imposter and I am just about to show it?"

> *Artists are the monks of the bourgeois state.*
>
> CESARE PAVESE

> *For good and evil, man is a free creative spirit.*
>
> JOYCE CARY

Morning Pages do not talk back, but they do give us a place to ventilate. They do give us one way to keep grounded. They do give us the privacy we crave and the intimacy we need to spit out what it is that is troubling us now, just when we "should" be grateful.

Now that the stakes are real, we do well to steal away for a head-clearing walk. A footfall at a time, the walk will also ground us. We can walk our way out of paranoia and into perspective.

"If the contracts vet out, then I am officially in preproduction," the writer-director marveled. "It all feels so fast."

On the days when we are just soldiering on, it seems impossible that any project could come to fruition too fast. Haven't we already been waiting "forever"? But breaks, when they come, seem to come just as we can barely handle them. The young writer-director has been working two years toward the goal of a go picture. Now that the light is green, the terrain seems threatening.

It is difficult when we are constricted by fear to allow ourselves the expansion of an Artist Date, and yet this is the very medicine we need. On an Artist Date we sense that we are part of a larger world. In this larger world, our dreams and ambitions have their place.

"I need to find a horse," confessed the writer-director. "I need to take some Artist Dates where I can just stroke a velvety nose."

I told the writer-director that her self-diagnosis sounded accurate. What she needed was a dose of regular life. "Find a horse to pet or a dog to walk. Find something that soothes and comforts you."

> *Nothing great was ever achieved without enthusiasm.*
>
> RALPH WALDO EMERSON

"I think I'll do that. What's that noise?"

I explained about the renovation. A former New Yorker, the writer-director hooted with laughter. "Gee. I guess there are worse things than suddenly having a million-dollar deal." When we got off the phone, the hammering mysteriously stopped.

Divining Rod

When we are faced with a heady change, there is warning in that word "heady." There is nothing like a success to bring on a misery-inducing bout of self-centered fears. To enjoy our triumph, we must not feel that it isolates us from our peers. A long sought accomplishment can be very alienating. Who are we now? Who can understand us? (More people than we think.) Despite our newly won victory, we must connect to those we love. In other words, we must move from our heads back into our hearts.

One more time, consult your list of friends. Who among them is going through a hard time? That is the person you need to talk with now—and not so much to talk as to listen. You need a strong dose of regular life and that is what your troubled friend offers you. Rather than calling with dramatic tales of your new triumph and the fears that it raises for you, call with an agenda of empathy. Say, simply, "I have been wondering how you are?" Coax from your friend the details of life-at-the-moment. Lose yourself in the play by play that greets your ear. It is grounding to listen to the cares and concerns of others. As you reach out to them, you also reach within yourself. Your heady fears diminish, replaced again by the reminder that we are all in "this" together.

CHECK-IN

1. **How many days this week did you do your Morning Pages?** If you skipped a day, why did you skip it? How was the experience of writing them for you? Are you experiencing more clarity? A wider range of emotions? A greater sense of detachment, purpose, and calm? Did anything surprise you? Is there a "repeating" issue asking to be dealt with?

2. **Did you do your Artist Date this week?** Did you note an improved sense of well-being? What did you do and how did it feel? Remember, Artist Dates can be difficult and you may need to coax yourself into taking them.

3. **Did you get out on your Weekly Walk?** How did that feel? What emotions or insights surfaced for you? Were you able to walk more than once? What did your walk do for your optimism and sense of perspective?

4. **Were there any other issues this week that felt significant to you in your self-discovery?** Describe them.

Uncovering a Sense of Perspective

Creativity requires that we focus on both the large and the small, the grand and the particular. Remember, the Grand Canyon was carved a drop at a time. This week's essays and tasks concern expansion. You are asked to imagine yourself larger and more surefooted than you may feel yourself to be. You are asked to focus on ways in which you can increase your conscious contact with the Great Artist. It is by feeling yourself connected to a larger Something that God can work through you. You are seeking to forge an artist-to-artist bond with your Creator.

Seasons

The cherry blossoms are spent. The trees that were bouffant pink clouds are now softly misted with green. The showy blooms are gone for another year. Spring moves toward summer. The London plane trees are the last to reveal their leaves, but even they are unfurling. Dandelions laze across the lawns and some have already passed into fluff. The joggers turn out earlier now to avoid the heat. Today simmers.

Books are the bees which carry the quickening pollen from one to another mind.

JAMES RUSSELL LOWELL

When we are incubating something creatively, we, too, follow a cycle of seasons. We begin locked in winter, when we look and feel devoid of ideas, although the ideas are there for us, simply dormant. Our wintry hearts lurch toward spring and suddenly an idea puts out a hopeful bud. The idea may be as festive as the buoyant pink cherry blossoms. It may be as determined as the forsythia flaring bravely into bloom. Make no mistake, our idea is bright and indisputable. We blossom as the landscape does. And then what happens? As surely as the seasons turn, our brightly budded ideas must now ripen and mature. Spring turns the corner into summer. Showy pink and gold give way to industrious green. Now come the long days of labor. We must work to bring forth the fruit of what we have envisioned.

Last night, in Los Angeles, there was a reading done of a play of mine, *Love in the DMZ*. This morning, I got the first of several feedback calls. The play was brilliant, the first caller said, but perhaps too demanding, perhaps a little long. She couldn't tell me exactly where, or how, but the play needed some pruning. I had to consider the attention span of the audience. Could I see my way clear to making some changes?

I waited for caller number two. This time, there was no talk of cutting. The play had played and played well, this caller believed. It was a timely play, set in the Vietnam era but echoing our misgivings about involvement with Iraq. This play had a future, the caller assured me. What were my intentions for the piece? How could it go forward?

Although I didn't say this to my callers, I had been waiting a long time to find a proper unfolding for this play. It was a piece of work that I had completed and then been unable to harvest. There had been no one waiting to pluck the play from the vine. It had lain in the field, ripe and ready, but no one had taken it to heart. I was delighted by the wave of interest in it now.

Each of us is in charge of cultivating our own talent. We have ideas that we are charged with bringing to fruition. Some of us remain locked in winter, unable to go forward because we doubt the strength of our ideas. Others of us make it to spring, shooting forward with rapid growth but unable to bring things to fulfillment, unable to put in the heavy labor necessary to cultivate our crop. Still others, myself included here, bring work all the way to completion but lack the resolution and bravado necessary to sell the work that we have done. A critical failure of nerve at the last moment causes us to doubt the worthiness of projects we have birthed. Novels go into desk drawers. Plays languish on shelves. The pumpkin rots on the vine.

How can we go forward from here? What is necessary to successfully harvest the fruits of our labors? We must believe, first of all, in the worth of our brainchildren.

We must not abandon them. We must keep them a priority. Faced with rejection, we must keep trying. At root, it comes back to being a matter of faith. We must see our work as divine in origin. We must believe there is a divine path of goodness ahead in its unfolding. When we are rejected, we must ask, "What next?" and not, "Why me?"

There is always a way to move forward. We may be blinded at times by our own belief in conventions. We may say, "I cannot go forward without a producer," or "I cannot go forward without a director," but the truth is that God is both a producer and a director and often we can move forward if we are willing, one more time, to trust a wing and a prayer.

Many playwrights have moved ahead by renting a venue and raising their own money for a production. Worried lest these "vanity" productions be exactly that, we fail to see that if we want others to believe in us we must first be totally committed to ourselves. If creativity is an act of faith, we must move out on faith and be willing to take action to

> *Experience is the name everyone gives to their mistakes.*
>
> OSCAR WILDE

make our dreams into concrete reality. Independent films are often made on a shoestring. Where does the faith, the sheer chutzpah, come from to take such an action? It can, and often does come, from prayer.

"God, grant me the serenity to accept the things I cannot change, courage to change the things I can, and wisdom to know the difference" 12-steppers are taught to pray. This prayer has value for us all. Very often we accept "no" for an answer where courage might tell us to look for a different way forward.

Left to my own devices, I am far too easily discouraged. This flaw in my own creative makeup is why I see so clearly that a lack of faith is often the sticking point. All too often our lack of faith is a personal matter. While we can easily muster belief in other peoples' projects, it is in our very own that we lack tenacity.

"What would I be willing to do for someone I love?" we might ask ourselves. The answer may surprise us. We may find that we are willing to rent a venue for the play written by a beloved. We might discover we have the daring to self-publish. We might rent a space for a dance recital or organize a gallery space for a group show. There are many things we might do.

Willing to go to bat for others, we must become willing to go to bat for ourselves. We must become willing to put cash on the barrelhead. When I directed my feature film, *God's Will,* I bankrolled the production with monies I received writing for *Miami Vice.* I could have put that money in the bank, saving it for a rainy day. Instead I placed a bet on myself and my talent. I look back on that film with satisfaction. The harvest was worth the labor.

Divining Rod

You are asked to write rapidly to evade your Censor. Take pen in hand. Number from one to ten. Very quickly fill in the blank ten times. "If it weren't so risky, I would try_____."

Now number from one to five. Fill in the blanks again. "If it weren't so conceited, I would try_____."

A third time, go to the page. Number again from one to five. Fill in the blanks. "If it weren't so expensive, I would try_____."

The responses to these questions should give you a portrait of your fears and the ways that they keep you crippled. Scanning your lists, select one risk that seems possible to take. Take one concrete step in its direction.

Ebb and Flow

The pink blossoms are gone from underfoot and overhead. The cherry trees are anonymous citizens now clothed in green. There are few flowering trees and bushes left, chiefly mock orange. For the most part, the trees are garbed in green as spring gives way to summer. At the westernmost reach of the reservoir, a man is schooling a Burmese mountain dog puppy. The puppy is not much of a learner, splay-footed and cuddly, flopping to the grass wanting to wrestle. On the cinder bridle path, adult dogs trot past the puppy busily resisting its blandishments. One German shepherd, a recent puppy itself, bounds closer in a playful crouch. "No, no," its master carols out and the dog, chastened, goes back to a dutiful trot. For Tiger Lily, my cocker spaniel, the puppy is irresistible. She leaps toward it, growling with bravado. The puppy scampers a retreat.

So much of a creative life is knowing when to go forward and when to retreat. So much of winning through in the long haul boils down to knowing when to push forward and when to hang back. There is wisdom to working on having multiple projects simultaneously so that a "no" on one can send you back to work on another. At the moment, my collaborator Emma and I are back at work on *Magellan*. The news—or lack of news—around our musical *The Medium at Large* was too daunting to push forward there.

So much of the feedback we get as artists is heartless or simply thoughtless. Our last round on *The Medium at Large* qualified as both. "You're really onto something with the idea of guidance from the afterworld," one producer's feedback began. "And you've got some really good music. But the story about two sisters . . . well, it's just too narrow. You need to tell a different story." Listening politely to this advice, we did not run from the room shrieking, "Our lives are overrun by idiots!" But we felt that way.

> *We are born believing. A man bears beliefs as a tree bears apples*
>
> RALPH WALDO EMERSON
>
> *It is not the language of painters, but the language of nature which one should listen to.*
>
> VINCENT VAN GOGH

We didn't choose to throw away our whole show based on this feedback but we did decide the time had come for us to let the world spin a few times before we pushed forward again. Here is what happened when we stopped trying. Another producer unexpectedly stepped forward. This time there was no talk of throwing away our whole story line. This time the elements seemed more right. "I would like to help you," this producer said. We listened eagerly. We were more than ready to be helped.

But we were also balanced. While taking time out from submissions on *The Medium at Large,* we had put ourselves back to work on *Magellan*. I had written new music for the opening. We had restructured the opening sequence. We had made the show more lean and focused. With the ballast of *Magellan* to help us hold steady, we were ready to take in more feedback on *The Medium at Large*.

In the first days following our backer's audition, our friend Bruce Pomahac had advised us to start to work again at something creative. "You girls are lucky you have multiple projects. That's what's going to save you," he said. Bruce reminded us of the story about director Hal Prince, the way he always schedules a meeting about a new project for the morning after he opens a show.

"What you are after is stamina," Bruce reminded us. And stamina is exactly what it felt like we were exercising the first time we tried to work again in the wake

Art, like nature, has her monsters, things of bestial shape and with hideous voices.

OSCAR WILDE

Art is a vast, ancient, interconnected web-work.

CAMILLE PAGLIA

of our disappointment. Fortunately, synchronicity was at hand. The precise place we needed to enter Magellan's story was the point at which he was the most discouraged and disheartened. Scooping the inner creative barrel, we did not have far to look for inspiration.

Once we accept that creativity is a spiritual act, it doesn't seem like such a far jump to expect such synchronicity to be at hand. There is a benevolent Something that is kindly toward ourselves and our art. The Great Creator is an artist and loves other artists. The Divine does play a hand in what it is we are making. We can consciously choose to invite divine participation. We can ask for and receive divine help and guidance.

We do not need to feel that our dreams and God's will for us are at opposite ends of the table. We can consider the possibility that our dreams come from God and that God has a plan for their proper unfolding. When we seek daily spiritual guidance, we are guided toward the next step forward for our art. Sometimes the step is very small. Sometimes the step is, "Wait. Not now." Sometimes the step is, "Work on something else for a while." When we are open to Divine Guidance, we will receive it. It will come to us as the hunch, the inkling, the itch. It will come to us as timely conversations with others. It will come to us in many ways—but it will come to us.

We are not alone and unpartnered in our desire to make art. Art is an act of expansion and faith. We are the children of an expansive power that interacts with us when we act on faith. When we are open to good things, good things come to us. Sometimes, in order for something good to happen, something apparently bad must happen first. This is when we are asked to have faith. This is when we are required to search for the silver lining. "Bad" feedback on a project helps us to know and appreciate "good" feedback on a project. A "no" from person A allows us to receive a "yes" from person B. We are always being brought along. Our dreams may feel thwarted when in reality they are being tempered. We are being shaped to fit a divine purpose. We can cooperate or we can resist.

Last night, on my final night of teaching down in SoHo, I received a letter from one of the members of my class. "I am very well connected in the theater world and I would love to help you with *The Medium at Large,*" the letter ran. "If it seems appropriate to you, please contact me."

Emma and I read the letter, laughing to ourselves. We had so despaired of finding help and here was the very help we were needing right under our very noses. We couldn't wait to place the call.

Divining Rod

When we become clear about what it is we need and hope for, help comes to hand. Clarity triggers manifestation. A lack of clarity prevents our good from coming to us. Very often, when we feel cut off from helping resources, it is because we have prematurely closed a door that needs to be reopened. We have decided, for example, that writers' workshops are not for us—when that is the next step necessary to move forward the play that we have been working on. We must be willing, one more time, to be a beginner. We must ask, "What venture could I take if my ego would just allow it?"

In order to move ahead creatively, we must be flexible. We must open our minds to the opportunities that abound around us. Before we say, "I would never," we need to ask, "What can I be humble enough to try?" Humility opens the door to diversity. Our help can come to us from any quarter.

Take pen in hand. Number from one to five. List five things you could be willing to try if you were openminded.

Companionship

We are midway through May and the weather is rapturous. Today is a day to swoon for. Baby carriages are out in droves, their bonnets tipped back so that little citizens can catch the sun. It's a workday but you would barely know it to see the park. It is crowded with joggers playing hooky. The reservoir is hip to hip with revelers in the day. On my block, a boxer dog and a Pomeranian make each other's acquaintance with

There is nothing stable in the world; uproar is your only music.

JOHN KEATS

> *Music is the mediator between the spiritual and the sensual life.*
>
> LUDWIG VAN BEETHOVEN

courtesy and barely throttled eagerness. The snow-white Samoyed bobs a near curtsy to a handsome rottweiler. Out for their morning walk, Tiger Lily and Charlotte lurch the length of their leashes, wriggling merrily at the approach of a Harlequin Great Dane. On a day like today, high spirits are the rule. Manhattan is a friendly village.

This morning, I walked over to see my friend Therese. She greeted me warmly, her face still flushed from her own trip to the gym. "Make yourself comfortable," she said, showing me to a loveseat. "Something to drink?"

"I'm fine," I told her. "It's such a beautiful day." Sitting in Therese's comfortable sitting room, I felt a flush of well-being. Perhaps, just perhaps, I thought, I may be coming somewhat back on the beam. Therese seemed to sense this.

"Do you have a sense of companionship?" Therese wanted to know. "Do you sense as you are working that a higher force is working with you?"

"On my good days," I told her.

"You know you can talk to God as a friend," she continued, her eyes gently twinkling. "You do not need to be alone. You can reach out."

"I try to do that," I answered. Therese was teaching me what I knew but what had seemed to be beyond my reach in my dark times.

"Conscious contact isn't a feeling," Therese went on. "It's a decision on our part to be in touch. We must make the effort, but if we do, God is there."

"I believe that," I said. And I do. In my dark night of the soul, I could not feel the comfort of my beliefs but I still had them. Every Wednesday night as I taught a classroom full of seekers, I would speak the good news of our spiritual connection even if at the moment I couldn't feel it. I might have been at the edge of the abyss emotionally but I knew there was a great invisible net waiting to catch me. Even if I couldn't see the net, I knew it was there. This was my experience, strength, and hope.

As a sober alcoholic, I was taught not to drink "five minutes before the miracle." I was taught to just hold on, that the dark night of the soul would pass if I just didn't drink. I was taught that my sobriety was a power of example. That each day that I managed to live without a drink was something to be proud of. And so, talking with Therese, I reiterated my determination not to drink.

"The liquor stores are pulsating at me," I complained. "They are whispering my name and I hate that." I told Therese that I was working with a newly sober alcoholic, that I was trying to teach her what I had been taught.

"You're a very sober lady," Therese told me. "You work hard at your sobriety. You really try to stay in the solution."

"The solution, as you call it, is the truth," I told Therese. "Despair is the great lie, and I should know better than to believe it." Just at the moment, despair felt at a safe remove. I could one more time feel myself connecting emotionally to the comfort of what I knew. My sobriety and my creativity were both safeguarded by a Higher Power.

As artists, we are ever companioned by the Great Artist. We are being nudged ever so gently forward, urged to continue making what it is that we make. There is no moment at which we are alone, even though our mythology makes much of artists as loners. We are not loners—certainly not spiritually. There is a higher octave that is always available to us. We need only to keep one ear cocked. There it is: the still, small voice. It comes to us as the hunch or the inkling. It comes to us as the lucky guess. It comes to us in all times at all places. We are never unpartnered, never solitary although we may, to the casual eye, make our art "alone."

> *Wishing to be friends is quick work, but friendship is a slow-ripening fruit.*
>
> ARISTOTLE

We can forget that we have such accompaniment available. We can cut ourselves off from the sunlight of the Spirit. We can work at working so relentlessly that the joy of working leaves us. We can enter a dark time, as I have recently. We can lose heart and as we do, our losses multiply.

We can forget to ask for inspiration. We can convince ourselves that we need to draw upon our own stores of inspiration. We can scoop at our hearts until they are as hollow as empty gourds. What happens if we work this way? We become desperate and desolate. We become hardened and disheartened. We forget that there is a Great Creator and that we are its creations, intended to be creative ourselves. Forgetting the proper order of things, forgetting that there is a divine plan of goodness for us and our work, we can strain ourselves striving for "more." And is there ever enough? When we compare ourselves to others rather than to ourselves, we come up lacking. There is always someone who has achieved more of what we desire. Sick at heart, truly soul sick, we forget to count our blessings. We may not even see that we have any to count. The glorious day, the friendly nods of strangers, all these pass us by unnoted. We are bent on achieving our aims. We are blinded to all around us.

And what happens when for a moment we remember?

When we remember that we are partnered, an ease enters our work. We begin to write more freely. We begin to paint with an inspired brush. Something or Someone larger than ourselves is striving to enter the world through us. We are the portal, the entryway, the gate. Through us great things come to pass. We are the conduits of a higher will. We are "humble" in the words of Piet Mondrian, essentially a "channel." When we cooperate, we feel a sense of right action, an ease.

Cooperating with a Higher Power, rather than striving to conquer, we find ourselves carried along by the tide of what we are creating. There is an energy flow that moves us forward. There is a propulsion to what it is we would create. It is as though all the plays, stories, songs, dances, paintings, and sculptures have a life of their own. They are our brainchildren and they actively seek birth through us. We are merely the doorway through which they enter the world. We open our hearts to what wishes to be born. We are receptive and what we receive is miraculous.

Tell me thy company and I'll tell thee what thou art.

MIGUEL DE CERVANTES

Friendship ought to be a gratuitous joy, like the joys afforded by art.

SIMONE WEIL

Any painter will tell you of time "lost" at the easel. A dancer will speak of being "lost" in the dance. Writers become absorbed and immersed and lose track of what it is they are writing. True artists become pawns and the hand that moves them is Art itself.

This morning Therese wondered if I had ever felt exalted, if I ever felt a submersion of self in the work that I create.

"On my good days," I answered her. "When I am in a dark time, I can remember my connection to God, but I cannot feel it."

We can elect to remember that we are partnered. We can ask a divine force to work through us. We can request the ability to erase ourselves as the conscious architects of what we create. We can strive to serve by what we make and, in that quality of service, we can attain a degree of egoless anonymity that is the midwife of good work.

"So you lose your sense of self?" Therese asked.

"Yes, the self becomes absorbed by something larger."

"I've had that experience when I'm helping someone," Therese volunteered.

"Yes. It's the experience of being in service to something other than our ego."

Therese goes to the gym and loses herself in the rhythm of her body. As artists we can lose ourselves in the rhythm of our souls. We can make what seems to want to be made. We can approach our day's work with a childlike glee. When we remember that there is a Great Creator we can begin to experience ourselves as children.

We can begin by thinking, "Something larger and grander than I made all that I see." We can look then at the boxer and the Pomeranian. We can look at the Harlequin Great Dane as it gaily sidesteps its tiny attackers, Tiger Lily and Charlotte. Even taking just this small survey of dogs, we can see the hand of something marvelous. Who made that rottweiler with its placid dignity? Who invented the feisty dachshund, so certain of its own number-one ranking in the world? Clearly there is Something or Someone at work who has great imagination and verve. This great Something waits to befriend us. We need only speak the word: help me.

And so I pray as I pass through my difficult passage. I lie in bed at night, awake with my fears, and I try to remember what I know. I know that God is good. I can ask that good God for mercy. I can pray:

> *It's not what you look at that matters, it's what you see.*
> HENRY DAVID THOREAU

Help me to become more teachable. Help me to become more open. Help me to see your face in every face; your hand in every hand. Give me a child's delight in the world that you have fashioned. Help me to know that I can work with you and play with you to fashion the world still further. Give me a sense of your power and your majesty. Give me a graceful heart that acknowledges the Great Maker in all that has been made. Help me to know that I am an artist companioned by the Great Artist. Allow me to make my inventions as part of a greater whole.

Help me to feel companioned always. Help me to make all days, good days. Help me to create knowing that in fact I cocreate. Help me to be small that I may be a part of Something very large. We are midway through May and the weather is rapturous. Help me to revel in its God-made delight.

"Yes, on my good days I feel companioned," I told Therese.

Divining Rod

All of us pass through periods when we do not feel companioned. We feel cut adrift, lost at sea, friendless, isolated, and alone. What has happened? As Therese warned, we fall prey to self-sufficiency. We unconsciously try to go it alone without God's help and aid. Because our human resources are always limited, we sooner or later reach a wall. We are brought up short by our own feelings of lack. At such times, we must reach out both to God and to others who can hold a lantern to our path. In such times, I seek out Bernice or Therese, Julie or Ed or Sonia or Larry or Libby or Elberta. When I feel really bankrupt, I seek out all of them. "Help me," I ask. "Put me in your prayers." My friends are believers. I want to be reminded there is a God.

Take pen in hand. Consciously draw to mind some of the dark nights of the soul that you have already survived. What did you do to help yourself through these bleak periods? What were your stratagems for making it through? How did you seek God? Or did God seem to seek you?

Number from one to five. List five things you could do to improve your conscious contact. For example, take more walks, read spiritual reading at bedtime, ask one of your friends to pray for you, make it a practice to write out a daily prayer. Choose one action and execute it. Remember that "conscious contact" is a decision and one you can make at any time.

Do a Little

The wind in the trees whispers secrets. The park has long green corridors hushed by the overarching trees. The weather is "perfect" yet another day. On the bridle path, horses are absent but pigeons pick their way among the hoof prints. Tiny finches dart amid the mock orange. A huge heron suddenly crosses the sky. It is headed south to the wilder "lake" where it makes its home. All along the trail, songbirds pipe from the bushes. Last night's heavy rain stands glistening in puddles. It's a good day for walking.

The possible's slow fuse is lit by the imagination.

EMILY DICKINSON

Tiger Lily and Charlotte take to the cinder bridle path. When a pigeon strays too close, Tiger Lily gives chase. Charlotte is too busy with the smells and sights to be bothered. Walking toward us comes a lady with two small poodles, one underfoot and one cradled in her arms.

"Charlotte, do you want to be that spoiled?" Emma asks. She confesses to having once carried Charlotte around the reservoir: "She was doing a lot of Westie position, balking, and so I had to drag her forward. I finally couldn't stand it anymore."

Just last night, a handsome stranger stopped Emma on the street. "Do you know why it is that Westies do that dragging thing?" he asked. "I once had two of them and they both did it."

"Maybe they're just stubborn," Emma replied.

Charlotte is now demonstrating her brakes-on "Westie position." There is no apparent reason for it. "Charlotte, come on," Emma begs.

As artists, our creative progress is also characterized by stubborn legs. It is for this reason that we do best to go forward slowly and steadily. There will be days when we are working uphill, tugging at our artist for cooperation. Not all days will be filled with eager forward motion. Our artist is willful.

If we hew to a course of "easy does it," we will do best. If we set our jumps too high, we may take them one day and fail miserably the next. Better to set modest jumps, jumps we can navigate even on the days our artists are acting up.

In order to succeed as an artist we must have two well-developed functions: our artist and its trainer. The trainer is steady and adult. It keeps its eye on the course and the long run. It coaxes, wheedles, begs, cajoles, and occasionally disciplines our artist which, Westie-like, proceeds in spurts and sometimes not at all.

> *Things won are done; joy's soul lies in the doing.*
> WILLIAM SHAKESPEARE

The trick is setting the jumps low enough that our artist can be lured into action. If I am writing nonfiction, I set my goal at a modest three pages. Almost anyone can write three pages of something and my artist knows that. On days that it digs in its heels and refuses to budge, I can drag it, kicking and screaming, for three pages. On most days, when it sprints ahead, three pages are easy. And the same kinds of goals can be set in all of the arts. A musician might set a goal of playing for fifteen minutes. Some days, that is an eternity, but most days, it is over in a blink. A dancer might set a certain set of warm-up exercises. An actor might tackle a monologue; a singer, a song.

If we set our jumps low enough, our artist can be lured into cooperation. It helps to think of our artist as an inner youngster, one susceptible to bribes. The promise of a treat can often induce a bout of good behavior. Our artist does best coaxed and cajoled. "If you write three pages, then you can talk with Sonia," I might promise, knowing that Sonia is one of my artist's favorite adults because she, too, is playful. "Write for three pages and then you can go for a walk," I might wheedle.

There are those who feel an artist should be treated with more dignity. In my experience, dignity doesn't go very far. Emma jokes that she was once told of her Westie, Charlotte, "I am afraid we can't do much with a terrier, ma'am." The same can be said of artists, "I am afraid we can't do much with an artist, ma'am." This is why artists are so frustrating to nonartists. It is not that we set out to be rebellious.

> *The deed is all, the glory nothing.*
>
> JOHANN WOLFGANG
> VON GOETHE

It is simply a part of our nature. Sometimes it is a part of our nature despite our desires to the contrary. Ask any artist who has been suddenly derailed just when he has the most to lose—the director who is having trouble delivering film number two, the novelist who is having trouble delivering a follow-up to a promising debut.

"Just do a little," is the medicine that most artists respond to. A novelist can manage to eke out a sentence or two. A singer can manage a set of scales. The whole trick is to think small, not large, although our adult "trainer" knows that all the smalls do add up to a large.

"You just write all the time, don't you?" a doctor recently exclaimed to me.

"Yes," I told him, "I do. I have noticed that writers who try to take down time are often very unhappy. Writers simply need to write and if we do it just a little at a time, it does add up."

"It does add up" is the phrase that everything boils down to. Whether we are talking about writing, singing, dancing, or acting. Whether we are talking about sculpting, designing, sewing, or cooking. No matter what our art form is, if we just do a little of it, we will find that all of our littles add up. "Fifteen minutes at the easel and then you can have an ice cream" may not strike you as the most adult way to make art. It does, however, make art.

Divining Rod

You will need to set aside an hour and take yourself out to a café or coffee shop where you can write unimpeded. Order a good cup of tea or perhaps a cappuccino and take your pen to the page. You are asked to write a letter to your artist from your trainer.

This letter will look at your life with objectivity, talking with you about the ways in which your care of your artist could be improved. You might find, for example, that your trainer thinks you set your jumps too high. You may be urged to lower your daily quota so that you will not be too discouraged to try to meet it.

Your trainer may want to help you dismantle your perfectionist. Or tell you need more Artist Dates. Or that you could benefit from joining a writers' support group, something that you have heretofore scorned.

Your trainer has your best interests at heart and may come up with actions that move you out of your comfort zone. You might be told to join an online Artist's Way group—or start one in your neighborhood. Your trainer might think you are falling short on your walks or are not really using your list of believing mirrors. Alternatively, your trainer might feel that you are doing better than you think. You might be urged to write a positive inventory.

Checking in with your trainer is a tool that you may wish to repeat at regular intervals. My trainer tells me when I have let my piano practice slide or when I am procrastinating on a script. Like many of us, I may wish for an outer mentor but having an inner mentor can be enough.

CHECK-IN

1. **How many days this week did you do your Morning Pages?** If you skipped a day, why did you skip it? How was the experience of writing them for you? Are you experiencing more clarity? A wider range of emotions? A greater sense of detachment, purpose, and calm? Did anything surprise you? Is there a "repeating" issue asking to be dealt with?

2. **Did you do your Artist Date this week?** Did you note an improved sense of well-being? What did you do and how did it feel? Remember, Artist Dates can be difficult and you may need to coax yourself into taking them.

3. **Did you get out on your Weekly Walk?** How did that feel? What emotions or insights surfaced for you? Were you able to walk more than once? What did your walk do for your optimism and sense of perspective?

4. **Were there any other issues this week that felt significant to you in your self-discovery?** Describe them.

Uncovering a Sense of Safety

Contrary to our mythology, creativity is not a dangerous pursuit. The creative flow is both normal and healthy. We have the safety net of both our friends and our Creator to fall back on. Our trepidations fade as we focus on the many positive resources available to us. As we "count coup," enumerating for ourselves our creative accomplishments, we see that more accomplishment is possible. Focused on small actions on our own behalf, we experience a sense of ourselves as our own friend and comrade.

Risk

The sky was a dark, coppery green. Raindrops the size of dimes pelted down. It was a tropical deluge—and this was midtown Manhattan, mid-May. Emma and I stood underneath a theater marquis watching as the rain created torrents on the street. We were on Forty-second Street. We had just seen *Twentieth Century* starring Alec Baldwin and Anne Heche. We were elated.

"They were good, weren't they?" Emma exclaimed. "I could almost go see the show one more time just to watch the direction." The snappy direction was by Walter Bobbie of *Chicago* fame. Physical comedy abounded. Performances went over the top and stayed there, taking the audience's spirits right along with them.

"He did such great things with his hands," I said. "I hadn't expected him to be funny physically."

> *When you go in search of honey you must expect to be stung by bees.*
>
> KENNETH KAUNDA

Yes, art is dangerous. Where it is chaste, it is not art.

PABLO PICASSO

"Yes, but he certainly was."

"Wasn't he, though?"

Twentieth Century is a play about theater people. Baldwin plays a larger-than-life impresario, down on his luck. Heche plays the leading lady he created. At no time did Baldwin or Heche seem like Hollywood actors, unused to life on the stage. They both seized the stage as if born to it. They leaned into Bobbie's boisterous direction. When they finally went for a clinch, it was a humdinger, a good case of chemistry requited. You could almost feel their actorly glee knowing that they were pushing the envelope, pulling out stops and gears that no one knew were there.

The play was the thing and "play" was what they were doing. The actors' high spirits leapt across the footlights. Theirs were big, risky performances. The joy of the show was that no one was playing it safe.

In order to grow as artists, we must be willing to risk. We must try to do something more and larger than what we have done before. We cannot continue indefinitely to replicate the successes of our past.

There are some risks that we cannot avoid taking. These adventures whisper to the heart, "Wouldn't it be fun to try . . .?" and don't let up until they are fulfilled. Careers are made by following the star of what our heart calls us to do. This means we may fly in the face of safety and convention. An actor like Baldwin moves from tragedy to comedy. He does not rest on the dignity of his darkly brilliant performances in films like *The Cooler*. He takes a chance the best may be yet to come.

Great careers are characterized by great risks. It takes courage to jettison the mantle of what we have done well for the chance to grab at the cape of what we might do even better.

Robert De Niro has crafted a career filled with brave choices. Known for the stark intensity of his dramatic work, he has insisted that he also can do comedy. His audience was at first reluctant to take the leap of faith with him: "Robert De Niro in a comedy?" But De Niro persisted and the audience eventually followed. Now a Robert De Niro comedy can be a must-see ticket. *Analyze That* followed the success of *Analyze This*. It took courage for De Niro to insist on playing comedy.

How do we know when a risk is right for us? We must learn to listen to the heart and not the head. The head is always full of second thoughts and second-guessing. It will arrive at a thousand reasons that we should not risk. "Why, you'll look like a fool," the head will start in. "Everyone knows you and respects you for doing X. If you try

Y, you'll never get away with it." Then the heart enters, "Come on. Lighten up. What's the worst thing that can happen? You fail. Wouldn't you like yourself better for failing at trying than you would like yourself for playing it safe?"

We cannot play it safe and expand as artists at the same time. We must risk expanding our territory—and we will survive if we are shot down for it. There are certain risks that come with pursuing an artistic career. All artists working in public run the risk of bad—even patently unfair—reviews. Even Baldwin and Heche, for all the fun they are having, are having it in the face of mixed reviews. It is for this reason that our reward must lie in the risk itself, in the self-esteem we feel for undertaking it. Looking back on our careers, we may have rueful laughter at the chances that we took, but we will not have regrets.

If you don't risk anything, you risk even more.

ERICA JONG

You aim for what you want and if you don't get it, you don't get it, but if you don't aim, you don't get anything.

FRANCINE PROSE

Divining Rod

Many times we do not want to take a risk with our creativity because we want a guarantee of a positive outcome. This is very American of us. We think that risks have to be large and noteworthy. We want a "product" to show for our process. We want a payoff in terms of our career. In order to free up our creativity, we need to be able to do some creativity for free, that is, with no guaranteed outcome. We need to practice some creativity that is not goal-oriented. Put simply, we need to let ourselves play.

Take pen in hand. Number from one to ten. List ten tiny creative actions that you could take that have no bearing on getting ahead in the world. (These actions are often things you tell yourself you are "too busy" to do.) For example, you might manicure your nails bright red; you might sit at the piano and noodle for ten minutes; you might write a short poem; you might do your mending; you might paint the inside of your closet chartreuse; you might sketch your boyfriend; you might bake a colleague a birthday cake;

you might send a postcard to your ailing aunt; you might brush the dog; you might make a collage; or you might bake a batch of chocolate-chip cookies or mix up some Jell-O.

None of these risks is earth-shattering, but they are sufficient to shatter your "boredom" or depression. An intellectual friend of mine scornfully calls such risks, "Martha Stewart risks." He has forgotten the joy that can come from practicing a hobby or handicraft. He has forgotten, too, that small risks train us to take larger ones. Think of your tiny risks as a form of self-training. You are learning to say, "Yes, I can" instead of "No, I can't."

Reviews

It is mid-May and the temperatures are in the mideighties. Summer is not yet here, but it is already upon us. Yesterday's torrential storm leaves today's simmering puddles. Yesterday's risks, well taken, leave today's self-respect.

Only those that risk going too far can possibly find out how far one can go.

T. S. ELIOT

It takes courage to be an artist. The part of us that creates is youthful and vulnerable. We make our art with high hopes. While we may not make our art with reviews in mind, they are always lurking. It is an artist's job to survive reviews and live to work another day.

I have a friend, actress Julianna McCarthy, who says that good reviews are as dangerous to an actor as bad reviews. She warns that if something is singled out for praise, an actor may end up trying to play that something, with the result that his performance becomes hopelessly skewed.

"If you're going to believe your good reviews," Julianna warns, "then you have to also believe your bad reviews." It's better not to believe any reviews and to try to work for the sake of the work.

"What is it with friends always wanting to make sure you know about reviews?" wonders another friend of mine. She tries not to read reviews, positive or negative, until the run of a show is safely over with.

Actors are not the only ones who run the risk of spoiling their work by taking in reviews. Writers, too, suffer from undergoing the review process. Seldom are the reviews accurate in helping an artist to improve his work. When they are, when the critical arrow actually hits the mark, most artists respond with excitement, "Ah hah! This is how I can make the work better!"

Making the work better is the true goal of most artists. We have, at heart, a purity of intention that gets lost in the reviewing process. We are out to make something that can stand on its own as worthy and this often gets lost in the shuffle of the marketplace. As celebrity increases, so does vulnerability to the reviewing process. As fame enters the equation, judgment—good judgment—seems to leave. The artists now finds himself reviewed not as an artist but as a media phenomenon.

> *There is no happiness except in the realization that we have accomplished something.*
>
> HENRY FORD

> *Too many people overvalue what they are not and undervalue what they are.*
>
> MALCOLM FORBES

Artists at all levels run the risk of reviews. Small-town press can be just as hurtful as a bad review in *The New York Times*. At bottom, reviews often focus on what is lacking and not on what has been accomplished. It is as though critics carry in their heads an imaginary movie, book, play, or painting, against which the actual work is measured and found wanting. And it does not matter how popular an artist may be—in fact, popularity seems to increase the incidence of unfair reviews. There is almost a spoilsport aspect to reviewing that insists on pulling the feathers off.

Yesterday I went to visit a famous writer. The writer lives in a sprawling sun-filled apartment overlooking Central Park. A full room was set aside to hold the writer's first editions. Everything about the place spoke of success. "I've had only one *New York Times* review," the writer told me. "That was two years ago and it was so mean that my friends advised me not to read it—which I haven't." This writer is so successful that new books debut at number one on *The New York Times* bestseller list.

"A book launch is like a NASA launch," the writer continued. "They will call me and say, 'We're going for the seventh. There's a two-day window between Grisham and Clancy. We're aiming for that.' I just let them aim where they see fit. My job has to be writing the books, not marketing them."

As artists it is our difficult job to do the work for the work's sake and to retain a healthy level of detachment from sales. This is easier said than done. I recently spoke with a best-selling author who was at her wit's end regarding her latest book. "They just dumped it into the stores. There was no thought, no publicity, nothing to help the book along. It was sink or swim and good luck to you."

We may put years of work into a project that a reviewer dismisses in a few quick paragraphs. Reviews now often come graded like grammar-school papers. A film that was three years in the making may garner a scanty two stars. An album that was five years in the writing may get three stars if the artist is lucky. It is very rare to see a full four-star review. That takes a generosity of spirit that critics are hard put to come by. As artists, how do we survive such stinginess?

> None think the great unhappy but the great.
>
> EDWARD YOUNG

> Envy is a kind of praise.
>
> JOHN GAY

Work is the best antidote for savaged work. If we are engaged in making something new, we are less invested in the reception of something old. If we remember to keep our own counsel—"How did *I* like the work?"—then we are less likely to be blown apart by the judgment of others. Having a healthy forum of before, during, and after friends is also an enormous help. We need those who love us and our work for the long haul and not for a hot-off-the-presses pick or pan.

It pays to remember that the reviewing process is historically misguided and often unfair. Wonderful work, work that has stood the test of time, was often savaged when it first appeared. The artist had to muster inhuman amounts of fortitude to keep going in the face of such discouragement—and yet, artists have kept going. We are stronger than we think.

"My success has to lie with my readers and not with my reviewers," the bestselling author concluded. "I need to go to my desk excited by what I have to share. It's up to me to try to retain some optimism and to do so in the face of tough reviews. I need to ask myself, 'Do people enjoy my books?' 'Do I enjoy making them?' If both answers are 'Yes,' then I am doing all right no matter what the critics say. And you know what? I am doing all right."

Divining Rod

As working artists we deserve credit for sheer courage. We need to applaud ourselves for having the fortitude to continue making our art.

Every scrap of art that we make deserves our encouragement. In addition to our believing mirrors, we ourselves need to cheer our progress. In Native American terms, this is called "counting coup." To 12-steppers it is called "taking a positive inventory."

Take pen in hand. Number from one to five. Enumerate five creative accomplishments. (These may have been included on your list of things you were proud of.) For example: I learned how to work with gouache; I wrote a one-act play; I learned a new monologue; I did a basic jazz dance course; I made my own Halloween costume.

In listing your accomplishments, allow yourself to look at process and not product. Even if it hasn't sold yet, you deserve credit for having written that romantic novel. Although you are still looking for a proper venue, you deserve points for having written a one-man show. Remember it is the making of art, not the reception of your art that makes you an artist. Van Gogh and Gauguin were both outcasts. Beethoven's later work was a century ahead of his time. Respect lies in the doing. Focus on that.

Receptivity

The tree beneath my writing-room window is a mystery to me. It has four-cornered leaves and large yellow flowers that are gold to the swarms of yellow jackets that feed and cruise and feed again amid its branches. This is the first summer that I have stayed on in New York rather than going on out to Taos, New Mexico. It is the first season when the tree has become a part of my story. I write at an IBM Selectric typewriter set on a small Chinese desk, up against a large window. The bees come to the window. They are large yellow jackets and they soar menacingly close. I remind myself that there is a pane of glass between them and me. I am grateful for the window.

> No theoretician, no writer on art, however interesting he or she might be, could be as interesting as Picasso. A good writer on art may give you an insight to Picasso, but, after all, Picasso was there first.
>
> DAVID HOCKNEY

> *A critic is a man who knows the way but can't drive the car.*
>
> KENNETH TYNAN

> *It is the weak and confused who worship the pseudosimplicities of brutal directness.*
>
> MARSHALL MCLUHAN

Very often in our creative lives we can feel ourselves in jeopardy. We may have a sudden and debilitating doubt that our work will continue to be supported by the Universe. We may have been earning a living so far, but that's so far—our fear says—and so far is no guarantee of tomorrow. Rather than trust that there is an unseen but benevolent web gently holding us in our place, we often panic and act like we have gotten where we have gotten entirely on our own. Panicked that we do not know how to go forward further, we flail in midair, caught between our fears and our projections.

But there is a benevolent web that holds us gently in our place. There *is* a larger power that wishes us well. We are led well and carefully. In order to be led further, we need only to ask for help. Help is always available to us. We need to open ourselves up. We need to be receptive.

For some of us, it is difficult to be receptive. We are used to self-propulsion and self-will. We count on ourselves and only on ourselves. When the chips fall our way, we do not thank a benevolent God, we thank our "lucky" stars.

The problem with depending on our luck is that luck is capricious. Our good luck can always change. Today we may be the darling of the gods and tomorrow we may be wailing at the gate, begging to be admitted one more time to paradise. How much better if there is something reliable on which we may build. How much better if there is a benevolent Something that is not capricious. To find such a Something, we need only look to the natural world. In God's world, the sun rises and the sun sets. The seasons appear each in their turn. Trees bud and bear leaves and flowers. Fruit grows heavy on the bough. There is a time of harvest.

It is our ego that tells us that we stand apart from nature. It is our ego that says we alone can force our growth. When we pray to be a part of the great unfolding plan, we are relieved of the burden of strategizing. We are relieved of the need to plot, to plan, to project. Each day we will be given what we need for that day. When we must act, we will have the clear knowledge of how it is we are to act. We will be guided. We will be shown. Is this a delusional fantasy?

Artists, when they speak candidly, almost always speak about higher forces. We may call it Guidance. We may call it Fate. We may call it Destiny or the Muse. Whatever we call it, it is the hand of a higher power at play in our lives. Artists will talk humbly about lucky breaks, about happening to be in the right place at the right time. We will speak of being led person to person, hand to hand. There is an invisible guiding force present in all of these transactions. Our destiny unfolds within a larger plan. When we set our hand to our work, something larger than us works through us. We sense that Something. Some of us call it God.

"When I write, I communicate with a greater Something," a writer friend of mine explains. "I am working at my plot but Something is working on me and through me. There is a truth that I am intended to express."

The truth that we are intended to express is that we are all larger than we know. We are part of a grand design. There is room for our expansion. The Universe falls in with worthy plans. As we strive to grow larger and more expansive, the Universe seeks to expand through us. When we reach for support, the support is there. Our expansion is planned for, even counted upon. If we do not expand, the Universe cannot expand. If we thwart our true nature, we also thwart God's.

And yet, all of us go through times when we doubt our capacity to expand. All of us go through times when we feel the Universe to be unsafe, when we are frightened about what will become of us. I have been weathering just

Man is least himself when he talks in his own person. Give him a mask and he will tell you the truth.

OSCAR WILDE

To have great poets, there must be great audiences too.

WALT WHITMAN

such a time. In times such as these, we turn, sick at heart, to prayer. "God, I believe. Help my disbelief," we pray, asking to be shown again how to trust. Our very prayers seem empty, based on an intimacy we no longer feel.

"I have a very intense, very meaningful relationship with God that comes and goes," one man jokes, kidding on the square. It is his experience that faith does not stay comfortable, that he is asked, again and again, to expand his faith beyond his comfort zone.

"It's not that I don't believe in God," he says. "It's just that sometimes I do not experience the relief of my belief. At times God feels like a fact of life to me and at other times God feels like a theory. During my theoretical times, I must act 'as if.' I must say to myself, '*If* I believed in a benevolent God, how would I act now?' and then I must act that way. Eventually, comfort returns."

"Faith will come back to you," another friend always assures me. "And then it will disappear again." I have had times of faith—even years of faith—but now my faith has gone glimmering. I know from experience that it will return again if I can simply keep on "faithfully" keeping on. It is ironic that I am one more time asked to grow larger by growing smaller. As Bernice advises, I must get tiny in order to be connected to the larger order. And so, on a sleepless night, I must pray, "Help me, God." And then I must lie there, knowing that I am in fact being helped.

Our relationship with God appears to be tidal. Sometimes it is at high tide, full of power and glory. Other times it is at low ebb, barely visible. Always, it is in the act of making art that contact again can be felt.

"I think of painting as prayer and meditation," one painter tells me. "I go to the canvas and I empty myself of me. I ask to paint and then I surrender control. I may take the first stroke but the strokes thereafter follow one upon the other with me hurrying along in obedience trying to paint what comes next. Time disappears when I am painting. I am hollowed out, empty of anything but a kind of listening. I have my skills but my skills are in service of something larger. That larger Something may be some sort of ideal. I paint toward that perfection. Reaching for perfection, I am reaching for God."

> *An audience is never wrong. An individual member of it may be an imbecile, but a thousand imbeciles together in dark—that is critical genius.*
>
> BILLY WILDER

Whether we call it reaching for God or reaching for the Muse, there is a humility to be found in the making of art. We strive to make what wants to be made. We open ourselves to inspiration and as we do so, we are led. We do not always *feel* that we are being led. We must affirm it in the face of our own doubt. We must go forward acting "as if." When we are willing to do that, we get a sense of our place in the greater scheme of things.

"When I am procrastinating about my art, it always feels risky to me," says one writer. "I always think I will be dropped on my ear. I think, 'I cannot believe I am really going to spend another day doing that.' And then I start working and suddenly the world all around me begins to make sense again. It is as though by working at my art I am given faith in the proper unfolding of things."

Divining Rod

You will need an hour's time and a notebook. Once again, seek out a space that feels sacred to you. It might be a church or synagogue. It might be a library or reading room. It could be a grove of trees. What is important is that the place hold a sense of the transcendent. Seat yourself comfortably. Do not turn immediately to your notebook. You are asked to sit quietly and see what thoughts and feelings come to you.

This is an exercise in receptivity. You are seeking to receive Guidance. Your Guidance may be diffuse—a sense of well-being—or it may be very particular. Try focusing on your breath or on something beautiful in your environment. Allow your everyday world to slip gently away. It may take a little while for you to become calm and quiet. Once your thoughts have slowed, deeper insights can swim to the fore. What thoughts come to you?

You have your notebook on your lap. You may wish to use it now to write a prayer—or to simply note the insights that you are receiving. What you "get" may be very simple: call your sister more often, remember to buy stamps, get yourself a good houseplant, let yourself buy some Joni Mitchell albums again. Alternatively, your Guidance might concern larger issues: "I really can't stay in this job."

You might receive "marching orders" that pertain to any area of your life. What you take in may be a fleeting impression: "I am doing better than I think," or "I really need to change a few things." Listen closely to what it is that you receive. Record what you will need to jog your memory. You are simply checking in. You may wish to make a daily practice of such stolen quiet moments. Many of us find that a lunch hour can afford us a spare quarter hour. Some students keep a special journal just for their quiet times. In that journal, they may use leading phrases to nudge themselves into greater introspection. They might write, "I wish" and complete the phrase twenty times. They might try, "I could try" and finish the phrase ten times. Alternatively, they might simply ask, "What do I need to know?" and record the answer that comes to them. You are seeking to "tag base" with a source of wisdom greater than your own.

Productivity

"It looks like a koi pond," my sister Libby has announced to me about her trout-covered kitchen table. "I have ordered a sheet of glass to protect it and I have signed it, which is fun." Over the phone line her voice bubbles with enthusiasm. She has had a very good time painting a school of trout just for fun. I picture her table in my mind's eye. I ask her to take some shots of it and e-mail me.

It has been fifteen years since my sister and I last lived in close proximity to each other. We have kept in touch by phone, e-mail, and mail. It is important to me that Libby be current with the events of my life. She is also a great inspiration to me and I like knowing just what portraits she has in process. What exactly is she painting in her studio on "Fairietale Farm"?

I like knowing that this month she is painting the tricky, thick coat of an elkhound. I like imagining the work she has done getting an aging thoroughbred exactly right. Long distance, I walk through the steps with her from the initial photo session through the client consultations, the decisions about size and medium that will be used. My sister works in colored pencils, watercolors, and oils. She especially loves oils.

When my sister is at work on a large oil, I can feel her concentration over the phone line. Always aware that for her client, the portrait represents a considerable cash outlay, Libby is determined to give good value and she does. Still, she is always on pins and needles waiting to see the client's response. She always has jitters before she delivers a commission. Do they like it? Yes!

Working full time as a portrait artist, it is relatively rare for her to indulge in creating something sheerly for the glee of creation. When she does, her joy leapfrogs over the phone line. Last year, she sculpted an eight-foot-tall poodle. It was kelly green and lit by Christmas bulbs.

"I had the poodle right in the middle of my kitchen. Guests would come by and go, 'Gee. I guess you're up to something.' I love being up to something.

It gives me back a part of my artist identity. If I am too much the drone for hire, I stop respecting myself. It all starts feeling a little too corporate for me, I guess."

To the outside eye, there is nothing corporate about Libby's life unless it is the consistent productivity that she musters. At any given time, she may have as many as five portraits in varying stages of completion. Moving portrait to portrait keeps her from going stale and allows her to edge further along on each commission without freezing up.

"Like anyone, I get scared. I think, 'Is this one good enough?' Working on more than one work at a time allows me to postpone that block-inducing question. I just do a little more work each day on each commission and then I move on. It may be an eccentric way to work, but for me it is productive. I am never bored and I am seldom stymied. There is always a little more that can be done on something. You keep adding up those 'little mores' and you do get quite a bit accomplished."

Although she doesn't phrase it this way, I see that my sister has arranged her work life to keep her work fun for her. Each portrait offers its unique set of challenges. She must be true to her art, true to her own vision and yet accommodating, too, to the client's vision. Sometimes an angry jawline must be softened. Sometimes a waistline must be whittled in.

"My job is to paint not only what I see, but also how they see themselves," Libby explains. "I try to bear in mind that I am offering them a service. When I remember that, it keeps my ego out of it."

Working to keep her ego out of it, Libby finds that she is able to paint more freely. She is able to "listen" to each painting as it unfolds. She strives to be open to the painting that wants to happen, not just to the painting that she has planned. Some of her best works are what she describes as "happy accidents."

> *God does not compel the will. Rather, He sets the will free so that it wills not otherwise than what God Himself wills.*
>
> MEISTER ECKHART

"I sometimes seem to stumble upon an idea that is better than the idea I had. I do believe that when we are open to it, we are led. I try to be available to whatever higher force is striving to work through me. I ask to be of service, and I ask for inspiration. My paintings are really my answered prayers."

Divining Rod

In 12-step lingo, God is sometimes spoken of as "Good Orderly Direction." There is something about creating order that does put us in touch with a sense of the Divine. The task I ask you to do now is a humble one. Set aside one half hour and a stack of your mending.

Take needle and thread in hand and set to work. You may have buttons that need tightening; socks that have a hole. The seam on a pair of slacks may need some reinforcement. Quietly and calmly, allow yourself to work gently through your pile. Be alert for the sense of well-being that may steal over you. Be alert, too, for some flashes of creative inspiration. Needlework goads the imagination—think of the Brontë sisters hiding their novels under their handiwork. Many novelists have found that needlepoint, crocheting, and knitting help them to stitch up their plots as well.

Prayer

I decided that it was not wisdom that enabled poets to write their poetry, but a kind of instinct or inspiration, such as you find in seers and prophets who deliver all their sublime messages without knowing in the least what they mean.

SOCRATES

It is hot and hazy in New York. In Chicago, it is cool and rainy. I know the Chicago weather because my friend Sonia lives there, and I am, by phone, a regular part of her Chicago household. I am, too, a part of my friend Elberta's household in New Mexico and my friend Ed Towle's household in Los Angeles. Here in New York, I am often lonely, wishing that my friends lived in the same city. But I am grateful to have friends, carefully collected and nurtured over the years.

"You are in my prayers twice each day," says my friend Larry, who lives in Taos, New Mexico, where I myself lived for ten years. As the sun comes up over the mountain ridge, Larry rises to pray and meditate. "I think of you every morning," he assures me. I, for one, am glad to be thought of.

"I wake up at five-thirty and you are at the top of my prayer list," declares my sister Libby who lives in Racine, Wisconsin. "I pray for you every single morning, chiefly the Our Father, but a prayer that you will feel well and work well during the day to come." Libby lives on a horse farm and light comes to her through a bank of pine trees bordering her farm. I am grateful to think that as the dawn comes so do prayers for my well-being. I myself wake up with a prayer not far from my consciousness. I get to the page for my three pages of morning writing and after my three pages, I pray. I ask that my day be in the care of God and that I be made into what God needs for me to be. The answer to that prayer seems most often to boil down to: Be a writer. And so, I come to the typewriter and I write.

Art is an invention of aesthetics, which is in turn an invention of philosophers . . . What we call art is a game.

OCTAVIO PAZ

No artist is ahead of his time. He is his time, it's just that others are behind the times.

MARTHA GRAHAM

In our modern world, prayer is seldom discussed as a viable part of living. It smacks a little of esoterica. In previous ages we had the great bells tolling across the countryside, marking the days into intervals of prayer. In modern life, no bells toll. Prayers are elected, not suggested by the very fabric of the day. Someone like Larry, who rises to pray and to meditate, is rare. Most of us find our day gets under way willy-nilly. We are out of bed and into the great maw of onrushing events without the buffer of prayer to gird us for the day's events.

Prayer is profoundly useful but we seldom see it as such. Instead it seems somewhat arcane, a dubious pastime of those with nothing better to do. In point of fact, prayer is intensely practical. It works like a routing system, sending divine energy just where it is needed. As artists, we can pray to be of service. We can ask that our work serve the greater whole. We can pray for practical things, too. We can pray for an inspiration, for the ability to do justice to a certain idea, for an acknowledgment of our work.

As artists, when we pray, we are joining a long tradition. Throughout the centuries, great art has been born of great humility. Although the Sistine Chapel was commissioned, Michelangelo sought to serve both his patron and his God. We, too, can seek to serve.

"I believe that when we are writing, we are communicating with something higher than ourselves," states one best-selling author. "Working at art is really an act of communion. When I write, I am praying. When I miss a day's writing, I, in effect, miss a day's prayer—and I feel it.

He neither serves nor rules, he
transmits. His position is
humble and the beauty at the
crown is not his own. He is
merely a channel.

PAUL KLEE

The product of the artist has
become less important than the
fact of the artist.

DAVID MAMET

"I believe there are higher forces that we connect with
when we work," the writer continues. "I have been writing for twenty years. That has given me a spiritual life. I believe that I am intended to write, that when I write, I open
myself to Spirit."

When an artist is fully engaged in working, there is a
self-forgetting that happens. The artist becomes absorbed
in the service of the work that he is creating. The ego dis-
solves and the soul steps forward.

"I believe that I am guided," the writer speculates. "I
believe that I am a conduit for God to put forward some
truth. At times I am frightened. I feel that what I am writing or saying is uncomfortable, and yet I feel guided that it
is what I am intended to say. I do my best simply to cooperate. I am not saying I am without fear, but rather that I
try to set fear to one side."

When Larry and Libby pray for me, they pray that I, too, may set aside my fear
and do what it is God would have me do with my day. They are praying that my
personality might be malleable, teachable by the Great Teacher. I have come to depend upon their prayers. Many days, I ask for them.

"I don't feel very good about what I am trying to write. Can you stick me in
the prayer pot for some inspiration?" I might ask my sister. With Libby praying
for me from her studio in Racine, Wisconsin, I sit down to write at my desk in
New York, New York.

There is an uncanny Something that kicks in as the result of prayer. I may find
myself at my desk, writing for longer hours than is my usual wont. I may find myself writing with greater candor, risking a self-revelation that I might normally
have eschewed. Days when I am being prayed for, I find myself more willing to
keep myself at the typewriter. I find myself cocking an inner ear for what it is that
I am trying to write and then writing it out with more fluidity. I do not know that
I would say my style improves as a result of prayer, but my willingness to write and
therefore have a style improves. Writing would seem to be a secular activity and yet
it benefits from spiritual aid.

"I think that when we deal with Spirit, we are dealing in the realm of arche-
types," posits a renowned editor. "It is as though there is an ideal book that is striving to come forward and the writer and the editor are both in service of this larger

and better Something. In a sense, a book tells you what it wants to be. Perhaps the best books are the ones where the players are the most obedient to the book's demands."

"I pray for you to be willing to write what wants to be written," says my sister. As a painter herself, she is familiar with a piece of art having its own imperious sense of where it wants to go. "There are days when you write what I seem to need to hear. Is that because I am the one praying? I sometimes wonder."

"Wonder" seems to be at the heart of inspiration. We receive a small, inner prompt and although we wonder where it could be taking us, we obediently follow. In that sense, the writing seems to move one step ahead of a writer. We write not to display what we think but to discover what we think. More is always being revealed to us as we are open to higher input.

"I don't know about the word 'higher,'" a writer friend of mine interjects. "I think all people are guided always. I don't think artists have a lock on it. I just think that our guidance results in something tangible on the page or on the stage or on the easel, whereas for other people guidance may result in something more ephemeral, say a shift in direction or emphasis. My point is that inspiration is a very daily and matter-of-fact phenomenon. Artists simply have something to show for it. Our art can easily seem to be inspired. But we're all inspired when you come down to it."

If we are all inspired, perhaps prayer gives us the consciousness of that inspiration. If the universe is ready at all times to guide and mentor us, perhaps we can be more or less open to such tutelage.

The sun rises over brownstones and Central Park. Before it has arched very high in its course, prayers have been sent up for my benefit. I am grateful to be the recipient of such prayers. They are like added lanterns on my path so that when my own prayer goes up, "Lord, show me what you would have me do," there is already illumination of the task at hand. I pray daily, "God, grant me the serenity to accept the things I cannot change," and among those things I cannot change is the fact that I am a writer. And so, prayers said, I write.

I write at a small Chinese desk. I look out over the brownstones and I hope that God will send me words. Sometimes words come to me in a rush. I am grateful for such times. Other days, I know that I am to write and I do write but it is without

> *When you pray for anyone you tend to modify your personal attitude toward him.*
>
> NORMAN VINCENT PEALE

> *He must pull out his own eyes and see no creature before he can say he sees no God.*
>
> JOHN DONNE

comfort and ease. Those days, I feel myself dependent on grace and that grace is something that I ask for and my friends ask for for me.

On the mornings after I have spent a sleepless night, it is harder to write. I go to the page already weary. "Help me," I pray. "Please help me." Help then comes to me in the form of a small thought, a notion really of how it is that I might go forward. Sometimes I feel that my very thoughts limp and that I am lame following after them. At times like this, I must remind myself that prayers have been said and that my job is simply to trust, to take down what appears to be next. Sometimes I look out my window at the rooftops as though answered prayers might materialize there, like Santa Claus with a fully laden sleigh. I pray and I write. The gift is being given the words to do so, however haltingly. "Help me now," I pray. Then I must trust as help comes.

> *I searched for God and found only myself. I searched for myself and found only God.*
>
> SUFI PROVERB

Divining Rod

Prayer is always an exercise in open-mindedness. You could think of it as a scientific experiment: if I pray (action), what will happen (response)? Although we may give lip service to the idea that God is all seeing and all knowing, there are usually areas about which we do not pray. We may, for example, consider our finances too worldly a concern to involve God. And yet, those students who have experimented with financial prayers report that they have received very useful financial guidance.

Take pen in hand. Number from one to twenty. List twenty topics—people, places, and things—about which you could pray. Your prayers may range from the tiny, "Help me to find some good-looking stamps," to the large, "Help me to know how to help my sister through her husband's death." Be alert for areas that you do not pray about. Is your need for a new haircut fuel for prayer? Is your diet, or your willingness to exercise? Some students make a regular practice of prayer after their Morning Pages. Others report great comfort from an evening ritual. The time you pray matters less than that you do find the time to pray. Consider your list a preliminary prayer.

CHECK-IN

1. **How many days this week did you do your Morning Pages?** If you skipped a day, why did you skip it? How was the experience of writing them for you? Are you experiencing more clarity? A wider range of emotions? A greater sense of detachment, purpose, and calm? Did anything surprise you? Is there a "repeating" issue asking to be dealt with?

2. **Did you do your Artist Date this week?** Did you note an improved sense of well-being? What did you do and how did it feel? Remember, Artist Dates can be difficult and you may need to coax yourself into taking them.

3. **Did you get out on your Weekly Walk?** How did that feel? What emotions or insights surfaced for you? Were you able to walk more than once? What did your walk do for your optimism and sense of perspective?

4. **Were there any other issues this week that felt significant to you in your self-discovery?** Describe them.

Uncovering a Sense of Discipline

Nowhere is the phrase "Easy does it" more useful than in the pursuit of our creative endeavors. Small and gentle daily actions build upon themselves to make large accomplishments. A novel is written a page at a time. A painting proceeds brushstroke by brushstroke. By thinking small, we are able to become large. As we exercise our creative gifts, we experience the joy of artistic rigor. Like athletes, we keep ourselves in training. Our daily laps build stamina.

Twenty Minutes

The sky is pewter. Heavy drops hang from the fire escape. Down on the streets umbrellas are folded under arms. The sun pulses behind the clouds, threatening to break through the over cast. The news from Wisconsin is rain, rain, and more rain. As usual, we have inherited their used weather.

This morning's e-mail included photographs of my sister Libby's trout-pond kitchen table. The trout are beautiful, mixing with each other, swirling to the surface. The table, viewed at a glance, does look like a koi pond. It will be fun taking meals atop those fish.

The bird of paradise alights only on the hand that does not grasp.

JOHN BERRY

Trying to take in the idea of something "fun," I feel myself straining. I am still caught in the undertow of depression and "fun" remains largely theoretical to me. When I talk on the phone to my sister, I must work to be really present and accounted for in the conversation. Libby chats brightly and I must force myself to listen to her and not to the undercurrent of despair that is still my constant sound track. I must set a discipline for myself, a mental fence to contain my negativity. "Try to be positive," I lecture myself. "Try to show up and be of service. Take an interest in other people, not just in your own dilemma."

Last night, my friend Sonia phoned in from Chicago. She was overtired, overworked, and frustrated. She has a book to write and no window in her schedule in which to write it. She longs for an empty savannah of time. I don't think she's going to get it, and so I urge her to fly at the page in the minutes to spare that she has got. "Just start where you are," I tell her. "Put down something and then we will go from there."

I say, "we," because I am functioning as a believing mirror for Sonia's writing career. I see her books as finished and successful. When she has doubt, she needs only check in with me to know that the books are a reality and not a "mere" dream. This is Sonia's eighth book. Sooner or later, her identity as a working writer will catch up to her. At this point, she still regards each book as a fluke, something she is lucky to be able to pull off.

"I am going to try to write page one," she announces. She will wedge that page in between readings, teaching, and interviews. "This is supposed to be a small book. I ought to be able to do that, right?"

"Let's take this book a page at a time," I tell her.

> *I like trees because they seem more resigned to the way they have to live than other things do.*
>
> WILLA CATHER
>
> *The trick is to make time—not to steal it—and produce fiction.*
>
> BERNARD MALAMUD

Nobody wakes up to suddenly find themselves a bestselling author, a Tony Award–winning director, a Pulitzer Prize–winning playwright. Successful careers in the arts develop one step at a time. Books are written a page at a time. So are plays. A songwriting career unfolds song by song. An acting career involves each day's immersion in that craft. When we keep our sights trained on the small and doable, we are able to do the large and unthinkable. It is all a matter of breaking things down to a day-by-day practice: What can I manage today?

It is rare to have a day without twenty minutes to spare in it. That twenty minutes is enough to get down one page. It is enough to get to the keyboard. It is enough to run through a monologue. Ideally, we want more than twenty minutes and we often get that, too, but I have found that twenty minutes is the minimum time we need and that is nearly always available to us.

"But Julia," Sonia says to me, "in twenty minutes I will barely get started."

"My point precisely. You will get started. Getting started is what you need."

"Yes, I guess that's true," Sonia concludes reluctantly. "Right now I am writing in my head."

"Well, give it twenty minutes and try writing on the page," I advise her.

"Oh, all right. But it's just one of your cheap tricks."

I believe in cheap tricks. I believe in whatever makes you more productive. This means that I believe in twenty-minute windows where we hurl ourselves at the page. These are the creative equivalent of sexual quickies—another practice that isn't perfect but is still very good.

"Imagine that you are a famished lover," I tell Sonia. "You only have twenty minutes to see your beloved. Would you take it?"

"Of course I would," Sonia laughs.

"Well then . . ."

When we are hungering for our art, we are like famished lovers. We yearn for contact and even the smallest amount, while it leaves us craving more, still gives us the will to go on. Yesterday, I got to the piano for twenty minutes. I played through a little bit of *Magellan* and then I just fooled around. When I got up from the keys, my phone rang. It was a director with an interest in *Magellan*. He wanted to set a meeting time. Was I amenable to that? Because I had just tagged base with the project, I felt in synch with it. I was able to schedule a meeting and promise myself a few more miniature piano dates before the meeting. My relationship to music is a lot like Sonia's to writing: although I have written a great deal of music, I still consider it a fluke. I have to take my career as a musician in tiny little bites. A day at a time, a note at a time, it is possible.

When we are focused on the possible, we are able to ignore the probable. We are able to set aside that tricky question of odds. The odds stacked against us as an artist immediately lessen if we are in fact doing our work. The odds of publishing a novel are a hell of a lot higher if you have written a novel. In other words, when we can focus on what it is we are doing, then what it is we could do becomes a logical progression and not a wild fantasy.

> *A perfect poem is impossible. Once it had been written, the world would end.*
>
> ROBERT GRAVES

Just at the moment, I am writing this book and I am working on *Magellan*. I work on the book daily. My habits as a writer are long-standing. I must nudge myself to extend the same courtesy to my music. It, too, can benefit from a gentle, "Easy Does

It" approach. I touch the keys and Magellan sets to sea. He reaches for the wind, I reach for the next spate of notes. Outside, the sun breaks through the clouds.

Divining Rod

For one week, you are asked to spend twenty minutes daily on your art. Set a timer. It's "only" twenty minutes. Practice the piano. Work with your voice tape. Go to the page and write on that novel. Gesso a canvas and start to paint. Twenty minutes is not a long time. We all have twenty minutes if we look for them. Survey your day. When can you best squeeze them in?

You may find that you need the additional support of a believing mirror in order to pin yourself down about work. Go to your list of encouraging friends and select one as a colleague. Pick up the phone and explain that you will be working twenty minutes daily and that you need someplace to check in. When I am rewriting *Magellan,* I check in daily with my friend Daisy Press, an opera singer. "Hi, Daisy," my message might run. "I am just about to go to the keys." I find it is very grounding to call Daisy. Once I have actually committed to her, I don't seem to be so prone to wriggle out of my commitment. After all, it is "only" twenty minutes.

The Courage to Create

Without kindness, there can be no true joy.

THOMAS CARLYLE

Kindness is in our power, even when fondness is not.

SAMUEL JOHNSON

Outside the window, on Columbus Avenue, a siren whirls past. It is closely followed by another. For a moment, conversation is difficult. Then quiet returns, or relative quiet, and I am able to hear what my companion, Daisy, is saying.

"For me music is ecstatic," she says. "When I am singing well, I feel myself to be in complete communion with God. It's like nothing else. There is an intense connection."

"I know what you mean," I counter. "When I go to the piano and write music, I, too, feel connected to God. I have a sense of expansion. It is unlike the feeling I get any other way."

We are seated in a small Greek diner. The waiter knows me well. He offers me a bowl of soup and a cup of chamomile tea. My opera singer companion orders peppermint. It is late on a gilded evening and we are talking about the connection between God and our work. We both find God through music. This spooks us a little.

"So has your guidance been telling you that right now it is all about music?" Daisy nudges. She encourages my music.

"It told me I needed to spend time at the keys. That if I wanted to learn piano, I had to simply put in time. It frightens me to sit at the keys. I don't want to feel all that I feel."

"I know what you mean. When you sit at the keys you feel everything."

"I may not be ready to feel everything."

"No," she says, laughing. "Neither am I."

The waiter refills our tea water. We sit for a moment in companionable silence. We both admit after a minute that we are avoiding our work. It simply feels too daunting. Somehow talking about it seems to swing open a door of willingness.

Grief can take care of itself, but to get the full value of a joy you must have somebody to divide it with.

MARK TWAIN

"I think I could call your machine and say that I was going to go to the piano," I volunteer.

"I could call your machine and tell it that I am about to sit down and write some music."

"Would you be writing in the morning or in the afternoon?"

"I don't know but I will write. How about you?"

"Me, too."

And so, just like that it is settled between us. I will return to work again on *Magellan* and my companion will start working on music composition for the first time. A virtuoso singer, a fine soprano, she has always yearned to compose. Now she will give it a try. All it took was having a believing mirror. All it took was the willingness to allow ourselves to be helped. Wherever two or more are joined together . . .

So often as artists the blocks that we feel to be ours alone can be dissolved by being shared. We have the opportunity to help one another and when we are willing to take it, great things can come to pass.

So much of making art is like running a marathon. We may have to run the race ourselves but it is tremendously helpful to have friends who can cheer us on.

"You are doing better than you think," Sonia might tell me. "You may not like what you are writing but you *are* writing. You are showing up at the page despite your resistance, and that speaks volumes. Why do we talk so little about artists needing courage?"

Each time an actor acts, he does not hide, he exposes himself.

JEANNE MOREAU

You can only perceive real beauty in a person as they get older.

ANOUK AIMÉE

The courage to create is a courage to make something out of what we are feeling. Out of the swirl of emotions comes some cogent form of expression. It may be a daub of paint. It may be a poem. It may be a few measures of music. Whatever it is, it is the distillate of our human personality. We seek to express what it is that wants to be expressed through us. And sometimes that expression is not comfortable. Our ego will tell us it's not good enough and neither are we.

This afternoon, I got a phone call from an estimable writer. She is at the beginning of a new book and it is fighting her. "I found myself saying to myself, 'Start over.' But then I thought, 'No, don't do that. Try to trust.' I don't always think we are the best judge of what it is that is trying to come through us. I think sometimes we are very harsh. We cannot see the beauty that we create. I have written books that struck me as flat and without grace only to have those very books be the ones that people write to me about years later."

I think we have to admit that we do not own our art. It owns us. I think the sooner we admit that and try to relinquish control, the better off we are. For some reason, God has chosen some of us to write and we have little to do with it. I believe all people are creative, and that I have been given this form as my own. I have to try to set my ego aside and stop letting it vote on everything that I do. The ego's votes are so often incorrect. If only I could remember that.

Sitting in the homely booth at the Greek diner, making a plan to check in around our art, my companion and I are working to outmaneuver our egos. We are reaching for humility, which is always the way to outsmart a stubborn block. "I am willing to make bad art" allows us to make art, and often very good art at that. Tomorrow I will phone my friend and then I will sit down at the keys.

Divining Rod

When we are reaching for inspiration, we do well to reach first for humility. Very often a prayer to be of service will clear the channel and allow you to access your creative guidance. When we are focused on ourselves, on our need to be brilliant or original, we often constrict the flow of our art. How often, when we seek to help someone else, do good ideas flood us?

Take pen in hand. Number from one to five. List five ways in which you could use your talents to be of service. ("God, please let this work of mine be of service," you might ask.) When we try to be of service, our very syntax clears up. We begin to be clear and plain-spoken. When we ask to be of service, we are moved to feelings of generosity. We have a sense of largesse as we prepare to give something away. Rather than feeling pinched, we find ourselves feeling expansive. This brings us a sense of freedom and work flows more easily.

Resigning as Author

At the piano this morning, I began piecing together the new opening for *Magellan*. The music must reflect a stormy night at sea, thirteen months into the voyage. The sailors must be mutinous and Magellan must be resolute, determined to continue no matter what the cost. Seated at the keys, I hear scraps of melody. One theme argues with the next. I strive to get the tumult onto the page. I call out to Emma, "Can you hear this? What do you think?"

"I think that's good," Emma says.

I have been working on *Magellan* for more than six years. The initial melodies came to me in a rush, song upon song. I raced to get them down, hurrying along with tape recorder and crabbed notation, trying to make a record of what it is I heard. On the early *Magellan* tapes I have scraps of conversation in the background as the

I don't believe in aging. I believe in forever altering one's aspect to the sun. Hence my optimism.

VIRGINIA WOOLF

music overtook me again as I tried to grab a meal in a restaurant. I have one tape recorded as I was driving. Again, the music was imperious and came flooding in with no respect for whatever else it was I was trying to do. Emma has been working on *Magellan* for three years now. Its melodies have come to haunt her as thoroughly as they have haunted me. Between the two of us, we have studied biographies of the great mariner and we have examined closely the diary of his scribe Antonio Pigafetta. There is a great story to be told and we are laboring to tell it. We have eighty-five pieces of music that must be shaped into a whole.

Yesterday I spoke with a writer who has just begun a new novel. The work is coming at her in a halting form. So she took herself on a walk, ears cocked, listening for the story to start unspooling. "The work comes through us. We don't control it," she marveled to me. "There's something bigger than we are that's up to something, I think." She is waiting for that larger Something to show itself to her.

Working on *Magellan,* I have often felt there was something larger than myself striving to be born. The music revealed itself without regard for me and my limitations. It wanted to sound a certain way. I could hear that sound and chase it on the page, but I could not really create it. It seemed to come to me fully formed. I was its servant not its master. It had its own ideas.

> *People from a planet without flowers would think we must be mad with joy the whole time to have such things about us.*
>
> IRIS MURDOCH

Allowing the work to move through us without impediment means resigning as its author. The work must be allowed to author itself, to take on the shapes and colors that it prefers. I can plan a sequence, but then I must surrender to how the sequence plans itself. This is what we mean by inspiration, the willingness to surrender to a higher octave, the finer vibration that the work itself might hold.

Painter Robert Motherwell claims that while he may take the beginning brushstroke on a painting, the brush itself takes stroke after stroke once it is launched. It is the same with music. It is the same with performance. There is something trying to be born through us and we do best when we are able to allow its passage.

Art requires that we relinquish control. It asks us to move out on faith. In this regard, art itself is always one step ahead of the artist, calling us forward. Agnes de Mille summarizes the situation very well: "Living is a form of not being sure, not knowing what next or how. The moment you know how, you begin to die a little. The artist never entirely knows. We guess. We may be wrong, but we take leap after leap in the dark."

It takes humility to not know. It takes courage to re-main teachable by our art. Yesterday, I got a letter from a novelist. She wrote to me, "Creations are our mirror. They don't go well when we're not going well. They don't have time for us when we don't have time for them. They are tired when we are, and the powder comes off their wings when we handle them too much. The relationship is deli-cate and fierce, and without it we are truly miserable. So we must do whatever it needs."

"We must do whatever it needs" requires that we be vigilant about nurturing our art. We must do what our art requires because, as the novelist noted, "without it we are truly miserable." And so, for me, I do Morning Pages, Weekly Walks, and Artist Dates. I try to be attentive to what it is that wants to be born. I go to the page or to the keys and I wait to hear what wants to come into being. I try to be both delicate and diligent. I try to be alert. Because my art moves through me, I try to make cer-tain that the circuits are static-free and rested. I pray to be of service and to live one day at a time. Art is born moment by moment and day by day. I must be willing to go slowly because slow has its own velocity. "Easy does it" doesn't mean, "Oh, calm down." It means "easy accomplishes it."

Fighting my depression, I must also fight inertia. I need grace to put myself in mo-tion. I must ask for that grace daily. "Take away my difficulties," I pray. "Please remove from me now every single defect of character that stands in the way of my usefulness to you and my fellows." It takes daily discipline to keep my creative commitments. It is good that I have Daisy, the young opera singer, to call about my music. It is good I have the novelist to talk to about my book. From each of them, the question is the same, "Did you work today?" Just for today, I am able to answer, "Yes."

> *Just as the creative artist is not allowed to choose, neither is he permitted to turn his back on anything: a single refusal and he is cast out of the state of grace and becomes sinful all the way through.*
>
> RAINER MARIA RILKE

Divining Rod

The ego's hold on us is tenacious. To test this out, try the simple tool of finishing the following phrase ten times. Ready? Write: "The reason I can't let God author my work is _____." You will discover that you do not trust God. You will discover that you do not trust yourself. This very line of questioning may make you mad.

Take pen in hand again—or better yet, use a magic marker. Devise for yourself a small sign that you can post clearly visible in your work area. The sign reads: "Okay, God. You take care of the quality. I will take care of the quantity."

Joy

There's a difference between invention and what comes from inside of a painter.

EDWARD HOPPER

The unconscious creates, the ego edits.

STANLEY KUNITZ

The imagination has resources and intimations we don't even know about.

CYNTHIA OZICK

On Eighty-ninth Street and Amsterdam, a sliding door moves to one side and two horses pick their way carefully out to the street. Their riders frown in concentration. This is the tricky part, getting their mounts from the stable, Claremont Riding Academy, safely out to the park. It entails a three-block ride through traffic. It is a triumph just getting to the park where the bridal trails await.

Once inside the park's leafy domain, a crisp chirrup and a slap of the reins sends the horses briskly trotting forward. Rentals are for an hour at a crack. An hour is long enough to make a circuit of the reservoir and a loop through the woods to the north. When my daughter was a toddler, I kept an Appaloosa horse at Claremont. I would hoist my daughter up with me double and pilot our way to the park. Many mornings found us circling the reservoir, competing with joggers for the bridle path's right of way.

Mornings nowadays, as I walk the reservoir with Tiger Lily in tow, I still see my tiny daughter in my mind's eye. My daughter is twenty-nine now and she has just bought herself a horse. Daily, on the phone coast to coast, I get the horse report.

"Horses" are Domenica's answer to the question, "What brings you joy?" My daughter has learned that she needs to have a daily dose of joy to help counterbalance any disappointments in her career. It is not easy vying for parts with other actresses. Domenica's horse, Velocity, loves her for herself alone. His welcoming whinny is always the same whether she is winning parts or losing them.

A horse might be a large item to juggle in an artist's attempt to find a balanced life. My friend Tracy, a quilt restoration expert, managed to keep a horse for many years. She still rides every Wednesday morning, setting out from Claremont just as dawn is breaking in the city streets.

Alison, on a more modest budget, has a rescued greyhound. Mornings find her in Central Park as well. Before nine, it is legal to run your dog off its leash and Alison's dog does love to run.

"I worried that I wouldn't be able to keep up with her," Alison confesses. "Before Zephyr entered my life, I was kind of a coach potato. I was always thinking, 'I really should get more exercise.' Now I do."

For Nelson, joy came in the form of a pair of Rollerblades. "Before I got my blades, I was always snorting in contempt. Someone would whirl past and I would think, 'Who does he think he is?' Now I know that owning a pair of blades makes you feel that you own the world. I should also add that I have dropped twenty pounds and that helps, too. Now I am that smug guy that you spot whizzing past. It's obnoxious, but I love it. I'm just plain happy."

Caroline made the transition to a more joyful life without benefit of a single purchase. "I always felt I lived in the city but I wasn't really a part of it. I felt alienated, trapped on the outside. All of that changed when I began walking." For starters, Caroline got off of the subway one stop early and walked the remaining distance to her job. That felt so good to her, she began grabbing walks on her lunch hour. One balmy spring evening, she tried walking all the way home.

> *I write out of curiosity and bewilderment.*
>
> WILLIAM TREVOR

> *You must be unintimidated by your own thoughts because if you write with someone looking over your shoulder, you'll never write.*
>
> NIKKI GIOVANNI

"Now I walk several miles daily. I traded in my purse for a good leather backpack. I didn't set out walking as a fitness program, but I could have. Within a week, I had dropped a pound or two. More than that, my attitude shifted. I began to really feel a part of the city. My alienation slipped away. I also noticed that walks were really great for brainstorming. Walking makes me smarter and, God knows, I am all for that."

Down on the deck below my writing-room window, my neighbor the sunbather has been joined by a lover. They lie entwined in each others arms as the afternoon slips lower and the day begins to cool. As five o'clock nears, the horses in the park are due back at Claremont. Their hooves clip-clop through the streets as they wind their way home. It is twilight and I have yet to get in my day's walk.

Fighting depression, I fight lethargy as well. I know that a walk will make me feel better and yet it is hard to stir the muscles necessary. "Help me be willing," I pray. "Please remove from me now whatever defects of character stand in the way of my usefulness."

As I so often do when I am feeling weak, I piggyback my energy onto another's. "Would you like to walk the reservoir loop?" I ask Emma. When she says, "Yes," I call to the dogs who are delighted to be getting out even late in the day as it is. We enter the park with an hour of daylight remaining. Out on the trail, I note that the evening joggers seem to be more serious than their daytime counterparts. Lean and committed, they glide through the dusk. Tiger Lily pirouettes at leash's end, straining after a stray squirrel. I laugh at her antics and feel then a brief surge of optimism, the reward for putting my body into motion, an answered prayer.

Divining Rod

You have already made a list of things that you love. Now you are asked to make a list of ten actions that bring you joy. For example: making homemade vegetable soup, baking fruit pies, cooking a pot of rice pudding, getting my hair professionally conditioned. Your list may range from the homely to the grandiose. Choose an easily doable action and execute it. For the next week, try to take one joy-bringing action a day.

The 12-step program Arts Anonymous believes that for many of us, our resistance to making art is addictive. Like anorectics, we get high on deprivation. Not making art is habit-forming just as not eating is. This cycle must be broken and we can do this a day at a time. We can write our pages, make our Artist Dates, take our walks. We can call and enlist the support of our believing mirrors. It is sobering and grounding to take small creative actions. Allow your self the joy of such sober grounding.

Cycles

Today no sunbathers loll beneath my window. The day is cool and gray. It is Memorial Day and New York is calm and subdued. Yesterday, a bright and gala day, the park was filled with strollers picking their way past bathers who lay on blankets just adjacent to the cinder trails. Dogs bounded the lengths of their leashes, greeting one another with wagging tails. Tiger Lily and Charlotte, bonded to each other, pursued squirrels in tandem, tugging at their leashes and straining to be free. But that was yesterday. Today the dogs are content to stay indoors. They stretch out on the Oriental carpets, napping through the gray afternoon.

As artists, we, too, must learn to live within our seasons. We must learn when to expand and explore and when to nap our way through gray afternoons. There is a rhythm to creative life. It expands and then contracts. We must learn to move with it, listening to our psyches for what is required at any given time.

"Creations are like children. They pout and sulk," a famous writer recently told me. "If we neglect them they grow petulant. They want our attention."

Giving attention to our creations means learning to sense when it is that they need inflow and when it is that they need calm. When our lives become too frantic, our art retreats. It does not thrive on a life lived pell-mell.

When I am finishing a picture I hold some God-made object up to it—a rock, a flower, the branch of a tree or my hand— as a kind of final test. If the painting stands up to a thing that man cannot make, the painting is authentic.

MARC CHAGALL

Art, that great undogmatized church.

ELLEN KEY

Art is man's expression of his joy in labor.

WILLIAM MORRIS

I need calm and quiet if I am to work, but I need a certain amount of stimulation, too. It's really a juggling act. I must be a gatekeeper on the traffic in my life. Too much traffic and I grow overwhelmed. Too little and I grow stagnant. It's a balance that I am seeking and I must be attentive because my needs are always shifting.

One more time, my night was restless and sleep eluded me until two a.m. One more time, waking up tired, I found myself cloaked in pessimism, wreathed by despair. It was with effort that I prayed my morning prayers, asking to be rendered fit for the day ahead. I found myself thinking, "If I were feeling good, then what would I do?" It was from that thought that the notion of taking an Artist Date came to me. Manhattan is chock-full of adventures.

After a cup of coffee and Morning Pages, I took myself to the American Museum of Natural History. From October to May of every year, they have an exhibit of butterflies. "I let you in as a senior," the ticket taker told me. "You're not quite a senior, are you?"

"No, not quite." He waved me in.

The butterfly exhibit walks you through a great deal of information, some of it very basic: there are 250,000 species of what we think of as butterflies, but of those only 18,000 are genuine butterflies. The average lifespan of a butterfly is several weeks. In a carefully sealed-off hallway, laden with tropical plants, one hundred species of butterfly fluttered freely. There were orange striped butterflies, azure butterflies, and large velvety moths. Four museum employees, identified by their badges, stood ready to answer any questions. They talked freely even without questions.

Moths, I learned, are largely nocturnal. Butterflies woo and begin their mating dance midair. Vladimir Nabokov was a noted lepidopterist. A section from one of his scholarly treatises on butterflies made it into *Lolita*. In Africa, in the Dzanga-Sangha region, there are 950 species of butterfly, leaning heavily toward specimens that are aqua and cobalt. A glass specimen case showed a panoply of examples.

"We order perhaps a hundred different species," a worker told me. "We get them from butterfly farms who ship them to us in the pupa stage when they are easy to transport. Once they get to us, they hatch. They may mate while they are

Art—the one achievement of man which has made the long trip up from all fours seem well advised.

JAMES THURBER

Is there not an art, a music, and a stream of words that shall be life, the acknowledged voice of life?

WILLIAM WORDSWORTH

with us but we don't keep any host plants for their young. They live several weeks, unless they are a monarch or other migratory species. Those live up to nine months."

Wide-eyed children walk amidst the butterflies. "Don't be afraid if one lands on you," cautions a museum worker. "But don't try to touch them. If one lands on you, I will remove it." The children, oblivious to cautions, reach their plump hands toward the delicate creatures.

"Gentle, gentle," chides a mother.

"See how beautiful," entices a worker. "We put out special food for them and they like it very much."

Gently fluttering from floor to ceiling, the butterflies flit plant to plant and occasionally land on a visitor.

"Stay very still," coaches the worker. "Stay still and don't do anything sudden. I'll move our little friend along."

Artist Dates, like this one, fire the imagination. They spark whimsy. They encourage play. Since art is about "the play of ideas," Artist Dates feed our work. They gently replenish the inner well. Art is an image-using system and Artist Dates restock our supply of images. The softly folding brightly colored wings, like tiny stained-glass windows, may not be an image we will use directly but they feed our inner artist, awakening a sense of wonder.

The gray sky grows grayer still. No yellow jackets patrol the upper branches of the tree beneath my writing-room window. It is too cool for rooftop picnics. Holiday revelers stay indoors. Turned back upon myself, I leaf through a butterfly book, the booty of my recent Artist Date. As the gray day closes down to dusk, I let myself read.

> *The dignity of the artist lies in his duty of keeping awake the sense of wonder in the world.*
>
> G. K. CHESTERTON

> *Everybody's an artist. Everybody's God. It's just that they're inhibited.*
>
> YOKO ONO

> *I saw the angel in the marble and carved until I set him free.*
>
> MICHELANGELO

> *God is beauty.*
>
> ST. FRANCIS OF ASSISI

Divining Rod

Art is transformational. We do not make it as therapy and yet it is profoundly therapeutic. As we work with our creativity tools—Morning Pages, Artist Dates, walks—we are ourselves worked on by the Great Creator. Many of the changes that are wrought are very subtle, so subtle we may let them pass without noticing. Now you are asked to take note.

Take pen in hand. You are asked to witness your own transformation. I will give you a brief list of questions to start you off. Have you reorganized your living space? Have you thrown anything away? Has your color sense shifted? Has your relationship to music shifted? Do you find yourself being more plainspoken? Have there been any shifts in your intimate relationship? Have you experienced any difference in your energy? Have you experienced a weight gain or weight loss? Have you relinquished—or seriously thought about relinquishing—any other "bad" habit? Are you conscious of having more choices in your daily life? Has your relationship to a Higher Power altered? Are you more comfortable with your spirituality? Is it more a fact of your everyday life?

As you write, many other changes may occur to you. You may exercise more or differently. Your sleep habits may have shifted. You might be remembering dreams with more clarity. You might have lost your taste for junk food. Be alert for all forms of transformation. You are your own butterfly. What further changes can you envision?

CHECK-IN

1. **How many days this week did you do your Morning Pages?** If you skipped a day, why did you skip it? How was the experience of writing them for you? Are you experiencing more clarity? A wider range of emotions? A greater sense of detachment, purpose, and calm? Did anything surprise you? Is there a "repeating" issue asking to be dealt with?

2. **Did you do your Artist Date this week?** Did you note an improved sense of well-being? What did you do and how did it feel? Remember, Artist Dates can be difficult and you may need to coax yourself into taking them.

3. **Did you get out on your Weekly Walk?** How did that feel? What emotions or insights surfaced for you? Were you able to walk more than once? What did your walk do for your optimism and sense of perspective?

4. **Were there any other issues this week that felt significant to you in your self-discovery?** Describe them.

The outer world, with all its phenomena, is filled with divine splendor. But we must have experienced the divine within ourselves before we can hope to discover it within our environment.

RUDOLF STEINER

Uncovering a Sense of Perseverance

We are stronger than we know. Like deep wells, we have a capacity for sustained creative action. Our lost dreams can come home to us. By now you are familiar with the use of creativity tools. This week asks you to recommit to continued self-nurturance. Remember, creativity flourishes in a place of safety and acceptance. Focus this week on creating a healthy environment for your inner artist.

Dreams

By the calendar, summer is here. Tell that to the weather, which is cool, gray, and dim. In the Midwest, it is raining. Those storms move toward us. The sky this afternoon is "threatening." By evening, it will deliver on its threat. Rain will come and with it thunder and lightning. Char-

> *All writing is dreaming.*
> JORGE LUIS BORGES

lotte, Emma's little West Highland terrier, has recently developed a terror of storms. When the thunder starts, so will her shaking. She will shake and quake until the storm has spent itself. There is no consoling her. She knows the storm is bigger than we are and any words of consolation are just empty murmurings. "We are all right. We are fine," I can tell her, but she does not trust the fates. I cannot comfort her.

Trusting the fates is learned behavior for most of us. Like Charlotte, we shake in the face of forces greater than ourselves. And yet, as we suffer through storm after storm, it becomes apparent that our fears do nothing to make it better. The gods do not demand our fears as bribes for our survival. Our fears are just needless suffering. We may as well elect to have faith. We may as well choose to be optimists. We can and do survive our storms. "This will pass," I tell myself of my recent emotional turbulence.

For artists, optimism is a great advantage. It is too easy to buy into pessimism, to romance the many odds so clearly stacked against us. It is easy to give in and to give up. It is easy to declare ourselves beaten and to resign ourselves to a life of "if only's." But is it really so easy to let dreams die? Dreams are hardy. They are stubborn as weeds. We may think we have uprooted our dreams only to have a dream push upward again, daring us, one more time, to believe in the unbelievable. As long as a dream lives, so does a chance of its manifesting. We can cooperate with our dreams or we can fight them. Our dreams are tenacious. They don't just fade away.

Every time we make a piece of art, we dream of its coming to a fruitful maturity. We write the book in the hopes that it will be published. We paint the picture in hopes that it will be seen. Recently, I wrote a novel that has been making the rounds and "nearly" but not quite selling. My agent has finally given the novel back to me. "Something must be missing," she has said. "But I do not know quite what."

If I want the novel to live—and I do—then I must do the work necessary to help it. I have given the novel to four select readers. I have asked them all to look for ways in which the book could be better. I have read the book myself, searching for the same elusive something. All of us are like detectives, sleuthing to make the book better. Now my ego doesn't like any of this. My ego wants to say the book is fine the way it is and that the editors who are not buying it lack vision. Barring that, my ego would like to pack the book away, give up on it, give it a gentle burial in a bottom desk drawer and go on to other work. But that is not what is called for. What is called for is faith. Faith enough to work further. Faith enough to invest more. Faith enough to risk again. Dreams demand that we have faith in them. If they are brave enough to live, we must be brave enough to assist them. We must one more time try on their behalf. And so I spend my evenings reading my novel. I press my friends into service to help me improve.

"I don't see any big something to change," I complain to one friend.

"Maybe there is no one big something. Maybe what you are looking at is a series of tiny tweaks. Maybe there is no one monster scene to be rewritten. Maybe you just need to improve many places just a little bit. Tiny shifts in tone may be your answer."

"Oh, no. I hate that!"

My friend clucks a little in sympathy. She is herself a writer and she knows the difficulty of what she is asking me to do.

My literary agent calls me on the phone. She sounds cautious, as if she may have just phoned up someone as volatile as a hand grenade.

"I just want to know how it is going," she says cautiously. "I am wondering if you have found anything to change yet or if you are still looking."

"Still looking," I tell her. "Although I have read the book again and I am now in the process of making a detailed outline. My readers are all finishing up this week."

"Well, good. I just wanted to see if you were okay."

"I'm okay."

I want to explain to her that I am like Charlotte, the little dog. I am shaking and quaking faced with changes I do not know quite how to make. I am certain that this round of work will be the storm that does me in and so I quaver before the task at hand. On the other hand, what is my alternative? To just give up? To pack away the novel that is almost good enough and never give it the dignity of one last try? I have been writing for too long not to believe that with help I can write better. I have had too many books improve in the rewrite process. I have gone back to the drawing board too many times with good results. As much as my ego would love to claim that the novel was perfect as is, I know enough to know better and so I am willing, although I resent it, to try one more time.

> *Oh, one world at a time!*
> HENRY DAVID THOREAU

> *We do not write as we want, but as we can.*
> W. SOMERSET MAUGHAM

A storm moves in from the west. Right on queue, Charlotte starts shaking. I queue up my novel and start rolling through the pages, making a tweak here and a tweak there. "Charlotte," I tell the little dog, "we will be fine."

And I believe it, whether Charlotte does or not. This round of changes will not kill me and if I am very lucky, I will edge ahead a little bit. My novel will get stronger and better. It will survive this round of surgery and grow stronger from it.

In any case, I as an artist will grow stronger and better, having the self-respect that comes from being willing one more time to invest in my dreams.

Divining Rod

A life in the arts is not a life without detours and delays. Sometimes a project must be set to one side while another project—or projects—comes to the fore. Busy with our daily lives, we may let certain dreams go unattended. And yet, such dreams do not really die. They wait patiently, sometimes for many years, for us to one more time turn our focus their direction. Now is a time to excavate a "forgotten" dream. Expect your dreams to burn a little as they reawaken. We often feel a shock of pain as a dream reactivates.

Take pen in hand. Answer the following questions. Have you ever set aside a dream related to writing? Have you ever set aside a dream related to the visual arts? Have you ever set aside a dream related to music? Have you ever set aside a dream related to public speaking or theater? A dream related to film or television? Have you set aside a dream related to dance or movement? A dream related to the culinary arts? To a handicraft? To photography? These questions may spur you to remember a dream that is not covered by any of these topics.

Now ask yourself, what led you to set your dream aside? Are you ready to one more time pursue this dream? What gentle action could you take? If you once wrote many poems but for years have not written any, you might try your hand at a simple poem. Or you might attend an open mike and hear what other people are writing. You might buy yourself an anthology of new poets. You might go to hear an established poet read. Choose a first step for you that feels "doable." Be modest. In reentering an arena, do not set the jumps too high. You do not want to scare yourself. Allow yourself the grace of being an absolute beginner.

Company

Heavy clouds bank in the west. The sunset is a few stripes of cerise. It rained then cleared then rained again. More "weather" is moving toward us. The air smells of ozone. A pushy wind whips the trees. On the street people hurry home, eager to be "in" before the storm. It is a good night for reading.

The table by my bed is stacked high with books, many of them written by friends of mine. It gives me pleasure at night to curl up with a book written by someone I know. There they are on the page. It is almost like visiting with them. Lately, I have been rereading my friend Sonia Choquette. Her books brim with optimism. I long to brim with it myself. This morning, by e-mail, I heard from novelist Tim Farrington. Normally we write each other once a week, sometimes more. Recently, he has been radio silent for nearly six weeks. Now he has shown up with a good explanation. He writes:

Go oft to the house of thy friend, for weeds choke the unused path.

RALPH WALDO EMERSON

Sooner or later you've heard all your best friends have to say. Then comes the tolerance of real love.

NED ROREM

"Hi there, my long-lost comrade, and please forgive my disappearance. I've been homestretching it on this novel and good for not much else. Two short anticlimactic chapters left, I should be done by next week. Then I'll probably just cry for a week, and then take a good long look around and see what's left of my so-called life. I feel turned inside out, thrashed, and twisted like a wet shirt, but I'll be hung out to dry soon enough, God willing and the river don't rise. I'm looking forward to catching up with you. I've missed us."

The brief missive was good to get. I have missed Tim's company, too, although I did know where he was—"writing." My friend Sonia is just entering the tunnel known as "the next book." For the next several months her emotional weather will be determined by how it went during her day at the page. I am her "catcher's mitt." She calls me daily to check in on her progress. I cheer her on.

This morning, when I had my phone turned off, I got a message from another friend, another writer. "Ah, Julia. I am glad to hear you're not picking up. Mornings are sacred to us writers, I think . . ." She went on to propose a lengthy walk at midday tomorrow, a sortie to be sandwiched in between our writing schedules. I am eager to see her, eager for the easy intimacy of a longish walk. There is something comforting in spending a little time with another working writer. My friend has recently launched herself down the chute into another novel. On our walk, there will be four of us present: the writer and her novel, myself and my book in progress.

Our creations are like children. They can be pushy about what they want and what they need. If we neglect them, they neglect us. If we ignore them, they ignore us. Sometimes they sulk and pout and cry and squabble until they've got our attention. In the end, we have to do what they want. It's the only way to make peace with them.

Making peace with our creations is an artist's primary task. We may be mothers. We may be wives or husbands. We may be colleagues and friends but we are first and foremost artists and we owe our creations our loyalty. If they don't get it, they rebel.

"I was a low-maintenance husband," recalls Tim Farrington. "All that was really required to keep me happy was a few undisturbed hours of writing time. If I could get up early and get my hours in, I was a happy camper. I didn't ask for much more than that."

> *It's the friends you can call up at 4 A.M. that matter.*
>
> MARLENE DIETRICH

I am divorced now for ten years and my daughter is grown. My days revolve around writing. I get in two sessions daily, one in the morning, one in the late afternoon. If I miss a session, I feel it. My creation throws a tantrum until attended to.

Last week I had lunch with a fellow writer. She was a writer of the political persuasion. She often serves on committees for worthy causes. We met at the Popover Café, named for its specialty. She arrived looking a bit the worse for wear. She had just come from a meeting.

"How do you do it?" I asked her. "All that you do?"

"I write in Connecticut," she told me. "I go there for long, green weekends. It's very quiet there." She rubbed wearily at her eyes.

"But you live in New York most of the time, don't you?"

"Yes, but if I don't get to the country on the weekend, I really miss it. I need to write." And for her writing in New York is difficult.

Anywhere that becomes too pell-mell can become the enemy. New York, which tends to the pell-mell, can be difficult on the artists in its midst. They must learn to live defensively. They need to learn to set a productive schedule amid the many attractions vying for their attention.

I need to set my own pace. And that pace is not this city's. I need to take long walks and have great bolts of quiet and solitude. I need to turn off the phone and turn down most of my invitations. It can be very seductive, the business of acting like an artist rather than actually being one.

Rain is pelting down. The bed beckons with its piles of pillows and comforting blankets. From the bedside table, I select *Your Heart's Desire,* a book by my friend Sonia. In Chicago, tonight, she is writing. In New York, tonight, I read what she has written. It is a dark and stormy night, but I spend it happily.

I am treating you as my friend, asking you to share my present minuses in the hope that I can ask you to share my future plusses.

KATHERINE MANSFIELD

Divining Rod

It does us good to keep the company of our friends. It does us good to have them present even when they are absent. By consciously cherishing our connections, we strengthen those bonds.

Purchase a small photo album or scrapbook. You are out to create a gallery of your friends and their projects. Start with photographs. (If you find that you do not have pictures of certain friends, ask for them.) Mount a photo and set aside additional pages for other images that speak to you of that friend.

Set aside a stack of magazines and search through them for images that remind you of your friends. Label these images with your friend's name, clip the image and mount it in your album. You may wish to include postcards or letters that you have received. You might include a playbill from a joint night at the theater. Or the pass that allowed the two of you to go backstage at a concert. What you are after is a mental snapshot of your relationship. You are aiming at rounding up "company" for yourself and your artist. Like a yearbook for grown-ups, it will remind you of the good times you have had and the dreams that you shared.

Staying Green

The park is green and verdant. Swans glide on the lake. Flotillas of ducks poke amid the reeds. An egret stands one-legged. In Turtle Pond, turtles are plentiful, large ones and smaller ones, poking their heads above the water's surface, nosing for tidbits. I stand at water's edge, talking with a distinguished writer. We are discussing the need for refreshment, for self-nurturing in the writer's day.

"It is fantastic that we have this park," the writer begins. "It's a window back onto the natural world and when we are in synch with nature, it is easier to write. Back at home, I go for bike rides. I glide out daily and pedal along the shore. I can go twenty miles along the bike path. Then I head home again and write."

The writer's novels are known for their meticulous research, for their deep grounding in facts. It is easy to see how, with her love of the natural world, she could have a fondness for specificity, a hunger for the small, telling detail.

"The last time I wrote, I had an interesting experience," she continues. "My inner writer said to me, 'No more research.' I was alarmed. I thought it meant I was being lazy. 'Are you sure?' I asked myself. 'Trust me,' the answer came back. 'I know far more than you give me credit for. Let me use a little bit of what I know.' And so, I wrote a book largely without research. I leaned into my imagination. I invented the kind of small facts I normally observed. It was challenging and it was fun. I had been looking for a way to put fun back into my work."

The distinguished writer's huge success has given a shape to her work life that occasionally feels onerous. Her books are contracted far ahead of time and eagerly awaited. Write them she must, not only to serve her public but also to serve her Muse. "I must write," she says. "When I am not writing, I am not happy. When I am writing well, everything else falls into place. I am a lot like a dog that turns around and around trying to get comfortable. I am like that until I settle into a writing routine. Once I do, I am fine."

Once a year, the writer produces a large novel. Her books typically debut at number one on *The New York Times* bestseller list. She is a cottage industry. There

> *Your lost friends are not dead, but gone before, advanced a stage or two upon that road which you must travel in the steps they trod.*
>
> ARISTOPHANES

> *To be capable of steady friendship or lasting love are the two greatest proofs, not only of goodness of heart, but of strength of mind.*
>
> WILLIAM HAZLITT

are numerous demands for her time and attention. She must battle to keep time and focus for her writing. She must keep the world at bay and live with her work.

"Right now I am at the beginning of a new book and my relationship with the book is rather formal. Every morning, I wake up and get properly dressed. I want to show the book I am respectful. Later on, once we know each other, I'll be able to tumble out of bed and write in pajamas, but not just yet."

The writer peers over the rail to see a flotilla of baby ducks cruise past. A butterfly flits close and lands on the back of my hand. "Will you look at that," the writer breathes, clearly delighted to take in whatever nature has to offer. Six times a week, the writer goes to a gym. There, solo, she works out for an hour, pushing her body through a grueling routine. As a result, the writer is lean and fit—just like her prose. "I found I needed the endorphins," she explains. She does not add that since the territory she writes about is dark, she may need endorphins more than most people. She must practice a gentle vigilance to keep positive energy around her. She does best, she has discovered, when she is able to keep the drama on the page.

"When I am not writing, I create chaos," she laughs ruefully. "I make all sorts of dramas to distract myself from the fact that I am not working. I buy and sell entire houses. I uproot myself—and it's all because I am not working well."

From under the surface of the pond, a dark bird suddenly bursts forth, a minnow clutched in its beak. The baby ducklings scatter. "Oooh," breathes the writer, "that is how it is in life, isn't it? Suddenly, from out of nowhere—" she breaks off and laughs. She has caught herself writing out loud.

In our era, the road to holiness necessary passes through the world of action.

DAG HAMMARSKJÖLD

"I think place is important," she volunteers suddenly. "Sometimes a book wants to be written in a certain place and nothing else will satisfy it. Take me last week. I was writing really well and I was holed up in a hotel room where I didn't care if the furniture was scratched." This week, she was in her posh New York apartment and she found herself circling again, just like a dog trying to make a bed.

"I want to learn to be comfortable here," she said firmly. "I want to learn to settle in. I don't want to keep it up anymore, this business of coming to New York and driving myself frantic so I just have to flee. This time, I need to set my own pace."

That pace will involve park time and gym time. It will involve steering clear of too many "boast and toast" high-powered dinners. It will mean turning off the phone and turning down the volume. The writer recognizes this and is prepared.

"I can't do too many extroverted things. As a writer, I need to be alone—alone with my character. Lately, I have been saying to myself, instead of thinking of writing as something that you must do by yourself, why not think of it as time that you get to spend with your character? I love my character. Sometimes I wish she were real so that we could just hang out."

To the writer's many fans, her character is real. They send long personal letters wanting her professional advice and guidance. Sometimes at book signings, lips tremble and tears are shed—the character is so present and so real to people. The writer goes home drained.

"I am really determined to get it right," said the writer. "I think I have to find a way to find compassion for myself, for all my fears."

Meanwhile, to the casual eye, the writer is larger than life, jetting here and there, place to place, restlessly, always seeking out the right spot to write the next book, the place that her writer wants to stay in for a while.

"You know, New York is not a bad place, if you get to the park enough," I tell her.

Divining Rod

Our inner artist likes to be courted. Remember that no matter how mature our work may be, our artist is still like a youngster, vulnerable and easily discouraged. As our artist's adult trainer, we must be alert for any signs that our artist is feeling soured and out of sorts. It is up to us to coddle our artist when that is what's called for.

When our work feels difficult, it is sometimes good to feel a little spoiled. In a perfect world, our friends would spoil us and so would our family or significant other. Ours is not a perfect world but we can make it feel much better by taking small actions in our own behalf.

Take pen in hand. Number from one to ten. List ten small actions or purchases that you could make that would tell you in no uncertain terms that you were "seen" and cared about. Be specific. What precisely makes you feel spoiled? This list need not be expensive or extravagant, merely thoughtful. Most of my students find they are cheap with themselves about money or time or both. This exercise asks you to spend a little of both commodities on your own behalf. For example: I could buy good new stationery; I could take a really long hot bath; I could get a pint of raspberries; I could buy a fast-writing pen; I could take myself to the pet store and spend time with the birds; I could let myself call my friend Laura just to catch up . . .

Working

The day is silvery gray. Rain is one more time moving in from the west. I have spent the morning receiving Midwestern reports of all kinds. My friend Sonia is in the water on her new book, writing up a blue streak, two chapters in two days. My sister Libby is painting despite her sore arm, working on a new oil portrait with a new technique she doesn't feel she has totally mastered. Both of them report in that the weather they are experiencing is fine—particularly the emotional weather. There is nothing that makes an artist happier than a good day spent working.

There should be less talk . . . Take a broom and clean someone's house. That says enough.

MOTHER TERESA

When I say artist, I don't mean in the narrow sense of the word—but the man who is building things—creating, molding the earth—whether it be the plains of the west—or the iron ore of Penn, it's all a big game of construction—some with the brush—some with the shovel—some choose a pen.

JACKSON POLLOCK

"I am so relieved that I am finally writing," Sonia says. "This morning I had to spend an hour and a half in a waiting room, waiting for a doctor's appointment. Instead of being bored or angry, I just started to write. I wrote nearly twenty longhand pages, most of an entire new chapter and, I think, a good one. Then, after all that writing, the appointment went well, too. I am having an excellent day. I may just sit out on my front porch and write a little more."

"I got the glass yesterday for my trout table," Libby says. "With the glass in place, it really is like looking into a koi pond. Then, too, I said to myself that I really needed to get past my reticence regarding my new oil technique. I was sort of waiting for the day when it would be suddenly easy." She laughs at herself, a little embarrassed. "I decided to stop waiting for it to get easy and to just let myself do it. The minute I did that, of course it did all become easier. I hate to be the one to say it, but I really like the work I did today. I feel that I am really getting somewhere, and that feels great."

Art is good when it springs from necessity.

NEAL CASSADY

Art is an absolute mistress; she will not be coquetted with or slighted; she requires the most entire self-devotion, and she repays with grand triumphs.

CHARLOTTE SAUNDERS CUSHMAN

I would love to feel great, but I do not. Last night was another sleepless night, and so today I face my workday already fatigued. I prefer writing when I am fresh, but I have learned to write no matter what. And so, I head myself to the page and put in my time there. I scoop the barrel for images to use and I remind myself that it is time for me to take another Artist Date in order to keep the images fresh. On the phone with my opera singer friend Daisy, I am able to report in that work on *Magellan* is going well and that my piano time has now extended itself to include a half hour's practicing. I am still working in Level One books, but I am learning now to read bass clef, which is a triumph for me. I am ever so slowly and ever so slightly edging ahead. My Morning Pages are wan and fragmented these days, but not so wan that they fail to note my tiny scintilla of progress.

For artists, few things feel better than a sense of propulsion. The feeling of forward motion in our art brings us a deep and abiding happiness, carrying with it feelings of self-esteem. When we are procrastinating—"waiting for it to become easier"—we inevitably feel bad about ourselves. Nothing takes the place of actually doing the work, of being able to say at day's end, "I accomplished that."

So much of being an artist boils down to: "Just do it." There is little point in analyzing our resistance, searching out deep reasons for why we cannot work. It is far better to face the resistance directly, to call a friend and say, "I need to work and I don't want to work, and I am going to work now for fifteen minutes." Signing up for a modest fifteen or twenty minutes usually gets us past our Inner Censor. It is such a slight amount of time that the Censor can be hoodwinked into thinking that it doesn't really matter. If we were to say to our Censor, "Now I am going to work for an hour or two," we would have a real fight on our hands. Because we say, "I'm just going to try a few minutes," our Censor can be gulled into letting us get to the page or the easel. A Censor has a great sense of self-importance. When we make our work small, humble, and doable, the Censor doesn't know how to fight us.

In order to be a good artist, I need to be willing to be a bad artist. Stalled on my book, I have to be willing finally to write anything—good, bad, or indifferent. The minute I am willing to write badly instead of well, then I am able to write freely.

Libby at her easel, facing down her mastery of her new technique, was eye to eye with the same ogre. As soon as she was willing to paint badly, she was freed to paint very well. Humility was the door to mastery as it often is.

As artists we must remember that our work is about "the play of ideas." When we become too serious about our work, when we demand perfection, our work rebels. It is when we are able to play a little that our work takes on verve and elasticity.

"I think our artist is naughty," explains my friend the distinguished writer. "I think the part of us that creates is mischievous and defiant. When we put our artist on too tight a leash, it fights us like a spirited animal. When we allow it a little rope, it often cooperates with us nicely."

In other words, our artist can be tricked.

I think of my own arrangement with Daisy. We have made a deal with each other that we will both go to the keys and write a little bit of new music every day. I call her and say, "Daisy, I am on my way to the keys," and then I go to the keys. I am working on *Magellan*, filling in little gaps in the story line. I go to the keys and listen for melody. I am seldom at the keys for more than a few minutes before something, some tendril of music begins seeping through my resistance. Willing to settle for the tiniest scraps, I take down what I am hearing. There are many days when the small Something reveals itself to be a part of a much larger Something. *Magellan*, after all, is a grand story and its scope has room for large as well as small.

When I have finished with my time at the keys, I phone Daisy back. Usually, I get her service. "Daisy, I have just gone to the keys," I tell her. A little later, my phone will ring. "It's Daisy. I have written my two measures for the day." For the most part, our messages are snared by machines and we do not get to actually talk to each other and yet there is a delicious feeling of complicity. Daisy is setting fragments of poetry to music. She is building a scaffolding for her own soaring voice. It is wonderful to be a part of her architecture, and she tells me that it is thrilling to her to be a part of *Magellan*.

As artists, we make things out of nothing. We invent from the whole cloth of our imaginations. When I allow myself, I can feel the magic in this. When I allow myself, I can fall just a little bit in love with the artist that I am.

Rain moves in from the west. Charlotte, the little West Highland terrier, begins to shake at the approach of thunder and lightning. Tiger Lily, taking in the weather, gives

If we are to change our world view, images have to change. The artist now has a very important job to do. He is not a little peripheral figure entertaining rich people, he is really needed.

DAVID HOCKNEY

an ominous growl. My plan at the moment is to use the storm for verisimilitude. I will go to the keys where Magellan is caught in a storm at sea. We will make music together.

Divining Rod

Very often our progress is made in such tiny increments that we fail to see and note it. Focused on what we "should" do and what we haven't done yet, we often turn a blind eye to our own ongoing accomplishments. It is a rare day that passes without our having done something right.

Take pen in hand. Number from one to five. Finish the phrase, "I am doing better at _____" five times. Your changes for the positive can be very slight. They will still make a large difference over time.

Take pen in hand again. Answer the following questions. Are you writing your Morning Pages? Taking your Artist Dates? Getting out for walks? Are you taking the time to check in with yourself? Are you doing better at contact with your friends? Has your comfort level with spiritual tools improved? Do you find yourself striving more consciously to be optimistic? Are you aware of having more choices? Do you find yourself playing the victim less often? Learn to give yourself credit where credit is due—and, in many cases, overdue.

Consistency

The reward of art is not fame or success but intoxication.

CYRIL CONNOLLY

At last, a warm, clear, and sunny day. The park is filled with casual strollers. Up by the reservoir, the runners make their rounds, nodding hello to one another. Many of them run at the same time each day and they know one another by sight. A number of runners have dogs in tow. Tiger Lily and Charlotte eye the running dogs with interest but no envy. They prefer the more leisurely pace that Emma and I set as we walk our slower circuit. Squirrels scamper near. Our dogs take the bait, skittering to the end of their long leashes. They cannot quite catch the squirrels who chatter busily from halfway up a tree trunk. Frustrated, the dogs leap at the tree's base. We walk on.

As artists, we do well to practice consistency. Our mad dashes after the squirrels of inspiration leave us frustrated and at our wits' end. There is much to be said for a slower and more leisurely pursuit of ideas. There is so much talk of creative "breakthroughs" that many of us expect our creativity to be dramatic. This is seldom the case. Very occasionally, we will have a flash of insight or intuition but more often we will experience a slow and steady course. Our creativity resembles sunlight more than lightning. Even in dark times, this is true.

My own dark time seems to be reaching an end. Despite my laundry list of fears, I am sleeping most nights. Despite my still turbulent emotions, my Morning Pages have more coherence. I am not yet optimistic, but my days do seem to be lit by a steadier lamp. One more time, the simple slogans of sobriety have done their good service. One day at a time, practicing "Easy does it," I have managed to muddle through. Now the light at the end of the tunnel is visible to me. I am on the mend. I am growing steadier. With every night's sleep and every day's writing, the abyss seems further and further removed. I am grateful. I focus on the light. "The key is consistency," my Guidance assures me. Every day when I listen for right action, the message is the same. "Be consistent. Stick to your grid." Obedient, I write, walk, and listen for further instructions.

> *We work in the dark—we do what we can—we give what we have. Our doubt is our passion, and our passion is our task. The rest is the madness of art.*
>
> HENRY JAMES

> *I believe we are free, within limits, and yet there is an unseen hand, a guiding angel, that somehow, like a submerged propeller, drives us on.*
>
> RABINDRANATH TAGORE

Obedient, I try to write three pages a day. I listen for insight and write down what it is that I hear. The process is much more like taking dictation than it is like thinking something up. The directions are important here. When I take something *down*, it is an easy process. When I strain to think something *up*, I am striving for something that may be beyond my reach. And so it is that I write three pages daily. My job is less writing than listening. I keep an appointment with the Muse. We meet for an agreed upon time and quantity.

When I teach creative writing, I urge my students to write Morning Pages, the daily three pages of longhand writing that primes the pump. Morning Pages miniaturize the Censor and train it to stand aside. When the Pages are completed, there is time for creative writing to step to the fore. The Censor is quiet. The Muse becomes talkative. We meet the Muse and take down what it has to say.

As a rule, I urge my students to try for three pages of new writing a day. It is not too daunting an amount. The key to its success is its gentle consistency. No mad gallops after elusive quarry, just a simple, doable routine.

"Julia, you make it so nondramatic," a student once complained. A poet, he had a long history of drama around his writing and he resisted the idea that writing could be consistent and even easy. Against his better judgment, he began the practice of Morning Pages and he quickly became hooked on them. From there, it was just a short step to trying his "real" writing. Imagine his surprise when good ideas began to come to him easily and daily. Where was his drama?

"I am writing on a regular basis now and I have to say that I cannot really tell the difference in caliber between one of the poems that was 'easy' to catch and one of the poems crafted my old way in a sudden fit of inspiration. To tell the truth, I think the new poems hold up very well. And it's sort of a relief not to have to 'act like' a poet in order to be a poet."

When we commit to creation on a consistent basis, we begin to dismantle some of our old ideas about artists. For one thing, regular work tends to improve the mood. We are less tortured and may even catch ourselves being sunny and optimistic. No longer restless, irritable, and discontent, we find ourselves suddenly user-friendly.

"Julia, you have wrecked my tantrums and tamed my temper," one writer, a recent convert to the Morning Pages, complains. "I used to be able to work myself up into a good fit when I wasn't writing. Now I am at least writing three pages daily and that seems to be enough to siphon off steam. I usually write three pages in the morning and then later, in early afternoon, I settle in and do my 'real' writing. In the interim, I no longer get on the phone and cause trouble. Some of my friends think I have had a spiritual awakening."

When artists are working regularly, they are spiritually centered. The act of making art is a spiritual act and our daily exposure to this realm does have an impact on our personality. It does not matter what language we use to describe it. Art puts us in touch with a power greater than ourselves. This conscious contact brings us a sense of optimism and grace. As we sense that there is a benevolent Something inclined toward helping us and our work, we begin to feel a sense of companionship. Higher forces are at our side. We are not alone.

There is a light evening wind. The runners around the reservoir lift their faces to the breeze. Fireflies glint in the undergrowth. The evening's light is turning golden. Skyscrapers are gilded by the setting sun. For the second time today, we have taken our dogs to the park. Tiger Lily is living up to her nickname, "Tiger." When a Jack Russell puppy makes its way toward us, Tiger Lily crouches, ready to spring. "No, girl," I tell her and give a tug at her leash. Reluctantly, she allows the puppy to pass, but not without a growl and a quick pirouette at the end of her lead.

> *Nothing in the world can take the place of persistence. Persistence and determination are omnipotent.*
>
> CALVIN COOLIDGE

Out of the crowd of joggers, a neighbor comes striding toward us. Her face is flushed and she is grinning. "I had the *best* run," she announces. I give her a grin of recognition. With a gay little wave, she is on her way. She runs daily, just as I write. In our own way, we are each athletes. For us both, a gentle consistency is key.

Divining Rod

Over the period of time you have spent with this book, you have experimented with a variety of tools, some familiar to you already and some new. It is my hope that you have been able to experience a growing sense of your own creative power. This may manifest as excitement or restlessness, optimism, or irritability. You have freed up considerably more creative energy, and it is up to you to channel it productively. Choose now a selection of tools that you believe you will be able to work with consistently.

Take pen in hand. On paper, in writing, commit yourself to the tools that you will continue to use. "I commit myself to the continued use of Morning Pages," you might write. Or, "I commit myself to continued Artist Dates." Or, "I vow to continue my walks." Beyond the big tools, you may have benefited from some of the smaller and homelier ones. If so, pledge to continue their use. "I will continue to take quiet times in a sacred space." "I will make a regular practice of mending." "I will continue to call my friends for prayers and encouragement." "I will continue to call my friends and listen actively to their dreams and hopes."

When you have completed your list of choices for continued work, contact one of your "believing mirrors." Enlist your friend's support in what it is you plan to undertake. You might wish to inaugurate a further course of creative studies—perhaps in the company of your friend.

A little sleuthing will usually yield an Artist Way group in your area. A search on the Web will reveal communities working together on *The Artist's Way, The Vein of Gold, Walking in This World*, and *The Right to Write*. Any of these courses can be pursued through the combination of essays and tasks that you have just mastered. Additionally, you may find yourself devising your own creativity tasks.

When I go out to teach, I am frequently met by students who offer, "I used your tools and I made this _____." I have been presented with novels, children's books, gift cards, DVD's, jewelry, and CD's. It is my delight that tools from my creativity kit have so often proved useful to others. It is my hope that you, in turn, will share these tools with still others. The Artist's Way is tribal and we all can contribute.

Just Do It

What I did have, which others perhaps didn't, was a capacity for sticking at it, which really is the point, not the talent at all. You have to stick at it.

DORIS LESSING

A classic is a book that has never finished saying all it has to say.

ITALO CALVINO

The day is back to cool and gray. Resolute runners make their way around the reservoir, pigeons flapping from their path. When breezes stir the trees, a shower of silvery drops fall to earth. It rained all night and in the early hours of the morning. Not to be deterred the runners are out in bright yellow slickers. They are ready to run in any weather and some of their best runs occur on days like today. It is a matter of grit. They do not ask to be coddled by sunshine.

As artists, we, too, need to work through many kinds of weather. It is lovely when we have a day of halcyon weather, when we wake up eager to work and have a day stretching out ahead of us filled with space and time. More often, we will feel resistant. We will move grudgingly and under half steam. Some of our best work is done under the least favorable conditions. We grab twenty minutes to write, telling ourselves it is barely worth the attempt and our sentences come flying to the page with winged feet. We go to the easel knowing we are going to be grabbing a few quick strokes before another interruption looms, but with those quick strokes we execute a tricky part of the portrait. It is done before we know it.

So much of being an artist involves that Nike slogan, "Just do it." So much good comes from our just showing up. Of course it is seductive, the idea that we will one day be in the mood, and we will work that day like a "real" artist. But a great deal of real art is made under the radar. We barely know we are working. We just suit up and show up and grab what moments we can, and it is only in cozy retrospect that we see the level of skill we were able to muster. It is humbling, the degree to which we are like automatons. Our art moves through us despite us.

So much of being an artist has to do with consistency and continuity. It isn't very glorious, the day-in-and-day-out labor of art. Books are made a page at a time which means a page at a time we must go to the typewriter. Symphonies are written measure by measure. "Just do it" works for all arts, lowbrow to highbrow. Right now, my friend the opera singer is learning to write music. I get a message on my machine, just checking in, "I wrote my two measures." Two measures doesn't seem like much but by the end of a month, the fragments will add up to a song cycle—glorious music that did not exist before my friend became humble enough to "try."

There is art in humility. There is art in the attempt to make art. Daily, I go to the keyboard and work on writing the saga of *Magellan*. Yesterday, I wrote a storm at sea. Waves crashed. Timbers groaned. The deck was slippery and the footing treacherous. I tried to convey all of this a note at a time. I could hear the music in my head. Whether I could get it to the page was the question. The task seemed daunting—but I could try and I did. When Emma, my collaborator, came in she could hear the storm I was striving for. "It just needs some of this," she said and laid down a few tumultuous chords. Magellan walked the decks.

The best, most beautiful things in the world cannot be seen, or even touched. They must be felt with the heart.

HELEN KELLER

As an artist, I write Morning Pages daily. After I have finished writing them, I sit quietly asking for Guidance. Again and again the Guidance comes back to me, "You need to stay steady as she goes." Again and again I am sent back to the page to try one more time to take down what I hear. There is no dramatic breakthrough where I say, "Ah hah! I have made it!" Instead, my work unfolds a page at a time, edging forward just a little. I listen, learn, and write.

"How are you doing?" my friend Natalie Goldberg, the famed writing teacher, often asks me. I tell her that I am soldiering on, putting in a day at a time, a page at a time at my craft. "The important part is not to get tossed away," Natalie tells me. "The important part is to just keep at the work, no matter how hard or how daunting the work may feel."

Out at the reservoir, the runners move with heads bent, arms and legs smoothly pumping. Some of them are running through stiffness. Some of them are recovering from injuries. Not all of them are running easily or freely, but run they do. As a result of their running, many of them are lean and fit. Fitness is the by-product of their commitment, just as art is the by-product of an artist's commitment. Our skills are honed by the doing. What is done is often excellent, but it is excellent in passing. We take care of the quantity, leaving it to the Great Creator to take care of the quality. When we labor so in humility, great art is often born. Very often the work that will later seem to be our best will be the most hard won.

The Infinite has written its name on the heavens in shining stars, and on Earth in tender flowers.

JEAN PAUL RICHTER

My friend the distinguished writer works daily. She loves to write, but it is not always easy for her. She writes as the runners run, in all weather.

"I just work"—that is the ethic that serves us best as artists. Although we seldom talk about it, so much of an artistic career is the long hours of duty, the hours where we simply show up. In this regard, artists are very much like athletes. We must learn to work despite mood. We must learn to work despite conditions. We must learn to work day in and day out because that is our commitment. Just as the runners circle the reservoir daily, I go to the typewriter. It is a luxury to be in the mood to write. It is a good day's work to simply write.

I have been simply writing for nearly four decades. Writing is a habit for me and that habit has been my saving grace as I have fought with my depression and my alcoholism. One day at a time, I have managed to get to the page. I have written, not always well, but faithfully. In black periods, even my Morning Pages have been difficult, fragmented, and sad. I have written them anyway, trusting that if I just didn't drink, and I just kept writing, something good would come of it. And it has.

What has come of it is a writer's life, a productive life characterized by steady productivity despite my breakdowns, despite my stretches of fragility when the hospital has loomed close. There are the "real" breakdowns and then there are the shadow breakdowns, like this one, when I have felt myself to have been unhinged but have managed to avoid hospitalization.

"Just show up," I have learned and I have practiced this advice in all types of emotional weather. It is daunting, sometimes, to glance back through Morning Pages and see how close I have teetered to the abyss, only backing off with the greatest of difficulty. But back off I have, hewing to my gentle grid of Morning Pages, Artist Dates, and Weekly Walks, getting myself to the page and to the piano. Working daily, I have managed to have a life that works. I have come to know myself as very tough and very delicate. My friends know me the same way.

> *The creation of a thousand forests is in one acorn.*
>
> RALPH WALDO EMERSON

And so it goes. A day at a time, my friends and I egg one another on a little bit. We cannot make art by committee, but we can enlist one another's support. We may work alone, but we are in it together—"it" being the artist's life.

Divining Rod

On my right-hand third finger, I wear a silver ring. I bought it many years ago in New Mexico, and it was purchased to symbolize my commitment to the artist's life. "To thine own self be true," my ring signifies. It is a constant, subtle reminder to myself to always live by my own values.

Art is a language of symbols. Gift yourself with a symbolic something that speaks to you of your identity as an artist. Choose the symbol that suits you personally. It may be a ring, a pendant, or a bracelet. It may be something else entirely. The dragon is the Chinese symbol for creativity. You might want a dragon shirt or robe or paperweight. You might designate an acorn as a symbol of creativity or a satiny river rock or seashell. There are as many symbols of creativity as there are forms of creativity. Select the symbol that speaks most clearly to your heart.

CHECK-IN

1. **How many days this week did you do your Morning Pages?** If you skipped a day, why did you skip it? How was the experience of writing them for you? Are you experiencing more clarity? A wider range of emotions? A greater sense of detachment, purpose, and calm? Did anything surprise you? Is there a "repeating" issue asking to be dealt with?

2. **Did you do your Artist Date this week?** Did you note an improved sense of well-being? What did you do and how did it feel? Remember, Artist Dates can be difficult and you may need to coax yourself into taking them.

3. **Did you get out on your Weekly Walk?** How did that feel? What emotions or insights surfaced for you? Were you able to walk more than once? What did your walk do for your optimism and sense of perspective?

4. **Were there any other issues this week that felt significant to you in your self-discovery?** Describe them.

EPILOGUE

AS WE REACH THE END of this collection of essays and tasks, it is clear that there is no real end to the creative path. It is a spiral path. You circle back through the same issues, over and over, just at slightly different altitudes. You now have a spiritual toolkit, which you can use in perpetuity. The simplest of tools—Morning Pages, Artist Dates, and Walks—will yield large, ongoing benefits. The smaller tools, when repeated alone or in a cluster, will bring surprising new results.

It's a great relief to me to know that I can actually be creative and be happy at the same time.

JAMES W. HALL

I have long envisioned The Artist's Way as a movement more than a solitary journey. It is easy to found a group and easy to find one, as well. Groups proliferate in cyberspace as well as in your very own neighborhood. Using this book or others I have written on the creative process, join together to support each other's unfolding. There are Artist's Way groups which have been meeting for more than a decade and a half. As their members flourish, it is like watching a great garden grow. As we find the spiritual water necessary to our growth, we are far more colorful than we know.

INDEX

Creative Clusters Guide

and

Suggested Reading

CREATIVE CLUSTERS GUIDE

When *The Artist's Way* was first published, I expressed a wish for Artist's Way groups to spring into being. I envisioned them as peer-run circles—"creative clusters"—where people would serve one another as believing mirrors, uniting with the common aim of creative unblocking. It was my vision that such circles would be free of charge, that anyone could assemble one, using the book as a guide and a text. Many such peer-run circles did form and many more are forming still. Such artist-to-artist, heart-to-heart help and support are the heart of *The Artist's Way* movement.

Not surprisingly, many therapists, community colleges, wellness centers, universities, and teachers soon began running facilitated Artist's Way groups, for which they charged a fee. The Artist's Way groups were led rather than simply convened. To the degree to which they adhered to the spiritual principles of creative recovery and introduced people to the use of the tools, they were—and are—valuable. Any group that starts with such a leader should, however, rapidly become autonomous, "graduating" to a peer-run, nonprofit status.

There are no "accredited" Artist's Way teachers. I chose not to franchise *The Artist's Way* but to offer it as a gift, free of charge. It is my belief that creative recovery at its best is a nonhierarchical, peer-run, collective process. In this it differs from the academic and therapeutic modes. Any professional using *The Artist's Way* should realize that autonomous, peer-run creative clusters must remain the eventual goal. Facilitated groups can serve as a sort of bridge to this end.

In my years of teaching and traveling, I have frequently encountered excellent results from peer-group clusters. On occasion, I have encountered situations where *The Artist's Way* has been unduly modified. Whenever there is a misplaced emphasis on intellectual "analysis" or therapeutic "processing," there is the risk of undermining creative unfolding. Very often, what could be interpreted as "neurosis" or a deep-seated problem is simply creative resistance.

The Artist's Way and all my other "teaching" books are experiential books. They are intended to teach people to process and transform life through acts of creativity. Both books and *all* creative clusters should be practiced through creative action, not through theory. As an artist, I know this. *The Artist's Way* and other books are the distillate of thirty years of artistic practice.

It is my belief and my experience as a teacher that all of us are healthy enough to practice creativity. It is not a dangerous endeavor requiring trained facilitators. It is our human birthright and something we can do gently and collectively. Creativity is like breathing—pointers may help, but *we do the process ourselves.* Creative clusters, where we gather as peers to develop our strength, are best regarded as tribal gatherings, where creative beings raise, celebrate, and actualize the creative power which runs through us all.

GUIDELINES

1. *Use a Twelve-Week Process with a Weekly Gathering of Two to Three Hours.* The Morning Pages and Artist Dates are required of everyone in the group, including facilitators. The exercises are done in order in the group, with everyone, including the facilitator, answering the questions and then sharing the answers in clusters of four, one chapter per week. Do not share your Morning Pages with the group or anyone else. Do not reread your Morning Pages until later in the course, if you are required to do so by your facilitator or your own inner guidance.

2. *Avoid Self-Appointed Gurus.* If there is any emissary, it is the work itself, as a collective composed of all who take the course, at home or otherwise. Each person is equally a part of the collective, no one more than another. While there may be "teachers," facilitators who are relied on during the twelve-week period to guide others down the path, such facilitators need to be prepared to share their own material and take their own creative risks. This is a dialectic rather than a monologue—an egalitarian group process rather than a hierarchical one.

3. *Listen.* We each get what we need from the group process by sharing our own material and by listening to others. We do not need to comment on another person's sharing in order to help that person. We must refrain from trying to "fix" someone else. Each group devises a cooperative creative "song" of artistic recovery. Each group's song is unique to that group—like that of a pod or family of whales, initiating and echoing to establish their position. When listening, go around the circle without commenting unduly on what is heard. The circle,

as a shape, is very important. We are intended to witness, not control, one another. When sharing exercises, clusters of four within the larger groups are important: five tends to become unwieldy in terms of time constraints; three doesn't allow for enough contrasting experience. Obviously, not all groups can be divided into equal fours. Just try to do so whenever you can.

4. *Respect One Another.* Be certain that respect and compassion are afforded equally to every member. Each person must be able to speak his own wounds and dreams. No one is to be "fixed" by another member of the group. This is a deep and powerful internal process. There is no one right way to do this. Love is important. Be kind to yourself. Be kind to one another.

5. *Expect Change in the Group Makeup.* Many people will—some will not—fulfill the twelve-week process. There is often a rebellious or fallow period after the twelve weeks, with people returning to the disciplines later. When they do, they continue to find the process unfolding within them a year, a few years, or many years later. Many groups have a tendency to drive apart at eight to ten weeks (creative U-turns) because of the feelings of loss associated with the group's ending. Face the truth as a group; it may help you stay together.

6. *Be Autonomous.* You cannot control your own process, let alone anyone else's. Know that you will feel rebellious occasionally—that you won't want to do all of your Morning Pages and exercises at times in the twelve weeks. Relapse is okay. You cannot do this process perfectly, so relax, be kind to yourself, and hold on to your hat. Even when you feel nothing is happening, you will be changing at great velocity. This change is a deepening into your own intuition, your own creative self. The structure of the course is about safely getting across the bridge into new realms of creative spiritual awareness.

7. *Be Self-Loving.* If the facilitator feels somehow "wrong" to you, change clusters or start your own. Continually seek your own inner guidance rather than outer guidance. You are seeking to form an artist-to-artist relationship with the Great Creator. Keep gurus at bay. You have your own answers within you.

A Word to Therapists, Teachers, Writing Instructors and Other Artist's Way Group Leaders. Thank you for the wonderful work you do. While I know that many of you are using *The Artist's Way* to run groups, I hope and expect that you will go on to explore your own interests using *The Artist's Way* for your process also. I encourage you to follow your own creative vision, to strive for your own True North. You will find that the facilitation process continues your own growth experience.

I cannot state emphatically enough that *The Artist's Way* fame and path should not be used in ways that differ substantially from the Artist's Way techniques as spelled out in the book. I have tested the tools for a decade and a half in order to find them roadworthy. I ask that you refrain from presenting yourselves publicly as Artist's Way "experts," though you may use the book within your practice. I ask that you remember that the wisdom of *The Artist's Way* is a collective, nonhierarchical experience. I have heard of abuses of this principle, such as a group leader's requiring the Morning Pages to be read in the group. This is not in the spirit of the book. Facilitated groups should "graduate" into free, peer-run clusters.

A Word to Therapeutic Clients. Please remember that the book itself remains the primary source of the Artist's Way teachings, and that it is your interpretation, and your work with the book and its tools, that are central to you in your recovery. I remind you that the work is your own, not just something done under the influence of a magic teacher. Please "own" your recovery as your recovery.

Thank you. I am delighted *The Artist's Way* is used in the many contexts in which it is (such as in colleges and universities, by therapists, and by peer-run clusters). I again offer the reminder that the Artist's Way is intended to be used in keeping with the spirit of the book, as written. There is always the book itself to refer to. This is an individual's journey that may be facilitated by the group process. If you cannot find or start a group, consider you and the book to constitute one!

Pass It On. To those forming a peer-run cluster, you do not need to make the Artist's Way a moneymaking venture, for me or for you. If you follow the spiritual practice of tithing, I recommend buying the book and passing it on.

SUGGESTED READING

My experience as a teacher tells me that those who read this book are better off doing something, rather than reading another book, but I have included many of my favorites just in case you feel compelled to research further. These books represent some of the very best in their fields. To keep it simple, try to finish Artist's Way work before adding this input.

Aftel, Mandy. *The Story of Your Live—Becoming the Author of Your Experience.* New York: Simon & Schuster, 1996. Persuasive and useful.

Ban Breathnach, Sarah. *Simple Abundance.* New York: Warner Books, 1995. Grounded in my own work and expanding on it, this is a profoundly touching book.

Berendt, Joachim-Ernst. *The World Is Sound: Nada Brahma.* Rochester, VT.: Destiny Books, 1991. Eloquent and persuasive book on sound theory.

Bolles, Richard Nelson. *What Color Is Your Parachute?* Berkeley: Ten Speed Press, 1970. Whimsical and pragmatic guide to goal-setting.

Bonny, Helen. *Music and Your Mind.* Barrytown, N.Y.: Helen A. Bonny and Louis M. Savary, 1973, 1970. An explicit guide to using music as an antidote for mental and emotional pain.

Bradley, Marion Zimmer. *The Mists of Avalon.* New York: Ballantine Books, 1982. A powerfully evocative novel of female spirituality in pre-Christian England. A mesmerizing novel of goddess worship in Arthurian times.

Brande, Dorothea. *Becoming a Writer.* 1934. Reprint. Los Angeles: Jeremy P. Tarcher, 1981. The best book on writing I've ever found.

Burnham, Sophy. *A Book of Angels.* New York: Ballantine Books, 1991. An elegant, deeply felt exploration of the spiritual powers and forces at play in our lives.

Bush, Carol A. *Healing Imagery and Music.* Portland, Oreg.: Rudra Press, 1995. A profoundly useful guide to listening for healing.

Came to Believe. New York: Alcoholics Anonymous World Series, 1973. Useful and touching book about embryonic faith.

Campbell, Don G. *The Roar of Silence.* Wheaton, Ill.: The Theosophical Publishing House, 1994. Seminal book on sound healing—clear, passionate and useful. All of Campbell's many books are important and persuasive, but this one remains a primer.

Cassou, Michelle, and Steward Cubley. *Life, Paint, and Passion: Reclaiming the Magic of Spontaneous Expression.* New York: Jeremy P. Tarcher/Putnam, 1996. Passionate and experienced into-the-water book for visual artists.

Chatwin, Bruce. *Songlines.* New York: Penguin Books, 1987. An exquisite, mysterious and powerful book.

Choquette, Sonia. *The Psychic Pathway.* New York: Random House. Crown Trade Paperbacks, 1994, 1995. Safe, grounded, practical guide to opening to spiritual gifts.

Choquette, Sonia. *Your Heart's Desire.* New York: Random House. Crown Trade Paperbacks, 1997. An extremely clear, step-by-step guide for manifesting dreams as working reality.

Eisler, Raine. *The Chalice and the Blade.* San Francisco: Harper & Row Publishers, 1987. Seminal book on the differences in masculine and feminine life approaches.

Fassel, Diane. *Working Ourselves to Death.* San Francisco: HarperCollins, 1990. A strong-minded intervention for workaholic personalities.

Fox, Matthew. *Original Blessing.* Santa Fe, N.M.: Bear & Company, 1983. An important corrective book on Christian tradition; brilliant, impassioned, compassionate.

Franck, Frederick. *Zen Seeing, Zen Drawing.* New York: Bantam Books, 1993. A fine treatise on the value of "attention" in the creative life.

Gawain, Shakti. *Creative Visualization.* Mill Valley, Cal.: Whatever Publishing, 1986. Helpful in learning to create and hold a vision.

Goldberg, Bonni. *Room to Write: Daily Invitations to a Writer's Life.* New York: Jeremy P. Tarcher/Putnam, 1996. A masterfully provocative and wise writer's tool.

Goldberg, Natalie. *Writing Down the Bones.* Boston, Mass.: Shambhala Publications, 1986. The best pen-to-paper writing book ever written.

Goldman, Jonathan. *Healing Sounds: The Power of Harmonics.* Rockport, Mass.: Element Books, Inc., 1992. Powerful and gentle teaching book on sound healing techniques.

Grof, Christina, and Stanislav Grof. *The Stormy Search for the Self.* Los Angeles: Jeremy P. Tarcher, 1990. A provocative book about the misunderstanding of spiritual experience in our culture.

Harmon, Willis, and Howard Rheingold. *Higher Creativity.* Los Angeles: Jeremy P. Tarcher, 1984. A valuable and often instructive book on creativity in frontline famous authors and others.

Hart, Mickey. *Drumming at the Edge of Magic.* San Francisco: HarperCollins, 1990. A great book on music as a spiritual experience.

Heywood, Rosalind. *ESP: A Personal Memoir.* New York: E. P. Dutton & Co., Inc., 1964. A delightful book of personal encounters with higher forces.

Holmes, Ernest. *Creative Ideas.* Los Angeles: Science of Mind Communications, 1973. A tiny, powerful and important book of spiritual law as applied to creative manifestation.

James, William. *The Varieties of Religious Experience.* Boston: Mentor Books, 1902. Seminal fountainhead describing different forms of spiritual awakening, much insight into creativity as a spiritual matter.

Jeffers, Susan. *Feel the Fear and Do It Anyway.* New York: Fawcett Columbine, 1987. An into-the-water book for getting past fear.

Leonard, Jim. *Your Fondest Dream.* Cincinnati: Vivation, 1989. Another into-the-water book; many brainstorming techniques.

Lewis, C. S. *Miracles.* New York: Macmillan, 1947. Inspirational, prickly, and provocative. A challenge in open-mindedness.

Lingerman, Hal A. *The Healing Energies of Music.* Wheaton, Ill.: The Theosophical Publishing House, 1983. Excellent book on music as medicine, learned yet friendly.

London, Peter. *No More Secondhand Art: Awakening the Artist Within.* Boston: Shambhala Publications, Inc., 1989. A manifesto for personal art as process, not product.

McClellan, Randall, Ph.D. *The Healing Sources of Music.* Rockport, Mass.: Element Books, Inc., 1994. A kindly yet wide-ranging source.

Maclean, Dorothy. *To Hear the Angels Sing.* Hudson, N.Y.: Lindisfarne Press, 1990. A lovely book, a fascinating spiritual autobiography by one of the founders of Findhorn.

Mathieu, W. A. *The Listening Book: Discovering Your Own Music.* Boston: Shambhala Publications, Inc., 1991. A companionable book that demystifies music as a life path.

Matthews, Caitlin. *Singing the Soul Back Home: Shamanism in Daily Life*. Rockport, Mass.: Element Books, Inc., 1995. A wonderfully rich book for grounded spiritual practice.

Miller, Alice. *The Drama of the Gifted Child*. New York: Basic Books, 1981. Seminal book on how toxic family dynamics dampen creativity.

Nachmanovitch, Stephen. *Free Play*. Los Angeles: Jeremy P. Tarcher, 1991. A wonderful book on creative freedom.

Noble, Vicki. *Motherpeace—A Way to the Goddess Through Myth, Art, and Tarot*. San Francisco: Harper & Row Publishers, 1983. Creativity through the lens of the goddess religion.

Norwood, Robin. *Women Who Love Too Much*. Los Angeles: Jeremy P. Tarcher, 1985. Seminal work on codependency.

Peck, M. Scott. *The Road Less Traveled*. New York: Simon & Schuster, 1978. A book for early spiritual skeptics.

Shaughnessy, Susan. *Walking on Alligators*. New York: HarperCollins, 1993. A companionable, savvy guide for anyone working to appreciate the worth of process as well as product.

Sher, Barbara, with Annie Gottleib. *Wishcraft: How to Get What You Really Want*. New York: Ballantine Books, 1979. A potent, catalytic book for creative living, similar to my own work and my current thinking.

Starhawk. *The Fifth Sacred Thing*. New York: Bantam Books, 1994. Mesmerizing novel of spiritual ecology.

Starhawk. *The Spiritual Dance*. New York: Harper and Row, 1979. Brilliant on creativity and god/goddess within.

Tame, David. *The Secret Power of Music*. New York: Destiny Books, 1984. A lucid introductory overview of the healing powers of music.

Ueland, Brenda. *If You Want to Write*. 1938. St. Paul, Minn.: Schubert, 1983. The care and maintenance of the writer as a creative artist. Shrewd, personal and pragmatic.

W., Bill. *Alcoholics Anonymous: The Story of How More Than One Hundred Men Have Recovered from Alcoholism*. Akron, Ohio: Carry the Message, 1985.

Wegscheider-Cruse, Sharon. *Choicemaking: For Co-dependents, Adult Children and Spirituality Seekers*. Pompano Beach, Fla.: Health Communications, 1985. Recommended for dismantling co-dependent workaholism.

Woititz, Janet. *Home Away from Home: The Art of Self-Sabotage*. Pompano Beach, Fla.: Health Communications, 1987. Important for arresting the mechanism of aborting success.

Wright, Machaelle Small. *Behaving As If the God in All Life Mattered*. Jeffersonton, Va: Perelandra. Ltd., 1987. A spiritual autobiography about work with "earth" and other energy forms.

Special Interest

These books are intended as special help on issues that frequently block creativity.

Alcoholics Anonymous. *The Big Book*. New York: Alcoholics Anonymous World Services. Care and maintenance of a sane and sober lifestyle for alcoholic and nonalcoholic alike. Inspirational guide.

Alcoholics Anonymous. *Came to Believe*. New York: Alcoholics Anonymous World Services, 1973. Useful and touching book about embryonic faith.

The Augustine Fellowship. *Sex and Love Addicts Anonymous.* Boston: The Augustine Fellowship, Sex and Love Addicts Anonymous Fellowship-Wide Services, 1986. One of the best books on addiction. The chapters on withdrawal and building partnership should be required reading.

Beattie, Meloy. *Codependent No More.* San Francisco: Harper & Row, 1987. Excellent for breaking the virtue trap.

Cameron, Julia, and Mark Bryan. *Money Dunk, Money Sober.* New York: Ballantine Books, 1992. A hands-on toolkit for financial freedom. This book creates new language and a new lens for money management. It grew out of *The Artist's Way* because money is the most often cited block.

Hallowell, Edward M., M.D., and John J. Ratey, M.D. *Driven to Distraction.* New York: Touchstone Books/ Simon & Schuster, 1994; first Touchstone edition, 1995. Invaluable book on attention deficit disorder.

Louden, Jennifer. *The Women's Comfort Book (A Self-Nurturing Guide for Restoring Balance in Your Life).* San Francisco: HarperSanFrancisco, 1992. Applicable to either sex as a practical guide to self-nurturing.

Mundis, Jerrold. *How to Get Out of Debt, Stay Out of Debt, and Live Prosperously.* New York: Bantam Books, 1990.

Osborn, Carol. *Enough Is Enough: Exploding the Myth of Having It All.* New York: G. P. Putnam's Sons, 1986. Excellent for helping dismantle the heroic workaholic personality.

ABOUT THE AUTHOR

Julia Cameron has been an active artist for more than thirty years. She is the author of twenty-four books, fiction and nonfiction, including her bestselling works on the Creative process: *The Artist's Way, Walking in This World, The Vein of Gold, The Right to Write,* and *The Sound of Paper.* A novelist, playwright, songwriter, and poet, she has multiple credits in theater, film, and television.